济南统计年鉴

JINAN STATISTICAL YEARBOOK

2022

（总第40期 NO.40）

济 南 市 统 计 局
国家统计局济南调查队 编

Jinan Municipal Bureau of Statistics
NBS Survey Office In Jinan

图书在版编目（CIP）数据

济南统计年鉴. 2022 = Jinan Statistical Yearbook 2022 : 汉英对照 / 济南市统计局, 国家统计局济南调查队编. -- 北京 : 中国统计出版社, 2022.10
ISBN 978-7-5037-9922-8

Ⅰ. ①济… Ⅱ. ①济… ②国… Ⅲ. ①社会经济统计—统计资料—济南—2022—年鉴—汉、英 Ⅳ. ①C832.521-54

中国版本图书馆 CIP 数据核字 (2022) 第 157047 号

济南统计年鉴 2022

作　　者 / 济南市统计局　国家统计局济南调查队
责任编辑 / 钟钰
装帧设计 / 山东麦德森文化传媒有限公司
出版发行 / 中国统计出版社有限公司
地　　址 / 北京市丰台区西三环南路甲 6 号
邮政编码 / 100073
电　　话 / 邮购（010）63376909　书店（010）68783171
网　　址 / http://www.zgtjcbs.com
印　　刷 / 山东麦德森文化传媒有限公司
经　　销 / 新华书店
开　　本 / 890mm×1240mm　1/16
字　　数 / 826 千字
印　　张 / 24.25　彩页 1.25
版　　别 / 2022 年 10 月第 1 版
版　　次 / 2022 年 10 月第 1 次印刷
定　　价 / 396.00 元　Price:396.00yuan(RMB)

如有印装差错，由本社发行部调换。

编辑委员会及编辑工作人员

Editorial Board and Editorial Staff

编 辑 说 明

一、《济南统计年鉴 2022》是一部全面反映济南市国民经济和社会发展情况的资料性统计年刊。本书收录了济南市及所辖县、区 2021 年经济和社会发展各方面大量的统计数据，以及历史重要年份的主要统计数据，是认识和研究济南市情、经济和社会发展，制定宏观政策、指导工作的重要工具书。

二、本年鉴以丰富、翔实的统计资料为主，辅以直观的统计图、特载，全面反映了济南市国民经济和社会发展状况。全书统计资料共分为二十二个部分，即：1．行政区划；2．人口；3．综合；4．国民经济核算；5．劳动就业；6．固定资产投资；7．城市公用事业和环境保护；8．财政和金融保险；9．物价；10．人民生活；11．农业；12．工业；13．建筑业；14．运输与邮电；15．国内贸易；16．对外贸易与国际旅游；17．科技；18．教育与文化；19．体育卫生；20．民政司法和其他；特载和附录。各篇末附有《主要统计指标解释》，对主要统计指标的含义、统计范围、统计方法以及历史变动情况作了简要说明。

三、本年鉴中使用的度量衡均采用国际统一标准计量单位，统计口径除特别注明外，均包括济南市区、平阴县、商河县。资料取自济南市统计局、国家统计局济南调查队及有关部门的统计报表。

四、本年鉴中部分数据合计数或相对数由于计量单位取舍不同而产生的计算误差，均未做机械调整。

五、本年鉴表中的符号使用说明：

“空格”表示该项统计指标数据不足本表最小单位数、数据不详或无该项数据；

“-”表示无此项事实；

“#”表示其中的主要项；

“*”或“①”表示本表下有注解。

《济南统计年鉴》自出版以来，受到了社会各界的关心和支持，对此我们深表感谢。同时，欢迎使用《济南统计年鉴 2022》，敬请广大读者提出宝贵意见，帮助我们进一步提高统计年鉴编辑工作，更好的为社会各界服务，谢谢！（网址：http://jntj.jinan.gov.cn/）

编　者

2022 年 10 月

EDITOR'S NOTES

Ⅰ. *Jinan Statistical Yearbook2022* is a statistical reference book published yearly that comprehensively reflects the development of Jinan's national economy and society. With a vast amount of statistical data on various aspects of economic and social development in Jinan and the counties and districts under its jurisdiction in 2021, as well as the main statistical data of important historical years, the yearbook is an important reference book for people to understand and study Jinan and its economic and social development, for government to formulate macro policies and guidance work.

Ⅱ. The yearbook is centered on rich and detailed statistical data with intuitive statistical charts and special articles added, comprehensively reflecting Jinan's economic and social development. Statistical data of the yearbook contains 22 parts, namely:1. Division of Administrative Areas;2. Population;3. General Survey;4. National Accounts;5. Labor and Employment;6. Investment in Fixed Assets;7. Urban Public Utilities and Environmental Protection;8. Government Finance and Financial Insurance;9. Prices;10. People's Livelihood;11.Agriculture;12. Industry;13. Construction;14. Transportation, Post and Telecommunications;15. Domestic Trade;16. Foreign trade and International Tourism;17. Science and Technology;18. Education and Culture;19. Sports and Public Health;20. Social Welfare Civil Administration and Justice; Special Published and Appendices. We edit *Exploratory Notes on Main statistical Indicators* at the end of every article, briefly explaining the meaning, statistical scope, methods and historical changes of the main statistical indicators.

Ⅲ. The units of measurement used in this yearbook are internationally unified and standard measurement units. The statistical caliber includes Jinan City, Pingyin County and Shanghe County unless otherwise noted. The data in this yearbook are from the statistical reports of Jinan Municipal Bureau of Statistics, Jinan Investigation Team of National Bureau of Statistics and relevant departments.

Ⅳ. The statistical discrepancies caused by the unit of measurement in the total or relative numbers of some data in this yearbook are not adjusted.

Ⅴ. Notations used in this yearbook:

"Blank Space" indicates that the statistical index data is not large enough to be measured with the smallest unit in this table, or data are unknown or not available;

"–" means that there is no such fact;

"#" indicates the main item;

"*" or "①" means there are annotations in this table.

Since its publication, *Jinan Statistical Yearbook* has received the concern and support of all sectors of society, for which we are deeply grateful. At the same time, welcome to use *Jinan Statistical Yearbook2022* and offer valuable suggestions, so as to help us further improve the editing of statistical yearbooks and better serve all sectors of society, thank you! (Website: http://jntj.jinan.gov.cn/)

Editor

October 2022

目　　录

特载　Special Report

一　行政区划　Divisions of Administrative Areas

二　人　口　Population

三　综　合　General Survey

四　国民经济核算　National Accounts

五　劳动就业　Labor and Employment

六　固定资产投资　Investment in Fixed Assets

七　城市公用事业和环境保护 Urban Public Utilities and Environmental Protection

八　财政和金融保险　Government Finance and Financial Insurance

九 物 价 Price

十　人民生活　People's Livelihood

十一　农　业　Agriculture

十二 工 业 Industry

十三 建筑业 Construction

十四 运输与邮电 Transportation Post and Telecommunication

十五 国内贸易 Domestic Trade

十六　对外贸易与国际旅游　Foreign Trade and International Tourism

十七　科　技　Science and Technology

十八 教育与文化 Education and Culture

十九 体育与卫生 Sports and Public Health

二十　民政、司法和其他 Social Welfare Civil Administration and Others

附　录　Appendix

特载

SPECIAL REPORT

济南概况

济南是中国东部沿海经济文化大省—山东省的省会，全国文明城市，黄河流域中心城市、全国副省级城市之一，是全省的政治、经济、科创、金融、贸易、文化、教育和交通中心，是山东半岛城市群和省会经济圈核心城市。与德州、滨州、淄博、泰安、聊城等市相邻，辖历下、市中、槐荫、天桥、历城、长清、章丘、济阳、莱芜、钢城十区和平阴、商河二县。2021 年末常住人口 933.6 万，现有汉、回、蒙古、满、苗、壮、朝鲜等 55 个民族。

济南位于山东省中部，地理位置介于北纬 36° 01′ 至 37° 32′、东经 116° 11′ 至 117° 44′ 之间，面积 10244 平方公里。南依泰山，北跨黄河，地处鲁中南低山丘陵与鲁西北冲积平原的交接带上，地势南高北低。境内矿产资源丰富，主要有煤、石油、天然气、铁、地热和建筑材料等。

自然景色秀丽，名胜古迹众多，是中国历史文化名城之一。尤以泉水遍布、清冽甘美而闻名于世，有“济南泉水甲天下”和“泉城”之美誉。主要风景名胜有趵突泉、黑虎泉、珍珠泉、五龙潭、百脉泉五大泉群，大明湖、千佛山、灵岩寺等文化遗址。

文化底蕴厚重，是中华文明的重要发祥地之一，是齐鲁文化和儒家文化传承弘扬的重要承载地。龙山文化、泉水文化、诗词文化等特色文化融汇交织，拥有城子崖遗址、齐长城遗址等 30 处全国重点文物保护单位，是中国非物质文化遗产博览会永久落户地。

综合实力雄厚。2021 年，全市地区生产总值达到 11432.2 亿元，比上年增长 7.2%，较 2020 年增长逾 1290 亿元，首次实现“千亿级”的 GDP 年增量。其中，第一产业增加值 408.8 亿元，增长 7.1%；第二产业增加值 3964.1 亿元，增长 3.6%；第三产业增加值 7059.4 亿元，增长 9.2%，三次产业构成比为 3.6 ∶ 34.7 ∶ 61.7。一般公共预算收入 1007.6 亿元。年末金融机构本外币各项存款余额 23437.0 亿元，比上年增长 11.3%；金融机构本外币各项贷款余额 23313.2 亿元，增长 12.5%。全年社会消费品零售总额 5126.1 亿元，比上年增长 14.7%。市场主体总量达到 145.5 万户，“四上”企业数量达到 12001 家。

区位优势突出。济南北接京津冀、南连长三角、东承环渤海经济圈、西通中原经济区，具有承东启西、衔南接北的区位优势。2021 年年末，公路通车里程 18200.1 公里，比上年增长 0.5%。其中，高速公路里程 737.8 公里，与上年持平。公路货运量 2.5 亿吨，增长 8.8%；货运周转量 577.4 亿吨公里，增长 11.8%。公共交通旅客运输量 5.9 亿人次，增加 0.6 亿人次。济南机场全年累计完成航班起降 11.3 万架次，增长 10.1%；旅客吞吐量 1361.6 万人次，增长 9.9%；货邮吞吐量 16.8 万吨，增长 14.7%。全年货物进出口总额 1944.2 亿元，比上年增长 40.1%。

创新资源富集。2021 年，济南拥有山东大学等驻济高校 52 所，全日制在校大学生 69.4 万人。新认定国家级企业技术中心 1 家，总数达到 30 家，新认定省级企业技术中心 16 家，总数达到 221 家。齐鲁科创大走廊、中科院济南科创城、济南国际医学科学中心等一批重大创新载体加快建设。

产业活力较强。2021 年，“四新”经济增加值达到 4306.2 亿元，占 GDP 比重提高到 37.7%。现代高效农业增加值 70.7 亿元，比上年增长 18.8%，占农林牧渔业增加值比重 16.5%。高新技术产业产值增长 7.6%，占规模以上工业总产值比重达到 54.7%。现代服务业实现增加值 4202.7 亿元，增长 8.5%，占服务业增加值比重提高到 59.5%。

民生福祉增强。全年居民人均可支配收入 46725 元，比上年增长 8.5%。其中，城镇居民人均可支配收入 57449 元，增长 7.7%；农村居民人均可支配收入 22580 元，增长 10.5%。年末拥有卫生机构 7530 个，比上年增加 16 个。城市居民最低生活保障标准每月 904 元；农村居民最低生活保障标准每月 676 元。

Special Report-1

Introduction of Jinan

Jinan is the capital of Shandong Province, a major coastal economic and cultural province in eastern China, and listed as a national civilized city, a central city in the Yellow River Basin and one of the sub-provincial cities in China. It is the political, economic, technological innovation, financial, trade, cultural, educational and transportation center of the whole province, and the core city of urban agglomeration in Shandong Peninsula and provincial economic circle. Adjacent to Dezhou, Binzhou, Zibo, Tai' an, Liaocheng and other cities, it has jurisdiction over 10 districts including Lixia, Shizhong, Huaiyin, Tianqiao, Licheng, Changqing, Zhangqiu, Jiyang, Laiwu and Gangcheng, and two counties of Pingyin and Shanghe. At the end of 2021, the number of permanent residents was 9.336 million, with 55 ethnic groups including Han, Hui, Mongolia, Manchu, Miao, Zhuang and Chinese Korean, among others.

Jinan, located in the middle of Shandong Province, lies between 36° 01′ to 37° 32′ north latitude and 116° 11′ to 117° 44′ east longitude, covering an area of 10,244 square kilometers. Resting on Mount Tai in the south, across the Yellow River in the north, Jinan is located at the junction of low hills in central and southern Shandong and alluvial plain in northwestern Shandong, and the terrain is high in the south and low in the north. The territory is rich in mineral resources, including coal, among others, oil, natural gas, iron, geothermal and building materials.

With beautiful natural scenery and numerous scenic spots and historical sites, it is one of the famous historical and cultural cities in China. Especially, it is famous all over the world for its pervading, clear and sweet springs, and has the reputation of "Jinan Spring is the finest over the world" and "Spring City". The main scenic spots are Baotu Spring, Black Tiger Spring, Pearl Spring, Five Dragons Pool and Baimai Spring, and cultural sites such as Daming Lake, Qianfo Mountain and Lingyan Temple.

Rich in cultural deposits, it is one of the important birthplaces of Chinese civilization, and an important bearing place for the inheritance and promotion of Qilu culture and Confucian culture. Longshan culture, spring culture, poetry culture and other characteristic cultures are intertwined. It has 30 national key cultural relics protection units such as Chengziya Site and Great Wall of Qi remains, and is the permanent settlement of China Intangible Cultural Heritage Expo.

Great comprehensive strength. In 2021, the GDP of the whole city reached 1,143.22 billion yuan, an increase of 7.2% over the previous year, and up by over 129 billion yuan over 2020, achieving an annual GDP increase of "hundreds of billions" for the first time. Among them, the added value of the primary industry was 40.88 billion yuan, an increase of 7.1%; the added value of the secondary industry was 396.41 billion yuan, up by 3.6%; the added value of the tertiary industry was 705.94 billion yuan, an increase of 9.2%, and the ratio of the three industries was 3.6 : 34.7 : 61.7. The general budget revenue was 100.76 billion yuan. At the end of 2021, the balance of local and foreign currency deposits of financial institutions was 2,343.70 billion yuan, an increase of 11.3% over the previous year; the balance of local and foreign currency loans of financial institutions was 2,331.32 billion yuan, up by 12.5%. The total retail sales of consumer goods in 2021 were 512.61 billion yuan, an increase of 14.7% over the previous year. The total number of market players reached 1.455 million, and the number of "four-top" enterprises reached 12,001.

Outstanding location advantages. Jinan is bordered by Beijing-Tianjin-Hebei Region in the north, the Yangtze River Delta in the south, the Bohai Economic Circle in the east and the Central Plains Economic Zone in the west. It has the geographical advantages of connecting the east with the west and linking the south with the north. By the end of 2021, the highway mileage was 18,200.1 kilometers, an increase of 0.5% over the previous year. Among them, the mileage of expressways was 737.8 kilometers, which was the same as the previous year. Road freight volume was 250 million tons, up by 8.8%; the freight turnover was 57.74 billion tons kilometers, an increase of 11.8%. The number of public transport passengers was 590 million, an increase of 60 million. Jinan International Airport completed a total of 113,000 flights in 2021, an increase of 10.1%; the passenger throughput was 13.616 million, an increase of 9.9%; the postal throughput was 168,000 tons, up by 14.7%. The total import and export volume of goods in 2021 was 194.42 billion yuan, an increase of 40.1% over the previous year.

Extensive and concentrated innovative resources. In 2021, there were 52 universities in Jinan, including Shandong University, with 694,000 full-time college students. There was 1 new national enterprise technology center, contributing to a total of 30, and 16 new provincial enterprise technology centers, constituting a total of 221. A number of major innovation carriers such as Qilu Science and Technology Corridor, Jinan Science and Technology City of Chinese Academy of Sciences, and Jinan International Medical Science Center have been accelerated.

Strong Industry vitality. In 2021, the added value of the "new technologies, new industries, new forms of business and new models" economy reached 430.62 billion yuan, accounting for 37.7% of GDP. The added value of modern agriculture was 7.07 billion yuan, an increase of 18.8% over the previous year, accounting for 16.5% of the added value of agriculture, forestry, animal husbandry and fishery. The output value of high-tech industries increased by 7.6%, accounting for 54.7% of the total output value of industrial enterprises above designated size. The modern service industry realized an added value of 420.27 billion yuan, an increase of 8.5%, accounting for 59.5% of the added value of the service industry.

Enhanced wellbeing of the people. The per capita disposable income of residents in 2021 was 46,725 yuan, an increase of 8.5% over the previous year. Among them, the per capita disposable income of urban households was 57,449 yuan, an increase of 7.7%; the per capita disposable income of rural households was 22,580 yuan, up by 10.5%. At the end of 2021, there were 7,530 health institutions, up by 16 over the previous year. The minimum living guarantee standard of urban residents was 904 yuan per month; that for rural residents was 676 yuan per month.

2021 年济南市 国民经济和社会发展统计公报[1]

济　南　市　统　计　局
国家统计局济南调查队

2021 年，在市委、市政府坚强领导下，全市各级各部门坚持以习近平新时代中国特色社会主义思想为指导，全面贯彻落实党的十九大和十九届历次全会精神，深入落实习近平总书记对山东、对济南工作的重要指示要求，锚定“走在前列、全面开创”“三个走在前”总遵循、总定位、总航标，抢抓黄河流域生态保护和高质量发展重大国家战略机遇，完整、准确、全面贯彻新发展理念，主动服务和融入新发展格局，加快落实“强省会”战略，统筹疫情防控和经济社会发展，全力推进“六稳”“六保”政策落地见效，经济社会稳定健康发展，主要指标处于合理区间，呈现稳中向好、量质齐升态势，高质量发展迈出坚实步伐，实现“十四五”良好开局。

一、综合

初步核算，全年全市生产总值[2]11432.2 亿元，比上年增长 7.2%，两年平均增长[3]6.0%。其中，第一产业增加值 408.8 亿元，增长 7.1%，两年平均增长 4.6%；第二产业增加值 3964.1 亿元，增长 3.6%，两年平均增长 5.3%；第三产业增加值 7059.4 亿元，增长 9.2%，两年平均增长 6.4%。三次产业构成比为 3.6 ∶ 34.7 ∶ 61.7。

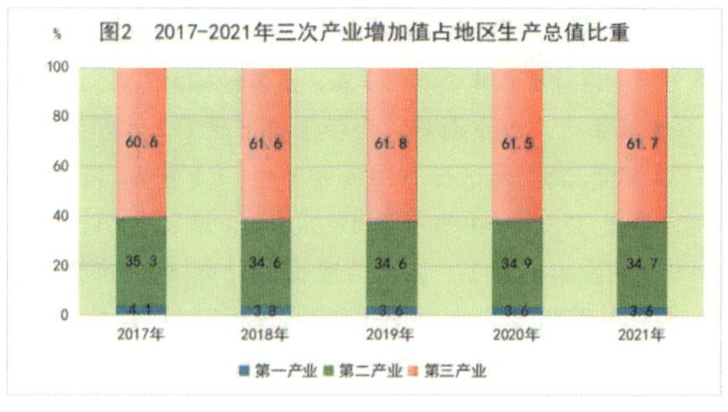

年末常住人口 933.6 万人，比上年末增长 1.0%。其中，城镇常住人口 692.8 万人，占总人口比重（常住人口城镇化率）为 74.2%，比上年末提高 0.75 个百分点。户籍人口 816.6 万人，增长 1.2%。全年申报出生率为 8.2‰，申报死亡率为 5.5‰，人口自然增长率为 2.8‰。

全年新增城镇就业 17.8 万人，比上年增长 9.2%，超额完成全年 14 万人的目标任务。

全年居民消费价格指数（CPI）上涨 1.5%，比上年缩小 0.9 个百分点，保供稳价成效显著。新建商品住宅销售价格同比指数整体趋势微涨后逐步回稳，环比指数涨幅基本保持稳定。

表 1　2021 年居民消费价格比上年涨跌幅度

指标	比上年增长（%）
居民消费价格指数	1.5
食品烟酒	1.5
衣着	1.5
居住	1.9
生活用品及服务	-1.2
交通和通信	4.7
教育文化和娱乐	-0.3
医疗保健	0.7
其他用品和服务	-0.1

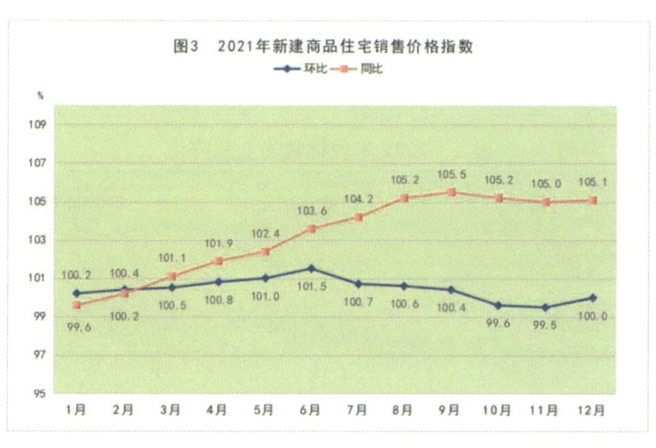

黄河重大国家战略落地见效。新旧动能转换起步区加速崛起，中科新经济科创园38栋建筑主体封顶，济南先进动力研究所投入运营并完成20兆瓦燃气轮机点火试验，填补国内技术空白。新能源乘用车及零部件产业园项目落地智能制造产业园，光大照明智慧产业园建成投产。黄河体育中心、山大二院北院区、省实验中学鹊华校区顺利推进。“万里黄河第一隧”——济南黄河济泺路隧道提前建成通车，凤凰大桥正式通车。

动能转换提档加速。“四新”经济成为增长重要引擎，“四新”经济增加值达到4306.2亿元，占GDP比重为37.7%，比上年提高1.6个百分点。“四新”经济领域投资不断提速，其中，科学研究和技术服务业投资增长2倍以上，卫生和社会工作投资增长1倍以上。“智造济南”赋能工业升级，规模以上工业高技术制造业增加值增长17.2%，高于规模以上工业11.3个百分点，对增长的贡献率为49.9%。规模以上工业高端装备制造业增加值增长13.5%，重点产品工业机器人、光缆产量分别增长25.6%、68.7%。“济南造”首列地铁列车下线，8英寸高功率半导体顺利通线。服务业新经济蓬勃发展，规模以上高技术服务业实现营业收入1077.8亿元，增长21.8%，高于规模以上服务业1.9个百分点。现代服务业[4]实现增加值4202.7亿元，增长8.5%，占服务业增加值比重为59.5%。

“六稳”“六保”扎实推进。坚持在发展中保障和改善民生，22件民生实事圆满完成，发放稳岗补贴1.4亿元。改造老旧小区624万平方米、惠及居民6.75万户。财政金融支撑有力，一般公共预算收入突破千亿元大关，民生支出占比达到79.8%，获批建设全国首个科创金融改革试验区。对外开放门户作用增强，全年开行中欧班列764列次，增长41.0%。新开通国际（地区）航线4条，济南机场国际（地区）货邮吞吐量6.0万吨，增长45.4%。市场主体活力进一步提升，总量达到145.5万户，“四上”企业[5]数量达到12001家。成功举办首届国际粮食减损大会，发出了“济南倡议”，坚决守牢粮食安全底线，农业生产形势稳定。重点行业产业链供应链运行顺畅，规模以上工业企业[6]流动资产合计增长9.3%，总资产周转比上年加快3.7天，产成品存货下降11.4%，产成品存货周转比上年加快2.7天。

二、农业、农村

农业稳步增长。全年农林牧渔业总产值758.4亿元，比上年增长8.4%。其中，农业总产值502.0亿元，增长4.0%；畜牧业总产值171.0亿元，增长23.4%。农林牧渔业增加值427.9亿元，增长7.1%。

表2　2021年农林牧渔业总产值

指标	产值（亿元）	比上年增长(%)
农林牧渔业总产值	758.4	8.4
农业	502.0	4.0
林业	34.4	16.1
畜牧业	171.0	23.4
渔业	8.2	39.0
农林牧渔服务业	42.8	7.8

粮食生产喜获丰收。粮食播种面积、单产、总产实现“三增”，全年粮食播种面积725.4万亩，比上年增加4.8万亩，增长0.7%；粮食平均单产404.0公斤/亩，增加0.5公斤/亩，增长0.1%；粮食总产量58.6亿斤，增加0.5亿斤，增长0.8%。

“菜篮子”供保能力稳中有升。全年新建“菜篮子”保供园区29个，直通车达到287辆，完成新改扩建生猪养殖场项目32个。蔬菜总产量691.8万吨，比上年增长2.7%；油料总产量6.6万吨，下降3.2%；水果总产量61.9万吨，下降2.1%。

表3　2021年主要农产品种植面积和产量

指标	单位	面积/产量	比上年增长(%)
粮食总播种面积	万亩	725.4	0.7
棉花种植面积	万亩	4.9	-8.0
油料种植面积	万亩	26.3	-3.2
蔬菜种植面积	万亩	146.0	-1.3
实有果园面积	万亩	57.5	-2.9
粮食总产量	万吨	293.1	0.8
棉花产量	万吨	0.4	-9.8
油料产量	万吨	6.6	-3.2
蔬菜产量	万吨	691.8	2.7
水果产量	万吨	61.9	-2.1

林业平稳发展。全年完成造林面积0.6万公顷，森林抚育面积0.3万公顷，建设生态廊道91公里、绿道170公里，绿化黄河堤防淤背区4466亩。创建市级绿化示范村100个，创建全国森林康养基地试点建设单位3家，省乡村林场3家。

畜牧业生产稳中向好。全年生猪出栏192.0万头，肉产量15.4万吨，比上年增长20.4%；牛出栏13.8万头，肉产量2.9万吨，增长37.1%；牛奶产量42.1万吨，增长1.6%；羊出栏126.8万头，肉产量1.9万吨，增长20.5%；禽肉产量7.2万吨，禽蛋产量30.5万吨，增长11.0%。水产品产量1.4万吨，增长5.8%。

特色农产品品牌知名度提升。省级以上农业知名品牌达到50个，全市农产品区域公用品牌“泉水人家”授权产品达到

230个，新认证“三品一标”农产品165个。长清茶叶、章丘大葱、莱芜生姜、仁风西瓜、曲堤黄瓜、历城草莓等特色农产品不断发展向好。全年全市茶叶产量59.0万公斤，大葱74.0万吨，生姜31.5万吨，西瓜29.5万吨，黄瓜115.6万吨，草莓8.3万吨。

现代高效农业发展较快。全年现代高效农业增加值70.7亿元，比上年增长18.8%，增速比上年提高0.3个百分点，现代高效农业增加值占农林牧渔业增加值比重为16.5%，提高1.6个百分点。

全面推进乡村振兴初见成效。产业发展深度融合，新建市级田园综合体5个，总数达到11个，新认定市级以上示范性新型农业经营主体203家，市级以上农业龙头企业发展到492家，10家企业入选国家级农业产业化重点龙头企业。家庭农场发展到7258个，农民专业合作社11780家。致力打造“中国北方种业之都”，全国种子“双交会”永久落户济南。建成省市两级种质资源库，入库种质资源5万余份，全市持证农作物良种企业数量达到75家，比上年增加6家，工厂化蔬菜年育苗量突破10亿株。持续巩固脱贫攻坚成果，做好困难群众帮扶工作，投入衔接补助资金6.3亿元。全面强化兜底保障，18万余名困难群众纳入救助保障范围。

三、工业和建筑业

工业生产运行平稳。全年全部工业增加值2746.0亿元，比上年增长5.7%。规模以上工业增加值增长5.9%，分经济类型看，公有制经济下降0.2%，非公有制经济增长9.8%；分轻重工业看，轻工业增长15.7%，重工业增长3.2%。41个大类行业中，31个行业实现增加值同比增长，增长面为75.6%，比上年提高19.5个百分点。增加值占比超过1%的17个大类行业中，13个行业保持增长，12个行业增速领先全市平均水平，9个行业增速高于10.0%。高新技术产业产值增长7.6%，占规模以上工业产值的比重为54.7%。

企业经营状况稳定。全年规模以上工业企业完成营业收入8335.8亿元，比上年增长10.0%；利润总额382.7亿元，下降7.6%；营业收入利润率为4.6%。41个大类行业中，营业收入超百亿的行业达到15个，合计占规模以上工业企业营业收入比重为91.5%。黑色金属冶炼和压延加工业、汽车制造业营业收入超过千亿规模。

表4　2021年规模以上工业重点行业营业收入

行业名称	比上年增长（%）
黑色金属冶炼和压延加工业	15.1
汽车制造业	-13.3
计算机、通信和其他电子设备制造业	14.8
非金属矿物制品业	13.8
电气机械和器材制造业	6.1
通用设备制造业	15.9
石油、煤炭及其他燃料加工业	14.1
金属制品业	13.1
化学原料和化学制品制造业	21.6
医药制造业	24.3
专用设备制造业	19.0
电力、热力生产和供应业	11.2
食品制造业	20.3

工业产品供应充足。全年规模以上工业产品产销率为97.4%。所生产的296种工业产品中，有181种产品产量实现增长，增长面为61.1%。其中，增幅超过20%的产品有82种，占比为27.7%，比上年提高1.7个百分点。光纤、集成电路、液晶显示屏实现1倍以上增长，数控金属切削机床、光缆、充电桩产量实现50%以上增长。

表5　2021年规模以上工业企业主要产品产量

产品名称	单位	产量	比上年增长（%）
服务器	万台	113.7	-20.8
载货汽车	万辆	31.9	-18.9
发动机	万千瓦	4085.1	-33.8
钢材	万吨	2105.7	-12.1
水泥	万吨	1530.3	13.3
石墨及碳素制品	万吨	186.6	7.5
数控金属切削机床	台	5531	72.1
工业机器人	套	2604	25.6
鲜、冷藏肉	万吨	11.6	-22.9
乳制品	万吨	53.7	9.7
饮料酒	万千升	25.7	-1.7
合成氨（无水氨）	万吨	45.0	-25.0
聚丙烯树脂	万吨	10.5	-9.4
初级形态塑料	万吨	33.5	-19.6
中成药	吨	7299.2	20.9

产品名称	单位	产量	比上年增长（%）
锻件	万吨	118.0	4.5
粉末冶金零件	万吨	1.3	2.2
变压器	万千伏安	15298.6	12.2
气动元件	万件	939.1	-36.7
矿山专用设备	万吨	8.2	28.1
铁路货车	辆	3119.0	-8.7
太阳能热水器	万平方米	166.0	13.4

建筑业平稳发展。全市具有总承包和专业承包资质的有工作量建筑业企业1182家，比上年增加149家。全年签订合同额11321.5亿元，增长34.9%。其中，本年新签合同额6388.5亿元，增长40.9%。实现建筑业总产值4126.0亿元，增长10.1%。其中，国有及国有控股企业产值3103.6亿元，增长9.2%。房屋施工面积19410.0万平方米，增长13.6%。

四、服务业

服务业支撑作用持续显现。全年服务业实现增加值7059.4亿元，比上年增长9.2%，占全市生产总值（GDP）比重为61.7%，对经济增长贡献率为79.1%。规模以上服务业[7]营业收入增长19.9%。新兴行业增长较快，互联网和相关服务、科技推广和应用服务业分别增长59.4%、57.2%。物流运力不断提升，重点物流企业实现营业收入807.6亿元，增长22.9%。其中，多式联运和运输代理业、装卸搬运和仓储业分别增长29.6%、29.2%。

交通运输综合承载能力提升。年末公路通车里程数18200.1公里，比上年增长0.5%。其中，高速公路里程数737.8公里，与上年持平。公路货运量2.5亿吨，增长8.8%；货运周转量577.4亿吨公里，增长11.8%[8]。年末拥有民用机动车344.7万辆，增长9.8%。其中，民用汽车302.5万辆，增长8.3%。公交线路763条，比上年增加113条，线路总长度15852.3公里，增加2647.6公里，旅客运输量5.9亿人次，增加0.6亿人次。全年累计完成航班起降11.3万架次，增长10.1%；旅客吞吐量1361.6万人次，增长9.9%；货邮吞吐量16.8万吨，增长14.7%。

邮政业、电信业健康发展。邮政行业全年业务收入（不包括邮政储蓄银行直接营业收入）99.2亿元，比上年增长16.6%；业务总量[9]89.3亿元，增长30.1%。快递服务企业业务收入77.5亿元，增长16.1%；业务量8.0亿件，增长22.0%。年末移动电话用户1216.3万户，增长5.4%。其中，5G移动电话用户463.7万户，增长1.7倍。宽带互联网接入用户463.0万户，增长10.0%。

旅游业、会展业发展向好。全年接待游客8192.7万人次，比上年增长35.0%。实现旅游总收入983.9亿元，增长40.0%。A级旅游景区86家，其中，5A级旅游景区1家，4A级旅游景区17家。省级旅游度假区2家。全年举办会展120场，增长12.1%，展览面积260万平方米，增长44.0%。

五、固定资产投资

固定资产投资总体平稳。全年固定资产投资比上年增长11.5%。其中，第一产业投资下降1.5%，第二产业投资下降4.2%，第三产业投资增长14.7%。高技术服务业投资增长35.0%，民间投资增长24.9%，基础设施投资下降5.2%。年末亿元以上固定资产投资项目1535个，比上年增加192个，完成投资增长11.6%。其中，50亿元以上项目44个，增加8个，完成投资增长15.0%。

表6　2021年三次产业投资增速及占比

产业	比上年增长(%)	占固定资产投资比重（%）
固定资产投资	11.5	100
第一产业	-1.5	0.4
第二产业	-4.2	14.0
第三产业	14.7	85.6

房地产投资持续增长。全年房地产开发完成投资1928.0亿元，比上年增长12.9%。其中，住宅完成投资1351.4亿元，增长12.2%。房屋施工面积10156.5万平方米，下降1.9%。其中，住宅施工面积6577.4万平方米，下降1.8%。房屋竣工面积1115.7万平方米，下降12.4%。其中，住宅竣工面积787.6万平方米，下降13.8%。商品房销售面积1548.2万平方米，增长15.9%。其中，住宅销售面积1300.2万平方米，增长13.5%。商品房销售额1957.0亿元，增长24.5%。其中，住宅销售额1721.7亿元，增长22.4%。

六、国内贸易

消费品市场平稳复苏。全年社会消费品零售总额5126.1亿元，比上年增长14.7%。其中，商品零售4390.1亿元，增长13.8%；餐饮收入736.0亿元，增长20.5%。分城乡看，城镇社会消费品零售额4609.3亿元，增长14.9%；乡村社会消费品零售额516.8亿元，增长13.4%。限额以上单位[10]实现零售额1809.9亿元，增长14.5%。

升级类商品增势较好。限额以上单位商品零售额中，化妆品类、金银珠宝类和新能源汽车分别比上年增长22.6%、57.1%和147.1%；可穿戴智能设备、智能家用电器和音像器材、智能手机分别增长18.3%、17.9%和34.7%。

基本生活类消费保持稳定。限额以上单位商品零售额中，粮油食品类商品全年实现零售额160.6亿元，比上年增长4.2%；服装鞋帽针纺织品类商品实现零售额118.6亿元，增长29.6%；

日用品类商品实现零售额 53.3 亿元，增长 33.1%。

线上消费快速拓展。限额以上单位通过公共网络实现的商品零售额 271.0 亿元，比上年增长 57.9%，占限额以上单位商品零售额比重为 15.0%，比上年提高 5.9 个百分点。

表 7　2021 年限额以上单位主要商品零售额

商品类别	零售额（亿元）	比上年增长 (%)
粮油、食品类	160.6	4.2
服装、鞋帽、针纺织品类	118.6	29.6
日用品类	53.3	33.1
文化办公用品类	50.0	-3.7
烟酒类	41.1	19.3
家用电器和音像器材类	130.8	39.2
通讯器材类	85.0	17.1
金银珠宝类	50.2	57.1
化妆品类	44.7	22.6
书报杂志类	92.7	9.7
中西药品类	62.6	3.5
汽车类	584.1	14.9
石油及制品类	189.6	2.6

七、开放型经济

进出口快速增长。全年货物进出口总额 1944.2 亿元，比上年增长 40.1%。其中，出口 1174.1 亿元，增长 55.6%；进口 770.1 亿元，增长 21.5%。对东盟进出口增长 31.3%，对欧盟（不含英国）进出口增长 9.0%，对拉丁美洲进出口增长 56.2%，对非洲进出口增长 44.7%。对“一带一路”沿线国家进出口增长 37.7%，占进出口总额的 34.1%。出口商品中，机电产品出口 661.8 亿元，增长 60.8%；钢材出口 77.4 亿元，增长 72.1%；集成电路出口 12.5 亿元，增长 47.6%。全年经济外向度 17.0%，比上年提高 3.4 个百分点。

利用外资规模提升。全年实际使用外资 26.6 亿美元，比上年增长 38.1%。其中，制造业使用外资 2.7 亿美元，增长 73.9%；第三产业使用外资 20.9 亿美元，增长 42.9%。全年实现合同外资 96.9 亿美元，增长 65.5%。新批外商投资项目 330 个，总投资过亿美元的项目 46 个，总投资过亿美元项目合同外资 61.3 亿美元。

对外合作积极拓展。全年对外承包工程新签合同额 66.1 亿美元，比上年增长 50.1%；完成营业额 41.0 亿美元，下降 4.0%。备案设立境外企业（机构）60 家，实际完成投资 17.4 亿美元，下降 8.9%。派出各类劳务人员 8608 人，下降 28.1%。

八、财政和金融

全财政收支执行情况总体良好。全年一般公共预算收入 1007.6 亿元，比上年增长 11.2%。其中，税收收入 776.5 亿元，增长 11.5%，占一般公共预算收入比重为 77.1%，比上年提高 0.2 个百分点。一般公共预算支出 1292.7 亿元，增长 8.4%。其中，社会保障和就业支出 203.8 亿元，增长 19.4%；卫生健康支出 111.7 亿元，增长 21.0%；城乡社区支出 293.4 亿元，增长 9.7%。

存、贷款保持较快增长。年末金融机构本外币各项存款余额 23437.0 亿元，比上年增长 11.3%；金融机构本外币各项贷款余额 23313.2 亿元，增长 12.5%。

金融市场活跃度提升。年末上市公司数量达到 52 家，股票 54 只，全年新增上市及过会企业 10 家。完成证券交易额 5.6 万亿元，比上年增长 17.0%；期货交易额 18.5 万亿元，增长 68.7%；新增直接融资 3716.0 亿元，增长 63.7%。在中国证券投资基金业协会登记的私募基金管理机构 205 家，管理基金 585 只，管理基金规模 1065.4 亿元，增长 7.3%。

保费收入稳步回升。全年保险业实现保费收入 598.5 亿元，比上年增长 2.3%。其中，财产险公司保费收入 131.8 亿元，下降 11.5%；人身险公司保费收入 466.7 亿元，增长 7.1%。各项赔款与给付 212.5 亿元，增长 37.3%。

信贷资产质量不断提升。年末金融机构不良贷款余额 197.1 亿元，比年初减少 38.2 亿元。不良贷款率为 0.85%，比年初下降 0.3 个百分点。

九、科技、教育、文化、卫生和体育事业

创新驱动力不断增强。全年研究与试验发展（R&D）经费投入[11] 265.5 亿元，比上年增长 17.7%。其中，基础研究 18.5 亿元，增长 6.4%；应用研究 41.4 亿元，增长 36.1%；试验发展 205.6 亿元，增长 15.7%。R&D 经费投入占 GDP 比重为 2.6%，比上年提高 0.2 个百分点。新认定国家级企业技术中心 1 家，总数达到 30 家，新认定省级企业技术中心 16 家，总数达到 221 家。

科技发明成果丰硕。全年万人有效发明专利拥有量 38.36 件，比上年增长 15.6%。发明专利授权量 8208 件，增长 40.7%。技术合同实现交易额 473.5 亿元，增长 40.2%。获得省级科技进步一等奖 16 项，二等奖 50 项。获得省级自然科学一等奖 1 项，二等奖 17 项。全市国家知识产权示范企业、优势企业共计 80 家。

教育事业高质量发展。全年开工新建、改扩建中小学校（幼儿园）97 所，新投入使用中小学校、幼儿园 101 所，普惠性幼儿园覆盖率为 88.5%，义务教育阶段集团化建设率为 85.2%。立项市校融合发展战略工程项目 95 个，签约引进高等教育项目 15 个。

表 8　2021 年教育事业基本情况

学校类别	学校数量（所）	全日制在校生（万人）	专任教师（人）
驻济高等学校	52	69.4	41894

学校类别	学校数量（所）	全日制在校生（万人）	专任教师（人）
中等职业学校（不含技工学校）	41	6.4	4040
技工学校	31	8.5	4471
普通中学	332	40.7	35587
小学	641	61.0	38467
特殊教育学校	13	0.1	505

文化生活更加丰富。年末有国有艺术表演团体14个，文化馆（站）174个，公共博物馆13个，公共图书馆14个。市级以上文物保护单位435处，其中，国家级30处。城市可统计票房数字影院65家，观众996.5万人次，票房收入4.1亿元。广播人口混合覆盖率为100%，电视人口混合覆盖率为99.7%。建成泉城书房38处，基层综合性文化服务中心覆盖率为100%。

卫生服务水平不断提升。年末拥有卫生机构7530个，比上年增加16个，其中，医院、卫生院338个。卫生机构床位7.3万张，增长5.7%。各类卫生技术人员10.8万人，增长5.8%；执业（助理）医师4.2万人，增长5.3%。稳妥有序推进新冠病毒疫苗接种，全年累计接种2042.3万剂次，覆盖878.3万人。

全民健身稳步推进。全年新成立体育社会组织9个，培训社会体育指导员2544人。组织各类全民健身活动（赛事）536次，参与人数300万人次（含线上活动）。获省级及以上金牌341枚，银牌190枚，铜牌253枚。

十、能源、环境、城市建设[12]和安全生产

能源转型和绿色低碳发展初见成效。清洁能源消费占比逐步提高，全年规模以上工业煤炭消费2799.9万吨，比上年增长1.1%，天然气消费9.2亿立方米，增长14.7%。新能源发电占比稳步提升，发电结构深度调整，风力发电、垃圾发电、生物质发电均有显著提高，火力发电量占发电总量比重比上年下降2.7个百分点。规模以上企业风力发电21.9亿千瓦时，占发电总量比重为7.0%，增长86.2%；垃圾发电9.5亿千瓦时，占发电总量比重为3.0%，增长37.7%；生物质发电5.1亿千瓦时，占发电总量比重为1.6%，增长86.2%。

表9　2021年规模以上企业能源生产情况

指标	单位	生产量	比上年增长（%）
原煤	万吨	72.9	-7.5
发电量	亿千瓦时	315.1	11.7
火力发电量	亿千瓦时	290.8	8.5
风力发电量	亿千瓦时	21.9	86.2
太阳能发电量	亿千瓦时	2.4	1.2

表10　2021年规模以上工业能源消费情况

指标	单位	消费量	比上年增长（%）
煤炭	万吨	2799.9	1.1
天然气	亿立方米	9.2	14.7
焦炭	万吨	897.1	-12.6
汽油	万吨	0.4	-7.5
柴油	万吨	3.9	1.5

全社会用电稳步增长。全年全社会用电475.3亿千瓦时，增长9.5%。其中，居民生活用电86.5亿千瓦时，增长8.6%。分产业看，第一产业用电3.3亿千瓦时，增长2.7%；第二产业用电267.0亿千瓦时，增长7.4%；第三产业用电118.4亿千瓦时，增长15.7%。工业用电256.6亿千瓦时，占全社会用电量比重为54.0%，增长7.1%。

表11　2021年全市用电情况

指标	累计用电（亿千瓦时）	比上年增长（%）
全社会用电	475.3	9.5
城乡居民生活用电	86.5	8.6
第一产业	3.3	2.7
第二产业	267.0	7.4
第三产业	118.4	15.7

生态环境质量进一步改善。全市空气质量综合指数为4.7，首次降至5以下，市区空气质量良好以上天数达到229天，优良天数占比为62.7%，成功退出全国重点城市空气质量排名后20名。全年城区环境空气中可吸入颗粒物（PM_{10}）年均浓度78微克/立方米，细颗粒物（$PM_{2.5}$）40微克/立方米，二氧化硫11微克/立方米，二氧化氮33微克/立方米[13]。小清河出境断面辛丰庄化学需氧量浓度14.6毫克/升，氨氮浓度0.78毫克/升，达到地表水Ⅲ类水质标准，为历史最好水平。区域环境噪声昼间平均等效声级54.9分贝，市区道路交通噪声昼间平均等效声级68.7分贝。

城市建设水平进一步提升。年末城市建成区面积841.2平方公里，比上年增加1.4平方公里。建成区绿化覆盖率为41.7%，人均公园绿地面积12.8平方米。全年天然气供气量

18.0亿立方米，增长11.7%；液化石油气供气量2.5万吨，下降34.4%。集中供热面积3.0亿平方米，增长9.8%。自来水供水量5.0亿吨，增长10.0%。完成市民泉水直饮工程建设20处，实现年供水量3.7万吨，累计服务用户3.5万户，供水人口10余万人。生活垃圾无害化处理率为100%。

社会治安持续稳定。全年共破获刑事案件17316起，命案现案破案率保持100%，连续11年实现命案全破，八类严重暴力案件破现案率达99.6%；抓获各类逃犯1442名，增长25.0%，追逃总成绩列全省第一。

安全生产形势平稳。全年共发生各类生产安全事故264起、死亡161人，分别比上年下降30.3%、41.7%，事故起数、死亡人数"双下降"，安全生产形势总体稳定。

十一、居民生活和社会保障

居民收入稳定增长。全年居民人均可支配收入46725元，比上年增长8.5%。其中，城镇居民人均可支配收入57449元，增长7.7%；农村居民人均可支配收入22580元，增长10.5%。居民人均消费支出30016元，增长8.4%。其中，城镇居民人均消费支出36866元，增长7.2%；农村居民人均消费支出14591元，增长12.7%。城乡居民收入比由上年的2.6：1缩小至2.5：1。城镇居民恩格尔系数为[14]23.5%，农村居民恩格尔系数为30.5%。

表12　2021年居民人均可支配收入

指标	全市居民		城镇居民		农村居民	
	绝对量（元）	比上年增长（%）	绝对量（元）	比上年增长（%）	绝对量（元）	比上年增长（%）
可支配收入	46725	8.5	57449	7.7	22580	10.5
工资性收入	27050	8.8	33546	8.0	12423	10.9
经营净收入	4728	9.2	3146	9.4	8291	10.1
财产净收入	6887	7.7	9732	7.0	482	8.9
转移净收入	8060	8.0	11025	7.2	1383	9.8

表13　2021年末每百户居民家庭主要耐用消费品拥有量[15]

指标	单位	城镇居民	农村居民
家用汽车	辆	62.1	40.6
电冰箱（柜）	台	100.9	96.2
洗衣机	台	98.1	91.5
热水器	台	99.5	89.3
空调	台	172.6	93.5
彩色电视机	台	104.8	104.3
照相机	台	23.5	4.1
计算机	台	80.2	41.7
移动电话	部	227.6	230.3

社会保障范围更加广泛。年末城镇职工基本养老保险参保人数472.7万人，比上年增加35.4万人；职工医疗保险参保人数336.2万人，增加22.7万人；失业保险参保人数226.9万人，增加13.3万人；工伤保险参保人数293.5万人，增加14.9万人；生育保险参保人数235.8万人，增加22.6万人。居民养老保险和医疗保险参保人数分别达到308.4万人和506.9万人。

居民生活保障稳步提升。城市居民最低生活保障标准每月904元，保障城镇居民0.9万户、1.3万人，发放保障金及各类补贴1.3亿元；农村居民最低生活保障标准每月676元（其中，市中区、槐荫区、天桥区、历城区、济南高新区为904元），保障农村居民5.9万户、8.4万人，发放保障金及各类补贴5.7亿元。城市特困人员基本生活标准每月1356元，农村特困人员基本生活标准每月1179元（其中，市中区、槐荫区、天桥区、济南高新区为1356元），城市特困保障745人，农村特困保障1.4万人，共发放特困供养救助金及补贴2.9亿元。照料护理标准按照自理、半自理和完全不能自理分三种档次，自理标准提高到231元/月，半自理标准提高到385元/月，完全不能自理标准提高到770元/月。

救助帮扶工作趋步向稳。全市共有救助管理站2处，未成年人救助保护中心1处。培训残疾人4116人次，安置残疾人员就业2102人，帮扶救助残疾人投入资金2.8亿元。

注释：

[1]2021年统计数据为统计快报数或初步核算数，正式数据以出版的《济南统计年鉴2022》为准。部分数据因四舍五入影响，存在总计与分项合计不等情况。

[2]全市地区生产总值、各产业增加值绝对数按现价计算，增长速度按不变价格计算，当年数据为初步核算数。根据第四次全国经济普查结果，对国内生产总值、各产业增加值等相关指标的历史数据进行了修订。

[3]两年平均增速是指以2019年同期数为基数，采用几何平均的方法计算的增速。

[4]现代服务业包括：信息传输、软件和信息技术服务业，金融业，房地产业，租赁和商务服务业，科学研究和技术服务业，水利、环境和公共设施管理业，居民服务、修理和其他服务业，教育，卫生和社会工作，文化、体育和娱乐业。

[5]"四上"企业指规模以上工业、有资质的建筑业、限额以上批发和零售业、限额以上住宿和餐饮业、房地产开发经营业、规

模以上服务业。

[6] 规模以上工业企业指年主营业务收入2000万元及以上的工业法人单位。

[7] 规模以上服务业包括：交通运输、仓储和邮政业，信息传输、软件和信息技术服务业，房地产业，租赁和商务服务业，科学研究和技术服务业，水利、环境和公共设施管理业，居民服务、修理和其他服务业，教育，卫生和社会工作，文化、体育和娱乐业。

[8] 2021年交通运输部采用新的公路货运统计方法，对2020年公路货运数据进行了修正，2021年增速根据2020年修正后数据得出。

[9] 邮政行业业务总量按2020年不变单价计算，同比增长按照可比口径计算。

[10] 限额以上单位是指年主营业务收入2000万元及以上的批发业单位、500万元及以上的零售业单位、200万元及以上的住宿和餐饮业单位。单位包括法人企业、产业活动单位和个体户。

[11] 研究与试验发展（R&D）经费投入相关指标错年使用2020年数据。

[12] 城市建设指标来源于住建部城市建设统计年报，为初步上报数，口径为包含两县的整个济南地区。

[13] 2021年生态环境相关数据以国家新调整的“十四五”国控站点统计。

[14] 恩格尔系数是指食品支出在消费支出中的比重。

[15] 数据来自住户收支与生活状况调查。

资料来源：本公报中企业技术中心数据来自发展改革部门；教育数据来自教育部门；科技数据来自科技部门；电信相关数据来自工业和信息化部门；户籍、社会治安、民用机动车数据来自公安部门；城乡最低生活保障、特困人员救助供养相关数据来自民政部门；财政数据来自财政部门；城镇新增就业、城镇职工保险参保数据来自人力资源和社会保障部门；环境保护相关数据来自生态环境部门；城市建设相关数据来自住房和城乡建设部门；交通运输数据来自交通运输部门；泉水直饮工程建设数据来自城乡水务部门；水产品产量、农业数据来自农业农村部门；林业数据来自园林和林业部门；进出口、展会、新设境外企业、外派劳务人员数据来自商务部门；旅游、文化数据来自文化和旅游部门；卫生数据来自卫生健康部门；安全生产数据来自应急管理部门；知识产权数据来自市场监管部门；体育数据来自体育部门；医疗保险类数据来自医疗保障部门；金融数据来自地方金融监督管理部门；招商引资、外资数据来自投资促进部门；市场主体数据来自行政审批服务部门；物流数据来自口岸物流部门；残疾人保障数据来自残联；邮政、快递数据来自邮政管理部门；居民收入与支出数据、恩格尔系数、价格指数、粮食畜牧数据、城乡家庭主要耐用消费品拥有量来自国家统计局济南调查队；济南新旧动能转换起步区数据来自济南起步区管委会；其他数据均来自市统计局。

STATISTICAL COMMUNIQUÉ OF THE JINAN MUNICIPAL ON THE 2021 NATIONAL ECONOMIC AND SOCIAL DEVELOPMENT [1]

Jinan Municipal Bureau of Statistics
NBS Survey Office in Jinan

In 2021, under the strong leadership of Jinan Municipal Party Committee and the Jinan Municipal People' s Government, Jinan City all levels and departments took Xi Jinping Thought on Socialism with Chinese Characteristics for a New Era as the guideline, fully implemented the spirits of the 19th CPC National Congress and the Plenary Sessions of the 19th Central Committee of the CPC. All levels and departments deeply implemented the principles of General Secretary Xi Jinping' s important speeches and instructions during his inspection tour to Shandong Province and Jinan City, anchored the general compliances, general positions and general navigation marks of "going ahead, new advances on all fronts" and "three items of going ahead" , followed and served the major national strategies of the ecological conservation and high-quality development of the Yellow River Basin, and fully and faithfully implemented the new development philosophy on all fronts. We actively served and integrated into the new development pattern, accelerated the implementation of the strategy of "strengthened provincial capital" , made overall plans for COVID-19 prevention and control and economic and social development, and fully promoted the implementation of the "stability on the six fronts and security in the six areas" . The effect was a stable and healthy economic and social development, with main indicators in a reasonable range, showing a steady and positive trend, both quantity and quality going up. Solid progress has been made in high-quality development, achieving a good starting with the 14th Five-Year Plan.

I. General

According to the preliminary calculations, the regional gross domestic product (GDP) of the whole city [2] in 2021 was 1,143.22 billion yuan, up by 7.2% over the previous year with the average two-year growth [3] of 6.0%. Of this total, the value added of the primary industry was 40.88 billion yuan, up by 7.1% with the average two-year growth of 4.6%; that of the secondary industry was 396.41 billion yuan, up by 3.6% with the average two-year growth of 5.3%; that of the tertiary industry was 705.94 billion yuan, up by 9.2% with the average two-year growth of 6.4%. The ratio of three industries is 3.6 : 34.7 : 61.7.

Figure 1 Gross Domestic Product Between 2017 to 2021

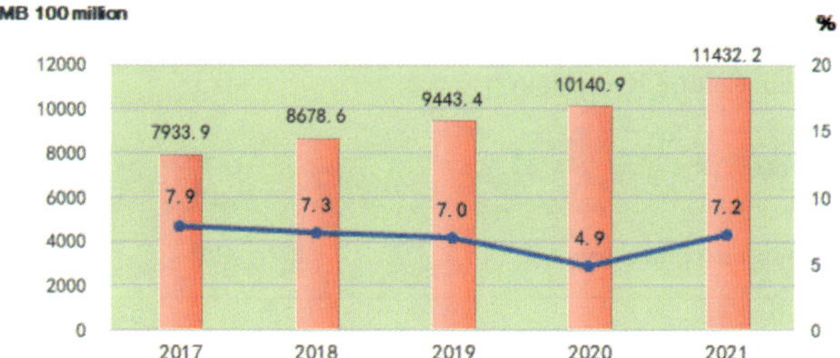

Figure 2 Ratio of Value Addition to the Gross Domestic Product of Primary, Secondary and Tertiary Industries 2017-2021

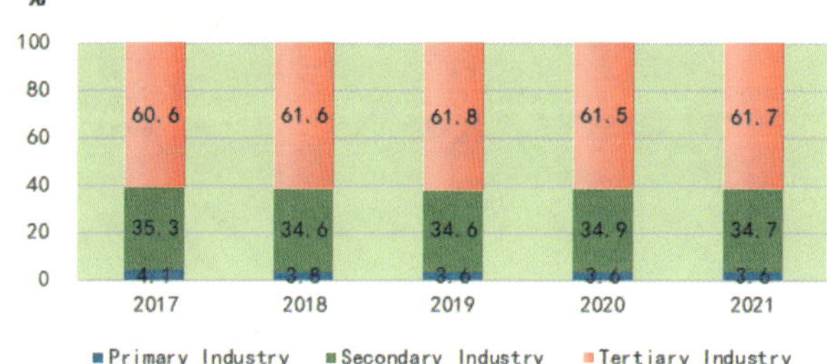

By the end of 2021, the number of permanent residents was 9.336 million, with an increase of 1.0% over the previous year. Of this total, urban permanent residents numbered 6.928 million, accounting for 74.2% of the total population (urbanization rate of permanent residents), up by 0.75 percentage points over that at the end of last year. The number of registered population was 8.166 million, with an increase of 1.2%. The declared birth rate in 2021 was 8.2‰ , the declared death rate was 5.5‰ and the natural population growth rate was 2.8‰ .

In 2021, employed urban people increased by 178,000, with an increase of 9.2% over the previous year, exceeding the target of 140,000 people in the whole year.

The annual consumer price index (CPI) went up by 1.5%, 0.9 percentage point lower than that of the previous year, and The supply guarantee and price stability effects were remarkable. A slight year-on-year index rise that then became stable was seen in the sales price of new commercial residential buildings. The month-on-month index rise remained basically stable.

Table 1 Year-on-Year Growth/Decrease Rate of Consumer Prices Index In 2021

Item	Year-on-year Growth Rate(%)
Consumer Price Index	1.5
Food,Tobacco and Liquor	1.5
Clothing	1.5
Residence	1.9
Daily Necessities and Services	-1.2
Transport Communication	4.7
Education Culture Recreation	-0.3
Health Care	0.7
Other Supplies and Services	-0.1

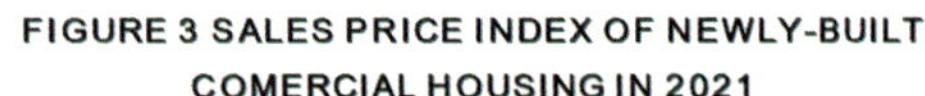
FIGURE 3 SALES PRICE INDEX OF NEWLY-BUILT COMERCIAL HOUSING IN 2021

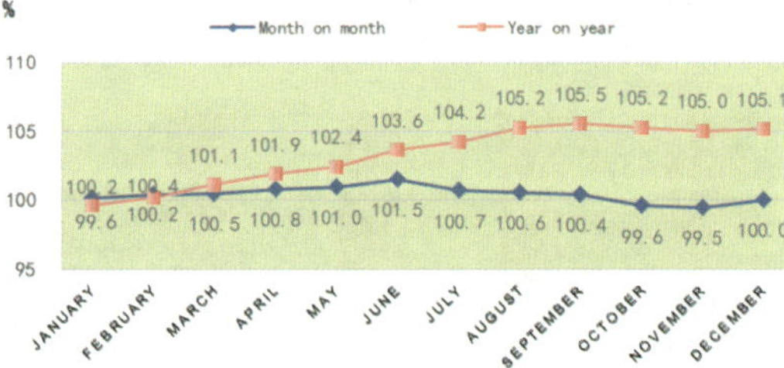

The important national strategy of the Yellow River has achieved significant effects. The construction of Jinan Start-up Area for Growth Driver Transformation will also be accelerated, 38 buildings in Zhongke New Economic Science and Technology Park were capped, and Jinan Advanced Power Research Institute was put into operation and completed the ignition test of 20 MW gas turbine, filling the domestic technical gap. The new energy vehicle and parts industrial park project was landed in the intelligent manufacturing industrial park, and Everbright Lighting Intelligent Industrial Park was completed and put into operation. The Yellow River Sports Center, North District of the Second Hospital of Shandong University and Quehua Branch of Shandong Experimental High School were progressed smoothly. "The First Tunnel of the Yellow River" - Jiluo Road Jinan Yellow River Tunnel was completed and opened to traffic ahead of schedule, and Fenghuang Bridge was officially opened to traffic.

Transformation from old growth drivers to new ones has been accelerated and upgraded. The "new technologies, new industries, new forms of business and new models (four news)" economy has become an important engine of growth, with the added value up to 430.62 billion yuan, accounting for 37.7% of GDP, with an increase of 1.6 percentage points over the previous year. Investment in the "four news" economy has been continuously accelerated, among which investment in scientific research and technical services has increased by more than 2 folds, and that in health and social work has increased by more than 1 fold. "Intellectual Jinan" enables industrial upgrading, with the added value of high-tech manufacturing industry above designated size up by 17.2%, which was 11.3 percentage points higher than that of industries above designated size, and its contribution rate to growth was 49.9%. The added value of high-end equipment manufacturing industry in industries above designated size increased by 13.5%, and the output of key products including industrial robots and optical cables increased by 25.6% and 68.7%, respectively. The first subway train "made in Jinan" rolled off the assembly line, and the 8-inch high-power semiconductor was successfully connected. The new economy in service industry has been booming, and the operating income of high-tech services above designated size reached 107.78 billion yuan, with an increase of 21.8%, which was 1.9 percentage points higher than that of services above designated size. The modern service industry [4] realized an added value of 420.27 billion yuan, with an increase of 8.5%, accounting for 59.5% of the added value of the service industry.

The "stability on the six fronts and security in the six areas" have been steadily promoted. By adhering to guarantees and improvements of people's livelihood in the course of development, 22 events related to people's livelihood have been successfully completed, and a subsidy of 140 million yuan has been paid to stabilize posts. A total of 6.24 million square meters of old residential areas have been renovated, benefiting 67,500 households. Under strong financial supports, general public budget revenue has exceeded 100 billion yuan, and expenditures for people's livelihood accounted for 79.8%. Jinan was approved to build the first science and technology financial reform pilot zone in China. Opening the door to the outside world has brought strengthened effects, Jinan tallies 764 China-Europe freight train trips the whole year, with an increase of 41.0%. Four new international (regional) routes were opened, cargo and mail throughput of Jinan Airport International (regional) reached 60,000 tons, with an increase of 45.4%. Market entities became more dynamic, with the total number up to 1.455 million, and the number of "four-top" enterprises [5] up to 12,001. Jinan successfully held the first international conference on grain losses, launched the "Jinan Initiative", firmly adhered to the bottom line of food security, and maintained the stable agricultural production situation. The industrial and supply chains of key industries were running smoothly. The total current assets of industrial enterprises above designated size [6] increased by 9.3%, the turnover of total assets was shortened by 3.7 days compared with that of the previous year, the inventory of finished products decreased by 11.4%, and the turnover of finished products inventory was shortened by 2.7 days compared with that of the previous year.

II. Agriculture and Rural Areasl

Agriculture was growing steadily. Gross output value of agriculture, forestry, animal husbandry and fishery in the whole year was 75.84 billion yuan, up by 8.4% over the previous year. Among them, gross output value of agriculture was 50.20 billion yuan, up by 4.0%; Gross output value of animal husbandry was 17.10 billion yuan, up by 23.4%. The Value-added of agriculture, forestry, animal husbandry and fishery was 42.79 billion yuan, up by 7.1%.

Table 2 Gross Output Value of Agriculture, Forestry, Animal Husbandry and Fishery In 2021

Item	Output value (100 million yuan)	Year-on-year Growth Rate(%)
Gross output value of agriculture,forestry, animal husbandry and fishery	758.4	8.4
Agriculture	502.0	4.0
Forestry	34.4	16.1
Animal husbandry	171.0	23.4
Fishery	8.2	39.0
Agriculture, forestry, animal husbandry and fishery services	42.8	7.8

A bumper harvest of grain production has been achieved. The sown area, unit yield and total output of grain have all increased. The sown area of grain in 2021 was 7.254 million mu, with an increase of 48,000 mu or 0.7% over the previous year. The average grain yield per unit area is 404.0 kg/mu, with an increase of 0.5 kg/mu or 0.1%; The total grain output was 5.86 billion Jin (a unit of weight), with an increase of 50 million Jin or 0.8%.

The ability of "vegetable basket" to guarantee supplies has increased steadily. In 2021, 29 "vegetable basket" guarantee parks were built with 287 direct vehicles, and renovated and expanded 32 new pig farm were completed. The total output of vegetables was 6.918 million tons, with an increase of 2.7% over the previous year; The total output of oil was 66,000 tons, down by 3.2%; The total output of fruits was 619,000 tons, down by 2.1%.

Table 3 Planting Area and Output of Main Agricultural Products In 2021

Item	Unit	Area/output	Year-on-year Growth Rate(%)
Total sown are of grain	10,000 mu	725.4	0.7
Cotton planting area	10,000 mu	4.9	-8.0
Oil planting area	10,000 mu	26.3	-3.2
Vegetable planting area	10,000 mu	146.0	-1.3
Actual orchard area	10,000 mu	57.5	-2.9
Total grain output	10,000 tons	293.1	0.8
Cotton yield	10,000 tons	0.4	-9.8
Oil yield	10,000 tons	6.6	-3.2
Vegetable yield	10,000 tons	691.8	2.7
Fruit yield	10,000 tons	61.9	-2.1

Forestry has been developed steadily. The afforestation area in 2021 was 6,000 hectares, the forest tending area was 3,000 hectares, 91 kilometers of ecological corridors and 170 kilometers of greenways were built, and 4,466 mu of silted back area of the Yellow River embankment was afforested. The number of municipal greening demonstration villages reached 100, with 3 pilot construction units of national forest rehabilitation bases and 3 provincial and rural forest farms.

Animal husbandry production has kept stable and improved. In 2021, 1.92 million pigs were slaughtered, and the meat output was 154,000 tons, up by 20.4% over the previous year. In addition, 138,000 cattle were slaughtered, and the meat output was 29,000 tons, up by 37.1%; The output of milk was 421,000 tons, up by 1.6%; Slaughtered sheep reached 1.268 million, and the meat output was 19,000 tons, up by 20.5%; The output of poultry was 72,000 tons, and that of poultry eggs was 305,000 tons, up by 11.0%. The output of aquatic products was 14,000 tons, up by 5.8%.

Brand awareness of characteristic agricultural products has gone up. There were 50 well-known agricultural brands at the provincial level or above, 230 authorized products of "QUAN SHUI REN JIA" brand, a regional public brand of agricultural products across the city, and 165 newly certified "SAN PIN YI BIAO" agricultural products. Changqing green tea, Zhangqiu green onion, Laiwu ginger, Renfeng watermelon, Qudi cucumber, Licheng strawberry and other characteristic agricultural products have been increasingly developed. The annual output of tea across the city in 2021 was 590,000 kilograms, with 740,000 tons of green onions, 315,000 tons of ginger, 295,000 tons of watermelon, 1.156 million tons of cucumbers and 83,000 tons of strawberries.

Modern and efficient agriculture has quickly grown. The added value of modern and efficient agriculture in 2021 was 7.07 billion yuan, up by 18.8%, at a growth rate 0.3 percentage points higher than that of the previous year. The added value of modern and efficient agriculture accounted for 16.5% of the added value of agriculture, forestry, animal husbandry and fishery, up by 1.6 percentage points.

Initial effects have been seen in promoting rural revitalization in

an all-round way. Industrial development was deeply integrated, 5 newly-built municipal pastoral complexes contributed to the total number of 11, with 203 new demonstration agricultural business entities above the city level and 492 leading agricultural enterprises above the city level, including 10 enterprises listed as national key leading agricultural industrialization enterprises. There were 7,258 family farms and 11,780 farmer professional cooperatives. Jinan is working to build "the seed industry capital of northern China" to make the National Seed Information Exchange Commodity Trading Fair permanently settled in Jinan. The provincial and municipal germplasm resource banks have been built, and more than 50,000 germplasm resources have been incorporated. There were 75 certified crop seed enterprises across the city, increased by 6 over the previous year, and the annual seedling production of factory vegetables has exceeded 1 billion. Our city will continue to consolidate the achievements in poverty alleviation, keep improved in helping the people in need, and invest 630 million yuan in bridging subsidy funds. Minimum guarantee was strengthened in all aspects, and more than 180,000 people in hardship were included in the scope of relief and assistance.

III. Industry and Construction Industry

Industrial production has been in a smooth operation. The total industrial value added in 2021 was 274.60 billion yuan, up by 5.7% over the previous year. The added value of industrial scale above designated size increased by 5.9%. According to the category of economy, the public-owned economy decreased by 0.2% and the non-public economy increased by 9.8%. In terms of light and heavy industries, light industry increased by 15.7% and heavy industry by 3.2%. Among 41 major industries, 31 industries achieved a year-on-year increase in added values, with a growth rate of 75.6%, up by 19.5 percentage points over the previous year. Among 17 major industries whose the proportion of added value exceeded 1%, 13 industries kept growing, 12 industries were ahead of the municipal average, and 9 industries had a growth rate higher than 10.0%. The output value of high-tech industries increased by 7.6%, accounting for 54.7% of the output value of industrial scale above designated size.

The business operation situation has kept stable. In 2021, the operating revenue of industrial enterprises above designated size reached 833.58 billion yuan, with an increase of 10.0% over the previous year; Total profit was 38.27 billion yuan, down by 7.6%; The profit margin of operating revenue was 4.6%. Among 41 major industries, there were 15 industries with operating revenue exceeding 10 billion yuan, accounting for 91.5% of the operating revenue of industrial enterprises above designated size. The operating revenue of smelting and pressing of ferrous metals as well as manufacture of automobiles exceeded 100 billion yuan.

Table 4 Operating Revenue of Key Industries Above Designated Size In 2021

Industry	Year-on-year Growth Rate(%)
Smelting and Pressing of Ferrous Metals	15.1
Manufacture of Automobiles	-13.3
Manufacture of Computers, Communication and Other Electronic Equipment	14.8
Manufacture of Non-metallic Mineral Products	13.8
Manufacture of Electrical Machinery and Apparatus	6.1
Manufacture of General Purpose Machinery	15.9
Processing of Petroleum, Coal and Other Fuels	14.1
Manufacture of Metal Products	13.1
Manufacture of Raw Chemical Materials and Chemical Products	21.6
Manufacture of Medicines	24.3
Manufacture of Special Purpose Machinery	19.0
Production and Supply of Electric Power and Heat Power	11.2
Manufacture of Foods	20.3

Industrial products were supplied adequately. The annual sales-output ratio of industrial products above designated size was 97.4%. Of 296 kinds of industrial products, 181 kinds of products achieved an increase in output, with an increase rate of 61.1%. Among them, there were 82 products with an increase of more than 20%, accounting for 27.7%, up by 1.7 percentage points over the previous year. Optical fibers, integrated circuits and liquid crystal displays have increased by more than 1 fold and the output of CNC Metal-cutting machine tools, optical cables and charging piles have increased by more than 50%.

Table 5 Output of Main Products of Industrial Enterprises Above Designated Size In 2021

Product Designation	Unit	Yield	Year-on-year Growth Rate(%)
Servers	10,000 units	113.7	-20.8
Trucks	10,000 vehicles	31.9	-18.9
Engine	10,000 kilowatts	4085.1	-33.8
Steel	10,000 tons	2105.7	-12.1
Cement	10,000 tons	1530.3	13.3

Product Designation	Unit	Yield	Year-on-year Growth Rate(%)
Graphite and Carbon Products	10,000 tons	186.6	7.5
CNC Metal-cutting Machine Tools	Set	5531	72.1
Industrial Robot	Set	2604	25.6
Frozen,Fresh Meat	10,000 tons	11.6	-22.9
Milk Products	10,000 tons	53.7	9.7
Liquor	10,000 liters	25.7	-1.7
Synthetic Ammonia	10,000 tons	45.0	-25.0
Poly propylene	10,000 tons	10.5	-9.4
Primary Plastic	10,000 tons	33.5	-19.6
Traditional Chemical Medicine	Ton	7299.2	20.9
Forge Piece	10,000 tons	118.0	4.5
Sintered Metal Products	10,000 tons	1.3	2.2
Transformers	10 000 KVA	15298.6	12.2
Pneumatic Components	10,000 pieces	939.1	-36.7
Mining Equipment	10,000 tons	8.2	28.1
Railway Freight Wagons	Unit	3119	-8.7
Solar Water Heater	10,000 square meters	166.0	13.4

The construction industry has been developed steadily. There were 1,182 workload-traceable construction enterprises with general contracting and professional contracting qualifications across the city, up by 149 over the previous year. The annual contract value was 1,132.15 billion yuan, up by 34.9%. Among them, the newly signed contract amount in 2021 was 638.85 billion yuan, with an increase of 40.9%. The total output value of the construction industry reached 412.60 billion yuan, with an increase of 10.1%. Of this total, the output value of state-owned and state-controlled enterprises was 310.36 billion yuan, with an increase of 9.2%. The house construction area was 194.1 million square meters, up by 13.6%.

IV. Service Industry

The service industry continues to play an increasingly supporting role. In 2021, the service industry realized an added value of 705.94 billion yuan, with an increase of 9.2% over the previous year, accounting for 61.7% of the municipal gross domestic product (GDP) and contributing 79.1% to economic growth. Operating revenue of the service industry above designated size [7] increased by 19.9%. Emerging industries were growing rapidly, with Internet and related services, technology promotion and application services increased by 59.4% and 57.2% respectively. Logistics capacity has been continuously improved, and key logistics enterprises have achieved operating revenue of 80.76 billion yuan, with an increase of 22.9%. Among them, multimodal transport and transportation agency, loading and unloading and warehousing increased by 29.6% and 29.2% respectively.

Comprehensive carrying capacity of transportation has been improved. At the end of 2021, the mileage of highway traffic was 18,200.1 kilometers, with an increase of 0.5% over the previous year. Among them, the mileage of expressway traffic was 737.8 kilometers as the same as that of last year. Highway freight volume was 250 million tons, up by 8.8%; The freight turnover was 57.74 billion tons kilometers, with an increase of 11.8%[8]. At the end of 2021, there were 3.447 million civil motor vehicles, with an increase of 9.8%. Among them, there were 3.025 million civil vehicles, with an increase of 8.3%. There were 763 bus lines, increased by 113 over the previous year, with a total length of 15,852.3 kilometers, up by 2,647.6 kilometers, and 590 million passengers, up by 60 million. A total of 113,000 flights took off and was landed in 2021, with an increase of 10.1%; The passenger throughput was 13.616 million people, with an increase of 9.9%; The cargo and mail throughput was 168,000 tons, up by 14.7%.

Sustainable and sound growth in the postal and telecommunications industries. The annual business income of post industry (excluding the direct business income of Postal Savings Bank of China) was 9.92 billion yuan, with an increase of 16.6% over the previous year; The total business volume [9] was 8.93 billion yuan, up by 30.1%. The business income of express delivery enterprises was 7.75 billion yuan, up by 16.1%; The business volume was 800 million pieces, up by 22.0%. At the end of 2021, there were 12.163 million mobile phone users, up by 5.4%. Among them, 5G mobile phone users reached 4.637 million, with an increase of 1.7 folds. There were 4.63 million broadband internet access users, increased by 10.0%.

Tourism and exhibition industry have been well developed. In 2021, 81.927 million tourists were received, with an increase of 35.0% over the previous year. The total tourism revenue reached 98.39 billion yuan, up by 40.0%. There were 86 A-level tourist attractions, including 1 5A-level tourist attraction and 17 4A-level tourist attractions. There were 2 provincial tourist resorts. In 2021, 120 exhibitions were held, up by 12.1%, with an exhibition area of 2.6 million square meters, up by 44.0%.

V. Investment In Fixed Assets

Investment in fixed assets has generally kept a stable pace. Investment in fixed assets in 2021 increased by 11.5% over the previous year. Among them, investment in primary industry decreased by 1.5%, that in secondary industry decreased by 4.2%, and that in tertiary industry increased by 14.7%. Investment in high-tech service industry increased by 35.0%, private investment increased by 24.9%, and infrastructure investment decreased by 5.2%. At the end of 2021, there were 1,535 investment projects in fixed assets of over 100 million yuan, with an increase of 192 over the previous year, and the completed investment increased by 11.6%. Among them, there are 44 projects with 5 billion yuan, up by 8, and the completed investment has increased by 15.0%.

Table 6 Growth Rate and Proportion of Investment In Three Industries In 2021

Industry	Year-on-year Growth Rate(%)	Proportion of investment in fixed assets (%)
Investment In Fixed Assets	11.5	100
Primary industry	-1.5	0.4
Secondary industry	-4.2	14.0
Tertiary industry	14.7	85.6

Investment in real estate continues to grow. The investment in real estate development in 2021 was 192.80 billion yuan, with an increase of 12.9% over the previous year. Among them, the investment in residential buildings was 135.14 billion yuan, with an increase of 12.2%. The construction area of houses was 101.565 million square meters, down by 1.9%. Among them, the residential construction area was 65.774 million square meters, down by 1.8%. The completed housing area was 11.157 million square meters, down by 12.4%. Of this total, the completed residential area was 7.876 million square meters, down by 13.8%. The sales area of commercial housing was 15.482 million square meters, up by 15.9%. Among them, the residential sales area was 13.002 million square meters, up by 13.5%. Sales of commercial housing reached 195.70 billion yuan, up by 24.5%. Among them, residential sales amounted to 172.17 billion yuan, up by 22.4%.

VI. Domestic Trade

The consumer goods market was resumed steadily. The total retail sales of social consumer goods in 2021 were 512.61 billion yuan, with an increase of 14.7% over the previous year. Among them, the retail sales of commodities amounted to 439.01 billion yuan, up by 13.8%; Food and beverage income was 73.60 billion yuan, up by 20.5%. In terms of urban and rural areas, the retail sales of urban social consumer goods reached 460.93 billion yuan, up by 14.9%; The retail sales of rural consumer goods amounted to 51.68 billion yuan, up by 13.4%. The retail sales of above-quota units [10] reached 180.99 billion yuan, with an increase of 14.5%.

Upgraded goods have been increasingly growing. Among the retail sales of commodities above the quota, cosmetics, gold and silver jewelry and new energy vehicles increased by 22.6%, 57.1% and 147.1% respectively over the previous year; Wearable smart devices, smart home appliances, audio-visual equipment and smart phones increased by 18.3%, 17.9% and 34.7% respectively.

Basic life consumption remained stable. Among the retail sales of commodities above quota units, the retail sales of cereals, oils and foods reached 16.06 billion yuan in 2021, with an increase of 4.2% over the previous year; The retail sales of costumes, shoes, hats, knitted fabrics and textiles reached 11.86 billion yuan, with an increase of 29.6%; The retail sales of daily necessities reached 5.33 billion yuan, with an increase of 33.1%.

Online consumption has been expanding rapidly. The retail sales of commodities above quota units reached 27.10 billion yuan through public network, with an increase of 57.9% over the previous year, accounting for 15.0% of the retail sales of commodities above quota units, with an increase of 5.9 percentage points over the previous year

Table 7 Retail Sales of Major Commodities Above Quota Units In 2021

Commodity classification	Retail sales (100 million yuan)	Year-on-year Growth Rate(%)
Grain and Oil, Food	160.6	4.2
Clothing, Shoes, Hats and Textiles	118.6	29.6
Articles for Daily Use	53.3	33.1
Cultural and Office Goods	50.0	-3.7
Tobacco and Liquor	41.1	19.3
Household Appliances and Audio-visual Equipment	130.8	39.2
Communication Appliances	85.0	17.1
Gold, Silver and Jewellery	50.2	57.1
Cosmetics	44.7	22.6
Newspapers and Magazines	92.7	9.7
Traditional Chinese and Western Medicine	62.6	3.5
Automobile	584.1	14.9
Petroleum and Related Products	189.6	2.6

VII. Open Economy

Imports and exports increased rapidly. The total import and export volume of goods in 2021 was 194.42 billion yuan, with an increase of 40.1% over the previous year. Among them, exports were 117.41 billion yuan, up by 55.6%; Imports reached 77.01 billion yuan, up by 21.5%. Imports and exports to ASEAN increased by 31.3%, imports and exports to the European Union (excluding UK) increased by 9.0%, those to Latin America increased by 56.2%, and those to Africa increased by 44.7%. Imports and exports to countries along the "Belt and Road Initiative" increased by 37.7%, accounting for 34.1% of the total imports and exports. Among the commodities, the export of mechanical and electrical products was 66.18 billion yuan, with an increase of 60.8%; Steel exports were 7.74 billion yuan, up by 72.1%; The export of integrated circuits was 1.25 billion yuan, up by 47.6%. The annual economic extroversion was 17.0%, with an increase of 3.4 percentage points over the previous year.

The scale of foreign capital utilization has come to a higher level. The actual use of foreign capital in 2021 was USD 2.66 billion, with an increase of 38.1% over the previous year. Among them, the manufacturing industry used foreign capital of USD 270 million, with an increase of 73.9%; Foreign capital used in the tertiary industry was USD 2.09 billion, with an increase of 42.9%. The contracted foreign investment reached USD 9.69 billion, with an increase of 65.5%. A total of 330 new foreign investment projects were approved, with 46 projects with a total investment of over USD 100 million involving the contracted foreign investment of USD 6.13 billion.

Actively expanded cooperation with foreign countries. The newly signed contract value of foreign contracted projects in 2021 was USD 6.61 billion, with an increase of 50.1% over the previous year; the turnover of USD 4.10 billion was completed, down by 4.0%. Sixty overseas enterprises (institutions) have been set up and filed for registration, and the actually completed investment was USD 1.74 billion, down by 8.9%. There were 8,608 dispatched labor workers of various types, down by 28.1%.

VIII. Fiscal and Financial Industry

The implementation of fiscal revenue and expenditure was generally in good condition. The general public budget revenue in 2021 was 100.76 billion yuan, with an increase of 11.2% over the previous year. Among them, tax revenue was 77.65 billion yuan, with an increase of 11.5%, accounting for 77.1% of the general public budget revenue, up by 0.2 percentage points over the previous year. The general budget expenditure was 129.27 billion yuan, with an increase of 8.4%. Among them, social security and employment expenditure was 20.38 billion yuan, up by 19.4%; Health expenditure was 11.17 billion yuan, up by 21.0%; Urban and rural community expenditure was 29.34 billion yuan, with an increase of 9.7%.

Deposits and loans maintained a rapid growth. At the end of 2021, the balance of local and foreign currency deposits in financial institutions was 2.34370 trillion yuan, with an increase of 11.3% over the previous year; The balance of local and foreign currency loans in financial institutions was 2.33132 trillion yuan, up by 12.5%.

Financial market became more active. At the end of 2021, the number of listed companies reached 52, with 54 stocks, and 10 new listed and approved enterprises were added throughout the year. The transaction volume of securities was 5.6 trillion yuan, with an increase of 17.0% over the previous year; The transaction volume of futures was 18.5 trillion yuan, with an increase of 68.7%; Direct financing increased by 371.60 billion yuan, up by 63.7%. There were 205 private fund management institutions registered in the Asset Management Association of China, with 585 managed funds and the managed fund size of 106.54 billion yuan, with an increase of 7.3%.

Premium income rose steadily. In 2021, the insurance industry realized premium income of 59.85 billion yuan, with an increase of 2.3% over the previous year. Among them, the premium income of property insurance companies was 13.18 billion yuan, down by 11.5%; The premium income of life insurance companies was 46.67 billion yuan, with an increase of 7.1%. Various indemnities and payments amounted to 21.25 billion yuan, up by 37.3%.

The quality of credit assets has been continuously improved. At the end of 2021, the balance of non-performing loans in financial institutions was 19.71 billion yuan, reduced by 3.82 billion yuan over that at the beginning of the year. The NPL ratio was 0.85%, down by 0.3 percentage points from the beginning of the year.

IX. Science and Technology, Education, Culture, Health and Sports

The driving force for innovation has constantly increased. Investment in the annual research and experimental development (R&D) was[11] 26.55 billion yuan, with an increase of 17.7% over the previous year. Among them, basic research was 1.85 billion yuan, with an increase of 6.4%; Applied research was 4.14 billion yuan, with an increase of 36.1%; The experimental development was 20.56 billion yuan, up by 15.7%. R&D investment accounted for 2.6% of GDP, with an increase of 0.2 percentage points over the previous year. One new state-level enterprise technology center was identified, contributing to the total of 30, and 16 provincial-level enterprise technology centers were newly identified, contributing to the total of 221.

Significant scientific and technological achievements have been made. In 2021, there were 38.36 valid invention patents owned by 10,000 people, with an increase of 15.6% over that the previous year. The number of invention patents granted was 8,208, with an increase of 40.7%. The transaction volume of technical contracts was 47.35 billion yuan, up by 40.2%. We were awarded 16 first prizes and 50 second prizes for provincial scientific and technological progress. This also included 1 first prize and 17 second prizes in the provincial natural science. There were 80 national intellectual property demonstration enterprises and superior enterprises across the city.

High-quality development of education. In 2021, 97 primary and secondary schools (kindergartens) were built, renovated and expanded, and 101 primary and secondary schools and kindergartens were newly put into use. The coverage rate of inclusive kindergartens was 88.5%, and the collectivization construction rate of compulsory education was 85.2%. There were 95 established strategic projects for the integration of cities and schools, with 15 signed projects for the introduction of higher education.

Table 8 Basic Situation of Education In 2021

School Categories	Number Of Schools (place)	Students At School (10 000 persons)	Full-time teacher (person)
Colleges and universities stationed in Ji' nan	52	69.4	41894
Secondary vocational schools (excluding technical schools)	41	6.4	4040
Vestibule school	31	8.5	4471
Ordinary middle school	332	40.7	35587
Elementary school	641	61.0	38467
Special education school	13	0.1	505

Cultural life became richer. At the end of 2021, there were 14 state-owned art performance groups, 174 cultural centers (stations), 13 public museums and 14 public libraries. There were 435 cultural relics protection units above the municipal level, including 30 at the national level. There were 65 digital cinemas whose box office can be statistical across the city, with 9.965 million visitors and box office income of 410 million yuan. The mixed coverage rate of radio broadcasting population was 100%, and that of TV population was 99.7%. There were 38 built Quan Cheng Study Rooms, and the coverage rate of comprehensive cultural service centers at the grass-roots level was 100%.

The health service level has been continuously improved. At the end of 2021, there were 7,530 health institutions, increased by 16 over the previous year, including 338 hospitals and health centers. There were 73,000 beds in health institutions, with an increase of 5.7%. The number of health technicians reached 108,000, with an increase of 5.8%; that of practicing (assistant) physicians reached 42,000, with an increase of 5.3%. COVID-19 vaccination was promoted in a stable and order manner, with a total of 20.423 million doses in 2021, covering 8.783 million people.

Public fitness program has been steadily advanced. In 2021, 9 new sports social organizations were established, and 2,544 social sports instructors were trained. In addition, 536 public fitness activities (competitions) were organized with 3 million participants (including online activities). In this aspect, we were awarded 341 provincial gold medals and above, 190 silver medals and 253 bronze medals.

X. Energy, Environment, Urban Construction [12] and Safety Production

Initial effects have been seen in energy transformation and green and low-carbon development. The proportion of clean energy consumption has gradually increased, with 27.999 million tons of coal consumption in industries above designated size, with an increase of 1.1% over the previous year, and 920 million cubic meters of natural gas, up by 14.7%. The proportion of new energy power generation steadily increased, and the power generation structure has been deeply adjusted. Significant improvement was seen in wind power generation, garbage power generation and biomass power generation. The proportion of thermal power generation in the total power generation decreased by 2.7 percentage points compared with that of the previous year. The wind power generation of enterprises above designated size was 2.19 billion kWh, accounting for 7.0% of the total power generation, with an increase of 86.2%; Garbage power was 950 million kWh, accounting for 3.0% of the total power generation, up by37.7%; Biomass power was 510 million kWh, accounting for 1.6% of the total power generation, with an increase of 86.2%.

Table 9 Energy Production of Enterprises Above Designated Size In 2021

Item	Unit	Production	Year-on-year Growth Rate(%)
Coal	10,000 tons	72.9	-7.5
Electricity Generation	100 million kWh	315.1	11.7
Thermal Power	100 million kWh	290.8	8.5
Wind Power	100 million kWh	21.9	86.2
Solar Power	100 million kWh	2.4	1.2

Table 10 Energy Consumption of Industrial Enterprises Above Designated Size In 2021

Item	Unit	Consumption	Year-on-year Growth Rate(%)
Coal	10,000 tons	2799.9	1.1
Natural Gas	100 million cu.m	9.2	14.7
Coke	10,000 tons	897.1	-12.6
Gasoline	10,000 tons	0.4	-7.5
Diesel Oil	10,000 tons	3.9	1.5

The electricity consumption of the whole society has increased steadily. The electricity consumption of the whole society in 2021 was 47.53 billion kWh, with an increase of 9.5%. Among them, household electricity consumption was 8.65 billion kWh, with an increase of 8.6%. In terms of industries, the electricity consumption of the primary industry was 330 million kWh, up by 2.7%; that of the secondary industry was 26.70 billion kWh, up by 7.4%; that of the tertiary industry was 11.84 billion kWh, up by 15.7%. Industrial electricity consumption was 25.66 billion kWh, accounting for 54.0% of the total electricity consumption of the whole society, with an increase of 7.1%.

Table 11 Electricity consumption of the whole city in 2021

Item	Cumulative Electricity Consumption (100 million kWh)	Year-on-year Growth Rate (%)
Total Electricity Consumption	475.3	9.5
Household Electricity Consumption	86.5	8.6
Primary industry	3.3	2.7
Secondary industry	267.0	7.4
Tertiary industry	118.4	15.7

The ecological quality has been further improved. Comprehensive air quality index of the city was 4.7, which dropped below 5 for the first time. The number of days with good air quality in urban areas reached 229, accounting for 62.7% of good days. It was not any longer listed in the bottom 20 air quality rankings of key cities in China. The annual average concentration of inhalable particulate matter (PM_{10}), fine particulate matter ($PM_{2.5}$), sulfur dioxide and nitrogen dioxide in urban ambient air was 78 μ g/m^3, 40 μ g/m^3, 11 μ g/m^3 and 33 μ g/m^3 respectively [13]. The concentration of chemical oxygen demand in Xinfengzhuang at Xiaoqinghe River fracture surface was 14.6 mg/L, and the concentration of ammonia nitrogen in Xinfengzhuang at Xiaoqinghe River fracture surface was 0.78 mg/L, reaching Class III water quality standard of surface water, which was the best level in history. The average daytime equivalent sound level of regional environmental noise was 54.9 dB, and that of urban road traffic noise was 68.7 dB.

The level of urban construction has been further improved. At the end of 2021, the urban built-up area was 841.2 square kilometers, with an increase of 1.4 square kilometers over the previous year. The green coverage rate of the built-up area was 41.7%, and the per capita park green area was 12.8 square meters. The annual natural gas supply was 1.80 billion cubic meters, with an increase of 11.7%; The supply of liquefied petroleum gas was 25,000 tons, down by 34.4%. The central heating area was 300 million square meters, with an increase of 9.8%. The tap water supply was 500 million tons, up by 10.0%. Completed direct spring drinking projects for citizens reached 20, with an annual water supply of 37,000 tons, serving 35,000 users and supplying a population of more than 100,000 people. The harmless treatment rate of domestic garbage was 100%.

Social security continued to be stable. In 2021, 17,316 criminal cases were solved, and the detection rate of current murder cases remained 100%. For 11 consecutive years, all murder cases were solved, and the detection rate of eight kinds of serious violence cases reached 99.6%. The arrested fugitives of all kinds reached 1,442, with an increase of 25.0%, and the overall performance of chasing escaped convict ranked first in the province.

The production safety was in a stable situation. In 2021, there were 264 production safety accidents and 161 deaths, which decreased by 30.3% and 41.7% respectively compared with that of the previous year. The number of both accidents and deaths decreased, and the situation of production safety was generally stable.

XI. Living and Social Security of Residents

Resident income has rose steadily. The per capita disposable income of residents in 2021 was 46,725 yuan, with an increase of 8.5% over the previous year. Among them, the per capita disposable income of urban residents was 57,449 yuan, with an increase of 7.7%; The per capita disposable income of rural residents was 22,580 yuan, up by 10.5%. Per capita consumption expenditure was 30,016 yuan, with an increase of 8.4%. Among them, the per capita consumption expenditure of urban residents was 36,866 yuan, with an increase of 7.2%; Per capita consumption expenditure of rural residents was 14,591 yuan, up by 12.7%. The income ratio of urban and rural residents decreased from 2.6 ： 1 in the previous year to 2.5 ： 1. The Engel coefficient of urban residents was [14]23.5%, and that of rural residents was 30.5%.

Table 12 Per Capita Disposable Income of Residents In 2021

Item	Residents of the Whole City		Urban Households		Rural Households	
	Number (yuan)	Year-on-year Growth Rate (%)	Number (yuan)	Year-on-year Growth Rate (%)	Number (yuan)	Year-on-year Growth Rate (%)
Disposable Income	46725	8.5	57449	7.7	22580	10.5
Income of Wages and Salaries	27050	8.8	33546	8.0	12423	10.9
Net Business Income	4728	9.2	3146	9.4	8291	10.1
Net Income from Property	6887	7.7	9732	7.0	482	8.9
Net Income from Transfer	8060	8.0	11025	7.2	1383	9.8

Table 13 At the End of 2021, Number of Major Durable Consumer Goods Owned Per 100 Households [15]

Item	Unit	Urban Households	Rural Households
Automobile	Unit	62.1	40.6
Refrigerator (cabinet)	Set	100.9	96.2
Washing Machine	Set	98.1	91.5
Water Heater	Set	99.5	89.3
Air Conditioner	Set	172.6	93.5
Colour Television Set	Set	104.8	104.3
Camera	Set	23.5	4.1
Computer	Set	80.2	41.7
Mobile Phone	Unit	227.6	230.3

The scope of social security became more extensive. At the end of 2021, 4.727 million of urban employees participated in the basic endowment insurance, with an increase of 354,000 over the previous year; The number of employees participating in medical insurance was 3.362 million, with an increase of 227,000; The number of unemployed insurance participants was 2.269 million, with an increase of 133,000; The number of employees participating in industrial injury insurance was 2.935 million, with an increase of 149,000; The number of maternity insurance participants was 2.358 million, with an increase of 226,000. The number of residents participating in endowment insurance and medical insurance reached 3.084 million and 5.069 million respectively.

Residents' living security has been improved steadily. The minimum living standard for urban residents was 904 yuan per month, providing guarantees to 9,000 households and 13,000 urban residents, and security funds and various subsidies reached 130 million yuan; The minimum living standard for rural residents was 676 yuan per month (904 yuan in Shizhong District, Huaiyin District, Tianqiao District, Licheng District and Jinan High-tech Zone), providing guarantees to 59,000 rural residents and 84,000 people, and security funds and various subsidies reached 570 million yuan. The basic living standard of urban residents in extreme poverty was 1,356 yuan per month, and that of rural residents in extreme poverty was 1,179 yuan per month (1,356 yuan in Shizhong District, Huaiyin District, Tianqiao district and Jinan High-tech Zone). There were 745 urban residents in extreme poverty and 14,000 rural residents in extreme poverty, and cumulative special support and subsidies reached 290 million yuan. Nursing standards are divided into three grades: self-care, semi-self-care and inability of self-care. Self-care standard was raised to 231 yuan/month, semi-self-care standard was raised to 385 yuan /month, and inability of self-care was raised to 770 yuan/month.

The support and assistance work became stable. There were 2 support management stations and 1 Rescue and Protection Center for minors across the city. A total of 4,116 physically disabled persons were trained, 2,102 physically disabled persons were placed for employment, and subsides of 280 million yuan were invested to help the disabled.

Notes:

[1] *Statistical Bulletin in 2021* are preliminary Statistics data, and the official data are subject to the published *Jinan Statistical Yearbook 2022*. Due to the effect of rounding, partial data are not equal in the total and itemized total.

[2] The city gross regional product and the absolute amount of the value added of various industries are calculated on current price, while the growth rate is calculated at a constant price. The data of that year are preliminary accounting data. According to the results of the fourth national economic census, the historical data on GDP, added value of various industries and other related indicators have been revised.

[3] Two-year average growth rate refers to the growth rate calculated by geometric average method based on the data in the same period in 2019.

[4] Modern service industry includes: Information transmission, software and IT, financial industry, real estate, leasing and business services, scientific research and technology services, water conservancy, environment and management of public facility, residential service, repair and other services, education, health and social work, culture, sports and entertainment.

[5] "Four-top" enterprises refer to industrial enterprises above designated size, qualified construction industries, wholesale and retail businesses above quota, accommodation and catering businesses, real estate development and management enterprise, and service industries above designated size.

[6] Industrial enterprises above designated size refer to industrial legal entities with annual major business revenue of 20,000,000 yuan and above.

[7] Service industry above designated size includes: transportation, warehousing and postal services, information transmission, software and information technology services, real estate, leasing and business services, scientific research and technical services, water conservancy, environment and public facilities management, residential services, repair and other services, education, health and social work, culture, sports and entertainment.

[8] In 2021 Ministry of Transport of the People's Republic of China adopted the new statistical method of road freight, and revised the road freight data in 2020. The growth rate in 2021 was obtained according to the revised data in 2020.

[9] The total postal business volume is calculated according to the constant unit price in 2020, and the year-on-year growth was calculated according to the comparable caliber.

[10] Units above quota refer to wholesale enterprises with annual major business revenue of 20,000,000 yuan and above, retail enterprises with annual major business revenue of 5,000,000 yuan and above, and accommodation and catering enterprises with annual major business revenue of 2,000,000 yuan and above. Unit includes corporate enterprises, industrial activity units and self-employed business.

[11] The indicators related to research and development (R&D) funds use the data of 2020.

[12] The urban construction indicator is derived from the annual statistical report of urban construction by the Ministry of Housing and Urban-Rural Development, which was a preliminary report and covered the whole Jinan area including two counties.

[13] Data related to ecological environment in 2021 are counted by the newly adjusted "14th Five-Year Plan" national control sites.

[14] Engel's coefficient refers to the proportion of food expenditure in consumption expenditure.

[15] The data came from the survey of household income and expenditure and living conditions.

Source: The data of enterprise technology center in this Communiqué comes from the development and reform department; data on education comes from the education department; data of science and technology comes from the science and technology department; data on telecommunications comes from the industrial and information departments; data on household registration, social security and civil motor vehicles come from public security departments; data on urban and rural minimum living security and assistance and support for residents in extreme poverty come from civil affairs departments; finance data comes from the finance department; data on new employment in cities and towns and insurance for urban employees come from human resources and social security departments; data related to environmental protection comes from the ecological environment department; data related to urban construction comes from the housing and urban–rural construction departments; data on transportation comes from the transportation department; data on the construction of direct spring drinking project comes from urban and rural water departments; data on outputs of aquatic products and agricultures come from agricultural and rural departments; forestry data comes from landscape and forestry departments; data of import and export, exhibitions, newly–established overseas enterprises and expatriates come from the commerce departments; data on tourisms and cultures come from the cultural and tourism departments; health data comes from health departments; safety data comes from emergency management department; intellectual property data comes from the market supervision department; data of sports comes from the sports department; medical insurance data comes from the medical security department; financial data comes from local financial supervision and management departments; data of attracting investment and foreign investment come from the investment promotion department; market data comes from the administrative examination and approval service department; logistics data comes from the port logistics department; data on the protection for disabled persons comes from Disabled Persons' Federation; postal and express data come from postal administration departments; data on residents' income and expenditure, Engel's coefficient, price index, grain data and holding quantity of major durable consumer goods in urban and rural households come from the NBS Survey Office in Jinan; data on the early adopting areas for replacing old growth drivers with new ones comes from Jinan Start–up Zone Management Committee; Other data are from the Municipal Bureau of Statistics.

2021 年的济南
Jinan in 2021

11432.2
地区生产总值（亿元）
Gross Domestic Product
(100 million yuan)

61.7
第三产业比重 (%)
Proportion of Tertiary
Industry(%)

933.6
常住人口（万人）
Permanent Population
(10 000 persons)

1007.6
一般公共预算收入（亿元）
General Public Budget
Revenue(100 million yuan)

11.5
全社会固定资产投资增长幅度 (%)
Growth Rate Total Investment in
Fixed Assets(%)

300.3
海关进出口总额（亿美元）
Total Value of Imports and
Exports(100 million USD)

123075
人均地区生产总值（元）
Per Capita Gross Domestic
Product(yuan)

5126.1
社会消费品零售总额（亿元）
Total Retail Sale of Consumer
Goods(100 million yuan)

57449
城镇居民人均可支配收入（元）
Per Capita Disposable Income of
Urban Households(yuan)

22580
农村居民人均可支配收入（元）
Per Capita Disposable Income of
Rural Households(yuan)

101.5
居民消费价格指数 (%)
Consumer Price Index(%)

济南一日

A Day in Jinan

每日创造

Daily Production

27605.5

一般公共预算收入（万元 / 天）

General Public Budget Revenue (10 000 yuan/day)

35427.4

一般公共预算支出（万元 / 天）

General Public Budget Expenditure (10 000 yuan/day)

8227.5

海关进出口总额（万美元 / 天）

Total Value of Imports and Exports (10 000 USD/day)

55452

公路客运量（人 / 天）

Highways Passenger Traffic (person/day)

11200.0

第一产业（万元 / 天）

Primary Industry(10 000 yuan/day)

313211.0

地区生产总值（万元 / 天）

Gross Domestic Product (10 000 yuan/day)

37304

民航客运量（人 / 天）

Civil Aviation Passenger Traffic (person/day)

108605.5

第二产业（万元 / 天）

Secondary Industry(10 000 yuan/day)

878

生产汽车（辆 / 天）

Automobile Manufacturing (unit/day)

193408.2

第三产业（万元 / 天）

Tertiary Industry(10 000 yuan/day)

8632

发电量（万千瓦时 / 天）

Power Generating Capacity (10 000 kWh/day)

18952

蔬菜产量（吨 / 天）

Output of Vegetables (ton/day)

8029

粮食产量（吨 / 天）

Output of Grain Crops (ton/day)

3115

生产服务器（台 / 天）

Server Manufacturing (unit/day)

每日生活
Daily Life

183
出生人口
（人/天）
Population of Birth
(person/day)

121
死亡人口
（人/天）
Population of Death
(person/day)

2370.7
城乡居民生活用电量
（万千瓦时/天）
Household Electricity Consumption of Urban and Rural Residents
(10 000 kWh/day)

135
登记结婚
（对/天）
Registered Marriages
(couple/day)

327
城镇非私营单位在岗职工平均工资
（元/天）
Average Wages of On-post Staff in Urban Non Private Entities(yuan/day)

65
离婚
（对/天）
Divorces
(couple/day)

157
城镇居民人均可支配收入
（元/天）
Per Capita Disposable Income of Urban Households(yuan/day)

136.2
自来水供水量
（万吨/天）
Volume of Water Supply
(10 000 tons/day)

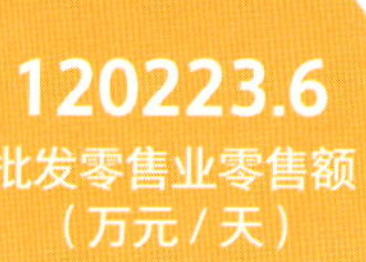

120223.6
批发零售业零售额
（万元/天）
Total Retail Sale of Wholesale and Retail Trades (10 000 yuan/day)

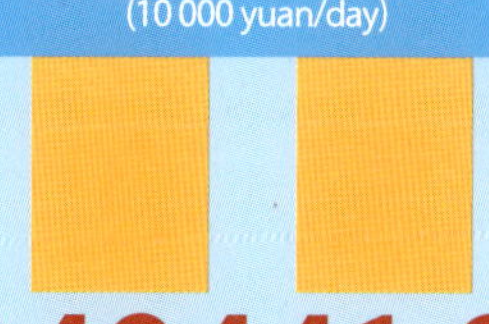

826.1
住宿业零售额（万元/天）
Total Retail Sale of Accommodation
(10 000 yuan/day)

19391.3
餐饮业零售额（万元/天）
Total Retail Sale of Catering Industry
(10 000 yuan/day)

140441.0
社会消费品零售总额（万元/天）
Total Retail Sale of Consumer Goods
(10 000 yuan/day)

492.9
天然气供气量
（万立方米/天）
Total Natural Gas Supply
(10 000 cu.m/day)

8136
生活垃圾清运量
（吨/天）
Domestic Waste Removed and Transported(ton/day)

40
农村居民人均消费支出
（元/天）
Per Capita Consumer Expenditure of Rural Households(yuan/day)

101
城镇居民人均消费支出
（元/天）
Per Capita Consumer Expenditure of Urban Households(yuan/day)

62
农村居民人均可支配收入
（元/天）
Per Capita Disposable Income of Rural Households(yuan/day)

综 合
General

地区生产总值（亿元）
Gross Domestic Product (100 million yuan)

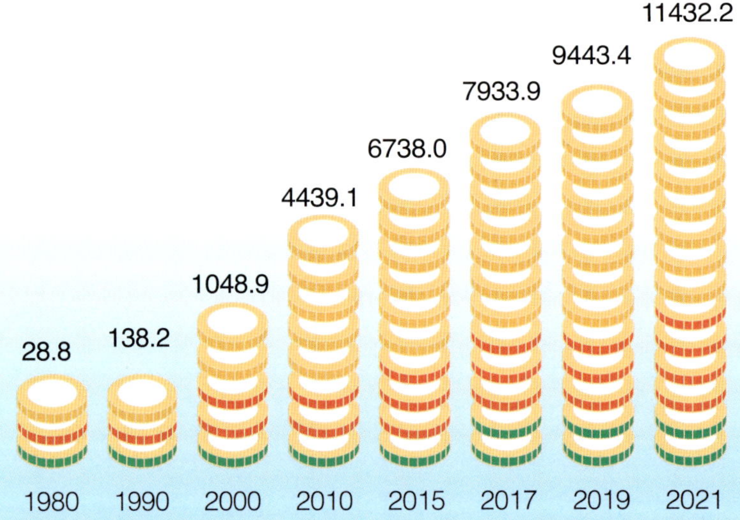

人均地区生产总值（元）
Per Capita Gross Domestic Product (yuan)

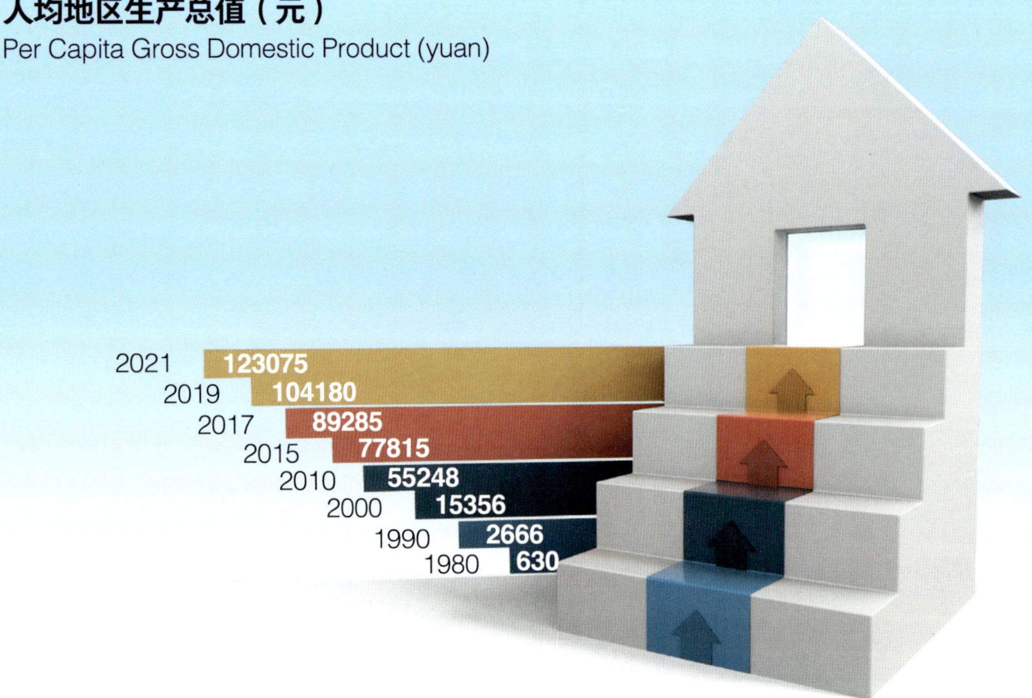

人口
Population

年末户籍总人口（万人）
Registered Population Year-end (10 000 persons)

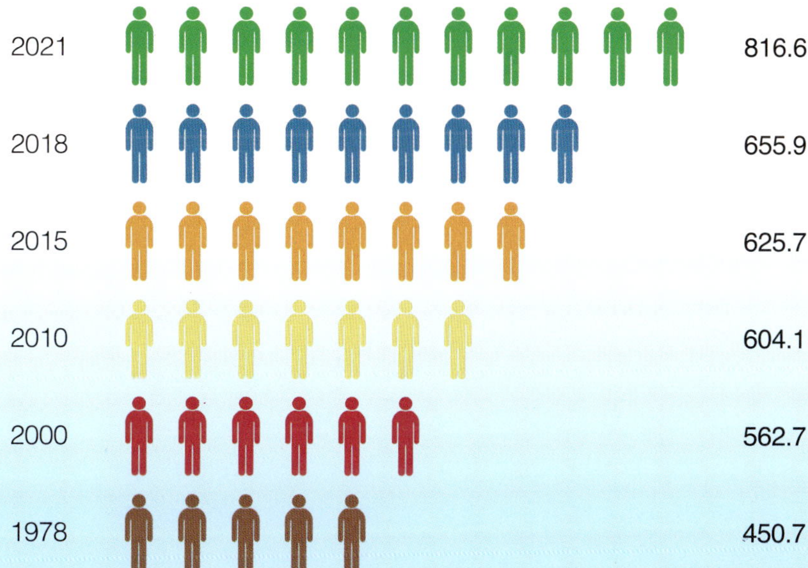

人口自然变动情况（‰）
Natural Changes of Population (‰)

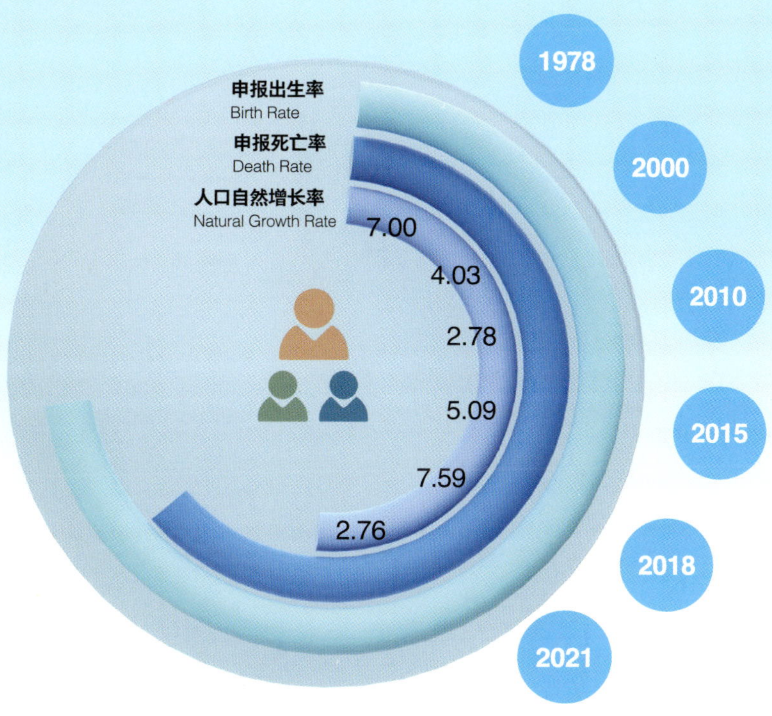

就 业
Employment

全社会从业人员（万人）
Total Employed Persons (10 000 persons)

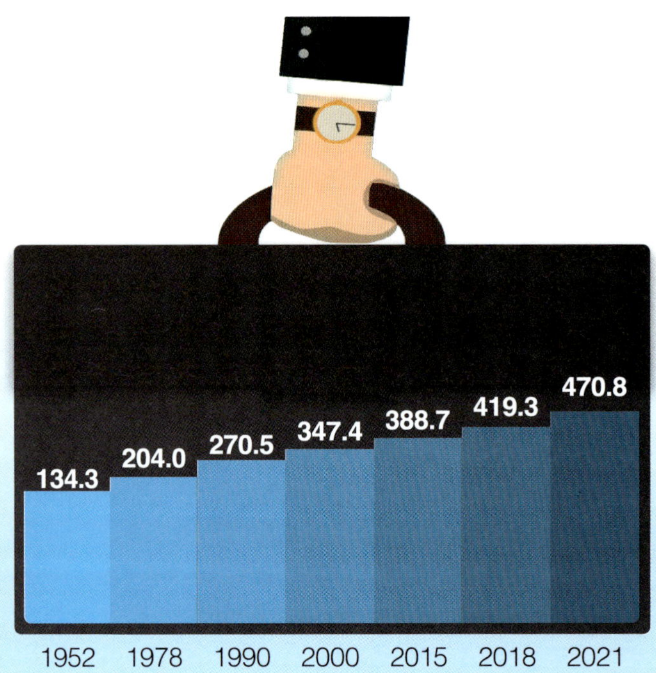

在岗职工平均工资（元）
Average Wage of Staff and Workers (yuan)

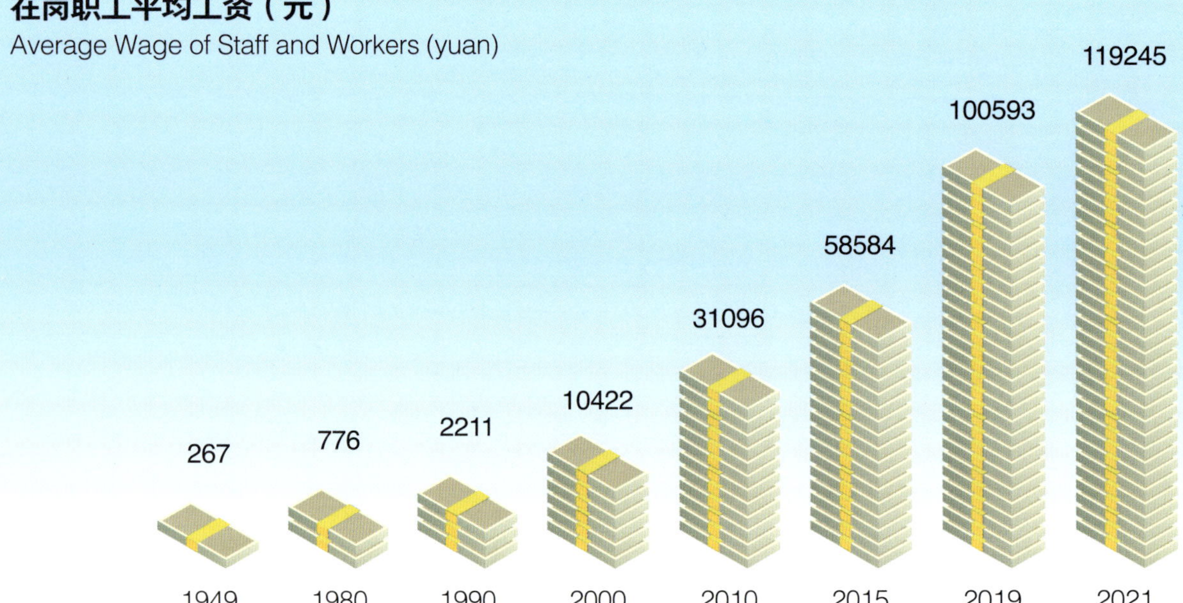

注：1．2006 年以后为法人单位在岗职工口径；2．2019 年以后为城镇非私营单位在岗职工口径。

Notes: 1.The data after 2006 are based on the caliber of on-the-job employees of legal entities.
2.The data after 2019 are based on the caliber of on-post staff in urban non private entities.

财政 金融
Government Finance Financial

一般公共预算收入支出（亿元）
General Public Budget Revenue and Expenditure (100 million yuan)

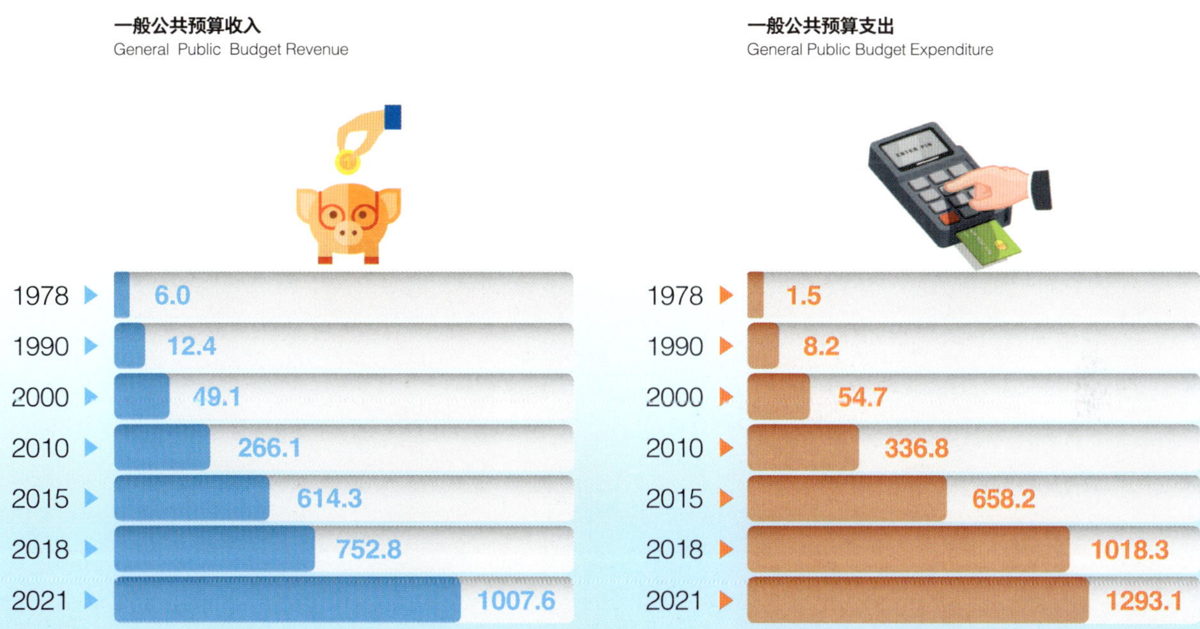

金融机构人民币存、贷款余额（亿元）
The Ending Balance of all Deposits and Loans in RMB of Financial Institutions (100 million yuan)

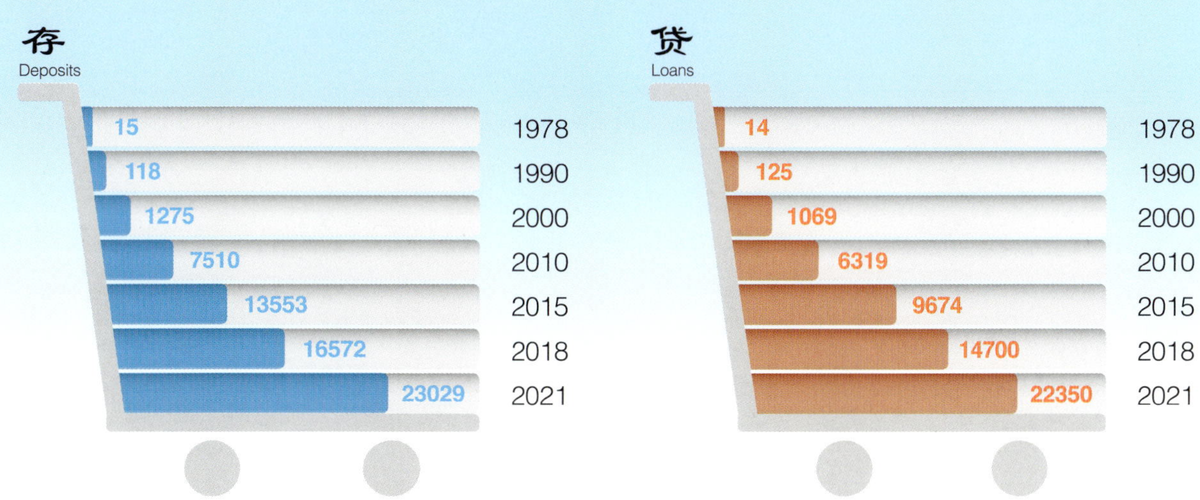

人民生活
People's Livelihood

城乡居民人均可支配收入（元）
Per Capita Disposable Income of Urban and Rural Households（yuan）

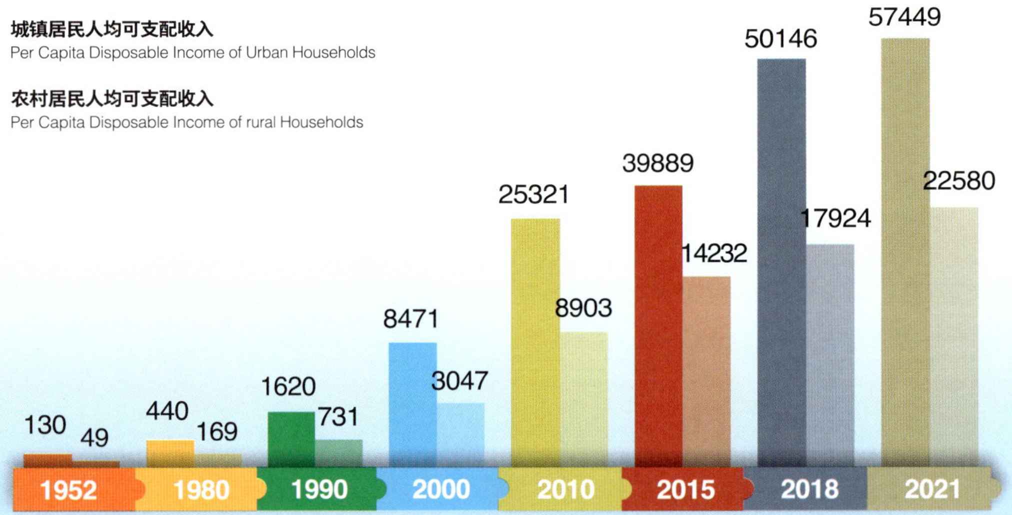

注：城乡一体化改革，2015 年起为城镇居民人均支配收入和农村居民人均可支配收入口径；之前年份为城市居民人均可支配收入和农民人均纯收入口径。
Note: The urban-rural integration reform has been based on the caliber of per capita disposable income of urban and rural households since 2015; the urban-rural integration reform in previous years was based on the caliber of per capita disposable income of urban households and the per capita net income of farmers.

城乡居民人均消费支出（元）
Per Capita Consumer Expenditure of Urban and Rural Households（yuan）

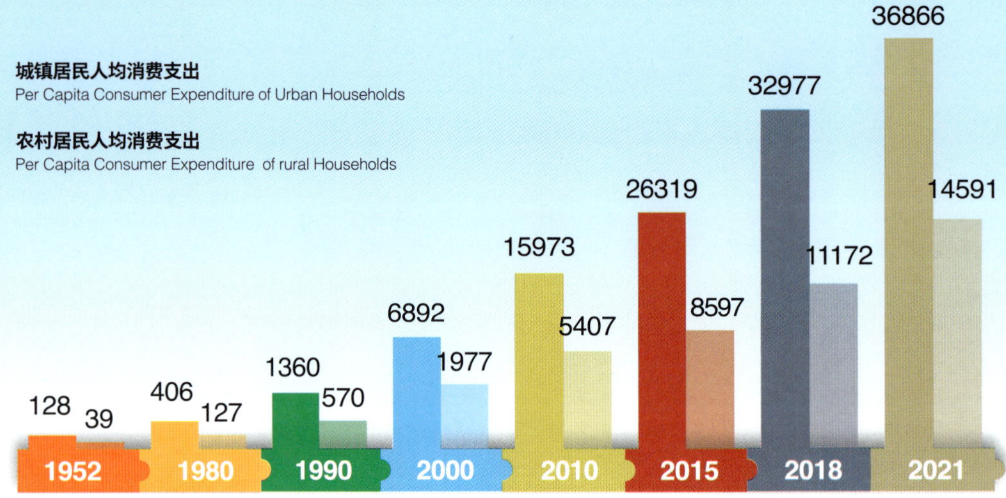

注：从 2015 年开始，本市居民收支调查指标采用新口径。“农村居民人均消费支出”2014 年以前为农民人均生活费支出口径。
Note: Starting from 2015, the city's residents' income and expenditure survey indicators adopt a new caliber. "Per capita consumption expenditure of Rural households" was the "per capita living expenses of farmers" before 2014.

城乡居民恩格尔系数（%）
Engel's Coefficient of Urban and Rural Households (%)

城镇居民恩格尔系数
Engel's Coefficient of Urban Households

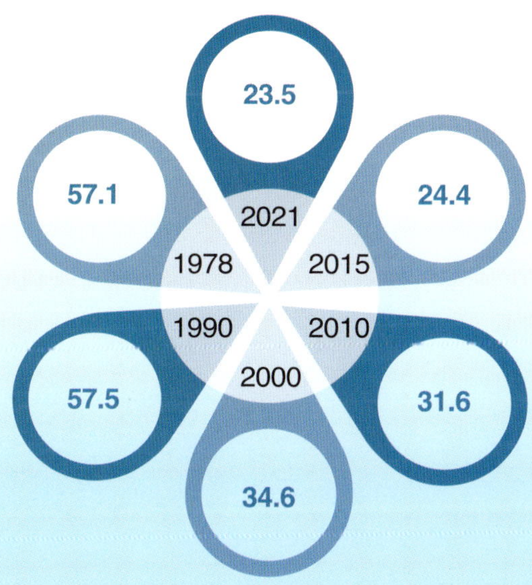

农村居民恩格尔系数
Engel's Coefficient of Rural Households

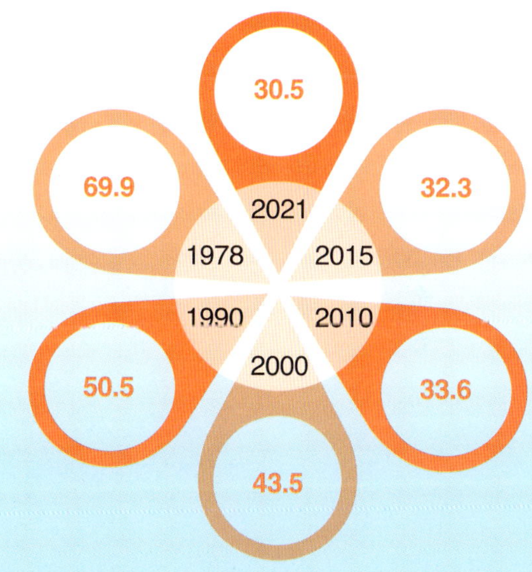

人民币住户存款余额（亿元）
The Balance RMB Household Deposits（100 millon yuan）

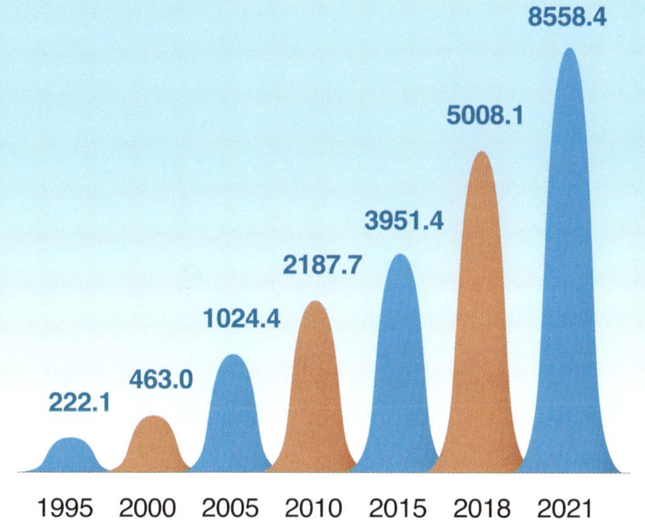

注：2015 年之前为城乡居民人民币储蓄存款余额口径，2015 年调整为住户存款余额口径。
Note: Before 2015, the caliber was the balance of saving deposit (RMB) of urban and rural Households, and has been adjusted to balance held on deposit of households since 2015.

城乡居民生活用电（亿千瓦时）
Household Electricity Consumption(100 million kWh)

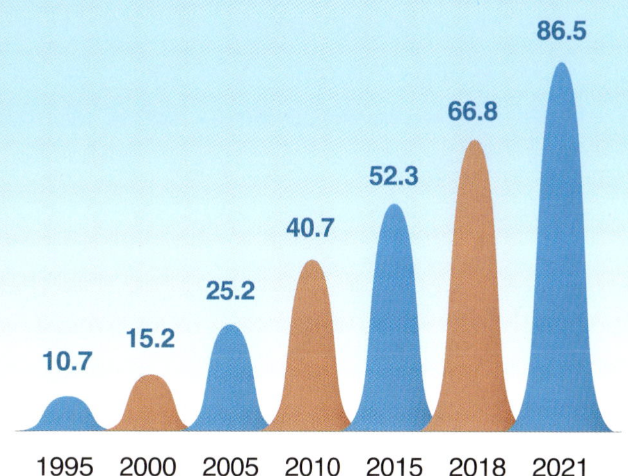

物 价
Price

居民消费价格指数与商品零售价格指数（以上年为 100）
Consumer Price Index and Retail Price Index (Preceding Last Year=100)

工业生产者出厂价格指数与工业生产者购进价格指数（以上年为 100）
Producer Price Index and Purchasing Price Index for Industrial Products (Preceding Last Year=100)

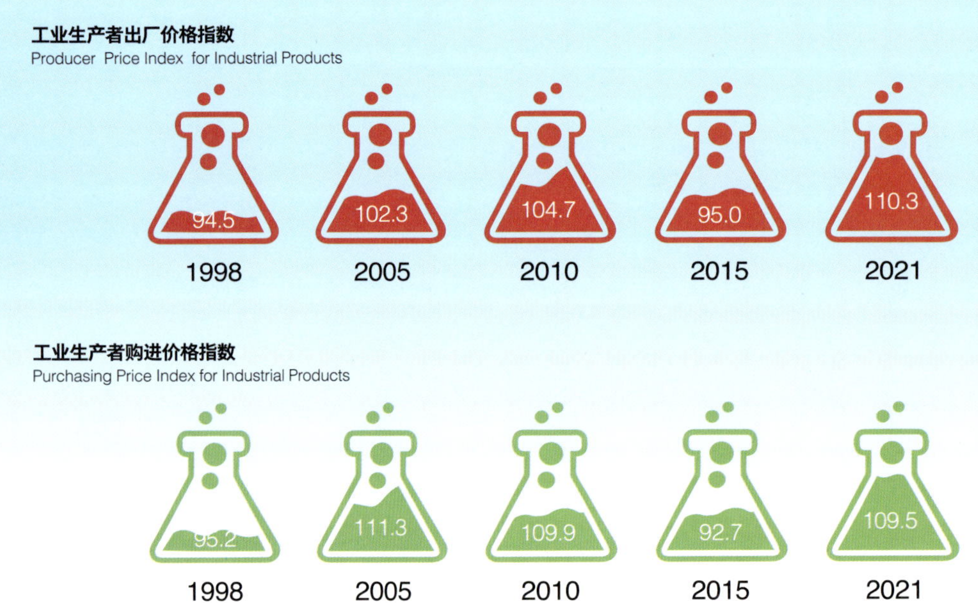

注：2020 年起，“工业生产者出厂价格指数”与“工业生产者购进价格指数”指标为全省数据。
Note: Starting in 2020, the “Producer Price Index ” and “Producer Purchasing Price Index ” are province-wide data.

农业
Agriculture

农林牧渔业总产值（亿元）
Gross Output Value of Agriculture, Forestry, Animal Husbandry and Fishery(100 million yuan)

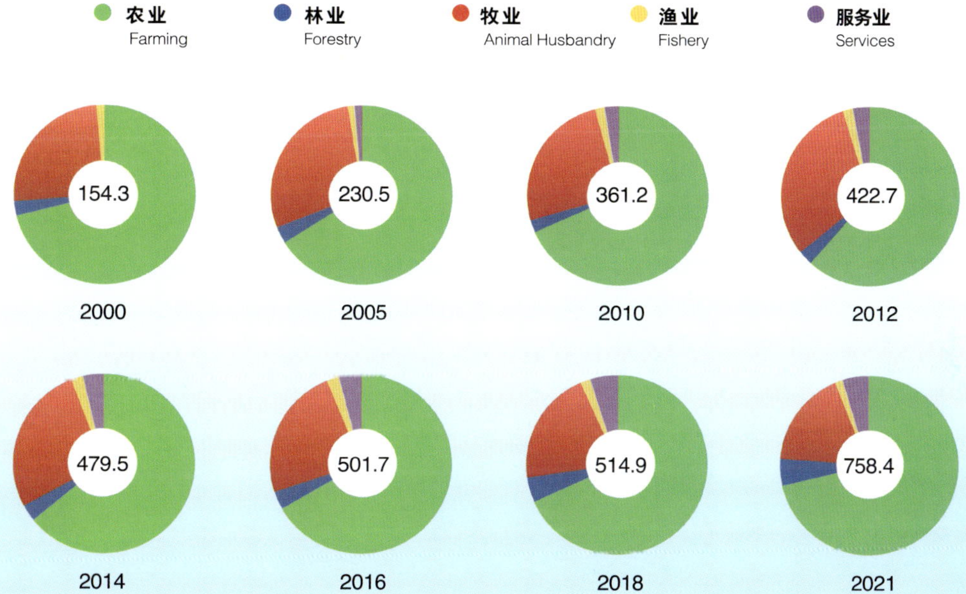

主要农产品产量（万吨）
Output of Main Agricultural Products (10 000 tons)

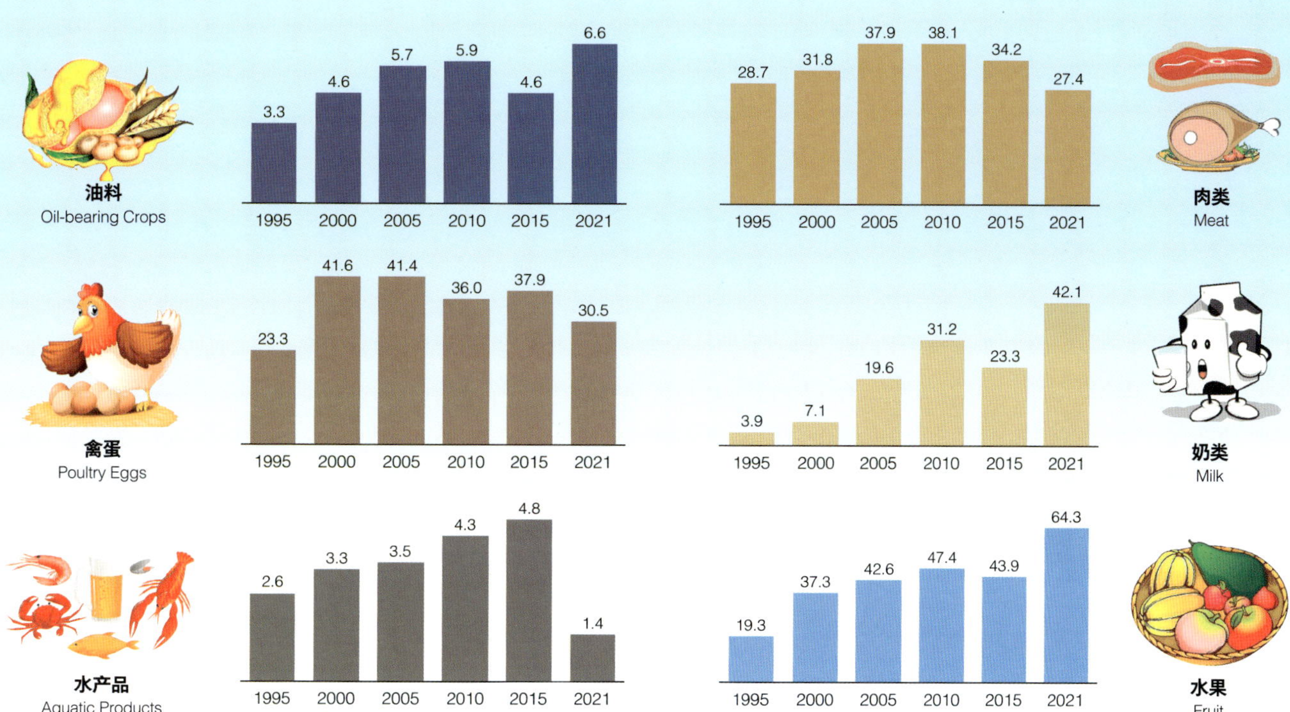

工 业
Industry

规模以上工业营业收入（亿元）
Business Revenue of Industrial Enterprises Above Designated Size (100 million yuan)

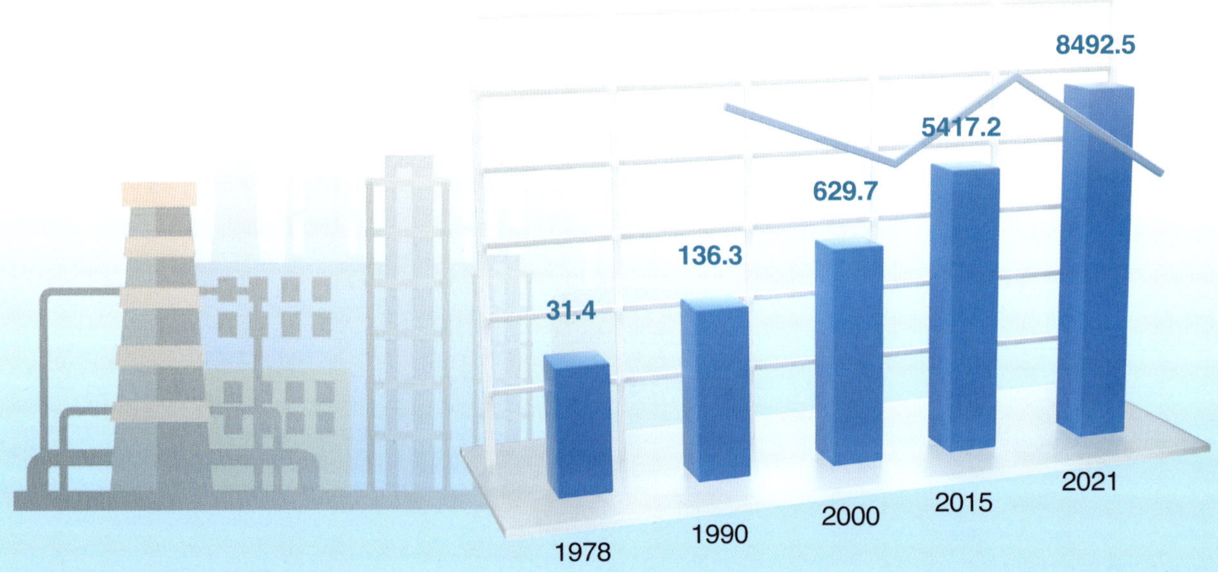

注：2018 年以前为主营业务收入口径。
Note: Before 2018, the caliber was revenue from principal business.Revenue from principal business.

规模以上工业利税总额（亿元）
Total Profits and Taxes of Industrial Enterprises Above Designated Size (100 million yuan)

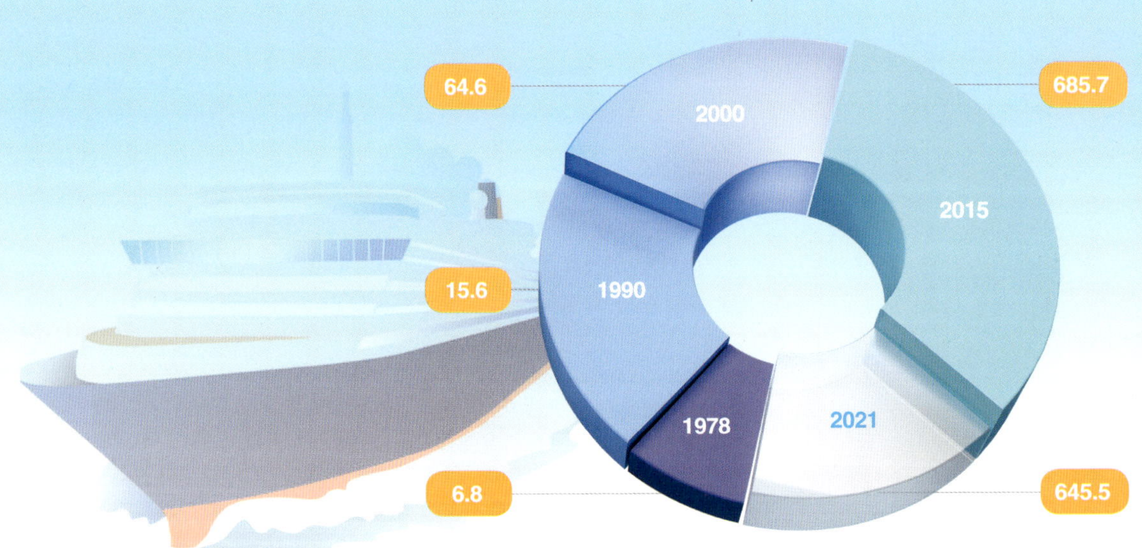

规模以上工业利润总额（亿元）

Total Profits of Industrial Enterprises Above Designated Size (100 million yuan)

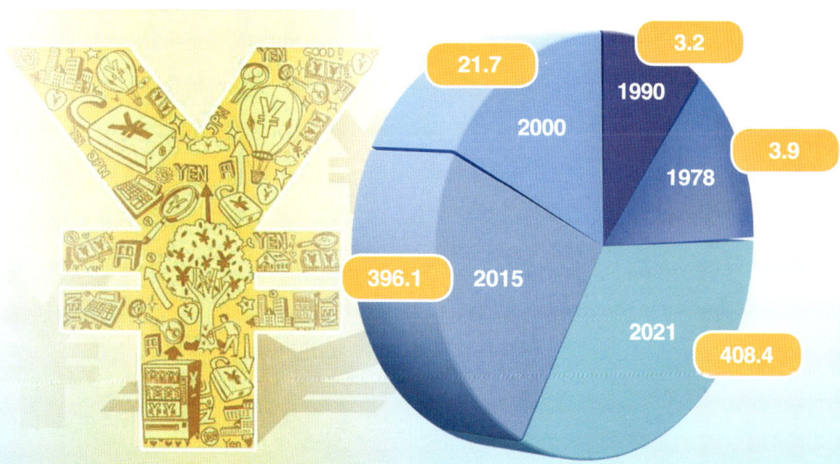

主要工业产品产量

Output of Major Industrial Products

发电量（亿千瓦时）
Power Generating Capacity (100 million kWh)

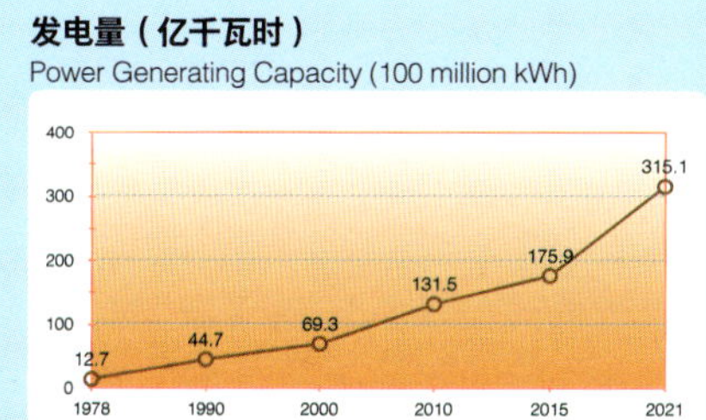

服务器（万台）
Servers (10 000 unit)

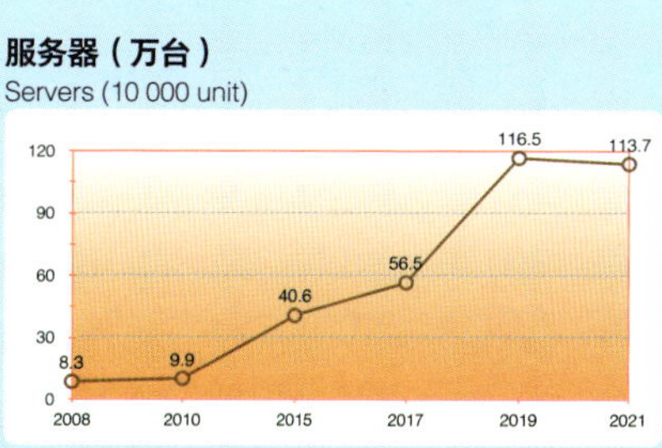

原油加工量（万吨）
Crude Processing Volume (10 000 tons)

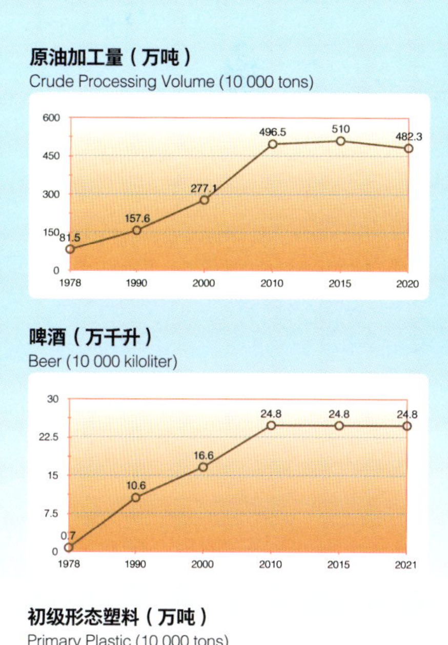

化肥（万吨）
Chemical Fertilizer (10 000 tons)

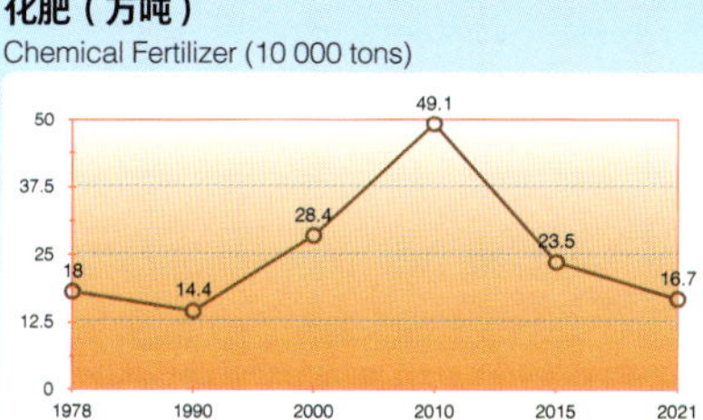

水泥（万吨）
Cement (10 000 tons)

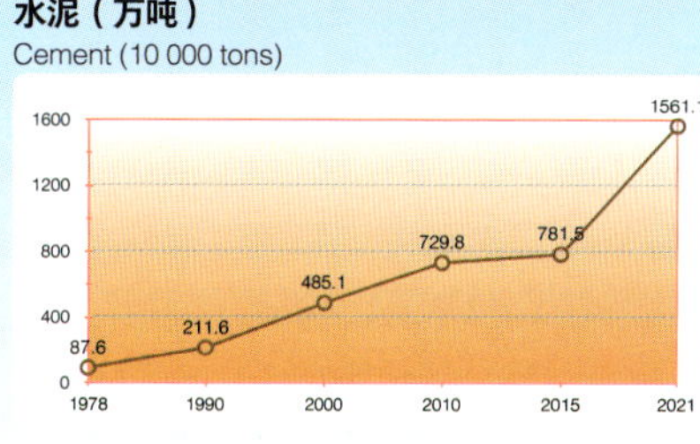

啤酒（万千升）
Beer (10 000 kiloliter)

30
22.5
15
7.5
0
0.7
10.6
16.6
24.8
24.8
24.8
1978
1990
2000
2010
2015
2021

汽车（辆）
Motor Vehicles (unit)

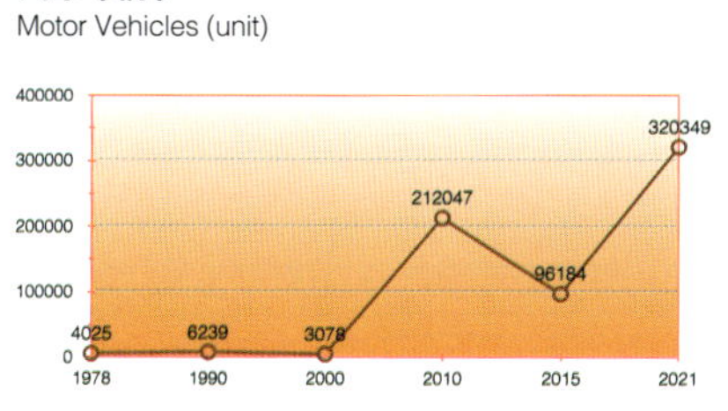

钢（万吨）
Steel (10 000 tons)

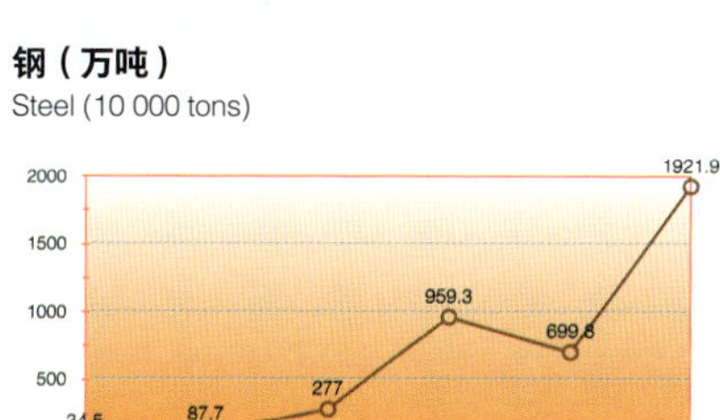

初级形态塑料（万吨）
Primary Plastic (10 000 tons)

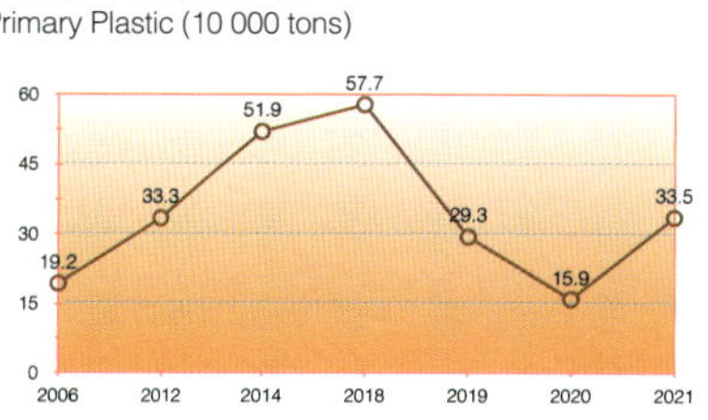

投资
Investment

固定资产投资总额（亿元）
Total Investment in Fixed Assets
(100 million yuan)

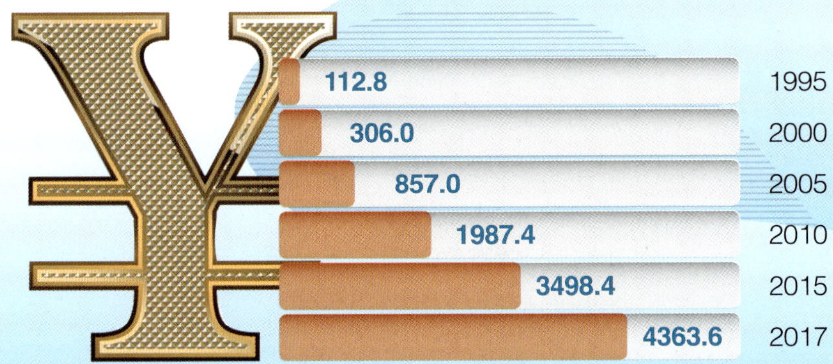

房地产开发投资总额（亿元）
Estate Development Investment
(100 million yuan)

贸易外经
Domestic and Foreign Trade

社会消费品零售总额（亿元）
Total Retail Sales of Consumer Goods (100 million yuan)

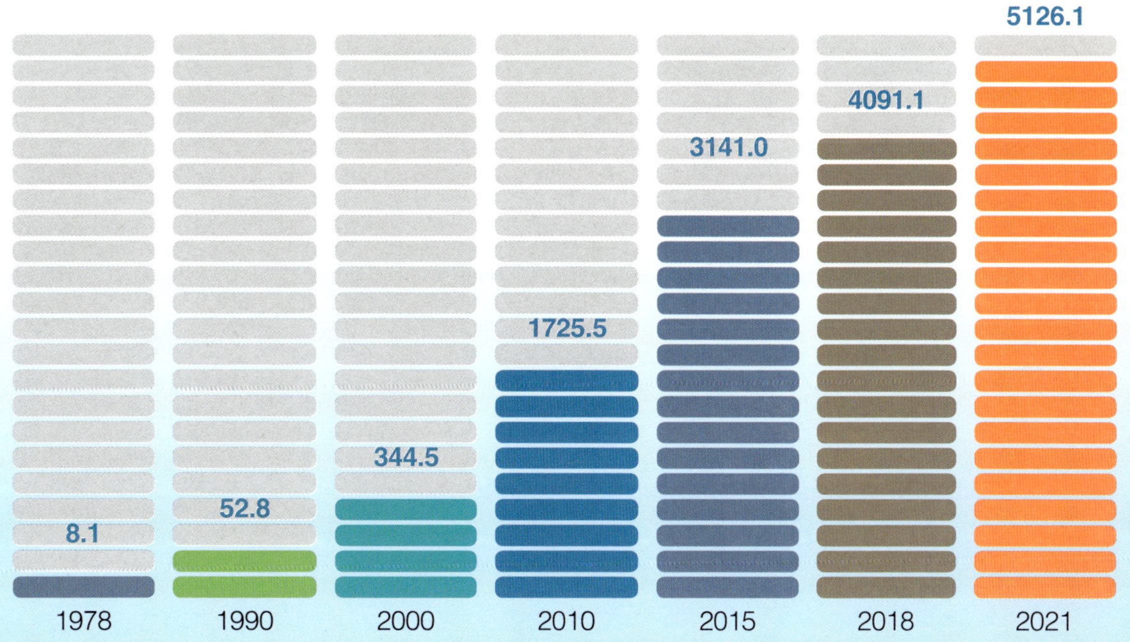

实际使用外资金额（万美元）
Actual Use of Foreign Capital (10 000 USD)

海关进出口总额（万美元）
Total Value of Imports and Exports (10 000 USD)

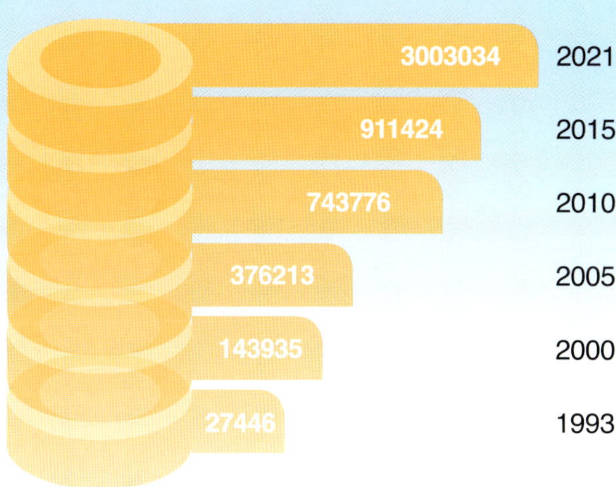

城市建设
Urban Public

全社会用电量（亿千瓦时）
Electricity Consumption (100 million kWh)

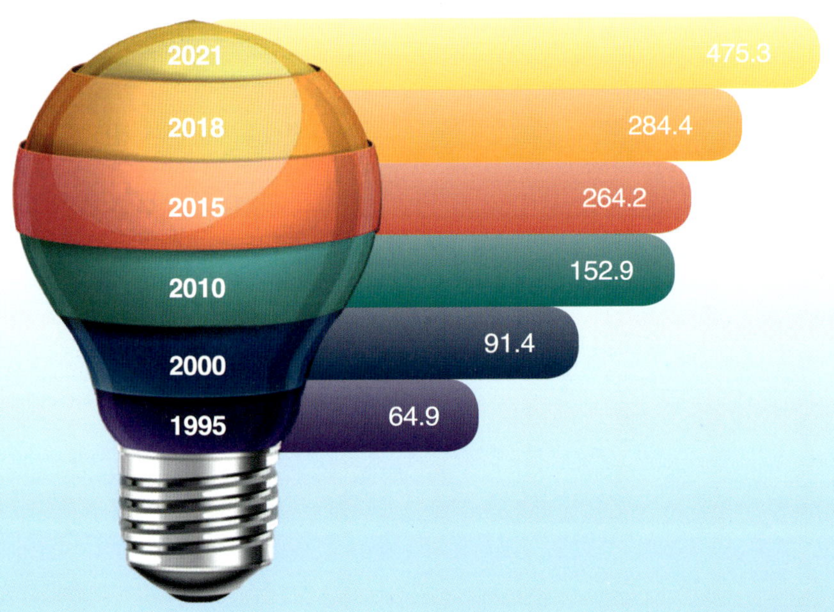

全社会供气量
Total Social Gas Supply

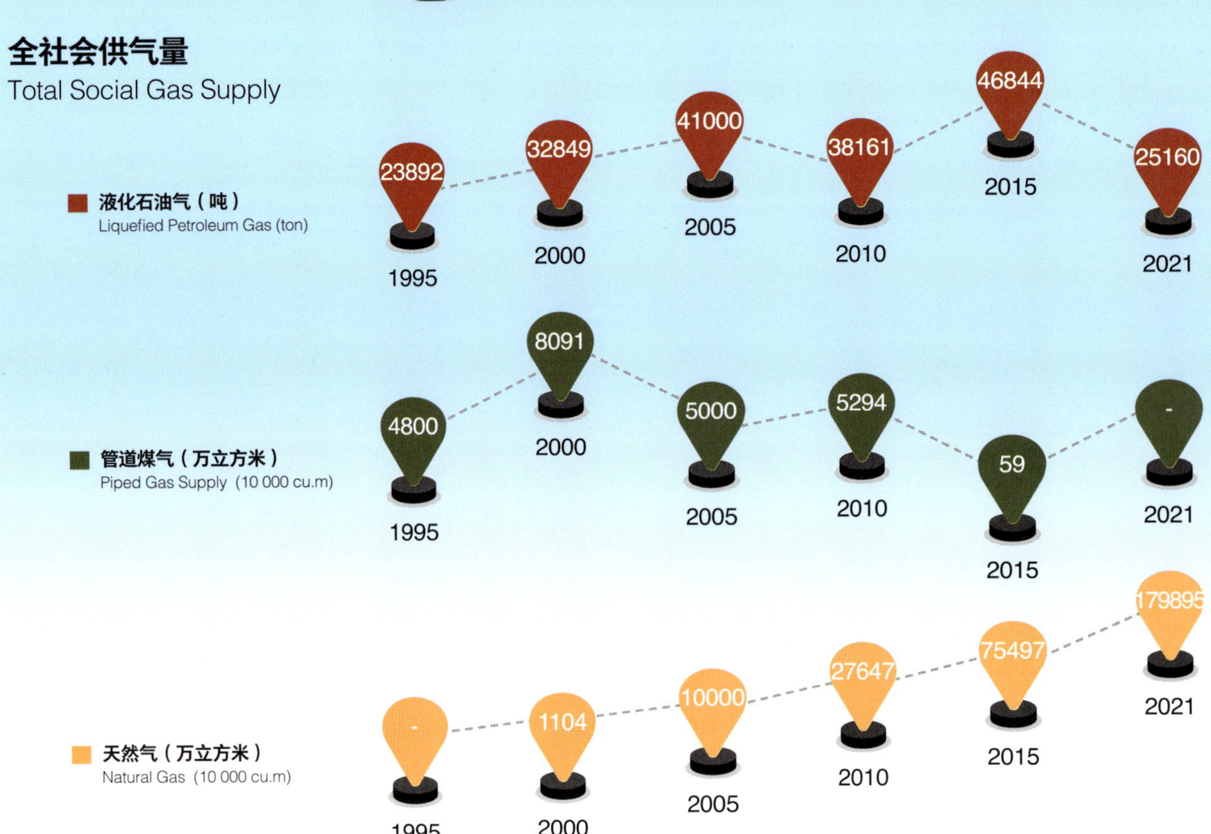

供热面积（万平方米）
Area of Central Heating (10 000 sq.m)

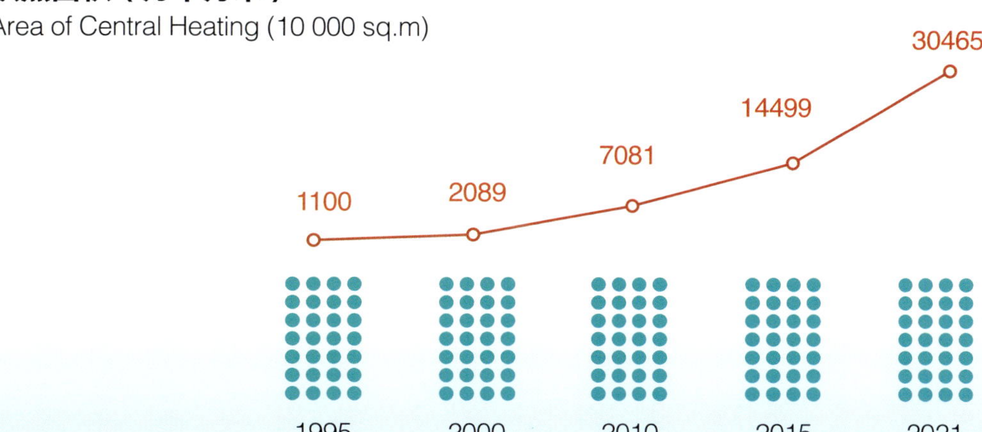

公共交通客运量（万人次）
Public Transportation of Passenger Traffic (10 000 person-times)

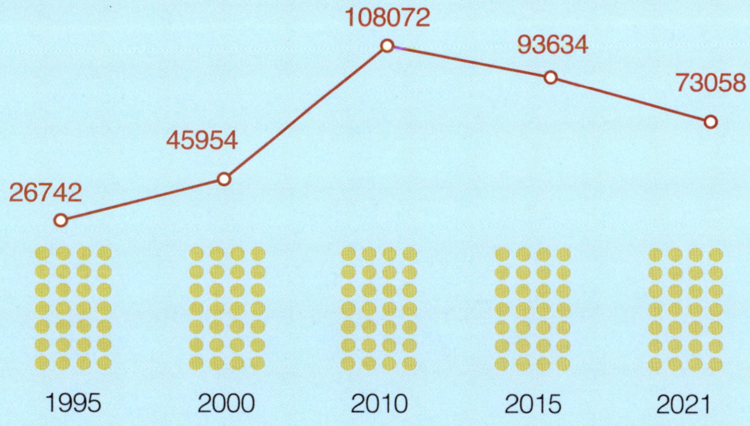

人均公园绿地面积（平方米/人）
Per Capita Public Green Area (sq.m/person)

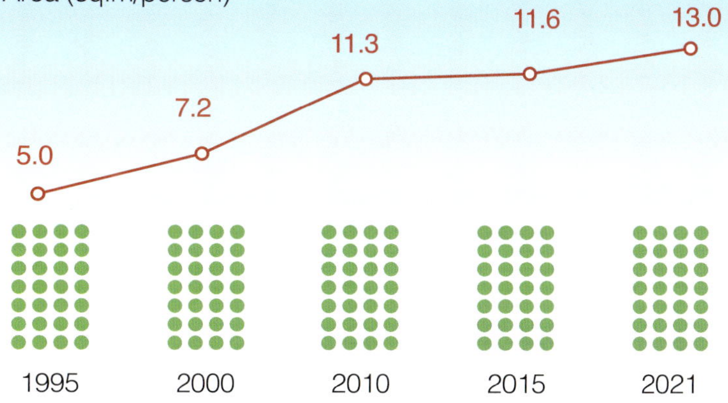

交通 邮电
Transportation Post and Telecommunication

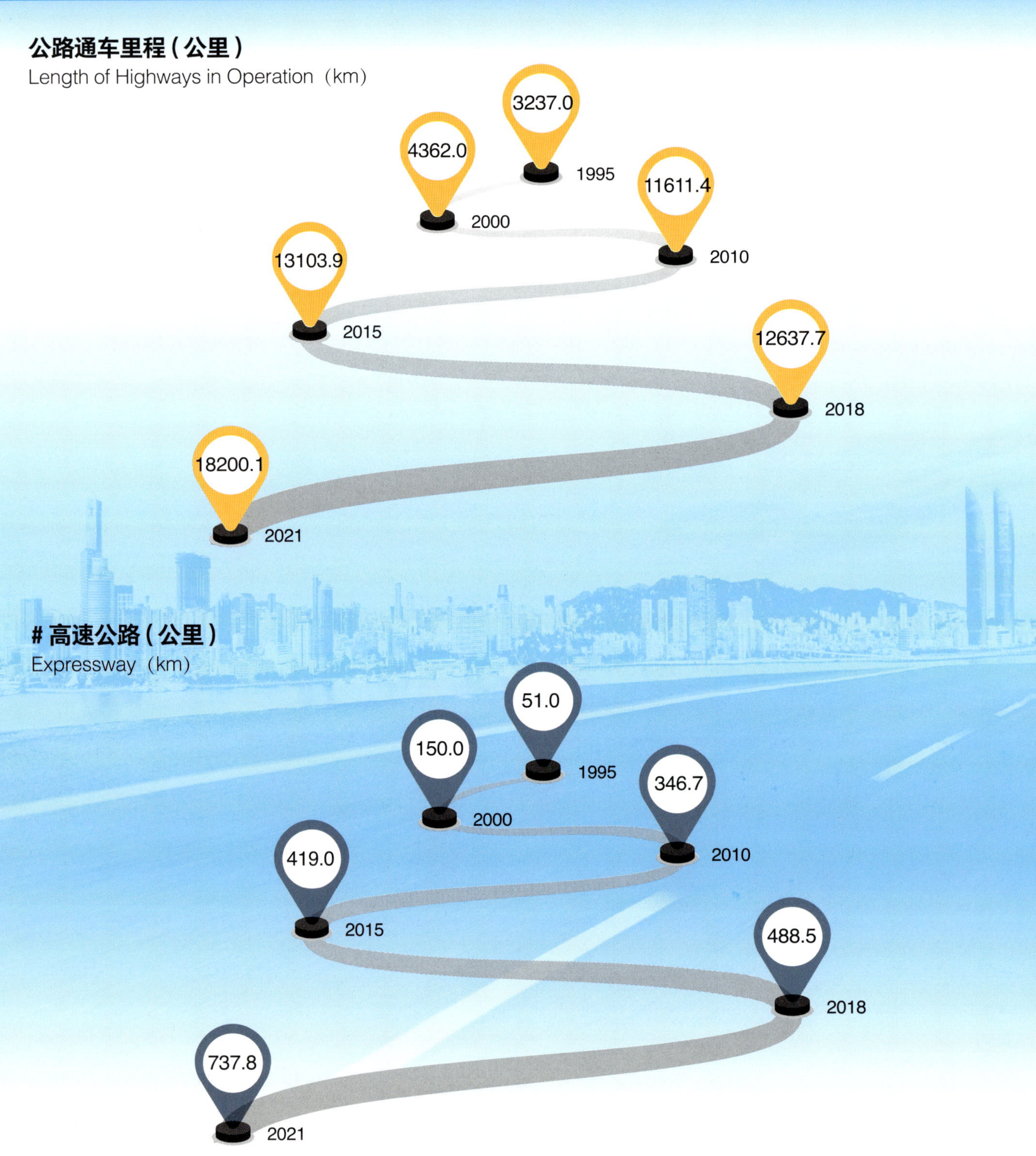

移动电话用户、宽带互联网接入用户数（万户）
Number of Mobile Telephone Subscribers, Subscribers of Broad Band Internet(10 000 subscribers)

移动电话用户（万户）
Number of Mobile Telephone Subscribers (10 000 subscribers)

宽带互联网接入用户数（万户）
Subscribers of Broad Band Internet (10 000 subscribers)

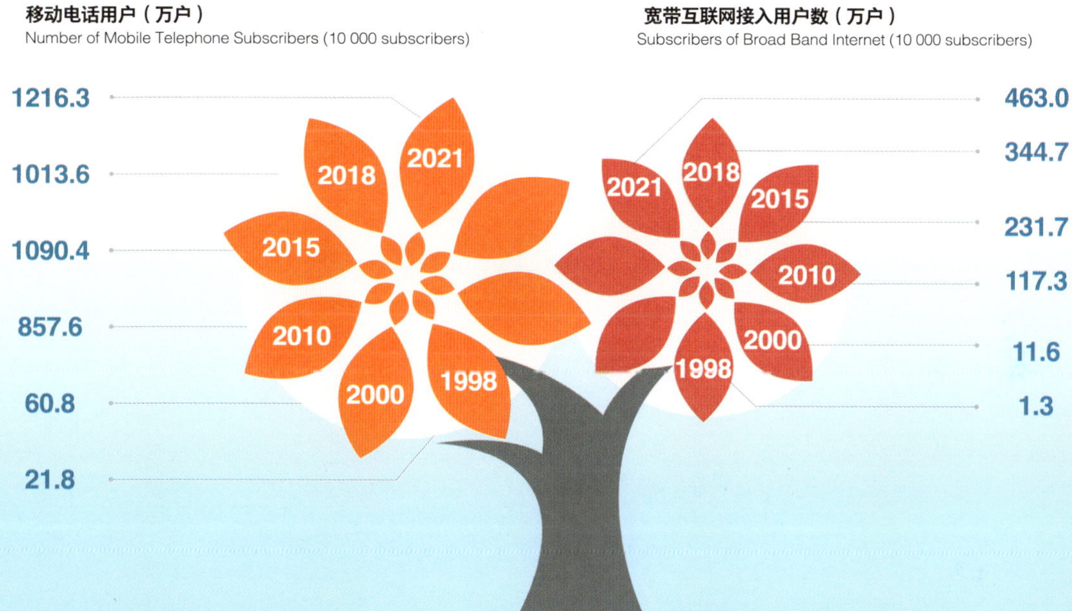

客运量（万人）
Passenger Traffic(10 000 persons)

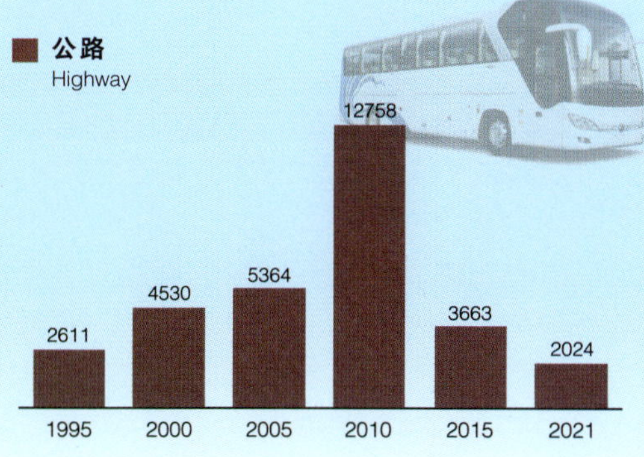

货运量（万吨）
Freight Traffic(10 000 tons)

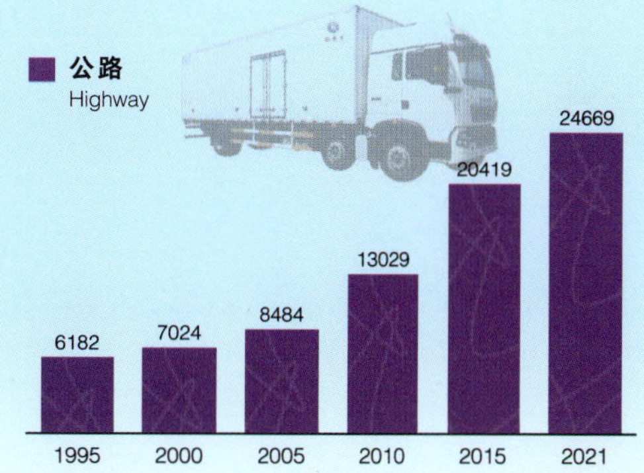

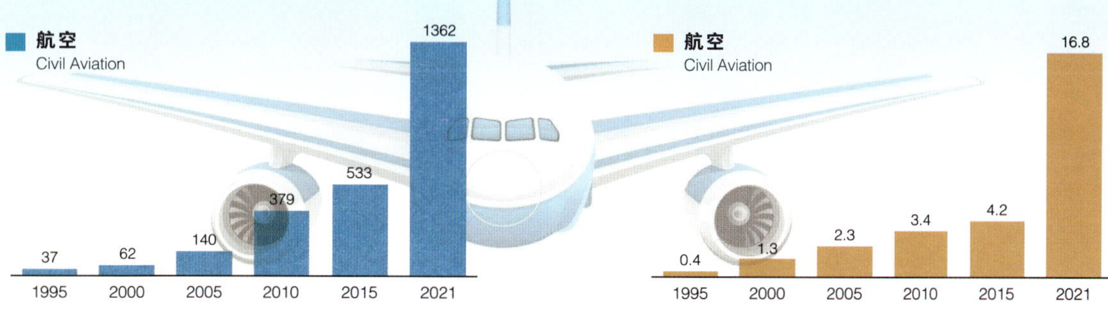

科技 教育 卫生
Science and Technology Education Health

发明专利授权量（件）
The number of invention patents granted(pieces)

各类学校专任教师(人)
Full-time Teachers (person)

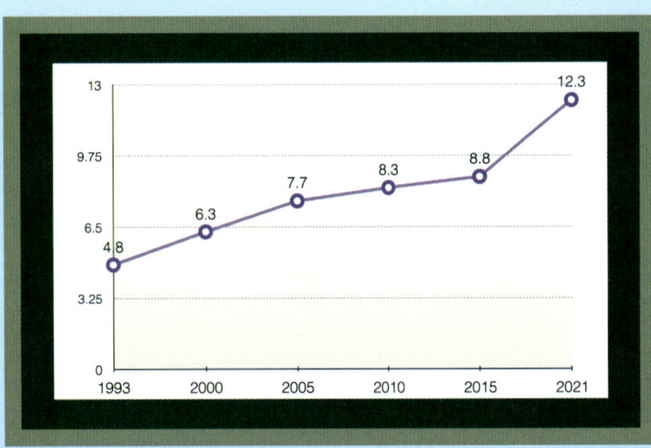

各类学校在校学生（万人）
Total Enrollment (10 000 persons)

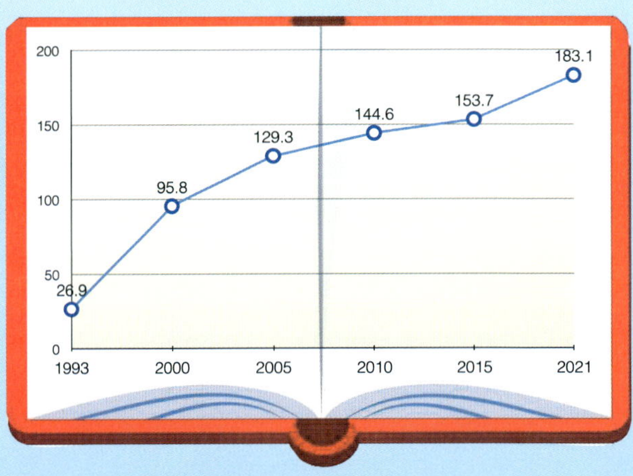

每万人拥有医院床位数（张）
Number of Hospitals Beds per 10000 Population (set)

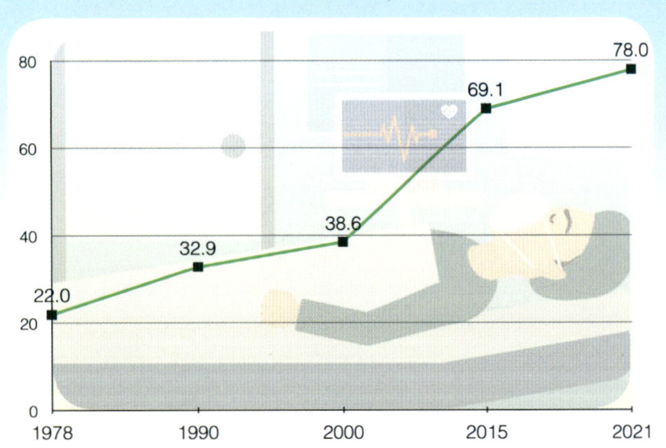

每万人拥有医生数（人）
Number of Doctors per 10000 Population (person)

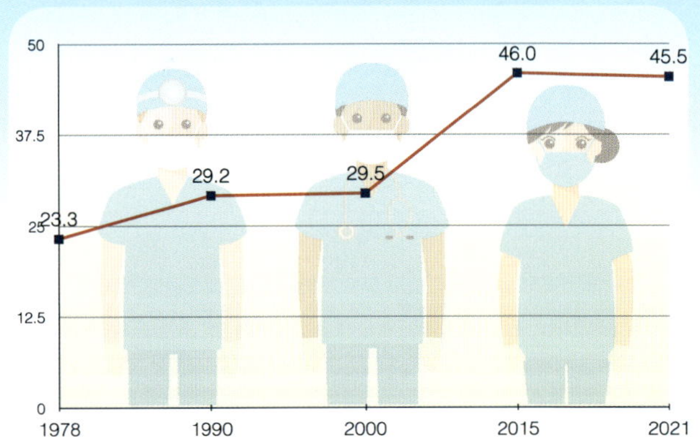

1

行政区划

DIVISIONS OF ADMINISTRATIVE AREAS

1-1 行政区划
Divisions of Administrative Areas

单位：个 (unit)

年份地区	Year and Region	乡 Townships	镇 Towns	街道 Street Communities	村 Village	居委会 Neighborhood committee	土地面积（平方公里）Land Area (sq.km)
全市主要年份							
1989		57	54	53	4710	702	8227
1990		57	54	48	4752	669	8227
1991		57	54	48	4752	670	8227
1992		57	54	48	4759	670	8227
1993		56	55	48	4756	670	8227
1994		55	56	48	4759	670	8227
1995		48	63	49	4723	721	8227
1996		42	68	49	4704	685	8154
1997		42	68	50	4696	616	8154
1998		42	69	50	4711	505	8154
1999		42	69	50	4714	468	8154
2000		42	69	50	4702	416	8154
2001		28	64	54	4677	417	8177
2002		27	65	54	4657	487	8177
2003		27	61	58	4657	487	8177
2004		27	61	58	4657	487	8177
2005		12	53	64	4628	400	8177
2006		11	53	64	4604	487	8177
2007		11	50	73	4563	500	8177
2008		11	50	73	4551	521	8177
2009		11	50	75	4553	522	8177
2010		6	49	86	4552	532	8177
2011		4	51	86	4538	556	8177
2012		4	51	86	4532	586	8177
2013		2	51	90	4548	597	7998
2014		2	51	90	4547	627	7998
2015		2	46	95	4546	641	7998
2016			39	104	4547	669	7998
2017			29	112	4548	711	7998
2018			29	112	4546	740	7998
2019			40	121	5551	847	10244
2020			29	132	5530	861	10244
2021			29	132	4699	992	10244
2021年分地区							
市区	Districts		29	132	4699	992	10244
历下区	Li xia			14		131	101
市中区	Shi zhong			17	77	128	281
槐荫区	Huai yin			16	93	107	152
天桥区	Tian qiao			15	48	153	259
历城区	Li cheng			21	266	99	1301
长清区	Chang qing		2	8	585	60	1209
章丘区	Zhang qiu		1	17	532	61	1719
济阳区	Ji yang		2	8	566	42	1099
莱芜区	Lai wu		7	8	793	69	1740
钢城区	Gang cheng			5	211	33	506
济南高新区	Ji'nan Gao xin				147	50	
济南起步区（直管）	Jinan Start-up Area (Directly under)				303	5	
南部山区	Nan shan				254		
平阴县	Ping yin		6	2	308	29	715
商河县	Shang he		11	1	516	25	1162

注：1. 指标“土地面积”2013年起为第二次全市土地调查数据。
2. 本表内数据由相关主管部门提供。

Notes:1.Indicator "land area" is the city land survey data for the second time as of 2013.
2.The data in this table are provided by the relevant authority departments.

1-2 县区所辖镇、街道办事处(2021 年末)
Town and Street Communities Under the Jurisdiction (End of 2021)

县区	Region	镇、街道办事处数量(个) Number of Towns and Street Communities (unit)	镇、街道办事处名称 Name of Towns and Street Communities
历下区	Li xia	14	解放路街道办事处　千佛山街道办事处　趵突泉街道办事处 泉城路街道办事处　大明湖街道办事处　东关街道办事处 文化东路街道办事处　建筑新村街道办事处　甸柳新村街道办事处 燕山街道办事处　姚家街道办事处　智远街道办事处　龙洞街道办事处 舜华路街道办事处
市中区	Shi zhong	17	大观园街道办事处　杆石桥街道办事处　四里村街道办事处 魏家庄街道办事处　二七新村街道办事处　七里山街道办事处 六里山街道办事处　舜玉路街道办事处　泺源街道办事处 王官庄街道办事处　舜耕街道办事处　白马山街道办事处　七贤街道办事处 十六里河街道办事处　兴隆街道办事处　党家街道办事处　陡沟街道办事处
槐荫区	Huai yin	16	振兴街道办事处　中大槐树街道办事处　道德街道办事处 西市场街道办事处　五里沟街道办事处　营市街道办事处 青年公园街道办事处　南辛庄街道办事处　段店北路街道办事处 张庄路街道办事处　匡山街道办事处　美里湖街道办事处 兴福街道办事处　玉清湖街道办事处　腊山街道办事处　吴家堡街道办事处
天桥区	Tian qiao	15	无影山街道办事处　天桥东街街道办事处　工人新村北村街道办事处 工人新村南村街道办事处　堤口路街道办事处　北坦街道办事处 制锦市街道办事处　宝华街街道办事处　官扎营街道办事处 纬北路街道办事处　药山街道办事处　北园街道办事处 泺口街道办事处　桑梓店街道办事处　大桥街道办事处
历城区	Li cheng	21	山大路街道办事处　洪家楼街道办事处　东风街道办事处　全福街道办事处 荷花路街道办事处　鲍山街道办事处　唐冶街道办事处　临港街道办事处 华山街道办事处　王舍人街道办事处　郭店街道办事处　港沟街道办事处 仲宫街道办事处　彩石街道办事处　董家街道办事处　柳埠街道办事处 遥墙街道办事处　巨野河街道办事处　孙村街道办事处　唐王街道办事处 西营街道办事处
长清区	Chang qing	10	文昌街道办事处　崮云湖街道办事处　平安街道办事处 五峰山街道办事处　归德街道办事处　张夏街道办事处 万德街道办事处　孝里街道办事处　马山镇　双泉镇
章丘区	Zhang qiu	18	明水街道办事处　双山街道办事处　枣园街道办事处　龙山街道办事处 埠村街道办事处　圣井街道办事处　普集街道办事处　绣惠街道办事处 相公庄街道办事处　文祖街道办事处　官庄街道办事处　曹范街道办事处 宁家埠街道办事处　高官寨街道办事处　白云湖街道办事处 刁镇街道办事处　黄河街道办事处　垛庄镇
济阳区	Ji yang	10	济阳街道办事处　济北街道办事处　孙耿街道办事处 回河街道办事处　崔寨街道办事处　太平街道办事处 垛石街道办事处　曲堤街道办事处　仁风镇　新市镇
莱芜区	Lai wu	15	凤城街道办事处　张家洼街道办事处　高庄街道办事处 鹏泉街道办事处　口镇街道办事处　羊里街道办事处 方下街道办事处　雪野街道办事处　牛泉镇　苗山镇 大王庄镇　寨里镇　杨庄镇　茶业口镇　和庄镇
钢城区	Gang cheng	5	艾山街道办事处　里辛街道办事处　汶源街道办事处 颜庄街道办事处　辛庄街道办事处
平阴县	Ping yin	8	榆山街道办事处　锦水街道办事处　东阿镇　孝直镇 孔村镇　洪范池镇　玫瑰镇　安城镇
商河县	Shang he	12	许商街道办事处　殷巷镇　怀仁镇　玉皇庙镇　龙桑寺镇 郑路镇　贾庄镇　白桥镇　孙集镇　韩庙镇　沙河镇　张坊镇

人 口

POPULATION

2-1 主要年份总户数、总人口（户籍人口）
Total Household and Population in Major Years(registered population)

年份 Year	年末总户数 （万户） Total year-end Households (10 000 households)	年末总人口 （万人） Total year-end Population (10 000 persons)	按性别分（万人） Grouped by Sex (10 000 persons)		性别比 （女=100） Sex Ratio (Female=100)	年平均人口 （万人） Annual Average Population (10 000 persons)	比上年增 (‰) Growth Rate (‰)	人口密度 （人/平方公里） Density of Population (Person/sq.km)
			男性 Male	女性 Female				
1952	70.19	318.66	157.68	160.98	97.95	315.94	3.30	387
1957	76.44	346.38	170.30	176.09	96.71	343.25	17.40	421
1962	81.45	351.44	174.55	176.89	98.68	350.18	–4.60	427
1965	83.01	373.22	186.08	187.14	99.43	370.24	19.50	454
1970	89.48	407.50	203.16	204.34	99.42	404.17	16.60	495
1975	96.54	437.73	217.82	219.91	99.05	435.15	9.90	532
1976	98.63	442.09	220.89	221.20	99.86	439.91	10.90	537
1977	100.60	445.05	222.46	222.59	99.94	443.57	8.30	541
1978	102.93	450.67	226.31	224.36	100.87	447.86	9.70	548
1979	105.34	456.37	228.57	227.80	100.34	453.52	12.60	555
1980	106.83	458.61	230.47	228.15	101.02	457.49	8.80	557
1981	110.52	467.93	235.35	232.58	101.19	463.27	12.60	569
1982	112.51	474.23	238.99	235.26	101.59	471.08	16.80	576
1983	114.92	479.38	242.02	237.36	101.54	476.81	12.20	583
1984	116.92	483.85	244.32	239.53	102.00	481.62	10.10	588
1985	120.19	488.39	246.86	241.53	102.21	486.12	9.30	594
1986	122.67	494.06	250.09	243.97	102.51	491.23	10.50	601
1987	125.43	501.03	253.95	247.08	102.78	497.55	12.90	609
1988	130.32	507.18	257.22	249.86	102.95	504.11	13.20	616
1989	134.77	513.39	260.79	252.61	103.24	510.29	12.30	624
1990	140.36	523.60	265.91	257.69	103.19	518.50	16.10	636
1991	143.42	527.43	267.78	259.65	103.13	525.52	13.50	641
1992	147.50	530.70	269.46	261.25	103.14	529.07	6.70	645
1993	149.42	533.53	270.77	262.76	103.05	532.12	5.80	649

2-1 续表 continued

年份 Year	年末总户数 (万户) Total year-end Households (10 000 households)	年末总人口 (万人) Total year-end Population (10 000 persons)	按性别分 (万人) Grouped by Sex (10 000 persons)		性别比 (女=100) Sex Ratio (Female=100)	年平均人口 (万人) Annual Average Population (10 000 persons)	比上年增 (‰) Growth Rate (‰)	人口密度 (人/平方公里) Density of Population (Person/sq.km)
			男性 Male	女性 Female				
1994	153.60	537.31	272.76	264.54	103.11	535.42	6.20	653
1995	156.45	542.12	274.98	267.14	102.93	539.72	8.00	656
1996	156.42	543.45	275.59	267.86	102.89	542.79	5.70	666
1997	157.66	549.20	278.30	270.90	102.73	546.33	6.50	674
1998	160.93	553.54	279.91	273.63	102.30	551.37	9.20	679
1999	163.52	557.63	281.71	275.93	102.09	555.59	7.70	684
2000	166.63	562.65	284.19	278.46	102.06	560.14	8.20	690
2001	168.46	569.00	287.39	281.61	102.06	565.83	10.20	696
2002	170.10	575.01	290.58	284.43	102.16	572.00	10.90	703
2003	172.18	582.56	294.04	288.52	101.91	578.78	11.90	712
2004	173.24	590.08	297.25	292.82	101.51	586.32	13.03	722
2005	177.69	597.44	300.42	297.02	101.15	593.76	12.69	731
2006	179.48	603.35	302.72	300.63	100.70	600.39	11.17	738
2007	181.88	604.85	302.87	301.98	100.29	604.10	6.17	740
2008	184.63	603.99	302.00	301.99	100.00	604.42	0.53	739
2009	187.70	603.27	301.26	302.01	99.75	603.63	-1.30	738
2010	190.65	604.08	301.28	302.80	99.50	603.68	0.08	739
2011	193.61	606.64	302.19	304.44	99.26	605.36	2.78	742
2012	195.79	609.21	303.30	305.91	99.15	607.92	4.23	745
2013	199.67	613.25	304.93	308.32	98.90	611.23	5.44	767
2014	201.93	621.61	309.09	312.52	98.90	617.43	15.64	777
2015	203.59	625.73	310.92	314.80	98.77	623.67	10.11	782
2016	205.45	632.83	314.28	318.55	98.66	629.28	9.00	791
2017	208.08	643.62	319.21	324.41	98.40	638.22	14.21	805
2018	216.64	655.90	324.74	331.15	98.06	649.76	19.08	820
2019	270.26	796.74	395.30	401.44	98.47	726.32	21.47	778
2020	276.35	806.72	399.61	407.11	98.16	801.73	12.45	788
2021	283.04	816.61	404.03	412.57	97.93	811.67		797

2-2 主要年份市区总户数、总人口（户籍人口）
Total Household and Population of Urban in Major Years(registered population)

年份 Year	年末总户数（万户） Total year-end Households (10 000 households)	年末总人口（万人） Total year-end Population (10 000 persons)	按性别分（万人） Grouped by Sex (10 000 persons)		年平均人口（万人） Annual Average Population (10 000 persons)
			男性 Male	女性 Female	
1952	26.46	124.96	63.95	61.01	123.83
1957	29.13	143.17	72.05	71.13	140.11
1962	32.25	153.35	78.52	74.83	154.18
1965	34.03	162.82	83.20	79.62	161.90
1970	37.21	167.82	85.61	82.21	168.51
1975	40.67	178.78	90.83	87.95	177.74
1976	41.59	180.99	91.83	89.16	179.88
1977	42.34	181.49	91.92	89.57	181.24
1978	43.79	186.43	94.70	91.73	183.96
1979	45.33	189.26	96.22	93.04	187.84
1980	46.12	190.01	97.22	92.79	189.63
1981	48.64	194.05	99.37	94.69	192.03
1982	50.60	201.31	101.44	99.87	197.68
1983	52.32	205.48	103.42	102.07	203.39
1984	54.30	209.55	105.57	103.99	207.52
1985	56.88	213.28	107.96	105.33	211.42
1986	58.65	216.98	111.54	105.43	215.13
1987	60.54	221.49	113.79	107.70	219.23
1988	63.03	225.00	115.51	109.39	223.25
1989	65.29	228.88	117.49	111.39	226.94
1990	81.22	283.66	145.29	138.36	
1991	83.30	286.20	146.55	139.65	284.93
1992	85.87	288.52	145.19	143.33	287.36
1993	88.02	291.24	149.07	142.17	289.88
1994	90.10	294.60	150.75	143.85	292.92
1995	92.04	299.20	152.97	146.23	296.90

2-2 续表 continued

年份 Year	年末总户数 (万户) Total year-end Households (10 000 households)	年末总人口 (万人) Total year-end Population (10 000 persons)	按性别分(万人) Grouped by Sex (10 000 persons)		年平均人口 (万人) Annual Average Population (10 000 persons)
			男性 Male	女性 Female	
1996	93.12	302.78	154.58	148.20	300.99
1997	93.90	306.98	156.54	150.44	304.88
1998	96.65	309.90	157.58	152.32	308.44
1999	97.74	313.18	159.19	153.99	311.54
2000	99.25	317.20	161.03	156.17	315.19
2001	100.53	322.45	163.73	158.72	319.83
2002	101.62	327.55	166.43	161.12	325.00
2003	102.71	334.80	169.84	164.96	331.18
2004	102.68	341.73	172.91	168.82	338.27
2005	104.87	347.87	175.41	172.45	344.80
2006	106.19	352.29	177.10	175.19	350.08
2007	107.55	352.71	176.70	176.01	352.50
2008	109.26	350.23	175.08	175.15	351.47
2009	111.07	348.24	173.71	174.53	349.24
2010	112.91	348.02	173.19	174.83	348.13
2011	114.75	349.44	173.51	175.93	348.73
2012	116.49	352.17	174.55	177.62	350.81
2013	118.50	355.38	175.86	179.52	353.78
2014	120.33	360.99	178.55	182.44	358.19
2015	121.96	364.54	180.12	184.42	362.77
2016	154.64	473.33	233.74	239.59	418.94
2017	157.42	483.75	238.48	245.27	478.54
2018	182.76	554.13	273.31	280.82	518.94
2019	236.31	695.09	343.90	351.19	689.31
2020	242.04	705.33	348.36	356.97	700.21
2021	248.66	715.55	352.90	362.66	710.44

注：1990 年以前的数据中不包括长清区。2016 年起数据包括章丘区。2018 年起数据包括济阳区。2019 年起数据包括莱芜区、钢城区。

Note:The data before 1990 excludes Changqing District. The data as of 2016 includes Zhangqiu District The data as of 2018 includes Jiyang District.Data after the year of 2019 involves Laiwu District and Gangcheng District.

2-3 主要年份人口自然变动情况
Natural Change of Population in Major Years

年份 Year	申报出生人口 （人） Population of Birth (person)	申报出生率 (‰) Birth Rate (‰)	申报死亡人口 （人） Population of Death (person)	申报死亡率 (‰) Death Rate (‰)	人口自然增长 （人） Population of Natural Growth (person)	人口自然增长率 (‰) Natural Growth Rate (‰)
1952	72861	23.06	29949	9.48	42912	13.58
1957	108432	31.59	38082	11.09	70350	20.50
1962	108029	30.85	44464	12.70	63565	18.15
1965	121364	32.78	39355	10.63	82009	22.15
1970	111861	27.68	29965	7.41	81896	20.27
1975	82939	19.06	33837	7.78	49102	11.28
1976	70065	15.93	34693	7.89	35372	8.04
1977	67413	15.20	33723	7.60	33690	7.60
1978	69541	15.53	31343	7.00	38198	8.53
1979	72596	16.01	30205	6.66	42391	9.35
1980	60336	13.19	32004	7.00	28332	6.19
1981	70327	15.18	31671	6.84	38656	8.34
1982	74147	15.74	28679	6.09	45468	9.65
1983	56454	11.84	30080	6.31	26374	5.53
1984	61156	12.70	32277	6.70	28879	6.00
1985	55386	11.39	31678	6.52	23708	4.87
1986	69901	14.23	30790	6.27	39111	7.96
1987	86752	17.44	30007	6.03	56745	11.41
1988	78922	15.66	32850	6.52	46072	9.14
1989	76380	14.97	30721	6.02	45659	8.95
1990	66806	12.88	33916	6.54	32890	6.34
1991	59374	11.30	32675	6.20	26699	5.10
1992	52825	9.98	34969	6.61	17856	3.37
1993	46007	8.65	35317	6.64	10690	2.01
1994	49940	9.30	35308	6.60	14632	2.70
1995	54132	10.03	34107	6.32	20025	3.71

2-3 续表 continued

年份 Year	申报出生人口 (人) Population of Birth (person)	申报出生率 (‰) Birth Rate (‰)	申报死亡人口 (人) Population of Death (person)	申报死亡率 (‰) Death Rate (‰)	人口自然增长 (人) Population of Natural Growth (person)	人口自然增长率 (‰) Natural Growth Rate (‰)
1996	58254	10.73	36452	6.71	21802	4.02
1997	62245	11.39	35768	6.55	26477	4.84
1998	62490	11.33	36497	6.64	25893	4.69
1999	55931	10.07	34956	6.29	20975	3.78
2000	62059	11.08	39499	7.05	22560	4.03
2001	55536	9.82	33816	5.98	21720	3.84
2002	57317	10.02	36234	6.33	21083	3.69
2003	54599	9.43	42539	7.35	12060	2.08
2004	60670	10.35	38158	6.51	22512	3.84
2005	60240	10.15	37782	6.36	22458	3.78
2006	57706	9.61	39040	6.50	18666	3.11
2007	58367	9.66	39752	6.58	18615	3.08
2008	59600	9.86	39887	6.60	19713	3.26
2009	56694	9.39	40911	6.78	15783	2.61
2010	67162	11.13	50380	8.35	16782	2.78
2011	66563	11.00	40310	6.66	26253	4.34
2012	71449	11.75	49148	8.08	22301	3.67
2013	69351	11.35	41713	6.82	27638	4.53
2014	110503	17.90	41887	6.78	68616	11.11
2015	73688	11.82	41999	6.73	31689	5.09
2016	91941	14.61	39460	6.27	52481	8.34
2017	113766	17.83	62958	9.86	50808	7.96
2018	94694	14.57	45374	6.98	49320	7.59
2019	101723	12.86	52396	6.62	49327	6.24
2020	83782	10.45	58568	7.31	25214	3.14
2021	66666	8.21	44228	5.45	22438	2.76

2-4 分地区户数、人口数(2021年)(户籍人口)
Household and Population by Region(2021)(registered population)

地区	Region	户数 (户) Households (household)	人口数 (人) Population (person)	按性别分(人) Grouped by Sex (person)	
				男性 Male	女性 Female
全市	Total City	2830448	8166065	4040349	4125716
市区	Districts	2486567	7155500	3528950	3626550
历下区	Li xia	261709	764725	372606	392119
市中区	Shi zhong	258205	692513	336264	356249
槐荫区	Huai yin	178916	482333	231798	250535
天桥区	Tian qiao	200945	545931	264573	281358
历城区	Li cheng	396840	1151885	565872	586013
长清区	Chang qing	187550	571347	284380	286967
章丘区	Zhang qiu	321540	1053942	520846	533096
济阳区	Ji yang	177539	600831	302218	298613
莱芜区	Lai wu	388157	993319	497495	495824
钢城区	Gang cheng	115166	298674	152898	145776
平阴县	Ping yin	136582	371062	185909	185153
商河县	Shang he	207299	639503	325490	314013

2-5 分地区人口机械变动情况 (2021 年)
Un-Natural Changes of Population by Region (2021)

地区	Region	迁入人口 (人) Move Into the Population (person)	迁入率 (‰) Move In Rate (‰)	迁出人口 (人) Move Out the population (person)	迁出率 (‰) Move Out Rate (‰)	人口机械增长 (人) Mechanical Growth of Population (person)	人口机械增长率 (‰) Mechanical Growth Rates of Population (‰)
全市	Total	114581	14.03	37539	4.60	77042	9.43
市区	Districts	108268	15.13	25882	3.62	82386	11.51
历下区	Li xia	20558	26.88	5406	7.07	15152	19.81
市中区	Shi zhong	13571	19.60	3590	5.18	9981	14.41
槐荫区	Huai yin	17120	35.49	2182	4.52	14938	30.97
天桥区	Tian qiao	12837	23.51	2028	3.71	10809	19.80
历城区	Li cheng	33071	28.71	4041	3.51	29030	25.20
长清区	Chang qing	3233	5.66	1434	2.51	1799	3.15
章丘区	Zhang qiu	3219	3.05	2318	2.20	901	0.85
济阳区	Ji yang	1697	2.82	1226	2.04	471	0.78
莱芜区	Lai wu	2251	2.27	2791	2.81	-540	-0.54
钢城区	Gang cheng	712	2.38	866	2.90	-154	-0.52
平阴县	Ping yin	2108	5.68	4249	11.45	-2141	-5.77
商河县	Shang he	4205	6.58	7408	11.58	-3203	-5.01

2-6 分地区人口自然变动情况 (2021 年)
Natural Changes of Population by Region (2021)

地区	Region	申报出生人口 (人) Population of Birth (person)	申报出生率 (‰) Birth Rate (‰)	申报死亡人口 (人) Population of Death (person)	申报死亡率 (‰) Death Rate (‰)	人口自然增长 (人) Population of Natural Growth (person)	人口自然增长率 (‰) Natural Growth Rate (‰)
全市	Total	66666	8.16	44228	5.42	22438	2.75
市区	Districts	59568	8.32	39243	5.48	20325	2.84
历下区	Li xia	7191	9.40	2543	3.33	4648	6.08
市中区	Shi zhong	5761	8.32	3231	4.67	2530	3.65
槐荫区	Huai yin	4680	9.70	2150	4.46	2530	5.25
天桥区	Tian qiao	4508	8.26	3080	5.64	1428	2.62
历城区	Li cheng	12715	11.04	6260	5.43	6455	5.60
长清区	Chang qing	4164	7.29	4429	7.75	-265	-0.46
章丘区	Zhang qiu	7064	6.70	7235	6.86	-171	-0.16
济阳区	Ji yang	5369	8.94	2665	4.44	2704	4.50
莱芜区	Lai wu	6354	6.40	6241	6.28	113	0.11
钢城区	Gang cheng	1762	5.90	1409	4.72	353	1.18
平阴县	Ping yin	2391	6.44	1110	2.99	1281	3.45
商河县	Shang he	4707	7.36	3875	6.06	832	1.30

2-7 结婚情况
Number of Marriages

单位: 对 (couple)

地区	Region	2016 年	2017 年	2018 年	2019 年	2020 年	2021 年
总计	Total	47457	52663	51383	52300	50521	49380
市直	Departments Directly Under the Municipal Government	82	67	90			
历下区	Li xia	5742	5830	5763	5456	5634	6196
市中区	Shi zhong	5364	5973	5699	5092	5074	4927
槐荫区	Huai yin	3445	3728	3863	3452	3434	3802
天桥区	Tian qiao	4447	4563	4874	4287	3869	3445
历城区	Li cheng	7296	7551	7419	6809	6094	5591
长清区	Chang qing	3649	4331	4003	3930	3547	3273
章丘区	Zhang qiu	6135	7613	6840	6000	6016	5315
济阳区	Ji yang	3615	4023	4248	3629	3154	2146
莱芜区	Lai wu				4514	4054	3970
钢城区	Gang cheng				1183	1117	1060
济南高新区	Ji'nan Gao xin	1593	2516	2621	2533	2783	2982
济南起步区（直管）	Jinan Start-up Area(Directly under)					560	1312
南部山区	Nan shan						816
平阴县	Ping yin	2563	2564	2330	1974	1881	1632
商河县	Shang he	3526	3904	3633	3441	3304	2913

2-8 离婚情况
Number of Divorces

单位: 对 (couple)

地区	Region	2016 年	2017 年	2018 年	2019 年	2020 年	2021 年
总计	Total	26915	32491	31611	35932	36515	23837
法院数	Divorce Case Handled	6909	6024	6228	7034	6887	6331
民政数	Divorces Handled through Civil	20006	26467	25383	28898	29628	17506
市直	Departments Directly Under the Municipal Government	17	25	19			
历下区	Li xia	2800	3474	3322	3644	3889	2331
市中区	Shi zhong	2327	3448	3288	3441	3785	2254
槐荫区	Huai yin	1720	2223	2362	2416	2530	1701
天桥区	Tian qiao	2224	2834	2810	3031	2936	1665
历城区	Li cheng	3177	4337	3664	4195	4398	2261
长清区	Chang qing	1422	1549	1801	1864	1953	1092
章丘区	Zhang qiu	2171	3303	2916	2793	2763	1633
济阳区	Ji yang	1434	1733	1783	1745	1587	652
莱芜区	Lai Wu				1418	1220	817
钢城区	Gang cheng				502	432	240
济南高新区	Ji'nan Gao xin	557	1097	1127	1322	1495	1005
济南起步区（直管）	Jinan Start-up Area(Directly under)					269	373
南部山区	Nan shan						319
平阴县	Ping yin	938	993	839	968	938	490
商河县	Shang he	1219	1451	1452	1559	1433	673

主要统计指标解释

人口统计资料主要有三个来源　人口普查、人口抽样调查和人口经常性登记。

人口普查　是在国家规定的统一时间内，用统一的方法，统一的调查项目，对全国或某一地区的人口进行的一种专门调查。

人口抽样调查　是从所要研究的总人口中，随机抽取部分人口，并根据对这些人口调查所得到的数据来推算该人口总体相应指标的方法。

人口经常性登记　是指对人口出生、死亡、婚姻、迁移等事件进行连续的、持久的、强制的全面登记制度。

人口数　指一定时点、一定地区范围内的有生命的个人的总和。

年度统计的年末人口数　指每年12月31日24时的人口数。

出生率（又称粗出生率）　指在一定时期内（通常为一年）平均每千人所出生的人数的比率，一般用千分率表示。计算公式为:

出生率＝年出生人数／年平均人数 ×1000‰

式中: 出生人数指活产婴儿，即胎儿脱离母体时(不管怀孕月数)，有过呼吸或其他生命现象。

出生人数　是指活产婴儿，即胎儿脱离母体时（不管怀孕月数），有过呼吸或其他生命现象。

年平均人数　是指年初、年底人口数的平均数，也可用年中人口数代替。

死亡率（又称粗死亡率）　指在一定时期内（通常为一年）一定地区的死亡人数与同期平均人数（或期中人数）之比，一般用千分率表示。计算公式为:

死亡率＝年死亡人数／年平均人数 ×1000‰

人口自然增长率　指在一定时期内（通常为一年）人口自然增加数（出生人数减死亡人数）与该时期内平均人数（或期中人数）之比，一般用千分率表示。计算公式为:

人口自然增长率＝（本年出生人数－本年死亡人数）／年平均人数 ×1000‰

人口自然增长率＝人口出生率－人口死亡率

机械增长率　是反映迁移变动的一个相对指标。它表明一个地区在一定时间内迁入人口数与迁出人口数相抵后的差额与总人口数的比率，一般用千分率表示。计算公式为:

机械增长率＝一定时期的迁入迁出人口差额／该时期的平均人口 ×100%

人口密度　指一定时点，一定地区的人口数与该时点、该地区的面积之比，即一定时点的单位土地面积上的人口数，通常以每平方公里的居民人数来表示:

人口密度＝该地区人口数／该地区土地面积 ×100%

性别比　反映两性人口间比例的指标，指在总人口中或各年龄组人口中，男性人数与女性人数之比。通常以每100个女性人口相对应的男性人口数。计算公式:

性别比＝男性人口／女性人口 ×100%

Explanatory Notes on Main Statistical Indicators

Source of Demographic Data population census, sample survey of population and recurrent registration of population.

Population Census refers to an official survey of total population nationwide or in a given region by an official method within a given period of time in China.

Sample Survey of Population refers to the method of calculating corresponding indicators of total population pursuant to the data originated from the survey of partial population randomly extracted from the total population to be researched.

Recurrent registration of population refers to continuous, persistent and enforced registration system for population birth, death, marriage, and migration , etc.

Total Population refers to the total number of people alive at a certain point of time within a given area.

The Annual Statistics on Total Population is taken at midnight, the 31st of December.

Birth Rate (or Crude Birth Rate) refers to the ratio of births per one thousand people during a certain period of time (generally a year), expressed in permillage. The following formula is used:

Birth rate = Number of births/Annual average population *1,000‰
Wherein: Births refer to liveborn infants, namely those with breath or other vital signs when breaking away from the mother (regardless of number of months of pregnancy).

Births refer to liveborn infants, namely those with breath or other vital signs when breaking away from the mother (regardless of number of months of pregnancy).

Annual Average Population refers to the mean value of the number of people at the beginning and ending of the year, which can be replaced with the number of people in the middle of the year.

Death Rate (or Crude Death Rate) refers to the ratio of the number of deaths to the average population (or mid period population) during a certain period of time (usually a year), expressed in ‰ . The following formula is used:

Death rate = number of deaths/annual average population *1,000‰

Natural Growth Rate of Population refers to the ratio of natural increase in population (number of births minus number of deaths) in a certain period of time (usually a year) to the average population (or mid period population) of the same period, expressed in ‰ . The following formula is used:

Natural Growth Rate of Population=(number of births – number of deaths)/ annual average population * 1,000‰

Natural Growth Rate of Population=Birth Rate–Death Rate

Mechanical Growth Rate is a relative indicator that reflects changes in the population migration. It shows the ratio of the balance (between the people count moving in and out of a given area) to total population during a certain period of time, expressed in permillage. The following formula is used:

Mechanical growth rate = the balance between people count moving in and out of a given area during a certain period of time/average population * 100%

Population Density refers to the ratio of total population in a given area at a certain point of time to the area at this point of time, namely total population per area of land at a certain point of time, expressed in number of residents per square kilometers:

Population density= Total population in the region/Land area in the region*100%

Sex ratio refers to the ratio of male to female population in total population or age groups, male population to per 100 female populations. The following formula is used:

Sex ratio= Male n population/Female population*100%

综合

GENERAL SURVEY

3-1 国民经济和社会发展总量指标
Principal Aggregate Indicators on National Economic and Social Development

指标	Item	单位 Unit	1978 年
面积	Area		
土地面积	Land Area	平方公里 (sq.km)	
#市内十区建成区面积	Built-up Area of Ten Districts in the City	平方公里 (sq.km)	85
人口	Population		
年末总户数（户籍人口）	Total year-end Households（Household Population）	万户 (10 000 households)	102.93
年末总人口	Total year-end Population	万人 (10 000 persons)	450.67
#市区	Population	万人 (10 000 persons)	186.43
#男性	Male	万人 (10 000 persons)	226.31
年末常住总人口	Total Resident Population at the Year-end	万人 (10 000 persons)	
就业	Employment		
全社会从业人员	Employed Persons	万人 (10 000 persons)	204.04
第一产业	Primary Industry	万人 (10 000 persons)	136.30
第二产业	Secondary Industry	万人 (10 000 persons)	46.06
第三产业	Tertiary Industry	万人 (10 000 persons)	21.68
职工平均工资	Average Wage of Staff and Workers	元 (yuan)	578
城镇非私营单位就业人员平均工资	Average Wage of Employed Persons in Urban Non Private Entities	元 (yuan)	
城镇非私营单位在岗职工平均工资	Average Wage of Staff and Workers in Urban Non Private Entities	元 (yuan)	
城镇私营单位就业人员平均工资	Average Wage of Employed Persons in Urban Private Entities	元 (yuan)	
城镇登记失业人员数	Registered Urban Unemployed Persons	万人 (10 000 persons)	
城镇登记失业率	Registered Urban Unemployment Rate	%	
国民经济核算	National Accounting		
地区生产总值	Gross Domestic Product	亿元 (100 million yuan)	23.60
#非公有制经济	Non-public Economy	亿元 (100 million yuan)	
第一产业	Primary Industry	亿元 (100 million yuan)	4.16
第二产业	Secondary Industry	亿元 (100 million yuan)	13.32
第三产业	Tertiary Industry	亿元 (100 million yuan)	6.12
人均地区生产总值	Per Capita GDP	元 (yuan)	527
固定资产投资	Investment in Fixed Assets		
固定资产投资	Investment in Fixed Assets	亿元 (100 million yuan)	3.19
第一产业	Primary Industry	亿元 (100 million yuan)	0.55
第二产业	Secondary Industry	亿元 (100 million yuan)	1.15
#工业	Industry	亿元 (100 million yuan)	0.75
第三产业	Tertiary Industry	亿元 (100 million yuan)	1.29
#房地产投资	Real Estate Investment	亿元 (100 million yuan)	0.00
财政税收	Fiscal Tax Revenue		
一般公共预算收入	General Public Budget Revenue	亿元 (100 million yuan)	5.90
一般公共预算支出	General Public Budget Expenditure	亿元 (100 million yuan)	1.50
地域税收收入	Regional Tax Revenue	亿元 (100 million yuan)	
国税税收收入	National Tax Revenue	亿元 (100 million yuan)	
地税税收收入	Land Tax Revenue	亿元 (100 million yuan)	

1990 年	1995 年	2000 年	2005 年	2010 年	2015 年	2018 年	2019 年	2020 年	2021 年
8227	8227	8154	8177	8177	7998	7998	10244	10244	10244
103	114	120	295	347	393	524	716	794	841
140.36	156.45	166.63	177.69	190.65	203.59	216.64	270.26	276.35	283.04
523.60	542.12	562.65	597.44	604.08	625.73	655.90	796.74	806.72	816.61
232.30	247.57	317.20	347.87	348.02	458.16	554.13	695.09	705.33	715.55
265.91	274.98	284.19	300.42	301.28	310.92	324.74	395.30	399.61	404.03
				681.80	713.20	746.04	890.87	924.16	933.61
270.54	324.22	347.37	360.00	373.70	388.70	419.27	492.36	468.90	470.78
125.73	116.13	109.98	99.10	76.66	71.80	68.80	77.42	–	–
87.75	106.68	110.81	114.20	120.20	124.70	132.17	154.27	–	–
57.06	101.41	126.58	146.70	176.84	192.20	218.30	260.67	–	–
2211	5851	10422	20866	31096	58578	71142	–	–	–
							97482	104990	114596
							100593	108391	119245
							51530	60348	60914
	2.45	3.90	5.75	5.97	3.20	3.49	3.53	–	–
	2.30	3.70	3.86	3.84	2.04	2.06	2.01	2.03	–
138.24	473.52	944.13	1846.28	3910.53	6100.23	7856.56	9443.37	10140.91	11432.22
		238.32	768.50	1664.43	2599.60	3237.50			
23.93	67.64	96.02	134.34	215.17	305.39	272.42	343.06	361.66	408.77
67.36	220.37	414.74	847.47	1637.45	2307.00	2829.31	3265.22	3530.67	3964.06
46.95	185.51	433.38	864.47	2057.90	3487.84	4754.83	5835.09	6248.58	7059.39
2666	8773	16855	28900	57947	85919	106302	106416	110199	123075
30.60	112.76	305.95	857.00	1987.44	3498.42	–	–	–	–
0.52	3.24	13.57	38.28	68.08	102.52	–	–	–	–
14.62	46.26	73.14	362.05	677.28	1217.39	–	–	–	–
2.05	45.35	67.72	352.27	667.35	1147.87	–	–	–	–
13.94	63.27	219.24	456.67	1242.08	2178.51	–	–	–	–
2.18	16.46	50.53	121.09	484.50	1014.14	1369.35	1576.93	1707.63	1928.00
12.40	16.99	49.05	106.15	266.13	614.32	752.82	874.19	906.08	1007.61
8.20	19.63	54.72	120.66	336.80	658.20	1018.32	1197.32	1288.80	1293.08
	53.49	112.35	231.34	527.70	959.33	1240.20	1419.58	1369.16	1555.89
	39.55	72.54	144.20	309.87	494.43	755.63	–	–	–
	13.94	39.80	87.14	217.82	464.90	484.58	–	–	–

3-1 续表 1 continued 1

指标	Item	单位 Unit	1978 年
金融保险	Finance and Insurance		
金融机构人民币存款余额	RMB Deposits Balance of Financial Institutions	亿元 (100 million yuan)	15.43
# 住户存款	Deposits of Households	亿元 (100 million yuan)	1.14
金融机构人民币贷款余额	RMB Loans Balance of Financial Institutions	亿元 (100 million yuan)	14.08
# 短期贷款	Short-term Loans	亿元 (100 million yuan)	-
保险金额	Insured Amount	亿元 (100 million yuan)	
保费收入	Premium Income	万元 (10 000 yuan)	
赔付支出	Claim Payment	万元 (10 000 yuan)	
农业	Agriculture		
农林牧渔业总产值	Gross Output Value of Farming Forestry,Animal Husbandry and Fishery	亿元 (100 million yuan)	6.57
农用机械总动力	total power of agricultural machinery	万千瓦 (10 000kW)	69.70
年末实有耕地面积	Actual cultivated Area at Year-end	千公顷 (1000 ha)	373.19
粮食总产量	Total Output of Grain	万吨 (10 000 tons)	115.38
蔬菜总产量	Total Output of Vegetable	万吨 (10 000 tons)	49.19
肉类总产量	Total Output of meat	万吨 (10 000 tons)	2.50
奶类总产量	Total Output of Milk	万吨 (10 000 tons)	0.40
棉花总产量	Total Output of Cotton	万吨 (10 000 tons)	0.51
规模以上工业	Industry Enterprises above Designated Size		
单位数	Number of Enterprises	个 (unit)	1319
工业总产值	Gross Industrial Output Value	亿元 (100 million yuan)	37.67
营业收入	Revenue from Principal Business	亿元 (100 million yuan)	31.39
利税总额	Total Profits and Taxes	亿元 (100 million yuan)	6.80
利润总额	Total Profits	亿元 (100 million yuan)	3.88
资产总计	Total Assets	亿元 (100 million yuan)	25.68
所有者权益	Owner's Equities	亿元 (100 million yuan)	7.47
建筑业	Construction		
资质以上企业个数	Number of Qualification Enterprises	个 (unit)	10
建筑业总产值	Gross Output Value of Construction Enterprises	亿元 (100 million yuan)	0.68
施工面积	Floor Space under Construction	万平方米 (10 000 sq.m)	
竣工面积	Floor Space of Completed	万平方米 (10 000 sq.m)	49
其中：住宅	Residential	万平方米 (10 000 sq.m)	
交通运输	Transport		
货运量	Freight Traffic		
铁路	Railways	万吨 (10 000 tons)	2191
公路	Highways	万吨 (10 000 tons)	1670
航空	Airways	万吨 (10 000 tons)	

1990年	1995年	2000年	2005年	2010年	2015年	2018年	2019年	2020年	2021年
117.95	438.01	1274.96	3483.34	7510.44	14174.72	16571.87	18303.20	20714.97	23029.20
51.08	222.06	463.04	1024.42	2187.68	3951.42	5008.08	6438.09	7584.12	8558.43
124.76	337.26	1069.31	3259.86	6319.09	11356.78	14700.07	17624.21	19704.88	22349.91
98.50	239.31	527.31	1240.49	1898.61	2692.81	2865.97	3400.21	3829.14	4329.33
						256399	438422	927748	659267
						4155535	5322643	6280398	5984712
						1033980	1219250	1603108	2124574
36.92	114.07	154.30	230.46	361.24	493.04	514.90	637.30	671.66	758.41
183.40	241.20	349.47	426.76	509.68	584.98	454.62	543.48	543.48	570.10
347.56	339.30	333.72	366.99	362.30	358.57	353.65	353.65	426.04	342.29
181.47	252.48	240.27	260.11	289.43	264.55	251.42	285.46	290.81	293.07
126.09	253.54	405.95	529.37	572.05	626.23	527.22	671.24	673.73	691.76
11.38	28.68	31.82	37.93	31.79	34.18	29.82	35.86	23.92	27.36
1.87	3.48	7.09	19.61	31.20	23.27	32.84	32.13	41.43	42.10
5.00	2.91	2.73	3.55	2.94	0.74	0.29	0.54	0.42	0.38
2008	2648	1038	1670	2021	2021	1889	2153	2215	2543
174.89	526.48	680.04	2237.51	4485.61	5339.97	4992.28	5839.18	6765.08	7591.25
136.29	432.17	629.72	2142.84	4497.17	5417.16	5192.15	6512.66	7575.34	8492.55
15.57	53.59	64.62	244.61	584.53	685.71	535.39	545.70	659.87	645.49
3.23	16.30	21.69	131.30	339.76	396.13	307.98	310.86	423.31	408.38
125.25	578.55	958.10	1868.06	3904.42	4987.76	5892.64	6663.13	7724.85	8494.19
36.82	180.86	363.37	630.06	1481.75	2159.78	2386.75	2743.28	2967.31	3380.30
46	141	569	737	739	463	507	895	1033	1182
12.56	58.78	141.92	462.65	894.30	1663.83	2823.47	3513.98	3748.12	4126.03
269	1030	1611	3298	4655	10189	12984	14955	17090	19410
170	306	701	1400	1306	2039	2366	3418	3323	3730
77	141	396	884	773	1178	1502	2170	1916	2247
3416	3877	5168	7211	9913	15794	18728	20870	23189	22895
3970	6182	7024	8484	13029	20419	25571	28064	22677	24669
	0.4	1.3	2.0	3.4	4.2	5.6	6.7	14.7	16.8

3-1 续表 2 continued 2

指标	Item	单位 Unit	1978 年
客运量	Passenger Traffic		
铁路	Railways	万人 (10 000 persons)	1302
公路	Highways	万人 (10 000 persons)	505
航空	Airways	万人 (10 000 persons)	
民用汽车拥有量	Possession of Private Vehicles	辆 (unit)	1684
# 载客	Passenger Vehicles	辆 (unit)	1353
# 载货	Trucks	辆 (unit)	224
邮电通信	Post and Telecommunication Services		
固定电话	Fixed Telephone	万户 (10 000 households)	2.68
# 城市	Urban	万户 (10 000 households)	2.27
移动电话	Mobile Telephone	万户 (10 000 households)	
互联网用户	Internet Broad Band	万户 (10 000 households)	
国内贸易	Domestic Trade		
社会消费品零售总额	Total Retail Sales of Consumer Goods	亿元 (100 million yuan)	8.13
# 批发零售业	Wholesale and Retail Trade	亿元 (100 million yuan)	7.07
# 餐饮业	Catering Services	亿元 (100 million yuan)	0.29
对外经济和国际旅游	Foreign Economy and Trade,Tourism		
全年货物进出口总额（海关）	Total Value of Imports and Exports（Customs）	万美元 (10 000 USD)	
进口	Imports	万美元 (10 000 USD)	
出口	Exports	万美元 (10 000 USD)	
全年货物进出口总额	Total Value of Imports and Exports	亿元 (100 million yuan)	
进口	Imports	亿元 (100 million yuan)	
出口	Exports	亿元 (100 million yuan)	
全年实际使用外资	Total Amount of Foreign Capital Actually Utilized	万美元 (10 000 USD)	
全年实现合同外资	Total Amount of Contracted Foreign Capital	万美元 (10 000 USD)	
入境游客人数	International Tourists	人 (person)	
外国人	Foreigners	人 (person)	
港澳台同胞	Compatriots from Hong Kong Macao and Taiwan	人 (person)	
国际旅游（外汇）收入	Foreign Exchange Earnings	亿美元 (100 million USD)	
教育	Education		
普通高等学校在校生	Total Enrollment of Regular Institutions of Higher Education	万人 (10 000 persons)	1.09
普通高等学校专任教师	Full-time Teachers of Regular Institutions of Higher Education	人 (person)	2947
中等专业学校在校生	Total Enrollment of Secondary Professional Schools	万人 (10 000 persons)	0.68
中等专业学校专任教师	Full-time Teachers of Secondary Professional Schools	人 (person)	1020
普通中学在校生	Total Enrollment of Regular Senior Secondary Schools	万人 (10 000 persons)	30.61
普通中学专任教师	Full-time Teachers of Regular Senior Secondary Schools	人 (person)	19275
小学在校生	Total Enrollment of Regular Primary Schools	万人 (10 000 persons)	60.91
小学专任教师	Full-time Teachers of Regular Primary Schools	人 (person)	24926
文化	Culture		
图书馆藏书量	Number of Books in Library	万册 (10 000 copies)	341.0
图书出版种数	Number of Publication	种 (kind)	389
图书量	Books	万册 (10 000 copies)	20166
报纸量	Newspapers	万册 (10 000 copies)	25055
杂志量	Magazines	万份 (10 000 copies)	2209

1990 年	1995 年	2000 年	2005 年	2010 年	2015 年	2018 年	2019 年	2020 年	2021 年
1438	1519	1693	1924	3327	10681	14548	15745	9797	12164
1801	2611	4530	5364	12758	3663	3149	3244	1209	2024
2.6	37.0	62.0	140.0	379.2	533.1	894.1	936.1	1238.5	1361.6
39748	86766	129204	347687	807378	1541045	2160748	2584278	2794278	3025326
26032	33968	68625	196415	627849	1400588	1978951	2370437	2556622	2759683
12141	47790	56627	71588	117994	123801	166277	194957	224713	250200
9.87	39.18	106.34	258.90	213.30	165.30	135.27	148.82	144.78	145.31
9.12	36.48	83.08	206.30	177.40	141.00	118.70	136.30	127.65	–
	2.3	60.8	239.0	857.6	1090.4	1013.7	1122.9	1154.1	1216.3
		11.57	74.34	117.30	231.66	344.70	392.62	445.48	463.04
52.82	183.76	344.45	772.65	1725.46	3141.04	4091.08	4420.41	4469.13	5126.10
38.20	134.53	228.75	657.55	1402.27	2648.44	3452.14	3760.47	3857.01	4388.16
2.56	13.35	37.76	108.44	308.11	473.23	614.10	632.37	586.62	707.78
	66587	143935	376213	743776	911424	1318209	1630123	1998749	3003034
	29812	143935	198370	338888	311763	463119	695064	909323	1184182
	36775	143935	177843	404888	599661	855090	935059	1089426	1818852
						825.0	1103.3	1382.7	1944.2
						305.7	480.8	627.6	770.1
						519.3	622.5	755.0	1174.1
	25294	31981	54158	104011	157851	272847	224249	192456	265840
	47449	44074	112072	120903	303100	556119	683441	585244	968530
20583	54468	103990	120164	230985	332942	398721	456585	108524	–
12705	30011	40990	69762	153327	205477	247086	285071	90926	–
7878	24457	63000	50402	77658	127465	151635	171514	17700	–
0.15	0.19	0.32	0.42	1.14	1.84	2.23	2.75	0.33	–
3.73	5.66	9.30	38.04	50.53	53.62	79.63	76.20	89.85	69.40
7245	7500	8267	18434	26870	30873	37539	40627	42202	41894
2.51	4.79	5.75	4.79	2.12	1.57	5.16	5.68	6.28	6.40
2890	2890	2916	1578	1334	763	3711	4058	3642	4040
22.45	27.15	33.82	30.91	30.18	30.16	31.18	39.35	39.84	40.70
16065	17621	20585	21915	21943	23643	26588	34177	34796	35587
47.57	49.23	41.40	37.88	38.40	41.44	46.66	54.14	57.01	61.00
26922	27417	27417	25201	24801	25795	30605	36067	37219	38467
476.0	524.6	591.7	725.1	941.2	1195.0	1442.3	–	–	–
2001	2603	3851	5389	6586	10234	–	–	–	–
31685	39025	38471	27919	26603	43860	–	–	–	–
46930	54460	109199	113751	184706	136480	–	–	–	–
3321	4579	11177	7195	6995	8572	–	–	–	–

3-1 续表 3 continued 3

指标	Item	单位 Unit	1978 年
卫生	Public Health		
卫生机构数	Number of Health Institutions	个 (unit)	1017
# 医院及卫生院	Hospitals and Township Hospitals	个 (unit)	148
卫生机构床位数	Number of Beds	张 (bed)	11496
# 医院及卫生院	Hospitals and Township Hospitals	张 (bed)	9856
卫生工作人员	Medical Personnel	人 (person)	24949
# 卫生技术人员	Medical Technical Personnel	人 (person)	19198
人民生活	People's Livelihood		
城镇居民人均可支配收入	Per Capita Disposable Income of Urban Households	元 (yuan)	337.8
城镇居民人均消费支出	Per Capita Life Consumption Expenditure of Urban Households	元 (yuan)	317.9
# 食品	Food	元 (yuan)	181.6
农村居民人均可支配收入	Per Capita Disposable Income of Rural Households	元 (yuan)	110.5
农村居民人均消费支出	Per Capita Life Consumption Expenditure of Rural Households	元 (yuan)	83.2
# 食品	Food	元 (yuan)	58.2
农民人均住宅居住面积	Rural Residential Area Per Capita	平方米 (sq.m)	9.6
社会治安	Public security		
交通事故起数	Number of Traffic Accidents	起 (case)	
交通事故死伤人数	Deaths and Injuries from Traffic Accidents	人 (person)	
交通事故损失折款	Property Losses from Traffic Accidents	万元 (10 000 yuan)	
火灾事故起数	Number of Fire Accidents	起 (case)	
火灾事故死伤人数	Deaths and Injuries from Fire Accidents	人 (person)	
火灾事故损失折款	Property Losses from Fire Accidents	万元 (10 000 yuan)	

注：1.“职工平均工资”2006 年以前为在岗职工口径，2006 年及以后为法人单位在岗职工口径。
2.“市内十区建成区面积”，2018 年为市内八区口径，2017 年以前为市内七区口径，2015 年以前为市内六区口径。
3. 工业统计指标 1997 年及以前统计口径为乡及乡以上工业企业，1998 年及以后为全部国有及年销售收入 500 万元以上工业企业，2011 年及以后为年主营业务收入 2000 万元及以上工业法人单位。
4. 货运量、客运量中的“铁路”指标，2013 年 3 月铁路系统改革，铁路系统统计数据按新口径执行；“公路指标”自 2014 年起交通部门执行新的公路运输量统计方案，调查范围较老口径有所缩小，2014 年及 2013 年数据均为新口径下交通部反馈数据。
5. 从 2015 年起，全市居民收支调查指标采用新口径。“农村居民人均可支配收入”2014 年以前为农民人均纯收入口径；“农村居民人均消费支出”2014 年以前为农民人均生活费支出口径。
6. 规模以上工业“营业收入”，2018 年以前为“主营业务收入”口径。

1990 年	1995 年	2000 年	2005 年	2010 年	2015 年	2018 年	2019 年	2020 年	2021 年
1300	1185	1414	2138	5086	5947	6030	7487	7514	7515
178	216	231	246	277	269	293	351	343	336
18214	20747	21698	24695	31947	49311	57460	66623	68831	72832
17216	19534	20830	23524	29844	45195	51207	59697	62072	66258
41444	43648	45166	41499	54711	89117	104347	122370	126681	131269
31130	32848	35669	34129	39366	71778	82834	97532	102172	108401
1619.5	4720.6	8471.3	13578.5	25321.1	39888.7	50146.5	51912.6	53328.6	57449
1360.1	3830.4	6891.8	9226.6	15973.3	26318.7	32977.1	33438.7	34390.8	36866
781.6	1823.6	2387.1	3046.9	5051.2	6415.0	7758.0	7956.3	8071.9	8654
731.1	1812.7	3046.8	4812.3	8903.3	14231.8	17924.4	19454.2	20432.1	22580
569.8	1373.6	1976.8	2902.8	5406.6	8597.2	11172.3	12300.3	12946.9	14591
287.7	770.8	860.0	1134.8	1818.3	2775.5	3409.0	3702.6	3931.3	4446
22.5	24.7	28.6	33.8	40.2	52.6	54.3	51.1	50.3	49.8
509	1231	1306	911	774	2946	3071	3334	3313	3317
518	1345	1364	1186	1121	3885	3618	3925	3747	3631
64	369	357	316	189	840	947	905	1006	1207
309	110	1281	1071	791	2609	1539	4577	4319	5907
67	87	26	3	9	12	12	12	16	35
166	925	471	76	462	1571	827	1529	2153	6232

Notes:1.The average salary of employees is the caliber data of employees in the post before 2006, and the caliber data of employees in the legal entity in 2006 and later.

2."The area of the built-up area in the eight districts of the city", before 2017 adopts the statistical scale of the seven districts in the city, six districts in the city before 2015, and eight districts in the city in 2018.

3.Industrial statistical indicators In 1997 and before, the statistical caliber was industrial enterprises at or above the township level. In 1998 and after, they were all state-owned and with an annual sales income of more than 5 million yuan. In 2011 and beyond, the annual main business income was 20 million yuan and above industrial enterprises legal entities.

4.The "railway" indicator in freight volume and passenger volume, the railway system reform in March 2013, the railway system statistics are implemented according to the new caliber; the "road indicators" since 2014, the transportation department has implemented a new road traffic statistics program. The scope of the survey has been narrower than that of the old one. The data for 2014 and 2013 are the feedback data of the Ministry of Communications under the new caliber.

5.Starting from 2015, the city's residents' income and expenditure survey indicators adopt a new caliber. "per capita disposable income of Rural Residents" was the "per capita net income of Rural Residents" before 2014; "Per capita consumption expenditure of Rural Residents"was the "per capita living expenses of farmers" before 2014.

6."Main operating revenue" of industrial enterprises above designated size adopts the statistical scale of "main operating revenue" before 2018.

3-2 国民经济和社会发展比例和效益指标
Indicators on Proportions and Efficiency in National Economic and Social Development

指标	Item	单位 Unit	1978 年	1985 年
人口	Population			
申报出生率	Birth Rate	‰	15.53	11.39
申报死亡率	Death Rate	‰	7.00	6.52
自然增长率	Natural Growth Rate	‰	8.53	4.87
就业	Employment			
就业者负担人口	Dependency of Employed Population	人 (person)	2.21	1.99
三次产业从业者比例	Composition of Employed Population			
第一产业	Primary Industry	%	66.8	47.5
第二产业	Secondary Industry	%	22.6	31.0
第三产业	Tertiary Industry	%	10.6	21.5
城镇登记失业率	Registered Unemployment Rate in Urban Areas	%		
国民经济核算	National Accounting			
三次产业增加值比例	Composition of Gross Domestic Product			
第一产业	Primary Industry	%		21.1
第二产业	Secondary Industry	%		51.8
第三产业	Tertiary Industry	%		27.1
人均生产总值	Per Capita GDP	元 (yuan)		1263
资本形成率（投资率）	Capital Formation Rate	%		
最终消费率（消费率）	Final Consumption Rate	%		
固定资产投资	Investment in Fixed Assets			
固定资产投资占生产总值比重	Proportion of Fixed Assets Investment in GDP	%		23.7
财政	Finance			
一般公共预算收入占生产总值比重	Proportion of General Public Budget Revenue in GDP	%	25.2	14.5
一般公共预算支出占生产总值比重	Proportion of General Public Budget Expenditure in GDP	%	6.3	5.6
农业	Agriculture			
人均耕地面积	Per Cultivated Area	亩 (mu)	1.24	1.10
每公顷耕地化肥施用量（折纯）	Consumption of Chemical Fertilizers per Hectare	千克 (kg)		225
每公顷播种面积粮食产量	Grain Yield Per Hectare of Sown Area	千克 (kg)	2475	3864
机耕率	Machine-cultivated Rate	%		

1990 年	1995 年	2000 年	2010 年	2015 年	2018 年	2019 年	2020 年	2021 年
12.88	10.03	11.08	11.13	11.82	14.57	12.77	10.45	8.21
6.54	6.32	7.05	8.35	6.73	6.98	6.58	7.31	5.45
6.34	3.71	4.03	2.78	5.09	7.59	6.19	3.14	2.76
1.94	1.67	1.62	1.62	1.61	1.4	1.5	1.3	1.4
46.5	35.8	31.7	20.5	18.5	16.4	15.7	–	–
32.4	32.9	31.9	32.2	32.1	31.5	31.3	–	–
21.1	31.3	36.4	47.3	49.4	52.1	52.9	–	–
	2.45	3.70	3.84	2.04	2.06	2.01	2.03	–
17.3	14.3	10.0	5.5	5.0	3.5	3.6	3.6	3.6
48.7	46.5	43.9	41.9	37.8	36.0	34.6	34.8	34.7
34.0	39.2	46.1	52.6	57.2	60.5	61.8	61.6	61.7
2666	8773	15356	55248	77815	96682	104180	110681	123075
39.1	39.5	40.2	52.6	63.0	–	–	–	–
37.8	41.9	56.9	46.9	52.3	–	–	–	–
22.1	23.8	32.1	50.8	57.3	–	–	–	–
9.0	3.6	5.2	15.2	10.1	9.6	9.3	8.9	8.8
5.9	4.1	5.8	16.9	10.8	13.0	12.7	12.7	11.3
1.00	0.94	0.88	0.90	0.87	0.82	–	–	0.63
330	569	641	646	626	564	–	–	584
4273	5512	5354	6192	6117	5659	5956	6053	6060
					96.7	92.0	94.1	96.5

3-2 续表 continued

指标	Item	单位 Unit	1978 年	1985 年
规模以上工业	**Industry Enterprises above Designated Size**			
产品销售率	Product Sales Rate	%		
总资产贡献率	Total Asset Contribution Rate	%		
流动资产周转次数	Turnover of Current Asset	次 (times)		
邮电通讯业	**Post and Telecommunication Services**			
每百人拥有电话机	Number of phones Per 100 Population	部 (unit)	0.60	1.26
国内商业	**Domestic Commerce**			
人均消费品零售总额	Total Sales of Consumption Good Per Capita	元 (yuan)	182	500
教育	**Education**			
学龄儿童入学率	School-age Children Enrollment Rate	%		99.44
学校教师负担人数	Teacher-student Ratio	人 (person)	21.28	16.75
高等教育	Higher Education	人 (person)	2.47	6.55
中等教育	Secondary Education	人 (person)	16.65	14.46
小学	Primary Schools	人 (person)	34.99	20.33
卫生	**Public Health**			
每万人拥有医院卫生院数	Number of Health Institutes per 10000 Population	个 (unit)	0.33	0.34
每万人拥有医生数	Number of Doctors per 10000 Population	人 (person)	23.3	26.3
每万人拥有医院床位数	Number of Hospitals Beds per 10000 Population	张 (bed)	22.0	28.2
市政建设	**City Construction**			
城市人口用水普及率	Coverage Rate of Water Supply	%	99.0	100.0
城市用气普及率	Coverage Rate of Natural Gas Supply	%	17.8	26.3
建成区绿化覆盖率	Coverage Rate of Urban Green Areas	%	12.0	23.0
生活	**Life**			
城镇居民恩格尔系数	Engel's Coefficient of Urban Households	%	57.1	56.5
农村居民恩格尔系数	Engel's Coefficient of Rural Households	%	69.9	51.8

注：1. "一般公共预算收入占生产总值比重" 2012 年 (含) 以前为 "地方财政收入" 口径； "一般公共预算支出占生产总值比重" 2012 年 (含) 以前为 "地方财政支出" 口径。
2. 由于第三次全国土地调查数据未反馈， "人均耕地面积" "每公顷耕地化肥施用量" 相关数据空缺。
3. 人均生产总值，2000 年及以后数据根据全国第四次经济普查修订。

1990 年	1995 年	2000 年	2010 年	2015 年	2018 年	2019 年	2020 年	2021 年
	97.12	98.24	98.71	98.23	97.50	96.80	–	–
	12.25	8.45	15.98	13.37	9.93	8.90	9.11	8.07
	1.69	1.52	2.11	1.82	1.38	1.65	1.61	1.63
1.89	7.23	18.98	35.31	26.48	20.82	18.81	18.06	17.90
1009	3389	6149	27343	50369	62963	55882	55744	63155
99.03	99.40	99.93	100.00	100.00	100.00	100.00	100.00	100.00
14.20	15.60	15.24	17.40	17.37	16.68	15.44	16.58	14.89
5.15	7.55	11.25	21.76	22.53	21.21	18.76	21.29	16.57
12.99	15.30	16.78	14.72	13.33	12.87	12.71	11.00	12.37
17.67	18.20	15.10	15.48	16.07	15.25	15.01	15.32	15.87
0.34	0.40	0.41	0.46	0.43	0.45	0.44	0.43	0.41
29.2	27.9	29.5	29.1	46.0	43.1	43.0	43.7	45.5
32.9	36.0	38.6	52.9	69.1	77.0	74.8	74.8	78.0
100.0	100.0	100.0	100.0	99.00	99.78	100.00	100.00	100.00
45.7	72.2	90.7	95.5	97.73	99.87	99.97	100.00	100.00
30.0	30.5	36.1	36.9	39.94	40.52	41.18	40.69	41.69
57.5	47.6	34.6	31.6	24.4	23.5	23.8	23.5	23.5
50.5	56.1	43.5	33.6	32.3	30.5	30.1	30.4	30.5

Notes:1."The proportion of general public budget revenue in total output value" was the caliber of "local financial revenue" before 2012 (inclusive); "The proportion of general public budget expenditure in total output value" was the caliber of "local financial expenditure"

2.Because the third national land survery data have not been released, the data of "arable land per capita" and "fertilizers per hectare of cultivated land" are blank.

3.Per Capita GDP, The data of 2000 and later are revised data after the Fourth National Economic Census.

3-3 平均每天主要社会经济活动
Selected Indicators on Average Daily Social and Economic Activities

指标	Item	单位 Unit	1978 年	1985 年
每天创造的财富				
地区生产总值（当年价）	Gross Domestic Product	万元 (10 000 yuan)	646	1682
第一产业	Primary Industry	万元 (10 000 yuan)	114	354
第二产业	Secondary Industry	万元 (10 000 yuan)	365	872
第三产业	Tertiary Industry	万元 (10 000 yuan)	167	456
一般公共预算收入	General Public Budget Revenue	万元 (10 000 yuan)	163	244
一般公共预算支出	General Public Budget Expenditure	万元 (10 000 yuan)	41	94
固定资产投资	Investment in Fixed Assets	万元 (10 000 yuan)		399
每天生产主要工、农业产品	Production of Major Industrial Product and Agricultural Products on Average Daily			
粮食	Grain	吨 (ton)	3161	4479
棉花	Cotton	吨 (ton)	14	136.2
蔬菜	Vegetable	吨 (ton)	1348	2304
猪肉	Pork	吨 (ton)	67	138
奶类	Milk	吨 (ton)	11	23
钢材	Steel	吨 (ton)	689	1197
发电量	Electric Energy Capacity	万千瓦时 (10 000 kWh)	347	724
水泥	Cement	吨 (ton)	2399	3699
化肥	Chemical Fertilizer	吨 (ton)	494	313
金切机床	Metal-cutting Machine Tools	台 (unit)	10	18
汽车	Motor Vehicles	辆 (unit)	12	31
服务器	Server	台 (unit)	-	-
布	Cloth	万米 (10 000 m)	38	50

1990 年	1995 年	2000 年	2010 年	2015 年	2018 年	2019 年	2020 年	2021 年
3787	12973	26087	107138	167130	215248	258722	277074	313211
656	1853	2603	5895	8367	7464	9399	9881	11200
1845	6257	11469	44862	63205	77515	89458	96466	108605
1286	5082	12015	56381	95557	130269	159865	170726	193408
339	465	1344	7291	16831	20625	23950	24757	27605
224	537	1499	9227	18032	27899	32803	35213	35427
838	3089	8382	54450	95847				
4972	6917	6583	7930	7248	6888	7820	7946	8030
137	79.7	74.7	81	20.2	8	15	12	10
3455	6946	14733	16478	17157	14444	18390	18408	18953
215	390	478	597	508	425	467	350	422
51	95	194	855	638	900	880	1132	1153
1576	2856	6507	26857	19852	6118	61793	63839	57690
1225	1884	1898	3601	4818	4189	8086	7560	8633
5796	11644	13291	19994	21411	16557	35283	36290	42770
396	384	778	1345	644	569	463	577	458
14	11	8	6	10	16	20	29	38
17	16	8	581	263	636	481	1077	874
–	–	–	271	1112	2729	3192	3921	3115
55	41	45	22	44	11	11	3	3

3-3 续表 continued

指标	Item	单位 Unit	1978 年	1985 年
每天其他经济活动	**Other Economic Activity on Average Daily**			
最终消费量	Final Consumption	万元 (10 000 yuan)		780
居民消费	Households Expense	万元 (10 000 yuan)		638
农业居民	Rural Households	万元 (10 000 yuan)		367
城镇居民	Urban Households	万元 (10 000 yuan)		271
政府消费	Government Expense	万元 (10 000 yuan)		142
社会消费品零售总额	Total Sales of Consumption Good Per Capita	万元 (10 000 yuan)	261	640
公路货运量	Highways Freight Traffic	万吨 (10 000 tons)	3.2	6.9
公路客运量	Highways Passenger Traffic	万人 (10 000 persons)	1.4	3.1
自来水供水量	Water Supply	万吨 (10 000 tons)	36.9	40
用电量	Electricity Consumption	万千瓦时 (10 000 kWh)	754	747
市内公共车辆乘客人数	Number of City Bus Passengers	万人次 (10 000 person-times)	34.0	62.2
实际使用外资额	Total Amount of Foreign Capital Actually Utilized	万美元 (10 000 USD)		
港澳台及外国来济旅游人数	Compatriots from Hong Kong Macao and Taiwan	人 (person)		27
每天人口变动和婚姻	**Daily Population Changes and Marriages**			
出生	Birth	人 (person)	191	152
死亡	Death	人 (person)	86	87
结婚	Marriages	对 (couple)		
离婚	Divorces	对 (couple)		

注：1. “一般公共预算收入” 指标 1978 年到 1995 年为“地方财政收入”口径，“一般公共预算支出”指标 1978 年到 1995 年为“地方财政支出”口径。
2. 按照国家统计局经济普查年度数据使用规定，部分涉及国民经济核算的指标数据空缺。

1990 年	1995 年	2000 年	2010 年	2015 年	2018 年	2019 年	2020 年	2021 年
1580	5524	14833	50253	87412	–	–	–	–
1274	4567	11098	39460	55221	–	–	–	–
624	1938	3596	5142	7120	–	–	–	–
650	2629	7502	34317	48101	–	–	–	–
306	957	3735	10794	32192	–	–	–	–
1447	5151	9718	49382	93433	120670	121107	122107	140441
10.9	16.9	19.2	35.7	55.9	70.1	94.2	76.5	67.6
4.9	7.2	12.4	35.0	10.0	8.6	8.9	3.3	5.5
45.3	57.5	76.7	64.5	87.2	107.5	121.8	123.0	136.2
1255	1779	2505	6713.3	7238.5	7790.8	11350.8	11855.2	13020.9
73.3	73.3	125.9	296.1	256.5	245.5	232.1	144.8	200.2
8.5	69.3	87.6	285.0	432.5	747.5	614.4	524.6	728.3
56	149	285	633	912.2	1092.0	1251.0	298.0	–
183	148	170	184	202	259	279	230	183
93	94	108	138	115	124	144	160	121
103	137	120	153	138	141	143	138	135
	17	20	50	70	87	98	100	65

Notes:1.The indicator–"general public budget revenue" was the caliber of "local financial revenue" from 1978 to 1995 and the indicator–"general public budget expenditure" was the caliber of "local fiscal expenditure" from 1978 to 1995.

2.Part of index data regarding national economic accounting is missing according to economic census year data use provisions of National Bureau of Statistics.

3-4 国民经济人均指标
Per Indicators of National Economic

指标	Item	单位 Unit	1978 年	1985 年
地区生产总值	**Gross Domestic Product**	元 (yuan)	527	1263
主要农产品产量	**Output of Major Agricultural Products**			
粮食	Grain	千克 (kg)	258	336
棉花	Cotton	千克 (kg)	1.14	10.22
猪肉	Pork	千克 (kg)	5.44	10.33
水果	Fruits	千克 (kg)	12.65	14.70
禽蛋	Eggs	千克 (kg)		
蔬菜	Vegetable	千克 (kg)	109.84	173.02
牛奶	Milk	千克 (kg)	0.88	1.76
水产品	Aquatic Products	千克 (kg)	0.29	0.41
主要工业产品产量	**Output of Major Industrial Products**			
钢材	Steel	千克 (kg)	48.1	69.6
发电量	Electric Energy Capacity	千瓦时 (kWh)	282.5	543.9
水泥	Cement	千克 (kg)	195.5	277.9
化肥	Chemical Fertilizer	千克 (kg)	29.5	18.7
服务器	Server	台 (unit)	–	–
布	Cloth	米 (m)	30.8	37.2
其他经济活动	**Other Economic Activity**			
社会消费品零售总额	Total Sales of Consumption Good Per Capita	元 (yuan)	182	500
一般公共预算收入	General Public Budget Revenue	元 (yuan)	133	183
一般公共预算支出	General Public Budget Expenditure	元 (yuan)	33	70
城乡居民人民币储蓄存款余额	RMB Deposits Balance of Urban and Rural Households	元 (yuan)	33	236
城镇居民人均可支配收入	Per Capita Disposable Income of Urban Households	元 (yuan)	338	732
城镇居民人均消费支出	Per Capita Life Consumption Expenditure of Urban Households	元 (yuan)	318	704
农村居民人均可支配收入	Per Capita Disposable Income of Rural Households	元 (yuan)	111	439
农村居民人均消费支出	Per Capita Life Consumption Expenditure of Rural Households	元 (yuan)	83	330

注：1. “一般公共预算收入” 指标 1978 年到 1995 年为 “地方财政收入” 口径。“一般公共预算支出” 指标 1978 年到 1995 年为 “地方财政支出” 口径。
2. 从 2015 年起，全市发布城乡住户调查一体化改革新口径数据，居民收支调查指标与 2014 年前分别实施的城镇和农村住户调查的调查范围、方法、指标口径、名称有所不同。
3. 根据年末反馈人口数据，修订 2020 年相关数据。

1990 年	1995 年	2000 年	2010 年	2015 年	2018 年	2019 年	2020 年	2021 年
2666	8773	16999	57966	85919	106302	106416	110681	123075
350	468	429	479	424	340	322	320	316
9.64	5.38	4.87	4.87	2.36	0.39	0.61	0.47	0.41
15.13	26.33	31.15	36.10	36.46	20.97	19.22	14.11	16.58
12.88	35.81	66.56	78.58	61.89	57.08	70.93	69.64	66.64
18.27	41.29	74.29	59.68	56.86	44.96	41.22	30.27	32.83
243.10	469.77	960.06	996.29	1041.79	713.35	756.41	742.39	744.76
3.46	6.44	12.65	51.68	46.75	44.43	36.21	45.65	45.32
1.80	4.72	5.87	7.06	7.63	4.32	1.82	1.46	1.51
169.1	195.7	424.0	1623.8	1161.8	302.1	2541.7	2574.6	2266.9
862.3	1237.0	1231.5	2177.5	2819.9	2068.8	3326.0	3049.0	3392.2
408.0	728.4	866.1	1208.9	1253.1	817.7	1451.2	1463.6	1680.6
23.6	23.0	46.5	80.3	37.7	28.1	19.1	23.3	18.0
–	–	–	0.016	0.065	0.1	0.1	0.2	0.1
38.9	19.9	29.5	13.6	25.7	5.5	4.6	1.2	1.2
1009	3468	6332	25577	44243	55353	49812	49245	55186
239	315	876	4409	9850	10186	9851	9984	10847
158	363	977	5579	10553	13778	13492	14201	13921
985	4115	8266	36239	63358	67761	72550	83570	92136
1620	4721	8471	25321	39889	50146	51913	53329	57449
1369	3830	6892	15973	26319	32977	33439	34391	36866
731	1813	3047	8903	14232	17924	19454	20432	22580
570	1374	1977	5407	8597	11172	12300	12947	14591

Notes:1.The indicator–"general public budget revenue" was the caliber of "local financial revenue" from 1978 to 1995 and the indicator–"general public budget expenditure"was the caliber of "local fiscal expenditure" from 1978 to 1995.

2.From 2015, new caliber data about urban and rural household survey integration reform was published by the city and the survey index of residents' income and expenditure was different from survey scope, method, indicator caliber and name of urban and rural residents implemented before 2014.

3.Relevant data in 2020 was revised according to population data at the end of the year.

3-5 国民经济主要指标及占全国、全省比重(2021年)
Main Indicators of National Economy and Their Proportion in China and Shandong Province(2021)

指标	Item	单位 Unit	全国 Country
区划面积	Area	万平方公里 (10 000 sq.km)	960
年末总人口	Total year-end Population	万人 (10 000 persons)	141260
生产总值(当年价)	Gross Domestic Product	亿元 (100 million yuan)	1143670.0
第一产业	Primary Industry	亿元 (100 million yuan)	83086.0
第二产业	Secondary Industry	亿元 (100 million yuan)	450904.0
第三产业	Tertiary Industry	亿元 (100 million yuan)	609680.0
规模以上工业营业收入	Revenue from Business of Industrial Enterprises above Designated Size	亿元 (100 million yuan)	1279226.5
规模以上工业利润总额	Total Profits of Industrial Enterprises above Designated Size	亿元 (100 million yuan)	87092.1
粮食总产量	Total Output of Grain	万吨 (10 000 tons)	68285.0
棉花总产量	Total Output of Cotton	万吨 (10 000 tons)	573.0
固定资产投资额	Investment in Fixed Assets	亿元 (100 million yuan)	552884.0
公路货物周转量	Highways Freight Turnover	亿吨公里 (100 million ton-km)	69087.7
社会消费品零售总额	Total Sales of Consumption Good Per Capita	亿元 (100 million yuan)	440823.0
实际使用外资	Total Amount of Foreign Capital Actually Utilized	亿美元 (100 million USD)	1735.0
一般公共预算收入	General Public Budget Revenue	亿元 (100 million yuan)	202539.0
一般公共预算支出	General Public Budget Expenditure	亿元 (100 million yuan)	246322
普通本专科在校学生	Enrollment of Regular Institutions of Higher Education	万人 (10 000persons)	3496.1
中等职业教育在校学生	Enrollment of Secondary Professional Schools	万人 (10 000persons)	1739
卫生机构数	Number of Health Institutions	个 (unit)	1031000
卫生技术人员	Medical Technical Personnel	万人 (10 000persons)	1123.0
#执业(助理)医师	Licensed Doctors	万人 (10 000persons)	427.0
城镇居民人均可支配收入	Per Capita Disposable Income of Urban Households	元 (yuan)	47412
农村居民人均可支配收入	Per Capita Disposable Income of Rural Households	元 (yuan)	18931

全省 Province	济南 Ji'nan	济南占全国比重 (%) Ji'nan Account for Proportion of Country (%)	济南占全省比重 (%) Ji'nan Account for Proportion of Province (%)
15.8	1.0244	0.11	6.49
10170.0	933.6	0.66	9.18
83095.9	11432.22	1.00	13.76
6029.0	408.77	0.49	6.78
33187.2	3964.06	0.88	11.94
43879.7	7059.39	1.16	16.09
102271.5	8335.9	0.65	8.15
5268.8	382.7	0.44	7.26
5500.7	293.07	0.43	5.33
14.0	0.4	0.07	2.86
7517.60	577.40	0.84	7.68
33714.5	5126.1	1.16	15.20
215.2	26.6	1.53	12.36
7284.5	1007.6	0.50	13.83
11709.1	1293.1	0.52	11.04
243.0	69.4	1.99	28.56
84	6.4	0.37	7.63
85775	7515	0.73	8.76
84.6	10.8	0.96	12.76
33.98	4.20	0.98	12.36
47066	57449		
20794	22580		

主要统计指标解释

几点说明：

1. 生产总值及一、二、三次产业增加值，历史数据有所调整，以本年鉴所列数据为准。

2. 生产总值及一、二、三次产业增加值，全部工业增加值，农业总产值等指标的增长速度均以可比价格计算。

3. 由于国家在 1994 年开始财税体制改革，1994 年及以后各年的财政收支与以前年份不可比。另外，2000 年财政收入统计口径也有微调。

4. 工业统计口径调整。1998 年以前工业统计范围为乡及乡以上独立核算工业企业，1998 年，统计范围调整为规模以上工业，即全部国有及年销售收入500万元以上的非国有工业单位，2011 年，调整为年主营业务收入 2000 万元以上。

5. 建筑业统计范围变化。建筑业统计范围 1994-1995 年为县及县以上单位，1996-1997 年为资质等级四级及以上独立核算建筑业企业，1998 年起为资质等级五级及以上独立核算建筑业企业。

登记注册类型　企业单位的登记注册类型，依据在市场监管部门登记注册的类型填写。机关、事业单位和社会团体及其他组织的登记注册类型，依据主要经费来源和管理方式，根据实际情况，比照《关于划分企业登记注册类型的规定》确定。

市场监管部门对企业（单位）登记注册的类型分为以下几种:

1. 国有企业：指企业全部资产归国家所有，并按《中华人民共和国企业法人登记管理条例》规定登记注册的非公司制的经济组织。不包括有限责任公司中的国有独资公司。

2. 集体企业：指企业资产归集体所有，并按《中华人民共和国企业法人登记管理条例》规定登记注册的经济组织。

3. 股份合作企业：指以合作制为基础，由企业职工共同出资入股，吸收一定比例的社会资产投资组建，实行自主经营，自负盈亏，共同劳动，民主管理，按劳分配与按股分红相结合的一种集体经济组织。

4. 联营企业：指两个及两个以上相同或不同所有制性质的企业法人或事业单位法人，按自愿、平等、互利的原则，共同投资组成的经济组织。联营企业包括国有联营企业、集体联营企业、国有与集体联营企业和其他联营企业。

5. 有限责任公司：指根据《中华人民共和国公司登记管理条例》规定登记注册，由两个以上，五十个以下的股东共同出资，每个股东以其所认缴的出资额对公司承担有限责任，公司以其全部资产对其债务承担责任的经济组织。有限责任公司包括国有独资公司以及其他有限责任公司。

6. 股份有限公司：指根据《中华人民共和国公司登记管理条例》规定登记注册，其全部注册资本由等额股份构成并通过发行股票筹集资本，股东以其认购的股份对公司承担有限责任，公司以其全部资产对其债务承担责任的经济组织。

7. 私营企业：指由自然人投资设立或由自然人控股，以雇佣劳动为基础的营利性经济组织。包括按照《公司法》《合伙企业法》以及《个人独资企业法》规定登记注册的私营独资企业、私营合伙企业、私营有限责任公司、私营股份有限公司和个人独资企业。

8. 其他内资企业：指上述第（1）条至第（7）条之外的其他内资经济组织。

9. 与港澳台商合资经营企业：指港澳台地区投资者与内地的企业依照原《中华人民共和国中外合资经营企业法》及有关法律的规定，按合同规定的比例投资设立，分享利润、分担风险和亏损的企业。

10. 与港澳台商合作经营企业：指港澳台地区投资者与内地企业依照原《中华人民共和国中外合作经营企业法》及有关法律的规定，依照合作合同的约定进行投资或提供条件设立，分配利润、分担风险和亏损的企业。

11. 港澳台商独资经营企业：指依照原《中华人民共和国外资企业法》及有关法律的规定，在内地由港澳台地区投资者全额投资设立的企业。

12. 港澳台商投资股份有限公司：指根据国家有关规定，经商务部（原外经贸部）批准设立，并且其中港、澳、台商的股本占公司注册资本的比例达 25% 以上的股份有限公司。凡其中港、澳、台商的股本占公司注册资本的比例小于 25% 的，属于内资中的股份有限公司。

13. 其他港、澳、台商投资企业：指在中国境内参照原《外国企业或个人在中国境内设立合伙企业管理办法》和《外商投资合伙企业登记管理规定》，依法设立的港、澳、台商投资合伙企业等。

14. 中外合资经营企业：指外国企业或外国人与中国内地企业依照原《中华人民共和国中外合资经营企业法》及有关法律的规定，按合同规定的比例投资设立，分享利润、分担风险和亏损的企业。

15. 中外合作经营企业：指外国企业或外国人与中国内地企业依照原《中华人民共和国中外合作经营企业法》及有关法律的规定，依照合作合同的约定进行投资或提供条件设立，分配利润、分担风险和亏损的企业。

16. 外资企业：指依照原《中华人民共和国外资企业法》及有关法律的规定，在中国内地由外国投资者全额投资设立的企业。

17. 外商投资股份有限公司：指根据国家有关规定，经商务部（原外经贸部）批准设立，并且其中外资的股本占公司注册资本的比例达 25% 以上的股份有限公司。凡其中外资股本占公司注册资本的比例小于 25% 的，属于内资中的股份有限公司。

18. 其他外商投资企业：指在中国境内依照原《外国企业或个人在中国境内设立合伙企业管理办法》和《外商投资合伙企业登记管理规定》，依法设立的外商投资合伙企业等。

机关、事业单位和社会团体及其他组织的登记注册类型，依据主要经费来源和管理方式，根据实际情况，比照《关于划分企业登记注册类型的规定》确定。

（1）各级机关，各级直属事业单位、各级机关所属事业单位，机构编制部门管理的群众团体，为“国有”。

（2）各种社团组织、民办非企业单位和基金会，若经费来源清楚，则比照《企业登记注册类型与代码》确定；若经费来源不清楚的，为“其他”。

（3）社区（居委会）、村委会、农民专业合作社的登记注册类型为“其他”。

（4）农村集体经济组织的登记注册类型为“集体”。

（5）如单位登记注册类型改变，但未重新办理变更登记，按原登记注册类型。

平均增长速度 平均增长速度表明社会经济现象在一个较长的时期内逐期平均增长变化的程度，它不能根据各个环比增长速度直接求得，但与平均发展速度之间存在着一定的数量关系：平均增长速度＝平均发展速度－1。

平均发展速度是一种根据环比发展速度计算的序时平均数，由于各时期对比的基础不同，所以计算平均发展速度不能采用一般的序时平均数的计算方法，计算方法分为水平法和累计法。水平法，又称几何平均法，即将环比发展速度按连乘法用几何平均数公式计算。累计法，也称方程法，根据一段时期内各年发展水平总和与基期水平的关系，列出方程式计算平均发展速度。水平法着重考虑最后一年所达到的发展水平；累计法着重考虑整个时期累计发展水平的总量。

本《年鉴》内所列的平均增长速度，除固定资产投资用“累计法”计算外，其余均用“水平法”计算。从某年到某年平均增长速度的年份，均不包括基期年在内。如建国四十三年的平均增长速度是以 1949 年为基期计算的，则写为 1950–1992 年平均增长速度，其余类推。

Explanatory Notes on Main Statistical Indicators

Some explanations:

1. Historical data regarding total output value and value added of the primary industry, the secondary industry and the tertiary industry is adjusted and the data listed in the yearbooks shall prevail.

2. The growth rate of such indicators as total output value, value added of the primary industry, the secondary industry and the tertiary industry, total industrial added value and total value of agricultural output is calculated as per comparable price.

3. Because China started reform of fiscal and tax system from 1994, financial revenue and expenditure in 1994 and later are incomparable to those of previous years. Furthermore, fiscal revenue statistical caliber in 2000 was slightly adjusted.

4. Adjustment of industrial statistical caliber. Industrial statistical range before 1998 covered independent accounting industrial enterprises of township and above. The statistical range was adjusted to industrial enterprises above designated size in 1998, namely all state–owned industrial units and non–state–owned industrial units with annual sales revenue of above RMB 5 million and those with annual main business income of above RMB 20 million in 2011.

5. Change in statistical range in the construction industry. The statistical range in the construction industry covered county and above units from 1994 to 1995, construction enterprises with independent accounting whose qualification level was Level IV and above from 1996 to 1997 or construction enterprises with independent accounting whose qualification level was Level V and above from 1998.

Registration Status Enterprises are classified according to the registration status of an enterprise with the qualifications of legal person in according to the registration status of an enterprise in market supervision administration. Government agencies, institutions, social organizations and other economic organizations shall follow the above classification.

Enterprises (units) are classified into the following categories according to the registration status of an enterprise in market supervision administration:

1.State–owned Enterprises refer to non–corporation economic units where the entire assets are owned by the state and which have been registered in accordance with the *Regulation of the People' s Republic of China on the Management of Registration of Corporate Enterprises*. Not included from this category are state sole–proprietorship corporations in the limited liability corporations.

2.Collective–owned Enterprises refer to economic units where the assets are owned collectively and which have been registered in accordance with the *Regulation of the People' s Republic of China on the Management of Registration of Corporate Enterprises.*

3. Cooperative Enterprises refer to a form of collective economic units (enterprises) where capitals come mainly from employees as their shares, with certain proportion of capital from the outside, where production is organized on the basis of independent operation, independent accounting for profits and losses, joint work, democratic management, and a distribution system that integrates remuneration according to work with dividend according to capital share.

4.Joint Ownership Enterprises refer to economic units established by two or more corporate enterprises or corporate institutions of the same or different ownership, through joint investment on the basis of voluntary participation, equality, and mutual benefits. They include state joint ownership enterprises; collective joint ownership enterprises; joint state–collective enterprises; and other joint ownership enterprises.

5.Limited Liability Corporations refer to economic units established with investment from 2–50 investors and registered in accordance with the *Regulation of the People' s Republic of China on the Management of Registration of Corporations*, each investor bearing limited liability to the corporation depending on its share of investment, and the corporation bearing liability to its debt to the maximum of its total assets. Limited liability corporations include state sole–proprietorship corporations and other limited liability corporations.

6.Share–holding Corporations Ltd. refer to economic units registered in accordance with the *Regulation of the People' s Republic of China on the Management of Registration of Corporations*, with total registered capital divided into equal shares and additional capitals raised through issuing stocks. Each investor bears limited liability to the corporation depending on the holding of shares, and the corporation bears liability to its debt to the maximum of its total assets.

7.Private Enterprises refer to profit–making economic units invested and established by natural persons, or controlled by natural persons, using employed labour. Included in this category are private sole–proprietorship enterprise, private partnership enterprise, private limited liability companies, private limited–liability company by shares and individual sole–proprietorship enterprise registered in accordance with the *Company Law, the Law on Partnership Business and the Law on Individual Proprietorship Enterprises*.

8.Other Domestic–funded Enterprises refer to other domestic–funded economic organizations other than those specified from Article (1) to Article (7).

9.Joint Venture Enterprises with Hong Kong, Macao and Taiwan are enterprises jointly established by investors from Hong Kong, Macao and Taiwan with enterprises in the mainland of China in accordance with the former *Law of the People' s Republic of China on Sino–foreign Equity Joint Ventures* and other relevant laws, where the establishment of the investment and the sharing of profits, taking risks and loss are stipulated in joint venture contracts.

10. Cooperative Enterprises with Hong Kong, Macao and Taiwan

established by investors from Hong Kong, Macao and Taiwan with enterprises in the mainland of China in accordance with the former *Law of the People' s Republic of China on Sino-foreign Contractual Joint Venture* and other relevant laws, where the investment or provision of facilities and the sharing of profits and risks are stipulated under cooperative contracts.

11.Sole-proprietorship Enterprises with Investment from Hong Kong, Macao and Taiwan refer to enterprises established in the mainland of China with exclusive investment from investors from Hong Kong, Macao and Taiwan in accordance with the former *Law of the People' s Republic of China on Enterprises with Foreign Investment* and other relevant laws.

12.Share-holding Corporations Ltd. with Investment from Hong Kong, Macao and Taiwan refer to share-holding corporations Ltd. established with the approval from the Ministry of Commerce (the former Ministry of Foreign Trade and Economic Relations) in line with relevant state regulations, where the share of investment from Hong Kong, Macao or Taiwan businessmen exceeds 25% of the total registered capital of the corporation. In case the share of investment from Hong Kong, Macao or Taiwan is less than 25% of the total registered capital, the enterprise is to be classified as domestic-invested share-holding corporation Ltd.

13.Other Enterprises with Funds From Hong Kong, Macao and Taiwan refer to partnership enterprises with investments from Hong Kong, Macao and Taiwan established within the territory of China in accordance with former *Administrative Measures on the Establishment of Partnership Enterprises in China by Foreign Enterprises or Foreign Individuals and Regulations for the Administration of the Registration of Foreign-invested Partnership Enterprises.*

14.Joint Venture Enterprises with Foreign Investment refer to enterprises jointly established by foreign enterprises or foreigners with enterprises in the mainland of China in accordance with the former *Law of the People' s Republic of China on Sino-foreign Equity Joint Ventures* and other relevant laws, where the sharing of investment, profits and risks and loss are stipulated in contracts.

15.Cooperative Enterprises with Foreign Investment refer to enterprises jointly established by foreign enterprises or foreigners with enterprises in the mainland of China in accordance with the former *Law of the People' s Republic of China on Sino-foreign Contractual Joint Venture* and other relevant laws, where the investment or provision of facilities and the sharing of profits and taking risks and loss are stipulated in cooperative contracts.

16.Sole-proprietorship Enterprises with Foreign Investment refer to enterprises established in the mainland of China with exclusive investment from foreign investors in accordance with the former *Law of the People' s Republic of China on Enterprises with Foreign Investment* and other relevant laws.

17.Share-holding Corporations Ltd. with Foreign Investment refer to share-holding corporations Ltd. established with the approval from the Ministry of Commerce (the former Ministry of Foreign Trade and Economic Relations) in line with relevant state regulations, where the share of investment from foreign investors exceeds 25% of the total registered capital of the corporation. In case the share of foreign investment is less than 25% of the total registered capital, the enterprise is to be classified as domestic-invested share-holding corporation Ltd.

18.Other Enterprises with Foreign Funds refer to partnership enterprises established within the territory of China in accordance with former *Administrative Measures on the Establishment of Partnership Enterprises in China by Foreign Enterprises or Foreign Individuals and Regulations for the Administration of the Registration of Foreign-invested Partnership Enterprises.*

Government Agencies, Institutions and Social Organizations are classified into the following categories by source of funds and manner of management taking reference of the registration status and code of enterprises:

(1) Offices at all levels, directly affiliated institutions at all levels, institutions managing all levels of offices, and mass organizations managed by the organization department are "state-owned".

(2) All kinds of community organizations, private non-enterprise units and foundations, if the funding sources are clear, will be determined according to the Type and Code of Enterprise Registration; If the funding source is unclear, they are "others".

(3) The registration type of communities (neighborhood committees), village committees and farmers' professional cooperatives is "others".

(4) The registration type of rural collective economic organizations is "collective".

(5) If the registration type of the unit changes, but the change registration is not re-applied, the original registration type shall be applied.

Average Annual Growth Rate shows the average growth rate of social and economic development during a longer period. It can not be directly calculated by chain based growth rate. The relation is:

Average growth rate = average speed of development － 1

Average speed of development is the time series average of speed which is obtained through chain-based calculation. Because the reference bases during the different periods are different, average speed of development can not be calculated by the general method. Level approach and accumulative approach for calculating average speed of development rate are applied. The "level approach" , or geometric average approach, is derived by the formula of geometric average of the chain-based speeds of development by continuous multiplication. The other is called the "accumulative approach" or the "equation" method, which is derived by the summation of the actual figure of each year in the interval divided by the figure in the base year. The level approach focuses on the level of the last year, while the accumulative approach emphasizes the aggregate development for the entire duration.

The average annual growth rates listed in the Yearbook are calculated by the level approach except for the growth rate of investment in fixed assets. The base year is not listed in the duration for which average annual growth rates are computed. For instance, the average annual growth rate of the 43 years since 1949 is shown as the average annual growth rate of 1950–1992 without showing the base year 1949.

国民经济核算

NATIONAL ACCOUNTS

4-1 各时期生产总值（按当年价格计算）
Gross Domestic Product in Each Period(Calculated at Current Prices)

年份 Year	地区生产总值（亿元）Gross Domestic Product (100 million yuan)	其中 of which				
		第一产业 Primary Industry	第二产业 Secondary Industry	第三产业 Tertiary Industry	# 工业 Industry	人均生产总值（元）Per Capita GDP (yuan)
1952	3.83	1.45	1.13	1.25	1.09	121
1957	6.66	1.93	2.24	2.50	2.18	194
1962	6.21	1.03	2.43	2.74	2.36	177
1965	9.68	1.88	4.44	3.36	4.34	262
1970	13.61	2.16	7.69	3.76	7.56	337
1975	16.24	2.90	8.65	4.69	8.46	373
“五五”时期						
1976	18.18	3.34	9.98	4.85	9.72	413
1977	19.98	3.58	11.23	5.16	10.98	450
1978	23.60	4.16	13.32	6.12	12.89	527
1979	26.56	5.01	14.77	6.78	14.10	586
1980	28.80	5.96	15.86	6.98	14.24	630
“六五”时期						
1981	31.56	6.56	17.65	7.35	15.11	681
1982	36.06	8.80	18.55	8.70	15.79	765
1983	42.01	11.62	20.48	9.92	17.96	881
1984	47.99	10.35	25.47	12.18	20.10	997
1985	61.37	12.92	31.82	16.63	27.54	1263
“七五”时期						
1986	71.28	14.82	34.48	21.99	28.69	1451
1987	84.54	17.52	40.29	26.74	32.88	1699
1988	114.22	22.23	57.07	34.92	47.49	2266
1989	125.83	23.77	61.52	40.54	54.66	2466
1990	138.24	23.93	67.36	46.95	60.43	2666
“八五”时期						
1991	163.39	25.38	76.56	61.45	67.73	3109
1992	207.84	27.74	98.36	81.73	86.85	3928
1993	270.76	32.66	133.15	104.96	115.36	5088
1994	371.88	49.44	176.82	145.61	154.49	6946
1995	473.52	67.64	220.37	185.51	194.16	8773

4-1 续表 continued

年份 Year	地区生产总值 （亿元） Gross Domestic Product (100 million yuan)	其中 of which				
		第一产业 Primary Industry	第二产业 Secondary Industry	第三产业 Tertiary Industry	# 工业 Industry	人均生产总值 （元） Per Capita GDP (yuan)
“九五” 时期						
1996	580.84	74.24	274.93	231.67	238.31	10701
1997	709.95	82.52	327.97	299.46	278.87	12995
1998	802.16	90.20	366.43	345.53	298.41	14549
1999	881.32	92.52	399.80	389.00	318.80	15863
2000	1048.85	109.27	468.23	471.35	379.07	15356
“十五” 时期						
2001	1175.98	112.59	499.58	563.81	405.00	17062
2002	1323.06	114.79	572.55	635.72	465.89	19032
2003	1529.34	118.47	687.31	723.56	570.04	21765
2004	1827.84	135.60	858.25	833.99	725.46	25729
2005	2086.44	150.50	1005.54	930.40	859.24	27338
“十一五” 时期						
2006	2417.78	161.70	1134.84	1121.24	961.73	31390
2007	2811.23	169.67	1292.43	1349.13	1091.74	36071
2008	3378.97	194.87	1514.48	1669.62	1280.66	42931
2009	3705.96	206.20	1603.76	1896.00	1313.89	46735
2010	4439.05	238.19	1918.55	2282.31	1572.50	55248
“十二五” 时期						
2011	4931.10	259.32	2058.29	2613.49	1661.94	60207
2012	5328.00	272.85	2132.64	2922.51	1711.76	63988
2013	5765.76	302.08	2276.14	3187.54	1764.60	68343
2014	6330.51	315.73	2424.33	3590.45	1861.37	74028
2015	6738.01	326.09	2516.99	3894.93	1924.96	77815
“十三五” 时期						
2016	7274.94	328.42	2601.27	4345.25	1966.07	82820
2017	7933.87	323.08	2800.42	4810.37	2062.26	89285
2018	8678.64	332.73	2997.08	5348.83	2100.16	96682
2019	9443.37	343.06	3265.22	5835.09	2167.87	104180
2020	10140.91	361.66	3542.73	6236.52	2382.27	110681
“十四五” 时期						
2021	11432.22	408.77	3964.06	7059.39	2746.00	123075

注：2000 年及以后数据根据全国第四次经济普查修订。
Note:The data of 2000 and later are revised data after the Fourth National Economic Census.

4-2 各时期生产总值环比指数(以上年为100)

Circle Indices of Gross Domestic Product (preceding year=100)

年份 Year	地区生产总值 Gross Domestic Product	其中 of which				
		第一产业 Primary Industry	第二产业 Secondary Industry	第三产业 Tertiary Industry	工业 Industry	人均生产总值 Per Capita GDP
1957	97.5	91.7	89.0	112.7	92.3	95.7
1962	105.6	116.7	82.7	121.9	81.3	105.9
1965	120.8	120.4	138.8	105.3	132.9	120.7
1970	113.7	95.9	131.9	100.5	130.8	108.7
1975	139.0	121.5	160.4	117.6	167.8	133.9
"五五"时期						
1976	104.9	93.2	114.6	104.5	113.1	104.6
1977	106.8	95.0	112.3	106.3	113.9	104.7
1978	113.0	99.3	114.2	119.0	111.9	109.1
1979	112.1	120.0	110.5	110.4	109.0	110.8
1980	113.6	124.5	112.5	107.9	105.7	112.6
"六五"时期						
1981	109.5	110.1	111.2	105.1	106.1	108.0
1982	116.0	136.2	106.7	120.2	106.1	114.1
1983	117.0	132.5	110.8	114.5	114.2	115.6
1984	118.4	92.3	128.9	127.3	116.0	117.3
1985	105.4	102.9	103.0	112.6	112.9	104.4
"七五"时期						
1986	110.8	109.4	103.4	126.1	99.4	109.6
1987	112.2	111.9	110.5	115.0	108.4	110.8
1988	119.0	111.8	124.8	115.0	127.2	117.5
1989	103.2	100.1	101.0	108.8	107.8	101.9
1990	108.3	99.2	107.9	114.2	109.0	106.6
"八五"时期						
1991	112.8	101.2	108.5	124.9	107.0	111.3
1992	122.8	105.5	124.0	128.4	123.8	122.0
1993	121.4	109.7	126.1	119.7	123.8	120.7
1994	118.9	131.0	115.0	120.1	115.9	118.2
1995	113.3	121.7	110.9	112.3	111.8	112.4

4-2 续表 continued

年份 Year	地区生产总值 Gross Domestic Product	其中 of which				
		第一产业 Primary Industry	第二产业 Secondary Industry	第三产业 Tertiary Industry	工业 Industry	人均生产总值 Per Capita GDP
"九五"时期						
1996	114.9	102.8	116.9	117.0	115.0	114.3
1997	119.6	108.8	116.7	126.3	114.5	118.8
1998	113.8	110.1	112.6	116.3	107.8	112.8
1999	113.1	109.5	111.8	115.4	110.6	112.2
2000	112.1	106.1	110.8	114.9	112.2	111.2
"十五"时期						
2001	111.9	104.3	110.3	115.2	111.7	110.9
2002	113.2	102.7	114.8	113.9	115.2	112.2
2003	115.6	102.2	117.8	116.0	120.5	114.4
2004	115.8	108.8	118.9	113.9	122.2	114.5
2005	113.9	106.7	119.0	109.9	119.9	106.0
"十一五"时期						
2006	115.6	105.6	116.5	116.2	118.0	114.5
2007	115.7	100.4	114.9	118.7	115.3	114.3
2008	112.9	104.4	109.5	117.5	109.8	111.8
2009	112.1	104.9	111.2	113.8	109.2	111.3
2010	112.5	104.6	110.1	115.5	109.5	111.0
"十二五"时期						
2011	110.3	104.0	110.8	110.5	110.9	108.2
2012	109.5	104.7	108.9	110.5	108.9	107.7
2013	109.4	103.6	110.9	108.7	108.7	108.0
2014	108.6	103.9	108.0	109.5	107.4	107.1
2015	107.9	103.9	107.1	108.8	106.4	106.5
"十三五"时期						
2016	107.6	104.1	105.9	108.9	105.6	106.0
2017	107.9	103.4	106.8	109.1	106.7	106.7
2018	107.3	102.7	106.1	108.5	104.5	106.3
2019	107.0	101.3	107.8	107.0	104.1	106.0
2020	104.9	102.2	107.0	103.7	108.2	103.7
"十四五"时期						
2021	107.2	107.1	103.6	109.2	105.7	105.7

4-3 分地区生产总值 (2021 年)

Value of Gross Domestic Product by Region(2021)

单位：亿元 (100 million yuan)

指标	Item	济南市 Total City	历下区 Li xia	市中区 Shi zhong	槐荫区 Huai yin	天桥区 Tian qiao	历城区 Li cheng	长清区 Chang qing	章丘区 Zhang qiu	济阳区 Ji yang
地区生产总值	Gross Domestic Product	11432.2	2124.1	1161.7	701.1	642.6	1166.0	371.9	1120.4	223.9
第一产业	Primary Industry	408.8	0.0	1.7	2.4	1.5	23.8	39.1	94.0	38.2
第二产业	Secondary Industry	3964.1	439.3	229.5	195.2	234.1	310.7	173.4	580.8	103.9
第三产业	Tertiary Industry	7059.4	1684.8	930.5	503.5	407.0	831.5	159.4	445.5	81.7

4-3 续表 continued

指标	Item	莱芜区 Lai wu	钢城区 Gang cheng	济南高新区 Ji'nan Gao xin	济南起步区（直管）Jinan Start-up Area (Directly under)	南部山区 Nan shan	平阴县 Ping yin	商河县 Shang he
地区生产总值	Gross Domestic Product	908.8	338.3	1510.3	61.1	65.6	269.1	208.5
第一产业	Primary Industry	71.4	12.3	3.9	12.2	12.0	40.1	56.1
第二产业	Secondary Industry	353.0	224.4	736.8	28.7	13.7	153.1	64.2
第三产业	Tertiary Industry	484.5	101.7	769.6	20.2	39.9	75.8	88.2

4-4 生产总值(2021年)(分行业，按当年价格计算)
Value of Gross Domestic Product(2021)(Sub Industry,Calculated at Current Prices)

单位：亿元 (100 million yuan)

指标	Item	2021年
地区生产总值	Gross Domestic Product	11432.22
农、林、牧、渔业	Agriculture, Forestry, Animal Husbandry and Fishery	427.92
农、林、牧、渔服务业	Services of Agriculture,Forestry,Animal Husbandry and Fishing	19.15
工业	Industry	2746.00
#开采辅助活动	Mining Support Activities	0.01
#金属制品、机械和设备修理业	Metal Products, Machinery and Equipment Repair Industry	11.94
建筑业	Construction	1230.01
批发和零售业	Wholesale and Retail Trade	1568.90
批发业	Wholesale	875.13
零售业	Retail Trade	693.77
交通运输、仓储和邮政业	Transport, Storage and Post	607.66
住宿和餐饮业	Hotels and Catering Services	153.26
住宿业	Hotels	15.44
餐饮业	Catering Services	137.82
金融业	Financial Intermediation	992.06
房地产业	Real Estate	876.95
房地产业(K门类)	Real estate industry(K category)	643.44
自有房地产经营活动	Own Real Estate Operating Activities	233.51
其他服务业	Other Services	2829.46
营利性服务业	Profit service industry	1645.76
非营利性服务业	Non-Profit service industry	1183.70
第一产业	Primary Industry	408.77
第二产业	Secondary Industry	3964.06
第三产业	Tertiary Industry	7059.39

4-5 规模以上服务业企业分行业主要经济指标（2021年）
Main Economic Indicators of Service Enterprises Above Designated Size by Sector (2021)

单位：万元 (10 000 yuan)

指标	Item	单位数（个）Number of Enterprises (unit)	固定资产原价 Original Value of Fixed Assets	本年折旧 Depreciation in the Year	折旧率（%）Depreciation Rate (%)	营业收入 Business Revenue	税金及附加 Taxes and Other Surcharges
合计	Total	2250	57610204	2506390	4.4	34395045	170787
交通运输、仓储和邮政业	Transport, Storage and Post	366	45100035	1721543	3.8	14546788	41827
信息传输、软件和信息技术服务业	Information Transmission, Software and Information Technology	299	6742111	443745	6.6	6517460	24254
房地产业	Real Estate	273	1524869	80429	5.3	1637013	30873
租赁和商务服务业	Leasing and Business Services	534	1585127	94410	6.0	3900021	34269
科学研究和技术服务业	Scientific Research,Technical Services	446	998073	75344	7.5	5268107	25753
水利、环境和公共设施管理业	Management of Water Conservancy, Environment and Public Facilities	41	786891	36201	4.6	674129	3880
居民服务、修理和其他服务业	Services to Households, Repair and Other Services	87	78646	6282	8.0	261575	709
教育	Education	53	167684	9053	5.4	335079	1157
卫生和社会工作	Health and Social Work	67	218224	20482	9.4	496127	513
文化、体育和娱乐业	Culture, Sports and Recreation	84	408546	18902	4.6	758745	7551

4-5 续表 continued

指标	Item	营业利润 Profits from Business	利润总额 Total Profits	应付职工薪酬（本年贷方累计发生额）Total Wages Payable	期末用工人数（人）Number of employees at the end of the period (person)	人均工资（元）Per Capita Wages (yuan)	应交增值税 Value Added Tax Payable
合计	Total	2019134	2121001	7341480	563552	130272	864196
交通运输、仓储和邮政业	Transport, Storage and Post	123521	162724	3047295	180531	168796	348777
信息传输、软件和信息技术服务业	Information Transmission, Software and Information Technology	391070	409248	1500799	107424	139708	179505
房地产业	Real Estate	69072	81762	444004	65222	68076	65533
租赁和商务服务业	Leasing and Business Services	685206	684882	763525	86003	88779	89126
科学研究和技术服务业	Scientific Research,Technical Services	498577	516561	1054164	65515	160904	135592
水利、环境和公共设施管理业	Management of Water Conservancy, Environment and Public Facilities	92302	92736	86951	15199	57208	18200
居民服务、修理和其他服务业	Services to Households, Repair and Other Services	14602	15268	75706	13781	54935	4254
教育	Education	6129	-2507	112456	8556	131435	8696
卫生和社会工作	Health and Social Work	35372	35103	127857	12717	100541	1135
文化、体育和娱乐业	Culture, Sports and Recreation	103284	125223	128723	8604	149609	13379

主要统计指标解释

国内生产总值（GDP） 指按市场价格计算的一个地区所有常住单位在一定时期内生产活动的最终成果。地区生产总值有三种表现形态，即价值形态、收入形态和产品形态。从价值形态看，它是所有常住单位在一定时期内生产的全部货物和服务价值与同期投入的全部非固定资产货物和服务价值的差额，即所有常住单位的增加值之和；从收入形态看，它是所有常住单位在一定时期内形成的劳动者报酬、生产税净额、固定资产折旧、营业盈余等各项收入之和；从产品形态看，它是所有常住单位在一定时期内最终使用的货物和服务价值与货物和服务净流出价值之和。

生产法 生产法是从生产过程中生产的货物和服务总产品价值入手，剔除生产过程中投入的中间产品的价值，得到增加价值的一种方法。计算公式为：

增加值＝总产出－中间投入

将国民经济各行业的增加值相加，得到国内生产总值。

总产出、中间投入和增加值具有相同的生产范围，即常住生产单位货物和服务的生产。它不仅包括常住生产单位为其他单位提供的货物和服务的生产，而且包括为本单位使用的货物和服务的生产，但是，住户为自己最终消费生产的服务，只计算自有住房服务和付酬家庭雇员提供的服务，不包括住户成员为本住户最终消费而生产的自给性家庭服务。

收入法 收入法也称为分配法。按收入法计算生产总值是从生产过程创造收入的角度，对常住单位的生产活动成果进行核算。按照这种计算方法，增加值由劳动者报酬、生产税净额、固定资产折旧和营业盈余四个部分组成。计算公式为：

增加值＝劳动者报酬＋生产税净额＋固定资产折旧＋营业盈余

国民经济各部门的增加值之和等于生产总值。

在计算劳动者报酬时，需要注意作为劳动者报酬的实物性收入与中间消耗的界限。如果生产单位为其从事生产活动的劳动者提供的货物或服务，可以由劳动者在自己闲暇的时间里满足他们的需要，并且可以改善和提高他们的实际生活水平，同时，其他普通消费者也可以在市场上购买到这些货物和服务，那么就属于劳动者的实物收入。生产单位为了生产能正常进行，为劳动者购买的货物和提供的服务，如因特殊工作需要提供的服装或鞋，因公出差提供的运输和旅馆服务费用等，属于中间投入。

支出法 支出法是从最终使用的角度反映国内生产总值最终使用去向的一种方法。最终使用包括货物和服务的最终消费支出、资本形成总额、货物和服务净出口三部分，计算公式为：

国内生产总值＝最终消费支出＋资本形成总额＋货物和服务净出口

按支出法计算的生产总值，在计算最终消费支出，包括居民消费支出和政府消费支出时，是从支出的最终承担者的角度计算的，而不是从最终实际消费者的角度计算的；在计算资本形成总额时，固定资本形成总额只包括通过生产活动生产出来的固定资产，不包括自然资产，存货增加不包括由于价格因素影响产生的持有收益。

按三种方法计算的国内生产总值反映的是同一经济总体在同一时期的生产活动成果，因此，从理论上讲，三种计算方法所得到的结果应该是一致的。但是，在实践中，由于受资料来源的口径限制和计算方法的影响，要保证这三种计算方法所得到的结果完全相等几乎是不可能的。在国内生产总值的三种计算方法中，生产法和收入法都是对各产业部门的增加值进行核算，为了就每一产业部门取得一致的增加值数据，根据资料来源状况，我国在核算实践中，有的产业部门，如农业、工业的增加值，确定以生产法的计算结果为准，有的产业部门，如部分服务业增加值，确定以收入法的计算结果为准，因此，我国的生产法国内生产总值等于收入法国内生产总值。但是，支出法国内生产总值与生产法和收入法国内生产总值之间存在统计误差，有的年份支出法国内生产总值大于生产法和收入法国内生产总值，有的年份结果相反。我国通常以生产法和收入法国内生产总值数据为准，将上述统计误差控制在一定范围。各种公开发表的国内生产总值总量和增长速度数据均是生产法和收入法的计算结果。按三种方法计算的国内生产总值数据之间具有如下关系：

国内生产总值＝生产法国内生产总值

＝收入法国内生产总值

＝支出法国内生产总值＋统计误差

可比价格 指计算各种总量指标所采用的扣除了价格变动因素的价格，可进行不同时期总量指标的对比。按可比价格计算总量指标有两种方法：一种是直接用产品产量乘某一年的不变价格计算；另一种是用价格指数进行缩减。

不变价格 指以同类产品某年的平均价格作为固定价格，用于计算各年的产品价值。按不变价格计算的产品价值消除了价格变动因素，不同时期对比可以反映生产的发展速度。新中国成立后，随着工农业产品价格水平的变化，国家统计局先后九次制定了全国统一的工业产品不变价格和农业产品不变价格。从1952 年到1957 年使用1952 年工（农）业产品不变价格，从1957 年到1970 年使用1957 年不变价格，从1971 年到1980 年使用1970 年不变价格，从1981 年到1990 年使用1980 年不变价格，从1991 年到2000年使用1990年不变价格，从2001年到2005年使用2000年不变价格，从2006年到2010年使用2005年不变价格，从2011年到2015年使用2010年不变价格，从2016年开始使用2015年不变价格。

三次产业 根据社会生产活动历史发展的顺序对产业结构的划分，产品直接取自自然界的部门称为第一产业，对初级产品进行再加工的部门称为第二产业。为生产和消费提供各种服务的部门称为第三产业。它是世界上通用的产业结构分类，但各国的划分不尽一致。我国的三次产业划分是：

第一产业是指农、林、牧、渔业（不含农、林、牧、渔服务业）。

第二产业是指采矿业（不含开采辅助活动），制造业（不含金属制品、机械和设备修理业），电力、热力、燃气及水生产和供应业，建筑业。

第三产业即服务业，是指除第一产业、第二产业以外的其他行业。第三产业包括：批发和零售业，交通运输、仓储和邮政业，住宿和餐饮业，信息传输、软件和信息技术服务业，金融业，房地产业，租赁和商务服务业，科学研究和技术服务业，水利、环境和公共设施管理业，居民服务、修理和其他服务业，教育，卫生和社会工作，文化、体育和娱乐业，公共管理、社会保障和社会组织，国际组织，以及农、林、牧、渔业中的农、林、牧、渔服务业，采矿业中的开采辅助活动，制造业中的金属制品、机械和设备修理业。

规模以上服务业法人单位 包括：交通运输、仓储和邮政业，信息传输、软件和信息技术服务业，租赁和商务服务业，科学研究和技术服务业，水利、环境和公共设施管理业，居民服务业、修理和其他服务业，教育，卫生和社会工作，文化、体育和娱乐业；以及物业管理、房地产中介服务等行业。

Explanatory Notes on Main Statistical Indicators

GDP refers to the final products at market prices produced by all residents in a region during a certain period of time. Gross regional domestic product is expressed in three different forms, i.e., value, income, and products respectively. GDP in its value form refers to the total value of all goods and services produced by all resident units during a certain period of time, minus the total value of input goods of non–fixed assets and services; in other term, it is the sum of the value–added of all resident units. GDP in the form of income is the sum of incomes created by all resident units during a certain period of time, including remuneration for workers, net production tax, fixed asset depreciation and operating surplus, among others. GDP in the form of products refers to the sum of the values of all goods and services for final consumption by all resident units and the net outflow values of goods and services during a given period of time.

Production Approach focuses on the total value of goods and services produced in production activities. GDP by Production Approach equals the value of total output minus that of input consumed in production process. The calculation formula is:

GDP by Production Approach= gross output– intermediate input

The sum of value added made by different industries is GDP.

Gross output, intermediate input and value added have the same production scope, i.e., production of goods and services by resident units. It not only includes the production of goods and services by resident units for other units, but that used for the unit. However, services finally consumed and produced by households only include own housing services and services provided by paid family employees (excluding self–supporting family services produced by the household member for final consumption of the household).

Income Approach (also known as distribution approach): refers to the method measuring the final results of production activities from the perspective of income made by all residents. GDP of income approach includes laborers' remuneration, net taxes on production, depreciation of fixed assets and operating surplus. The calculation formula is:

GDP by income approach= laborers' remuneration + net taxes on production + depreciation of fixed assets+ operating surplus

The sum of value added made by different industries is GDP.

In the calculation of labourers' remunerations, it's necessary to define the limit between material incomes and intermediate consumption among labourers' remunerations. If goods or units provided by production units for its labourers engaging in production activity can be met by such labourers in their spare time, improve and raise their actual living level, and other ordinary consumers can purchase such goods and services in the market, these goods and services are classified into material incomes of labourers. Goods purchased by production units for labourers and relevant services for the purpose of successful production, such as clothes or shoes provided due to special work need and transportation and hotel service charges in the business trip, are classified into intermediate input.

Expenditure Approach refers to the method measuring the final results of production activities of a country during a given period from the perspective of final use. It includes final consumption expenditure, total capital formation and net export of goods and services.

GDP by expenditure approach = final consumption expenditure+ gross capital formation+ net export of goods and services

For GDP by expenditure approach, the final consumption expenditure, including household consumption expenditure and government consumption expenditure, is calculated from the perspective of final bearer of expenditure, not from the perspective of final consumers; in the calculation of gross capital formation, gross fixed capital formation only includes fixed assets produced by production activities, excluding natural assets, where increases in inventories do not include holding gains.

GDP by three approaches reflects the results of production activities of the same economic entity during the same period, so theoretically results from three calculation approaches shall be consistent. However, in practice, it's almost impossible to ensure results from these three approaches are completely equal due to the caliber limit of data source and the influence of calculation approaches. Among three calculation approaches of GDP, production approach and income approach are used for business accounting of the value added of each industry sector. For the purpose of consistent data regarding value added of each industrial sector, the value added of some industrial sectors (such as agriculture and industry) is subject to the calculation result of the production approach and the value added of some industry sectors (such as some service industries) is subject to the calculation result of the income approach in the accounting practice in China according to data source, thus China's GDP by production approach is equal to that by income approach. However, statistical error exists between GDP by expenditure approach and that by production approach and income approach. GDP by expenditure approach is more than that by production approach and income approach in some years and it turns out just the opposite in some other years. GDP by production approach and income approach prevail in China generally and the above statistical error shall be controlled to a certain range. Various data regarding total volume and growth rate of GDP published is the calculation result based on production approach and income approach. The following relationships between data regarding GDP calculated based on above–mentioned three methods are as follows:

GDP= GDP by production approach

= GDP by income approach

= GDP by expenditure approach+ statistical error

Constant Price refers to the price without the effect of price change.

By using constant price, total amount of indices of different periods can be compared. There are two methods in which total amount indices are obtained, one using current price of some year to multiply the physical volume of certain products and the other using price index.

Fixed Price refers to the average price of similar products in a given period, with which the product value of different period can be calculated. The product value calculated at fixed price can show the growth rate of production in different periods. Since 1949, NBS has framed the united industrial and agricultural fixed price 8 times, including the fixed price of 1952 used from 1952 to 1957, the fixed price of 1957 used from 1957 to 1970, the fixed price of 1970 used from 1971 to 1980, the fixed price of 1980 used from 1981 to 1990, the fixed price of 1990 used from 1991 to 2000, the fixed price of 2000 used from 2001 to 2005, the fixed price of 2005 used from 2006 to 2010, the fixed price of 2010 used from 2011 to 2015, and the fixed price of 2015 used from 2016.

Three Industries Classification of economic activities into three branches of industries is based on the development of production. Primary industry refers to the production activities that obtain products from nature. Secondary industry refers to the production activities that process primary goods. Tertiary industry refers to the production activities that provide primary and secondary industries with services. Classification of economic activities into three branches of industries is a common practice in the world, although the grouping varies to some extent from country to country.

Economic activities of China are categorized into following industries:

Primary industry refers to agriculture, forestry, animal husbandry and fishery (not contain agriculture, forestry, animal husbandry and fishery service industry).

Secondary industry refers to mining industry (not contain mining auxiliary activities), manufacturing industry (not contain metal products, machinery and equipment repair industry), electricity, heat, gas and water production and supply industry and construction industry.

The tertiary industry is the service industry, refers to all other economic activities not included in primary or secondary industry. According to the economic condition in China, tertiary industry includes Wholesale and Retail Trades, Transport, Storage and Post, Information Transmission, Computer Services and Software, Hotels and Catering Services, Financial Intermediation, Real Estate, Leasing and Business Services, Scientific Research, Technical Services and Geologic Prospecting, Management of Water Conservancy, Environment and Public Facilities, Services to Households and Other Services, Education, Health and Social Security and Social Welfare, Culture, Sports and Entertainment, Public Management and Social Organization, and International Organizations, as well as agriculture, forestry, animal husbandry and fishery services in the agriculture, forestry, animal husbandry and fishery, mining auxiliary activities in the mining industry, metalware, machinery and equipment repair industry in the manufacturing industry.

Above State Designated Scale Service Industry Legal Entities include: transportation, warehousing and postal services, information transmission, software, and information technology service industry, leasing and business service, scientific research and technological services, water conservancy, environment and public facility management, resident service, repair and other service industries, education, health and social work, culture, sports and entertainment as well as property management, real estate agency service.

5

劳动就业

LABOR AND EMPLOYMENT

5-1 按三次产业分从业人员及构成
Number of Employed Persons and Structure by Type of Industry

年份 Year	从业人员（万人） Total Employed Persons (10 000 persons)				构成（合计=100） Composition in Percentage (Total=100)		
	合计 Total	第一产业 Primary Industry	第二产业 Secondary Industry	第三产业 Tertiary Industry	第一产业 Primary Industry	第二产业 Secondary Industry	第三产业 Tertiary Industry
1952	134.26	109.87	5.86	18.53	81.8	4.4	13.8
1957	144.29	118.65	13.12	12.52	82.2	9.1	8.7
1962	137.58	106.50	16.45	14.63	77.4	12.0	10.6
1965	143.67	107.68	20.96	15.03	74.9	14.6	10.5
1970	161.18	118.15	30.32	12.71	73.3	18.8	7.9
1975	192.59	135.95	41.56	15.08	70.6	21.6	7.8
1978	204.04	136.30	46.06	21.68	66.8	22.6	10.6
1980	214.21	135.16	51.30	27.75	63.1	23.9	13.0
1985	245.32	116.59	76.08	52.65	47.5	31.0	21.5
1990	270.54	125.73	87.75	57.06	46.5	32.4	21.1
1991	276.18	130.36	87.99	57.83	47.2	31.9	20.9
1992	280.19	127.09	85.59	67.51	45.4	30.5	24.1
1993	285.69	124.25	89.91	71.53	43.5	31.5	25.0
1994	303.46	122.62	91.64	89.20	40.4	30.2	29.4
1995	324.22	116.13	106.68	101.41	35.8	32.9	31.3
1996	332.33	107.70	113.91	110.72	32.4	34.3	33.3
1997	337.43	108.17	113.93	115.33	32.0	33.8	34.2
1998	341.63	109.32	113.38	118.93	31.9	33.2	34.9
1999	344.48	109.56	112.98	121.94	31.8	32.8	35.4
2000	347.37	109.98	110.81	126.58	31.7	31.9	36.4
2001	350.10	109.99	109.24	130.87	31.4	31.2	37.4
2002	352.70	108.01	109.14	135.55	30.6	30.9	38.5
2003	355.30	104.90	110.60	139.80	29.5	31.1	39.4
2004	358.50	99.30	113.30	145.90	27.7	31.6	40.7
2005	360.00	99.10	114.20	146.70	27.5	31.7	40.8
2006	361.80	99.00	115.20	147.60	27.4	31.8	40.8
2007	364.30	98.80	116.30	149.20	27.1	31.9	41.0
2008	367.36	98.01	116.95	152.40	26.7	31.8	41.5
2009	372.25	97.80	119.15	155.30	26.3	32.0	41.7
2010	373.70	76.66	120.20	176.84	20.5	32.2	47.3
2011	375.50	74.95	120.70	179.85	20.0	32.1	47.9
2012	379.30	74.30	123.10	181.90	19.6	32.5	47.9
2013	382.30	73.40	122.19	186.71	19.20	32.00	48.80
2014	385.70	72.50	123.30	189.90	18.80	31.97	49.24
2015	388.70	71.80	124.70	192.20	18.47	32.08	49.45
2016	394.93	70.90	126.90	197.13	17.95	32.13	49.92
2017	405.38	69.50	129.35	206.53	17.14	31.91	50.95
2018	419.27	68.80	132.17	218.30	16.41	31.52	52.07
2019	492.36	77.42	154.27	260.67	15.72	31.33	52.94
2020	468.90						
2021	470.78						

注：2020年起，山东省统计局不再反馈从业人员分产业相关数据。
Note:Since 2020, Shandong Provincial Bureau of Statistics will no longer provide relevant data of practitioners by industry.

5-2 主要年份职工工资
Wage of Staff and Workers in Major Years

年份 Year	职工工资总额 (万元) Total Wages of Staff and Workers (10 000 yuan)				职工平均工资 (元) Average Wage of Staff and Workers (yuan)			
	合计 Total	国有经济 State-owned Units	城镇集体经济 Urban ollective-owned Units	其他经济 Others	合计 Total	国有经济 State-owned Units	城镇集体经济 Urban ollective-owned Units	其他经济 Others
1952	4881	4587	294	–	442	453	324	–
1957	14553	11654	2899	–	586	621	480	–
1962	19412	16409	3003	–	577	607	451	–
1965	20367	16821	3546	–	617	664	461	–
1970	21226	17314	3912	–	549	578	449	–
1975	29239	22662	6577	–	557	615	420	–
1978	37840	28733	9107	–	578	626	465	–
1980	55900	41809	14091	–	776	821	668	–
1985	92092	67756	24330	6	1104	1169	954	894
1986	111934	84269	27643	22	1298	1384	1092	882
1987	126263	96322	29673	268	1422	1515	1185	1603
1988	166206	130287	35515	404	1806	1946	1427	2304
1989	190106	150899	38654	553	2037	2199	1577	2614
1990	210618	166250	43003	1365	2211	2370	1751	2460
1991	229540	181185	46091	2264	2368	2535	1872	2658
1992	267295	214311	49565	3419	2710	2938	2020	2919
1993	327226	264252	54442	8532	3323	3547	2524	3553
1994	465966	371403	67351	27212	4736	5209	2975	4922
1995	581432	465311	79932	36189	5851	6561	3623	5663
1996	700636	562645	89126	48865	7031	7839	4290	6875
1997	792368	636694	67999	57675	7896	8761	4954	7303
1998	717927	578788	68455	70684	8326	9022	5459	7410
1999	756696	608052	67273	81371	9083	9929	5766	7818
2000	857337	639312	59468	158557	10422	11761	6211	8651
2001	950851	713222	60818	176811	11980	13462	7061	9945
2002	1120837	846978	74672	199187	14395	16362	8188	11729
2003	1256160	930392	69554	256214	16027	18197	9331	12942
2004	1420491	1049033	73150	298308	18029	20759	10587	13974
2005	1966782	1126918	77722	762142	20866	24626	11890	18164
2006	2459044	1326412	140974	991658	21808	26550	12332	19305
2007	3086928	1680494	166960	1239474	26085	31910	15763	22500
2008	3735956	2049453	202995	1483509	30798	37191	19296	26645
2009	4241838	2227992	177020	1836825	34544	41239	21365	30368
2010	4695402	2462874	179365	2053164	36833	43339	22593	32740
2011	5569118	2647111	169476	2752531	41959	49342	26646	37851
2012	6458632	2811390	161513	3485729	45924	52845	32180	42294
2013	7927677	2766005	170176	4991497	53650	58842	37264	51891
2014	8464904	2912941	148424	5403539	59534	66810	40170	56945
2015	8885256	3282169	143078	5460009	67112	78733	47013	62283
2016	10068893	3715397	162695	6190800	74834	88887	51370	69107
2017	10694345	3776127	124702	6793516	82192	98770	54790	75814
2018	11496722	3869498	98327	7528898	89168	109052	62941	81935
2019	14170697	4846897	87776	9236024	97482	123249	66047	88204
2020	16196772				104990			
2021	18110031				114596			

注：1. 本表中 1998 年及以后年份数据均为在岗职工口径，国有、集体、其他分组按 1998 年新标准。2006 年及以后年份数据为非私营单位从业人员口径。
2. 2020 年起，国家统计局修订劳动工资统计报表制度，山东省统计局未反馈国有经济、城镇集体经济、其他经济相关分类数据。

Notes:1.In this table, the data for 1998 and subsequent years are the caliber of on-the-job workers, and the data of state-owned, collective and other groups base the new standard in 1998. Data for 2006 and subsequent years are the caliber of employees in non-private units.
2.Since 2020, the National Bureau of Statistics has revised the statistical system of labor wages and salaries, and the Provincial Bureau of Statistics has not given classified data of state-owned economy, urban collective economy and other economies.

5-3 城镇非私营单位就业人员人数 (2021 年)

Number of Employed Persons in Urban Non Private Entities(2021)

单位：人 (person)

指标	Item	就业人员 Employed Persons	# 在岗职工 Staff and Workers
合计	Total	1587351	1476853
按国民经济行业分组	Grouped by Sector		
农、林、牧、渔业	Agriculture,Forestry,Animal Husbandry and Fishing	866	866
采矿业	Mining	13015	12888
制造业	Manufacturing	259781	256932
电力、热力、燃气及水生产和供应业	Production and Distribution of Electricity, Heating Power, Gas and Water	17937	17585
建筑业	Construction	287901	243314
批发和零售业	Wholesale and Retail Trade	88037	86051
交通运输、仓储和邮政业	Traffic,Transport,Storage and Post	71549	68941
住宿和餐饮业	Hotels and Catering Services	26122	22949
信息传输、软件和信息技术服务业	Information Transfer, Software and Information Technology Services	95086	94920
金融业	Financial Intermediation	100111	63101
房地产业	Real Estate	62433	61248
租赁和商务服务业	Leasing and Business Services	52375	51515
科学研究和技术服务业	Scientific Research and Development,Technical Services	70840	69367
水利、环境和公共设施管理业	Management of Water Conservancy, Environment and Public Facilities	19321	17886
居民服务、修理和其他服务业	Services to Households, Repair and Other Services	7901	7710
教育	Education	164044	159786
卫生和社会工作	Health and Social Work	103926	97736
文化、体育和娱乐业	Culture,Sports and Entertainment	20869	19897
公共管理、社会保障和社会组织	Public Administration, Social Security and Social Organizations	125235	124159

5-4 城镇非私营单位就业人员工资总额（2021年）

Total Wage of Employed Persons in Urban Non Private Entities(2021)

单位：万元 (10 000 yuan)

指标	Item	就业人员工资总额 Wage Bill of Employed Persons	# 在岗职工工资总额 Total Wage of Staff and Workers
合计	Total	18110031	17498491
按国民经济行业分组	Grouped by Sector		
农、林、牧、渔业	Agriculture,Forestry,Animal Husbandry and Fishing	7206	7206
采矿业	Mining	129922	128044
制造业	Manufacturing	2645630	2623325
电力、热力、燃气及水生产和供应业	Production and Distribution of Electricity, Heating Power, Gas and Water	197892	196787
建筑业	Construction	2825241	2556628
批发和零售业	Wholesale and Retail Trade	741244	730280
交通运输、仓储和邮政业	Traffic,Transport,Storage and Post	840574	830170
住宿和餐饮业	Hotels and Catering Services	135195	131640
信息传输、软件和信息技术服务业	Information Transfer, Software and Information Technology Services	1106895	1105774
金融业	Financial Intermediation	1446071	1259324
房地产业	Real Estate	504862	500029
租赁和商务服务业	Leasing and Business Services	514864	509921
科学研究和技术服务业	Scientific Research and Development,Technical Services	953077	932941
水利、环境和公共设施管理业	Management of Water Conservancy, Environment and Public Facilities	128299	125314
居民服务、修理和其他服务业	Services to Households, Repair and Other Services	51531	50823
教育	Education	2115045	2090509
卫生和社会工作	Health and Social Work	1630630	1590703
文化、体育和娱乐业	Culture,Sports and Entertainment	262651	259314
公共管理、社会保障和社会组织	Public Administration, Social Security and Social Organizations	1873202	1869760

5-5 城镇非私营单位就业人员平均工资(2021年)
Average Wage of Employed Persons in Urban Non Private Entities(2021)

单位：元 (yuan)

指标	Item	就业人员平均工资 Average Wage of Employed Persons	#在岗职工平均工资 Average Wage of Total Wage of Staff
合计	Total	114596	119245
按国民经济行业分组	Grouped by Sector		
农、林、牧、渔业	Agriculture,Forestry,Animal Husbandry and Fishing	84756	84756
采矿业	Mining	99321	98876
制造业	Manufacturing	101929	102226
电力、热力、燃气及水生产和供应业	Production and Distribution of Electricity, Heating Power, Gas and Water	110346	111512
建筑业	Construction	98619	104765
批发和零售业	Wholesale and Retail Trade	85375	86049
交通运输、仓储和邮政业	Traffic,Transport,Storage and Post	116497	118979
住宿和餐饮业	Hotels and Catering Services	53393	59449
信息传输、软件和信息技术服务业	Information Transfer, Software and Information Technology Services	118024	118132
金融业	Financial Intermediation	138617	201591
房地产业	Real Estate	80540	81187
租赁和商务服务业	Leasing and Business Services	101969	102784
科学研究和技术服务业	Scientific Research and Development,Technical Services	134599	135640
水利、环境和公共设施管理业	Management of Water Conservancy, Environment and Public Facilities	66393	70420
居民服务、修理和其他服务业	Services to Households, Repair and Other Services	62968	64200
教育	Education	129571	131286
卫生和社会工作	Health and Social Work	160913	166431
文化、体育和娱乐业	Culture,Sports and Entertainment	127906	132515
公共管理、社会保障和社会组织	Public Administration, Social Security and Social Organizations	151763	152754

5-6 社会保障基本情况
Basic Conditions of Social Security

单位：万人 (10 000 persons)

指标	Item	2015 年	2016 年	2017 年	2018 年	2019 年	2020 年	2021 年
职工基本养老保险参保人数	Urban Basic Pension Insurance	266.14	284.28	304.63	331.66	408.33	437.30	472.68
# 企业	Enterpris	241.07	259.26	279.65	306.59	378.63	345.26	441.90
事业机关	Institution and Government Agency	25.08	25.02	24.98	25.06	29.70	18.99	30.78
职工基本医疗保险参保人数	Medical Care Insurance	208.09	214.48	228.68	241.54	288.04	313.52	336.20
参加失业保险人数	Unemployment Insurance	130.08	135.78	147.19	158.29	189.70	213.60	226.91
工伤保险参保人数	Work Injury Insurance	144.46	161.22	187.51	220.47	262.56	278.60	293.47
生育保险参保人数	Maternity Insurance	136.43	142.17	152.73	163.97	201.24	213.10	235.77

注：1.“职工基本养老保险参保人数”“企业”及“事业机关”包含离退休人员。
2.2019 年职工基本养老保险参保人数中事业机关数据修订为 29.7 万人。

Notes:1.The caliber "number of employees with basic endowment insurance", " enterprise" and "business organ" contains the retired after.
2.In 2019, data related to the state-owned organizations in the number of employees participating in basic endowment insurance was revised to 297,000 people.,

主要统计指标解释

从业人员 指在本单位工作，并取得工资或其他形式劳动报酬的人员。

在岗职工 指在本单位工作且与本单位签订劳动合同，并由单位支付各项工资和社会保险、住房公积金的人员，以及上述人员中由于学习、病伤、产假等原因暂未工作仍由单位支付工资的人员。

在岗职工工资总额 指本单位在报告期内直接支付给本单位全部在岗职工的劳动报酬总额。

在岗职工平均工资 指本单位在岗职工在报告期内平均每人所得的工资额。

Explanatory Notes on Main Statistical Indicators

Employees refer to persons who work in the unit and receive remuneration payment or other forms of payment.

Fully Employed staff and Workers refer to persons who work in the unit and sign a labor contract with working units for whom working units pays various wages, social insurances and housing provident fund, and persons who have their work posts, but are temporarily absent from work for reasons of study or on sick, injury or maternal leave and still receive wages from their working units.

Total Wages Bill refers to the total remuneration payment to staff and workers in working units during the reporting period.

Average Wage refers to average wage per person within the reporting period for staff and workers in working units.

6

固定资产投资

INVESTMENT IN FIXED ASSETS

6-1 固定资产投资
Total Investment in Fixed Assets

单位：万元 (10 000 yuan)

指标	Item	2011 年	2012 年	2013 年	2014 年	2015 年	2016 年	2017 年
固定资产投资额	Investment in Fixed Assets	19343389	21860756	26383337	30634425	34984158	39743278	43635821
按管理渠道分	By Management Channels							
城镇集体以上投资	Above Urban Collective Investment	13059328	14005706	18189147	20297503	23817574	27091510	30334660
房地产开发投资	Real Estate Development Investment	5271575	6633153	7211744	9173706	10141433	11639381	12325712
农村投资	Rural Investment	1012486	1221898	982446	1163216	1025151	1012387	975449
按经济类型分	Registration Status							
国有经济	State-owned	7334983	6595774	8770551	6421555	8236033	7175934	8700130
集体经济	Collective-owned	1802483	1920132	2165782	2309282	1809902	1298005	1458316
联营经济	Joint Ownership Units		195897	100213	17820	30882	1808	
股份制经济	Share-holding	5682038	1234405	1448535	5814573	7403146	10826143	12722943
外商投资经济	Fund from Overseas	408736	466383	336618	384940	284944	771449	410019
港澳台投资经济	Fund from Hong Kong,Macao and Taiwan	586347	634574	546675	177167	270022	961601	1129955
个体经济	Self-employed	2956158	3318099	30342	4423319	4447149	6788160	39804
其他经济	Others	572644	1169661	2044857	1912063	2360647	1683680	1002734
按投资用途分	By Investment Purpose							
第一产业	Primary Industry	486482	624114	982446	1163216.064	1025151	1012387	975449
第二产业	Secondary Industry	6073178	7337047	9078831	10985385.51	12173905	13019930	14418169
#工业	Industry	5767374	7018465	8060463	10410562.18	11478708	12373806	13176351
第三产业	Tertiary Industry	12783729	13899596	16322060	18485823.43	21785102	25710961	28242203
投资资金来源	Fund of Different Sources							
国家资金	State Appropriations	1317777	1693582	1302138	1240862	691574	1360695	1353707
国内贷款	Domestic Loans	1579846	517431	2173131	341374	73212	3656032	3343213
债券	Bond							40902
利用外资	Overseas Funds	68300	226374	262823	32757	44835	327727	250555
自筹资金	Self-raised Fund	14843051	16405182	19166006	19058000	23594834	28216931	28042143
其他资金	Others	3469710	4139026	5741361	454265	342083	10839004	10267805

注：自 2011 年起固定资产投资统计口径由 50 万元调整为 500 万元。
Note:Statistical caliber of fixed-asset investment as of 2011 was adjusted to RMB 5 million from 0.5 million..

6-2 固定资产投资分类(2021年)
Classification of Investment in Fixed Assets(2021)

指标	Item	固定资产投资额比上年增长(%) Growth rate of Investment in Fixed Assets(%)
本年完成投资	**Investment Completed This Year**	11.5
按构成分	**Investment by Structure**	
建筑安装工程	Construction and Installation	-0.8
设备工器具购置	Purchase of Equipment and Instruments	-32.6
#购置旧设备	Purchase of Second-hand Equipment	-17.4
其他费用	Others	60.8
按产业分	**Grouped by Three Strata of Industry**	
第一产业	Primary Industry	-1.5
第二产业	Secondary Industry	-4.2
第三产业	Tertiary Industry	14.7
按登记注册类型分	**By Status of Registration**	
内资	**Domestic Invested**	10.9
国有	State-owned	-2.7
集体	Collective-owned	46.8
股份合作	Cooperative Enterprises	22.5
私营个体	Private Enterprises	3.2
港澳台投资	**Investment from Hong Kong,Macao and Taiwan**	1.5
#港澳台股份有限公司	Share-holding	-2.4
外商投资	**Foreign Invested**	53.1
#外商合资经营	Joint Venture	55.0
#外商独资	Enterprises with Sole Fund	1.2
其他	Others	69.8
按建设性质分	**Investment by Type of Construction**	
新建	New Construction	13.3
扩建	Expansion	-9.3
改建和技术改造	Reconstruction and Technical Transformation	7.2
其他	Others	13.6
按国民经济行业分	**by Sector**	

6-2 续表 continued

指标	Item	固定资产投资额比上年增长（%）Growth rate of Investment in Fixed Assets（%）
农、林、牧、渔业	Farming, Forestry, Animal Husbandry and Fishery	-11.8
采矿业	Mining	-45.9
制造业	Manufacturing	1.2
电力、热力、燃气及水生产和供应业	Production and Supply of Electricity, Heat, Gas and Water	-21.7
建筑业	Construction	-
批发和零售业	Wholesale and Retail Trade	-26.3
交通运输、仓储和邮政业	Transport, Storage and Post	9.6
住宿和餐饮业	Hotels and Catering Services	-1.2
信息传输、软件和信息技术服务业	Information Transmission, Software and Information Technology	-28.2
金融业	Financial Intermediation	145.6
房地产业	Real Estate	16.9
租赁和商务服务业	Leasing and Business Services	46.5
科学研究和技术服务业	Scientific Research and Technical Services	216.7
水利、环境和公共设施管理业	Management of Water Conservancy,Environment and Public Facilities	-15.4
居民服务、修理和其他服务业	Service to Households, Repair and Other Service	58.2
教育	Education	-2.0
卫生和社会工作	Health and Social Service	110.2
文化、体育和娱乐业	Culture, Sports and Entertainment	13.7
公共管理、社会保障和社会组织	Public Management,Social Security and Social Organizations	-38.9
新增固定资产（万元）	Newly Increased Fixed Assets(10 000 yuan)	13413908
施工项目个数（个）	Number of Project under Construction(unit)	4104
# 新开工	Started This Year	1660
竣工项目个数（个）	Number of Buildings Completed(unit)	916
施工房屋面积（万平方米）	Project under Construction(10 000 sq.m)	10156.5
# 住宅	Residential Buildings	6577.4
竣工房屋面积（万平方米）	Project Completed and Put into Use(10 000 sq.m)	1115.7
# 住宅	Residential Buildings	787.6

6-3 房地产开发投资分类(2021年)
Classification of Estate Development Investment(2021)

指标	Item	房地产开发投资 Estate Development Investment
本年完成投资额(万元)	Investment Completed This Year(10 000 yuan)	19280018
按构成分	Investment by Structure	
建筑工程	Construction	9012796
安装工程	Installation	828597
设备、工器具购置	Purchase of Equipment and Instruments	44903
其他费用	Others	9393722
按登记注册类型分	By Status of Registration	
内资	Domestic Fund	18002095
国有	State-owned	418501
集体	Collective-owned	
股份合作	Cooperative Enterprises	5358
联营	Joint Ownership	
国有联营	State Joint Ownership	
集体联营	Collective Joint Ownership	
其他联营企业	Other Joint Ownership	
有限责任公司	Limited Liability Corporations	13170973
国有独资公司	State Sole-proprietorship Corporations	1220135
其他有限责任公司	Other Limited Liability Corporations	11950838
股份有限公司	Share-holding Corporations Ltd.	212644
私营	Private	3873805
其他内资	Other Domestic Fund	320814
港澳台投资	Investment from Hong Kong,Macao and Taiwan	1057819
港澳台商合资经营	Joint-venture	640379
港澳台商合作经营	Cooperative	
港澳台商独资	Sole-proprietorship	346696
港澳台股份有限公司	Share-holding Corporations Ltd.	
外商投资	Foreign Invested	220104
外商合资经营	Joint-venture	145869
外商合作经营	Cooperative	
外商独资	Sole-proprietorship	65323
外商股份有限公司	Share-holding Corporations Ltd.	8912
其他外商投资企业	Other Foreign Funded Enterprises	
个体经营	Self-employed	
新增固定资产(万元)	Newly Increased Fixed Assets (10 000 yuan)	7149999
施工项目个数(个)	Number of Project under Construction(unit)	815
#新开工	Started This Year	121
竣工项目个数(个)	Number of Buildings Completed(unit)	92
施工房屋面积(万平方米)	Project under Construction(10 000 sq.m)	10156.54
#住宅	Residential Buildings	6577.38
竣工房屋面积(万平方米)	Project Completed and Put into Use(10 000 sq.m)	1115.66
#住宅	Residential Buildings	787.62

6-4 固定资产投资资金来源(2021 年)
Investment by Source of Funds (2021)

指标	Item	固定资产投资额比上年增长 (%) Growth rate of Investment in Fixed Assets (%)	房地产开发投资(万元) Estate Development Investment (10 000 yuan)
本年资金来源合计	Total Funds of All Sources	8.5	33315678
上年末结余资金	Fund Left from Last Year	27.7	8986890
本年资金来源小计	Fund of All Sources in Current Year	5.0	24328788
国家预算资金	State Budget	-35.5	
国内贷款	Domestic Loans	-12.9	3658302
债券	Bond	39.9	
利用外资	Foreign Investment	-27.0	19099
其中：外商直接投资	Foreign Direct Investment		
自筹资金	Self-Raising Funds	15.7	7439314
其中：企、事业单位自有资金	Enterprise and Intitutions Own Funds		
其他资金来源	Other Funds	11.8	451104

6-5 新增主要生产能力和效益(2021 年)
Newly Increased Production Capacity and Administrative(2021)

项目 Item	单位 Unit	新增生产能力 Newly Increased This Year
年产 5 万辆新能源商用车项目	辆 / 年 (unit/year)	50000
山东华盛铝业科技有限公司铝材精加工项目	吨 / 年 (ton/year)	1500
山东山和铝业科技有限公司铝板带深加工(汽车轻量化、轨道交通及建筑用铝板)项目	吨 / 年 (ton/year)	400
智能钣金件生产线技术改造项目	辆 / 年 (unit/year)	400
山东永合铝业科技有限公司 7500 吨铝加工项目	吨 / 年 (ton/year)	300
济南泰山阳光冶金有限公司高炉煤气综合利用节能环保技改项目	万吨 / 年 (10 000 tons/year)	35
济南泰山阳光冶金有限公司高炉鼓风机节能改造提升项目	万吨 / 年 (10 000 tons/year)	35
山东山水水泥集团有限公司商河分公司 100 万吨粉磨线	万吨 / 年 (10 000 tons/year)	30

6-6 历年房地产开发建设情况
Basic Situations of Real Estate Development in Major Years

指标	Item	单位 Unit	2016 年	2017 年	2018 年	2019 年	2020 年	2021 年
计划总投资	Intended Investment	万元 (10 000 yuan)	65080572	75662272	90392774	111989855	120132064	122030897
本年完成投资	Investment Completed in Current Year	万元 (10 000 yuan)	11639381	12325712	13693456	15769302	17076304	19280018
按构成分	Grouped by Use of Funds							
建筑工程	Construction	万元 (10 000 yuan)	7329570	8643701	7920264	9183871	10195398	9012796
安装工程	Installation	万元 (10 000 yuan)	1614742	1446801	1409538	1606223	1172528	828597
设备、工器具购置	Purchase of Equipment and Instruments	万元 (10 000 yuan)	152443	172327	178895	406018	265076	44903
其他费用	Others	万元 (10 000 yuan)	2542621	2062883	4184759	4573190	5443302	9393722
#旧建筑物购置费	Purchase of Used Building	万元 (10 000 yuan)	35444	4742	196	9701	6041	2211
土地购置	Value of Land Purchased	万元 (10 000 yuan)	2241602	1683185	3780143	4231601	5040479	8497926
按工程用途分	Grouped by Use of Buildings							
住宅	Residential Buildings	万元 (10 000 yuan)	8055689	8227871	9285419	11356997	12043120	13513858
#安居工程	Comfortable Housing Project	万元 (10 000 yuan)						
办公楼	Office Buildings	万元 (10 000 yuan)	1112954	1058113	1047097	1312853	1693130	1433323
商业营业用房	Buildings for Business Use	万元 (10 000 yuan)	1665634	1907938	1879155	1662057	1693638	1734079
其他	Others	万元 (10 000 yuan)	805104	1131790	1481785	1437395	1646416	2598758
本年新增固定资产	Newly Increased Fixed Assets	万元 (10 000 yuan)	3770747	3061175	4698943	3988646	5297407	7149999
待开发土地面积	Space of Land to be Developed	万平方米 (10 000 sq.m)	225.80	138.80	302.35	455.30	278.98	349.94
本年购置土地面积	Space of Land Purchased in Current Year	万平方米 (10 000 sq.m)	170.34	144.77	265.91	280.40	106.04	189.99
房屋施工面积	Floor Space of Buildings under Construction	万平方米 (10 000 sq.m)	7912.30	8006.85	9112.05	9979.96	10353.04	10156.54
房屋竣工面积	Floor Space of Buildings Completed	万平方米 (10 000 sq.m)	1134.10	631.29	1203.81	1070.03	1272.97	1115.66
竣工房屋价值	Value of Buildings Completed	万元 (10 000 yuan)	2639414	1615213	3172322	2844724	3321996	3335553
竣工住宅	Residential Buildings Completed	套 (unit)	68682	45775	70120	60422	77790	64928

6-7 历年房地产开发公司经营情况
Real Estate Development and Managment in Major Years

指标	Item	单位 Unit	2016 年	2017 年	2018 年	2019 年	2020 年	2021 年
开发公司家数	Number of Real Estate Enterprises	家 (unit)	622	646	706	710	704	655
企业资本金	Enterprises Funds	万元 (10 000 yuan)	9270991	10505186	12994960	14920358	15884470	16394299
资产与负债	Assets and Liabilities							
资产总计	Total Assets	万元 (10 000 yuan)	72602423	85586496	113393735	128868654	136819137	142473813
负债总计	Total Liabilities	万元 (10 000 yuan)	58406976	68738188	93511277	106654306	113236782	117808688
所有者权益	Owners' Equity	万元 (10 000 yuan)	14195447	16848309	19882458	22214348	23582355	16394299
损益情况	Net Income or Loss							
经营收入	Business Revenue	万元 (10 000 yuan)	11913217	11218828	12495191	14411472	14853884	18351536
土地转让收入	Revenues from Land Transfer	万元 (10 000 yuan)	2409	1501	952885	150739	344311	339936
商品房销售收入	Revenues from Commercial Housing Sold	万元 (10 000 yuan)	11227539	10803498	11087179	11656310	11934688	15836088
房屋出租收入	Revenue from House Leasing	万元 (10 000 yuan)	106425	109982	90017	99996	109568	170083
其他收入	Others	万元 (10 000 yuan)	576844	302963	126592	134461	472363	877906
经营成本	Business Cost	万元 (10 000 yuan)	968896	8352620	8570149	10131040	11087743	14419864
经营税金及附加	Taxes and Other Charges	万元 (10 000 yuan)	706161	658995	951196	1036931	977022	989222
利润总额	Total Profits	万元 (10 000 yuan)	606344	875949	2177983	2287980	1719277	1715428
房屋销售与出租	House for Sales and Rent							
本年实际销售房屋面积	Floor Space of Commercial Buildings Sold	平方米 (sq.m)	14242514	12152665	12346236	12464708	13357486	15481974
# 住宅	Residential Buildings	平方米 (sq.m)	12316804	9737162	9636143	10206808	11452394	13001987
本年房屋实际销售额	Total Sale of Commercial Buildings	万元 (10 000 yuan)	11750932	11725660	14737908	13807789	15719460	19569740
# 住宅	Residential Buildings	万元 (10 000 yuan)	10357228	9462791	11728181	11738543	14065259	17216533
待售房屋面积	Floor Space of Waiting For Sold	平方米 (sq.m)	1720232	1398451	980301	1064915	1474183	2100169
# 住宅	Residential Buildings	平方米 (sq.m)	931437	740636	542047	635088	906322	1203741
出租房屋面积	Floor Space of House Leasing	平方米 (sq.m)	182137	66089	1794	39132	2385	1165

6-8 房地产开发公司经营情况(2021年)
Real Estate Development and Management(2021)

单位：万元 (10 000 yuan)

指标	Item	合计 Total	内资企业 Domestic Invested Enterprises 小计 Total	# 国有 State-owned	港、澳、台商投资企业 Enterprises with Investment from Hong Kong,Macao and Taiwan	外商投资企业 Foreign Invested Enterprises
开发公司家数（家）	Number of Real Estate Enterprises(unit)	655	623	153	22	10
按资质分	by Qualification Criteria					
#一级资质	First Grade	32	31	20	1	0
二级资质	Second Grade	64	61	24	2	1
三级资质	Third Grade	74	71	13	1	2
四级资质	Forth Grade	7	6	3	1	0
企业资本金	Enterprises Funds	16394299	14155411	6772814	2063688	175200
资产与负债	Assets and Liabilities					
资产总计	Total Assets	142473813	136390650	66849103	4745469	1337694
负债总计	Total Liabilities	117808688	114249640	52899311	2609233	949815
所有者权益	Owners' Equity	24665125	22141010	13949792	2136236	387879
损益情况	Net Income or Loss					
经营收入	Business Revenue	18351536	16379634	674970	1946864	25038
土地转让收入	Revenues from Land Transfer	339936	339936	121	0	0
商品房销售收入	Revenues from Commercial Housing Sold	15836088	13974006	660186	1837186	24897
房屋出租收入	Revenue from House Leasing	170083	78569	3578	91514	0
其他收入	Others	877906	866924	3810	10981	0
经营成本	Business Cost	14419864	12791466	488212	1623360	5039
经营税金及附加	Taxes and Other Charges	989222	928391	66516	60099	733
利润总额	Total Profits	1715428	1542787	83507	195690	-23049

主要统计指标解释

固定资产投资额 指以货币形式表现的在一定时期内建造和购置固定资产的工作量以及与此有关的费用的总称。

房地产开发投资 指各种登记注册类型的房地产开发法人单位统一开发的住宅、厂房、仓库、饭店、宾馆、度假村、写字楼、办公楼等房屋建筑物，配套的服务设施，土地开发工程（如道路、给水、排水、供电、供热、通讯、平整场地等基础设施工程）和土地购置的投资；不包括单纯的土地开发和交易活动。

固定资产投资的资金来源 根据固定资产投资的资金来源不同，分为国家预算内资金、国内贷款、债券、利用外资、自筹资金和其他资金来源。

（1）国家预算内资金：指各级政府用于固定资产投资的财政资金，包括中央预算资金和地方预算资金。

（2）国内贷款：指报告期固定资产投资项目单位向银行及非银行金融机构借入用于固定资产投资的各种国内借款，包括银行利用自有资金及吸收存款发放的贷款、上级拨入的国内贷款、国家专项贷款，地方财政专项资金安排的贷款、国内储备贷款、周转贷款等。

（3）债券：指企业或金融机构为筹集用于固定资产投资的资金向投资者出具的承诺按一定发行条件还本付息的债务凭证，包括金融债券和企业债券。

（4）利用外资：指报告期收到的境外（包括外国及港澳台地区）资金（包括设备、材料、技术在内）。包括对外借款（外国政府贷款、国际金融组织贷款、出口信贷、外国银行商业贷款、对外发行债券和股票）、外商直接投资、外商其他投资（包括补偿贸易、加工装配由外商提供的设备价款、国际租赁，外商投资收益的再投资资金）。不包括我国自有外汇资金（国家外汇、地方外汇、留成外汇、调剂外汇和中国境内银行自有资金发放的外汇贷款等）。各类外资按报告期的外汇牌价（中间价）折成人民币计算。

（5）自筹资金：指在报告期内筹集的用于项目建设和购置的资金。包括自有资金、股东投入资金和借入资金，但不包括各类财政性资金、从各类金融机构借入资金和国外资金。

（6）其他资金来源：指在报告期收到的除以上各种资金之外的用于固定资产投资的资金。包括社会集资、个人资金、无偿捐赠的资金及其他单位拨入的资金等。

固定资产投资按建设性质分 建设项目的性质一般分为新建、扩建、改建和技术改造、单纯建造生活设施、迁建、恢复、单纯购置。

（1）新建：指从无到有"平地起家"开始建设的项目。现有企业、事业、行政单位投资的项目一般不属于新建。但如有的单位原有基础很小，经过建设后新增的固定资产价值超过该企业、事业、行政单位原有固定资产价值（原值）三倍以上的，也应作为新建。

（2）扩建：指为扩大原有产品的生产能力（或效益）或增加新的产品生产能力，而增建的生产车间（或主要工程）、分厂、独立的生产线等项目。行政、事业单位在原单位增建业务性用房（如学校增建教学用房、医院增建门诊部、病房等）也作为扩建。

（3）改建和技术改造：指对原有设施进行技术改造或更新（包括相应配套的辅助性生产、生活福利设施）的建设项目。

（4）单纯建造生活设施：指在不扩建、改建生产性工程和业务用房的情况下，单纯建造职工住宅、托儿所、子弟学校、医务室、浴室、食堂等生活设施的项目。

（5）迁建：指为改变生产能力布局或由于城市环境保护和安全生产的需要等原因而搬迁到另地建设的项目。在搬迁另地的建设过程中，不论是维持原来规模还是扩大规模都按迁建来统计。

（6）恢复：指因自然灾害、战争等原因，使原有固定资产全部或部分报废，以后又投资恢复建设的项目。不论是按原规模恢复还是在恢复的同时进行扩建的都按恢复项目统计。尚未建成投产的建设项目因自然灾害而损坏重建的，仍按原有建设性质划分。

（7）单纯购置：指单纯购置不需要安装的设备、工具、器具而不进行工程建设的项目。有些调查单位当年虽然只从事一些购置活动，但其设计中规定有建筑安装活动，应根据设计文件的内容来确定建设性质，不得作为单纯购置统计。

固定资产投资按构成分 固定资产投资活动按其工作内容和实现方式分为建筑工程、安装工程、设备工器具购置、其他费用三个部分。

（1）建筑工程：指各种房屋、建筑物的建造工程，又称建筑工作量。这部分投资额必须兴工动料，通过施工活动才能实现，是固定资产投资额的重要组成部分。

（2）安装工程：指各种设备、装置的安装工程，又称安装工作量。

（3）设备工器具购置：指报告期内购置或自制的，达到固定资产标准的设备、工具、器具的价值。

（4）其他费用：指在固定资产建造和购置过程中发生的，除建筑安装工程和设备、工器具购置投资完成额以外的应当分摊计入固定资产投资项目的费用，不指经营中财务上的其他费用。

新增生产能力（或工程效益）名称 指建成投产项目或工程新增生产能力（或工程效益）的名称。

建设规模 指建设项目或工程设计文件中规定的全部设计能力（或工程效益）。包括已经建成投产和尚未建成投产的工程的生产能力（或工程效益）。它是以实物形态表示固定资产投资规模的指标，反映建设项目或工程全部建成投产（或交付使用）后，能够为社会提供多少设计能力（或工程效益）。

房屋施工面积 指报告期内施工的全部房屋建筑面积。

房屋竣工面积 指报告期内房屋建筑按照设计要求已全部完工，达到住人和使用条件，经验收鉴定合格或达到竣工验收标准，可正式移交使用的各栋房屋建筑面积的总和。

本年新增固定资产　指在报告期已经完成建造和购置过程，并已交付生产或使用单位的固定资产的价值，包括已经建成投入生产或交付使用的工程投资和达到固定资产标准的设备、工具、器具的投资及有关应摊入的费用。属于增加固定资产价值的其他建设费用，应随同交付使用的工程一并计入新增固定资产。

房地产开发本年完成投资　指各种登记注册类型的房地产开发法人单位本年内统一开发的住宅、厂房、仓库、饭店、宾馆、度假村、写字楼、办公楼等房屋建筑物，配套的服务设施，土地开发工程（如道路、给水、排水、供电、供热、通讯、平整场地等基础设施工程）和土地购置的投资；不包括单纯的土地开发和交易活动。

土地购置和开发情况

（1）待开发土地面积：指经有关部门批准，通过各种方式获得土地使用权，但尚未开工建设的土地面积。

（2）本年土地购置面积：指在本年内通过各种方式获得土地使用权的土地面积。

商品房屋销售与出租情况

（1）商品房销售面积：指报告期内出售商品房屋的合同总面积（即双方签署的正式买卖合同中所确定的建筑面积）。商品房销售面积由现房销售面积和期房销售面积两部分组成。

①现房销售面积：指在报告期内正式签订买卖合同、已经竣工达到入住条件的商品房屋建筑面积。包括以一次性付款方式和分期付款方式销售的现房建筑面积。

②期房销售面积：指在报告期内正式签订买卖合同、正在建设尚未竣工交付使用的商品房屋建筑面积。包括以一次性付款方式和分期付款方式销售的商品房屋建筑面积。期房销售建筑面积竣工后不再结转为现房销售建筑面积。

（2）待售面积：指报告期末已竣工的可供销售或出租的商品房屋建筑面积中，尚未销售或出租的商品房屋建筑面积，包括以前年度竣工和本期竣工的房屋面积，但不包括报告期已竣工的拆迁还建、统建代建、公共配套建筑、房地产公司自用及周转房等不可销售或出租的房屋面积。按照商品房待售时间的长短可以划分为待售一年以下、待售一到三年（含一年）和待售三年以上（含三年）。

（3）房屋出租面积：指在报告期末房屋开发单位出租的商品房屋的全部面积。

（4）商品房销售额：指报告期内出售商品房屋的合同总价款（即双方签署的正式买卖合同中所确定的合同总价）。该指标与商品房销售面积同口径，由现房销售额和期房销售额两部分组成。

①现房销售额：指报告期内销售的已竣工商品房屋的合同总价款。包括现房销售前期预收的定金、预收款、首付款及全部按揭贷款的本金等款项。该指标与现房销售面积同口径。

②期房销售额：指报告期内销售的正在建设尚未竣工的商品房屋的合同总价款。包括预售房屋前期预收的定金、预收款、首付款及全部按揭贷款的本金等项。该指标与期房销售面积同口径。

Explanatory Notes on Main Statistical Indicators

Total Investment in Fixed Assets refers to the volume of activities in construction and purchases of fixed assets and related fees during a certain period of time, expressed in monetary terms.

Investment in Real Estate Development refers to the investment by real estate development units of various types of ownership in buildings and structures (such as residence, factory, warehouse, restaurant, hotel, resort, office building and administration building), supporting service facilities and land development engineering (including infrastructure projects such as road, water supply, drainage, power supply, heat supply, communication and land grading) excluding activities in pure land transactions.

Source of Funds for Investment in Fixed Assets include national budgetary funds, domestic loans, foreign investment, self–raised funds, and others depending on the source of investment.

(1) National budgetary funds refers to financial funds used by governments at all levels for fixed–asset investment, including central budget funds and local budget funds.

(2) Domestic loans refer to loans of various forms borrowed by investing units from banks and non–bank financial institutions during the reference period for the purpose of investment in fixed assets, including the loan issued by the bank by self–owned funds and deposit taking, domestic loans appropriated by superior, national special loan, loan arranged by special funds for local finance, domestic reserve loan and revolving credit.

(3) Bonds: refer to the certificate of indebtedness issued by the enterprise or the financial institution to the investor for raising the capital of fixed–asset investment with capital and interest promised to be repaid as per certain issue terms, including financial bond and enterprise bond.

(4) Foreign investment: refer to overseas (including foreign countries, Hong Kong, Macau and Taiwan) funds (including equipment, materials and technology) received in the reporting period, including foreign borrowings (loans from foreign governments and international financial organizations, export credit, commercial loans from foreign banks and issue of bonds and stocks overseas), foreign direct investment and other foreign investments (including compensation trade, the price of processing and assembling the equipment provided by foreign business, international leasing, funds from foreign direct investment income that are reinvested in fixed assets domestically). Excluded from this category is capital in foreign exchanges owned by China (foreign exchanges owned by the central and local governments, foreign exchanges retained by enterprises, foreign exchanges by enterprises through the regulating mechanism, loans in foreign exchanges issued by the Bank of China with its own fund, etc.). In calculating the utilization of foreign capital, foreign currencies are converted into CNY applying the exchange rate (central parity rate) at the end of the reference period. .

(5) Self–raised funds: refer to the fund raised in the reporting period and used for construction and purchase of the project, including self–owned funds, capital invested by shareholders and borrowed funds other than various financial funds, capital borrowed from various financing institutions and offshore funds.

(6) Other refer to funds for investment in fixed assets received in the reporting period, except for the above–mentioned various capitals, including funds raised in society, personal money, voluntary donations and capital from other units.

Investment in Fixed Assets by Type of Construction The construction projects in general can be classified, by the type of construction, into new construction, expansion, reconstruction and technical transformation, simple construction of living facilities, relocation, recovery and simple purchase.

(1) New construction: refers to the project that started construction from scratch. Projects invested by the existing enterprises, institutions or agencies is not considered as new construction. In case the assets of the existing unit are quite small, and the value of newly added fixed assets exceeds the original value of assets by three times, the expansion will be considered as new construction.

(2) Expansion: refers to construction of new production workshops (or major projects), branch factories or independent production lines, for the purpose of increasing the production capacity (or improving efficiency) of the original products. Newly constructed houses for the operation of institutions and administrative organizations (such as the newly constructed buildings for teaching in schools, buildings for clinics or wards in hospitals, etc.) are also classified as expansion.

(3) Reconstruction and technical transformation: refer to the construction project for technical transformation or renewal for original facilities (including corresponding supporting auxiliary production and living welfare facilities).

(4) Simple construction of living facilities: refers to the project of simply constructing living facilities such as staff houses, nurseries, schools for children of employees, medical rooms, shower rooms and canteens, etc. without expanding or reconstructing productive engineering and business housing.

(5) Relocation: refer to the project moved to other place for construction for the purpose of changing production capacity layout or urban environment protection and safety production requirements. In the process of being moved to other places for construction, whether it is to maintain the original scale or augment the scale, it will be counted as relocation.

(6) Recovery: refers to the project with original fixed assets scrapped in whole or in part due to natural disaster or war which is invested to recover construction later. Regardless of recovery as per

original size or expansion at the time of recovery, it will be counted as recovery. If the construction project which has not been completed and gone into operation is reconstructed due to being damaged by natural disaster, it is still classified according to the original type of construction.

(7) Simple purchase: refers to the project of simply purchasing equipment, tools and appliances which do not need to be installed without engineering construction. Although some investigating units only engaged in some purchase activities in that year, construction and installation activities were specified in their design, so it is necessary to confirm the type of construction in line with the content of the design document, and should not be counted as simple purchase.

Investment in fixed assets by Structure Fixed-asset investment activities are divided into construction engineering, installation engineering, purchase of equipment & tools and other expenses in terms of working content and implementation model.

(1) Construction engineering: refers to the construction of various houses and buildings, also called as construction workload. Such investment volume must be implemented through construction activities based on utilization of materials, which is an important part of fixed investments.

(2) Installation engineering: refers to installation of various equipment and devices, also called as installation workload.

(3) Purchase of equipment and tools: refers to the value of purchased or home-made equipment, tools and appliances within the reporting period, which reach to fixed-asset standards.

(4) Other expenses: refer to expenses incurred in the construction and purchase process of fixed assets which shall be allocated and included into the fixed-asset investment project, except for the expenses of construction and installation engineering and purchase of equipment & tools, and not refer to other financial expenses in the operation.

Newly Increased Production Capacity (or Project Efficiency) refers to the name of new production capacity (or project benefit) of the project or the engineering completed and put into operation.

Scale of Construction refers to all design ability (or project benefit) specified in the design document for construction project or engineering, including production capacity (or project benefit) completed and put into production and not yet be completed and put into production. It is an indicator showing the scale of investment in fixed assets in the matter form and reflects the design capability (or project benefit) provided for the society after the construction project or engineering is completed and put into production (or delivered for use).

Construction area of the house refers to building area of all houses constructed in the reporting period.

Housing completion area refers to total building areas of all houses which have been completed in accordance with design requirements in the reporting period, reach to living and using conditions, pass acceptance and verification or reach to the completion acceptance standards and can be formally handed over for use.

New fixed assets in this year refer to the value of fixed assets having been delivered to the production or use unit with construction and purchase process completed in the reporting period, including investment in projects completed and put into production or delivered for use and investment in equipment, tools and appliances reaching to fixed-asset standards and related expenses which shall be included. Other construction costs falling into the added fixed-asset value shall be included into new fixed assets together with the project delivered for use.

Investment completed in current year in real estate development refers to buildings and structures (such as residence, factory, warehouse, restaurant, hotel, resort, office building and administration building), supporting service facilities and land development engineering (including infrastructure projects such as road, water supply, drainage, power supply, heat supply, communication and land grading) and investment in land purchase uniformly developed by real estate development legal entity in the current year based on all kinds of businesses; excluding simple land development and trading activities.

Land purchase and development

(1) Land area to be developed: refers to the area of the land approved by related department with land use right obtained by all means but not yet under construction.

(2) Land acquisition area in the current year: refers to the area of the land with land use right obtained by all means in the current year.

Sales and rental of the residential property

(1) Sales area of residential property: refers to the total area in the contract of residential properties sold within the reporting period (namely the building area set forth in the sales contract formally signed by both parties). Sales area of the residential property is composed by two parts -- sales area of completed houses and sales area of the property under construction.

① Sales area of completed houses: refers to the building area of the residential property which has been completed and reached to living conditions with the sales contract formally signed within the reporting period, including the building area of completed houses sold by one-off payment and installment payment.

② Sales area of property under construction: refer to the building area of residential properties under construction which has not yet been delivered for use with the sales contract formally signed within the reporting period, including the building area of residential properties sold by one-off payment and installment payment. The sales building area of the property under construction will not be transfered to the sales building area of the competed house after being completed.

(2) Area to be sold: refers to the building area of residential properties not sold or rented in the building area of residential properties available for sale or renting which has been completed at the end of the reporting period, including the area of houses completed before and in the current period, and other than the area of housings not available for sale or renting such as the housing built due to demolition, the housing uniformly

built by the government, public matching buildings, the housing used by the real estate company and the relocation housing in the reporting period. As per the waiting time for sales of the residential property, the housings can be divided into the one waiting for sales for less than one year, the one waiting for sales for more than one year (one year included) but less than three years and the one waiting for sales for more than three years (three years included).

(3) Area of rental housing: refers to all areas of the residential property rented out by the house development unit at the end of the reporting period.

(4) Sales amount of residential property: refers to the total price in the contract of residential properties sold within the reporting period (namely the total contract price set forth in the sales contract formally signed by both parties). The indicator shares the same caliber with the sales area of the residential property, and it consists two parts -- sales amount of completed houses and sales amount of the property under construction.

① Sales amount of completed houses: refer to total contract price of residential properties completed and sold within the reporting period, including deposits, prepayments and down payment as well as all principal of all mortgage loans. The indicator shares the same caliber with the sales area of the completed houses.

② Sales amount of property under construction: refer to total contract price of residential properties under construction sold within the reporting period, including deposits, prepayments and down payment as well as all principal of all mortgage loans. The indicator shares the same caliber with the sales area of the property under construction.

城市公用事业和环境保护

URBAN PUBLIC UNILITIES
AND ENVIRONMENTAL
PROTECTION

7-1 城市道路与公共交通
Basic Statistics on Muncipal Engineering and Public Transportation

指标	Item	2016 年	2017 年	2018 年	2019 年	2020 年	2021 年
城市道路	City Roads						
道路长度（公里）	Length of Roads (km)	5422	5663	5788	6987	7301	7847
道路面积（万平方米）	Area of Roads(10 000 sq.m)	9724	10224	10529	12653	13138	14212
城市桥梁（座）	Number of City Bridges(unit)	927	935	1021	1136	978	1004
# 立交桥（座）	Interchange(unit)	82	82	85	95	79	79
路灯（盏）	Number of Streetlights(unit)	170314	188598	195014	213259	185188	204404
人均拥有道路面积（平方米）	Per Capita Road Arae(sq.m)	26.20	22.96	23.03	20.30	20.66	20.88
公共交通	Public Transportation						
年末营运车辆（辆）	Number of Operating Vehicles(unit)	15539	16850	16644	19676	18915	19219
公共汽车	Buses	5846	7157	6951	8383	8188	8833
# 无轨电车	Trolley Buses	121	121	106	109	126	126
出租汽车	Number of Taxis	9693	9693	9693	11293	10727	10386
客运总量（万人次）	Total Passenger Traffic(10 000 person-times)	90776.1	90515.6	89619.7	99389.9	62425.9	73058.0
轨道交通	Rail Traffic						
配属车辆数（辆）	Number of Vehicles(unit)				204	204	408
运营里程（公里）	Length in Operatio(km)				47.7	47.7	84.1
客运总量（万人次）	Total Passenger Traffic(10 000 person-times)				573.5	867.6	5602.9

注：2020 年，“城市桥梁”使用新统计口径。
Note:In 2020, “Urban Bridge” will be subject to new statistic specifications.

7-2 水、电、气、热供应情况
Basic Statistics on Water,Electricity,Gas and Heating in Cities

指标	Item	单位 Unit	2016 年	2017 年	2018 年	2019 年	2020 年	2021 年
自来水	**Water**							
年末水厂生产能力	Production Capacity of Water Supply	万吨 / 日 (10 000 tons/day)	211.47	215.57	220.27	241.00	243.00	288.90
年末管线长度	Length of Water Supply Pioelines	公里 (km)	4241.04	4779.01	5277.13	5703.60	6033.59	7077.25
全年供水量	Volume of Water Supply	万吨 (10 000 tons)	33191.11	35865.07	39226.16	44452.30	45182.90	49712.36
人均日生活用水	Per Capita Daily Water Consumption	升 (litre)	142.78	139.58	140.37	134.79	131.58	141.07
城市人口用水普及率	Coverage Rate of Water Supply	%	99.57	99.64	99.78	100.00	100.00	100.00
用电量	**Electricity Consumption**							
全社会用电量	Total Electricity Consumption	万千瓦时 (10 000 kWh)	2799221	2762869	2843630	4143022	4338712	4752639
工业	Industrial Electricity Consumption	万千瓦时 (10 000 kWh)	1470794	1319975	1215034	2215281	2395876	2565881
城乡居民生活用电	Household Electricity Consumption	万千瓦时 (10 000 kWh)	554853	598578	667505	776162	796871	865304
液化石油气和天然气	**Liquefied Petroleum Gas and Gas**							
液化石油气全年供气量	Total Liquefied Petroleum Gas Supply	吨 (ton)	53086.2	49944.0	41110.0	45518.0	38353.0	25160.0
生活用	Residential Use	吨 (ton)	19771	23462	20458	25935	22119	12981
居民用气人口	Population Uses Gas	万人 (10 000 persons)	77.39	55.93	46.81	59.90	52.59	40.70
天然气供气量	Total Natural Gas Supply	万立方米 (10 000 cu.m)	79325.47	90724.36	113945.56	143576.00	161034.00	179895.21
生产用	Production Use	万立方米 (10 000 cu.m)	60994.42	69361.61	88821.02	96706.80	113916.82	100508.71
生活用	Residential Use	万立方米 (10 000 cu.m)	18331.05	21362.75	25124.54	46869.20	47117.18	79386.50
居民用气人口	Population Uses Gas	万人 (10 000 persons)	291.56	388.63	409.70	560.90	614.20	639.78
用气普及率	Coverage Rate of Gas Supply	%	99.42	99.85	99.87	99.97	100.00	100.00
集中供热	**Central Heating**							
管道长度	Pipe Length	公里 (km)	2742	6104	7010	8893	10426	12836
供热面积	Heating Area	万平方米 (10 000 sq.m)	14917	18174	19834	26073	27740	30465

7-3 环境状况及污染治理情况
Basic Statistics on Environment and Treatment of Pollution

指标	Item	单位 Unit	2017 年	2018 年	2019 年	2020 年	2021 年
环境质量状况	**Environment Condition**						
环境空气细颗粒物（$PM_{2.5}$）浓度年均值	Annual Average Concentration of $PM_{2.5}$	mg/m^3	0.063	0.052	0.053	0.047	0.04
环境空气二氧化硫浓度年均值	Annual Average Concentration of SO_2	mg/m^3	0.025	0.017	0.015	0.012	0.011
环境空气二氧化氮浓度年均值	Annual Average Concentration of NO_2	mg/m^3	0.046	0.045	0.041	0.035	0.033
环境空气可吸入颗粒物 (PM_{10}) 浓度年均值	Annual Average Concentration of PM_{10}	mg/m^3	0.130	0.112	0.103	0.086	0.078
集中式饮用水源地水质达标率	Standard rate of concentrate Water Source Area	%	100.00	100.00	100.00	100	100
区域环境噪声昼间平均等效声级	Area Whole-day Average Noise Value	分贝 (db)	53.7	53.3	54.9	54.4	53.8
道路交通噪声平均等效声级	Traffic Average Noise Value	分贝 (db)	69.7	69.5	69.6	69.1	68.8
污染物排放情况	**Discharge of Major Pollutants**						
废水排放总量	Volume of Waste Water Discharged	万吨 (10 000 tons)	34693	28714	29261	46493	
# 工业废水排放量	Volume of Industrial Waste Water Discharged	万吨 (10 000 tons)	5949	4770	5120	5886	
化学需氧量排放量	Volume of COD Emission	万吨 (10 000 tons)	28701	19756	19131	49922	
# 工业化学需氧量排放量	Volume of Industrial COD Emission	吨 (ton)	2594	1433	1425	1744	
氨氮排放量	Volume of Ammonia Nitrogen	吨 (ton)	4255	1497	1447	3016	
# 工业氨氮排放量	Volume of Industrial Ammonia Nitrogen	吨 (ton)	197	111	78	54	
二氧化硫排放量	Volume of Sulphur Dioxide Discharged	吨 (ton)	32502	20948	17124	15920	
# 工业二氧化硫排放量	Volume of Industrial Sulphur Dioxide Discharged	吨 (ton)	16545	16672	13353	11356	
氮氧化物排放量	Volume of Nitrogen Oxides Discharged	吨 (ton)	23316	43841	41533	52729	
# 工业氮氧化物排放量	Volume of Industrial Nitrogen Oxides Discharged	吨 (ton)	21254	41128	38022	25382	
机动车氮氧化物排放量	Volume of Vehicle Nitrogen Oxides	吨 (ton)				24814	
烟（粉）尘排放量	Volume of Soot and Dust Discharged	吨 (ton)	32794	31345	31258	25871	
# 工业烟（粉）尘排放量	Volume of Industrial Soot and Dust Discharged	吨 (ton)	25060	22497	22404	13414	

注：1. 生态环境部以第二次污染源普查成果为基准，依法组织对 2016–2019 年污染源统计初步数据进行更新，2018 年、2019 年数据为更新后的数据。根据统计规则，2020 年之前未对机动车氮氧化物排放量进行统计。

2. 根据生态环境部统一工作安排，2020 年开始统计农村生活污水污染物产排量；目前 2021 年环境统计工作只完成了工业源统计部分，生活源、机动车统计正在开展中，尚未定库。

Notes: 1. Based on the results of the Second Pollution Sources Census of China, the Ministry of Ecology and Environment organized to update preliminary statistic data of pollution sources from 2016 to 2019 under laws, and data in 2018 and 2019 are the updated data. According to the statistic rules, the emission of nitrogen oxides from motor vehicles was not counted before 2020.

2. According to the unified work arrangement of the Ministry of Ecology and Environment, the output and discharge of pollutants in rural domestic sewage have been counted since 2020; At present, the environmental statistics work in 2021 has only completed for the statistics of industrial sources, while the statistics of living sources and motor vehicles are undergoing, and the database has not yet been fixed.

7-4 城市园林绿化、环境卫生及其他
Basic Statistics on Parks Green Areas and Urban Sanitation in Cities

指标	Item	单位 Unit	2016 年	2017 年	2018 年	2019 年	2020 年	2021 年
园林绿化	Parks Gardens and Green Areas							
年末园林绿地面积	Garden Green Area at Year-end	公顷 (ha)	18162.9	19528.6	20701.0	28199.3	31087.8	31761.9
# 公园面积	Area of Parks	万平方米 (10 000 sq.m)	3190	3414	3930	3688	3754	4339
人均公园绿地面积	Per Capita Public Green Areas	平方米 / 人 (sq.m/person)	11.8	11.8	12.6	13.2	13.1	13.0
建成区绿化覆盖率	Coverage of Green Area	%	40.12	40.57	40.52	41.18	40.69	41.69
城市卫生	Urban Health							
污水集中处理率	Centralized Sewage Treatment Rate	%	96.33	95.98	96.59	97.73	98.17	98.20
清运垃圾	Garbage Clearance	万吨 (10 000 tons)	179.68	192.22	202.64	278.75	278.03	296.96
清运粪便	Garbage Disposal	万吨 (10 000 tons)	10.5	–	–	–	–	–
公共厕所	Public Lavatory	座 (unit)	1077	1075	1086	1122	1203	1267
城市维护费收支	Expenditure and Earning for City Maintenance							
维护费收入	Earning for City Maintenance	万元 (10 000 yuan)	1843784	–	–	–	–	
维护费支出	Expenditure for City Maintenance	万元 (10 000 yuan)	1571443	–	–	–	–	

注：本表指标为“–”的，部门相关统计制度中已经不在进行统计。
Note:The indicator “–” in this table means statistics are no longer in the relevant statistical system of the department.

主要统计指标解释

年末自来水生产能力 指年底城建部门管理的自来水厂和自备水源的社会单位取水、净化、送水、出厂输水干管等环节的实际生产能力。

年末供水管道长度 指从送水泵到用户水表之间所有管道的长度。

全年供水总量 指公用自来水厂和自备水源的社会单位全年的供水总量，包括有效供水量及损失水量。

生活用水量 指居民日常生活与公共福利设施的用水量，包括居民、饮食店、旅馆、医院、理发店、浴池、洗衣店、游泳池、商店、学校、机关、部队等单位的用水量。

城市人口用水普及率 指城市用水的非农业人口数（不包括临时人口和流动人口）与城市非农业人口总数之比。计算公式为:

用水普及率 = 城市用水的非农业人口数 / 城市非农业人口数 ×100%

城市用气普及率 指使用煤气（包括人工煤气、液化石油气、天然气）的城市非农业人口数（不包括临时人口和流动口）与城市非农业人口总数之比。计算公式为:

城市用气普及率 = 城市用气的非农业人口数 / 城市非农业人口总数 ×100%

年底实有铺装道路长度 指除土路外，路面经过铺装宽度在 3.5 米以上的道路，包括高级、次高级道路和普通道路。

城市桥梁 指城市范围内，修建在河道上的桥梁和道路与道路立交、道路跨越铁路的立交桥及人行天桥。包括永久性桥和半永久性桥，不包括临时性桥、铁路桥、涵洞。

城市污水日处理能力 指污水处理厂每昼夜处理污水量的设计能力。

年末实有公共汽（电）车 指年底可参加营运的全部车辆数，包括营运车辆数和库存查封未参加营运的车辆。不包括非营运车辆，如架线车、油罐车、工程车、货车及其他专用车辆和借入的客运车辆。

绿地面积 指报告期末用作园林和绿化的各种绿地面积。包括公园绿地、生产绿地、防护绿地、附属绿地和其他绿地的面积。

公园绿地 城市中向公众开放的、以游憩为主要功能，有一定的游憩设施和服务设施，同时兼有健全生态、美化景观、防灾减灾等综合作用的绿化用地。它是城市建设用地、城市绿地系统和城市市政公用设施的重要组成部分。

工业废水排放量 指报告期内经过企业厂区所有排放口排到企业外部的工业废水量。包括生产废水、外排的直接冷却水、废气治理设施废水、超标排放的矿井地下水和与工业废水混排的厂区生活污水，不包括独立外排的间接冷却水（清浊不分流的间接冷却水应计算在内）。

化学需氧量 (COD) 测量有机和无机物质化学分解所消耗氧的质量浓度的水污染指数。废气排放总量 指燃料燃烧和生产工艺过程中排放的各种废气总量，以标准状态下每年万标立方米表示。

二氧化硫排放量 指报告期内企业在燃料燃烧和生产工艺过程中排入大气的二氧化硫总质量。工业中二氧化硫主要来源于化石燃料（煤、石油等）的燃烧，还包括含硫矿石的冶炼或含硫酸、磷肥等生产的工业废气排放。

氮氧化物排放量 指报告期内企业在燃料燃烧和生产工艺过程中排入大气的氮氧化物总质量。

烟（粉）尘排放量 指报告期内企业在燃料燃烧和生产工艺过程中排入大气的烟尘及工业粉尘的总质量之和。烟尘或工业粉尘排放量可以通过除尘系统的排风量和除尘设备出口烟尘浓度相乘求得。

工业粉尘排放量 指企业在生产工艺过程中排放的颗粒物重量。如钢铁企业的耐火材料粉尘、焦化企业的筛焦系统粉尘、烧结机的粉尘、石灰窑的粉尘、建材企业的水泥粉尘等。不包括电厂排放大气的烟尘。

Explanatory Notes on Main Statistical Indicators

Year-end Tap Water Production Capacity refers to actual capacity of such links as water intaking, purification, water carriage and leaving factory water main pipe of the waterworks managed by urban construction department and social unit water source prepared at the end of the year.

Length of Water Supply Pipelines at the Year-end refers to the total length of all the pipelines between the water pumps and the user water meters.

Annual Volume of water supply refers to annual total water supply of public waterworks and social unit with water source prepared, including both the effective water supply and loss during the water supply.

Consumption of Water for Residential Use refers to water consumption in the daily life of residents and by public amenities and facilities, including water consumption by residents, eateries, hotels, hospitals, barber shops, common bathing pools, laundries, swimming pools, shops, schools, organs and troops, etc..

Urban Population Water Penetration Rate refers to the ratio between non-agricultural population of municipal water (excluding temporary and floating population) and total urban non-agricultural population. The calculation formula is:

Water penetration rate = non-agricultural population of municipal water / urban non-agricultural population * 100%

Urban Gas Popularizing Rate refers to the ratio between urban non-agricultural population (excluding temporary population and migrant population) using the coal gas (including manufactured gas, liquefied petroleum gas and natural gas) and total urban non-agricultural population. The calculation formula is:

Urban gas popularizing rate = non-agricultural population of municipal gas / total urban non-agricultural population * 100%

Year-end Actual Length of Paved Road refers to roads whose pavement width exceeds 3.5 m except for unsurfaced road (including senior, sub-senior and ordinary roads).

Urban Bridges refer to bridge and road built above the river, interchange between roads, highway interchange based on road spanning railway and pedestrian overpass, both permanent and semi-permanent bridges are included, other than temporary bridge, railway bridge and culvert in the scope of the city.

Daily Urban Sewage Treatment Capacity refers to the design capability of the sewage quantity treated by sewage treatment works every day and night.

Year-end Existing Buses (Public Trolleys) refer to all vehicles which can be put into operation at the end of the year, including number of vehicles put into operation and vehicles with inventory sealed up which are not put into operation other than non-operating vehicles, such as overhead line vehicle, oil tank truck, engineering vehicle, truck, other special vehicle and borrowed passenger service vehicle.

Green Area refers to a green area for gardening and greening. Including parks, green spaces, protective green, the accessory Greenbelt and other green areas at the end of referenced period.

Park Green Land refers to the green land which is open to the public for relaxation and has services facilities and is used for ecological protection, landscaping and disaster reduction. It is an important part of construction land, urban green space and municipal public facilities. public facilities.

Industrial Waste Water Discharged refers to the volume of industrial waste water discharged through all of the drainage system to the outside of factory complex by enterprises during the report period. It includes discharged waste water from production, direct cooling water, waste gas treatment facilities, mine groundwater beyond the standard and domestic sewage mixed with industrial waste water, does not include independently discharged indirect cooling water (voicing split-less indirect cooling water should be taken into account).

Chemical Oxygen Demand (COD) refers to index of water pollution measuring the mass concentration of oxygen consumed by the chemical breakdown of organic and inorganic matter. Total exhaust emission refers to total quantity of various exhaust gases discharged in the process of fuel burning and production which is expressed with 10,000 standard cubic meters each year under the standard state.

SO_2 Emission refers to total volume of SO_2 discharged into air during the process of fuel combustion and industrial production in enterprises in a given time, and is mainly caused by the combustion of fossil fuel, ore smelting and the discharge of industrial waste gas during the production of sulfuric acid and phosphate fertilizers.

Nitrogen Oxides Emission refers to total volume of nitrogen oxides discharged into air during the process of fuel combustion and industrial production.

Industrial Soot and Dust Emission refers to volume of soot and dust in smoke emitted in process of fuel burning and industrial production in premises of enterprises in the report period. It is calculated by multiplying exhaust volume of dust removal system by dust concentration.

Emission Load of Industrial Dust refers to the weight of particulate matters discharged in the process of production (such as fireproofing dust of the iron and steel enterprise, coke screening system dust of the coke making enterprise, dust of the sintering machine, dust of the lime kiln and cement dust of the building material industry), excluding smoke discharged by the power plant in to the atmosphere.

财政和金融保险

GOVERNMENT FINANCE AND FINANCIAL INSURANCE

8-1 各时期地方财政收支及指数
Local Government Revenue,Expenditures and Indices of Major Years

年份 Year	一般公共预算收入（万元）General Public Budget Revenue (10 000yuan)	一般公共预算支出（万元）General Public Budget Expenditure (10 000yuan)	指数(%)（以上年为 100）(%)(Preceding Year=100)	
			一般公共预算收入 General Public Budget Revenue	一般公共预算支出 General Public Budget Expenditure
1999	460690	497667	119.9	110.8
2000	490485	547210	110.5	110.4
“十五”时期				
2001	596061	703720	121.5	128.6
2002	662511	775046	115.4	110.2
2003	761064	884597	119.6	114.3
2004	890364	1016953	120.9	115.0
2005	1061547	1206643	120.7	118.7
“十一五”时期				
2006	1284388	1469762	121.0	121.8
2007	1570192	1799787	122.3	122.5
2008	1860155	2213190	118.5	123.1
2009	2101923	2599178	113.0	117.4
2010	2661314	3368037	126.6	129.6
“十二五”时期				
2011	3249315	3968831	122.1	117.8
2012	3808218	4656731	117.0	117.3
2013	4820722	5193190	113.9	111.5
2014	5431278	5714138	112.7	110.0
2015	6143172	6581813	113.1	115.2
“十三五”时期				
2016	6412167	7412641	104.4	112.6
2017	6772100	8340600	105.6	112.5
2018	7528162	10183179	111.2	122.1
2019	8741898	11973158	107.2	107.0
2020	9060751	12887953	103.6	107.6
“十四五”时期				
2021	10076073	12930814	111.2	108.4

注：1.2013 年财政部门对一般公共预算收入口径进行调整，2013 年一般公共预算收入指数为可比口径。2018 年以前为区划调整前数据。
2.“一般公共预算收入”与“一般公共预算支出”为预算数据，以下各表同。

Notes:1.In 2013, the financial department adjusted the caliber of general public budget revenue. In 2013, the index of general public budget income index was comparable caliber.Data before the year of 2018 are the data of administrative division before the adjustment.
2."General public budget revenue" and "general public budget expenditure" are estimates, the same for the following tables.

8-2 地方财政收入(2021 年)
Local Financial Revenue(2021)

单位：万元 (10 000yuan)

指标	Item	全市合计 Total	市本级 Cities				县区级 Counties
			小计 Total	市直 Departments Directly Under the Municipal Government	济南起步区（直管）Jinan Start-up Area (Directly under)	南部山区 Nanshan	
一般公共预算收入	General Public Budget Revenue	10076073	996451	913286	68788	14377	9079622
增值税	Value-added Tax	2680311	25328		18716	6612	2654983
企业所得税	Enterprise Income Tax	1320639	6890		6005	885	1313749
个人所得税	Personal Income Tax	427754	1569		965	604	426185
资源税	Resource Tax	65976	115		63	52	65861
城市维护建设税	Tax on City Maintenance and Construction	472017	10904	5759	3840	1305	461113
房产税	Tax on Real Estates	274076	1940		1633	307	272136
印花税	Stamp Tax	167302	2467		2362	105	164835
城镇土地使用税	Holding tax on urban and county land	253968	2582		2199	383	251386
土地增值税	Land Value Added Tax	1016281	5466		4604	862	1010815
车船税	Tax on vehicles and Their Registration	126378	3		2	1	126375
耕地占用税	Farmland Occupation Tax	54258	6712		6712		47546
契税	Contract tax	893406	11483		11439	44	881923
环境保护税	Environmental Protection Tax	10253	17		14	3	10236
专项收入	Specific Revenue	593364	269991	264500	4377	1114	323373
行政事业性收费收入	Income from Administrative Fees	519432	245631	244199	1343	89	273801
罚没收入	Penalty and Confiscatory Income	225083	105781	104971	368	442	119302
国有资本经营收入	Profits of State-owned Enterprises	42479					42479
国有资源（资产）有偿使用收入	Revenue of Compensable Use of State-owned Resources (Assets)	789347	176476	170783	4146	1547	612871
捐赠收入	Donation Income	11070	213	213			10857
政府住房基金收入	Government Housing Fund Income	128511	122850	122850			5661
其他收入	Others	2001	33	11		22	1968
政府性基金收入	Government Funds Income	10523414	8637815	8507798	129846	171	1885599
# 城市基础设施配套收入	Urban Infrastructure Supporting Income	778063	440765	425581	15013	171	337298

8-3 各区财政收入(2021 年)

Financial Revenue by District(2021)

单位：万元

指标	Item	合计 Total	历下区 Li xia	市中区 Shi zhong
一般公共预算收入	General Public Budget Revenue	8615500	1685203	1084922
增值税	Value-added Tax	2540734	493597	294946
企业所得税	Enterprise Income Tax	1271411	274835	181242
个人所得税	Personal Income Tax	415478	113092	68715
资源税	Resource Tax	56875	1291	8337
城市维护建设税	Tax on City Maintenance and Construction	448772	84058	51751
房产税	Tax on Real Estates	264415	73743	33394
印花税	Stamp Tax	159823	38703	21978
城镇土地使用税	Holding tax on urban and county land	231950	12979	13491
土地增值税	Land Value Added Tax	994020	291420	100704
车船税	Tax on vehicles and Their Registration	68911	22317	10474
耕地占用税	Farmland Occupation Tax	39553		579
契税	Contract tax	853552	126296	112369
环境保护税	Environmental Protection Tax	9096	385	302
专项收入	Specific Revenue	306933	52473	31923
行政事业性收费收入	Income from Administrative Fees	240149	7587	27820
罚没收入	Penalty and Confiscatory Income	92922	2341	8100
国有资本经营收入	Profits of State-owned Enterprises	42479		
国有资源（资产）有偿使用收入	Revenue of Compensable Use of State-owned Resources (Assets)	560533	89188	118579
捐赠收入	Donation Income	9631		14
政府住房基金收入	Government Housing Fund Income	5635	875	
其他收入	Others	1409	1	
政府性基金收入	Government Funds Income	1426932		
# 城市基础设施配套收入	Urban Infrastructure Supporting Income	286865		

(10 000yuan)

槐荫区 Huai yin	天桥区 Tian qiao	历城区 Li cheng	长清区 Chang qing	章丘区 Zhang qiu	济阳区 Ji yang	莱芜区 Lai wu	钢城区 Gang cheng	济南高新区 Ji'nan Gao xin
587613	467988	1243968	291698	770489	268165	501232	233980	1480242
164862	149690	276669	78065	240476	75916	180347	114698	471468
48261	56932	186306	24083	107893	30073	52244	14256	295286
24907	21606	41253	8286	18766	4834	13085	6939	93995
327	561	1842	4298	9439	764	17514	7399	5103
24895	21243	45163	12432	36068	10775	27977	16255	118155
20625	16187	17847	7414	17845	4809	11014	8041	53496
8328	8138	16228	4739	13991	3111	8820	4345	31442
12141	11150	32388	16678	49331	14938	26656	16268	25930
107676	34057	224140	25178	37873	17088	17477	-80	138487
2016	2289	8767	2449	4385	6751	7839	1519	105
2274	-654	7248	5535	2554	6062	5813	4128	6014
84591	60474	217404	35145	70524	20068	36081	3817	86783
109	159	545	93	1224	111	2768	3171	229
15119	12744	34247	14202	26916	8601	22798	12546	75364
15780	7126	77271	16300	26327	10121	33331	6934	11552
3214	2698	6510	3850	23373	32929	5712	1502	2693
41080						1149	250	
10271	63398	44416	29734	82826	20850	30092	11708	59471
25	68	5692	3200	2	363	267		
				422				4338
1105				188		18	97	
	6721		26155	683962	104936	419296	58806	127056
	6721		24167	60464	48960	19932	1576	125045

8-4 各县财政收入(2021 年)
Financial Revenue by County(2021)

单位：万元　(10 000yuan)

指标	Item	合计 Total	平阴县 Ping yin	商河县 Shang he
一般公共预算收入	General Public Budget Revenue	464122	263709	200413
增值税	Value-added Tax	114249	69779	44470
企业所得税	Enterprise Income Tax	42338	28037	14301
个人所得税	Personal Income Tax	10707	7588	3119
资源税	Resource Tax	8986	8716	270
城市维护建设税	Tax on City Maintenance and Construction	12341	6961	5380
房产税	Tax on Real Estates	7721	4907	2814
印花税	Stamp Tax	5012	3114	1898
城镇土地使用税	Holding tax on urban and county land	19436	8270	11166
土地增值税	Land Value Added Tax	16795	2432	14363
车船税	Tax on vehicles and Their Registration	57464	20648	36816
耕地占用税	Farmland Occupation Tax	7993	1871	6122
契税	Contract tax	28371	9902	18469
环境保护税	Environmental Protection Tax	1140	1037	103
专项收入	Specific Revenue	16440	8885	7555
行政事业性收费收入	Income from Administrative Fees	33652	25064	8588
罚没收入	Penalty and Confiscatory Income	26380	5810	20570
国有资本经营收入	Profits of State-owned Enterprises			
国有资源（资产）有偿使用收入	Revenue of Compensable Use of State-owned Resources (Assets)	52338	49187	3151
捐赠收入	Donation Income	1226	1178	48
政府住房基金收入	Government Housing Fund Income	26	26	
其他收入	Others	559	296	263
政府性基金收入	Government Funds Income	458667	195017	263650
# 城市基础设施配套收入	Urban Infrastructure Supporting Income	50433	11011	39422

8-5 地方财政支出(2021年)
Local Financial Expenditures(2021)

单位：万元 (10 000yuan)

指标	Item	全市合计 Total	市本级 Cities 小计 Total	市直 Departments Directly Under the Municipal Government	济南起步区(直管) Jinan Start-up Area (Directly under)	南部山区 Nanshan	县区级 Counties
一般公共预算支出	General Public Budget Expenditure	12930814	5126190	4594997	384469	146724	7804624
一般公共服务支出	General Public Service	1335633	331989	284640	26329	21020	1003644
国防支出	Defence Expenditure	32382	22824	22774		50	9558
公共安全支出	Public Security	629053	432751	431495	49	1207	196302
教育支出	Education	2128337	438467	394069	148	44250	1689870
科学技术	Science and Technology	411772	210954	203991	6891	72	200818
文化体育与传媒支出	Culture、Sports and Media	122443	76534	75553	606	375	45909
社会保障和就业支出	Social Security and Employment	2042176	812170	774640	11290	26240	1230006
医疗卫生与计划生育支出	Health and Family Planning	1116038	483000	468367	2029	12604	633038
节能环保支出	Energy-saving and Environment Protection	395382	312544	308693	1458	2393	82838
城乡社区支出	Urban and Rural Community Affairs	2930173	1410559	1129276	270079	11204	1519614
农林水支出	Farming、Forestry and Irrigation Affairs	672171	233615	170750	44200	18665	438556
交通运输支出	Transport	138332	67465	61754	50	5661	70867
资源勘探信息等支出	Exploration and Information Affairs	210092	25463	23570	1828	65	184629
商业服务业等支出	Commerce and Services Affairs	80326	12634	12596	38		67692
金融支出	Financial Supervision Affairs	31875	933	933			30942
援助其他地区支出	Aid to Other Area	38359	17813	17813			20546
自然资源海洋气象等支出	Natural Resources Marine Meteorological	162111	84110	83557	420	133	78001
住房保障支出	Housing Security Affairs	298501	89330	67737	18991	2602	209171
粮油物资储备支出	Grain and Oil Reserves	10931	6408	6408			4523
债务付息支出	Pay Principle and Interest for Public Debt	79854	26412	26412			53442
其他支出	Other Expenditure						
政府性基金支出	Government Funds Expenditure	13177333	6807682	5319550	1401013	87119	6369651
#城乡社区支出	Urban and Rural Community Affairs	9959498	4520359	3421946	1012255	86158	5439139

8-6 各区地方财政支出(2021年)
Local Financial Expenditures by District(2021)

单位：万元

指标	Item	合计 Total	历下区 Li xia	市中区 Shi zhong
一般公共预算支出	**General Public Budget Expenditure**	**6962607**	**808107**	**611619**
一般公共服务支出	General Public Service	913896	145491	110155
国防支出	Defence Expenditure	7550	3522	743
公共安全支出	Public Security	160190	25560	20831
教育支出	Education	1504607	183998	155614
科学技术	Science andTechnology	198257	16319	6866
文化体育与传媒支出	Culture、Sports and Media	39310	4459	2105
社会保障和就业支出	Social Security and Employment	1108141	126031	91653
医疗卫生与计划生育支出	Health and Family Planning	566499	48815	57800
节能环保支出	Energy-saving and Environment Protection	74753	5278	1439
城乡社区支出	Urban and Rural Community Affairs	1363254	178447	115873
农林水支出	Farming、Forestry and Irrigation Affairs	340881	8299	8225
交通运输支出	Transport	60445	4	48
资源勘探信息等支出	Exploration and Information Affairs	169811	3965	3730
商业服务业等支出	Commerce and Services Affairs	65267	5483	2330
金融支出	Financial Supervision Affairs	30740	15328	397
援助其他地区支出	Aid to Other Area	20183	3010	2407
国土海洋气象等支出	Land and Weather Affairs	65252	2220	2339
住房保障支出	Housing Security Affairs	193141	25227	23195
粮油物资储备支出	Grain and Oil Reserves	3984		
国债还本付息支出	Pay Principle and Interest for Public Debt	45588	24	1052
其他支出	Other Expenditure			
政府性基金支出	**Government Funds Expenditure**	**5851424**	**591651**	**626615**
#城乡社区支出	Urban and Rural Community Affairs	5012730	580721	602961

(10 000yuan)

槐荫区 Huai yin	天桥区 Tian qiao	历城区 Li cheng	长清区 Chang qing	章丘区 Zhang qiu	济阳区 Ji yang	莱芜区 Lai wu	钢城区 Gang cheng	济南高新区 Ji'nan Gao xin
465566	378980	765062	573206	820163	483586	855089	230296	970933
63971	56869	120481	86352	86186	45006	88313	31565	79507
823	164	253	817	428	38	186	466	110
16143	14447	15166	11658	11401	12760	13036	6642	12546
102021	114459	169323	128689	234568	87162	177975	43853	106945
6467	6277	28154	4187	3918	5276	6753	1031	113009
1831	1547	4711	7398	7637	4504	3523	1197	398
104779	77628	96029	97309	119335	88976	217417	33096	55888
48736	39334	45663	48683	73837	46881	90850	25791	40109
5184	4326	1630	10552	12216	9060	19139	5188	741
58830	42584	212545	29087	141959	93737	50703	27517	411972
12957	5732	28092	103473	37137	48316	62898	14376	11376
87	112	9102	6927	7136	6676	16749	7104	6500
14600	686	1256	2130	28981	4194	54886	1534	53849
4300	1400	3428	1529	1223	750	4565	504	39755
836		213	191	244		1634	124	11773
737	649	2213		5166	1955	511	1918	1617
2253	1502	6000	13233	3889	9267	12086	12121	342
16853	6885	18802	17904	36744	11791	11228	6671	17841
		388	855	1350	1308		83	
1847	2786	524	820	5456	3574	17127	7997	4381
91227	89051	846512	384419	1342458	326753	621937	118760	812041
44056	66182	762205	313641	1229757	236286	473128	73528	630265

8-7 各县地方财政支出(2021年)
Local Financial Expenditures by County(2021)

单位：万元 (10 000yuan)

指标	Item	合计 Total	平阴县 Ping yin	商河县 Shang he
一般公共预算支出	General Public Budget Expenditure	842017	407578	434439
一般公共服务支出	General Public Service	89748	41598	48150
国防支出	Defence Expenditure	2008	1824	184
公共安全支出	Public Security	36112	17029	19083
教育支出	Education	185263	83241	102022
科学技术	Science andTechnology	2561	1404	1157
文化体育与传媒支出	Culture、Sports and Media	6599	4479	2120
社会保障和就业支出	Social Security and Employment	121865	62024	59841
医疗卫生与计划生育支出	Health and Family Planning	66539	29944	36595
节能环保支出	Energy-saving and Environment Protection	8085	5338	2747
城乡社区支出	Urban and Rural Community Affairs	156360	68310	88050
农林水支出	Farming、Forestry and Irrigation Affairs	97675	43478	54197
交通运输支出	Transport	10422	6665	3757
资源勘探信息等支出	Exploration and Information Affairs	14818	9807	5011
商业服务业等支出	Commerce and Services Affairs	2425	910	1515
金融支出	Financial Supervision Affairs	202	56	146
援助其他地区支出	Aid to Other Area	363	231	132
自然资源海洋气象等支出	Natural Resources Marine Meteorological	12749	9946	2803
住房保障支出	Housing Security Affairs	16030	13307	2723
粮油物资储备支出	Grain and Oil Reserves	539	539	
国债还本付息支出	Pay Principle and Interest for Public Debt	7854	4790	3064
其他支出	Other Expenditure			
政府性基金支出	Government Funds Expenditure	518227	218378	299849
#城乡社区支出	Urban and Rural Community Affairs	426409	165223	261186

8-8 金融机构本外币各项存、贷款期末余额
The Ending Balance of all Deposits and Loans in RMB and Foreign Currencies of Financial Institutions

单位：万元 (10 000yuan)

指标	Item	2017 年	2018 年	2019 年	2020 年	2021 年
金融机构本外币各项存款余额	The Balance of RMB and Foreign Currencies Deposits in Financial Institutions	165605979	170601377	186460860	210649849	234369588
# 住户存款	Household Deposits	45241390	50672701	64970029	76475384	86204521
非金融企业存款	Non-financial Corporate Deposits	73973987	72213088	77067935	87238924	93393082
广义政府存款	General Government Deposits	35586733	36530329	35087861	36351481	41171421
非银行业金融机构存款	Non-bank Financial Intermediary Deposits	7083306	6729522	7629436	9239886	11598655
金融机构本外币各项贷款余额	The Balance of RMB and Foreign Currencies Loans in Financial Institutions	143502995	160599213	187687420	207202433	233132266
# 住户贷款	Household Loans	31418600	37617608	47041192	54682406	61126528
非金融企业及机关团体贷款	Non-financial Corporate and Institution Loans	98004377	109865593	129406853	142485017	162082669
短期贷款	Short-term Loans	30184576	29398790	34665784	38736145	43586160
中长期贷款	Medium and Long-term Loans	61606175	72421049	82655910	91489364	102739117
票据融资	Bill Financing	3896507	4995957	8682607	8566014	11195931
融资租赁	Finance Lease	2181289	2870478	3240815	3592611	3971136
各项垫款	Bill Financing	135831	179319	161737	100884	590324
非银行业金融机构贷款	Non-bank Financial Intermediary Loans	50000	0	200000	0	0

8-9 金融机构人民币各项存、贷款期末余额

The Ending Balance of all Deposits and Loans in RMB of Financial Institutions

单位：万元 (10 000yuan)

指标	Item	2017年	2018年	2019年	2020年	2021年
金融机构人民币各项存款余额	The Balance of RMB Deposits in Financial Institutions	159577448	165718671	183032033	207149738	230292028
#住户存款	Household Deposits	44657303	50080833	64380943	75841225	85584289
非金融企业存款	Non-financial Corporate Deposits	72288512	70776618	75805636	85613093	91691729
广义政府存款	General Government Deposits	35426387	36493478	34923450	36297466	41156864
非银行业金融机构存款	Non-bank Financial Intermediary Deposits	6942272	6630358	7571079	9193889	11550960
金融机构人民币各项贷款余额	The Balance of RMB Loans in Financial Institutions	128836570	147000678	176242063	197048849	223499074
#住户贷款	Household Loans	31417225	37616195	47038338	54680859	61124765
非金融企业及机关团体贷款	Non-financial Corporate and Institution Loans	96407415	108452714	128277535	141659442	161539618
短期贷款	Short-term Loans	29297325	28659735	34002100	38291441	43293345
中长期贷款	Medium and Long-term Loans	60896806	71747225	82190276	91128303	102488882
票据融资	Bill Financing	3896507	4995957	8682607	8566014	11195931
融资租赁	Finance Lease	2181289	2870478	3240815	3592611	3971136
各项垫款	Bill Financing	135488	179319	161737	81074	590324
非银行业金融机构贷款	Non-bank Financial Intermediary Loans	50000	–	200000	0	0

8-10 保险业务情况
Insurance Business

指标	Item	2017 年	2018 年	2019 年	2020 年	2021 年
保险金额（亿元）	Insurance Amount(100 million yuan)	162712	256399	438422	927748	659267
保费收入（万元）	Premium Income(10 000yuan)	3810660	4155535	5322643	6280398	5984712
财产险	Property Insurance	758326	843871	1174143	1255657	1091694
人身险	Life Insurance	3052334	3311664	4148500	5024741	4893017
赔付支出（万元）	Claim Payment(10 000yuan)	886699	1033980	1219250	1603108	2124574
财产险	Property Insurance	366337	421493	562261	683340	778634
人身险	Life Insurance	520363	612471	656989	919768	1345940

注：1. 数据由地方金融监管局提供。
2.2018 年以前为区划调整前数据。
Notes:1.Data are provided by the Data are provided by the Financial Regulatory Authority.
2.Data before the year of 2018 are the data of administrative division before the adjustment.

8-11 证券机构及证券交易情况
Institution and Trading Summary for Stocks

单位：亿元 (100 million yuan)

指标	Item	2016 年	2017 年	2018 年	2019 年	2020 年	2021 年
注册地在济南证券公司数（个）	Stocks Institutions in Ji'nan(Unit)	1	1	1	1	1	1
证券营业部（个）	Securities Business Department(Unit)	83	92	87	92	91	120
证券交易额	Trading Volume of Securities Business Department	34687	30975	28482	36453	47753	55847
股票	Stock	19183	15987	12126	18621	28606	35660
基金	Fund	1449	2361	2111	2197	3528	2872
债券	Bond	14045	12602	14119	15536	15444	17045
其他	Others	10	25	126	99	174	271

注：1. 数据由地方金融监管局提供。
2.2018 年以前为区划调整前数据。
Notes:1.Data are provided by the Data are provided by the Financial Regulatory Authority.
2.Data before the year of 2018 are the data of administrative division before the adjustment.

主要统计指标解释

一般公共预算收入 指国家财政参与社会产品分配所取得的收入，是实现国家职能的财力保证。主要包括：（1）各项税收：包括国内增值税、国内消费税、进口货物增值税和消费税、出口货物退增值税和消费税、营业税、企业所得税、个人所得税、资源税、城市维护建设税、房产税、印花税、城镇土地使用税、土地增值税、车船税、船舶吨税、车辆购置税、关税、耕地占用税、契税、烟叶税等。（2）非税收入：包括专项收入、行政事业性收费、罚没收入和其他收入。财政收入按现行分税制财政体制划分为中央本级收入和地方本级收入。

一般公共预算支出 指国家财政将筹集起来的资金进行分配使用，以满足经济建设和各项事业的需要。主要包括：一般公共服务、外交、国防、公共安全、教育、科学技术、文化体育与传媒、社会保障和就业、医疗卫生与计划生育、节能环保、城乡社区、农林水、交通运输、资源勘探信息等、商业服务业等、金融、援助其他地区、国土海洋气象等、住房保障、粮油物资储备、政府债务付息等方面的支出。财政支出根据政府在经济和社会活动中的不同职权，划分为中央财政支出和地方财政支出。

存款 指企业、机关、团体或居民根据资金必须收回的原则，把货币资金存入银行或其他信贷机构保管并取得一定利息的一种信用活动形式。根据存款对象或性质的不同可划分为企业存款、财政存款、机关团体存款、基本建设存款、储蓄存款、农村存款、委托存款、其他存款等科目。它是银行信贷资金的主要来源。

贷款 指银行或其他信贷机构根据资金必须归还的原则，按一定利率，为企业、个人等提供资金的一种信用活动形式。我国银行贷款分为短期贷款、中期流动资金贷款、中长期贷款、信托贷款、融资租赁、委托贷款、票据融资、各项垫款等。

保险金额 指保险人承担赔偿或者给付保险金责任的最高限额。

Explanatory Notes on Main Statistical Indicators

General Public Budget Revenue refers to the revenue of the government finance by means of participating in the distribution of the social products, which is the financial resources for ensuring the government to function. The contents of government revenue have been changed several times. Now it includes the following main items : (1) Various tax revenues: Include domestic value-added tax, domestic excise duty, value-added tax and consumption tax on imported goods, VAT refund and consumption tax on exports, business tax, corporate income tax, individual income tax, resource tax, urban maintenance and construction tax, building taxes, stamp duty, city and town land use tax, land value increment tax, vehicle and vessel tax, tonnage tax, vehicle purchase tax, tariff, farmland conversion tax, deed tax and tobacco taxes. (2) Non-tax revenues: Included in this category are special revenue, revenue from administrative and institutional fees, confiscated income and other income. Fiscal revenues are divided into revenue at the central level and local income pursuant to the current tax-sharing financial system.

General Public Budget Expenditure refers to the distribution and use of the funds the government finances has raised, so as to meet the needs of economic construction and various causes. It includes the following main items: expenditures regarding general public service, diplomacy, national defense, public security, education, science and technology, culture, sports and media, social security and employment, health care and family planning, energy conservation and environment protection, urban and rural communities, agroforestry water, transportation, resource exploration information, commercial service industry, finance, assistance to other areas, territorial marine meteorology, housing security, reserves of grain, oil and materials and payment of government debt interest, etc. Fiscal expenditure is divided into central fiscal expenditure and local fiscal expenditure in accordance with different function and power of government in economic and social activities.

Deposit is a form of credit by which enterprises, institutions, organizations or households can put money into banks and other credit institutions for safekeeping and interest earning under the principle of free withdrawal. According to different depositors, deposits are divided into enterprise deposits, treasury deposits, deposits of government agencies and organizations, capital construction deposits, savings deposits, rural saving deposits, entrusted deposits and other deposits. Deposits are major sources of the credit funds of banks.

Loan is a form of credit by which banks and other credit institutions provide funds at certain interest rate to enterprises and individuals in the light of the principle of unconditional repayment. Loans from Chinese Banks include circulating capital loans, fixed assets loans, loans to urban and rural individuals engaged in industrial and commercial business and agricultural loans.

Amount Insured refers to the maximum that the insurant will get for the claim of the case insured.

物价

PRICE

9-1 主要年份物价指数(以上年价格为100)
Price Indices of Major Years(Preceding Last Year=100)

年份 Year	居民消费价格指数 Consumer Price Index	# 食品 Food	# 服务项目 Services	零售物价指数 Retail Price Index
1951	108.5	105.3	98.7	109.8
1952	101.5	103.9	101.0	101.2
1955	101.6	101.3	103.4	101.4
1956	100.5	100.7	100.6	100.5
1965	107.3	111.5	97.5	108.0
1970	98.4	99.0	100.0	98.3
1971	100.0	100.5	100.0	100.0
1972	100.1	100.3	100.0	100.1
1973	99.5	99.6	97.9	99.7
1974	99.4	99.1	99.9	99.5
1975	100.2	100.0	100.0	100.2
1976	100.4	100.0	100.0	100.4
1977	99.2	99.9	91.2	100.0
1978	100.3	100.3	100.0	100.3
1979	101.1	101.7	100.5	101.1
1980	104.7	107.9	100.0	105.0
1981	101.9	102.2	100.1	102.0
1982	101.1	101.6	100.3	101.2
1983	100.1	100.3	100.9	100.1
1984	101.9	101.1	109.8	101.3
1985	108.7	112.2	103.3	109.1
1986	106.2	107.6	104.9	106.3
1987	109.5	111.9	104.9	109.8
1988	122.4	128.0	108.8	123.4
1989	116.2	111.2	113.5	116.4
1990	103.3	102.6	108.0	103.0
1991	106.7	107.6	106.9	106.7
1992	110.4	108.7	122.2	109.3
1993	114.7	109.8	138.0	112.1
1994	124.8	133.9	114.5	122.7
1995	117.3	123.0	115.1	113.2
1996	109.1	109.7	116.2	106.3
1997	102.9	101.8	107.8	101.5
1998	100.9	99.4	119.0	98.9
1999	99.1	97.3	127.6	96.9
2000	100.6	97.9	129.0	98.0
2001	100.3	100.8	106.1	98.8
2002	98.8	100.2	101.3	97.8
2003	99.9	103.6	100.3	98.0
2004	102.5	107.4	101.2	100.6
2005	101.1	102.7	101.2	100.4
2006	100.9	102.4	100.9	100.3
2007	103.9	111.6	101.8	102.2
2008	105.7	115.5	101.8	104.5
2009	100.3	102.7	102.4	98.7
2010	102.1	107.3	100.6	101.3
2011	105.4	111.3	104.4	104.6
2012	102.4	103.6	102.2	101.8
2013	102.8	104.9	102.7	101.3
2014	102.2	103.2	102.9	101.2
2015	101.9	101.4	101.6	100.3
2016	102.7	103.9	103.5	100.8
2017	102.0	98.5	104.2	101.0
2018	102.6	102.8	102.1	102.6
2019	103.3	112.0	101.4	102.5
2020	102.4	112.3	99.0	101.9
2021	101.5	100.5	101.4	101.3

9-2 主要年份物价指数（以1950年价格为100）
Price Indices of Major Years(Preceding 1950=100)

年份 Year	居民消费价格指数 Consumer Price Index	#食品 Food	#服务项目 Services	零售物价指数 Retail Price Index
1951	108.5	105.3	98.7	109.8
1952	110.1	109.4	103.7	111.1
1955	117.2	123.7	108.2	118.4
1956	117.8	124.6	108.8	119.0
1965	127.7	141.5	116.9	130.7
1970	123.0	141.6	110.1	126.0
1971	123.0	142.3	110.1	126.0
1972	123.1	142.7	110.1	126.1
1973	122.5	142.1	107.8	125.8
1974	121.8	140.9	107.7	125.1
1975	122.0	140.9	107.7	125.4
1976	122.5	140.9	107.7	125.9
1977	121.5	140.7	98.2	125.9
1978	121.9	141.1	98.2	126.3
1979	123.2	143.5	98.6	127.6
1980	129.0	154.9	98.6	134.0
1981	131.5	158.3	98.7	136.7
1982	132.9	160.8	99.0	138.3
1983	133.0	161.3	99.9	138.5
1984	135.6	163.1	109.7	140.3
1985	147.4	183.0	113.3	153.0
1986	156.5	195.8	118.9	162.7
1987	171.4	219.1	124.7	178.6
1988	209.8	280.4	135.7	220.4
1989	234.8	311.8	154.0	256.5
1990	251.8	319.9	166.3	264.2
1991	268.7	344.2	177.8	281.9

9-2 续表 continued

年份 Year	居民消费价格指数 Consumer Price Index	# 食品 Food	# 服务项目 Services	零售物价指数 Retail Price Index
1992	296.6	376.2	217.3	308.1
1993	340.2	413.1	299.8	345.4
1994	424.6	570.4	343.3	423.8
1995	498.1	709.7	395.1	479.7
1996	543.4	797.7	459.1	509.9
1997	559.2	782.5	494.9	551.6
1998	564.2	777.8	588.9	545.5
1999	559.1	756.8	751.4	528.6
2000	562.4	740.9	969.3	518.0
2001	564.1	746.8	1028.4	511.8
2002	557.3	748.3	1041.8	500.5
2003	556.7	775.2	1044.9	490.5
2004	570.6	832.6	1057.4	493.4
2005	576.9	855.1	1070.1	495.4
2006	582.1	875.6	1079.7	496.9
2007	604.8	977.2	1099.1	507.8
2008	639.3	1128.7	1118.9	530.7
2009	641.2	1159.2	1145.8	523.8
2010	654.7	1243.8	1152.7	530.6
2011	690.2	1384.7	1203.1	555.1
2012	706.8	1434.5	1229.5	565.1
2013	726.6	1504.8	1262.7	572.4
2014	742.6	1553.0	1299.3	579.3
2015	756.7	1574.7	1320.1	581.0
2016	777.1	1636.1	1366.3	585.6
2017	792.6	1611.6	1423.7	591.5
2018	813.3	1656.7	1453.6	606.8
2019	840.1	1855.5	1473.9	622.0
2020	860.3	2083.7	1459.2	633.8
2021	873.2	2094.1	1479.6	642.1

9-3 分月居民消费价格指数（2021 年，以上年同期价格为 100）
Consumer Price Indices by Month(2021， Preceding Last Year=100)

指标	Item	全年 Total	一月 January	二月 February
居民消费价格总指数	Consumer Price Index	101.5	99.3	100.4
非食品烟酒价格指数	Non-food,tobacco and alcohol Price Index	101.5	98.8	99.7
服务价格指数	Services Price Index	101.4	99.1	100.5
工业品价格指数	Industrial Products Price Index	101.6	98.3	98.8
消费品价格指数	Consumer Goods Price Index	101.5	99.4	100.3
扣除食品和能源价格指数	Excluding Food and Energy Price Index	101.1	99.6	100.5
一、食品烟酒	Food,Tobacco and Liquor	101.5	100.7	102.3
1. 食品	Food	100.5	100.0	101.2
(1) 粮食	Grain	98.7	98.5	98.3
(2) 薯类	Tuber	97.4	93.7	97.2
(3) 豆类	Beans	100.7	100.9	101.3
(4) 食用油	Edible Oil	109.4	105.5	104.3
食用植物油	Edible Vegetable Oil	109.7	105.5	104.1
(5) 菜及食用菌	Vegetable and Edible Fungi	106.3	101.5	102.8
鲜菜	Fresh Vegetable	106.8	102.3	103.2
(6) 畜肉类	Livestock Meat	82.8	98.5	95.5
猪肉	Pork	65.3	93.2	88.0
(7) 禽肉类	Poultry	99.2	98.2	97.3
(8) 水产品	Aquatic Products	115.4	101.2	113.8
(9) 蛋类	Eggs	105.5	97.7	96.2
鸡蛋	Hen's Eggs	106.5	99.2	96.7
(10) 奶类	Milk	102.8	99.7	99.5
(11) 干鲜瓜果类	Dried and Fresh Melons and Fruits	107.2	98.1	102.3
鲜果	Fresh Fruits	112.2	98.7	106.5
(12) 糖果糕点类	Candy and Cakes	104.5	103.4	103.2
(13) 调味品	Condiment	104.6	111.0	111.1
(14) 其他食品类	Other Foods	100.5	100.6	100.1
2. 茶及饮料	Tea and Beverages	101.2	102.5	100.2
3. 烟酒	Tobacco and Liquor	100.6	99.0	99.2
(1) 卷烟	cigarette	100.0	100.0	100.0
(2) 酒类	Liquor	101.1	98.0	98.5
4. 在外餐饮	Outside Catering	104.5	103.3	107.0
二、衣着	Clothing	101.5	100.4	100.0
1. 服装	Garments	102.7	101.8	101.3
(1) 男式服装	Men's Clothing	102.9	102.5	101.4
(2) 女式服装	Women's Clothing	103.4	102.0	101.8
(3) 儿童服装	Children's Clothing	100.2	100.0	99.3
(4) 衣着材料及配件	Clothing Material and Accessories	101.9	99.3	100.1
(5) 衣着服务费	Clothing service fee	102.9	104.1	104.1

三月 March	四月 April	五月 May	六月 June	七月 July	八月 August	九月 September	十月 October	十一月 November	十二月 December
101.1	101.7	102.0	101.8	102.0	101.6	101.4	102.3	102.9	101.6
100.9	101.6	101.8	102.1	102.3	102.3	102.2	102.3	102.4	101.8
101.7	102.0	101.6	101.6	101.7	102.2	101.9	101.5	101.5	101.4
99.9	101.2	102.0	102.5	103.0	102.4	102.6	103.3	103.4	102.4
100.7	101.4	102.2	102.0	102.1	101.1	101.0	102.9	103.8	101.7
101.0	101.3	101.3	101.5	101.6	101.6	101.5	101.3	101.2	101.1
101.9	101.7	102.5	101.2	101.0	99.5	98.9	102.4	104.5	100.9
100.5	100.6	101.9	100.1	99.9	97.8	96.7	102.1	105.2	99.8
97.4	98.1	96.2	97.7	98.0	97.6	96.2	100.1	104.6	102.3
94.3	92.4	90.2	95.5	95.9	97.7	100.2	109.1	108.5	101.8
102.1	99.0	95.1	98.1	99.9	100.1	101.3	102.6	103.8	105.2
105.9	108.0	110.9	115.9	113.4	113.1	108.6	106.9	109.7	109.8
105.7	108.0	111.0	116.2	113.9	113.8	109.3	107.7	110.5	110.7
96.8	101.5	111.7	94.5	97.0	92.1	101.5	133.0	143.6	107.4
97.3	102.7	114.1	93.3	95.7	90.3	99.8	135.9	146.9	109.0
93.0	89.6	88.4	81.2	74.8	73.1	71.1	73.2	79.5	75.4
83.0	75.9	71.9	59.1	51.5	48.9	46.2	49.3	60.0	54.3
100.1	100.3	100.5	100.8	99.3	98.7	99.1	99.7	99.1	97.9
113.3	114.5	121.8	121.7	121.1	117.8	115.4	112.7	114.1	117.2
95.8	98.8	102.7	114.3	108.4	108.8	108.2	109.2	117.6	111.8
94.0	99.4	103.6	117.6	109.3	110.5	109.6	110.4	119.3	112.4
101.8	104.8	103.1	102.6	104.2	103.2	104.1	104.5	105.6	100.9
107.0	105.4	105.0	110.8	124.5	117.8	103.9	106.4	103.8	108.2
113.2	111.2	109.8	119.6	140.7	128.2	108.9	108.3	104.1	110.7
101.0	101.2	98.2	103.1	109.6	109.5	109.6	108.8	106.0	101.6
105.4	103.9	103.3	104.1	102.7	103.4	103.4	104.9	102.7	100.5
100.4	99.8	99.0	99.5	99.0	100.5	97.7	101.1	102.7	105.4
102.9	100.7	102.9	101.2	100.4	100.4	100.4	102.5	99.6	100.9
99.3	99.9	100.9	101.5	101.2	101.0	101.1	101.1	101.0	102.1
100.0	100.0	100.0	100.0	100.0	100.0	100.0	100.0	100.0	100.0
98.7	99.8	101.6	102.8	102.3	101.9	102.2	102.0	101.9	104.0
106.8	105.6	104.6	104.0	103.8	103.7	104.0	103.9	104.0	103.3
100.8	102.1	103.4	102.5	102.8	102.6	101.6	101.2	100.4	100.1
102.3	103.6	105.5	103.9	104.1	103.6	102.3	102.1	101.4	100.8
102.5	104.6	106.2	104.2	104.5	104.0	102.0	101.6	101.0	100.1
102.7	104.1	107.3	104.8	104.6	103.9	103.0	102.9	102.1	101.8
100.6	100.6	100.4	100.9	102.4	102.0	99.8	99.3	98.8	98.2
100.7	100.7	100.7	102.1	102.1	103.2	104.6	104.4	103.4	102.0
104.1	104.1	104.1	104.1	101.7	101.7	101.7	101.7	101.7	101.7

9–3 续表 1 continued 1

指标	Item	全年 Total	一月 January	二月 February
2. 鞋类	Footwear	96.3	95.0	94.7
(1) 鞋	Shoes	96.2	94.8	94.6
(2) 鞋类服务	Footwear Services	100.4	100.0	100.0
三、居住	**Residence**	**101.9**	**100.0**	**100.4**
1. 租赁房房租	Rental Housing Rent	101.8	99.5	101.0
2. 住房保养维修及管理	Housing Maintenance	100.9	101.8	101.8
(1) 住房装潢材料	Housing Decoration Materials	101.2	102.2	102.2
(2) 住房维修管理费用	Housing Maintenance Management Fee	100.6	101.4	101.4
3. 水电燃料	Water, Electricity and Fuels	101.9	100.1	100.1
(1) 水	Water	100.0	100.0	100.0
(2) 电	Electricity	100.0	100.0	100.0
(3) 燃气	Gas	101.4	101.0	101.0
(4) 其他水电燃料类	Other Fuel	103.9	100.0	100.0
4. 自有住房	Self-owned House	102.0	99.6	100.2
四、生活用品及服务	**Daily Necessities and Services**	**98.8**	**98.0**	**97.6**
1. 家具及室内装饰品	Furniture and Interior Decorations	101.0	102.9	103.6
(1) 家具	Furniture and Interior Decorations	101.5	103.5	104.4
(2) 室内装饰品	Interior Decorations	97.8	99.0	99.0
2. 家用器具	Household Appliances	99.3	98.5	98.4
(1) 大型家用器具	Large Household Appliances	98.8	97.9	97.8
(2) 小家电	Small Household Appliances	102.2	101.8	102.2
3. 家用纺织品	Home Textiles	95.6	95.2	96.5
(1) 床上用品	Bedding Article	95.4	94.6	96.9
(2) 窗帘门帘	Curtain	100.0	100.0	100.0
(3) 其他家用纺织品	Other Household Textiles	92.7	94.3	89.6
4. 家庭日用杂品	The Family Daily Sundry Goods	99.0	97.0	95.0
(1) 洗涤卫生用品	Washing Sanitary Articles	100.7	100.6	95.7
(2) 厨具餐具茶具	Kitchenware, Tableware, Tea Set	97.1	95.1	95.9
(3) 其他家庭日用杂品	Other Household Articles For Daily Use	97.5	92.7	93.3
5. 个人护理用品	Personal Care Products	93.4	91.5	90.7
(1) 化妆品	Cosmetics	89.7	86.4	85.6
(2) 其他护理用品类	Other Nursing Products	99.9	101.3	100.3
6. 家庭服务	Family Services	104.6	103.7	103.8
五、交通通信	**Transport Communication**	**104.7**	**95.3**	**100.2**
1. 交通	Transport	105.9	93.4	99.4
(1) 交通工具	Transport Tools	99.4	96.5	96.6
(2) 交通工具用燃料	Transport Fuels	117.4	86.4	95.0
(3) 交通工具使用和维修	Vehicle Use and Maintenance	103.8	99.2	115.8
(4) 交通费	Travelling Expenses	107.6	92.3	104.0

三月 March	四月 April	五月 May	六月 June	七月 July	八月 August	九月 September	十月 October	十一月 November	十二月 December
94.5	95.9	94.9	96.5	97.5	98.6	98.4	97.5	96.0	96.9
94.4	95.8	94.8	96.5	97.4	98.5	98.3	97.4	95.9	96.7
100.0	100.0	100.0	100.0	100.0	100.0	100.0	100.0	100.0	104.6
102.8	102.5	102.5	102.4	102.4	102.5	102.4	101.8	101.4	101.3
103.5	102.7	101.5	101.9	101.6	102.2	102.2	101.5	102.2	102.0
101.8	101.4	101.3	100.5	100.5	100.2	100.2	100.2	100.2	100.6
102.2	101.3	101.1	101.1	101.1	100.4	100.4	100.4	100.4	101.2
101.4	101.4	101.4	100.0	100.0	100.0	100.0	100.0	100.0	100.0
100.1	100.9	101.7	101.7	102.0	102.5	103.3	103.5	103.5	103.5
100.0	100.0	100.0	100.0	100.0	100.0	100.0	100.0	100.0	100.0
100.0	100.0	100.0	100.0	100.0	100.0	100.0	100.0	100.0	100.0
101.0	100.0	100.0	100.0	100.0	100.0	102.0	104.1	104.1	104.1
100.0	101.9	103.8	103.8	104.4	105.6	106.7	106.7	106.7	106.7
103.6	103.2	103.1	103.1	102.9	102.9	102.6	101.6	100.9	100.6
97.1	97.2	97.2	99.1	99.6	99.5	99.8	100.5	100.2	100.6
101.9	102.1	101.7	100.5	100.6	99.8	99.7	99.6	99.6	99.8
102.3	102.3	102.3	101.1	101.1	100.2	100.2	100.2	100.2	100.1
99.0	100.5	98.1	96.8	97.1	97.3	96.7	96.1	96.1	97.7
96.6	98.2	98.5	98.4	99.4	99.9	100.2	100.3	101.4	102.2
95.7	97.5	97.9	97.8	98.7	99.7	100.0	100.1	101.1	102.1
102.2	102.3	102.4	101.7	103.6	101.2	101.4	101.5	103.2	102.7
96.5	97.0	97.5	93.9	94.8	94.2	93.2	95.8	99.0	93.5
96.2	97.4	96.6	91.9	94.4	94.1	92.4	96.1	100.2	93.9
100.0	100.0	100.0	100.0	100.0	100.0	100.0	100.0	100.0	100.0
94.9	91.7	102.0	103.2	93.0	88.8	92.2	90.0	90.0	84.1
94.9	94.6	95.7	100.5	101.1	99.4	102.8	105.0	102.1	101.0
96.5	95.3	96.2	104.6	103.0	98.2	106.4	110.6	102.6	100.4
94.1	96.6	96.3	94.7	98.6	97.7	97.8	98.2	100.1	100.6
92.9	92.1	94.4	97.7	99.9	102.6	100.3	101.0	102.4	102.2
92.2	90.9	89.8	95.2	94.6	96.8	94.1	94.4	93.8	97.2
87.8	85.8	85.1	93.6	92.3	95.1	90.4	90.3	90.5	94.9
100.2	100.5	98.5	97.8	98.5	99.6	100.3	101.5	99.3	101.0
103.8	103.8	102.5	105.3	105.3	105.3	105.3	105.3	105.3	105.8
103.7	105.9	105.4	106.0	106.7	106.0	105.9	107.5	108.7	105.9
104.6	107.5	106.6	107.5	108.4	107.5	107.5	109.9	111.6	107.8
96.9	98.0	98.6	100.1	101.1	100.6	100.8	101.2	101.7	101.2
111.8	119.9	121.9	124.2	125.3	122.5	123.1	132.0	136.4	122.7
117.4	116.8	103.3	99.4	100.0	100.0	100.0	100.0	100.0	100.0
105.5	109.0	110.1	111.1	110.6	110.7	109.3	109.6	111.8	109.9

9–3 续表 2 continued 2

指标	Item	全年 Total	一月 January	二月 February
2. 通信	Signal Communication	100.8	102.5	102.8
(1) 通信工具	Communication Tools	101.9	106.4	107.1
(2) 通信服务	Communication Services	100.0	100.0	100.0
(3) 邮递服务	Mailing Service	100.6	99.8	99.8
六、教育文化娱乐	**Education Culture Recreation**	**99.7**	**97.5**	**97.8**
1. 教育	Education	100.4	98.3	98.3
(1) 教育用品	Educational Supplies	100.7	100.1	100.1
(2) 教育服务	Education Services	100.4	98.2	98.2
2. 文化娱乐	Culture and Entertainment	98.5	96.3	97.0
(1) 文娱耐用消费品	Recreational Consumer Durables	98.1	95.2	96.8
(2) 其他文娱用品	Other Entertainment Products	99.8	100.0	98.7
(3) 文化娱乐服务	Cultural and Recreational Services	104.5	96.5	98.1
(4) 旅游	Tourism	92.2	94.7	95.3
七、医疗保健	**Health Care**	**100.7**	**99.9**	**99.8**
1. 药品及医疗器具	Drugs and Medical Devices	101.7	99.7	99.3
(1) 中药	Traditional Chinese Medicine	102.9	99.8	99.8
(2) 西药	West Medicine	101.1	97.8	99.3
(3) 滋补保健品	Western Medicine	103.6	101.6	100.8
(4) 医疗卫生器具	Medical and Health Equipment	95.6	105.5	91.4
(5) 保健器具	Healthcare Apparatus	101.7	100.7	102.2
2. 医疗服务	Medical Services	100.3	100.0	100.1
(1) 综合医疗类	Comprehensive Health Care	100.6	100.0	100.0
(2) 诊断类	Diagnostic	100.0	100.0	100.0
(3) 治疗类	Therapeutic	100.1	100.0	100.0
(4) 康复类	Rehabilitation	100.0	100.0	100.0
(5) 中医医疗服务类	Chinese Medicine Services	102.7	100.0	100.0
(6) 其他医疗保健服务	Other Medical Services	102.5	100.0	102.7
八、其他用品及服务	**Other Supplies and Services**	**99.9**	**103.6**	**103.0**
1. 其他用品	Other Articles	98.3	107.2	102.6
(1) 首饰手表	Jewelry Watches	97.3	110.9	103.2
(2) 母婴用品	Maternal and Infant Supplies	99.3	99.2	99.9
(3) 其他杂项用品	Other Miscellaneous Supplies	100.1	103.5	102.5
2. 其他服务	Other Services	101.5	100.3	103.3
(1) 在外住宿	Hotel Accommodation	106.1	98.4	121.8
(2) 美容美发洗浴	Hairdressing Bath	102.8	101.2	102.8
(3) 养老服务	Pension Services	100.8	102.2	102.2
(4) 金融及保险服务	Finance and Insurance Services	100.1	100.0	100.0
(5) 中介法律及其他服务	Legal Intermediary and Other Service	100.4	100.0	100.0

三月 March	四月 April	五月 May	六月 June	七月 July	八月 August	九月 September	十月 October	十一月 November	十二月 December
100.9	100.7	101.2	100.8	101.1	100.9	100.4	99.5	99.3	99.5
102.1	101.7	102.7	101.9	102.6	102.2	101.0	98.7	98.2	98.6
100.0	100.0	100.0	100.0	100.0	100.0	100.0	100.0	100.0	100.0
100.8	100.8	100.8	100.8	100.8	100.8	100.8	100.8	101.0	101.0
97.4	98.6	98.8	99.3	99.8	101.6	101.4	101.4	101.7	101.8
98.7	99.7	99.7	101.9	102.0	102.0	101.2	101.2	101.2	101.2
100.9	100.6	100.6	101.1	100.9	100.9	100.6	100.9	100.7	100.7
98.6	99.7	99.7	102.0	102.0	102.0	101.2	101.2	101.2	101.2
95.4	96.6	97.2	95.2	96.3	100.9	101.6	101.6	102.5	102.8
98.3	98.4	98.9	97.6	98.7	97.9	98.0	99.2	98.8	99.6
98.9	100.5	99.6	101.0	100.3	100.4	100.5	99.7	100.3	97.8
96.5	98.3	99.5	99.2	100.7	114.2	115.3	114.4	113.6	113.6
91.1	92.3	92.8	87.1	88.9	90.4	91.4	91.7	94.7	96.4
99.7	100.4	100.4	100.8	101.2	101.4	101.4	101.5	100.9	101.0
98.8	101.3	101.2	101.8	103.1	103.6	103.7	103.6	101.8	102.0
99.9	100.7	100.7	103.3	103.3	105.4	105.4	105.4	105.4	105.6
100.4	103.0	102.9	102.1	102.2	102.3	102.3	102.2	99.0	99.8
96.0	101.6	101.3	101.6	107.5	107.5	108.4	106.5	106.5	105.0
91.4	91.4	91.4	95.1	96.0	96.0	96.0	99.8	96.0	98.1
102.2	100.7	102.2	102.8	102.8	102.8	101.1	102.8	100.3	100.0
100.1	100.1	100.1	100.4	100.4	100.4	100.4	100.6	100.6	100.6
100.0	100.0	100.0	100.8	100.8	100.8	100.6	101.3	101.3	101.3
100.0	100.0	100.0	100.0	100.0	100.0	99.9	99.9	99.9	99.9
100.0	100.0	100.0	100.0	100.0	100.0	100.3	100.3	100.3	100.3
100.0	100.0	100.0	100.0	100.0	100.0	100.0	100.0	100.0	100.0
100.0	100.0	100.0	104.7	104.7	104.7	104.7	104.7	104.7	104.7
102.7	102.7	102.7	102.7	102.7	102.7	102.7	102.7	102.7	102.7
99.0	100.2	101.9	101.4	100.8	96.9	97.5	97.2	99.1	98.9
97.9	98.8	101.1	100.7	98.3	91.3	95.0	94.9	96.7	96.4
96.6	99.3	100.8	101.6	97.1	86.4	92.8	92.0	95.2	95.1
101.7	98.7	99.0	100.0	100.7	100.0	96.1	98.2	99.6	98.9
99.0	97.4	102.7	99.2	100.0	99.5	99.8	100.2	98.6	98.2
99.9	101.6	102.7	102.1	103.2	102.7	99.9	99.4	101.5	101.3
92.4	106.2	118.0	113.0	123.0	118.2	101.5	90.1	97.7	98.8
101.7	103.1	103.2	103.2	103.2	103.2	103.2	103.2	103.6	102.0
103.9	101.6	100.0	100.0	100.0	100.0	100.0	100.0	100.0	100.0
100.0	100.0	100.0	99.9	99.9	99.9	97.9	99.9	101.8	101.8
100.0	100.0	100.4	100.4	100.6	100.6	100.6	100.6	100.6	100.6

9-4 分月商品零售价格指数（2021 年，以上年同期价格为 100）
Retail Price Indices by Month(2021，Preceding Last Year=100)

指标	Item	全年 Total	一月 January	二月 February
商品零售价格指数	Retail Price Index	101.3	98.6	99.3
一、食品	Food	101.5	100.8	102.6
二、饮料、烟酒	Beverages, Tobacco and Liquor	100.8	99.9	99.5
三、服装、鞋帽	Garments, Shoes and Hats	101.5	100.4	99.9
四、纺织品	Textiles	97.2	95.9	97.9
五、家用电器及音像器材	Household Appliances, Music and Video Equipment	98.3	96.6	97.0
六、文化办公用品	Cultural and Office Appliances	98.8	99.4	100.1
七、日用品	Articles for Daily Use	99.2	98.5	97.3
八、体育娱乐用品	Sports and Recreation Articles	99.7	99.7	98.2
九、交通、通信用品	Transportation and Communication Appliances	99.5	98.6	98.5
十、家具	Furniture	101.5	103.5	104.4
十一、化妆品	Cosmetics	92.3	90.2	89.5
十二、金银饰品	Gold and Silver Ornaments	97.2	116.5	106.1
十三、中西药品及医疗保健用品	Traditional Chinese and Western Medicines and Health Care Articles	101.7	99.7	99.3
十四、书报杂志及电子出版物	Books, Newspapers, Magazines and Electronic Publications	99.2	99.7	99.7
十五、燃料	Fuels	115.7	89.3	96.6
十六、建筑材料及五金电料	Building Materials and Hardware	100.9	101.6	101.5

三月 March	四月 April	五月 May	六月 June	七月 July	八月 August	九月 September	十月 October	十一月 November	十二月 December
100.0	101.0	101.7	102.0	102.3	101.5	101.5	103.1	103.4	101.9
102.1	101.9	102.7	101.2	101.0	99.3	98.7	102.6	104.9	100.8
100.3	100.1	101.4	101.4	101.0	100.8	100.9	101.4	100.6	101.8
100.7	102.0	103.4	102.5	102.8	102.7	101.6	101.2	100.3	100.0
97.3	98.3	97.7	93.6	96.8	96.5	95.1	98.3	102.4	96.8
96.6	97.4	97.7	97.1	98.7	99.0	98.8	99.5	100.4	100.8
99.7	98.9	98.6	98.5	97.8	97.3	99.1	99.1	97.5	99.7
97.1	96.4	97.8	99.5	100.3	99.2	101.1	102.6	100.5	99.8
98.5	100.7	100.2	101.6	100.4	99.8	99.9	99.6	99.9	97.5
97.9	98.2	98.9	100.2	100.9	100.4	100.3	100.6	100.0	99.8
102.3	102.3	102.3	101.1	101.1	100.2	100.2	100.2	100.2	100.1
90.7	89.3	88.4	94.5	93.6	96.4	93.0	93.2	92.9	96.4
97.2	100.8	102.7	102.0	96.3	83.0	90.9	89.8	93.9	93.7
98.8	101.3	101.2	101.8	103.1	103.6	103.7	103.6	101.8	102.1
99.3	99.7	98.9	99.0	98.8	98.8	99.1	99.3	99.3	99.1
109.9	116.5	118.7	120.5	121.6	119.8	121.0	129.4	132.4	121.2
101.2	100.8	100.7	101.1	101.0	100.4	100.4	100.4	100.7	101.2

9-5 主要年份零售商品和服务项目年平均价格
Per Retail and Services Price of Major Years

商品名称	Name	规格等级牌号 Grade	单位 Unit	1978 年	1980 年	1985 年
面粉	Flour	特一	元 / 千克 (yuan/kg)	0.50	0.50	0.50
粳米	Japonica	标一	元 / 千克 (yuan/kg)	0.34	0.34	0.40
小米	Millet	一等	元 / 千克 (yuan/kg)	0.27	0.27	0.44
土豆	Potato		元 / 千克 (yuan/kg)	0.19	0.22	0.30
豆腐	Doufu	水豆腐	元 / 千克 (yuan/kg)	0.16	0.18	0.26
猪肉	Pork	净肉	元 / 千克 (yuan/kg)	1.72	1.95	2.65
牛肉	Beef	净肉	元 / 千克 (yuan/kg)	1.26	1.76	2.91
羊肉	Mutton	净肉	元 / 千克 (yuan/kg)	1.38	1.88	2.80
鸡蛋	Hen's Egg	新鲜完整	元 / 千克 (yuan/kg)	1.58	2.20	2.60
海带	Kelp	盐干一级	元 / 千克 (yuan/kg)	1.18	1.26	1.32
大白菜	Chinese Cabbage	一等	元 / 千克 (yuan/kg)	0.11	0.07	0.09
菠菜	Spinage	一等	元 / 千克 (yuan/kg)	0.08	0.09	0.28
油菜	Oilseed rape	一等	元 / 千克 (yuan/kg)	0.05	0.07	0.26
芹菜	Celery	一等	元 / 千克 (yuan/kg)	1.13	0.11	0.39
韭菜	Chinese Chives	一等	元 / 千克 (yuan/kg)	0.15	0.16	0.54
黄瓜	Cucumber	一等	元 / 千克 (yuan/kg)	0.19	0.18	0.47
西红柿	Tomato	一等	元 / 千克 (yuan/kg)	0.15	0.18	0.53
茄子	Eggplant	一等	元 / 千克 (yuan/kg)	0.14	0.11	0.27
青椒	Green Pepper	一等	元 / 千克 (yuan/kg)	0.23	0.20	0.47
大葱	Allium Fistulosum	一等	元 / 千克 (yuan/kg)	0.11	0.12	0.28
黑木耳	Black Fungus	甲级	元 / 千克 (yuan/kg)	30.00	32.00	34.86
精盐	Salt	再制盐	元 /500 克 (yuan/500g)	0.16	0.16	0.14
酱油	Soy Sauce	二级	元 / 千克 (yuan/kg)	0.22	0.22	0.34
味精	Aginomoto	含麸酸钠 80% 以上	元 / 千克 (yuan/kg)	10.80	9.68	12.60
绵白糖	Soft Sugar	国产机制一级	元 / 千克 (yuan/kg)	1.60	1.70	1.70
红糖	Brown Sugar	一级	元 / 千克 (yuan/kg)	1.30	1.30	1.30
啤酒	Beer	熟 12 度瓶装	元 / 瓶 (yuan/unit)	0.58	0.58	0.73
苹果	Apple	一级	元 / 千克 (yuan/kg)	0.82	0.90	1.19
桔子	Orange	一级	元 / 千克 (yuan/kg)	1.30	1.52	2.35
西瓜	watermelon	一级	元 / 千克 (yuan/kg)	0.24	0.28	0.32
香蕉	Banana	一级	元 / 千克 (yuan/kg)	1.46	1.65	1.82
自来水	Tap Water	生活用水	元 / 吨 (yuan/tons)	0.08	0.08	0.09
照明用电	Lighting Electricity	民用 220V	元 / 度 (yuan/kWh)	0.18	0.18	0.18
平信	Ordinary Mail	外埠	元 / 封 (yuan/unit)	0.08	0.08	0.08
注射费	Injection Fees	肌肉注射	元 / 次 (yuan/unit)	0.10	0.10	0.10
住院费	Hospitalization Fees	普通床位	元 / 天 (yuan/day)			
学杂费	Tuition and Fees	高中学生	元 / 学期 (yuan/semester)	2.50	2.50	2.50
公园门票	Park Tickets	大明湖	元 / 张 (yuan/unit)	0.03	0.03	0.03
理发	Haircut	男理一级全活	元 / 次 (yuan/unit)	0.30	0.30	0.45
洗澡	Bath		元 / 次 (yuan/unit)	0.24	0.24	0.30
课本	Textbook	高中语文一年级	元 / 本 (yuan/unit)			
银花	Silver	一等	元 / 千克 (yuan/kg)	6.65	8.00	18.00

注：1. 大明湖景区 2017 年开始免费入园。
2. 由于居民消费价格是指数比较，所以理发和洗澡所选的规格品与上年不一致，绝对价格无可比性。
3. 因消费升级，商品和服务规格变化较大，零售商品和服务项目年平均价格自 2019 年起停止更新。

1990 年	1995 年	2000 年	2005 年	2010 年	2013 年	2014 年	2015 年	2016 年	2017 年	2018 年
0.50	2.24	1.78	2.86	4.14	5.07	5.41	5.43	5.46	5.64	8.54
1.04	3.33	2.03	3.08	4.76	5.91	5.91	6.04	6.05	6.00	6.06
1.32	2.66	2.07	3.26	6.99	8.58	14.10	14.63	10.51	11.49	10.87
0.36	1.48	1.48	1.92	4.53	3.61	3.72	3.80	3.84	3.53	3.84
0.70	1.43	1.55	2.14	4.31	5.21	5.99	6.24	5.97	5.88	6.11
5.52	12.91	12.87	14.90	25.18	33.04	30.57	32.37	35.78	35.49	32.88
5.43	12.06	10.99	16.34	36.47	64.52	65.00	66.58	69.02	69.46	69.25
5.91	15.49	15.04	22.07	44.80	75.33	79.23	76.29	76.85	69.67	79.86
4.96	5.99	3.99	5.72	7.48	8.52	10.87	9.25	8.41	8.18	9.75
3.60	5.35	5.36	8.76	19.29	30.35	33.43	32.50	28.87	27.15	25.51
0.13	0.72	0.91	1.64	3.23	2.77	2.29	2.84	2.80	2.41	2.93
0.50	0.90	1.57	2.21	6.69	7.61	6.53	7.91	8.53	7.41	8.81
0.63	1.11	1.26	1.83	5.05	5.84	5.17	6.43	7.14	6.08	7.46
0.60	1.22	1.25	2.28	4.99	5.46	4.07	5.62	5.06	5.13	5.68
1.01	1.80	1.98	2.99	6.55	7.05	6.47	7.42	5.33	4.97	5.59
0.99	2.45	2.53	3.16	5.67	6.26	5.36	5.96	6.03	5.67	7.53
1.02	2.66	2.07	2.90	6.01	6.60	6.37	7.02	6.97	7.24	7.69
0.89	2.67	2.51	3.07	6.05	6.34	5.60	6.14	6.66	6.14	7.48
1.34	4.13	3.15	4.10	6.45	7.48	6.38	8.07	7.61	7.00	9.03
0.54	1.46	1.31	2.51	6.16	6.95	5.94	6.56	9.59	6.44	6.19
48.95	59.16	68.57	65.13	86.80	121.45	128.14	122.59	118.11	122.67	128.34
0.31	0.70	1.10	2.02	1.50	3.83	3.84	4.28	5.17	5.97	6.18
0.68	1.83	2.40	4.53	6.74	7.04	6.75	6.61	7.14	7.05	8.69
16.50	22.81	14.26	15.67	19.33	21.02	21.34	22.19	21.94	22.56	22.92
2.60	6.89	6.12	5.43	9.75	15.15	15.89	16.08	14.38	14.25	15.39
2.21	6.32	5.90	5.54	9.80	15.62	15.54	14.70	15.68	18.29	21.07
1.41	2.13	2.30	2.42	2.61	2.68	2.77	2.76	2.72	2.49	2.62
2.48	3.86	2.72	3.19	8.93	12.04	14.96	15.11	10.86	11.86	11.85
2.27	3.37	2.35	3.30	7.45	10.29	11.97	9.06	10.72	13.86	11.96
0.58	3.20	2.70	3.06	4.72	5.56	5.88	5.57	5.16	5.60	5.26
2.93	4.78	4.05	4.02	6.39	7.28	9.70	7.01	7.04	6.63	8.24
0.19	0.51	1.60	2.78	3.15	3.15	3.15	4.00	4.21	4.21	4.21
0.18	0.29	0.43	0.53	0.55	0.55	0.56	0.56	0.56	0.56	0.56
0.13	0.20	0.80	0.80	1.20	1.20	1.20	1.20	1.20	1.20	1.20
0.20	0.25	1.67	2.00	2.00	2.00	2.00	2.00	2.00	2.00	2.00
2.50	4.00	7.67	15.00	26.67	26.67	23.33	23.33	33.89	36.67	36.67
12.00	49.00	600.00	800.00	800.00	800.00	800.00	800.00	800.00	800.00	800.00
0.30	4.33	13.48	15.63	30.00	30.00	30.00	30.00	30.00		
1.30	5.63	10.00	17.50	20.50	25.00	25.21	25.21	32.38	25.10	27.70
0.58	5.00	8.00	12.00	30.00	38.00	53.00	58.00	58.00	68.00	68.00
2.00	2.55	6.41	4.60	6.47	6.47	6.47	6.47	6.47	6.44	6.39
28.00	70.00	93.00	87.22	325.00	314.10	361.17	352.71	325.00	324.39	403.83

Notes:1.Daming Lake Scenic spot has been free since 2017.

2.Because the consumer price of residents is an index comparison, the standard products selected for haircut and bath are inconsistent with the previous year, and the absolute price is incomparable.

3.Because of consumption upgrading and large exchanges in commodity and service specifications, the annual average price of retail commodity and service items has not been updated since 2019.

9-6 住宅销售价格指数 (2021 年，以上月价格为 100)

Sales Price of Residential Buildings(2021,Preceding last month=100)

指标	Item	1 月 January	2 月 February	3 月 March	4 月 April	5 月 May	6 月 June
新建住宅	New Residential Buildings	100.2	100.4	100.5	100.8	101.0	101.5
新建商品住宅	New Commercial Residential Buildings	100.2	100.4	100.5	100.8	101.0	101.5
90 平方米及以下	Buildings below 90sq.m	100.3	100.2	100.3	100.0	101.4	102.2
90–144 平方米	Buildings 90–144 sq.m	100.1	100.5	100.5	101.1	100.9	101.3
144 平方米以上	Buildings above 144sq.m	100.2	100.0	100.8	100.3	101.2	101.7
二手住宅	Second-hand House	100.4	99.8	100.1	100.6	100.5	100.5
90 平方米及以下	Buildings below 90sq.m	100.6	99.6	100.1	100.1	100.6	100.8
90–144 平方米	Buildings 90–144 sq.m	100.3	99.8	100.2	100.8	100.7	100.3
144 平方米以上	Buildings above 144sq.m	100.5	99.9	100.0	100.8	100.0	100.7

9-6 续表 continued

指标	Item	7 月 July	8 月 August	9 月 September	10 月 October	11 月 November	12 月 December
新建住宅	New Residential Buildings	100.7	100.6	100.4	99.6	99.5	100.0
新建商品住宅	New Commercial Residential Buildings	100.7	100.6	100.4	99.6	99.5	100.0
90 平方米及以下	Buildings below 90sq.m	100.4	100.6	101.0	99.9	99.0	100.1
90–144 平方米	Buildings 90–144 sq.m	100.7	100.5	100.2	99.4	99.5	100.0
144 平方米以上	Buildings above 144sq.m	101.0	100.7	100.4	99.9	99.5	99.9
二手住宅	Second-hand House	100.4	100.2	99.7	99.8	99.5	99.9
90 平方米及以下	Buildings below 90sq.m	100.3	100.1	99.9	99.7	99.3	99.7
90–144 平方米	Buildings 90–144 sq.m	100.4	100.2	99.6	99.7	99.7	99.8
144 平方米以上	Buildings above 144sq.m	100.5	100.2	99.7	99.9	99.6	100.1

9-7 住宅销售价格指数(2021年，以上年同期价格为100)
Sales Price of Residential Buildings (2021,Preceding last year=100)

指标	Item	1月 January	2月 February	3月 March	4月 April	5月 May	6月 June
新建住宅	New Residential Buildings	99.6	100.2	101.1	101.9	102.4	103.6
新建商品住宅	New Commercial Residential Buildings	99.6	100.2	101.1	101.9	102.4	103.6
90平方米及以下	Buildings below 90sq.m	98.9	100.0	100.0	101.0	101.9	103.1
90–144平方米	Buildings 90–144 sq.m	100.0	100.3	101.4	102.5	103.0	104.0
144平方米以上	Buildings above 144sq.m	98.8	99.7	100.7	100.3	100.8	102.5
二手住宅	Second-hand House	97.7	98.0	98.2	98.9	99.2	100.0
90平方米及以下	Buildings below 90sq.m	98.4	97.9	98.0	98.5	99.5	99.8
90–144平方米	Buildings 90–144 sq.m	97.5	98.0	98.4	99.1	99.2	100.4
144平方米以上	Buildings above 144sq.m	97.2	98.0	98.0	98.8	98.8	99.3

9-7 续表 continued

指标	Item	7月 July	8月 August	9月 September	10月 October	11月 November	12月 December
新建住宅	New Residential Buildings	104.2	105.2	105.5	105.2	105.0	105.1
新建商品住宅	New Commercial Residential Buildings	104.2	105.2	105.5	105.2	105.0	105.1
90平方米及以下	Buildings below 90sq.m	104.0	105.1	105.7	105.3	105.2	105.6
90–144平方米	Buildings 90–144 sq.m	104.5	105.3	105.5	105.1	104.8	104.8
144平方米以上	Buildings above 144sq.m	103.1	104.7	105.5	105.5	105.4	105.6
二手住宅	Second-hand House	100.2	100.9	101.0	101.1	101.1	101.5
90平方米及以下	Buildings below 90sq.m	100.0	100.8	101.0	101.3	100.7	101.0
90–144平方米	Buildings 90–144 sq.m	100.6	101.1	101.2	101.0	101.2	101.6
144平方米以上	Buildings above 144sq.m	99.6	100.4	100.8	100.9	101.5	102.0

9-8 主要年份工业生产者出厂、购进价格指数（以上年价格为100）
Producer Price Index for Industrial Products and Purchasing Price Index for Industrial Producers in Main Years(Preceding last year=100)

年份 Year	工业生产者出厂价格指数 Producer Price Indices for Industrial Products	工业生产者购进价格指数 Purchasing Price Index for Industrial Producers
1998	94.5	95.2
1999	98.9	97.6
2000	104.8	114.5
2001	99.8	101.4
2002	97.9	100.4
2003	103.2	111.2
2004	106.7	116.4
2005	102.3	111.3
2006	100.2	105.6
2007	103.9	105.0
2008	109.2	116.9
2009	96.2	94.3
2010	104.7	109.9
2011	105.3	108.2
2012	98.4	99.4
2013	98.8	97.8
2014	99.0	98.0
2015	95.0	92.7
2016	99.8	99.0
2017	105.7	113.9
2018	104.8	108.3
2019	100.3	98.6
2020	98.1	97.5
2021	110.3	109.5

注：2020年起，“工业生产者出厂价格指数”与“工业生产者购进价格指数”指标为全省数据。
Note: Starting in 2020,the “Producer Price Index” and “Producer Purchasing Price Index” are province-wide data.

主要统计指标解释

居民消费价格 是指城乡居民购买并用于日常生活消费的商品和服务项目的价格。

居民消费价格指数 反映一定时期内居民所消费商品及服务项目的价格水平变动趋势和变动程度的相对数。居民消费价格水平的变动率在一定程度上反映了通货膨胀（或紧缩）的程度。编制居民消费价格指数的目的，是了解全国各地价格变动的基本情况，分析研究价格变动对社会经济和居民生活的影响，满足各级政府制定政策和计划、进行宏观调控的需要，以及为国民经济核算提供参考依据。

调查内容是城乡居民购买并用于日常生活消费的商品和服务项目的价格。调查内容根据全国城乡居民家庭消费支出调查资料以及居民消费结构和消费习惯确定，按用途划分为8个大类，268个基本分类，包括食品烟酒、衣着、居住、生活用品及服务、交通通信、教育文化娱乐、医疗保健、其他用品及服务。

商品零售价格 是商品在流通过程中最后一个环节的价格，是工业、商业、餐饮业和其他零售企业向城乡居民、机关团体出售生活消费品和办公用品的价格。

商品零售价格指数 反映市场商品零售价格的变动趋势和变动程度。其目的在于掌握商品价格的变动趋势，为国家宏观调控和国民经济核算提供参考依据。

调查内容是工业、商业、餐饮业和其他行业的零售商品价格。包括食品、饮料烟酒、服装鞋帽、纺织品、家用电器及音像器材、文化办公用品、日用品、体育娱乐用品、交通通信用品、家具、化妆品、金银饰品、中西药品及医疗保健用品、书报杂志及电子出版物、燃料、建筑材料及五金电料等16个大类，197个基本分类的商品零售价格。

工业生产者价格 工业生产者价格包括工业企业产品第一次出售时的出厂价格和企业作为中间投入的原材料、燃料、动力购进价格（简称工业生产者购进价格）。工业生产者价格调查的目的在于及时、准确、科学地反映各工业行业产品价格水平及其变动趋势和幅度，为国民经济核算、计算工业发展速度、宏观经济分析和调控、理顺价格体系等提供科学、准确的依据。

工业生产者价格指数 是由工业生产者出厂价格指数和工业生产者购进价格指数两部分组成。

工业生产者出厂价格指数 是反映一定时期内全部工业产品第一次出售时的出厂价格总水平的变动趋势和变动幅度的相对数。

工业生产者购进价格指数 是反映作为中间投入的原材料、燃料、动力购进价格总水平的变动趋势和变动幅度的相对数。

住宅销售价格 指房产所有权转移时买卖双方实际成交的价格（合同价格）。房产买卖时，买房人购买的是房产的所有权，卖房人将房产所有权出让，同时要获得房产所有权出让的价格补偿。它主要包括新建住宅销售和二手住宅销售两部分。

住宅销售价格指数 是综合反映住宅商品价格总体变化趋势和变化幅度的相对数。各市住宅销售价格指数是由新建住宅销售价格指数和二手住宅销售价格指数组成。

Explanatory Notes on Main Statistical Indicators

Consumer Price refers to the price of goods and services purchased and used for daily life consumption by urban and rural residents.

Consumer Price index reflects the price changing trend of commodities and services consumed by residents in a certain period, and the relative number of the changing degree. The change rate of Consumer Price Index may reflect the degree of inflation (deflation) to a certain extent. The purpose for preparing Consumer Price Index is to get a basic known about the price variation across the country, analyze the influence of price variation upon social economy and residential livings, satisfy the requirements of government at all levels for preparing policies and plans, and carrying out macroeconomic regulation, and provide a reference basis for national economic accounting.

The investigation content is the price of goods and services purchased and used for daily life consumption by urban and rural residents. The investigation content is confirmed pursuant to survey data regarding national urban and rural residents' household consumption expenditure and resident consumption structure as well as consumption habit which is divided into 8 categories (268 basic types) as per purpose, including food, alcohol and tobacco, clothing, housing, daily necessities and services, transportation and communication, education, culture and entertainment, health care and other goods and services.

Retail Price refers to the prices in the last link of the production circulation process. It is the prices that industrial, commercial, catering and other retail enterprises sell daily consumer goods and products for office use to urban and rural residents and institutions and social organizations.

Retail Price Indices reflects the changing trend and degree of the retail prices of commodities in the market to master the changing trend of commodity retail prices and provide a reference basis for state macro-control and national economic accounting.

The investigation content involves the prices of retail goods in industry, business, catering and other industries, including the commodities of 16 categories (including 197 basic types) -- food, beverage alcohol & tobacco, clothing & shoes, textile, household appliances and audio & video equipment, cultural & office goods, daily necessities, sports & entertainment goods, transportation & communication supplies, furniture, cosmetics, gold & silver accessories, traditional Chinese and western medicines & healthcare supplies, newspapers & magazines and electronic publications, fuel, building materials & hardware.

Industrial Producer Price covers the ex-factory price when products of industrial enterprises are sold for the first time and the purchase price (called as industrial producer purchase price for short) of raw materials, fuels and power which are intermediate inputs of the enterprise. The investigation of industrial producer price is aimed at timely, accurately and scientifically reflecting the price level of products and the corresponding trend and range of changing in various industries, and providing scientific and accurate basis for national economic accounting, computing industry development speed, macroeconomic analysis and regulation and straightening out the price system, etc.

Industrial Producer Price Index is constituted by Producer Price Indices for Industrial Products and Purchasing Price Indices for Industrial Producers.

Producer Price Indices for Industrial Products reflect the trend and degree of changes in general ex-factory prices of all manufactured goods for first sale during a given period.

Purchasing Price Indices for Industrial Producers reflect changes in the level and degree of purchasing prices such as intermediate input such as raw materials, fuels and power.

The Sales Price of Residential refers to the actual price (contract price) of the transaction between the buyer and the seller when the house ownership is transferred. When the house property is sold, the house buyer purchases the ownership of the house property and the house seller transfers the ownership of the house property with price compensation for house property ownership transfer obtained at the same time. Housing sales mainly include sales of newly built house and sales of second-hand house.

Price Index for Residential reflects the trend and degree of changes in prices of real estate. The price index for real estate is constituted by the price index for the new houses and the price index for the second-hand house.

10

人民生活

PEOPLE´ S LIVELIHOOD

10-1 人民物质文化生活提高情况
Improvement in People's Material and Cultural Life

指标	Item	单位 (unit)	1978 年	1990 年
就业	**Employment**			
每一农村劳动力负担人数	Average Dependents Per Labor Force	人 (person)	1.70	1.61
每一城镇就业者负担人数	Dependents Per Urban Employee	人 (person)	1.89	1.72
城镇登记失业率	Registered Urban Unemployment Rate	%		
收入与支出	**Income and Expenditure**			
农村居民人均可支配收入	Per Capita Disposable Income of Rural Households	元 (yuan)	111	731
农村居民人均消费支出	Per Capita Consumer Expenditure of Rural Households	元 (yuan)	83	570
农村居民恩格尔系数	Engel's Coefficient of Rural Households	%	69.9	50.5
城镇居民人均可支配收入	Per Capita Disposable Income of Urban Households	元 (yuan)	338	1620
城镇居民人均消费支出	Per Capita Consumer Expenditure of Urban Households	元 (yuan)	318	1360
城镇居民恩格尔系数	Engel's Coefficient of Urban Households	%	57.1	57.5
居民储蓄	**Household Savings**			
城乡居民年末储蓄存款余额	Deposits of Urban and Rural Households	亿元 (100 million yuan)	1.3	51.1
人均储蓄存款余额	Per Capita Savings Balance	元 (yuan)	28.5	975.5
住房面积	**Area of Building**			
农村人均住房建筑面积	Rural Per Capita Living Space	平方米 (sq.m)	9.6	22.5
城镇人均住房建筑面积	Urban Per Capita Living Space	平方米 (sq.m)	4.1	7.5
交通通讯	**Traffic and Communication**			
农村每百户拥有摩托车	Number of Motorcycles Owned by Per 100 Rural Households	辆 (unit)		4.0
城市每百户拥有摩托车	Number of Motorcycles Owned by Per 100 Urban Households	辆 (unit)		7.7
城市公用事业	**Urban Utilities**			
城市人口用水普及率	Urban water Penetration Rate	%	99	100
每万人拥有公园绿地面积	Green Area of Park Per 10 000 Population	公顷 (ha)	1.6	4
文化生活	**Culture Life**			
城市每百户拥有彩色电视机	Number of Color TV Sets Owned by Per 100 Urban Households	台 (set)	-	61.3
农村每百户拥有彩色电视机	Number of Color TV Sets Owned by Per 100 Rural Households	台 (set)	-	70.0
教育卫生	**Education and Public Health**			
每万人口中在校大学生数	Number of College Students Per 10 000 Population	人 (person)	22	71
每万人拥有卫生技术人员	Number of Health Technical Personnel Per 10 000 Population	人 (person)	10.98	59.45
每万人拥有医院病床	Number of Beds of Hospitals and Health Centers Per 10 000 Population	张 (unit)	22.01	32.88

注：1. “城镇居民人均消费支出”1990 年以前为“生活费支出”。
2. “人均住宅建筑面积”，2009 年以前（不含）为“使用面积”口径，2002 年以前（不含）为“居住面积”口径。
3. 从 2015 年起，全市发布城乡住户调查一体化改革新口径数据，居民收支调查指标与 2014 年前分别实施的城镇和农村住户调查的调查范围、方法、指标口径、名称有所不同。（以下相关表同）。
4. “农村居民人均可支配收入”2014 年以前为“农民人均纯收入”口径。

2000 年	2010 年	2016 年	2017 年	2018 年	2019 年	2020 年	2021 年
1.40	1.35	1.42	1.31	1.4	1.4	1.4	1.3
1.71	1.67	1.87	1.35	1.4	1.5	1.3	1.4
3.70	3.84	2.17	2.08	2.06	2.01	2.03	–
3047	8903	15346	16594	17924	19454	20432	22580
1977	5407	9396	10327	11172	12300	12947	14591
43.5	33.6	32.2	31.5	30.5	30.1	30.4	30.5
8471	25321	43052	46642	50146	51913	53329	57449
6892	15973	28537	30729	32977	33439	34391	36866
34.6	31.6	24.2	23.5	23.5	23.8	23.5	23.5
463.0	2187.7	4279.9	4465.7	5008.1	6438.1	7584.1	8558.4
8229.6	36239.0	68012.6	69971.2	77076.2	81389.8	94596.7	105441.9
28.6	40.2	53.8	55.2	54.3	51.1	50.3	49.8
10.5	29.7	45.5	47.8	46.5	39.0	39.3	39.4
61.0	84.9	75.8	76.3	51.7	58.5	57.7	51.7
34.3	13.3	13.5	16.1	11.6	12.9	13.1	11.1
100	100	100	100	99.78	100.00	100.00	100.00
7.2	11.3	11.8	11.8	12.59	13.20	13.06	12.95
132.3	115.5	110.6	111.1	106.0	105.1	105.9	104.8
125.0	122.2	118.3	118.4	114.1	113.0	110.0	104.3
165	1064	1154	1241	1226	1040	1121	743
63.40	65.20	105.60	104.20	111.00	109.50	112.80	116.10
38.57	52.9	72.2	74.9	77.0	74.8	74.8	78.0

Notes:1."Per capita living expenditure of urban residents" was "cost of living expenses" before 1990.

2."Per capita housing area" was the caliber of "usable area" before 2009 (excluding) and was the caliber of "living area" before 2002 .

3.Since 2015, the city has released new caliber data for the integrated reform of urban and rural household surveys. The survey indicator of residents' income and expenditure was different from the survey scope, method, index caliber and name of urban and rural households carried out before 2014. (The same below) .

4."Per capita disposable income of rural residents" was the caliber of "rural per capita net income" before 2014.

10-2 各时期城镇居民生活情况

Basic Conditions of Urban Households in Each Period

年份 Year	人均可支配收入（元） Per Capita Disposable Income (yuan)	人均消费支出（元） Per Capita Consumer Expenditure(yuan)		就业者负担人数（人） Average Dependents Per Employee (person)	人均住宅建筑面积（平方米） Per Capita Floor Space (sq.m)
		小计 Total	# 人均食品支出 Per Capita Food Expenditure		
1949	64.53	61.30	37.39		4.09
1952	130.00	127.84	77.98		4.11
1957	206.50	194.15	117.69		3.64
1962	201.74	209.84	131.42		3.48
1965	219.51	212.82	131.59		3.31
1970					3.51
1975					3.66
1978	337.80	317.88	181.56	1.89	4.06
1980	440.09	405.53	230.11	1.67	4.22
“六五”时期					
1981	487.19	452.77	256.67	1.73	4.40
1982	502.97	468.03	275.30	1.70	4.57
1983	552.37	484.87	293.32	1.66	4.93
1984	671.89	537.27	326.97	1.69	5.10
1985	783.00	703.82	397.33	1.68	5.21
“七五”时期					
1986	946.46	836.50	474.62	1.70	7.40
1987	1057.48	943.58	534.12	1.73	7.30
1988	1272.83	1150.44	635.11	1.70	7.50
1989	1487.91	1355.64	745.32	1.71	7.50
1990	1619.50	1360.08	781.58	1.72	7.50
“八五”时期					
1991	1854.33	1569.26	896.62	1.71	7.60
1992	2148.49	1781.21	979.03	1.73	7.65
1993	2873.94	2394.03	1146.02	1.74	7.80
1994	3951.94	3224.73	1566.59	1.72	7.90
1995	4720.55	3830.38	1823.64	1.80	8.00
“九五”时期					
1996	5681.49	4422.91	2161.00	1.71	8.00

10-2 续表 continued

年份 Year	人均可支配收入（元） Per Capita Disposable Income (yuan)	人均消费支出（元） Per Capita Consumer Expenditure(yuan)		就业者负担人数（人） Average Dependents Per Employee (person)	人均住宅建筑面积（平方米） Per Capita Floor Space (sq.m)
		小计 Total	# 人均食品支出 Per Capita Food Expenditure		
1997	6261.21	5210.40	2185.11	1.62	8.10
1998	6757.12	5440.10	2179.99	1.61	9.89
1999	7162.48	6415.39	2204.76	1.66	10.00
2000	8471.32	6891.75	2387.06	1.71	10.50
"十五"时期					
2001	9564.99	7465.04	2386.84	1.74	10.70
2002	10094.13	7818.33	2575.21	1.72	17.83
2003	11012.86	8395.36	2610.75	1.68	18.85
2004	12005.06	8580.54	2784.87	1.65	19.50
2005	13578.46	9226.61	3046.93	1.73	19.55
"十一五"时期					
2006	15340.17	10713.13	3335.31	1.74	20.1
2007	18005.10	12389.69	3900.91	1.72	21.0
2008	20802.17	13904.59	4466.18	1.87	21.5
2009	22721.65	14764.28	4836.78	1.86	29.4
2010	25321.06	15973.32	5051.18	1.67	29.7
"十二五"时期					
2011	28891.97	18045.58	5722.65	1.71	30.3
2012	32569.75	20031.67	6162.16	1.72	–
2013	35647.59	21666.94	6624.32	–	–
2014	38762.77	22980.67	6814.14	2.04	–
2015	39888.71	26318.72	6415.00	1.80	44.9
"十三五"时期					
2016	43052.16	28536.93	6908.01	1.87	45.5
2017	46642.40	30728.60	7229.30	1.35	47.8
2018	50146	32977	7758	1.4	46.5
2019	51913	33439	7956	1.4	39.0
2020	53329	34391	8072	1.3	39.3
"十四五"时期					
2021	57449	36866	8654	1.4	39.4

注：1. 可支配收入 1983 年以前为生活费收入，消费支出 1992 年以前为生活费支出。
2. "人均住宅建筑面积"，2009 年以前（不含）为"使用面积"口径，2002 年以前（不含）为"居住面积"口径。

Notes:1.The disposable income was living expenditure income before 1983, and the consumption expenditure was previously the cost-of-living expenditure before 1992.
2."Per capita housing area", was the caliber of "usable area" before 2009 (excluding) and was the caliber of "living area" before 2002.

10-3 主要年份农村居民生活情况
Basic Conditions of Rural Households in Major Years

年份 Year	人均可支配收入（元） Per Capita Disposable Income (yuan)	人均消费支出（元） Per Capita Consumer Expenditure(yuan)		每一劳动力负担人数（人） Average Dependents Per Labor Force (person)	人均住宅建筑面积（平方米） Per Capita Floor Space (sq.m)
		小计 Total	# 人均食品支出 Per Capita Food Expenditure		
1952	49.4	39.2	29.2	1.8	7.5
1957	63.6	57.9	34.8	1.8	7.8
1962	67.7	59.9	36.3	1.8	8.0
1965	92.6	69.7	46.1	1.8	8.2
1970	82.7	67.2	42.2	1.7	8.5
1975	79.1	59.5	40.8	1.7	9.0
1978	110.5	83.2	58.2	1.7	9.6
1980	168.9	127.1	85.8	1.6	10.5
1985	439.2	330.5	171.1	1.6	16.9
1990	731.1	569.8	287.7	1.6	22.5
1991	810.1	610.6	303.7	1.6	23.7
1992	865.3	660.5	335.1	1.6	21.1
1993	1031.4	724.8	371.4	1.6	22.9
1994	1401.0	942.5	511.0	1.6	24.1
1995	1812.7	1373.6	770.8	1.4	24.7
1996	2328.1	1728.1	926.2	1.4	26.9
1997	2600.0	1799.7	922.0	1.4	27.1
1998	2826.4	1872.5	935.9	1.4	27.4
1999	2943.7	1841.2	876.7	1.4	28.3
2000	3046.8	1976.8	860.0	1.4	28.6
2001	3215.7	2057.8	852.5	1.5	29.9
2002	3355.8	2133.9	849.5	1.4	30.6
2003	3619.3	2316.2	900.7	1.4	32.5
2004	4198.7	2543.1	1040.4	1.4	32.9
2005	4812.3	2902.8	1134.8	1.4	33.8
2006	5480.0	3415.3	1199.8	1.4	35.3
2007	6300.1	3789.8	1423.0	1.4	37.3
2008	7180.2	4385.4	1628.2	1.4	38.7
2009	7804.8	4733.1	1686.3	1.4	39.4
2010	8903.3	5406.6	1818.3	1.4	40.2
2011	10411.8	5905.1	2147.3	1.4	41.2
2012	11786.2	6932.2	2465.4	1.4	42.9
2013	13247.6	7798.7	2640.8	1.4	43.9
2014	14726.0	8581.4	2831.4	1.4	–
2015	14231.8	8597.2	2775.5	1.4	52.6
2016	15345.6	9396.3	3028.0	1.4	53.8
2017	16593.8	10327.3	3253.2	1.3	55.2
2018	17924	11172	3409	1.4	54.3
2019	19454	12300	3703	1.4	51.1
2020	20432	12947	3931	1.4	50.3
2021	22580	14591	4446	1.3	49.8

注：1. "人均可支配收入" 2014 年以前为"农民人均纯收入"口径。
2. "人均住宅建筑面积"，2009 年以前（不含）为"使用面积"口径，2002 年以前（不含）为"居住面积"口径。

Notes:1."Per capita disposable income" was the caliber of "rural per capita net income" before 2014.
2."Per capita housing area" was the caliber of "usable area" before 2009 (excluding) and was the caliber of "living area" before 2002 (excluding).

10-4 城镇每百户居民家庭主要耐用消费品拥有量
Number of Major Durable Consumer Goods Owned Per 100 Urban Households in Major Years

商品名称	Item	单位 Unit	1995 年	2000 年	2005 年	2010 年	2015 年	2019 年	2020 年	2021 年
家用汽车	Automobile	辆 (Unit)			5.4	22.7	47.6	54.0	58.5	62.1
摩托车	Motorcycle	辆 (Unit)	13.0	34.3	30.1	13.3	15.1	12.9	13.1	11.1
洗衣机	Washing Machine	台 (set)	91.5	100.0	97.0	93.2	98.5	98.6	98.4	98.1
电冰箱	Refrigerator	台 (set)	92.0	99.3	97.0	96.7	101.8	104.0	104.0	100.9
彩色电视机	Color Television Set	台 (set)	95.0	132.3	126.8	115.5	110.5	105.1	105.9	104.8
空调器	Air Conditioner	台 (set)	16.0	65.0	104.4	121.5	146.3	166.6	166.4	172.6
热水器	Water Heaters	台 (set)	36.5	81.3	79.3	82.0	100.3	99.0	100.6	99.5
照相机	Camera	台 (set)	40.5	76.0	59.2	54.0	56.1	32.9	33.8	23.5
住宅电话	Fixed-line Phones	台 (set)	38.0	86.7	88.6	46.3	54.7	20.8	19.2	14.5
移动电话	Mobile Phones	台 (set)		28.7	145.2	179.7	213.5	222.9	225.7	227.6
计算机	Computer	台 (set)		20.0	54.2	81.0	90.8	81.8	83.2	80.2

10-5 农村每百户居民家庭主要耐用消费品拥有量
Number of Major Durable Consumer Goods Owned Per 100 Rural Households in Major Years

商品名称	Item	单位 Unit	2011 年	2012 年	2013 年	2015 年	2016 年	2019 年	2020 年	2021 年
家用汽车	Automobile	辆 (unit)						39	37	41
摩托车	Motorcycle	辆 (unit)	71	62	65	79	76	58	58	52
洗衣机	Washing Machine	台 (set)	82	86	88	86	90	93	91	91
电冰箱	Refrigerator	台 (set)	88	91	92	91	97	99	98	96
彩色电视机	Color Television Set	台 (set)	116	118	119	114	118	113	110	104
空调器	Air Conditioner	台 (set)	36	39	46	56	67	93	90	94
热水器	Water Heater	台 (set)	64	69	69	74	79	82	86	89
照相机	Camera	台 (set)	15	14	16	8	9	6	3	4
住宅电话	Fixed-line Phones	部 (set)	60	58	55	47	48	21	20	16
移动电话	Mobile Phone	部 (set)	175	186	195	214	224	232	229	230
计算机	Computer	台 (set)	36	39	43	40	43	39	43	42

10-6 居民人均可支配收入和消费支出（2021 年）
Per Capital Annual Income and Per Capital Annual Expenditure(2021)

单位：元 (yuan)

指标名称	Item	全体居民 All Households	城镇居民 Urban households	农村居民 Rural households
可支配收入	Disposable Income	46725	57449	22580
工资性收入	Income of Wages and Salaries	27050	33546	12423
经营净收入	Net Business Income	4728	3146	8291
财产净收入	Net Income from Properties	6887	9732	482
转移净收入	Net Income from Transfer	8060	11025	1383
消费支出	Consumption Expenditure	30016	36866	14591
食品烟酒	Food,Tobacco and liquor	7360	8654	4446
衣着	Clothing and Footwear	1728	2173	725
居住	Housing	8835	11339	3197
生活用品及服务	Household Equipments, Furnishings and Services	2113	2634	941
交通通信	Transport and Communications	3986	4773	2214
教育文化娱乐	Education, Culture and Recreation	3199	3969	1466
医疗保健	Health care and Medical Services	2178	2534	1378
其他用品和服务	Miscellaneous Goods and Services	617	792	223

主要统计指标解释

可支配收入 指调查户在调查期内获得的、可用于最终消费支出和储蓄的总和，即调查户可以用来自由支配的收入。可支配收入既包括现金，也包括实物收入。按照收入的来源，可支配收入包含四项，分别为：工资性收入、经营净收入、财产净收入、转移净收入。计算公式为：

可支配收入 ＝ 工资性收入＋经营净收入＋财产净收入＋转移净收入

其中：经营净收入 ＝ 经营收入－经营费用－生产性固定资产折旧－生产税

财产净收入 ＝ 财产性收入 － 财产性支出

转移净收入 ＝ 转移性收入 － 转移性支出

工资性收入 指就业人员通过各种途径得到的全部劳动报酬和各种福利，包括受雇于单位或个人、从事各种自由职业、兼职和零星劳动得到的全部劳动报酬和福利。

经营净收入 指住户或住户成员从事生产经营活动所获得的净收入，是全部经营收入中扣除经营费用、生产性固定资产折旧和生产税之后得到的净收入。

财产净收入 指住户或住户成员将其所拥有的金融资产、住房等非金融资产和自然资源交由其他机构单位、住户或个人支配而获得的回报并扣除相关的费用之后得到的净收入。财产净收入包括利息净收入、红利收入、储蓄性保险净收益、转让承包土地经营权租金净收入、出租房屋净收入、出租其他资产净收入和自有住房折算净租金等。

转移性收入 指国家、单位、社会团体对住户的各种经常性转移支付和住户之间的经常性收入转移。包括养老金或退休金、社会救济和补助、政策性生产补贴、政策性生活补贴、救灾款、经常性捐赠和赔偿、报销医疗费、住户之间的赡养收入，本住户非常住成员寄回带回的收入等。转移性收入不包括住户之间的实物馈赠。

转移性支出 指调查户对国家、单位、住户或个人的经常性或义务性转移支付。包括缴纳的税款、各项社会保障支出、赡养支出、经常性捐赠和赔偿支出以及其他经常转移支出等。

消费支出 指住户用于满足家庭日常生活消费需要的全部支出，包括用于消费品的支出和用于服务性消费的支出。根据用途不同，消费支出可划分为食品烟酒、衣着、居住、生活用品及服务、交通通信、教育文化娱乐、医疗保健、其他用品及服务八大类。根据来源不同，消费支出可划分为现金消费支出、实物消费支出（含自产自用、来自单位、来自政府和其他社会组织）。

食品烟酒 指用于各种食品和烟草、酒类的支出，包括食品和烟酒两个中类。

衣着 指与居民穿着有关的支出，包括服装、服装材料、鞋类、其他衣类及配件、衣着相关加工服务的支出。

居住 指与居住有关的支出，包括房租、水、电、燃料、物业管理等方面的支出，也包括自有住房折算租金。

生活用品及服务 指家庭及个人的各类生活品及家庭服务。包括家具及室内装饰品、家用器具、家用纺织品、家庭日用杂品、个人用品和家庭服务。

交通通信 指用于交通和通信工具及相关的各种服务费、维修费和车辆保险等支出。

教育文化和娱乐 指用于教育和文化娱乐方面的支出。

医疗保健 指用于医疗和保健的药品、用品和服务的总费用。包括医疗器具及药品，以及医疗服务。

其他用品及服务 指无法直接归入上述各类支出的其他用品与服务支出。

就业者负担人数 指家庭人口与就业人口之比。

城镇家庭可支配收入（老口径） 指家庭成员得到可用于最终消费支出和其他非义务性支出以及储蓄的总和，即居民家庭可以用来自由支配的收入。它是家庭总收入扣除交纳的所得税、个人交纳的社会保障支出以及记账补贴后的收入。计算公式为：

可支配收入＝家庭总收入－交纳所得税－个人交纳的社会保障支出－记帐补贴

农村居民纯收入（老口径） 指农村住户当年从各个来源得到的总收入相应地扣除所发生的费用后的收入总和。计算方法：

纯收入＝总收入－家庭经营费用支出－税费支出－生产性固定资产折旧

纯收入主要用于再生产投入和当年生活消费支出，也可用于储蓄和各种非义务性支出。“农民人均纯收入”按人口平均的纯收入水平，反映的是一个地区或一个农户农村居民的平均收入水平。

农村居民人均可支配收入与改革前的农民纯收入指标的主要区别是：可支配收入扣除了赠送农村以外亲友支出、农村居民用于购买住房、汽车等生活性贷款的利息支出，以及个人交纳的养老、医疗等社会保障支出，纯收入则不扣。同时，计算农村居民人均收入的分母调整为农村常住人口，调整了外出农民工寄带回收入的归类。

Explanatory Notes on Main Statistical Indicators

Disposable Income refers to the sum of households income that can be used for final consumption expenditure and savings during the period of investigation. Disposable income includes cash and real income. According to sources of income, disposable income includes the wage income, net operating income, net property income, and net transfer income. The formula for computing:

Disposable income = the wage income + net operating income + net property income + net transfer income

Net operating income = Income – operating costs – depreciation of productive fixed assets – production tax

Net property income = income from property – property expenditure

Net transfer income = income from transfer – transfer expenditure

Wage Income refers to income and all kinds of welfare obtained by labors employed by different establishments, working independently or part–time.

Net Operating Income refers to the net income from operation run by the members of households, and it equals to total income minus operating costs and depreciation of productive fixed assets and taxes on production.

Net Property Income refers to the net income obtained from the financial assets, non–financial assets such as housing and natural resources provided by its owners to other establishments, households or individuals. It includes net interest income, bonus, net income from saving insurance, net income from the transfer of the right to land contractual management, income from house renting, income from renting of other assets and net rental income of home ownership.

Net transfer income refers to the regular transfer received from governments, institutions, social organizations to households and between households. It includes old–age and retirement pension, disaster relief funds, regular donation and compensation, reimbursement of medical fees, supporting income between households, income from non–resident members of households, etc. Income from transfer do not include gifts in kinds between households.

Transfer Expenditure refers to the regular or obligatory expenditure provided by the households to governments, institutions, other households or residents. It includes taxes, social security expenditure, supporting expenditure, regular donation and compensation expenditure, etc.

Expenditure refers to the consumption of all expenditures needs to meet the family daily life, including the expenditures on consumer goods and services. According to different purposes, consumption can be divided into tobacco & food, clothing, housing, daily necessities & services, transportation & communication, education & culture & entertainment, health care, and other goods & services. According to different sources, consumption expenditures can be divided into cash consumption and physical consumption expenditures (including self–occupied, from the unit, from the government and other social organizations).

Tobacco & Food refers to all kinds of expenditure on foods, tobaccos and beverages, including food and tobacco.

Clothing refers to the expenditure on clothes, clothing materials, shoes, accessories and charges for clothing production process.

Housing refers to the expenditure related to residing, including the expenditure on rent, water, fuel, power and real estate management and net rental income of home ownership.

Daily Necessities & Services refer to the expenditure on daily necessities and home service, including the expenditure on furniture, decoration, appliance, textile, personal items and home service.

Transportation & Communication refer to the expenditure on transportation, communication, related service, maintenance, and vehicle insurance.

Education & Culture & Entertainment refer to the expenditure on education, culture and entertainment.

Health Care refers to the sum of the expenditure on health care, medicine, related products and service, including the medical devices, drug as well as medical services.

Other Services refer to the expenditure on the goods and services that cannot be included in the categories mentioned above.

Number of Dependents per Employee refers to the ratio between number of persons in households and the number of employers in the household.

Urban Households Disposable Income (in previous cope) refers to the sum of households' income used for final consumption expenditure and savings during the period of investigation, meaning the income that is disposable for households. Disposable income is the general income of households minus income tax, social security expenditure and subsidy for account–keeping. The formula for computing:

Disposable Income of Households = General income – income tax – personal social security expenditure – subsidy for account keeping

Rural Households Net Income (in previous cope) refers to the total income of rural households from all sources minus all corresponding expenses. The formula for calculation is as follows:

Net income = total income – household operation expenses – taxes and fees – depreciation of fixed assets for production

Net income is mainly used as input for reproduction and as consumption expenditure of the year, and also used for savings and non–compulsory expenses of various forms. "Per capita net income of farmers" is the level of net income averaged by population which reflects the average income level of rural households in a given area.

The main difference between rural household disposable income and rural household net income is that the disposable income does not include the expenditure of donations to urban relatives, the expenditure on houses and vehicles purchasing, interest expenditure on consumer loans, and expenditure on pension and health care, but the net income includes all the expenditure mentioned above. When calculating the average income of rural household, the denominator is changed to permanent rural residents, and the classification of income brought back by migrant workers is also changed.

农　业

AGRICULTURE

11-1 各时期农业主要经济指标
Major Economic Indicators of Agriculture in Each Period

年份 Year	农村劳动力（万人） Rural Labor (10 000 persons)	农林牧渔业总产值（亿元） Gross Output Value of Farming,Forestry, Animal Husbandry and Fishery (100 million yuan)	农业机械总动力（万千瓦） Total Agricultural Machinery Power (10 000 kW)	年末实有耕地面积（千公顷） Actual Cultivated Area (1000 ha)	粮食总产量（万吨） Output of Grain (10 000 tons)	蔬菜总产量（万吨） Output of Vegetable (10 000 tons)	肉类总产量（万吨） Output of Meat (10 000 tons)	粮食单产（千克/公顷） Output Per Hectare of Grain (kg/ha)
1949	106.51	1.50	–	469.85	51.63	10.72	0.24	825
1952	112.35	1.91	–	481.17	62.75	8.61	0.40	960
1957	121.09	2.79	0.32	479.58	67.92	15.86	0.66	1065
1962	108.44	1.33	2.98	412.34	39.74	27.67	0.72	765
1965	111.74	2.61	4.84	410.02	73.80	29.12	1.12	1350
1970	123.91	2.75	14.32	396.49	75.47	31.81	1.21	1470
1975	141.00	4.07	48.04	382.05	100.46	42.00	2.07	2025
1978	140.05	6.57	69.70	373.19	115.38	49.19	2.50	2475
1979	141.60	7.48	80.63	372.45	122.56	49.42	2.92	2610
1980	143.19	7.79	88.45	370.87	116.54	58.13	3.69	2565
“六五”时期								
1981	146.52	11.73	94.47	369.80	121.27	49.85	3.99	2865
1982	149.07	14.47	106.60	369.22	121.13	63.45	4.31	3060
1983	152.39	18.07	112.19	368.45	147.41	65.66	4.66	3570
1984	158.23	19.00	123.92	367.35	160.60	86.91	5.03	3915
1985	162.51	18.36	130.41	357.41	163.50	84.11	5.43	3915
“七五”时期								
1986	165.86	20.91	147.36	353.96	168.16	118.86	6.44	3855
1987	168.56	24.65	156.23	352.18	167.25	101.52	7.13	3945
1988	171.44	34.24	172.89	350.56	167.95	122.83	8.68	4080
1989	173.38	35.14	182.40	349.59	162.45	117.99	9.70	3945
1990	176.83	36.92	183.40	347.56	181.47	126.09	11.38	4273
“八五”时期								
1991	180.09	40.13	191.00	344.76	207.55	146.87	13.50	4779
1992	182.51	45.14	191.50	343.29	198.29	170.61	15.36	4655
1993	183.78	57.81	194.40	341.54	232.21	205.62	19.12	4963
1994	183.42	85.37	207.40	339.97	237.66	226.39	26.14	5237
1995	183.55	114.07	241.20	339.30	252.48	253.54	28.68	5512

注：1. 自 2005 年始年末实有耕地面积有国土资源局提供，暂无 2009 年数据。
2. 依据 2006 年农业普查数据，对 1997 年至 2007 年蔬菜面积、产量做了相应调整。
3. 粮食作物产量、播种面积自 2012 年开始由山东调查总队反馈。
4. 按照国务院农普办要求，由国家统计局山东调查总队根据第三次农业普查数据，对 2016-2017 年市县（区）粮食播种面积．单产和总产量等数据进行了修订。
5. 依据 2016 年农业普查数据，对 2007 年至 2017 年农林牧渔业总产值做了相应调整。
6. 依据 2016 年农业普查数据，对 2008 年至 2017 年蔬菜总产量、肉类总产量做了相应调整。
7. 2019 年农业数据为区划调整后的数据，以下各表同。
8. 由于第三次全国国土调查数据未反馈，“年末实有耕地面积”2019 年相关数据延用 2018 年数据。
9. 由于第三次全国国土调查数据未反馈，“年末实有耕地面积”2020 年相关数据延用 2018 年数据；2020 年数据为区划调整后数据。
10. 由于市农业农村局未提供农业机械类指标数据，延用 2019 年数据。以下相关各表同。

11-1 续表 continued

年份 Year	农村劳动力（万人）Rural Labor (10 000 persons)	农林牧渔业总产值（亿元）Gross Output Value of Farming,Forestry, Animal Husbandry and Fishery (100 million yuan)	农业机械总动力（万千瓦）Total Agricultural Machinery Power (10 000 kW)	年末实有耕地面积（千公顷）Actual Cultivated Area (1000 ha)	粮食总产量（万吨）Output of Grain (10 000 tons)	蔬菜总产量（万吨）Output of Vegetable (10 000 tons)	肉类总产量（万吨）Output of Meat (10 000 tons)	粮食单产（千克/公顷）Output Per Hectare of Grain (kg/ha)
“九五”时期								
1996	184.68	117.65	247.07	337.25	267.08	350.36	30.43	5602
1997	186.68	131.69	258.50	335.90	240.34	328.64	24.75	5064
1998	186.54	141.45	273.30	334.83	273.10	344.67	27.38	5634
1999	188.27	148.61	297.55	333.72	279.01	366.78	29.89	5752
2000	189.15	154.30	349.47	333.72	240.27	405.95	31.82	5354
“十五”时期								
2001	189.87	162.27	409.07	331.75	239.08	435.20	33.23	5480
2002	190.98	167.99	410.17	329.35	189.86	478.34	31.87	4440
2003	192.71	180.30	417.43	325.18	220.56	504.81	33.29	5448
2004	191.31	204.39	418.54	324.89	242.74	515.26	35.35	5807
2005	190.21	230.46	426.76	366.99	260.11	529.37	37.93	5932
“十一五”时期								
2006	190.80	247.70	429.62	361.74	267.91	536.28	38.74	6042
2007	191.16	262.51	446.60	358.80	268.01	522.24	31.85	6064
2008	190.45	302.00	466.00	361.33	281.50	520.25	30.22	6230
2009	195.56	318.06	486.00		289.47	560.83	31.39	6246
2010	196.85	361.24	509.68	362.30	289.43	572.05	31.79	6192
“十二五”时期								
2011	197.38	399.90	527.39	361.25	295.84	590.02	32.43	6315
2012	198.74	422.75	538.66	360.28	286.03	606.11	33.22	6285
2013	199.80	470.55	552.06	361.01	266.60	629.54	33.59	5997
2014	199.73	479.50	567.02	360.24	271.19	638.22	34.10	6109
2015	200.45	493.04	584.98	358.57	264.55	626.23	34.18	6117
“十三五”时期								
2016	200.46	501.72	447.83	357.60	275.43	611.25	31.72	5778
2017	198.91	505.08	442.90	355.66	255.57	591.63	32.50	5660
2018	189.10	514.90	454.62	353.65	251.42	527.22	29.82	5659
2019	239.03	637.30	543.48	353.65	285.46	671.24	35.86	5956
2020	222.13	671.66	543.48	426.04	290.81	673.73	23.92	6053
“十四五”时期								
2021	212.69	758.41	570.10	342.29	293.07	691.76	27.36	6060

Notes:1.Since 2005, the actual cultivated area has been provided by Land Resources Bureau. No data for 2009.

2.According to the data of the agricultural census in 2006, the area and yield of the vegetables from 1997 to 2007 were adjusted accordingly.

3.Grain crop yield and sown area have been reported by Shandong Survey Team since 2012.

4.According to the requirements of Agricultural Census Office of the State Council, Shandong Survey Team of National Bureau of Statistics revised the grain sown area, yield per unit and total yield of each city and country (district) from 2016–2017 based on the data from the third agricultural census.

5.According to the data of the agricultural census in 2016, the total output value of agriculture, forestry, animal husbandry and fishery in the period from 2007 to 2017 was adjusted accordingly.

6.According to the data of the agricultural census in 2016, the total output value of vegetable and meat in the period from 2008 to 2017 was adjusted accordingly.

7.The data of agriculture in 2019 is the adjusted data by the administrative division (the same below).

8."Actual cultivated area at the end of year " in 2019 uses the data in the year of 2018 because no data of the third national land survey has been reflected.

9.As the data of the Third National Territorial Survey has not been provided, the “existing agricultural acreage to year end” of 2020 adopts the data of 2018; the data of 2020 is collected after administrative division adjusting.

10.Due to the municipal bureau of agriculture and rural affairs didn’t provide data on agricultural machines index, thus the data of 2019 is adopted. The same for the following tables.

11-2 农村基层组织和农业基本情况
Basic Conditions of Rural Grassroots Units and Agriculture

指标	Item	单位 Unit	2016 年	2017 年	2018 年	2019 年	2020 年	2021 年
乡镇数量	Number of Towns	个 (Unit)	39	29	29	40	29	29
# 镇	Towns	个 (Unit)	39	29	29	40	29	29
村民委员会	Village Committee	个 (Unit)	4547	4548	4546	5551	5530	4699
乡村户数	Rural Households	万户 (10 000 households)	103.14	102.31	101.96	139.19	133.69	130.03
乡村人口	Rural Numbers	万人 (10 000 persons)	362.55	359.18	355.74	456.10	430.65	413.22
家庭从业人员	FamilyPractitioner	万人 (10 000 persons)	200.46	198.91	189.10	239.03	222.13	212.69
男	Male	万人 (10 000 persons)	106.06	105.38	99.96	127.55	119.06	113.34
女	Female	万人 (10 000 persons)	94.40	93.52	89.15	111.48	103.07	99.35
耕地	Cultivated Land	公顷 (ha)	357601	355659	353652	353652	426036	342289
其中：水浇地	Irrigated Land	公顷 (ha)	263310	261894	263885	263885	299089	268186
园地	Garden Land	公顷 (ha)	25957	25801	25675	25675	41361	102052
林地	Forest Land	公顷 (ha)	84484	84175	83947	83947	121243	247879
草地	Pasture Land	公顷 (ha)	57151	57018	56879	56879	88864	27300
城镇村及工矿用地	Land for Urban Village, Mining and Manufacturing	公顷 (ha)	144219	146819	149020	149020	183415	189766
交通运输用地	Land for Transport Facilities	公顷 (ha)	29319	29617	30216	30216	37537	31109
水域及水利设施用地	Land for Water Conservancy Facilities	公顷 (ha)	50875	50696	50531	50531	61157	58956
农业机械总动力	Total Agricultural Machinery Power	万千瓦 (10 000 kW)	447.83	442.90	454.62	543.48	543.48	570.10
农用大中型拖拉机	Large and Medium-sized Tractors	台 (set)	25574	24329	20208	23553	23553	25498
农用小型拖拉机	Small Tractors	台 (set)	35492	27179	30152	49911	49911	48261
谷物联合收割机	Combine Harvester	台 (set)	14365	13948	14380	15746	15746	16838
柴油机	Diesel Engine	台 (set)	84583	82173				
割晒机	Cutter-Rower	台 (set)	3103	2935				
脱粒机	Thresher	台 (set)	20450	19917	19660	27007	27007	25932
农用化肥使用量	Consumption of Chemical Fertilizer	吨（折纯）(ton convert to pure volume)	221167	209449	199591	214814	205007	199919
农药使用量	Pesticides mption	吨 (ton)	2933.0	2896.0	2692.9	3477.5	3231.4	2960.8
农作物总播种面积	Total Sown Area of Farm Crops	千公顷 (1000 ha)	598.9	566.1	549.0	615.6	614.3	614.8

注：1. 按照国务院农普办要求，由国家统计局山东调查总队根据第三次农业普查数据，对 2016-2017 年市、县（区）粮食播种面积数据进行了修订。
2. 由于第三次全国国土调查数据未反馈，“地类面积”2019 年相关数据延用 2018 年数据，以下相关各表同。
3. 由于第三次全国国土调查数据未反馈，“地类面积”2020 年相关数据延用 2018 年数据；2020 年数据为区划调整后数据。以下相关各表同。

Notes:1.According to the requirements of Agricultural Census Office of the State Council, Shandong Survey Team of National Bureau of Statistics revised the grain sown area, of each city and country (district) from 2016-2017 based on the data from the third agricultural census.
2."Land Category Area" data in 2019 uses the data of year 2018 because no data of the third national land survey has been reflected (the same below).
3.As the data of the Third National Territorial Survey has not been provided, the land data of 2020 adopts the data of 2018; the data of 2020 is collected after administrative division adjusting. The same for the following related tables.

11-3 分地区农村基层组织和农业基本情况 (2021 年)
Basic Conditions of Rural Grassrootsunits and Agriculture by Region(2021)

指标	Item	单位 Unit	济南市 Ji'nan	历下区 Li xia
乡镇数量	Number of Towns	个 (Unit)	29	
#镇	Towns	个 (Unit)	29	
村民委员会	Village Committee	个 (Unit)	4699	
乡村户数	Rural Households	万户 (10 000 households)	130.03	
乡村总人口	Rural Numbers	万人 (10 000 persons)	413.22	
乡村劳动力	Rural Labor Forces	万人 (10 000 persons)	212.69	
男	Male	万人 (10 000 persons)	113.34	
女	Female	万人 (10 000 persons)	99.35	
耕地	Cultivated Land	公顷 (ha)	342289	78
其中：水浇地	Irrigated Land	公顷 (ha)	268186	11
园地	Garden Land	公顷 (ha)	102052	84
林地	Forest Land	公顷 (ha)	247879	2596
草地	Pasture Land	公顷 (ha)	27300	86
城镇村及工矿用地	Land for Urban Village, Mining and Manufacturing	公顷 (ha)	189766	7103
交通运输用地	Land for Transport Facilities	公顷 (ha)	31109	113
水域及水利设施用地	Land for Water Conservancy Facilities	公顷 (ha)	58956	36
农业机械总动力	Total Agricultural Machinery Power	万千瓦 (10 000 kW)	570.1	3.0
农用大中型拖拉机	Large and Medium-sized Tractors	台 (set)	25498	50
农用小型拖拉机	Small Tractors	台 (set)	48261	511
谷物联合收割机	Combine Harvester	台 (set)	16838	27
脱粒机	Thresher	台 (set)	25932	18
农用化肥使用量	Consumption of Chemical Fertilizer	吨（折纯） (ton convert to pure volume)	199919	
农药使用量	Pesticides mption	吨（ton)	2960.8	
农作物总播种面积	Total Sown Area of Farm Crops	千公顷 (1000 ha)	614.76	

市中区 Shi zhong	槐荫区 Huai yin	天桥区 Tian qiao	历城区 Li cheng	长清区 Chang qing	章丘区 Zhang qiu	济阳区 Ji yang	莱芜区 Lai wu	钢城区 Gang cheng	平阴县 Ping yin	商河县 Shang he
				2	1	2	7		6	11
				2	1	2	7		6	11
77	93	48	266	585	532	566	793	211	308	516
4.77	2.21	2.44	17.07	12.45	24.41	11.73	25.83	6.15	8.81	14.16
15.75	8.07	8.29	52.37	41.43	80.30	41.10	66.64	16.60	30.01	52.67
6.96	3.10	3.39	26.28	17.01	46.34	21.09	35.20	9.26	16.23	27.83
3.79	1.64	1.72	13.74	8.70	24.51	11.60	18.89	5.07	8.44	15.23
3.17	1.46	1.67	12.54	8.31	21.83	9.49	16.31	4.18	7.79	12.60
3025	1500	8065	13460	30255	61488	64422	45620	11203	26884	76287
822	525	7941	9735	16602	44130	63719	25513	2240	20668	76281
2962	406	571	30173	18449	14284	1554	19645	5403	7927	593
9167	2110	3275	43709	41675	38431	10287	54268	15987	17211	9163
943	161	410	2674	3906	7832	459	7050	1965	1453	361
10220	7550	8523	29017	15873	31538	16374	26659	10178	10465	16266
1032	972	1134	4816	2907	4941	3631	5394	1336	2034	2798
351	2357	3764	4654	4071	8627	12540	8305	2040	2493	9717
12.9	4.0	3.9	51.1	51.3	98.7	116.1	69.2	19.3	47.4	93.2
378	242	225	1741	2999	3582	5469	2278	496	1842	6196
412	303	84	5383	3489	2243	5476	15360	4525	5010	5465
122	151	177	1241	1392	4067	3034	853	154	827	4793
121	2396	0	1227	886	2193	7214	6702	1291	705	3179
602	191	2828	13367	12023	44194	29692	24068	3504	13907	55543
30.4	4.4	29.2	282.0	326.6	393.2	605.6	570.1	215.9	130.4	373.0
4.08	2.37	12.87	25.21	56.47	139.94	115.73	59.51	10.79	49.25	138.54

11-4 各时期农林牧渔业总产值（按当年价格计算）
Gross Output Value of Agriculture, Forestry, Animal Husbandry and Fishery in Each Period(Calculated at Current Prices)

单位：亿元 (100 million yuan)

年份 Year	合计 Total	其中 of which 农业 Farming	林业 Forestry	牧业 Animal Husbandry	渔业 Fishery	农林牧渔服务业 Services of Agriculture,Forestry,Animal Husbandry and Fishing
1952	1.91	1.67	0.04	0.18	0.02	–
1957	2.79	2.41	0.09	0.28	0.01	–
1962	1.33	1.18	0.03	0.12	–	–
1965	2.61	2.25	0.07	0.28	0.01	–
1970	2.75	2.32	0.10	0.32	0.01	–
1975	4.07	3.48	0.13	0.44	0.02	–
1978	6.57	5.63	0.20	0.72	0.02	–
1980	7.78	6.66	0.18	0.93	0.01	–
1985	18.36	14.63	0.75	2.93	0.05	–
"七五"时期						
1986	20.91	16.81	0.79	3.23	0.08	–
1987	24.65	19.50	0.99	4.05	0.11	–
1988	34.24	24.83	1.42	7.67	0.32	–
1989	35.14	25.04	1.24	8.47	0.39	–
1990	36.92	24.70	1.41	10.36	0.45	–
"八五"时期						
1991	40.13	26.44	1.47	11.64	0.58	–
1992	45.14	29.01	1.70	13.71	0.72	–
1993	57.81	36.00	1.98	18.86	0.97	–
1994	85.37	52.36	2.80	29.38	0.83	–
1995	114.07	71.48	2.71	38.69	1.19	–
"九五"时期						
1996	117.65	77.16	3.35	35.25	1.89	–
1997	131.69	87.91	3.86	38.04	1.88	–
1998	141.45	93.56	3.55	42.17	2.17	–
1999	148.61	96.81	3.12	46.27	2.41	–
2000	154.30	100.18	3.64	48.34	2.14	–
"十五"时期						
2001	162.27	105.54	3.27	51.16	2.30	–
2002	167.99	106.27	3.51	55.84	2.37	–
2003	180.30	109.41	4.11	60.90	2.05	3.83
2004	204.39	121.28	4.49	71.87	2.50	4.25
2005	230.46	137.01	5.56	80.56	2.69	4.64

11-4 续表 continued

年份 Year	合计 Total	其中 of which 农业 Farming	林业 Forestry	牧业 Animal Husbandry	渔业 Fishery	农林牧渔服务业 Services of Agriculture,Forestry,Animal Husbandry and Fishing
"十一五"时期						
2006	247.72	147.98	6.44	84.86	2.89	5.55
2007	262.51	154.32	7.28	91.33	3.18	6.41
2008	302.00	173.32	10.63	104.53	4.54	8.97
2009	318.06	192.96	11.16	98.96	4.79	10.18
2010	361.24	231.08	6.87	106.40	5.31	11.58
"十二五"时期						
2011	399.90	240.80	7.98	131.55	6.05	13.51
2012	422.75	251.57	9.00	139.90	6.88	15.39
2013	470.55	284.66	10.34	149.46	8.01	18.07
2014	479.50	291.94	11.19	147.57	8.76	20.03
2015	493.04	296.93	12.15	153.12	9.32	21.52
"十三五"时期						
2016	501.72	298.63	13.20	156.28	9.88	23.74
2017	505.08	296.75	15.25	159.23	7.80	26.06
2018	514.90	318.55	17.72	141.48	7.28	29.88
2019	637.30	424.04	24.99	144.53	6.79	36.96
2020	671.66	447.15	29.82	149.14	6.10	39.46
"十四五"时期						
2021	758.41	501.98	34.41	170.99	8.20	42.83
2021 年分地区 Region						
历下区 Li xia						
市中区 Shi zhong	3.20	0.72	0.21	2.08	0.00	0.19
槐荫区 Huai yin	4.34	2.74	0.65	0.27	0.54	0.13
天桥区 Tian qiao	6.04	3.11	0.51	1.89	0.27	0.27
历城区 Li cheng	75.04	53.19	9.33	5.91	0.36	6.25
长清区 Chang qing	71.60	47.06	3.22	18.11	0.66	2.55
章丘区 Zhang qiu	176.27	118.73	5.26	39.61	1.39	11.29
济阳区 Ji yang	88.05	64.71	2.78	15.83	1.10	3.63
莱芜区 Lai Wu	128.30	89.24	3.49	30.34	1.64	3.59
钢城区 Gang Cheng	22.61	11.58	1.94	8.02	0.13	0.95
平阴县 Ping yin	76.19	47.79	2.63	19.14	0.53	6.10
商河县 Shang he	106.77	63.12	4.38	29.78	1.60	7.90

注：依据 2016 年农业普查数据，对 2007 年至 2017 年农林牧渔业总产值做了相应调整。
Note:According to the data of the agricultural census in 2016, the total output value of agriculture, forestry, animal husbandry and fishery in the period from 2007 to 2017 was adjusted accordingly.

11-5 各时期农林牧渔业总产值定基指数(以1952年为100)

Gross Output Value Indices of Agriculture, Forestry, Animal Husbandry and Fishery in Each Period(1952=100)

年份 Year	合计 Total	其中 of which			
		农业 Farming	林业 Forestry	牧业 Animal Husbandry	渔业 Fishery
1952	100.00	100.00	100.00	100.00	100.00
1957	116.18	114.55	170.35	119.90	109.96
1962	73.32	74.42	69.10	69.25	20.68
1965	123.31	121.76	147.34	141.38	28.95
1970	151.35	146.28	254.82	184.02	58.65
1975	201.09	196.80	317.61	226.74	78.38
"五五"时期					
1976	198.67	185.64	340.19	269.52	118.70
1977	197.95	190.19	373.20	218.87	56.26
1978	208.10	203.90	304.32	239.93	57.89
1979	233.93	224.05	316.47	293.89	53.70
1980	264.53	259.07	286.30	330.80	43.98
"六五"时期					
1981	279.36	279.29	281.28	377.56	55.36
1982	312.68	308.75	346.83	460.13	51.95
1983	402.03	369.18	434.91	460.59	57.98
1984	493.28	436.59	572.67	651.29	69.52
1985	505.48	460.68	992.56	841.94	161.47
"七五"时期					
1986	531.29	488.47	964.62	857.25	229.32
1987	560.14	506.85	1075.00	960.76	291.92
1988	585.14	510.86	992.11	1191.92	383.08
1989	571.95	483.32	886.96	1320.55	495.30
1990	607.77	449.63	1126.99	1931.15	695.49
"八五"时期					
1991	670.19	488.17	1189.04	2204.93	830.45
1992	712.62	491.78	1298.34	2574.55	1007.33
1993	844.31	566.55	1420.51	3221.58	1209.21
1994	945.74	603.90	1671.10	2864.71	1064.29
1995	1093.57	657.49	1508.72	4905.57	1945.11

11-5 续表 continued

年份 Year	合计 Total	其中 of which			
		农业 Farming	林业 Forestry	牧业 Animal Husbandry	渔业 Fishery
"九五"时期					
1996	1197.20	727.03	1818.36	5258.95	2224.25
1997	1273.56	820.27	2002.99	5116.96	2202.07
1998	1426.28	914.05	1858.14	5907.41	2516.54
1999	1486.09	934.64	2110.21	6277.65	2639.47
2000	1569.90	991.58	2255.81	6620.62	2441.73
"十五"时期					
2001	1599.32	1005.16	1700.16	6905.18	2646.43
2002	1638.09	997.16	1826.57	7349.57	2712.97
2003	1711.88	1072.24	1977.78	7726.93	2324.25
2004	1804.32	1132.29	1979.76	8121.00	2803.05
2005	1930.62	1188.90	2237.13	8770.68	2802.30
"十一五"时期					
2006	2046.15	1249.31	2454.25	9245.35	3003.10
2007	2046.15	1334.26	2610.83	9006.43	3540.65
2008	2148.45	1422.32	2783.14	9231.59	3204.85
2009	2260.17	1524.73	2964.04	9342.35	3323.43
2010	2367.76	1584.02	1815.08	10311.68	3416.48
"十二五"时期					
2011	2471.94	1658.47	2016.56	10600.40	3508.72
2012	2588.12	1724.80	2216.20	11151.62	3768.36
2013	2689.05	1762.74	2491.01	11809.56	3877.64
2014	2801.99	1845.58	2724.66	12116.60	3916.41
2015	2919.67	1924.93	2986.23	12540.68	4033.90
"十三五"时期					
2016	3045.21	2007.70	3317.70	12967.06	4187.19
2017	3157.88	2126.15	3689.28	13278.26	4203.93
2018	3095.96	2215.44	4105.56	12733.85	4330.04
2019	3123.82	2290.76	5037.52	11587.80	3814.77
2020	3205.04	2361.77	5979.54	11460.33	3715.59
"十四五"时期					
2021	3474.26	2456.24	6942.25	14142.05	5164.67

11-6 主要农作物播种面积及产量
Sown Areas and Output of Main Farm Crops

指标	Item	2016 年	2017 年	2018 年	2019 年	2020 年	2021 年
农作物总播种面积（万公顷）	Total Sown Area of Crops(10 000 ha)	59.89	56.61	54.90	61.56	61.43	61.48
粮食作物	Grain Crops	47.67	45.15	44.43	47.93	48.04	48.36
谷物	Cereals	46.05	43.79	43.25	46.33	46.38	46.74
小麦	Wheat	22.00	21.58	21.38	21.89	21.73	21.95
稻谷	Rice	0.20	0.18	0.14	0.14	0.06	0.08
玉米	Corn	22.93	21.07	20.84	23.18	23.53	23.64
谷子	Millet	0.86	0.91	0.86	1.09	1.03	1.04
高粱	Jowar	0.05	0.05	0.02	0.01	0.01	0.01
其他	Others	0.01	0.00	0.01	0.01	0.01	0.01
豆类	Beans	0.85	0.70	0.62	0.77	0.77	0.75
薯类	Tubers	0.77	0.66	0.56	0.83	0.90	0.88
油料作物	Oil-bearing Crops	1.00	1.00	1.02	1.92	1.81	1.75
# 花生	Peanuts	0.88	0.87	0.90	1.81	1.67	1.62
棉花	Cotton	0.62	0.20	0.28	0.38	0.35	0.33
蔬菜	Vegetable	9.13	8.86	7.89	10.03	9.86	9.74
果用瓜	Melon	1.20	1.16	1.07	0.98	0.96	1.00
其他作物	Other Farm Crops	0.26	0.25	0.21	0.32	0.40	0.30
果园种植面积（万公顷）	Orchard Area(10 000 ha)	3.20	3.16	3.09	3.89	3.95	3.83
# 苹果	Apple	1.18	1.18	1.13	1.24	1.20	1.20
梨	Pear	0.14	0.14	0.16	0.18	0.19	0.21
葡萄	Grape	0.10	0.10	0.11	0.11	0.11	0.11
桃	Peach	0.49	0.49	0.72	1.00	1.03	0.97
农作物总产量（万吨）	Total Output of Farm Crops(10 000 tons)						
粮食作物	Grain Crops	275.43	255.57	251.42	285.46	290.81	293.07
谷物	Cereals	268.30	249.47	246.12	276.48	280.74	283.22
小麦	Wheat	127.31	123.79	121.78	135.31	137.37	139.25
稻谷	Rice	1.55	1.36	1.18	1.21	0.52	0.63
玉米	Corn	136.65	121.25	119.82	136.11	139.16	139.56
谷子	Millet	2.64	2.97	3.27	3.80	3.64	3.73
高粱	Chinese Sorghum	0.11	0.11	0.04	0.03	0.02	0.03
其他	Other Cereals	0.04	0.00	0.03	0.03	0.03	0.03
豆类	Beans	2.25	1.82	1.67	2.12	2.13	2.05
薯类	Tubers	4.87	4.28	3.63	6.86	7.93	7.80
油料作物	Oil-bearing Crops	3.53	3.59	4.15	6.57	6.82	6.60
# 花生	Peanuts	3.25	3.31	3.87	6.31	6.48	6.29

11-6 续表 continued

指标	Item	2016 年	2017 年	2018 年	2019 年	2020 年	2021 年
棉花	Cotton	0.69	0.20	0.29	0.54	0.42	0.38
蔬菜	Vegetable	611.25	591.63	527.22	671.24	673.73	691.76
果用瓜	Melon	70.74	67.51	59.65	48.02	49.49	50.54
水果总产量(万吨)	**Output of Fruits(10 000 tons)**	**41.08**	**43.15**	**42.19**	**62.95**	**63.20**	**61.90**
# 苹果	Apple	18.33	18.59	16.00	20.22	18.92	19.26
梨	Pear	4.26	3.98	3.40	4.19	3.80	4.16
葡萄	Grape	2.86	3.00	3.00	3.13	3.21	3.33
桃	Peach	11.08	13.10	11.86	21.40	21.87	20.12
杏	Apricot	0.78	0.75	3.02	4.11	4.01	3.47
枣(鲜)	Jujube	1.02	1.02	0.89	1.21	1.01	0.97
柿子(鲜)	Persimmon	0.23	0.23	1.24	2.29	2.51	2.63
山楂	Hawthorn	0.55	0.55	0.63	2.19	2.80	3.15
樱桃	Cherry	1.49	1.45	1.51	2.78	3.82	3.60
其他	Others	0.48	0.47	0.64	1.19	0.98	0.90
农作物单位面积产量(公斤/公顷)	**Output per Hectare of Farm Crops(kg/ha)**						
粮食作物	Grain Crops	5778	5660	5659	5956	6053	6060
谷物	Cereals	5826	5697	5690	5968	6053	6060
小麦	Wheat	5787	5736	5696	6181	6321	6344
稻谷	Rice	7698	7645	8288	8334	8250	7771
玉米	Corn	5960	5754	5748	5872	5914	5903
谷子	Millet	3071	3252	3809	3490	3522	3586
高粱	Chinese Sorghum	2097	2228	2074	1941	1958	2324
其他	Others	2716		3062	2750	2813	2838
豆类	Beans	2659	2614	2716	2747	2784	2738
薯类	Tubers	6371	6462	6462	8248	8835	8886
油料作物	Oil-bearing Crops	3531	3609	4083	3418	3761	3761
# 花生	Peanuts	3713	3795	4327	3495	3878	3883
棉花	Cotton	1106	1037	1029	1410	1193	1170
蔬菜	Vegetable	66918	66798	66852	66895	68337	71058
果用瓜	Melon	46939	58724	55628	48797	51472	50569

注：1. 依据 2006 年农业普查数据，对 1997 年至 2007 年蔬菜面积、产量做了相应调整。
2. 按照国务院农普办要求，由国家统计局山东调查总队根据第三次农业普查数据，对 2016–2017 年市、县(区)粮食播种面积、单产和总产量等数据进行修订。
3. 依据 2016 年农业普查数据，对 2008 年至 2017 年种植业相关品种面积、产量做了相应调整。

Notes:1.According to the data of the agricultural census in 2006, the area and yield of the vegetables from 1997 to 2007 were adjusted.
2.According to the requirements of Agricultural Census Office of the State Council, Shandong Survey Team of National Bureau of Statistics revised the grain sown area, yield per unit and total yield of each city and country (district) from 2016–2017 based on the data from the third agricultural census.
3.According to the agricultural census data in 2016, the area and yield of planting related varieties from 2008 to 2017 were adjusted.

11-7 林、牧、渔业生产情况
Basic Statistics on Forestry,Animal Husbandry and Fishery

指标	Item	单位 Unit	2016 年	2017 年	2018 年	2019 年	2020 年	2021 年
林业生产	Production of Forestry							
造林面积	Forested Area	公顷 (ha)	3504	3809	4902	10758	10939	5333
四旁植树	Surrounding Tree Planting	万株 (10000 trees)	1312	1301	1306	1576	1527	845
育苗面积	Area of Nursery Garden	公顷 (ha)	11773	10645	10174	11579	10750	7781
果品产量	Output of Fruits	吨 (ton)	539475	596994	555042	686868	653290	643282
木材采伐量	Timber Cut	立方米 (cu.m)	157238	214946	283354	355596	298532	223579
牧业生产	Production of Animal Husbandry							
大牲畜存栏	Stocked Large Livestock	万头 (10 000 heads)	28.97	31.63	26.30	24.42	15.26	17.18
#役畜	Draught Animal	万头 (10 000 heads)	0.19	0.02	0.02			
#牛	Cattle	万头 (10 000 heads)	28.69	31.36	26.17	24.27	15.20	17.16
猪存栏	Stocked Pigs	万头 (10 000 heads)	116.73	120.13	102.95	129.26	122.86	131.95
羊存栏	Stocked Sheep	万只 (10 000 heads)	93.27	96.60	87.61	100.13	66.01	73.56
家禽存栏	Stocked Poultry	万只 (10 000 heads)	2743.90	2467.54	2300.42	3440.94	2523.33	2763.07
猪出栏数	Slaughtered Pigs	万头 (10 000 heads)	194.15	198.43	185.59	217.66	157.03	192.00
羊出栏数	Slaughtered Sheep	万只 (10 000 heads)	149.03	153.23	143.84	164.26	86.91	126.84
肉类总产量	Output of Meat	吨 (ton)	317201	325036	298180	358655	239186	273577
#猪牛羊肉	Meat	吨 (ton)	235990	246561	223735	236601	164537	201638

11-7 续表 continued

指标	Item	单位 Unit	2016 年	2017 年	2018 年	2019 年	2020 年	2021 年
猪肉	Pork	吨 (ton)	162114	168054	155005	170584	128052	154189
牛肉	Beef	吨 (ton)	53203	57206	46438	40698	21020	28807
羊肉	Mutton	吨 (ton)	20673	21301	22292	25319	15465	18642
禽肉	Poultry Meat	吨 (ton)	80447	77809	74164	120194	73887	71686
奶类	Milk	吨 (ton)	214620	263642	328412	321323	414297	420987
# 牛奶	Cow Milk	吨 (ton)	214617	263638	328410	321321	414297	420987
禽蛋	Poultry Eggs	吨 (ton)	386440	394001	332303	365810	274673	304983
# 鸡蛋	Hen's Eggs	吨 (ton)	368636	375517	313234	343650	–	–
渔业生产	Aquatic Products							
水产品产量	Total Aquatic Products	吨 (ton)	46709	41279	31911	16167	13294	14068
捕捞	Fishing	吨 (ton)	465	186	289	3513	3291	1187
养殖	Cultured	吨 (tons)	46244	41093	31622	12654	10003	12881
养殖面积	Breeding Area of Aquatic Products	公顷 (ha)	7079	6673	5228	4380	4304	4336
养殖单产	Aquaculture Yield	公斤 / 公顷 (kg/ha)	6533	6158	6049	2889	2324	2971

注：依据 2016 年农业普查数据，对 2008 年至 2017 年牧业生产有关指标做了相应调整。
Note:According to the data of agricultural census in 2016, the relevant indicators of animal husbandry production from 2008 to 2017 were adjusted accordingly.

11-8 分地区主要农作物播种面积及产量(2021 年)
Sown Areas and Output of Main Farm Crops by Region(2021)

指标	Item	济南市 Total City	历下区 Li xia	市中区 Shi zhong
农作物播种总面积(公顷)	**Total Sown Area of Crops(ha)**	**614760**		**4076**
粮食	Grain	483616		3996
谷物	Cereals	467351		3960
小麦	Wheat	219510		1429
稻谷	Rice	806		
玉米	Corn	236414		2363
谷子	Millet	10398		169
高粱	Jowar	121		
其他	Others	102		
豆类	Beans	7486		28
薯类	Tubers	8779		8
油料作物	Oil-bearing Crops	17541		5
# 花生	Peanuts	16207		5
棉花	Cotton	3257		8
蔬菜	Vegetable	97352		59
果用瓜	Melon	9994		9
其他作物	Other Farm Crops	3000		
果园种植面积(公顷)	**Orchard Area(ha)**	**38347**		**247**
# 苹果	Apple	12033		51
梨	Pear	2112		1
葡萄	Grape	1135		17
桃	Peach	9694		117
农作物产量(吨)	**Total Output of Farm Crops(ton)**			
粮食作物	Grain Crops	2930705		19050
谷物	Cereals	2832198		18931
小麦	Wheat	1392481		8397
稻谷	Rice	6260		
玉米	Corn	1395596		10197
谷子	Millet	37289		338
高粱	Jowar	282		
其他	Other Cereals	290		
豆类	Beans	20500		50
薯类	Tubers	78007		69

槐荫区 Huai yin	天桥区 Tian qiao	历城区 Li cheng	长清区 Chang qing	章丘区 Zhang qiu	济阳区 Ji yang	莱芜区 Lai Wu	钢城区 Gang Cheng	平阴县 Ping yin	商河县 Shang he
2367	12866	25210	56469	139943	115726	59513	10795	49250	138543
2147	12374	19757	44227	107515	100814	31475	4321	35270	121719
2022	12374	19135	41502	102745	99812	29342	3757	31130	121571
858	5686	5806	16772	52130	53740	6069	533	17053	59434
409			22	47	327				
717	6688	11951	21026	48053	45639	22224	2975	12641	62137
		1377	3579	2436	107	1048	249	1433	
37			1	79				3	
			102						
95		287	1105	2688	978	250	38	1912	107
31		335	1620	2082	24	1883	526	2228	42
34	18	313	3870	1790	353	5199	3631	2314	14
	18	312	3560	1595	331	5168	3631	1574	14
	43	20	110	682	133	569	239	1057	395
181	385	3194	7992	24891	12968	22075	2542	8861	14204
5	16	1879	113	5060	1383	188	62	1021	257
	30	48	157	4	75	7		726	1954
11	375	10321	3359	6059	832	5586	3236	7752	568
	43	2981	128	2513	121	708	331	5042	115
5	104	883	50	289	112	251	274	59	84
	13	68	17	364	46	237	20	295	58
3	108	3861	936	827	444	1030	2004	207	158
13160	70025	104134	264462	624821	622646	194700	24180	196438	797090
12752	70025	100466	244779	599502	619677	174860	19675	175166	796365
5250	34173	34662	98453	327653	344614	38347	3166	95969	401798
3100			182	335	2644				
4319	35852	61258	128562	264173	271915	134273	15676	74804	394567
		4545	17288	7156	504	2239	833	4386	
84		1	3	187				7	
			290						
224		869	3156	7439	2773	630	103	4939	317
184		2798	16527	17880	196	19210	4402	16332	408

11-8 续表 continued

指标	Item	济南市 Total City	历下区 Li xia	市中区 Shi zhong
油料作物	Oil-bearing Crops	65957		12
# 花生	Peanuts	62930		12
棉花	Cotton	3810		9
蔬菜	Vegetable	6917627		2899
果用瓜	Melon	505365		432
水果总产量(吨)	**Output of Fruits(ton)**	**618972**		**3737**
# 苹果	Apple	192585		1572
梨	Pear	41635		34
葡萄	Grape	33287		528
桃	Peach	201225		1188
杏	Apricot	34662		331
枣(鲜)	Jujube	9667		14
柿子(鲜)	Persimmon	26255		1
山楂	Hawthorn	31458		1
樱桃	Cherry	35968		53
其他	Others	9044		
农作物单位面积产量(公斤/公顷)	**Output per Hectare of Farm Crops(kg/ha)**			
粮食作物	Grain Crops	6060		4767
谷物	Cereals	6060		4780
小麦	Wheat	6344		5877
稻谷	Rice	7771		
玉米	Corn	5903		4316
谷子	Millet	3586		1997
高粱	Jowar	2324		
其他	Others	2838		
豆类	Beans	2738		1800
薯类	Tubers	8886		8400
油料作物	Oil-bearing Crops	3760		2290
# 花生	Peanuts	3883		2290
棉花	Cotton	1170		1114
蔬菜	Vegetable	71058		49419
果用瓜	Melon	50569		50174

注：粮食作物产量、播种面积自 2012 年开始由山东调查总队反馈。
Note:Grain crop yield and sown area have been reported by Shandong Survey Team since 2012.

槐荫区 Huai yin	天桥区 Tian qiao	历城区 Li cheng	长清区 Chang qing	章丘区 Zhang qiu	济阳区 Ji yang	莱芜区 Lai Wu	钢城区 Gang Cheng	平阴县 Ping yin	商河县 Shang he
	54	1621	17899	5650	1785	19946	9550	9412	28
	54	1619	17171	5330	1738	19719	9550	7709	28
	71	25	153	730	155	709	304	1157	498
11251	13738	166985	549528	1861622	1189918	1220409	208299	673140	1019838
210	685	82509	4840	253621	71884	7326	3141	67718	12999
125	8315	119239	58385	72911	22374	110276	105602	101186	16821
	1160	23236	3017	38151	3746	20084	17547	81223	2849
25	3269	17984	1607	2820	2841	5866	1262	1714	4213
5	303	2268	458	11102	1354	4662	678	7663	4267
90	3053	52591	14828	11016	11232	24232	75575	3544	3876
5	185	3427	15373	517	506	12102	1087	267	863
	150	227	296	5517	911	1323	274	402	552
		3067	5555	135	865	14062	2120	417	34
		12907	134	580	113	13871	3152	685	16
	80	2688	16974	2830	5	10285	2101	881	71
	115	685	13	59	775	1365	1600	4350	81
6128	5659	5271	5980	5811	6176	6186	5596	5570	6549
6306	5659	5250	5898	5835	6208	5959	5237	5627	6551
6118	6010	5970	5870	6285	6413	6318	5945	5628	6760
7572			8385	7080	8079				
6020	5361	5126	6114	5498	5958	6042	5269	5918	6350
		3300	4830	2938	4725	2137	3345	3062	
2250		2400	2723	2365				2055	
			2838						
2365		3030	2857	2768	2835	2520	2701	2583	2969
6000		8347	10200	8588	8250	10200	8370	7331	9805
	3000	5173	4625	3156	5051	3837	2630	4068	2090
	3000	5192	4824	3342	5246	3816	2630	4899	2090
	1650	1265	1389	1069	1165	1245	1274	1094	1260
62067	35702	52286	68758	74790	91758	55285	81954	75964	71800
41981	41587	43919	42858	50121	51980	38902	50444	66321	50553

11-9 分地区林、牧、渔业生产情况 (2021 年)
Basic Statistics on Forestry,Animal Husbandry and Fishery by Region(2021)

指标	Item	单位 Unit	济南市 Total City	历下区 Li xia
林业生产	Production of Forestry			
造林面积	Forested Area	公顷 (ha)	5333	
四旁植树	Surrounding Tree Planting	万株 (10 000 trees)	845	
育苗面积	Area of Nursery Garden	公顷 (ha)	7781	
果品产量	Output of Fruits	吨 (ton)	643282	
木材采伐量	Timber Cut	立方米 (stere)	223579	
牧业生产	Production of Animal Husbandry			
大牲畜存栏	Stocked Large Livestock	万头 (10 000 heads)	17.18	
# 役畜	Draught Animal	万头 (10 000 heads)		
# 牛	Cattle	万头 (10 000 heads)	17.16	
猪存栏	Stocked Pigs	万头 (10 000 heads)	131.95	
羊存栏	Stocked Sheep	万只 (10 000 heads)	73.56	
家禽存栏	Stocked Poultry	万只 (10 000 heads)	2763.07	
猪出栏数	Slaughtered Pigs	万头 (10 000 heads)	192.00	
羊出栏数	Slaughtered Sheep	万只 (10 000 heads)	126.84	
肉类总产量	Output of Meat	吨 (ton)	273577	
# 猪牛羊肉	Meat	吨 (ton)	201638	
猪肉	Pork	吨 (ton)	154189	
牛肉	Beef	吨 (ton)	28807	
羊肉	Mutton	吨 (ton)	18642	
禽肉	Poultry Meat	吨 (ton)	71686	
奶类	Milk	吨 (ton)	420987	
# 牛奶	Cow Milk	吨 (ton)	420987	
禽蛋	Poultry Eggs	吨 (ton)	304983	
渔业生产	Aquatic Products			
水产品产量	Total Aquatic Products	吨 (ton)	14068	
捕捞	Fishing	吨 (ton)	1187	
养殖	Cultured	吨 (ton)	12881	
养殖面积	Breeding Area of Aquatic Products	公顷 (ha)	4336	
养殖单产	Aquaculture Yield	公斤 / 公顷 (kg/ha)	2971	

市中区 Shi zhong	槐荫区 Huai yin	天桥区 Tian qiao	历城区 Li cheng	长清区 Chang qing	章丘区 Zhang qiu	济阳区 Ji yang	莱芜区 Lai Wu	钢城区 Gang Cheng	平阴县 Ping yin	商河县 Shang he
27			1547	733	1333		1073	140	80	400
151	10		60	133	190	70	175			56
24	33	15	1456	3085	753	693	565	43	84	1028
8492		674	366080	56098	22502	7734	89011	52525	25360	14806
299	996	2412	2892	72326	31929	34665	6996	37737	18391	14937
0.10	0.04	0.08	0.50	2.27	0.92	1.56	1.13	0.34	2.91	7.33
0.10	0.04	0.08	0.49	2.26	0.92	1.56	1.13	0.34	2.91	7.33
0.85	0.06	2.02	4.16	19.28	18.39	9.34	23.91	13.84	16.08	24.02
4.77	0.20	4.59	1.75	5.99	8.80	5.41	17.98	7.49	5.47	11.11
22.95	4.47	91.89	154.70	300.51	653.53	192.42	544.06	187.58	290.45	320.52
1.27	0.09	2.47	5.86	23.99	27.96	13.73	40.34	21.07	22.10	33.11
5.84	0.51	8.78	3.24	8.64	12.31	13.05	28.87	15.40	9.81	20.39
2949	398	5599	9762	28998	45015	21147	57497	26071	29069	47072
2597	285	3636	6977	25061	27830	15418	40843	21116	21081	36793
1007	81	1988	4657	20224	23086	10363	31543	17130	17084	27026
723	128	373	1783	3497	2922	3466	4923	1668	2582	6744
867	77	1275	537	1340	1822	1590	4376	2319	1415	3024
352	112	1963	2779	3898	17140	5726	16531	4955	7950	10279
329	31	1175	8936	69547	5921	37707	1427	1066	70357	224491
329	31	1175	8936	69547	5921	37707	1427	1066	70357	224491
4339	876	10951	31289	47263	57939	19262	38007	21602	35647	37809
	1256	414	368	903	1620	3180	3610	217	741	1759
		30	18	89		33	919			98
	1256	384	350	814	1620	3147	2691	217	741	1661
	120	69	50	346	360	659	1720	270	446	296
	10467	5565	7000	2353	4500	4775	1565	804	1661	5611

11-10 主要农副产品产量与上年和历史最高年份比较
Output of Major Agricultural Products in Comparision with Last Year and Maximum Year

单位：万吨 (10 000 tons)

指标	Item	2021 年	2020 年	历史最高年 Maximum Year 年份 Year	历史最高年 Maximum Year 产量 Output	2021 年为历史最高年的% 2021 Account for Historic High	2021 年为 2020 年的% 2021 Account for 2020
农产品产量	Total Output of Farm Crops						
粮食总产量	Output of Grain Crops	293.07	290.81	2011	295.84	99.1	100.8
#小麦	Wheat	139.25	137.37	2021	139.25	100.0	101.4
稻谷	Rice	0.63	0.52	2000	9.89	6.4	121.2
玉米	Corn	139.56	139.16	2011	143.96	96.9	100.3
薯类	Tubers	7.80	7.93	1995	23.10	33.8	98.4
经济作物	Commercial Crop						
#棉花	Cotton	0.38	0.42	1999	5.00	7.6	90.5
油料花生	Peanuts	6.29	6.48	2020	6.48	97.1	97.1
蔬菜总产量	Output of Vegetable	691.76	673.73	2020	673.73	102.7	102.7
水果总产量	Output of Fruits	61.90	63.20	2020	63.20	97.9	97.9
水产品总产量	Total Aquatic Products	1.4	1.3	2015	4.80	29.2	107.7

主要统计指标解释

乡村户数 指长期（一年以上）居住在乡镇（不包括城关镇）行政管理区域内的住户，还包括居住在城关镇所辖行政村范围内的农村住户。户口不在本地而在本地居住一年及以上的住户也包括在本地农村住户内；有本地户口，但举家外出一年以上的住户，无论是否保留承包耕地都不包括在本地农村住户范围内。不包括乡村地区内的国有经济的机关、团体、学校、企业、事业单位的集体户。

乡村人口数 指乡村地区常住居民户数中的常住人口数，即经常在家或在家居住6个月以上，而且经济和生活与本户连成一体的人口。外出从业人员在外居住时间虽然在6个月以上，但收入主要带回家中，经济与本户连为一体，仍视为家庭常住人口；在家居住，生活和本户连成一体的国家职工、退休人员也为家庭常住人口。但是现役军人、中专及以上（走读生除外）的在校学生以及常年在外（不包括探亲、看病等）且已有稳定的职业与居住场所的外出从业人员，不应当作家庭常住人口。

农林牧渔业总产值 是以货币表现的农、林、牧、渔业全部产品的总量，它反映一定时期内农林牧渔业生产的总规模和总成果。

农、林、牧、渔四业的统计范围是辖区内各种经济组织类型、各个系统的全部农林牧渔业生产单位和非农行业单位附属的农林牧渔业生产活动单位。不包括农业科学试验机构进行的农业生产。

农林牧渔业总产值的核算范围是本辖区内在一定时期内生产的农业、林业、牧业、渔业产品的价值和对农林牧渔业生产活动进行的各种支持性服务活动的价值总和，执行日历年度。

（1）农业产值，包括谷物和其他作物产值：蔬菜，园艺作物产值：水果，坚果，饮料和香料产值；中药材产值。其中谷物和其他作物产值包括谷物、薯类、豆类、棉花、油料，糖料，麻类、烟叶和其他农作物的产值。其他农作物包括青饲料，绿肥、牧草、桑叶及采集的野生植物。

（2）林业，包括林木的培育和种植（不包括茶园、桑园和果园的栽培，管理和收获等活动）。林产品的采集和竹木采伐。

（3）牧业，包括除渔业养殖以外的一切动物饲养和放牧以及捕猎野兽野禽产值。

（4）渔业，包括水生动物和海藻类植物的养殖和捕捞。

（5）农林牧渔服务业，包括灌溉，农产品初加工。农机服务，病虫害防治、森林防火、兽医服务、鱼苗及鱼种场等对农林牧渔业生产活动进行的各种支持性服务活动。但不包括各种科学技术和专业技术服务活动。农林牧渔业总产值核算采用“产品法”进行计算，即用产品产量乘以价格以求出各种产品产值，然后加总求得各业产值，最后各业相加求得农林牧渔业总产值。

1957 年以前的农业总产值中包括了厩肥和农民自给性手工业（如农民自制衣服、鞋、袜，自己从事粮食初步加工等）。1958 年及以后的农业总产值，林业中增加了村及村以下竹木采伐产值；牧业中取消了厩肥产值；副业中取消了农民自给性手工业产值，增加了村及村以下办的工业产值；渔业中增加了海洋捕捞水产品产值。1980 年及以后的农业总产值，在副业中增加了农民家庭兼营工业商品性部分的产值。从1984 年起村及村以下办工业产值划归工业。从1993 年起取消副业，将采集野生植物产值和农民家庭兼营商品性工业产值划归农业产值，捕猎野兽、野禽产值划入牧业产值。2003 年根据新的国民经济行业分类，农林牧渔服务业划归第一产业。原农业产值中的农民家庭兼营商品性工业产值划归工业产值；林业中竹木采伐产值统计范围由村及村以下改为全社会。

农林牧渔业增加值 是指农、林、牧、渔及农林牧渔服务业生产货物或提供服务活动而增加的价值，为农林牧渔业现价总产值扣除农林渔业现价中间投入后的余额。

农林牧渔业增加值的核算范围同农林牧渔业总产值的核算范围相同。

农林牧渔业增加值的计算方法：采用生产法和分配法（收入法）两种。

1. 生产法计算公式：

农林牧渔业增加值 = 农林牧渔业总产值 - 农林牧渔业中间消耗

2. 分配法计算公式：

农林牧渔业增加值 = 固定资产折旧 + 劳动者报酬 + 生产税净额 + 营业盈余

其中：生产税净额 = 生产税收 - 生产补贴

粮食产量 指日历年度内生产的全部粮食数量。按收获季节包括夏收粮食、早稻和秋收粮食，按作物品种包括谷物、薯类和豆类。其产量计算方法：谷物按脱粒后的原粮计算，豆类按去豆荚后的干豆计算；薯类（包括甘薯和马铃薯，不包括芋头和木薯）1964 年以前按每 4 公斤鲜薯折 1 公斤粮食计算，从1964 年开始改为按 5 公斤鲜薯折 1 公斤粮食计算；城市郊区作为蔬菜的薯类（如马铃薯等）按鲜品计算，并且不作粮食统计。1989 年以前全国粮食产量数据主要靠全面报表取得，1989 年开始使用抽样调查数据。

油料产量 指全部油料作物的生产量。包括花生、油菜籽、芝麻、向日葵籽、胡麻籽（亚麻籽）和其他油料。不包括大豆、木本油料和野生油料。花生以带壳干花生计算。

水产品产量 指人工养殖的水产品和天然生长的水产的捕捞量。包括海水的鱼类、虾蟹类、贝类和藻类以及淡水的鱼类、虾蟹类和贝类，不包括淡水水生植物。

猪、牛、羊肉产量 指当年出栏并已屠宰的猪、牛、羊的肉产量。即屠宰后除去头蹄下水后带骨肉（即胴体重）的重量。

耕地面积 指年初可以用来种植农作物、经常进行耕锄的田地，包括熟地、当年新开荒地、连续撂荒未满三年的耕地和当年的休闲地（轮歇地），还包括以种植农作物为主并附带种植桑树、茶树、果树和其他林木的土地，以及沿海、沿湖地区已围垦利用的“海涂”“湖田”等面积。

不包括属于专业性的桑园、茶园、果园、果木苗圃、林地、芦苇地、天然或人工草地面积。

农作物播种面积 指实际播种或移植有农作物的面积。凡是实际种植有农作物的面积，不论种植在耕地上还是种植在非耕地上，均包括在农作物播种面积中。在播种季节基本结束后，因遭灾而重新改种和补种的农作物面积，也包括在内。

农用化肥施用量 指本年内实际用于农业生产的化肥数量，包括氮肥、磷肥、钾肥和复合肥。化肥施用量要求按折纯量计算数量。折纯量是指把氮肥、磷肥、钾肥分别按含氮、含五氧化二磷、含氧化钾的百分之一百成份进行折算后的数量。复合肥按其所含主要成分折算。

农业机械总动力 指主要用于农、林、牧、渔业的各种动力机械的动力总和。包括耕作机械、排灌机械、收获机械、农产品加工机械、运输机械、植物保护机械、牧业机械、林业机械、渔业机械和其他农业机械（内燃机按引擎马力折成瓦（特）计算），电动机按功率折成瓦特计算。不包括专门用于乡办工业、基本建设、非农业运输、科学试验和教学等非农业生产方面用的动力机械与作业机械。

Explanatory Notes on Main Statistical Indicators

Number of rural households refers to the households living within the administrative management regions of villages and towns (excluding counties) for a long term (more than one year), including rural households living in administrative villages under the jurisdiction of counties. The households who have no local census register but live locally for one year and above are also included in local rural households; those households who move out for more than one year are excluded from local rural households, although they have local census register, whether they retain contracted lands. This excludes collective households of state-owned economy organs, organizations, schools, enterprises and public institutions within rural regions.

Number of rural populations refers to the number of permanent residents in permanent households living in rural regions, which means the population who are often at home or for more than 6 months, and have local economic and living activities. Migrant workers are also deemed as household permanent population because their incomes are taken back and economic activities are linked with the household, although they live outside for more than six months; This also includes national employees and retirees who live at home and whose economic activities are linked with the households. However, military personnel in active service, students in technical secondary schools and above (other than non-resident students) and migrant workers who live outsides for years (excluding visiting relatives and seeking for medical treatment, etc.) and have stable occupations and living places are excluded.

Gross Output Value of Farming, Forestry, Animal Husbandry and Fishery refers to the total volume of products of farming, forestry, animal husbandry and fishery in monetary expression, which reflects the total scale and the total result of farming, forestry, animal husbandry and fishery production during a given period.

The scope of statistics of farming, forestry, animal husbandry and fishing covers various economic organizations in the area under administration as well as agriculture, forestry, animal husbandry and fishery production activity units which all agriculture, forestry, animal husbandry and fishing production units and units in non-agricultural industries of all systems are subordinate to, excluding agricultural production by agricultural science experiment organization.

The scope of accounting of the gross output value of farming, forestry, animal husbandry and fishery is the sum of the value of agriculture, forestry, animal husbandry and fishery products produced in the area under administration within a certain period and the value of various supportive service activities in agriculture, forestry, animal husbandry and fishery production activities based on a calendar year.

(1) The value of agricultural production includes the output value of cereal and other crop: output value of vegetables and horticultural plants: output value of fruits, nuts, beverages and spices; output value of traditional Chinese medicinal materials. Output value of cereal and other crops includes that of cereal, potato, bean, cotton, oil plants, sugar, bast fiber plants, tobacco and other crops. Other crops include green feed, green manure, pasture, folium mori and collected wild plants.

(2) Forestry includes cultivation and plantation of the forest (excluding cultivation, management and harvesting of tea plantation, mulberry plantation and orchard). Acquisition of forest products and bamboo and wood cutting.

(3) Animal husbandry includes output value of animal feeding and grazing and hunting wild animals and wildfowls except for fishery breeding.

(4) Fishery includes breeding and fishing of aquatic animals and seaweed plants.

(5) Farming, forestry, animal husbandry and fishery service industry include irrigation and primary processing of agricultural products. Various supportive service activities (such as agricultural machinery service, pest control, forest fire prevention, veterinary service and fry and seed farm) for agriculture, forestry, animal husbandry and fishery production activities, excluding various service activities of scientific technology and professional technology. The gross output value of farming, forestry, animal husbandry and fishery is calculated by "product approach", which means the gross output value of agriculture, forestry, animal husbandry and fishery is obtained after adding the output value of all industries obtained by adding the output value of various products originating from the production output multiplying by the price.

Gross output value of farming before 1957 includes animal manure and peasant self-catering handicraft industry (including homemade clothes, shoes and socks of farmers as well as preliminary processing of grain by farmers). As for the gross output value of agriculture in 1958 and later, the output value of bamboo and wood cutting of the village and below is added in the forestry; output value of animal manure is cancelled in the animal husbandry; output value of peasant self-catering handicraft industry is cancelled and output value of the industry of the village and below is added in the sideline; output value of aquatic products based on marine fishing is added in the fishery. As for gross output value of agriculture in 1980 and later, output value of industrial commodities concurrently operated by the peasant family is added in the sideline. Output value of the industry of the village and below from 1984 was incorporated into value of industrial output. The sideline was cancelled from 1993. The output value of wild plants acquired and output of commercial industry concurrently operated by peasant family are classified into value of agricultural production and output of wild animals and wild birds hunted is included into output of animal husbandry. Agriculture, forestry, animal husbandry and fishery service industry was classified into the primary industry in 2003 pursuant to the new classification of national economy industries. Output value of the commercial industry concurrently operated by the peasant family in the original value of agricultural production is included into value of industrial output; the scope of statistics of the output value of bamboo and wood cutting in the forestry is changed to the whole society.

Value added of agriculture, forestry, animal husbandry and fishery refers to the value added due to production of goods or provision of service in agriculture, forestry, animal husbandry and fishing and agriculture, it is the balance of the total output value at the current price of agriculture, forestry, animal husbandry and fishery minus by intermediate input at the current price of agriculture, fishing and forestry.

The scope of accounting of the value added of agriculture, forestry, animal husbandry and fishery is the same to the gross output value of farming, forestry, animal husbandry and fishery.

The method for computing the value added of farming, forestry, animal husbandry and fishery: Production approach and distribution approach (income approach) are adopted:

1. Calculation formula of production approach:

Value added of agriculture, forestry, animal husbandry and fishery = gross output value of agriculture, forestry, animal husbandry and fishery – intermediate consumption of agriculture, forestry, animal husbandry and fishery

2. Calculation formula of distribution approach:

Value added of agriculture, forestry, animal husbandry and fishery = depreciation of fixed assets + remuneration for workers + net production tax + operating surplus

Wherein: Net production tax = production tax – production subsidy

Grain output refers to the total output of grains produced within a calendar year. It includes summer crops, early rice and autumn crops by harvest seasons; and covers cereals, tubers and beans by type of crops. Output of cereals cover husked grain only. Output of beans refers to dry beans without pods. The output of tubers (sweet potatoes and potatoes, not including taros and cassava) are converted with the ratio of 4:1, i.e. 4 kilograms of fresh tubers were equivalent to 1 kilogram of grain before 1964. Since 1964 the ratio has been changed to 5:1. Tubers consumed as vegetables (such as potatoes) in cities and suburbs are calculated as fresh vegetables and their output is not included in the output of grain. Data on grain production before 1989 were obtained through the comprehensive statistical reporting system. Since 1989, data from sample surveys are used.

Output of Oil–bearing Crops refers to the total production of oil bearing crops of various kinds, including peanuts, sesame, sunflower seeds, flax seeds, and other oil bearing crops. Soybeans, oil bearing woody plants, and wild oil–bearing crops are not included. Only shelled dry peanuts are included.

Output of Aquatic Products refers to catches of both artificially cultured and naturally grown aquatic products, including fish, shrimps, crabs, shellfish and algae in sea and fish, shrimps, crabs and shellfish in fresh water. Freshwater plants are not included.

Output of Pork, Beef, and Mutton refers to the output of meat of slaughtered hogs, cattle, sheep and goats with head, feet, and offal taken away.

Cultivated Area refers to area of the farmland used to plant crops at the beginning of the year which is often plowed, including cultivated land, new cultivated land that very year, arable land abandoned for less than three years consecutively, fallow land (rotation land) that very year, the land mainly planting crops complemented by plantation of white mulberry, tea tree, fruit tree and other forest as well as "shoal" and "shoaly land" having been subject to reclamation and utilization in coastal and lake–side areas.

Excluded from this category are professional mulberry field, tea garden, orchard, nurseries of young plants, woods, reeds, natural or artificial grass area.

Sown Area of Crops refers to area of land sown or transplanted with crops regardless of being in cultivated area or non–cultivated area. Area of land re–sown due to natural disasters is also included.

Consumption of Chemical Fertilizers in Agriculture refers to the quantity of chemical fertilizers applied in agriculture in the year, including nitrogenous fertilizer, phosphate fertilizer, potash fertilizer, and compound fertilizer. The consumption of chemical fertilizers is required in calculation to convert the gross weight into weight containing 100% effective component (e.g. 100% nitrogen content in nitrogenous fertilizer, 100% phosphorous pent oxide contents in phosphate fertilizer, 100% potassium oxide contents in potash fertilizer). Compound fertilizer is converted with its major component.

Total Power of Farm Machinery refers to total mechanical power of machinery used in farming, forestry, animal husbandry, and fishery, including ploughing, irrigation and drainage, harvesting, transport, plant protection, stock breeding, forestry and fishery. The power of internal combustion engines is required to convert horsepower into watts and the power of electric motors is required to be converted into watts. Machinery employed for non– agricultural purposes, such as the machines used in township run and village run industry, construction, non–agricultural transport, scientific experiments and teaching, is excluded.

工 业

INDUSTRY

12-1 各时期全部工业基本情况
Basic Statistics on Total Industry in Each Period

年份 Year	全部工业单位数（个）Number of Industial Enterprises (Unit)		工业总产值（亿元）Gross Industrial Output Value (100 million yuan)		工业增加值（亿元）Value Added of Industry Enterprises (100 million yuan)		国有独立核算工业（万元）State-owned Independent Accounting Industrial (10 000 yuan)	
	合计 Total	# 国有单位 State-owned	合计 Total	# 国有单位 State-owned	合计 Total	# 国有单位 State-owned	利润总额 Total Profits	利税总额 Total Profits and Taxes
1949	52	-	1.20	0.52	0.40	0.15	190	541
1952	92	-	2.97	1.65	1.09	0.52	1616	2761
1957	399	-	6.90	6.13	2.18	1.84	5742	10065
1962	847	286	6.67	5.61	2.36	1.80	3293	8242
1965	724	247	11.99	10.09	4.34	3.39	16246	22906
1970	828	285	23.12	17.93	7.56	5.64	19347	31834
1975	1041	326	26.41	18.87	8.46	5.50	11555	27846
1978	1319	398	39.06	25.87	12.89	7.11	28852	53031
1979	1353	359	42.95	28.90	14.10	8.01	31875	57532
1980	1535	356	45.31	30.37	14.24	8.85	32909	59572
“六五”时期								
1981	1538	350	47.61	31.72	15.11	9.47	35077	62657
1982	1619	357	51.98	33.91	15.79	10.01	32062	64673
1983	1674	369	59.06	36.99	17.96	11.49	35870	60308
1984	1981	325	66.96	39.78	20.10	13.17	45869	83520
1985	2584	477	74.41	44.66	27.54	16.97	61274	112154
“七五”时期								
1986	3005	369	86.93	48.71	28.69	17.53	54804	115006
1987	3957	361	107.63	56.16	32.88	19.40	58715	125775
1988	5252	372	138.05	68.58	47.49	25.09	80173	156056
1989	7655	380	158.53	76.19	54.66	30.51	76571	170703
1990	11020	394	222.63	116.92	60.43	37.11	25084	125522
“八五”时期								
1991	12211	376	245.73	131.35	67.73	43.35	36715	151718
1992	15374	373	303.33	162.35	86.85	48.97	55463	193000
1993	19392	376	448.25	230.93	115.36	69.65	57984	223445
1994	22009	366	614.08	236.40	154.49	69.64	60393	240473
1995	24621	495	752.23	279.16	194.16	83.12	65335	316289
“九五”时期								
1996	32902	425	834.45	260.16	238.31	91.30	79615	337807
1997	33000	325	897.59	263.34	278.87	92.99	95267	343426
1998	32793	227	966.62	234.03	298.41	94.28	42152	292991

12-1 续表 continued

年份 Year	全部工业单位数（个）Number of Industial Enterprises (Unit)		工业总产值（亿元）Gross Industrial Output Value (100 million yuan)		工业增加值（亿元）Value Added of Industry Enterprises (100 million yuan)		国有独立核算工业（万元）State-owned Independent Accounting Industrial (10 000 yuan)	
	合计 Total	# 国有单位 State-owned	合计 Total	# 国有单位 State-owned	合计 Total	# 国有单位 State-owned	利润总额 Total Profits	利税总额 Total Profits and Taxes
1999	29319	211	981.78	212.95	318.80	79.51	-2340	254619
2000	30899	195	994.00	237.14	336.61	81.00	34824	292198
"十五"时期								
2001	34135	169	1090.70	140.44	356.72	64.69	49222	226242
2002	30064	155	1302.00	144.78	410.98	49.16	28011	234986
2003	30258	126	1544.50	167.30	494.55	68.80	53363	302975
2004	31163	115	1981.80	150.70	620.14	37.21	-3943	72684
2005	31370	102	2447.51	177.00	786.11	66.49	268573	354111
"十一五"时期								
2006	35370	86	2806.94	193.10	861.48	73.95	315323	458191
2007	36112	76	3389.09	283.32	985.78	103.65	364790	751182
2008	36416	80	4829.16	338.24	1140.14	136.55	418265	853091
2009	37656	77	5096.98	345.44	1191.36	166.36	422898	885006
2010	37521	66	5800.39	404.38	1352.42	284.75	643216	1162785
"十二五"时期								
2011	36750	54	5544.60	478.10	1507.88		561683	1217350
2012	35917	52	5535.25	491.20	1603.08		646193	1401892
2013	38443	30	5711.48	280.63	1690.63		551967	665206
2014	38753	25	5861.98	246.26	1822.11		507491	611865
2015	38793	24	5877.28	204.79	1844.37		517575	571354
"十三五"时期								
2016	34310	16	6059.16	157.83	1878.83		540739	622714
2017	33725	12	6395.21	147.27	2003.10		583734	589999
2018	31270	13	5641.61	15.50	2145.10			5014
2019					2167.87			
2020					2360.48			
"十四五"时期								
2021					2746.00			

注：1. 工业增加值、工业总产值按当年价格计算。
2. 1985 年、1995 年因工业普查对教育局校办工厂统计方法的规定，故国有单位较多。
3. 2001 年后炼油、浪潮、将军等原国有企业陆续改制，故国有数字较以前年份有所减小。
4. 2004 年第一次经济普查后，统计年鉴包含济南供电公司年报数据。
5. 非经济普查年度，除"工业增加值"外，其他指标空缺。

Notes:1.Industrial value added and total industrial output value are calculated according to the current year' s prices.
2.There were many state-owned units in 1985 and 1995 due to the provisions regarding statistical approach for school-run factories of Education Bureau from industrial census.
3.Original state-owned enterprises such as Oil Refining, Inspur and General were subject to restructuring in succession after 2001, so the quantity of state-owned enterprises decreased in comparison to that of previous years.
4.After the economic census for the first time in 2004, statistical yearbook includes annual report data of Ji' nan Power Supply Company.
5.In years other than the year of economic census, indicators are blank, excluding "Value Added of Industrial Enterprises".

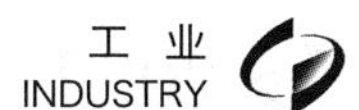

12-2 各时期规模以上工业基本情况

Basic Statistics of Industrial Enterprises Above Designated Size in Each Period

单位：亿元 (100 million yuan)

年份 Year	单位数 （个） Number of Enterprises (unit)	工业总产值 Gross Industrial Output Value	工业增加值 Value Added of Industry Enterprises	营业收入 Business Revenue	利税总额 Total Profits and Taxes	利润总额 Total Profits	资产总计 Total Assets	所有者权益 Owner's Equities
1949	52	1.06	0.40	0.91	0.07	0.03	0.58	0.17
1952	92	2.83	1.02	2.40	0.32	0.18	1.89	0.55
1957	399	6.04	2.08	5.85	1.04	0.60	2.85	0.83
1962	847	6.65	2.15	6.87	0.92	0.39	5.66	1.65
1965	724	11.89	4.07	9.49	2.47	1.73	5.93	1.73
1970	828	22.94	7.29	19.30	3.66	2.22	10.67	3.10
1975	1041	26.16	7.94	19.70	3.47	1.55	17.21	5.01
1978	1319	37.67	9.94	31.39	6.80	3.88	25.68	7.47
1979	1353	38.79	11.18	35.51	7.21	4.13	27.19	7.91
1980	1535	43.60	12.15	36.90	7.51	4.26	29.22	8.50
“六五”时期								
1981	1538	42.26	12.77	39.84	7.98	4.37	31.49	9.20
1982	1619	45.58	13.63	42.94	8.13	4.18	34.52	10.08
1983	1674	49.64	14.86	46.38	8.84	4.74	38.09	11.12
1984	1981	55.95	17.91	52.16	10.46	5.82	41.66	12.16
1985	1915	66.98	23.10	64.76	13.98	7.62	47.09	13.75
“七五”时期								
1986	2036	75.67	24.54	73.98	14.38	7.07	56.79	16.70
1987	2004	88.17	27.24	86.19	15.88	7.52	64.21	18.88
1988	1984	107.76	35.39	113.84	19.65	10.37	81.67	24.01
1989	1993	118.88	43.20	131.86	20.88	9.73	104.34	30.68
1990	2008	174.89	41.63	136.29	15.57	3.23	125.25	36.82
“八五”时期								
1991	1985	194.29	44.84	160.58	18.46	4.97	138.34	40.81
1992	1941	236.37	60.16	200.54	23.48	7.84	167.44	49.39
1993	2156	319.49	104.43	309.91	31.88	10.26	338.15	99.61
1994	2202	414.81	113.71	346.13	41.69	13.61	462.34	136.14
1995	2648	526.48	130.88	432.17	53.59	16.30	578.55	180.86
“九五”时期								
1996	2301	549.40	175.21	494.99	66.82	27.83	705.50	225.53

注：1. 工业增加值、工业总产值按当年价格计算。
2. 1997 年及以前统计口径为乡及乡以上工业企业，1998 年及以后为全部国有及年销售收入 500 万元以上工业企业，2011 年及以后为年主营业务收入 2000 万元以上工业企业。
3. 1991 年及以前“工业增加值”指标为“工业净产值”指标。
4. 2018 年及以前“营业收入”“营业成本”“税金及附加”指标为“主营业务收入”“主营业务成本”及“主营业务税金及附加”指标。以下相关各表同。
5. 自 2019 年起，不再包含省直单位相关数据。以下相关各表同。
6. 自 2019 年起，数据为济南市、莱芜市区划调整后合并数据，之前年度数据为原济南市数据。以下相关各表同。
7. 表中的合计数和部分计算数据因小数取舍而产生的误差，均未作机械调整。以下相关各表同。

12-2 续表 continued

年份 Year	单位数（个）Number of Enterprises (unit)	工业总产值 Gross Industrial Output Value	工业增加值 Value Added of Industry Enterprises	营业收入 Business Revenue	利税总额 Total Profits and Taxes	利润总额 Total Profits	资产总计 Total Assets	所有者权益 Owner's Equities
1997	1843	603.30	194.42	605.81	70.12	26.99	882.36	286.59
1998	1060	593.83	189.88	539.29	58.56	18.62	882.38	297.81
1999	1064	628.59	201.38	579.64	59.17	15.97	931.22	302.21
2000	1038	680.04	219.19	629.72	64.62	21.69	958.10	363.37
“十五”时期								
2001	1015	786.70	252.61	746.92	77.79	28.45	984.71	369.40
2002	1125	1009.04	325.98	917.31	92.71	32.13	1120.60	407.36
2003	1319	1318.54	426.30	1223.76	132.84	54.71	1312.97	440.85
2004	1512	1781.78	560.15	1677.93	175.98	83.68	1473.90	507.63
2005	1670	2237.51	722.11	2142.84	244.61	131.30	1868.06	630.06
“十一五”时期								
2006	1752	2591.65	797.70	2490.94	289.78	153.74	2000.62	702.78
2007	1820	3189.09	926.58	3086.85	358.87	199.73	2337.09	903.87
2008	2016	3862.64	1052.48	3766.93	425.72	220.79	2899.47	1123.03
2009	2156	3950.77	1154.01	3868.70	500.63	275.85	3478.94	1572.11
2010	2021	4485.61	1313.00	4497.17	584.53	339.76	3904.42	1481.75
“十二五”时期								
2011	1417	4028.49	–	4165.19	453.47	242.63	3932.90	1407.89
2012	1647	4248.29	–	4454.97	498.24	253.06	4109.29	1582.77
2013	1901	4777.47	–	4926.11	539.49	312.95	4249.79	1671.91
2014	1984	5253.05	–	5406.67	606.60	357.82	4564.86	1846.32
2015	2021	5339.97	–	5417.16	685.71	396.13	4987.76	2159.78
“十三五”时期								
2016	1962	5486.56	–	5714.29	729.75	421.11	5501.88	2301.94
2017	2051	5770.91	–	5810.16	686.80	415.23	6319.64	2268.27
2018	1889	4992.28	–	5192.15	535.39	307.98	5892.64	2386.75
2019	2153	5839.18	–	6512.66	545.70	310.86	6663.13	2743.28
2020	2215	6765.08	–	7575.34	659.87	423.31	7724.85	2967.31
“十四五”时期								
2021	2543	7591.25	–	8492.55	645.49	408.38	8494.19	3380.30

Notes:1.The value added and total output of industrial enterprises are calculated as per the price of the years.

2.The statistic scale of year 1997 and before involves industrial enterprises in rural areas and above level, that of year 1998 and onwards involves all state-owned industrial enterprises and industrial enterprises with the annual sales revenue of RMB 5 million, and that of year 2011 and onwards involves industrial enterprises with the annual main operating income of RMB 20 million.

3."Value added of industrial enterprises" in year 1991 and before refers to the indicator of "net value of industiral output".

4."Operating income", "operating cost" and "taxes and surcharges" indicators in year 2019 and before refer to "main operating income", "main operating cost" and "main operating taxes and surcharges" (the same below).

5.Since 2019, statistics does not include data of units directly under provincial jurisdiction (the same below).

6.Since 2019, the data used refer to the combined data after the adjustment of administrative division between Jinan City and Laiwu City, and the data before 2019 are data of original Jinan City (the same below).

7.Errors in totals and part of calculations in the table are produced by decimal trade-offs, not mechanically adjusted (the same below).

12-3 各时期主要工业产品产量
Output of Major Industrial Products in Each Period

年份 Year	钢 (万吨) Steel (10 000 tons)	发电量 (亿千瓦小时) Electricity Generation (100 million kWh)	水泥 (万吨) Cement (10 000 tons)	化肥 (万吨) Chemical Fertilizer (10 000 tons)	金切机床 (台) Metal-cutting Machine Tools (unit)	汽车 (辆) Motor Vehicles (unit)	服务器 (万台) Servers (10 000 unit)	布 (万米) Cloth (10 000 m)
1949	–	0.29	0.15	–	40	–	–	2682
1952	–	0.55	1.08	1.62	565	–	–	5104
1957	0.03	1.07	1.29	0.48	2312	–	–	5573
1962	0.57	4.20	4.85	0.81	1140	12	–	2160
1965	0.54	5.65	19.24	3.79	2061	335	–	4853
1970	7.01	11.28	38.06	4.87	4718	1775	–	11665
1975	22.81	11.07	58.48	9.06	3994	3507	–	12547
1978	34.54	12.65	87.55	18.02	3610	4025	–	13806
1979	33.19	11.92	93.77	11.07	3771	4515	–	14300
1980	36.34	11.95	98.86	12.78	4414	5641	–	15236
"六五"时期								
1981	34.23	11.12	96.50	11.62	3336	5099	–	16290
1982	34.96	11.15	104.64	13.23	4262	5993	–	17657
1983	41.24	13.01	112.38	15.37	4816	7249	–	17963
1984	43.80	23.49	117.17	14.53	5533	7947	–	16522
1985	52.64	26.44	135.10	11.44	6686	9400	–	18082
"七五"时期								
1986	57.24	27.01	154.51	12.31	7472	7600	–	12346
1987	64.09	28.83	158.92	13.00	7007	5225	–	20137
1988	75.23	42.97	182.80	13.69	7280	6741	–	19374
1989	81.58	43.98	198.95	14.48	6806	7701	–	21744
1990	87.68	44.71	211.56	14.44	5121	6239	–	20155
"八五"时期								
1991	105.42	56.43	248.33	14.90	5330	7096	–	20119
1992	113.34	61.46	335.61	14.64	7443	8544	–	14896
1993	139.35	69.00	340.35	14.47	6724	10132	–	13205
1994	166.19	66.87	384.00	15.62	3297	9380	–	16062
1995	172.72	68.75	425.02	14.03	4109	5657	–	15046
"九五"时期								
1996	205.49	63.50	379.32	13.73	3855	7125	–	13710

12-3 续表 continued

年份 Year	钢 (万吨) Steel (10 000 tons)	发电量 (亿千瓦小时) Electricity Generation (100 million kWh)	水泥 (万吨) Cement (10 000 tons)	化肥 (万吨) Chemical Fertilizer (10 000 tons)	金切机床 (台) Metal-cutting Machine Tools (unit)	汽车 (辆) Motor Vehicles (unit)	服务器 (万台) Servers (10 000 unit)	布 (万米) Cloth (10 000 m)
1997	237.70	59.14	392.23	13.89	2526	5656	–	14213
1998	267.33	60.06	379.40	17.29	1508	3615	–	11286
1999	265.29	64.24	474.47	22.91	1955	3738	–	14782
2000	277.04	69.29	485.12	28.41	2908	3078	–	16493
"十五"时期								
2001	293.83	69.81	572.28	28.71	3528	7395	–	14107
2002	394.41	69.12	867.71	28.29	4522	12152	–	16027
2003	507.70	77.60	925.20	28.50	6751	19989	–	17040
2004	688.30	74.70	1343.90	40.30	8904	29648	–	16336
2005	1046.60	90.80	1595.70	28.90	7166	42214	–	14018
"十一五"时期								
2006	1131.26	100.14	1960.64	31.44	10057	59242	–	22852
2007	1214.90	130.37	733.98	40.31	9473	100133	–	27469
2008	1123.20	124.25	734.58	48.52	5110	109107	8.3	11786
2009	1051.67	128.76	761.72	57.77	2400	129900	9.7	7500
2010	959.33	131.45	729.79	49.09	2165	212047	9.9	8191
"十二五"时期								
2011	835.80	154.48	824.70	44.20	2024	170717	13.0	11461
2012	694.50	156.60	776.00	55.20	4237	141269	14.7	14908
2013	711.14	162.55	782.20	33.29	4297	165963	17.1	14574
2014	746.20	178.47	832.40	28.60	4902	139751	28.1	14070
2015	699.80	175.87	781.50	23.50	3807	96184	40.6	15539
"十三五"时期								
2016	805.70	177.20	719.80	32.50	4679	124200	46.8	15585
2017	452.03	160.12	604.48	21.00	6013	201883	56.5	16407
2018	160.92	152.90	604.32	20.77	5964	232082	99.6	4032
2019	2144.18	295.10	1287.82	16.91	7237	175488	116.5	4095
2020	2228.91	276.70	1335.88	21.09	8998	394133	143.5	1144
"十四五"时期								
2021	1921.86	315.1	1561.13	16.66	14049	320349	113.7	1099

注：按经济普查规定汽车产量不含底盘。
Note:The automotive output excludes chassis in line with the provisions of economic census.

12-4 规模以上工业主要经济指标(2021 年)
Main Economic Indicators of Industrial Enterprises Above Designated Size(2021)

指标	Item	企业单位数（个）Number of Enterprises (unit)	亏损企业数（个）Loss Enterprises (unit)	工业总产值（现价）（亿元）Gross Industrial Output Value (Current Prices) (100 million yuan)	平均用工人数（万人）Annual Average Employees (10 000 persons)
总计	Total	2543	490	7591.25	41.13
按登记注册类型分组	by Status of Registration				
内资企业	Domestic Invested Enterprises	2397	474	6438.04	35.03
国有企业	State-owned Enterprises	37	13	119.76	0.69
中央企业	Central Enterprises	8	2	38.95	0.20
地方企业	Local Enterprises	29	11	80.81	0.48
集体企业	Collective-owned Enterprises	7	2	7.09	0.08
股份合作企业	Cooperative Enterprises	4	1	1.68	0.05
联营企业	Joint Ownership Enterprises	2		1.96	0.02
国有联营企业	State Joint Ownership Enterprises				
集体联营企业	Collective Joint Ownership Enterprises	1		1.20	0.02
国有与集体联营企业	Joint State-collective Enterprises	1		0.77	
其他联营企业	Other Joint Ownership Enterprises				
有限责任公司	Limited Liability Corporations	631	161	2196.63	13.76
国有独资公司	State Sole Funded Corporations	36	13	162.45	1.37
其他有限责任公司	Other Limited Liability Corporations	595	148	2034.18	12.39
股份有限公司	Share-holding Corporations Ltd.	86	13	2013.95	5.03
私营企业	Private Enterprises	1630	284	2096.96	15.39
私营独资企业	Private-funded Enterprises	49	6	23.10	0.25
私营合伙企业	Private Partnership Enterprises	6		2.35	0.02
私营有限责任公司	Private Limited Liability Corporations	1496	266	1943.43	14.09
私营股份有限公司	Private Share-holding Corporations Ltd.	79	12	128.08	1.03
其他企业	Other Enterprises				
港、澳、台商投资企业	Enterprises with Funds from Hong Kong,Macao and Taiwan	58	4	789.95	3.68
合资经营企业	Joint-venture Enterprises	30	4	295.79	1.75
合作经营企业	Cooperative Enterprises				
港澳台商独资经营企业	Enterprises with Sole Investment	27		492.47	1.92
港澳台商投资股份有限公司	Share-holding Corporations Ltd.				
其他港澳台商投资企业	Other Enterprises with Funds from Hong Kong,Macao and Taiwan	1		1.69	0.01
外商投资企业	Foreign Funded Enterprises	88	12	363.25	2.43

12–4 续表 1 continued 1

指标	Item	企业单位数（个）Number of Enterprises (unit)	亏损企业数（个）Loss Enterprises (unit)	工业总产值（现价）（亿元）Gross Industrial Output Value (Current Prices) (100 million yuan)	平均用工人数（万人）Annual Average Employees (10 000 persons)
中外合资经营企业	Joint–venture Enterprises	39	5	160.73	1.23
中外合作经营企业	Cooperation Enterprises	2		2.80	0.03
外资企业	Enterprises with Sole Fund	44	7	157.39	1.13
外商投资股份有限公司	Share–holding Corporations Ltd.	3		42.34	0.05
其他外商投资企业	Other Foreign Funded Enterprises				
按轻重工业分	**by Light & Heavy Industry**				
轻工业	Light Industry	654	140	1167.53	11.19
重工业	Heavy Industry	1889	350	6423.72	29.94
按企业规模分	**by Enterprise Size**				
大型企业	Large–sized Enterprises	65	9	4258.13	15.67
中型企业	Medium–sized Enterprises	163	28	1220.47	8.00
小型企业	Small–sized Enterprises	2007	383	1937.15	16.74
微型企业	Micro–sized Enterprises	308	70	175.50	0.73
按工业行业分	**by Sector**				
煤炭开采和洗选业	Mining and Washing of Coal	3	2	7.83	0.26
石油和天然气开采业	Extraction of Petroleum and Natural Gas	3		8.06	0.04
黑色金属矿采选业	Mining and Processing of Ferrous Metal Ores	12	1	134.56	0.80
有色金属矿采选业	Mining and Processing of Non–Ferrous Metal Ores				
非金属矿采选业	Mining and Processing of Non–metal Ores	10	1	19.50	0.09
开采专业及辅助性活动	Professional and Support Activities for Mining				
其他采矿业	Mining of Other Ores				
农副食品加工业	Processing of Food from Agricultural Products	101	22	153.05	0.94
食品制造业	Manufacture of Foods	74	17	151.41	1.68
酒、饮料和精制茶制造业	Manufacture of Liquor, Beverages and Refined Tea	20	6	65.05	0.52
烟草制品业	Manufacture of Tobacco	1		1.50	0.02
纺织业	Manufacture of TextileV	50	14	43.87	0.51
纺织服装、服饰业	Manufacture of Textile, Wearing Apparel and Accessories	23	5	14.01	0.55
皮革、毛皮、羽毛及其制品和制鞋业	Manufacture of Leather, Fur, Feather and Related Products and Footwear	4	1	2.99	0.03
木材加工和木、竹、藤、棕、草制品业	Processing of Timber, Manufacture of Wood, Bamboo, Rattan,Palm and Straw Products	11	1	7.74	0.07
家具制造业	Manufacture of Furniture	15	6	10.12	0.20

12–4 续表 2 continued 2

指标	Item	企业单位数（个）Number of Enterprises (unit)	亏损企业数（个）Loss Enterprises (unit)	工业总产值（现价）（亿元）Gross Industrial Output Value (Current Prices) (100 million yuan)	平均用工人数（万人）Annual Average Employees (10 000 persons)
造纸和纸制品业	Manufacture of Paper and Paper Products	46	10	46.18	0.43
印刷和记录媒介复制业	Printing and Reproduction of Recording Media	43	7	47.38	0.62
文教、工美、体育和娱乐用品制造业	Manufacture of Articles for Culture, Education, Arts and Crafts,Sport and Entertainment Activities	24	5	16.47	0.29
石油、煤炭及其他燃料加工业	Processing of Petroleum, Coal and Other Fuels	14		313.88	0.34
化学原料和化学制品制造业	Manufacture of Raw Chemical Materials and Chemical Products	119	23	335.62	1.54
医药制造业	Manufacture of Medicines	73	6	366.95	3.20
化学纤维制造业	Manufacture of Chemical Fibres	10	3	14.30	0.12
橡胶和塑料制品业	Manufacture of Rubber and Plastics Products	68	12	38.38	0.46
非金属矿物制品业	Manufacture of Non–metallic Mineral Products	312	72	473.08	3.24
黑色金属冶炼和压延加工业	Smelting and Pressing of Ferrous Metals	44	16	1440.14	3.19
有色金属冶炼和压延加工业	Smelting and Pressing of Non–ferrous Metals	37	8	41.02	0.22
金属制品业	Manufacture of Metal Products	284	39	343.14	3.08
通用设备制造业	Manufacture of General Purpose Machinery	299	52	380.07	4.12
专用设备制造业	Manufacture of Special Purpose Machinery	248	38	289.23	2.58
汽车制造业	Manufacture of Automobiles	128	26	1197.00	4.64
铁路、船舶、航空航天和其他运输设备制造业	Manufacture of Railway, Ship, Aerospace and Other Transport Equipments	26	5	70.44	0.69
电气机械和器材制造业	Manufacture of Electrical Machinery and Apparatus	150	28	387.97	1.89
计算机、通信和其他电子设备制造业	Manufacture of Computers, Communication and Other Electronic Equipment	80	15	732.12	1.63
仪器仪表制造业	Manufacture of Measuring Instruments and Machinery	81	6	88.01	0.90
其他制造业	Other Manufacture	6		3.61	0.03
废弃资源综合利用业	Utilization of Waste Resources	9	4	23.77	0.24
金属制品、机械和设备修理业	Repair Service of Metal Products, Machinery and Equipment	6	1	12.40	0.20
电力、热力生产和供应业	Production and Supply of Electric Power and Heat Power	56	24	180.84	1.08
燃气生产和供应业	Production and Supply of Gas	32	8	101.27	0.34
水的生产和供应业	Production and Supply of Water	21	6	28.28	0.36

12-5 规模以上国有及国有控股工业主要经济指标(2021 年)
Main Economic Indicators of State-Owned and State-Controlled Industrial Enterprises Above Designated Size(2021)

指标	Item	企业单位数(个) Number of Enterprises (unit)	亏损企业数(个) Loss Enterprises (unit)	工业总产值(现价)(亿元) Gross Industrial Output Value (Calculated at Current Prices) (100 million yuan)	平均用工人数(万人) Annual Average Employees (10 000 persons)
总计	Total	252	61	3267.21	11.22
按登记注册类型分组	by Status of Registration				
内资企业	Domestic Invested Enterprises	235	60	3048.99	10.10
国有企业	State-owned Enterprises	37	13	119.76	0.69
中央企业	Central Enterprises	8	2	38.95	0.20
地方企业	Local Enterprises	29	11	80.81	0.48
集体企业	Collective-owned Enterprises				
股份合作企业	Cooperative Enterprises				
联营企业	Joint Ownership Enterprises	1		0.77	
有限责任公司	Limited Liability Corporations	177	42	1146.83	6.37
国有独资公司	State Sole Funded Corporations	36	13	162.45	1.37
其他有限责任公司	Other Limited Liability Corporations	141	29	984.38	5.00
股份有限公司	Share-holding Corporations Ltd.	20	5	1781.63	3.04
私营企业	Private Enterprises				
其他企业	Other Enterprises				
港、澳、台商投资企业	Enterprises with Funds from Hong Kong,Macao and Taiwan	8		157.16	0.75
合资经营企业	Joint-venture Enterprises	8		157.16	0.75
合作经营企业	Cooperative Enterprises				
港澳台商独资经营企业	Enterprises with Sole Investment				
港澳台商投资股份有限公司	Share-holding Corporations Ltd.				
其他港澳台商投资企业	Other Enterprises with Funds from Hong Kong,Macao and Taiwan				
外商投资企业	Foreign Funded Enterprises	9	1	61.06	0.37
中外合资经营企业	Joint-venture Enterprises	8	1	58.66	0.35
中外合作经营企业	Cooperation Enterprises	1		2.40	0.02
外资企业	Enterprises with Sole Fund				
外商投资股份有限公司	Share-holding Corporations Ltd.				
其他外商投资企业	Other Foreign Funded Enterprises				
按轻重工业分	by Light & Heavy Industry				

12-5 续表 1 continued 1

指标	Item	企业单位数(个) Number of Enterprises (unit)	亏损企业数(个) Loss Enterprises (unit)	工业总产值(现价)(亿元) Gross Industrial Output Value (Calculated at Current Prices) (100 million yuan)	平均用工人数(万人) Annual Average Employees (10 000 persons)
轻工业	Light Industry	39	12	106.36	1.14
重工业	Heavy Industry	213	49	3160.85	10.08
按企业规模分	**by Enterprise Size**				
大型企业	Large-sized Enterprises	26	6	2526.51	6.74
中型企业	Medium-sized Enterprises	48	11	399.32	2.40
小型企业	Small-sized Enterprises	155	41	298.08	1.77
微型企业	Micro-sized Enterprises	23	3	43.29	0.30
按工业行业分	**by Sector**				
煤炭开采和洗选业	Mining and Washing of Coal	1		6.37	0.21
石油和天然气开采业	Extraction of Petroleum and Natural Gas	3		8.06	0.04
黑色金属矿采选业	Mining and Processing of Ferrous Metal Ores	3		25.25	0.43
有色金属矿采选业	Mining and Processing of Non-Ferrous Metal Ores				
非金属矿采选业	Mining and Processing of Non-metal Ores	3		10.18	0.05
开采专业及辅助性活动	Professional and Support Activities for Mining				
其他采矿业	Mining of Other Ores				
农副食品加工业	Processing of Food from Agricultural Products	1		0.28	
食品制造业	Manufacture of Foods	6	3	15.02	0.17
酒、饮料和精制茶制造业	Manufacture of Liquor, Beverages and Refined Tea	3	1	23.11	0.21
烟草制品业	Manufacture of Tobacco	1		1.50	0.02
纺织业	Manufacture of Textile	3	2	3.18	0.06
纺织服装、服饰业	Manufacture of Textile, Wearing Apparel and Accessories	3	1	3.20	0.14
皮革、毛皮、羽毛及其制品和制鞋业	Manufacture of Leather, Fur, Feather and Related Products and Footwear				
木材加工和木、竹、藤、棕、草制品业	Processing of Timber, Manufacture of Wood, Bamboo, Rattan,Palm and Straw Products				
家具制造业	Manufacture of Furniture				
造纸和纸制品业	Manufacture of Paper and Paper Products	2	1	3.55	0.02
印刷和记录媒介复制业	Printing and Reproduction of Recording Media	6	1	7.16	0.14

12-5 续表 2 continued 2

指标	Item	企业单位数（个）Number of Enterprises (unit)	亏损企业数（个）Loss Enterprises (unit)	工业总产值（现价）(亿元) Gross Industrial Output Value (Calculated at Current Prices) (100 million yuan)	平均用工人数（万人）Annual Average Employees (10 000 persons)
文教、工美、体育和娱乐用品制造业	Manufacture of Articles for Culture, Education, Arts and Crafts,Sport and Entertainment Activities				
石油、煤炭及其他燃料加工业	Processing of Petroleum, Coal and Other Fuels	1		244.46	0.15
化学原料和化学制品制造业	Manufacture of Raw Chemical Materials and Chemical Products	13	3	97.33	0.49
医药制造业	Manufacture of Medicines	3		21.75	0.18
化学纤维制造业	Manufacture of Chemical Fibres	2		4.53	0.04
橡胶和塑料制品业	Manufacture of Rubber and Plastics Products				
非金属矿物制品业	Manufacture of Non-metallic Mineral Products	22	3	62.96	0.40
黑色金属冶炼和压延加工业	Smelting and Pressing of Ferrous Metals	5	3	796.36	1.74
有色金属冶炼和压延加工业	Smelting and Pressing of Non-ferrous Metals	1		14.75	0.02
金属制品业	Manufacture of Metal Products	15	2	59.36	0.35
通用设备制造业	Manufacture of General Purpose Machinery	14	3	79.39	0.95
专用设备制造业	Manufacture of Special Purpose Machinery	13	4	34.75	0.32
汽车制造业	Manufacture of Automobiles	12	1	651.15	1.65
铁路、船舶、航空航天和其他运输设备制造业	Manufacture of Railway, Ship, Aerospace and Other Transport Equipments	10	1	56.27	0.49
电气机械和器材制造业	Manufacture of Electrical Machinery and Apparatus	25	7	141.57	0.50
计算机、通信和其他电子设备制造业	Manufacture of Computers, Communication and Other Electronic Equipment	11	1	632.79	0.60
仪器仪表制造业	Manufacture of Measuring Instruments and Machinery	6		23.18	0.16
其他制造业	Other Manufacture	1		2.21	0.01
废弃资源综合利用业	Utilization of Waste Resources				
金属制品、机械和设备修理业	Repair Service of Metal Products, Machinery and Equipment	3		10.07	0.19
电力、热力生产和供应业	Production and Supply of Electric Power and Heat Power	34	16	160.45	0.94
燃气生产和供应业	Production and Supply of Gas	12	3	47.64	0.22
水的生产和供应业	Production and Supply of Water	14	5	19.39	0.32

12-6 规模以上私营工业企业主要经济指标(2021年)
Main Economic Indicators of Private Industrial Enterprises Above Designated Size(2021)

指标	Item	企业单位数(个) Number of Enterprises (unit)	亏损企业数(个) Loss Enterpriss (unit)	工业总产值(现价)(亿元) Gross Industrial Output Value (Calculated at Current Prices) (100 million yuan)	平均用工人数(万人) Annual Average Employees (10 000 persons)
总计	Total	1630	284	2096.96	15.39
按登记注册类型分组	by Status of Registration				
内资企业	Domestic Invested Enterprises	1630	284	2096.96	15.39
私营企业	Private Enterprises	1630	284	2096.96	15.39
私营独资企业	Private-funded Enterprises	49	6	23.10	0.25
私营合伙企业	Private Partnership Enterprises	6		2.35	0.02
私营有限责任公司	Private Limited Liability Corporations	1496	266	1943.43	14.09
私营股份有限公司	Private Share-holding Corporations Ltd.	79	12	128.08	1.03
其他企业	Other Enterprises				
按轻重工业分	by Light & Heavy Industry				
轻工业	Light Industry	414	88	494.22	5.16
重工业	Heavy Industry	1216	196	1602.74	10.23
按企业规模分	by Enterprise Size				
大型企业	Large-sized Enterprises	11	1	645.96	3.04
中型企业	Medium-sized Enterprises	44	5	334.63	2.01
小型企业	Small-sized Enterprises	1338	228	1013.56	9.99
微型企业	Micro-sized Enterprises	237	50	102.82	0.36
按工业行业分	by Sector				
煤炭开采和洗选业	Mining and Washing of Coal	1	1	0.46	
石油和天然气开采业	Extraction of Petroleum and Natural Gas				

12-6 续表 1 continued 1

指标	Item	企业单位数（个）Number of Enterprises (unit)	亏损企业数（个）Loss Enterpriss (unit)	工业总产值（现价）(亿元) Gross Industrial Output Value (Calculated at Current Prices) (100 million yuan)	平均用工人数（万人）Annual Average Employees (10 000 persons)
黑色金属矿采选业	Mining and Processing of Ferrous Metal Ores	5	1	81.53	0.06
有色金属矿采选业	Mining and Processing of Non-Ferrous Metal Ores				
非金属矿采选业	Mining and Processing of Non-metal Ores	7	1	9.32	0.04
开采专业及辅助性活动	Professional and Support Activities for Mining				
其他采矿业	Mining of Other Ores				
农副食品加工业	Processing of Food from Agricultural Products	68	16	87.88	0.61
食品制造业	Manufacture of Foods	44	10	46.46	0.69
酒、饮料和精制茶制造业	Manufacture of Liquor, Beverages and Refined Tea	5	2	2.52	0.02
烟草制品业	Manufacture of Tobacco				
纺织业	Manufacture of Textile	36	8	21.42	0.24
纺织服装、服饰业	Manufacture of Textile, Wearing Apparel and Accessories	15	3	5.38	0.15
皮革、毛皮、羽毛及其制品和制鞋业	Manufacture of Leather, Fur, Feather and Related Products and Footwear	3	1	1.64	0.01
木材加工和木、竹、藤、棕、草制品业	Processing of Timber, Manufacture of Wood, Bamboo, Rattan,Palm and Straw Products	11	1	7.74	0.07
家具制造业	Manufacture of Furniture	12	4	8.81	0.19
造纸和纸制品业	Manufacture of Paper and Paper Products	36	7	24.10	0.28
印刷和记录媒介复制业	Printing and Reproduction of Recording Media	28	4	22.58	0.32
文教、工美、体育和娱乐用品制造业	Manufacture of Articles for Culture, Education, Arts and Crafts,Sport and Entertainment Activities	19	4	14.08	0.24
石油、煤炭及其他燃料加工业	Processing of Petroleum, Coal and Other Fuels	9		42.33	0.13
化学原料和化学制品制造业	Manufacture of Raw Chemical Materials and Chemical Products	72	15	120.44	0.61
医药制造业	Manufacture of Medicines	37	3	203.23	1.72

12-6 续表 2 continued 2

指标	Item	企业单位数（个）Number of Enterprises (unit)	亏损企业数（个）Loss Enterpriss (unit)	工业总产值（现价）(亿元) Gross Industrial Output Value (Calculated at Current Prices) (100 million yuan)	平均用工人数（万人）Annual Average Employees (10 000 persons)
化学纤维制造业	Manufacture of Chemical Fibres	4	2	1.25	0.02
橡胶和塑料制品业	Manufacture of Rubber and Plastics Products	53	9	29.08	0.31
非金属矿物制品业	Manufacture of Non-metallic Mineral Products	220	48	267.13	1.84
黑色金属冶炼和压延加工业	Smelting and Pressing of Ferrous Metals	31	10	385.20	0.73
有色金属冶炼和压延加工业	Smelting and Pressing of Non-ferrous Metals	33	8	20.00	0.14
金属制品业	Manufacture of Metal Products	201	29	127.40	1.40
通用设备制造业	Manufacture of General Purpose Machinery	213	34	131.53	1.62
专用设备制造业	Manufacture of Special Purpose Machinery	170	19	197.90	1.56
汽车制造业	Manufacture of Automobiles	83	17	67.76	0.94
铁路、船舶、航空航天和其他运输设备制造业	Manufacture of Railway, Ship, Aerospace and Other Transport Equipments	6	1	4.63	0.06
电气机械和器材制造业	Manufacture of Electrical Machinery and Apparatus	84	11	71.06	0.49
计算机、通信和其他电子设备制造业	Manufacture of Computers, Communication and Other Electronic Equipment	35	5	22.45	0.28
仪器仪表制造业	Manufacture of Measuring Instruments and Machinery	59	2	39.69	0.50
其他制造业	Other Manufacture	5		1.40	0.02
废弃资源综合利用业	Utilization of Waste Resources	7	3	15.01	0.05
金属制品、机械和设备修理业	Repair Service of Metal Products, Machinery and Equipment	2	1	0.30	
电力、热力生产和供应业	Production and Supply of Electric Power and Heat Power	7	2	8.33	0.04
燃气生产和供应业	Production and Supply of Gas	7	2	5.77	0.01
水的生产和供应业	Production and Supply of Water	2		1.16	0.01

12-7 规模以上工业资产实力（2021 年）
Capital Power of Industrial Enterprises Above Designated Size(2021)

单位：亿元

指标	Item	流动资产合计 Current Assets	其中 of which 应收账款 Accounts Receivable	存货 Inventories
总计	Total	5224.97	1429.69	1115.06
按登记注册类型分组	by Status of Registration			
内资企业	Domestic Invested Enterprises	4385.46	1286.06	959.54
国有企业	State-owned Enterprises	126.42	26.13	11.40
中央企业	Central Enterprises	22.05	6.53	2.94
地方企业	Local Enterprises	104.37	19.61	8.46
集体企业	Collective-owned Enterprises	3.15	0.65	1.14
股份合作企业	Cooperative Enterprises	2.16	0.44	0.47
联营企业	Joint Ownership Enterprises	0.97	0.60	0.05
国有联营企业	State Joint Ownership Enterprises			
集体联营企业	Collective Joint Ownership Enterprises	0.36	0.24	0.03
国有与集体联营企业	Joint State-collective Enterprises	0.60	0.36	0.02
其他联营企业	Other Joint Ownership Enterprises			
有限责任公司	Limited Liability Corporations	1733.50	377.78	328.65
国有独资公司	State Sole Funded Corporations	258.31	47.13	51.21
其他有限责任公司	Other Limited Liability Corporations	1475.19	330.65	277.44
股份有限公司	Share-holding Corporations Ltd.	1041.65	267.79	307.56
私营企业	Private Enterprises	1477.60	612.67	310.27
私营独资企业	Private-funded Enterprises	9.73	5.53	1.55
私营合伙企业	Private Partnership Enterprises	0.73	0.40	0.15
私营有限责任公司	Private Limited Liability Corporations	1354.37	570.80	279.87
私营股份有限公司	Private Share-holding Corporations Ltd.	112.78	35.94	28.70
其他企业	Other Enterprises			
港、澳、台商投资企业	Enterprises with Funds from Hong Kong,Macao and Taiwan	612.57	85.01	99.56
合资经营企业	Joint-venture Enterprises	242.35	39.44	34.83
合作经营企业	Cooperative Enterprises			
港澳台商独资经营企业	Enterprises with Sole Investment	369.70	45.54	64.58
港澳台商投资股份有限公司	Share-holding Corporations Ltd.			
其他港澳台商投资企业	Other Enterprises with Funds from Hong Kong,Macao and Taiwan	0.51	0.02	0.15
外商投资企业	Foreign Funded Enterprises	226.95	58.63	55.96
中外合资经营企业	Joint-venture Enterprises	100.35	25.34	29.18
中外合作经营企业	Cooperation Enterprises	1.80	0.23	1.26
外资企业	Enterprises with Sole Fund	93.46	25.63	22.33
外商投资股份有限公司	Share-holding Corporations Ltd.	31.34	7.43	3.20
其他外商投资企业	Other Foreign Funded Enterprises			
按轻重工业分	by Light & Heavy Industry			
轻工业	Light Industry	924.68	224.65	179.24
重工业	Heavy Industry	4300.29	1205.05	935.82
按企业规模分	by Enterprise Size			
大型企业	Large-sized Enterprises	2438.53	542.36	555.94
中型企业	Medium-sized Enterprises	986.15	287.59	213.99
小型企业	Small-sized Enterprises	1669.80	558.55	323.95
微型企业	Micro-sized Enterprises	130.49	41.19	21.18

(100 million yuan)

固定资产净额 Net Fixed Assets	固定资产原价 Original Value of Fixed Assets	流动负债合计 Current Liabilities Total	非流动负债合计 Non-Current Liabilities Total	所有者权益合计 Total Owner' s Equities	其中 of which: 实收资本 Paid- up Capital	其中 of which: 国家资本 Official Capital
1778.16	3316.02	4449.43	664.46	3380.30	1491.51	325.32
1580.36	2895.99	3829.18	604.89	2716.86	1184.39	312.39
67.52	150.29	116.13	40.63	68.81	37.81	15.78
41.02	73.39	35.29	19.32	19.68	20.40	2.91
26.50	76.90	80.84	21.31	49.13	17.41	12.87
2.60	5.25	2.25	0.93	2.82	0.52	
0.42	0.90	1.19	0.61	1.65	0.16	
0.95	1.55	1.21	0.08	0.80	0.22	
0.39	0.95	0.20	0.08	0.56	0.02	
0.56	0.61	1.01		0.24	0.20	
933.97	1564.45	1741.75	364.85	1145.69	625.28	198.16
194.60	297.94	290.55	120.36	172.47	116.75	30.75
739.37	1266.51	1451.20	244.49	973.22	508.53	167.41
248.74	542.51	754.31	97.04	738.16	200.32	96.31
326.15	631.04	1212.34	100.76	758.94	320.07	2.14
3.75	5.77	10.43	2.15	3.29	2.30	
0.15	0.34	0.73		0.23	0.15	
290.47	575.75	1140.60	82.18	656.99	283.62	2.06
31.78	49.18	60.57	16.43	98.42	34.00	0.08
120.14	256.95	478.04	33.67	448.07	205.58	8.34
62.22	130.44	146.13	18.14	222.93	88.74	8.34
57.79	126.36	331.72	15.52	224.41	116.15	
0.13	0.15	0.19	0.01	0.73	0.68	
77.66	163.08	142.21	25.90	215.37	101.55	4.58
30.88	74.75	76.68	13.52	70.94	40.56	3.95
0.66	1.81	1.33	0.02	1.18	0.70	0.64
45.23	85.01	46.73	12.13	109.26	52.02	
0.89	1.50	17.47	0.23	33.99	8.27	
289.19	517.46	581.01	51.70	875.32	292.63	9.54
1488.97	2798.56	3868.41	612.77	2504.97	1198.88	315.77
928.35	1782.50	2104.92	278.89	1737.13	587.63	180.84
351.66	647.47	845.45	144.23	615.92	259.66	72.97
429.11	795.17	1397.20	178.21	969.37	601.54	60.59
69.05	90.89	101.86	63.13	57.87	42.68	10.91

12-7 续表 continued

指标	Item	流动资产合计 Current Assets	其中 of which 应收账款 Accounts Receivable	存货 Inventories
按工业行业分	by Sector			
煤炭开采和洗选业	Mining and Washing of Coal	7.23	1.31	0.56
石油和天然气开采业	Extraction of Petroleum and Natural Gas	30.62	2.36	0.06
黑色金属矿采选业	Mining and Processing of Ferrous Metal Ores	55.75	3.32	5.42
有色金属矿采选业	Mining and Processing of Non-Ferrous Metal Ores			
非金属矿采选业	Mining and Processing of Non-metal Ores	12.39	3.16	2.56
开采专业及辅助性活动	Professional and Support Activities for Mining			
其他采矿业	Mining of Other Ores			
农副食品加工业	Processing of Food from Agricultural Products	68.88	24.33	15.94
食品制造业	Manufacture of Foods	65.28	9.72	16.65
酒、饮料和精制茶制造业	Manufacture of Liquor, Beverages and Refined Tea	53.82	4.97	10.24
烟草制品业	Manufacture of Tobacco	2.62	0.17	0.28
纺织业	Manufacture of Textile	30.09	7.76	11.53
纺织服装、服饰业	Manufacture of Textile, Wearing Apparel and Accessories	11.60	2.15	3.34
皮革、毛皮、羽毛及其制品和制鞋业	Manufacture of Leather, Fur, Feather and Related Products and Footwea	2.34	0.17	0.59
木材加工和木、竹、藤、棕、草制品业	Processing of Timber, Manufacture of Wood, Bamboo, Rattan,Palm and Straw Products	3.45	0.59	1.44
家具制造业	Manufacture of Furniture	5.81	2.75	1.52
造纸和纸制品业	Manufacture of Paper and Paper Products	24.47	5.86	9.69
印刷和记录媒介复制业	Printing and Reproduction of Recording Media	32.74	8.56	6.46
文教、工美、体育和娱乐用品制造业	Manufacture of Articles for Culture, Education, Arts and Crafts,Sport and Entertainment Activities	13.72	2.35	8.06
石油、煤炭及其他燃料加工业	Processing of Petroleum, Coal and Other Fuels	128.53	62.01	14.94
化学原料和化学制品制造业	Manufacture of Raw Chemical Materials and Chemical Products	226.14	32.50	43.39
医药制造业	Manufacture of Medicines	391.95	104.93	57.30
化学纤维制造业	Manufacture of Chemical Fibres	11.20	1.62	4.05
橡胶和塑料制品业	Manufacture of Rubber and Plastics Products	23.04	9.18	5.27
非金属矿物制品业	Manufacture of Non-metallic Mineral Products	435.15	208.85	61.13
黑色金属冶炼和压延加工业	Smelting and Pressing of Ferrous Metals	407.63	102.41	128.69
有色金属冶炼和压延加工业	Smelting and Pressing of Non-ferrous Metals	22.28	8.54	5.26
金属制品业	Manufacture of Metal Products	257.22	80.16	50.80
通用设备制造业	Manufacture of General Purpose Machinery	358.61	98.40	86.81
专用设备制造业	Manufacture of Special Purpose Machinery	296.24	98.06	75.05
汽车制造业	Manufacture of Automobiles	793.73	126.60	150.04
铁路、船舶、航空航天和其他运输设备制造业	Manufacture of Railway, Ship, Aerospace and Other Transport Equipments	69.87	14.04	10.27
电气机械和器材制造业	Manufacture of Electrical Machinery and Apparatus	428.99	129.51	82.51
计算机、通信和其他电子设备制造业	Manufacture of Computers, Communication and Other Electronic Equipment	493.22	173.99	192.97
仪器仪表制造业	Manufacture of Measuring Instruments and Machinery	83.97	29.50	18.93
其他制造业	Other Manufacture	2.77	2.06	0.27
废弃资源综合利用业	Utilization of Waste Resources	7.62	2.17	1.75
金属制品、机械和设备修理业	Repair Service of Metal Products, Machinery and Equipment	10.43	4.33	3.15
电力、热力生产和供应业	Production and Supply of Electric Power and Heat Power	246.48	38.25	19.04
燃气生产和供应业	Production and Supply of Gas	62.48	13.22	6.93
水的生产和供应业	Production and Supply of Water	46.59	9.84	2.16

固定资产净额 Net Fixed Assets	固定资产原价 Original Value of Fixed Assets	流动负债合计 Current Liabilities Total	非流动负债合计 Non-Current Liabilities Total	所有者权益合计 Total Owner's Equities	其中 of which 实收资本 Paid-up Capital	其中 of which 国家资本 Official Capital
3.13	7.29	17.59	0.01	-6.21	1.42	0.30
3.65	31.66	0.76	3.23	33.08	5.18	3.50
32.48	74.01	84.34	12.51	19.28	32.93	3.10
8.84	11.17	17.54	2.63	10.05	5.72	0.50
13.58	22.93	72.23	8.27	18.99	14.37	
49.47	87.51	50.64	5.18	79.20	40.07	0.59
25.10	53.71	39.33	2.88	59.11	45.77	0.37
0.92	1.54	0.55		3.11	0.95	0.95
14.81	25.03	32.76	2.91	17.35	10.36	0.93
11.79	16.89	12.92	1.88	11.29	4.99	
0.27	0.54	2.04	0.23	0.41	0.18	
1.36	2.23	4.43	0.14	0.96	0.55	
1.69	2.64	8.01	0.15	3.37	2.31	
12.98	22.99	26.22	2.38	14.22	9.54	1.44
17.61	37.69	26.39	3.20	32.24	17.68	1.36
3.98	6.12	12.27	1.84	6.62	4.72	
42.09	111.60	122.87	13.38	47.28	33.48	27.25
108.85	181.36	233.90	66.87	156.85	54.67	9.75
94.05	163.27	170.24	16.25	427.29	85.00	2.08
7.77	11.93	9.08	0.37	15.57	13.20	0.85
7.38	16.54	18.56	1.36	12.82	12.48	
91.10	184.25	340.93	25.04	217.90	71.84	4.05
384.56	773.96	555.28	51.55	310.02	176.90	113.72
4.72	8.62	21.42	0.28	8.72	4.15	0.88
71.59	125.81	194.12	17.22	191.09	63.76	3.47
91.30	156.77	239.40	12.23	248.71	151.14	7.30
50.01	75.56	225.33	27.25	158.55	69.14	4.10
99.24	222.50	665.03	18.81	396.40	152.86	17.97
11.43	26.46	56.19	7.98	46.51	32.00	2.05
67.22	118.46	375.04	15.97	221.80	121.14	34.93
29.86	53.20	321.43	25.48	248.96	58.32	9.79
10.99	19.90	44.55	2.79	62.16	22.05	2.18
0.99	1.22	2.01	0.14	1.63	1.19	
3.68	5.90	9.34	2.00	4.34	1.87	
3.44	7.22	6.84	0.03	8.44	3.75	2.25
321.47	519.80	305.47	221.14	182.07	120.24	60.81
25.66	49.66	57.61	16.74	67.01	24.14	3.36
49.11	78.10	66.76	74.16	43.10	21.48	5.49

12-8 规模以上国有及国有控股工业资产实力(2021年)
Capital Power of State-Owned and State-Controlled Industrial Enterprises Above Designated Size(2021)

单位：亿元

指标	Item	流动资产合计 Current Assets	其中 of which 应收账款 Accounts Receivable	存货 Inventories
总计	Total	1948.35	422.33	453.89
按登记注册类型分组	by Status of Registration			
内资企业	Domestic Funded Enterprises	1801.22	404.31	430.32
国有企业	State-owned Enterprises	126.42	26.13	11.40
中央企业	Central Enterprises	22.05	6.53	2.94
地方企业	Local Enterprises	104.37	19.61	8.46
集体企业	Collective-owned Enterprises			
股份合作企业	Cooperative Enterprises			
联营企业	Joint Ownership Enterprises	0.60	0.36	0.02
有限责任公司	Limited Liability Corporations	906.15	182.84	164.05
国有独资公司	State Sole Funded Corporations	258.31	47.13	51.21
其他有限责任公司	Other Limited Liability Corporations	647.84	135.71	112.84
股份有限公司	Share-holding Corporations Ltd.	768.04	194.97	254.85
私营企业	Private Enterprises			
其他企业	Other Enterprises			
港、澳、台商投资企业	Enterprises with Funds from Hong Kong,Macao and Taiwan	111.36	10.95	12.51
合资经营企业	Joint-venture Enterprises	111.36	10.95	12.51
合作经营企业	Cooperative Enterprises			
港澳台商独资经营企业	Enterprises with Sole Investment			
港澳台商投资股份有限公司	Share-holding Corporations Ltd.			
其他港澳台商投资企业	Other Enterprises with Funds from Hong Kong,Macao and Taiwan			
外商投资企业	Foreign Funded Enterprises	35.77	7.07	11.07
中外合资经营企业	Joint-venture Enterprises	34.30	6.92	9.95
中外合作经营企业	Cooperation Enterprises	1.47	0.16	1.12
外资企业	Enterprises with Sole Fund			
外商投资股份有限公司	Share-holding Corporations Ltd. with Foreign Investment			
其他外商投资企业	Other Foreign Funded Enterprises			
按轻重工业分	by Light & Heavy Industry			
轻工业	Light Industry	90.03	12.97	20.44
重工业	Heavy Industry	1858.31	409.36	433.46
按企业规模分	by Enterprise Size			
大型企业	Large-sized Enterprises	1217.64	231.60	306.99
中型企业	Medium-sized Enterprises	352.50	83.83	86.42
小型企业	Small-sized Enterprises	321.74	99.10	49.90
微型企业	Micro-sized Enterprises	56.46	7.80	10.59
按工业行业分	by Sector			
煤炭开采和洗选业	Mining and Washing of Coal	3.72	0.57	0.55
石油和天然气开采业	Extraction of Petroleum and Natural Gas	30.62	2.36	0.06
黑色金属矿采选业	Mining and Processing of Ferrous Metal Ores	11.56	0.79	1.09

(100 million yuan)

固定资产净额 Net Fixed Assets	固定资产原价 Original Value of Fixed Assets	流动负债合计 Current Liabilities Total	非流动负债合计 Non-Current Liabilities Totall	所有者权益合计 Total Owner's Equities	其中 of which 实收资本 Paid- up Capital	其中 of which 国家资本 Official Capital
939.21	1754.52	1941.83	420.90	1174.07	599.83	316.86
907.26	1671.39	1830.02	402.93	1064.11	553.21	304.37
67.52	150.29	116.13	40.63	68.81	37.81	15.78
41.02	73.39	35.29	19.32	19.68	20.40	2.91
26.50	76.90	80.84	21.31	49.13	17.41	12.87
0.56	0.61	1.01		0.24	0.20	
664.13	1096.93	1096.58	296.42	561.37	395.60	194.73
194.60	297.94	290.55	120.36	172.47	116.75	30.75
469.53	798.99	806.03	176.06	388.90	278.86	163.98
175.05	423.56	616.30	65.87	433.69	119.59	93.86
24.97	62.86	82.45	15.19	90.18	35.10	8.33
24.97	62.86	82.45	15.19	90.18	35.10	8.33
6.98	20.27	29.37	2.78	19.79	11.52	4.16
6.36	18.56	28.06	2.76	18.95	10.88	3.52
0.62	1.71	1.31	0.02	0.84	0.64	0.64
35.78	62.63	71.60	8.65	71.82	27.32	8.51
903.43	1691.89	1870.23	412.25	1102.25	572.51	308.36
621.70	1184.39	1260.58	233.08	749.06	332.62	179.21
189.47	326.35	360.98	92.27	203.68	130.41	70.52
95.11	204.71	273.71	62.15	199.60	120.93	56.27
32.92	39.08	46.55	33.41	21.74	15.86	10.87
2.65	6.42	12.62		-5.57	1.05	0.30
3.65	31.66	0.76	3.23	33.08	5.18	3.50
16.44	41.31	11.58	11.58	25.61	26.83	1.99

12-8 续表 continued

指标	Item	流动资产合计 Current Assets	其中 of which	
			应收账款 Accounts Receivable	存货 Inventories
有色金属矿采选业	Mining and Processing of Non-Ferrous Metal Ores			
非金属矿采选业	Mining and Processing of Non-metal Ores	4.99	0.55	0.37
开采专业及辅助性活动	Professional and Support Activities for Mining			
其他采矿业	Mining of Other Ores			
农副食品加工业	Processing of Food from Agricultural Products	0.30	0.03	0.19
食品制造业	Manufacture of Foods	9.99	2.43	1.46
酒、饮料和精制茶制造业	Manufacture of Liquor, Beverages and Refined Tea	12.58	1.22	2.65
烟草制品业	Manufacture of Tobacco	2.62	0.17	0.28
纺织业	Manufacture of Textile	2.15	0.45	1.02
纺织服装、服饰业	Manufacture of Textile, Wearing Apparel and Accessories	5.54	0.43	1.23
皮革、毛皮、羽毛及其制品和制鞋业	Manufacture of Leather, Fur, Feather and Related Products and Footwear			
木材加工和木、竹、藤、棕、草制品业	Processing of Timber, Manufacture of Wood, Bamboo, Rattan,Palm and Straw Products			
家具制造业	Manufacture of Furniture			
造纸和纸制品业	Manufacture of Paper and Paper Products	3.26	0.16	1.22
印刷和记录媒介复制业	Printing and Reproduction of Recording Media	5.39	1.68	0.85
文教、工美、体育和娱乐用品制造业	Manufacture of Articles for Culture, Education, Arts and Crafts,Sport and Entertainment Activities			
石油、煤炭及其他燃料加工业	Processing of Petroleum, Coal and Other Fuels	35.49	3.66	5.35
化学原料和化学制品制造业	Manufacture of Raw Chemical Materials and Chemical Products	69.10	3.53	12.53
医药制造业	Manufacture of Medicines	23.04	3.13	2.93
化学纤维制造业	Manufacture of Chemical Fibres	3.10	0.16	2.18
橡胶和塑料制品业	Manufacture of Rubber and Plastics Products			
非金属矿物制品业	Manufacture of Non-metallic Mineral Products	54.01	25.70	7.16
黑色金属冶炼和压延加工业	Smelting and Pressing of Ferrous Metals	131.17	0.53	36.28
有色金属冶炼和压延加工业	Smelting and Pressing of Non-ferrous Metals	6.99	3.46	0.91
金属制品业	Manufacture of Metal Products	31.25	9.49	9.84
通用设备制造业	Manufacture of General Purpose Machinery	135.32	25.11	28.32
专用设备制造业	Manufacture of Special Purpose Machinery	72.67	17.27	18.72
汽车制造业	Manufacture of Automobiles	382.34	60.54	72.03
铁路、船舶、航空航天和其他运输设备制造业	Manufacture of Railway, Ship, Aerospace and Other Transport Equipments	59.03	9.93	7.05
电气机械和器材制造业	Manufacture of Electrical Machinery and Apparatus	161.79	57.11	43.34
计算机、通信和其他电子设备制造业	Manufacture of Computers, Communication and Other Electronic Equipment	388.33	143.94	163.86
仪器仪表制造业	Manufacture of Measuring Instruments and Machinery	21.19	6.79	5.66
其他制造业	Other Manufacture	1.90	1.62	0.04
废弃资源综合利用业	Utilization of Waste Resources			
金属制品、机械和设备修理业	Repair Service of Metal Products, Machinery and Equipment	9.25	3.69	2.96
电力、热力生产和供应业	Production and Supply of Electric Power and Heat Power	192.25	25.36	17.09
燃气生产和供应业	Production and Supply of Gas	40.29	3.51	4.89
水的生产和供应业	Production and Supply of Water	37.13	6.93	1.77

固定资产净额 Net Fixed Assets	固定资产原价 Original Value of Fixed Assets	流动负债合计 Current Liabilities Total	非流动负债合计 Non-Current Liabilities Totall	所有者权益合计 Total Owner's Equities	其中 of which 实收资本 Paid- up Capital	其中 of which 国家资本 Official Capital
6.23	6.75	10.02	1.47	7.13	4.25	0.50
0.14	0.25	0.39		0.18	0.30	
3.13	7.23	7.28	0.07	9.32	1.08	0.46
6.32	13.32	8.47	0.80	11.06	6.13	0.37
0.92	1.54	0.55		3.11	0.95	0.95
2.09	3.22	4.05		1.44	0.74	0.69
5.49	7.20	9.28	0.21	3.39	0.55	
1.16	2.31	3.54	0.02	1.60	1.44	1.44
3.35	9.53	2.89	1.44	5.54	4.20	0.77
33.09	91.58	36.94	7.18	36.09	27.25	27.25
57.26	88.25	137.88	34.39	17.59	15.22	9.15
5.94	8.94	17.93	4.78	15.43	2.94	2.00
3.56	4.29	2.15	0.32	7.59	5.91	0.85
15.18	34.09	53.54	1.45	26.98	10.79	3.75
280.23	542.89	303.94	44.05	155.23	114.07	113.72
2.02	2.98	8.22		1.55	0.88	0.88
9.22	16.98	33.40	1.36	12.07	7.39	3.28
35.99	61.82	70.34	3.57	101.28	67.62	5.36
15.33	20.78	70.81	10.24	19.00	18.12	3.28
34.98	77.04	279.79	8.91	173.75	36.18	17.96
9.55	20.96	50.36	7.38	38.28	27.68	2.05
30.83	57.70	172.72	6.88	75.09	54.15	33.60
6.26	13.48	261.03	18.13	153.06	25.39	9.71
3.58	6.39	13.36	0.38	14.60	6.06	2.18
0.66	0.84	1.11		1.45	1.00	
3.34	6.93	5.97		7.79	3.23	2.25
277.63	457.01	255.08	173.25	142.11	95.75	59.93
14.97	34.49	36.77	16.53	52.27	19.01	3.23
48.01	76.33	59.05	63.31	26.98	8.49	5.46

12-9 规模以上工业损益及分配(2021年)

Profit, Loss and Distribution of Industrial Enterprises Above Designated Size(2021)

单位：亿元

指标	Item	营业收入 Business Revenue	营业成本 Business Cost	税金及附加 Taxes and Other Charges
总计	Total	8492.55	7270.71	99.05
按登记注册类型分组	by Status of Registration			
内资企业	Domestic Invested Enterprises	7328.18	6333.65	93.35
国有企业	State-owned Enterprises	130.42	122.72	1.77
中央企业	Central Enterprises	38.18	41.16	0.35
地方企业	Local Enterprises	92.24	81.56	1.42
集体企业	Collective-owned Enterprises	6.90	6.61	0.04
股份合作企业	Cooperative Enterprises	1.58	1.10	0.01
联营企业	Joint Ownership Enterprises	1.93	1.05	0.06
国有联营企业	State Joint Ownership Enterprises			
集体联营企业	Collective Joint Ownership Enterprises	1.19	0.49	0.06
国有与集体联营企业	Joint State-collective Enterprises	0.74	0.56	0.01
其他联营企业	Other Joint Ownership Enterprises			
有限责任公司	Limited Liability Corporations	2555.95	2248.93	16.49
国有独资公司	State Sole Funded Corporations	192.49	193.25	1.56
其他有限责任公司	Other Limited Liability Corporations	2363.46	2055.68	14.93
股份有限公司	Share-holding Corporations Ltd.	2269.58	1999.61	65.44
私营企业	Private Enterprises	2361.81	1953.64	9.53
私营独资企业	Private-funded Enterprises	21.02	19.06	0.07
私营合伙企业	Private Partnership Enterprises	2.23	2.01	
私营有限责任公司	Private Limited Liability Corporations	2220.98	1843.62	8.64
私营股份有限公司	Private Share-holding Corporations Ltd.	117.58	88.95	0.82
其他企业	Other Enterprises			
港、澳、台商投资企业	Enterprises with Funds from Hong Kong,Macao and Taiwan	810.97	661.75	3.53
合资经营企业	Joint-venture Enterprises	322.05	250.97	1.68
合作经营企业	Cooperative Enterprises			
港澳台商独资经营企业	Enterprises with Sole Investment	487.56	409.79	1.85
港澳台商投资股份有限公司	Share-holding Corporations Ltd.			
其他港澳台商投资企业	Other Enterprises with Funds from Hong Kong,Macao and Taiwan	1.36	1.00	
外商投资企业	Foreign Funded Enterprises	353.39	275.30	2.17
中外合资经营企业	Joint-venture Enterprises	154.33	121.33	1.05
中外合作经营企业	Cooperation Enterprises	2.83	1.78	0.03
外资企业	Enterprises with Sole Fund	156.15	119.19	1.00
外商投资股份有限公司	Share-holding Corporations Ltd.	40.09	33.00	0.10
其他外商投资企业	Other Foreign Funded Enterprises			
按轻重工业分	by Light & Heavy Industry			
轻工业	Light Industry	1193.66	814.47	8.42
重工业	Heavy Industry	7298.89	6456.23	90.63
按企业规模分	by Enterprise Size			
大型企业	Large-sized Enterprises	4900.90	4240.82	76.88
中型企业	Medium-sized Enterprises	1412.94	1199.76	9.29
小型企业	Small-sized Enterprises	1993.92	1664.87	12.20
微型企业	Micro-sized Enterprises	184.79	165.27	0.69

(100 million yuan)

销售费用 Selling Expenses	管理费用 Management Expenses	利息费用 Interest Expenses	利润总额 Total Profits	所得税费用 Income Tax Payable	亏损企业亏损总额 Total Loss of Loss Enterprises	利税总额 Total Profits and Taxes	应交增值税 Value-added Tax Payable
264.19	**251.00**	**56.23**	**408.38**	**63.51**	**63.24**	**645.49**	**138.06**
218.67	211.17	49.45	292.86	46.89	62.21	502.11	115.90
0.86	4.58	1.60	−1.66	0.67	9.34	2.75	2.64
0.06	1.47	1.29	−5.95	−0.73	7.28	−4.87	0.73
0.80	3.11	0.31	4.29	1.39	2.06	7.62	1.91
0.05	0.33	0.01	−0.18	0.02	0.31	−0.04	0.10
0.17	0.28	0.02	−0.05		0.12	0.02	0.06
0.04	0.15	0.01	0.62	0.01		0.82	0.14
	0.10		0.54			0.70	0.11
0.04	0.05	0.01	0.08	0.01		0.11	0.02
62.36	77.70	28.00	92.65	17.94	37.02	148.25	39.11
4.44	9.40	2.25	−3.21	0.29	5.83	−1.90	−0.25
57.92	68.30	25.75	95.86	17.65	31.19	150.15	39.35
49.04	46.54	8.58	66.97	9.64	4.98	161.12	28.71
106.16	81.60	11.24	134.50	18.61	10.44	189.19	45.15
0.74	0.81	0.04	−0.05	0.04	0.34	0.40	0.37
0.03	0.06	0.01	0.08			0.10	0.02
99.27	73.64	9.94	128.08	17.70	9.63	177.28	40.56
6.12	7.09	1.25	6.39	0.88	0.47	11.41	4.20
28.00	23.24	5.28	73.59	9.64	0.04	92.83	15.71
13.46	10.46	0.67	44.23	9.07	0.04	53.70	7.80
14.42	12.66	4.60	29.31	0.57		39.06	7.90
0.11	0.11	0.01	0.05			0.06	0.01
17.53	16.59	1.49	41.93	6.97	0.99	50.55	6.45
7.88	6.39	0.93	13.59	2.06	0.34	17.42	2.79
0.02	0.33		0.56	0.09		0.68	0.10
5.38	9.05	0.56	19.55	4.30	0.65	23.75	3.20
4.24	0.82		8.24	0.52		8.70	0.36
120.36	53.49	5.58	167.30	25.61	5.73	206.78	31.07
143.84	197.51	50.64	241.08	37.90	57.51	438.71	106.99
131.90	102.77	26.43	247.70	38.41	17.27	394.35	69.77
53.04	45.15	13.66	65.14	9.26	19.40	99.45	25.02
75.70	98.62	13.67	89.61	14.97	24.73	141.89	40.08
3.56	4.46	2.47	5.93	0.87	1.84	9.80	3.18

12-9 续表 continued

指标	Item	营业收入 Business Revenue	营业成本 Business Cost	税金及附加 Taxes and Other Charges
按工业行业分	by Sector			
煤炭开采和洗选业	Mining and Washing of Coal	7.55	4.71	0.38
石油和天然气开采业	Extraction of Petroleum and Natural Gas	8.11	4.45	0.86
黑色金属矿采选业	Mining and Processing of Ferrous Metal Ores	207.35	182.26	2.17
有色金属矿采选业	Mining and Processing of Non-Ferrous Metal Ores			
非金属矿采选业	Mining and Processing of Non-metal Ores	18.73	11.19	0.79
开采专业及辅助性活动	Professional and Support Activities for Mining			
其他采矿业	Mining of Other Ores			
农副食品加工业	Processing of Food from Agricultural Products	169.04	156.96	0.29
食品制造业	Manufacture of Foods	152.64	117.15	1.00
酒、饮料和精制茶制造业	Manufacture of Liquor, Beverages and Refined Tea	62.68	49.76	2.01
烟草制品业	Manufacture of Tobacco	1.26	0.66	0.01
纺织业	Manufacture of Textile	46.87	42.56	0.18
纺织服装、服饰业	Manufacture of Textile, Wearing Apparel and Accessories	16.47	13.57	0.19
皮革、毛皮、羽毛及其制品和制鞋业	Manufacture of Leather, Fur, Feather and Related Products and Footwear	2.73	2.43	0.01
木材加工和木、竹、藤、棕、草制品业	Processing of Timber, Manufacture of Wood, Bamboo, Rattan,Palm and Straw Products	7.67	6.78	0.03
家具制造业	Manufacture of Furniture	12.05	10.52	0.07
造纸和纸制品业	Manufacture of Paper and Paper Products	48.80	40.85	0.26
印刷和记录媒介复制业	Printing and Reproduction of Recording Media	47.15	38.74	0.27
文教、工美、体育和娱乐用品制造业	Manufacture of Articles for Culture, Education, Arts and Crafts,Sport and Entertainment Activities	17.67	14.02	0.12
石油、煤炭及其他燃料加工业	Processing of Petroleum, Coal and Other Fuels	348.74	262.99	60.28
化学原料和化学制品制造业	Manufacture of Raw Chemical Materials and Chemical Products	364.01	301.89	1.81
医药制造业	Manufacture of Medicines	368.42	143.93	2.75
化学纤维制造业	Manufacture of Chemical Fibres	13.79	10.88	0.09
橡胶和塑料制品业	Manufacture of Rubber and Plastics Products	38.27	32.63	0.17
非金属矿物制品业	Manufacture of Non-metallic Mineral Products	483.97	405.42	3.22
黑色金属冶炼和压延加工业	Smelting and Pressing of Ferrous Metals	1956.17	1876.47	4.29
有色金属冶炼和压延加工业	Smelting and Pressing of Non-ferrous Metals	52.62	49.16	0.12
金属制品业	Manufacture of Metal Products	358.51	302.09	1.81
通用设备制造业	Manufacture of General Purpose Machinery	378.39	297.34	2.12
专用设备制造业	Manufacture of Special Purpose Machinery	301.34	229.50	1.33
汽车制造业	Manufacture of Automobiles	1250.93	1112.11	4.70
铁路、船舶、航空航天和其他运输设备制造业	Manufacture of Railway, Ship, Aerospace and Other Transport Equipments	74.03	61.41	0.59
电气机械和器材制造业	Manufacture of Electrical Machinery and Apparatus	420.88	360.01	1.74
计算机、通信和其他电子设备制造业	Manufacture of Computers, Communication and Other Electronic Equipment	785.37	690.11	1.13
仪器仪表制造业	Manufacture of Measuring Instruments and Machinery	88.86	59.95	0.52
其他制造业	Other Manufacture	3.34	2.74	0.01
废弃资源综合利用业	Utilization of Waste Resources	30.59	28.83	0.24
金属制品、机械和设备修理业	Repair Service of Metal Products, Machinery and Equipment	12.89	9.93	0.17
电力、热力生产和供应业	Production and Supply of Electric Power and Heat Power	191.55	208.14	1.66
燃气生产和供应业	Production and Supply of Gas	109.73	99.91	0.16
水的生产和供应业	Production and Supply of Water	33.38	28.63	1.48

销售费用 Selling Expenses	管理费用 Management Expenses	利息费用 Interest Expenses	利润总额 Total Profits	所得税费用 Income Tax Payable	亏损企业亏损总额 Total Loss of Loss Enterprises	利税总额 Total Profits and Taxes	应交增值税 Value-added Tax Payable
0.08	0.78	0.45	1.17		0.01	2.29	0.73
	0.04	0.02	2.73	0.68		4.30	0.71
0.13	5.77	2.40	12.99	2.15	0.63	19.98	4.82
0.44	2.35	0.37	3.22	0.78		4.85	0.83
5.06	3.50	0.83	2.72	0.25	0.90	4.12	1.11
8.20	7.66	0.58	16.67	3.34	0.54	21.25	3.57
4.76	2.21	0.28	4.17	1.07	0.39	7.66	1.48
	0.13		0.38	0.06		0.48	0.08
0.93	1.98	0.35	–0.20	0.03	0.87	0.33	0.36
1.44	1.44	0.09	0.18	0.07	0.41	0.89	0.53
0.01	0.09		–0.06		0.16		0.05
0.32	0.15	0.10	0.12		0.02	0.21	0.06
0.41	0.54	0.01	0.37	0.08	0.05	0.76	0.32
2.01	2.27	0.30	1.79	0.39	0.32	2.95	0.90
1.52	2.74	0.25	3.45	0.41	0.31	4.82	1.10
1.56	0.96	0.30	0.37	0.02	0.08	0.86	0.37
1.05	6.34	0.78	17.59	4.03		89.50	11.62
14.86	11.35	6.11	17.05	2.09	1.77	24.82	5.96
70.41	19.31	1.82	110.60	15.94	0.12	128.46	15.11
0.34	0.64	0.10	1.02	0.12	0.16	1.03	–0.08
1.33	1.99	0.15	–1.09	0.28	2.46	–0.21	0.71
18.68	19.89	3.61	24.59	4.80	2.73	39.80	11.99
4.49	28.40	11.33	9.96	4.50	5.13	28.67	14.42
0.53	1.43	0.25	0.21	0.02	0.18	0.67	0.35
11.12	12.14	2.30	19.15	3.63	1.56	28.27	7.32
20.36	23.24	1.04	24.62	3.38	3.27	34.91	8.16
18.67	15.03	2.45	22.95	2.94	4.65	30.78	6.50
26.19	22.90	6.10	59.43	7.72	2.36	85.42	21.29
2.00	5.56	0.20	3.14	0.79	0.28	5.09	1.36
15.69	14.36	2.69	20.88	2.08	4.38	28.40	5.78
17.90	14.45	2.80	26.97	1.18	1.81	33.10	5.00
7.32	6.49	0.22	10.11	0.95	0.25	13.34	2.71
0.09	0.13	0.01	0.25			0.37	0.11
0.29	0.54	0.03	1.57	0.06	0.19	3.61	1.80
0.11	1.67	0.05	0.80	0.09	0.01	1.36	0.39
1.26	7.02	6.27	–17.60	–2.11	26.29	–16.75	–0.81
2.93	2.80	0.43	4.51	1.30	0.30	5.17	0.50
1.70	2.72	1.18	1.60	0.36	0.63	3.93	0.84

12-10 规模以上国有及国有控股工业损益及分配(2021年)
Profit、Loss and Distribution of State-Owned and State-Controlled Industrial Enterprises Above Designated Size(2021)

单位：亿元

指标	Item	营业收入 Business Revenue	营业成本 Business Cost	税金及附加 Taxes and Other Charges
总计	Total	3635.12	3250.35	77.17
按登记注册类型分组	by Status of Registration			
内资企业	Domestic Invested Enterprises	3411.35	3071.12	75.84
国有企业	State-owned Enterprises	130.42	122.72	1.77
中央企业	Central Enterprises	38.18	41.16	0.35
地方企业	Local Enterprises	92.24	81.56	1.42
集体企业	Collective-owned Enterprises			
股份合作企业	Cooperative Enterprises			
联营企业	Joint Ownership Enterprises	0.74	0.56	0.01
有限责任公司	Limited Liability Corporations	1247.34	1112.38	10.33
国有独资公司	State Sole Funded Corporations	192.49	193.25	1.56
其他有限责任公司	Other Limited Liability Corporations	1054.85	919.12	8.77
股份有限公司	Share-holding Corporations Ltd.	2032.85	1835.46	63.73
私营企业	Private Enterprises			
其他企业	Other Enterprises			
港、澳、台商投资企业	Enterprises with Funds from Hong Kong,Macao and Taiwan	164.78	129.60	0.87
合资经营企业	Joint-venture Enterprises	164.78	129.60	0.87
合作经营企业	Cooperative Enterprises			
港澳台商独资经营企业	Enterprises with Sole Investment			
港澳台商投资股份有限公司	Share-holding Corporations Ltd.			
其他港澳台商投资企业	Other Enterprises with Funds from Hong Kong,Macao and Taiwan			
外商投资企业	Foreign Funded Enterprises	58.99	49.64	0.46
中外合资经营企业	Joint-venture Enterprises	56.57	48.11	0.44
中外合作经营企业	Cooperation Enterprises	2.41	1.53	0.02
外资企业	Enterprises with Sole Fund			
外商投资股份有限公司	Share-holding Corporations Ltd.			
其他外商投资企业	Other Foreign Funded Enterprises			
按轻重工业分	by Light & Heavy Industry			
轻工业	Light Industry	105.57	67.29	1.80
重工业	Heavy Industry	3529.55	3183.06	75.37
按企业规模分	by Enterprise Size			
大型企业	Large-sized Enterprises	2807.55	2539.33	69.17
中型企业	Medium-sized Enterprises	445.62	379.30	4.56
小型企业	Small-sized Enterprises	326.98	284.60	3.21
微型企业	Micro-sized Enterprises	54.97	47.12	0.23
按工业行业分	by Sector			
煤炭开采和洗选业	Mining and Washing of Coal	6.05	3.37	0.33
石油和天然气开采业	Extraction of Petroleum and Natural Gas	8.11	4.45	0.86
黑色金属矿采选业	Mining and Processing of Ferrous Metal Ores	25.05	14.44	1.22

(100 million yuan)

销售费用 Selling Expenses	管理费用 Management Expenses	利息费用 Interest Expenses	利润总额 Total Profits	所得税费用 Income Tax Payable	亏损企业 亏损总额 Total Loss of Loss Enterprises	利税总额 Total Profits and Taxes	应交增值税 Value-added Tax Payable
66.17	82.03	27.88	92.47	19.46	37.46	219.42	49.78
54.97	74.49	27.36	70.46	14.14	37.21	191.25	44.95
0.86	4.58	1.60	-1.66	0.67	9.34	2.75	2.64
0.06	1.47	1.29	-5.95	-0.73	7.28	-4.87	0.73
0.80	3.11	0.31	4.29	1.39	2.06	7.62	1.91
0.04	0.05	0.01	0.08	0.01		0.11	0.02
27.76	37.58	19.30	30.49	6.29	24.02	59.85	19.03
4.44	9.40	2.25	-3.21	0.29	5.83	-1.90	-0.25
23.32	28.18	17.05	33.70	6.00	18.18	61.75	19.28
26.32	32.29	6.45	41.55	7.17	3.86	128.53	23.25
9.61	4.17	0.39	18.99	4.69		23.83	3.98
9.61	4.17	0.39	18.99	4.69		23.83	3.98
1.59	3.36	0.14	3.02	0.63	0.25	4.34	0.86
1.58	3.08	0.14	2.56	0.56	0.25	3.75	0.76
0.01	0.28		0.47	0.07		0.59	0.10
21.16	4.99	0.78	9.44	1.40	0.70	14.86	3.62
45.01	77.04	27.11	83.03	18.07	36.76	204.55	46.16
36.92	52.47	17.54	68.50	14.18	14.94	172.53	34.86
20.26	15.48	6.22	9.62	0.07	14.02	22.77	8.59
7.39	13.32	3.03	10.76	4.59	8.38	19.87	5.91
1.60	0.76	1.10	3.59	0.63	0.12	4.25	0.42
0.08	0.76	0.35	1.18			2.07	0.56
	0.04	0.02	2.73	0.68		4.30	0.71
	2.41	0.50	5.29	0.40		8.78	2.27

12-10 续表 continued

指标	Item	营业收入 Business Revenue	营业成本 Business Cost	税金及附加 Taxes and Other Charges
有色金属矿采选业	Mining and Processing of Non-Ferrous Metal Ores			
非金属矿采选业	Mining and Processing of Non-metal Ores	10.38	5.21	0.47
开采专业及辅助性活动	Professional and Support Activities for Mining			
其他采矿业	Mining of Other Ores			
农副食品加工业	Processing of Food from Agricultural Products	0.27	0.17	
食品制造业	Manufacture of Foods	14.22	10.43	0.07
酒、饮料和精制茶制造业	Manufacture of Liquor, Beverages and Refined Tea	26.43	19.29	1.12
烟草制品业	Manufacture of Tobacco	1.26	0.66	0.01
纺织业	Manufacture of Textile	2.76	2.64	0.02
纺织服装、服饰业	Manufacture of Textile, Wearing Apparel and Accessories	3.42	2.84	0.04
皮革、毛皮、羽毛及其制品和制鞋业	Manufacture of Leather, Fur, Feather and Related Products and Footwear			
木材加工和木、竹、藤、棕、草制品业	Processing of Timber, Manufacture of Wood, Bamboo, Rattan,Palm and Straw Products			
家具制造业	Manufacture of Furniture			
造纸和纸制品业	Manufacture of Paper and Paper Products	3.57	2.61	0.03
印刷和记录媒介复制业	Printing and Reproduction of Recording Media	7.26	5.58	0.09
文教、工美、体育和娱乐用品制造业	Manufacture of Articles for Culture, Education, Arts and Crafts,Sport and Entertainment Activities			
石油、煤炭及其他燃料加工业	Processing of Petroleum, Coal and Other Fuels	244.89	166.89	59.85
化学原料和化学制品制造业	Manufacture of Raw Chemical Materials and Chemical Products	115.95	91.06	0.72
医药制造业	Manufacture of Medicines	19.35	8.13	0.24
化学纤维制造业	Manufacture of Chemical Fibres	4.37	3.94	0.03
橡胶和塑料制品业	Manufacture of Rubber and Plastics Products			
非金属矿物制品业	Manufacture of Non-metallic Mineral Products	64.49	53.34	0.65
黑色金属冶炼和压延加工业	Smelting and Pressing of Ferrous Metals	930.15	883.03	2.59
有色金属冶炼和压延加工业	Smelting and Pressing of Non-ferrous Metals	26.12	24.95	0.03
金属制品业	Manufacture of Metal Products	74.45	67.23	0.37
通用设备制造业	Manufacture of General Purpose Machinery	82.23	65.13	0.65
专用设备制造业	Manufacture of Special Purpose Machinery	36.98	33.01	0.19
汽车制造业	Manufacture of Automobiles	720.84	664.53	2.79
铁路、船舶、航空航天和其他运输设备制造业	Manufacture of Railway, Ship, Aerospace and Other Transport Equipments	60.03	50.28	0.49
电气机械和器材制造业	Manufacture of Electrical Machinery and Apparatus	175.41	158.17	0.76
计算机、通信和其他电子设备制造业	Manufacture of Computers, Communication and Other Electronic Equipment	689.15	623.16	0.46
仪器仪表制造业	Manufacture of Measuring Instruments and Machinery	24.87	18.19	0.15
其他制造业	Other Manufacture	2.01	1.63	0.01
废弃资源综合利用业	Utilization of Waste Resources			
金属制品、机械和设备修理业	Repair Service of Metal Products, Machinery and Equipment	10.76	8.07	0.16
电力、热力生产和供应业	Production and Supply of Electric Power and Heat Power	168.85	190.80	1.48
燃气生产和供应业	Production and Supply of Gas	50.51	44.18	0.09
水的生产和供应业	Production and Supply of Water	24.94	22.95	1.22

销售费用 Selling Expenses	管理费用 Management Expenses	利息费用 Interest Expenses	利润总额 Total Profits	所得税费用 Income Tax Payable	亏损企业亏损总额 Total Loss of Loss Enterprises	利税总额 Total Profits and Taxes	应交增值税 Value-added Tax Payable
0.01	1.46	0.37	2.62	0.66		3.69	0.60
0.03	0.05	0.02	0.01			0.02	0.01
0.68	0.91	0.03	1.44	0.14	0.21	1.47	–0.03
3.86	0.41	0.02	1.94	0.50	0.05	3.83	0.77
	0.13		0.38	0.06		0.48	0.08
0.03	0.16	0.01	–0.08		0.09	–0.04	0.02
0.16	0.63	0.02	0.26	0.03	0.06	0.45	0.16
0.06	0.33		0.39	0.07	0.08	0.52	0.10
0.24	0.66	0.01	0.70	0.07	0.03	1.17	0.37
0.20	3.33	0.44	14.03	3.54		83.43	9.55
7.98	2.98	3.66	6.13	0.26	0.83	8.31	1.46
8.42	0.71	0.66	2.27	0.27		3.77	1.26
0.07	0.12		0.11	–0.01		0.10	–0.05
2.50	2.17	0.43	4.78	0.91	0.27	7.33	1.90
1.41	20.89	9.08	0.62	2.16	3.32	10.85	7.64
0.08	0.77	0.13	0.09			0.26	0.13
1.10	1.70	0.39	1.55	0.21	0.13	3.08	1.16
3.05	5.31	0.13	7.25	1.03	0.94	9.84	1.95
1.26	1.92	1.55	–2.84	0.02	3.21	–2.14	0.51
11.13	5.56	1.54	34.09	8.54	0.04	49.76	12.88
1.72	4.47	0.15	2.45	0.62		4.03	1.09
3.96	4.99	1.19	0.50	0.33	3.35	3.50	2.25
11.43	6.35	2.26	17.38	0.71	0.24	19.37	1.53
1.48	1.25	0.02	2.91	0.33		3.54	0.49
0.01	0.07		0.21			0.32	0.10
0.06	1.59	0.04	0.76	0.09		1.27	0.35
0.93	5.81	3.91	–19.15	–2.96	24.05	–18.64	–0.96
2.50	1.89	0.31	2.28	0.67	0.12	2.60	0.22
1.69	2.19	0.63	0.18	0.14	0.43	2.11	0.71

12-11 分地区规模以上工业主要经济指标(2021年)
Main Economic Indicators of Industrial Enterprises Above Designated Size By Region(2021)

单位:亿元

指标	Item	全市 Total	历下区 Li xia	市中区 Shi zhong	槐荫区 Huai yin	天桥区 Tian qiao
企业单位数(个)	Number of Industial Enterprises(unit)	2543	49	60	75	130
工业总产值	Gross Industrial Output Value	7591.25	332.50	519.20	178.03	165.52
资产与负债	Assets and Liabilities					
资产总计	Total Assets	8494.19	410.81	504.76	318.72	303.02
流动资产合计	Current Assets	5224.97	192.71	360.75	229.58	151.87
存货	Inventories	1115.06	20.43	70.26	37.87	28.71
应收账款	Accounts Receivable	1429.69	28.17	86.21	49.54	39.75
固定资产净额	Net Fixed Assets	1778.16	113.86	58.06	29.45	92.79
流动负债合计	Current Liabilities Total	4449.43	204.21	255.76	143.67	182.65
非流动负债合计	Non-Current Liabilities Total	664.46	58.60	54.68	8.32	46.19
所有者权益合计	Total Owner's Equities	3380.30	148.00	194.32	166.73	74.17
实收资本	Paid- up Capital	1491.51	68.79	41.31	47.41	47.15
国家资本	Official Capital	325.32	35.89	18.07	5.00	14.12
损益及分配	Profit,Loss and Distribution					
营业收入	Business Revenue	8492.55	340.63	600.52	181.24	164.84
营业成本	Business Cost	7270.71	253.99	565.56	149.46	151.10
税金及附加	Taxes and Other Charges	99.05	60.24	2.56	0.93	0.94
管理费用	Management Expenses	251.00	9.66	8.77	8.89	8.87
利润总额	Total Profits	408.38	13.14	14.02	16.17	4.44
应交所得税	Income Tax Payable	63.51	4.30	1.57	1.59	0.66
亏损企业亏损总额	Total Loss of Loss Enterprises	63.24	4.23	0.22	0.68	3.16
利税总额	Total Profits and Taxes	645.49	83.83	25.59	20.95	6.50
本年应交增值税	Value-added Tax Payable	138.06	10.44	9.02	3.84	1.13

(100million yuan)

历城区 Li cheng	长清区 Chang qing	章丘区 Zhang qiu	济阳区 Ji yang	莱芜区 Lai wu	钢城区 Gang cheng	平阴县 Ping yin	商河县 Shang he	济南高新区 Ji'nan gao xin	济南起步区（直管） Ji'nan Start-up Area (Directly under)	南部山区 Nan shan
168	221	567	139	288	135	137	172	351	35	16
326.57	248.23	1385.02	181.98	1078.04	1001.06	336.68	174.40	1602.29	48.20	13.51
592.74	367.35	1524.07	249.01	1084.80	739.71	434.85	222.61	1668.03	50.02	23.68
409.04	235.52	907.36	151.40	663.03	258.96	266.37	127.49	1229.26	26.02	15.59
57.37	55.11	173.25	26.86	152.98	74.21	53.67	30.64	323.28	4.31	6.09
102.09	84.03	196.51	28.62	248.01	33.74	61.09	41.28	413.46	13.74	3.47
96.72	80.34	278.63	54.69	288.12	345.11	90.24	68.03	172.47	7.93	1.75
355.06	184.09	819.95	93.53	662.64	430.88	163.44	103.00	808.41	26.16	15.98
38.01	36.12	104.16	26.70	103.01	54.20	31.06	27.88	70.96	2.68	1.88
199.68	147.15	599.96	128.78	319.16	254.63	240.34	91.73	788.66	21.17	5.83
123.02	117.77	262.69	52.95	233.25	158.19	56.67	48.86	217.32	13.96	2.15
9.43	9.43	29.35	7.24	29.90	119.17	2.89	2.11	42.58	0.12	
350.72	256.30	1400.62	184.76	1582.18	1152.29	357.54	175.20	1681.54	51.36	12.81
285.78	211.16	1185.39	145.91	1488.24	1069.36	286.49	144.94	1280.76	42.79	9.78
1.78	1.64	8.02	1.78	5.85	4.22	2.46	1.06	6.72	0.31	0.55
17.80	14.29	41.90	8.41	26.77	27.89	15.31	7.97	51.76	1.90	0.81
27.25	12.26	66.55	14.44	19.79	17.78	30.09	11.42	157.12	3.35	0.57
3.36	1.72	6.49	3.04	4.22	4.16	6.65	1.65	22.84	1.17	0.09
8.55	2.96	6.88	2.64	18.14	4.49	2.41	1.31	7.31	0.11	0.14
36.87	19.67	100.84	20.86	43.53	33.97	40.48	15.10	191.06	4.93	1.32
7.84	5.77	26.28	4.65	17.89	11.98	7.93	2.62	27.21	1.27	0.20

12-12 规模以上大中型工业企业经营情况 (2021 年)
Main Indicators of Large and Medium-Sized Enterprises(2021)

单位：亿元

指标	Item	企业单位数（个）Number of Enterprises(unit)	亏损企业（个）Loss nterprises (unit)	工业总产值（现价）Gross Industrial Output Value (Current Prices)
总计	Total	228	37	5478.60
按登记注册类型分组	by Status of Registration			
内资企业	Domestic Invested Enterprises	183	36	4518.15
国有企业	State-owned Enterprises	2	1	65.18
中央企业	Central Enterprises	1	1	27.73
地方企业	Local Enterprises	1		37.45
集体企业	Collective-owned Enterprises			
股份合作企业	Cooperative Enterprises			
联营企业	Joint Ownership Enterprises			
有限责任公司	Limited Liability Corporations	97	24	1533.08
国有独资公司	State Sole Funded Corporations	10	4	110.29
其他有限责任公司	Other Limited Liability Corporations	87	20	1422.80
股份有限公司	Share-holding Corporations Ltd.	29	5	1939.29
私营企业	Private Enterprises	55	6	980.59
私营独资企业	Private-funded Enterprises	1	1	2.18
私营合伙企业	Private Partnership Enterprises			
私营有限责任公司	Private Limited Liability Corporations	48	5	907.71
私营股份有限公司	Private Share-holding Corporations Ltd.	6		70.70
其他企业	Other Enterprises			
港、澳、台商投资企业	Enterprises with Funds from Hong Kong,Macao and Taiwan	22		725.00
合资经营企业	Joint-venture Enterprises	13		258.47
合作经营企业	Cooperative Enterprises			
港澳台商独资经营企业	Enterprises with Sole Investment	9		466.53
港澳台商投资股份有限公司	Share-holding Corporations Ltd.			
其他港澳台商投资企业	Other Enterprises with Funds from Hong Kong,Macao and Taiwan			
外商投资企业	Foreign Funded Enterprises	23	1	235.45
中外合资经营企业	Joint-venture Enterprises	12		128.60
中外合作经营企业	Cooperation Enterprises			
外资企业	Enterprises with Sole Fund	11	1	106.85
外商投资股份有限公司	Share-holding Corporations Ltd.			
其他外商投资企业	Other Foreign Funded Enterprises			
按轻重工业分	by Light & Heavy Industry			
轻工业	Light Industry	69	7	685.97
重工业	Heavy Industry	159	30	4792.63
按企业规模分	by Enterprise Size			
大型企业	Large-sized Enterprises	65	9	4258.13
中型企业	Medium-sized Enterprises	163	28	1220.47
小型企业	Small-sized Enterprises			
微型企业	Micro-sized Enterprises			
按工业行业分	by Sector			
煤炭开采和洗选业	Mining and Washing of Coal	2	1	7.37

(100 million yuan)

资产总计 Total Assets	负债合计 Total Liabilities	营业收入 Business Revenue	利润总额 Total Profits	利税总额 Total Profits and Taxes	平均用工人数（万人） Annual Average Employees (10 000 persons)
5726.54	3373.49	6313.84	312.84	493.80	23.67
4644.78	2803.16	5361.35	222.01	379.26	18.70
60.01	45.67	63.59	–4.28	–2.33	0.33
42.65	31.18	27.73	–7.19	–6.29	0.15
17.37	14.49	35.86	2.91	3.96	0.17
2234.68	1429.26	1852.27	71.03	111.38	8.93
495.76	356.72	138.64	–3.83	–3.91	1.09
1738.92	1072.54	1713.63	74.86	115.29	7.85
1430.29	776.61	2192.94	59.02	149.98	4.39
919.80	551.62	1252.55	96.24	120.23	5.04
4.54	4.82	2.18	–0.24	–0.18	0.04
827.06	513.39	1191.85	93.59	114.47	4.67
88.20	33.41	58.52	2.89	5.94	0.33
862.65	467.66	725.69	65.99	83.71	3.33
345.05	149.01	265.45	40.34	48.82	1.58
517.60	318.65	460.24	25.65	34.89	1.74
219.11	102.67	226.80	24.84	30.82	1.64
122.32	70.46	122.21	11.49	14.51	0.92
96.79	32.21	104.59	13.35	16.31	0.73
956.11	347.90	705.31	136.88	165.13	6.59
4770.43	3025.58	5608.53	175.96	328.67	17.07
4120.94	2383.81	4900.90	247.70	394.35	15.67
1605.60	989.68	1412.94	65.14	99.45	8.00
10.62	16.94	7.09	1.17	2.24	0.26

12-12 续表 continued

指标	Item	企业单位数（个）Number of Enterprises(unit)	亏损企业（个）Loss nterprises (unit)	工业总产值（现价）Gross Industrial Output Value (Current Prices)
石油和天然气开采业	Extraction of Petroleum and Natural Gas			
黑色金属矿采选业	Mining and Processing of Ferrous Metal Ores	5	1	116.71
有色金属矿采选业	Mining and Processing of Non-Ferrous Metal Ores			
非金属矿采选业	Mining and Processing of Non-metal Ores	1		6.82
开采专业及辅助性活动	Professional and Support Activities for Mining			
其他采矿业	Mining of Other Ores			
农副食品加工业	Processing of Food from Agricultural Products	8	2	43.24
食品制造业	Manufacture of Foods	10	1	102.81
酒、饮料和精制茶制造业	Manufacture of Liquor, Beverages and Refined Tea	7	2	51.94
烟草制品业	Manufacture of Tobacco			
纺织业	Manufacture of Textile	4	1	14.89
纺织服装、服饰业	Manufacture of Textile, Wearing Apparel and Accessories	4	1	7.33
皮革、毛皮、羽毛及其制品和制鞋业	Manufacture of Leather, Fur, Feather and Related Products and Footwear			
木材加工和木、竹、藤、棕、草制品业	Processing of Timber, Manufacture of Wood, Bamboo, Rattan,Palm and Straw Products			
家具制造业	Manufacture of Furniture	2		4.86
造纸和纸制品业	Manufacture of Paper and Paper Products	3		13.91
印刷和记录媒介复制业	Printing and Reproduction of Recording Media	3		10.98
文教、工美、体育和娱乐用品制造业	Manufacture of Articles for Culture, Education, Arts and Crafts,Sport and Entertainment Activities	1		3.15
石油、煤炭及其他燃料加工业	Processing of Petroleum, Coal and Other Fuels	3		294.98
化学原料和化学制品制造业	Manufacture of Raw Chemical Materials and Chemical Products	9	1	178.66
医药制造业	Manufacture of Medicines	18		333.89
化学纤维制造业	Manufacture of Chemical Fibres			
橡胶和塑料制品业	Manufacture of Rubber and Plastics Products	1	1	1.93
非金属矿物制品业	Manufacture of Non-metallic Mineral Products	21	3	200.59
黑色金属冶炼和压延加工业	Smelting and Pressing of Ferrous Metals	8	2	1385.31
有色金属冶炼和压延加工业	Smelting and Pressing of Non-ferrous Metals	1		4.61
金属制品业	Manufacture of Metal Products	16	1	148.74
通用设备制造业	Manufacture of General Purpose Machinery	18	3	210.55
专用设备制造业	Manufacture of Special Purpose Machinery	13	2	146.42
汽车制造业	Manufacture of Automobiles	17	3	1061.91
铁路、船舶、航空航天和其他运输设备制造业	Manufacture of Railway, Ship, Aerospace and Other Transport Equipments	6		58.21
电气机械和器材制造业	Manufacture of Electrical Machinery and Apparatus	19	2	196.70
计算机、通信和其他电子设备制造业	Manufacture of Computers, Communication and Other Electronic Equipment	10	1	656.20
仪器仪表制造业	Manufacture of Measuring Instruments and Machinery	3		16.61
其他制造业	Other Manufacture			
废弃资源综合利用业	Utilization of Waste Resources	1		5.94
金属制品、机械和设备修理业	Repair Service of Metal Products, Machinery and Equipment	1		7.33
电力、热力生产和供应业	Production and Supply of Electric Power and Heat Power	7	7	139.21
燃气生产和供应业	Production and Supply of Gas	3		33.04
水的生产和供应业	Production and Supply of Water	3	2	13.76

资产总计 Total Assets	负债合计 Total Liabilities	营业收入 Business Revenue	利润总额 Total Profits	利税总额 Total Profits and Taxes	平均用工人数（万人） Annual Average Employees (10 000 persons)
103.91	89.89	190.86	10.88	16.97	0.72
14.23	9.25	6.61	1.94	2.82	0.04
39.94	34.15	56.52	1.82	2.47	0.35
77.73	27.34	101.77	11.51	14.26	1.04
46.82	25.88	49.04	3.63	6.33	0.40
15.95	11.36	18.44	–0.16	0.14	0.19
18.24	11.86	9.75	0.32	0.87	0.38
6.13	5.16	7.07	0.29	0.56	0.12
12.01	6.93	15.94	1.16	1.71	0.13
10.18	6.21	11.03	0.82	1.17	0.20
6.88	6.01	2.92	0.16	0.37	0.05
172.67	132.01	323.32	16.51	87.68	0.24
310.33	212.49	188.35	10.47	15.17	0.75
566.59	164.65	335.02	105.30	121.59	2.77
1.93	5.40	1.95	–2.34	–2.29	0.05
226.55	98.22	216.80	19.25	25.60	1.35
881.75	581.27	1898.83	10.18	28.68	3.01
7.52	4.26	4.24	0.08	0.11	0.05
199.24	76.14	148.31	14.72	19.16	1.31
302.81	134.94	212.58	18.58	24.39	1.90
225.97	155.86	154.48	13.48	16.16	0.87
912.87	550.14	1111.07	54.95	77.69	3.28
86.48	49.45	61.88	2.67	4.10	0.51
304.01	188.17	234.02	12.01	16.38	1.00
491.01	290.17	711.81	20.06	23.34	0.99
19.37	8.57	16.00	2.00	2.39	0.17
6.49	4.07	12.69	1.16	1.46	0.18
7.74	2.34	8.03	0.54	0.96	0.17
432.67	319.74	144.92	–21.68	–21.50	0.79
91.91	43.67	35.32	1.75	1.97	0.21
116.01	100.94	17.18	–0.39	0.84	0.20

12-13 规模以上大中型工业企业一览表(2021年)

Summary of Large and Medium-Sized Enterprises(2021)

企业名称 Name	登记注册类型 Status of Registration	企业规模 Enterprise Size	所属行业 Industry
浪潮电子信息产业股份有限公司	股份有限公司	大型	计算机整机制造
山东钢铁股份有限公司	股份有限公司	大型	钢压延加工
中国重汽集团济南卡车股份有限公司	股份有限公司	大型	汽柴油车整车制造
山东泰山钢铁集团有限公司	其他有限责任公司	大型	钢压延加工
莱芜钢铁集团银山型钢有限公司	其他有限责任公司	大型	钢压延加工
山东富伦钢铁有限公司	私营有限责任公司	大型	钢压延加工
中国重汽集团济南商用车有限公司	港澳台商独资	大型	汽柴油车整车制造
中国石油化工股份有限公司济南分公司	股份有限公司	大型	原油加工及石油制品制造
齐鲁制药有限公司	私营有限责任公司	大型	化学药品制剂制造
山东泰威冶金材料制造有限公司	私营有限责任公司	中型	铁矿采选
济南市九羊福利钢铁有限公司	私营有限责任公司	大型	炼铁
中国重汽集团济南动力有限公司	港澳台商独资	大型	汽车零部件及配件制造
重汽（济南）车桥有限公司	与港澳台商合资经营	大型	汽车零部件及配件制造
临工集团济南重机有限公司	私营有限责任公司	大型	矿山机械制造
山东闽源钢铁有限公司	其他有限责任公司	大型	钢压延加工
山东泰山轧钢有限公司	私营有限责任公司	中型	钢压延加工
玫德集团有限公司	其他有限责任公司	大型	建筑装饰及水暖管道零件制造
山东电力设备有限公司	国有独资公司	中型	变压器、整流器和电感器制造
华能莱芜发电有限公司	其他有限责任公司	中型	火力发电
山东圣泉新材料股份有限公司	私营有限股份公司	大型	初级形态塑料及合成树脂制造
山东宝鼎煤焦化有限公司	私营有限责任公司	中型	煤制液体燃料生产
济南圣泉集团股份有限公司	股份有限公司	中型	初级形态塑料及合成树脂制造
山东泰山焦化有限公司	其他有限责任公司	中型	炼焦
济南万瑞炭素有限责任公司	私营有限责任公司	中型	石墨及碳素制品制造
中国重汽集团济南橡塑件有限公司	其他有限责任公司	大型	汽车车身、挂车制造
山东中车风电有限公司	其他有限责任公司	中型	发电机及发电机组制造
重汽（济南）传动轴有限公司	国有	大型	汽车零部件及配件制造
济南澳海炭素有限公司	其他有限责任公司	中型	石墨及碳素制品制造
济南二机床集团有限公司	其他有限责任公司	大型	金属成形机床制造
费斯托气动有限公司	外资企业	大型	气压动力机械及元件制造
伊莱特能源装备股份有限公司	中外合资经营	大型	锻件及粉末冶金制品制造
山东晋煤明水化工集团有限公司	其他有限责任公司	大型	有机化学原料制造
齐鲁安替制药有限公司	与港澳台商合资经营	大型	化学药品原料药制造
济南伊利乳业有限责任公司	其他有限责任公司	大型	液体乳制造
大汉科技股份有限公司	其他有限责任公司	大型	生产专用起重机制造
华能济南黄台发电有限公司	国有	大型	火力发电
山东鲁碧建材有限公司	其他有限责任公司	大型	水泥制造
华熙生物科技股份有限公司	其他有限责任公司	大型	生物药品制造
济南轻骑铃木摩托车有限公司	中外合资经营	大型	摩托车整车制造
济南热力集团有限公司	国有独资公司	大型	热力生产和供应
山东旺旺食品有限公司	外资企业	大型	液体乳制造
华电章丘发电有限公司	其他有限责任公司	中型	热电联产
山东明泉新材料科技有限公司	其他有限责任公司	中型	有机化学原料制造
中国重汽集团济南特种车有限公司	其他有限责任公司	中型	汽柴油车整车制造

12-13 续表 1 continued 1

企业名称 Name	登记注册类型 Status of Registration	企业规模 Enterprise Size	所属行业 Industry
齐鲁动物保健品有限公司	私营有限责任公司	大型	兽用药品制造
济南邦德激光股份有限公司	股份有限公司	大型	其他金属加工机械制造
济南热电集团有限公司	国有独资公司	大型	热力生产和供应
山东安信制药有限公司	与港澳台商合资经营	大型	化学药品原料药制造
卧龙电气（济南）电机有限公司	与港澳台商合资经营	中型	微特电机及组件制造
中国石油集团济柴动力有限公司	国有独资公司	大型	内燃机及配件制造
中粮可口可乐饮料（济南）有限公司	与港澳台商合资经营	大型	果菜汁及果菜汁饮料制造
山东晋控日月新材料有限公司	其他有限责任公司	中型	有机化学原料制造
济南裕兴化工有限责任公司	其他有限责任公司	大型	专项化学用品制造
山东正泰电缆有限公司	其他有限责任公司	中型	电线、电缆制造
中车山东机车车辆有限公司	其他有限责任公司	大型	铁路机车车辆制造
济南港华燃气有限公司	与港澳台商合资经营	大型	天然气生产和供应业
山东省万兴食品有限公司	其他有限责任公司	中型	蔬菜加工
山东国舜建设集团有限公司	私营有限责任公司	大型	环境保护专用设备制造
济南达利食品有限公司	私营有限责任公司	大型	饼干及其他焙烤食品制造
鲁中矿业有限公司	其他有限责任公司	大型	铁矿采选
金雷科技股份公司	股份有限公司	大型	发电机及发电机组制造
山东山水水泥集团有限公司	港澳台商独资	大型	水泥制造
山东海鼎农牧有限公司	其他有限责任公司	中型	其他饲料加工
福士汽车零部件（济南）有限公司	外资企业	大型	汽车零部件及配件制造
平阴山水水泥有限公司	与港澳台商合资经营	中型	水泥制造
莱钢集团矿山建设有限公司	其他有限责任公司	中型	铁矿采选
山东阳光铸业有限公司	其他有限责任公司	中型	炼铁
山东省章丘鼓风机股份有限公司	股份有限公司	大型	风机、风扇制造
山东福瑞达生物股份有限公司	股份有限公司	中型	化妆品制造
济南龙山炭素有限公司	私营有限责任公司	中型	石墨及碳素制品制造
山东济华燃气有限公司	与港澳台商合资经营	中型	天然气生产和供应业
积成电子股份有限公司	股份有限公司	大型	配电开关控制设备制造
中国重汽集团济南专用车有限公司	其他有限责任公司	中型	改装汽车制造
莱芜钢铁集团泰东实业有限公司	其他有限责任公司	大型	金属废料和碎屑加工处理
山东水泥厂有限公司	私营有限责任公司	中型	水泥制造
莱芜钢铁集团莱芜矿业有限公司	其他有限责任公司	大型	铁矿采选
山东爱普电气设备有限公司	其他有限责任公司	中型	其他输配电及控制设备制造
济南迈科管道科技有限公司	港澳台商独资	中型	金属结构制造
山东鲁银新材料科技有限公司	其他有限责任公司	中型	锻件及粉末冶金制品制造
华润双鹤利民药业（济南）有限公司	其他有限责任公司	大型	化学药品制剂制造
山东电工电气日立高压开关有限公司	中外合资经营	中型	配电开关控制设备制造
济南西门子变压器有限公司	中外合资经营	中型	变压器、整流器和电感器制造
山东宏济堂制药集团股份有限公司	股份有限公司	大型	中成药生产
莱芜泰禾生化有限公司	其他有限责任公司	中型	食品及饲料添加剂制造
济南金威刻科技发展有限公司	其他有限责任公司	中型	其他非金属加工专用设备制造
山东齐发药业有限公司	其他有限责任公司	中型	兽用药品制造
济南水务集团有限公司	国有独资公司	大型	自来水生产和供应
科兴生物制药股份有限公司	股份有限公司	大型	生物药品制造
维达纸业（山东）有限公司	港澳台商独资	中型	机制纸及纸板制造
浪潮商用机器有限公司	与港澳台商合资经营	中型	计算机整机制造

12–13 续表 2 continued 2

企业名称 Name	登记注册类型 Status of Registration	企业规模 Enterprise Size	所属行业 Industry
山东宏业纺织股份有限公司	股份有限公司	中型	棉纺纱加工
济南佳宝乳业有限公司	其他有限责任公司	大型	液体乳制造
济南统一企业有限公司	与港澳台商合资经营	中型	茶饮料及其他饮料制造
济南海川投资集团有限公司	私营有限责任公司	中型	石墨及碳素制品制造
中孚安全技术有限公司	其他有限责任公司	大型	信息安全设备制造
国网智能科技股份有限公司	股份有限公司	中型	其他输配电及控制设备制造
山东力诺特种玻璃股份有限公司	股份有限公司	中型	日用玻璃制品制造
济南金麒麟刹车系统有限公司	私营有限责任公司	大型	汽车零部件及配件制造
山东力诺瑞特新能源有限公司	中外合资经营	中型	太阳能器具制造
山东汉方制药有限公司	私营有限责任公司	中型	中成药生产
济南森峰科技有限公司	其他有限责任公司	中型	其他专用仪器制造
泰富特钢悬架（济南）有限公司	其他有限责任公司	中型	弹簧制造
山东太古飞机工程有限公司	与港澳台商合资经营	大型	航空航天器修理
山东奥太电气有限公司	其他有限责任公司	中型	金属切割及焊接设备制造
济南黄河特钢有限责任公司	其他有限责任公司	中型	金属结构制造
济南重工股份有限公司	股份有限公司	中型	矿山机械制造
博世汽车转向系统（济南）有限公司	外资企业	中型	液压动力机械及元件制造
山东博士伦福瑞达制药有限公司	中外合资经营	中型	化学药品制剂制造
济南鲁冠混凝土有限责任公司	私营有限责任公司	中型	水泥制品制造
山东济钢环保新材料有限公司	其他有限责任公司	中型	石灰石、石膏开采
济南锅炉集团有限公司	其他有限责任公司	大型	锅炉及辅助设备制造
山东温岭精锻科技有限公司	私营有限责任公司	中型	锻件及粉末冶金制品制造
莱芜莱新铁矿有限责任公司	其他有限责任公司	中型	铁矿采选
山东朗进科技股份有限公司	股份有限公司	中型	制冷、空调设备制造
青岛啤酒(济南)有限公司	其他有限责任公司	中型	啤酒制造
山东福牌阿胶股份有限公司	私营有限股份公司	中型	中成药生产
山东晨熙智能科技有限公司	私营有限责任公司	大型	包装装潢及其他印刷
莱芜新希望六和食品有限公司	私营有限责任公司	中型	禽类屠宰
山东莱芜煤矿机械有限公司	国有独资公司	大型	矿山机械制造
济南轻骑标致摩托车有限公司	中外合资经营	中型	摩托车整车制造
西电济南变压器股份有限公司	股份有限公司	中型	变压器、整流器和电感器制造
济南沃德汽车零部件有限公司	中外合资经营	大型	汽车零部件及配件制造
济南迈克阀门科技有限公司	与港澳台商合资经营	中型	阀门和旋塞制造
山东万祥矿业有限公司	其他有限责任公司	大型	烟煤和无烟煤开采洗选
山东鲁中啤酒原料有限公司	私营有限责任公司	中型	其他未列明农副食品加工
安莉芳(山东)服装有限公司	港澳台商独资	大型	运动休闲针织服装制造
章丘重型锻造有限公司	私营有限责任公司	大型	锻件及粉末冶金制品制造
山推建友机械股份有限公司	股份有限公司	中型	建筑材料生产专用机械制造
济南顶津食品有限公司	外资企业	中型	瓶（罐）装饮用水制造
山东银鹭食品有限公司	港澳台商独资	中型	含乳饮料和植物蛋白饮料制造
山东桑乐集团有限公司	其他有限责任公司	中型	太阳能器具制造
济南泉华包装制品有限公司	与港澳台商合资经营	中型	纸和纸板容器制造
山东华凌电缆有限公司	私营有限责任公司	中型	电线、电缆制造
山东济南发电设备厂有限公司	国有独资公司	中型	发电机及发电机组制造
山东福贞金属包装有限公司	外资企业	中型	金属包装容器及材料制造
国机铸锻机械有限公司	其他有限责任公司	中型	铸造机械制造

12–13 续表 3 continued 3

企业名称 Name	登记注册类型 Status of Registration	企业规模 Enterprise Size	所属行业 Industry
山东天岳先进科技股份有限公司	股份有限公司	中型	电子专用材料制造
济南轻骑大韩摩托车有限责任公司	中外合资经营	中型	摩托车整车制造
山东福瑞达医药集团有限公司	其他有限责任公司	中型	生物药品制造
济南和盛热力有限公司	其他有限责任公司	中型	热力生产和供应
济南黄台煤气炉有限公司	私营有限责任公司	中型	气体、液体分离及纯净设备制造
济南新峨嵋实业有限公司	私营有限责任公司	中型	耐火陶瓷制品及其他耐火材料制造
山东天鹅棉业机械股份有限公司	股份有限公司	中型	棉花加工机械制造
济南京华金属制品有限公司	其他有限责任公司	中型	金属结构制造
济南中维世纪科技有限公司	其他有限责任公司	中型	集成电路制造
山东平阴丰源炭素有限责任公司	其他有限责任公司	中型	石墨及碳素制品制造
山东明化新材料有限公司	私营有限责任公司	中型	有机化学原料制造
山东华熙海御生物医药有限公司	外资企业	中型	生物药品制造
济南弘正科技有限公司	港澳台商独资	中型	摩托车零部件及配件制造
济南市莱芜燃气热力有限责任公司	其他有限责任公司	中型	天然气生产和供应业
山东欧克家具有限公司	私营有限责任公司	中型	木质家具制造
济南重工集团有限公司	其他有限责任公司	中型	隧道施工专用机械制造
山东山大电力技术股份有限公司	股份有限公司	中型	其他专用仪器制造
济南中燃科技发展有限公司	私营有限责任公司	中型	其他金属加工机械制造
山东北辰机电设备股份有限公司	私营有限股份公司	中型	金属压力容器制造
山东汇金股份有限公司	股份有限公司	中型	汽车零部件及配件制造
山东博科生物产业有限公司	其他有限责任公司	中型	医疗实验室及医用消毒设备和器具制造
济南市冶金科学研究所有限责任公司	其他有限责任公司	中型	有色金属合金制造
齐鲁宏业纺织集团有限公司	私营有限责任公司	中型	棉纺纱加工
济南三星灯饰有限公司	其他有限责任公司	中型	智能照明器具制造
北谷电子有限公司	其他有限责任公司	中型	其他电子器件制造
济南鲁东耐火材料有限公司	中外合资经营	中型	耐火陶瓷制品及其他耐火材料制造
济南晶恒电子有限责任公司	其他有限责任公司	中型	半导体分立器件制造
山东科源制药股份有限公司	股份有限公司	中型	化学药品原料药制造
山东大旺食品有限公司	外资企业	中型	饼干及其他焙烤食品制造
山东铂源药业有限公司	其他有限责任公司	中型	化学药品原料药制造
山东中天华泰新材料有限公司	私营有限责任公司	中型	石墨及碳素制品制造
中集车辆（山东）有限公司	中外合资经营	中型	汽车用发动机制造
章丘华明水泥有限公司	其他有限责任公司	中型	水泥制造
济南中船设备有限公司	私营有限责任公司	中型	船用配套设备制造
济南东区供水有限公司	其他有限责任公司	中型	自来水生产和供应
山东鲁信天一印务有限公司	其他有限责任公司	中型	包装装潢及其他印刷
济南宜和食品有限公司	中外合资经营	中型	酱油、食醋及类似制品制造
济南泓泉制水有限公司	其他有限责任公司	中型	自来水生产和供应
山东新升实业发展有限责任公司	国有独资公司	中型	热电联产
济南科盛电子有限公司	其他有限责任公司	中型	光电子器件制造
济南二机床铸造有限公司	国有独资公司	中型	黑色金属铸造
山东金钟科技集团股份有限公司	股份有限公司	中型	衡器制造
山东耀华玻璃有限公司	私营有限责任公司	中型	其他玻璃制造
山东上好佳食品工业有限公司	港澳台商独资	中型	饼干及其他焙烤食品制造
山东大鲁阁织染工业有限公司	外资企业	中型	棉纺纱加工
济南宇飞食品有限公司	私营有限责任公司	中型	禽类屠宰

12-13 续表 4 continued 4

企业名称 Name	登记注册类型 Status of Registration	企业规模 Enterprise Size	所属行业 Industry
济南超意兴餐饮配送有限公司	私营有限责任公司	中型	肉制品及副产品加工
济南世纪创新水泥有限公司	其他有限责任公司	中型	水泥制造
山东小鸭精工机械有限公司	其他有限责任公司	中型	汽车零部件及配件制造
济南圣都食品有限公司	私营有限责任公司	中型	肉制品及副产品加工
山东巧夺天工家具有限公司	私营有限责任公司	中型	其他工艺美术及礼仪用品制造
迈大食品（山东）有限公司	外资企业	中型	饼干及其他焙烤食品制造
中孚信息股份有限公司	股份有限公司	中型	信息安全设备制造
济南冶金化工设备有限公司	其他有限责任公司	中型	冶金专用设备制造
平阴鲁西装备科技有限公司	其他有限责任公司	中型	金属压力容器制造
莱芜朝阳电子有限公司	其他有限责任公司	中型	电力电子元器件制造
济南台有玻璃制品有限公司	其他有限责任公司	中型	日用玻璃制品制造
济南实达紧固件有限公司	私营有限责任公司	中型	紧固件制造
济南虫洞智能家居设施有限公司	私营有限责任公司	中型	木质家具制造
山东明仁福瑞达制药股份有限公司	股份有限公司	中型	中成药生产
山东华森建材集团有限公司	其他有限责任公司	中型	水泥制品制造
济南星辉数控机械科技有限公司	私营有限责任公司	中型	其他专用设备制造
神思电子技术股份有限公司	股份有限公司	中型	其他计算机制造
山东华氟化工有限责任公司	其他有限责任公司	中型	初级形态塑料及合成树脂制造
济南活力食品有限公司	私营独资	中型	肉制品及副产品加工
济南奥图自动化股份有限公司	私营有限股份公司	中型	工业机器人制造
山东力创科技股份有限公司	私营有限股份公司	中型	电力电子元器件制造
济南趵突泉酿酒有限责任公司	其他有限责任公司	中型	白酒制造
山东通发实业有限公司	私营有限责任公司	中型	建筑工程用机械制造
山东黑旋风锯业有限公司	其他有限责任公司	中型	切削工具制造
山东地矿慧通特种轮胎有限公司	其他有限责任公司	中型	轮胎制造
山东九龙新材料有限公司	私营有限责任公司	中型	耐火陶瓷制品及其他耐火材料制造
济南元首针织股份有限公司	股份有限公司	中型	运动休闲针织服装制造
山东宏达科技集团有限公司	私营有限责任公司	中型	金属压力容器制造
济南翼菲自动化科技有限公司	其他有限责任公司	中型	工业机器人制造
山东新华泰纺织有限公司	私营有限责任公司	中型	棉纺纱加工
济南明鑫制药股份有限公司	私营有限股份公司	中型	化学药品原料药制造
山东越宫钢构件有限公司	其他有限责任公司	中型	金属结构制造
金德利餐饮有限公司	其他有限责任公司	中型	米、面制品制造
山东百脉泉酒业有限公司	其他有限责任公司	中型	白酒制造
济南巨鑫机车车辆配件有限公司	私营有限责任公司	中型	锻件及粉末冶金制品制造
莱芜科林光电有限公司	其他有限责任公司	中型	光伏设备及元器件制造
山东新华印务有限公司	国有独资公司	中型	书、报刊印刷
济南双凤耐火材料有限公司	私营有限责任公司	中型	隔热和隔音材料制造
山东省莱芜市辛庄煤矿有限公司	其他有限责任公司	中型	烟煤和无烟煤开采洗选
济南市白象科技发展有限公司	其他有限责任公司	中型	冶金专用设备制造
济南思迈迩制衣有限公司	私营有限责任公司	中型	其他针织或钩针编织服装制造
济南金木铸造有限公司	私营有限责任公司	中型	汽车零部件及配件制造
莱芜环球汽车零部件有限公司	外资企业	中型	汽车零部件及配件制造
济阳元首针织有限责任公司	其他有限责任公司	中型	其他针织或钩针编织服装制造
山东博特生物资源制品有限公司	私营有限责任公司	中型	其他纸制品制造
山东豪驰新能源汽车有限公司	其他有限责任公司	中型	新能源车整车制造

12–14 主要工业产品生产量 (2021 年)
Output of Major Industrial Products(2021)

主要工业产品名称	Major Industrial Products above Designated Size	单位 Unit	生产量 Production
铁矿石原矿	Crude Iron ore	万吨 (10 000 tons)	593.6
铁矿石成品矿	Iron ore finished ore	万吨 (10 000 tons)	2068.9
铁精矿	Iron ore concentrate	万吨 (10 000 tons)	1997.1
石灰石	Lime Powder	万吨 (10 000 tons)	1622.4
饲料	Feed	万吨 (10 000 tons)	113.7
鲜、冷藏肉	Frozen,Fresh Meat	万吨 (10 000 tons)	11.6
乳制品	Milk Products	万吨 (10 000 tons)	53.7
液体乳	Liquid Milk	万吨 (10 000 tons)	52.3
酱油	Soy Sauce	万吨 (10 000 tons)	5.5
食品添加剂	Food Additives	万吨 (10 000 tons)	15.0
饲料添加剂	Feed Additive	万吨 (10 000 tons)	5.7
饮料酒	Liquor	万千升 (10 000 kiloliter)	25.7
白酒（折 65 度，商品量）	Liquor (65 degree discount, commercial quantity)	万千升 (10 000 kiloliter)	0.9
啤酒	Beer	万千升 (10 000 kiloliter)	24.8
饮料	Drinks	万吨 (10 000 tons)	244.4
碳酸型饮料（汽水）	Carbonated Drinks	万吨 (10 000 tons)	68.2
包装饮用水	Bottled Drinking Water	万吨 (10 000 tons)	54.8
果汁和蔬菜汁类饮料	Juice and Vegetable Juice Beverage	万吨 (10 000 tons)	46.8
布	Cloth	万米 (10 000 m)	1098.9
服装	Garments	万件 (10 000 pieces)	4899.5
家具	Furniture	万件 (10 000 pieces)	44.7
纸制品	Paper Products	万吨 (10 000 tons)	29.5
瓦楞纸箱	Corrugated Box	万吨 (10 000 tons)	16.6
单色印刷品	Monochrome Print	万令 (10 000 ream)	49.8
多色印刷品	Ploychrome Print	万对开色令 (10 000 color folio ream)	1138.6
纯苯	Purified Petroleum Benzin(e)	万吨 (10 000 tons)	9.7
精甲醇	Extracted Methanol	万吨 (10 000 tons)	69.1
硅	Silicon	万吨 (10 000 tons)	3.3
合成氨（无水氨）	Synthetic Ammonia	万吨 (10 000 tons)	45.0
农用氮、磷、钾化学肥料（折纯）	Chemical Fertilizer	万吨 (10 000 tons)	16.7
尿素（折含氮 100%）	Urea	万吨 (10 000 tons)	16.4
化学农药原药（折有效成分 100%）	Chemical Pesticide	吨 (ton)	5234
涂料	Paint	万吨 (10 000 tons)	10.7
初级形态塑料	Primary Plastic	万吨 (10 000 tons)	33.5
化学试剂	Chemical Reagent	万吨 (10 000 tons)	11.5

12-14 续表 1 continued 1

主要工业产品名称	Major Industrial Products above Designated Size	单位 Unit	生产量 Production
表面活性剂	Surface active agent	万吨 (10 000 tons)	3.5
化学药品原药	Chemical Medicine	吨 (ton)	9310
中成药	Traditional Chemical Medicine	吨 (ton)	7299
兽用药品	Veterinary Drugs	吨 (ton)	23362
化学纤维	Chemical Fiber	万吨 (10 000 tons)	8.4
橡胶轮胎外胎	Rubber Tyre Cover	万条 (10 000 tires)	19.6
塑料制品	Plastic Articles	万吨 (10 000 tons)	16.0
硅酸盐水泥熟料	Portland Cement Clinker	万吨 (10 000 tons)	630.3
水泥	Cement	万吨 (10 000 tons)	1561.1
石灰	Lime	万吨 (10 000 tons)	263.3
商品混凝土	Concrete	万立方米 (10 000 cu.m)	3139.4
水泥混凝土排水管	Cement and Concrete Drainage Pipes	千米 (km)	165.3
水泥混凝土压力管	Cement and Concrete Pressure Pipes	千米 (km)	114.1
砖	Brick	亿块 (100 million unit)	3.1
钢化玻璃	Stalinite	万平方米 (10 000 sq.m)	139.3
中空玻璃	Hollow Glass	万平方米 (10 000 sq.m)	193.1
耐火材料制品	Refractory Product	万吨 (10 000 tons)	59.0
石墨及碳素制品	Graphite and Carbon Products	万吨 (10 000 tons)	186.6
生铁	Cast Iron	万吨 (10 000 tons)	1914.6
粗钢	Crude Steel	万吨 (10 000 tons)	1921.9
钢材	Steel	万吨 (10 000 tons)	2105.7
钢结构	Steel Structure	万吨 (10 000 tons)	71.6
金属切削工具	Metal Cutting Tool	万件 (10 000 unit)	390.4
锻件	Forge Piece	万吨 (10 000 tons)	118.0
粉末冶金零件	Sintered Metal Products	万吨 (10 000 tons)	1.3
电站锅炉	Utility Boilers	蒸发量吨 (evaporation ton)	3412
发动机	Engine	万千瓦 (10 000kW)	4085.1
汽车用发动机	Automotive Engine	万千瓦 (10 000kW)	4014.4
金属切削机床	Metal-cutting Machine Tools	台 (unit)	14049
起重机	Lifting Equipment	万吨 (10 000 tons)	37.5
电梯、自动扶梯及升降机	Elevators, Escalators and Lifts	台 (unit)	11743
液压元件	Hydraulic Components	万件 (10 000 unit)	69.9
气动元件	Pneumatic Components	万件 (10 000 unit)	939.1
鼓风机	Air Blower	万台 (10 000 unit)	3.2
工商用制冷、空调设备	Commercial Refrigeration Equipment	万台 (10 000 unit)	3.0
金属紧固件	Metal Fastener	万吨 (10 000 tons)	4.8
弹簧	Spring	万吨 (10 000 tons)	7.1
矿山专用设备	Mining Equipment	万吨 (10 000 tons)	8.2

12-14 续表 2 continued 2

主要工业 产品名称	Major Industrial Products above Designated Size	单位 Unit	生产量 Production
金属冶炼设备	Metal Smelting Equipment	万吨 (10 000 tons)	4.2
炼油、化工生产专用设备	Special Equipment for Oil Refining and Chemical Protection	吨 (ton)	22985
农产品初加工机械	Agricultural Primary Processing Machinery	万台 (10 000 unit)	1.9
电子工业专用设备	Special Equipment for Electrionic Industry	万台 (10 000 unit)	18.0
棉花加工机械	Cotton Processing Machinery	台 (unit)	1115
医疗仪器设备及器械	Medical Instruments	万台 (10 000 unit)	7.0
工业机器人	Industrial Robot	套 (unit)	2604
汽车	Motor Vehicles	万辆 (10 000 unit)	32.0
载货汽车	Trucks	万辆 (10 000 unit)	31.9
改装汽车	Modified Cars	万辆 (10 000 unit)	2.2
铁路货车	Railway Freight Wagons	辆 (unit)	3119
摩托车整车	Motorcycles	万辆 (10 000 unit)	46.5
发电机组（发电设备）	Power Generating Equipment	万千瓦 (10 000kW)	387.5
电动机	Electromotor	万千瓦 (10 000kW)	280.3
变压器	Transformers	万千伏安 (10 000 KVA)	15298.6
高压开关设备（11 万伏以上）	High Voltage Switchgear (over 110,000 volts)	万台 (10 000 unit)	1.4
安全、自动化监控设备	Safety and Automatic Monitoring Equipment	台 (套)(unit)	49577
通信及电子网络用电缆	Cable for Communications and Electronic Network	万对千米 (10 000 couples.km)	5.0
电力电缆	Power Cable	万千米 (10 000 km)	12.7
太阳能热水器	Solar Water Heater	万平方米 (10 000 sq.m)	166.0
灯具及照明装置	Lamps and Lighting Fixtures	万套 (台个)(10 000 unit)	20.2
电子计算机整机	Computers	万台 (10 000 unit)	114.8
服务器	Servers	万台 (10 000 unit)	113.7
半导体分立器件	Discrete Semiconductor Devices	亿只 (100 million unit)	170.2
传感器	Transducer	万只 (10 000 unit)	1273.0
集成电路	Integrated Circuit	万块 (10 000 unit)	16972.2
电子元件	Eletronic Components	亿只 (100 million unit)	27.1
电声器件	Electroacoustic Device	万只 (10 000 unit)	1177.0
印制电路板	Print-circuit Board	万平方米 (10 000 sq.m)	178.4
工业自动调节仪表与控制系统	Industrial Automatic Instrument and Control System	台 (套)(unit)	122270
电工仪器仪表	Electrical Instrument	万台 (10 000 unit)	796.7
汽车仪器仪表	Automobile Instrument	万台 (10 000 unit)	117.4
钟	Clock	万只 (10 000 unit)	64.6
自来水生产量	Tap Water Production	亿立方米 (100 million cu.m)	8.1
发电量	Power Generating Capacity	亿千瓦时 (100 million kWh)	315.1
其中：火力发电量	Thermal Power Generation	亿千瓦时 (100 million kWh)	290.8
风力发电量	Wind Power Generation	亿千瓦时 (100 million kWh)	21.9
垃圾发电量	Garbage Power Generation	亿千瓦时 (100 million kWh)	9.5
煤气生产量	Gas Power Generation	亿立方米 (100 million cu.m)	219.6

12-15 工业企业能源购进、消费及库存（2021 年）
Purchases,Consumption and Invetory of Main Energy Source in Industrial Enterprises(2021)

能源名称	Type of Energy	计量单位 Unit	年初库存量 Beginning Stock	本年购进量 Purchases This Year	本年工业生产消费 Industrial Consumption of This Year	年末库存量 Year-end Stock
能源合计	Total Energy	吨标准煤 (tons of SCE)	0	0	50070032	0
原煤	Raw Coal	吨 (ton)	492947	17719987	17645579	1052805
洗精煤	Cleaned Coal	吨 (ton)	233888	6658876	6729204	163560
其他洗煤	Other Cleaned Coal	吨 (ton)	182339	3337319	3282995	215844
煤制品	Coal Product	吨 (ton)	64973	998401	1004130	71510
焦炭	Coke	吨 (ton)	203686	7934652	8970705	93830
天然气	Natural Gas	万立方米 (10 000 cu.m)	0	92243	91960	1
液化天然气	Liquefied Nutural Gas	吨 (ton)	58	16315	16312	22
氢气	Hydrogen	万立方米 (10 000 cu.m)	0	3434	3434	0
汽油	Gasoline	吨 (ton)	21	4169	4190	45
煤油	Kerosene	吨 (ton)	2	44	61	0
柴油	Diesel Oil	吨 (ton)	1145	44972	39433	1834
液化石油气	Liquefied Petroleum	吨 (ton)	42	1414	1414	0
石油焦	Petroleum coke	吨 (ton)	16794	2119821	2136615	0
热力	Heating	百万千焦 (mkj)	0	9391672	10451054	0
电力	Electricity	万千瓦时 (10 000 kWh)	0	1721624	2336600	0
城市生活垃圾（用于燃料）	Municipal household waste (for fuels)	吨 (ton)	41633	2564750	2348609	41605
生物燃料	Biofuel	吨标准煤 (tons of SCE)	15520	222405	235692	43399
余热余压	Residual heat and residual pressure	百万千焦 (mkj)	0	613679	22688156	0
其他燃料	Other Fuel	吨标准煤 (tons of SCE)	0	220	197	0

注：按照经济普查要求，免填能源合计中，年初库存、购进量、年末库存。

Note:According to requirements of economic census, it's unnecessary to fill in inventory and volume of purchase at the beginning of the year and the inventory at the end of the year in the total energy.

12-16 工业分行业主要能源消费量（2021年）
Consumption of Main Energy Source in Industrial Enterprises by Sector(2021)

指标	Item	原煤（吨） Coal (ton)	天然气（万立方米） Natural Gas (10 000 cu.m)	液化天然气（吨） Liquefied Nutural Gas (ton)	汽油（吨） Gasoline (ton)	柴油（吨） Diesel Oil (ton)	热力（百万千焦） Heating (mkj)	电力（万千瓦时） Electricity (10 000 kWh)
总计	Total	17645579	91960	16312	4190	39433	10451054	2336600
采矿业	Mining							
煤炭开采和洗选业	Mining and Washing of Coal	704134	0	0	0	179	0	5493
石油和天然气开采业	Extraction of Petroleum and Natural Gas	0	0	0	0	6	0	4309
黑色金属矿采选业	Mining and Processing of Ferrous Metal Ores	49701	0	0	53	2295	249630	66070
非金属矿采选业	Mining and Processing of Non-Ferrous Metal Ores	0	0	0	0	1606	0	7267
制造业	Manufacture							
农副食品加工业	Processing of Food from Agricultural Products	35013	1120	2612	13	74	32625	12703
食品制造业	Manufacture of Foods	0	4315	370	40	192	1180225	40001
酒、饮料和精制茶制造业	Manufacture of Wine, Drinks and Refined Tea	0	1594	0	55	184	51915	16758
纺织业	Manufacture of Textile	0	846	0	0	0	155024	32041
纺织服装、服饰业	Manufacture of Textile Wearing Apparel and Finery	0	260	0	13	6	31456	2853
皮革、毛皮、羽毛及其制品和制鞋业	Manufacture of Leather, Fur, Feather and Related Products and Footwear	0	182	0	0	0	0	390
木材加工及木、竹、藤、棕、草制品业	Processing of Timbers, Manufacture of Wood, Bamboo, Rattan, Palm, and Straw Products	0	0	0	0	0	0	7536
家具制造业	Manufacture of Furniture	0	0	0	18	77	0	2652
造纸及纸制品业	Manufacture of Paper and Paper Products	0	824	435	27	18	1089481	18102
印刷和记录媒介复制业	Printing and Reproduction of Recording Media	0	238	0	134	62	31234	13892
文教、工美、体育和娱乐用品制造业	Manufacture of Articles for Culture, Education, Arts and Crafts,Sport and Entertainment Activities	0	380	219	25	0	0	3042
石油、煤炭及其他燃料加工业	Processing of Petroleum, Coal and Other Fuels	0	2474	409	83	210	519013	59881
化学原料及化学制品制造业	Manufacture of Chemical Raw Material and Chemical Products	2001506	5514	1920	52	746	2823113	249262

12-16 续表 2 continued 2

指标	Item	原煤 (吨) Coal (ton)	天然气 (万立方米) Natural Gas (10 000 cu.m)	液化天然气 (吨) Liquefied Nutural Gas (ton)	汽油 (吨) Gasoline (ton)	柴油 (吨) Diesel Oil (ton)	热力 (百万千焦) Heating (mkj)	电力 (万千瓦时) Electricity (10 000 kWh)
医药制造业	Manufacture of Medicines	27242	3946	0	124	27	2176949	75607
化学纤维制造业	Manufacture of Chemical Fiber	9280	900	0	16	16	229646	8510
橡胶和塑料制品业	Manufacture of Rubber and Plastic	0	452	774	48	149	97302	16845
非金属矿物制品业	Manufacture of Non-metallic Mineral Products	934409	17960	2563	329	15353	361816	202554
黑色金属冶炼及压延加工业	Manufacture and Processing of Ferrous Metals	2128891	2522	448	48	6642	125689	739661
有色金属冶炼及压延加工业	Manufacture & Processing of Non-ferrous Metals	0	49	41	14	47	18920	5637
金属制品业	Manufacture of Metal Products	14457	10154	2930	319	714	0	149082
通用设备制造业	Manufacture of General Purpose Machinery	0	2861	116	739	1855	0	51682
专用设备制造业	Manufacture of Special Purpose Machinery	0	629	45	461	337	24646	31183
汽车制造业	Manufacture of Automotive	0	4525	7	117	5174	543895	101492
铁路、船舶、航空航天和其他运输设备制造业	Manufacture of Railroad,Marine,Aerospace and Other Transportation Equipment	0	179	20	179	104	45757	11358
电气机械及器材制造业	Manufacture of Electrical Machinery & Equipment	0	3684	2	306	44	0	38041
计算机、通信和其他电子设备制造业	Manufacture of Computer, Communications and Other Electronic Equipment	0	44	0	249	29	2449	19906
仪器仪表制造业	Manufacture of Measuring Instrument	0	3	0	498	38	1752	2484
其他制造业	Other Manufacture	0	0	0	8	0	0	750
废弃资源综合利用业	Utilization of Waste Resources	0	0	0	0	339	0	9087
金属制品、机械和设备修理业	Metal Products, Machinery and Equipment Repair Industry	0	0	0	0	0	0	554
电力、热力、燃气及水生产和供应业	**Production and Supply of Electric Power and Heat Power**							
电力、热力生产和供应业	Production and Supply of Electric Power and Heat Power	11740946	26306	3401	20	2842	658517	290813
燃气生产和供应业	Production and Supply of Gas	0	0	0	93	23	0	1640
水的生产和供应业	Production and Supply of Water	0	0	0	109	46	0	37464

主要统计指标解释

按照国家统计方法制度规定，1998 年独立核算工业统计范围由原乡及乡以上调整为全部国有及年销售收入500 万元以上非国有工业企业，2011 年规模以上工业企业统计范围调整为年主营业务收入2000 万元以上。同时，统计分类中的原经济组织类型分组相应地调整为按企业登记注册类型分组。

工业 指从事自然资源的开采，对采掘品和农产品进行加工和再加工的物质生产部门。具体包括：(1) 对自然资源的开采，如采矿、晒盐等（但不包括禽兽捕猎和水产捕捞）；(2) 对农副产品的加工、再加工，如粮油加工、食品加工、缫丝、纺织、制革等；(3) 对采掘品的加工、再加工，如炼铁、炼钢、化工生产、石油加工、机器制造、木材加工等，以及电力、自来水、煤气的生产和供应等；(4) 对工业品的修理、翻新，如机器设备的修理、交通运输工具（如汽车）的修理等。

工业统计调查单位为独立核算法人工业企业。

独立核算法人工业企业指从事工业生产经营活动的单位。独立核算法人工业企业应同时具备以下条件：①依法成立，有自己的名称、组织机构和场所，能够承担民事责任；②独立拥有和使用资产，承担负债，有权与其他单位签订合同；③独立核算盈亏，并能够编制资产负债表。

国有控股企业 即原来的国有及国有控股企业，根据企业实收资本中国有经济成分的出资人的实际投资情况，或国有经济成分的出资人对企业资产的实际控制、支配程度进行分类。以下情况为国有控股：（1）在企业的全部实收资本中，国有经济成分的出资人拥有的实收资本（股本）所占企业全部实收资本（股本）的比例大于50%的国有绝对控股。（2）在企业的全部实收资本中，国有经济成分的出资人拥有的实收资本（股本）所占比例虽未大于50%，但相对大于其他任何一方经济成分的出资人所占比例的国有相对控股；或者虽不大于其他经济成分，但根据协议规定拥有企业实际控制权的国有协议控股。（3）投资双方各占50%，且未明确由谁绝对控股的企业，若其中一方为国有经济成分的，一律按国有控股处理。

本篇涉及的企业登记注册类型的解释详见综合篇。

轻工业 指主要提供生活消费品和制作手工工具的工业。按其所使用的原料不同，可分为两大类：(1) 以农产品为原料的轻工业，是指直接或间接以农产品为基本原料的轻工业。主要包括食品制造、饮料制造、烟草加工、纺织、缝纫、皮革和毛皮制作、造纸以及印刷等工业；(2) 以非农产品为原料的轻工业，是指以工业品为原料的轻工业。主要包括文教体育用品、化学药品制造、合成纤维制造、日用化学制品、日用玻璃制品、日用金属制品、手工工具制造、医疗器械制造、文化和办公用机械制造等工业。

重工业 指为国民经济各部门提供物质技术基础的主要生产资料的工业。按其生产性质和产品用途，可以分为下列三类：(1) 采掘（伐）工业，是指对自然资源的开采，包括石油开采、煤炭开采、金属矿开采、非金属矿开采等工业；(2) 原材料工业，指向国民经济各部门提供基本材料、动力和燃料的工业。包括金属冶炼及加工、炼焦及焦炭、化学、化工原料、水泥、人造板以及电力、石油和煤炭加工等工业；(3) 加工工业，是指对工业原材料进行再加工制造的工业。包括装备国民经济各部门的机械设备制造工业、金属结构、水泥制品等工业，以及为农业提供的生产资料如化肥、农药等工业。

根据上述划分原则，修理业中以重工业产品为修理作业对象的划为重工业，反之划为轻工业。

工业总产值 是以货币表现的工业企业在一定时期内生产的已出售或可供出售工业产品总量，它反映一定时间内工业生产的总规模和总水平。它包括：在本企业内不再进行加工，经检验、包装入库（规定不需包装的产品除外）的成品价值，对外加工费收入，自制半成品、在产品期末初差额价值。工业总产值采用“工厂法”计算，即以工业企业作为一个整体，按企业工业生产活动的最终成果来计算，企业内部不允许重复计算，不能把企业内部各个车间（分厂）生产的成果相加。但在企业之间、行业之间、地区之间存在着重复计算。

轻重工业总产值的划分也是按“工厂法”计算的，即一个工业企业在正常情况下生产的主要产品的性质属于轻工业，则该企业的全部总产值作为轻工业总产值。如生产的主要产品的性质属于重工业，则该企业的全部总产值作为重工业总产值。

工业增加值 是指工业行业在报告期内以货币表现的工业生产活动的最终成果。

实收资本 指企业实际收到的投资人投入的资本。按投资主体可分为国家资本、集体资本、法人资本、个人资本、港澳台资本和外商资本等。

资产总计 指企业拥有或控制的能以货币计量的经济资源。包括各种财产、债权和其他权利。资产按其流动性划分为流动资产、长期投资、固定资产、无形及递延资产和其他资产。

（1）流动资产指企业可以在一年内或者超过一年的一个生产周期内变现或耗用的资产合计。包括现金及各种存款、短期投资、应收及预付款项、存货等。

（2）固定资产指企业固定资产净值、固定资产清理、在建工程、待处理固定资产损失所占用的资金合计。

（3）无形资产指企业长期使用而没有实物形态的资产。包括专利权、非专利技术、商标权、著作权、土地使用权、商誉等。

负债合计　指企业承担的能以货币计量，将以资产或劳务偿付的债务。负债一般按偿还期长短分为流动负债和长期负债、递延税项等。

（1）流动负债指企业在一年内或者超过一年的一个营业周期内需要偿还的债务合计，其中包括短期借款、应付及预收款项、应付工资、应交税金和应交利润等。

（2）长期负债指企业在一年以上或者超过一年的一个营业周期以上需要偿还的债务合计，其中包括长期借款、应付债务、长期应付款项等。

所有者权益 指企业投资人对企业净资产的所有权。企业净资产等于企业全部资产减去全部负债后的余额，其中包括投资者对企业的最初投入，以及资本公积金、盈余公积金和未分配利润，对股份制企业即为股东权益。

固定资产原价 指企业在建造、购置、安装、改建、扩建、技术改造某项固定资产时所支出的全部货币总额。它一般包括买价、包装费、运杂费和安装费等。

营业收入 指企业从事销售商品、提供劳务和让渡资产使用权等生产经营活动形成的经济利益流入。营业收入包括“主营业务收入”和“其他业务收入”。来源于会计“利润表”中“营业收入”项目的本年累计数。

营业成本 指企业从事销售商品、提供劳务和让渡资产使用权等生产经营活动发生的实际成本。包括企业（单位）在报告期内从事销售商品、提供劳务等日常活动发生的各种耗费。包括“主营业务成本”和“其他业务成本”。来源于会计“利润表”中“营业成本”项目的本年累计数。

税金及附加 指企业因从事生产经营活动按税法规定应缴纳的消费税、城市维护建设税、资源税、环境保护税、教育费附加及房产税、土地使用税、车船使用税、印花税等相关税费。

利润总额 指企业在一定会计期间的经营成果，是生产经营过程中各种收入扣除各种耗费后的盈余，反映企业在报告期内实现的盈亏总额。

平均用工人数 是指报告期平均实际拥有的，参与本企业生产经营活动的人员数。

利税总额 指企业产品销售税金及附加、利润总额和应交增值税之和。

本年应交增值税 指按照税法规定，以销售货物、服务、无形资产、不动产或提供加工、修理修配劳务的增值额和货物进口金额为计税依据而课征的一种流转税。

Explanatory Notes on Main Statistical Indicators

As per provisions of national system of statistical method, the scope of statistics of the independent accounting industry in 1998 was adjusted to all state-owned enterprises and non-state industrial enterprises with above RMB 5 million annual sales revenue from those of village and above and the scope of statistics of above state designated scale industrial enterprises in 2011 was adjusted to above RMB 20 million annual income of main business. Meanwhile, grouping of original economic organizations in the statistical classification is adjusted to grouping based on enterprise registration type accordingly.

Industry refers to the material production sector which is engaged in extraction of natural resources and processing and reprocessing of minerals and agricultural products, including (1) extraction of natural resources, such as mining, salt production (but not including hunting and fishing); (2) processing and reprocessing of farm and sideline produces, such as rice husking, flour milling, wine making, oil pressing, silk reeling, spinning and weaving, and leather making; (3) manufacture of industrial products, such as steel making, iron smelting, chemicals manufacturing, petroleum processing, machine building, timber processing; water and gas production and electricity generation and supply; (4)repairing of industrial products such as the repairing of machinery and means of transport (including cars).

Units of industrial statistics survey corporate are industrial enterprises with independent accounting system.

Corporate industrial enterprises with independent accounting system refer to enterprises engaging in industrial production activities, which meet the following requirements: (1)They are established legally, having their own names, organizations, location, able to take civil liability; (2)They possess and use their assets independently, assume liabilities, and are entitled to sign contracts with other units; (3)They are financially independent and compile their own balance sheets.

State-holding Enterprises cover the original state-owned enterprises and state-holding enterprises. They are classified according to the actual investment made by the contributors of state-owned part in the paid-in capital of the enterprises, or the degree of control or dominance of the contributor on the assets of the enterprises. The following cases are regarded as state-holding: (1) Absolute state-holding in which the contributors of state-owned parts possess more than 50% of all the paid-in capital (stocks) of the enterprises; (2) Relative state-holding in which the contributors of state-owned parts possess no more than 50% of the paid-in capital (stocks) of the enterprises, but more than that of any other contributors; or agreed state-holding in which the contributors of state-owned parts possess no more than other contributors but have actual control over the enterprises according to agreements; (3) In case both contributors possess 50% and it is not clear which one is in absolute holding position, the enterprise is regarded as state-holding enterprise if one of the contributor has state-owned elements.

For explanation of types of registration covered in this chapter, please refer to Chapter 1 on General Survey.

Light industry refers to the industry that produces consumer goods and hand tools. It consists of two categories, depending on the materials used: (1) Industries using farm products as raw materials. These are branches of light industry which directly or indirectly use farm products as basic raw materials, including the manufacture of food and beverages, tobacco processing, textile, clothing, fur and leather manufacturing, paper making, printing, etc.(2) Industries using non-farm products as raw materials. These are branches of light industry which use manufactured goods as raw materials, including the manufacture of cultural, educational articles and sports goods, chemicals, synthetic fiber, chemical products for daily use, glass products for daily use, metal products for daily use, hand tools, medical apparatus and instruments, and the manufacture of cultural and clerical machinery.

Heavy Industry refers to the industry which produces capital goods, and provides various sectors of the national economy with necessary material and technical basis. It consists of the following three branches according to the purpose of production or the use of products: (1) Mining, quarrying and logging industry refers to the industry that extracts natural resources, including extraction of petroleum, coal, metal and non-metal ores. (2) Raw materials industry refers to the industry that provides various sectors of the national economy with raw materials, fuels and power. It includes smelting and processing of metals, coking and coke chemistry, chemical materials, cement, plywood, power, petroleum refining and coal dressing. (3) Manufacturing industry refers to the industry that processes raw materials. It includes machine building industry which equips sectors of the national economy, industries of metal structure and cement products, industries producing means of agricultural production, such as chemical fertilizers and pesticides.

According to the above principle of classification, the repairing trades, which are engaged primarily in repairing products of heavy industry are classified into heavy industry while these engaged in repairing products of light industry are classified into light industry.

Gross Industrial Output Value refers to total industrial products which were sold or are available for sale produced by industrial enterprise within a certain period of time and expressed with currency and reflects total scale and total level of industrial production within a certain period of time. It includes: value of finished product not processed in the enterprise which are put in storage after inspection and packaging (except products specified not to be packaged), external processing fee income and the value of the difference between the end of the period and the beginning of the period of self-made semi-manufactured goods. Gross industrial output value is calculated as per "factory approach", that is to say that gross industrial output value is calculated according to final result of industrial production activities of enterprises based on industrial enterprise as a whole. Repeated calculation in the enterprise and adding production results of all workshops (branch factories) in the enterprise are forbidden. However, the repeated calculation between enterprises, industries and regions exists.

Gross output value of light and heavy industries is also calculated according to "factory approach", that is to say that total output value of the enterprise is used as gross output of the light industry if major products produced by an industrial enterprise under normal circumstances fall into light industry. Gross output value of the enterprise is use as gross output value of heavy industry if major products produced fall into heavy industry.

Value–added of Industry refers to the final results of industrial production of industrial enterprises in currency during the reference period

Paid–up capital refers to the capital actually received by the enterprise and invested by the investor. Paid–up capital can be divided into national capital, collectively owned capital, corporate capital, personal capital, Hong Kong, Macao and Taiwan capital and foreign capital as per investors.

Total Assets refer to all economic resources, in monetary terms, that is owned or controlled by enterprises, including properties, creditors equity and other economic rights of all forms. Classified by the degree of equitability, total assets include circulating assets, long–term investment, fixed assets, intangible assets and deferred assets, and other assets.

(1) Current assets refer to assets that an enterprise can convert into cash or use during one year or one production cycle that may exceeds one year, including cash and savings deposits of various forms, short–term investment, receivable and prepaid money, inventories, etc..

(2) Fixed assets refer to the total amount of net fixed assets of the enterprise, disposal of fixed assets, project under construction and losses on pending fixed assets.

(3) Intangible assets refer to the assets without physical form used by the enterprise for a long time. It consists of patent right, non–patent technology, trademark right, copyright, chartered right, land use right, etc..

Total Liabilities refer to the liabilities borne by the enterprise which can be measured with currency and repaid by assets or labor services. Liabilities are generally divided into current liabilities, long–term liabilities and deferred tax on the basis of repayment period.

(1) Current liabilities (also called quick liabilities or immediate liabilities) refer to enterprises' total debt payable within an operating cycle of one year or over one year, including short term loans, payables and advance payments, wages payable, taxes payable and profit payable, etc..

(2) Long–term liabilities refers enterprises' total debt payable within an operating cycle of one year or over one year, including long–term loans, payable liabilities, long–term payables, etc..

Owner's Equity refers to the ownership of net assets of enterprise by its investors. The net assets equal the total assets minus total liabilities of the enterprise, including the actual assets invested into the enterprise by investors, accumulation of capitals and operating surplus and non–distributed profits (namely stockholders' equity for corporate enterprise).

Original Value of Fixed Assets refers to the total value, in monetary terms, that an enterprise spent on fixed assets, through construction, purchase, installation, transformation, expansion or technical upgrading. Generally, it covers cost of purchase, packing, transportation and installation, etc..

Business Revenue refers to the inflow of economic benefits through production and operation activities of enterprises, such as selling commodities, providing labor services and transferring the right to use of assets. Business revenue includes "revenue from principal business" and " revenue from other business". It comes from current year' s cumulative report of "business revenue" items from the "income statement".

Business Cost refers to the actual costs incurred by the enterprises in such production and operation activities as selling commodities, providing labor services and transferring the right to use of assets. It includes various expenditures incurred by enterprises (units) in their daily activities of selling goods and providing labour services during the reporting period. It includes "cost of principal business" and "cost of other business". It comes from current year' s cumulative report of "operating cost" items from the "income statement".

Taxes and Surcharges refers to the consumption tax, urban maintenance and construction tax, resource tax, environmental protection tax, education surcharges, and real estate tax, land use tax, vehicle and vessel use tax, stamp tax and other related taxes and fees due in accordance with the tax law for their production and business activities .

Total Profits refer to the operating result of the enterprise during a certain accounting period, they are the balance of the production and operation process after all incomes are deducted by various costs, reflect the total amount of profit and loss achieved within the reporting period. Total profit is the amount after operating profit plus non–business income and then minus non–business expenditure, which shall be filled in and reported pursuant to the cumulative data in the current year in the item "total profit" in the "profit statement".

Annual Average Employees refer to the number of persons engaged in the production and operation activities of enterprises in the reporting period, which are actually employed by the enterprises.

Total Profits and Taxes refer to the sum of sales taxes, charges, revenues and VAT of the products in the enterprise.

VAT payable this year refers to a turnover tax that pursuant to the VAT of goods and services sales, invisible assets, real estate, machining provided, repair services and to the amount of goods import in accordance with the taxes laws.

13

建筑业

CONSTRUCTION

13-1 建筑业主要指标
Main Indicators of Construction Enterprises

指标	Item	单位 Unit	2016 年	2017	2018 年	2019 年	2020 年	2021 年
汇总单位数	Number of Enterprises	个 (unit)	460	504	507	895	1033	1182
建筑业总产值	Gross Output Value	万元 (10 000 yuan)	18647972	22189343	28234734	35139777	37481222	41260343
按隶属关系分	by Ownership							
中央属	Central	万元 (10 000 yuan)	9079591	11379540	14747883	17350365	20148118	21677643
地方属	Local	万元 (10 000 yuan)				11793174	10596000	10417195
省属	Provincial	万元 (10 000 yuan)	1853736	2391026	3039149			
市属	Region	万元 (10 000 yuan)	3676145	5195869	6391344			
县及县以下	County	万元 (10 000 yuan)	1711315	570463	641220			
其他	Others	万元 (10 000 yuan)	2327185	2652445	3415138	5996238	6737105	9165505
按工程性质分	by Sector							
建筑工程	Building and Civil Engineering Construction	万元 (10 000 yuan)	16291789	19476820	25182882	31199367	33447869	35981015
安装工程	Construction Installation	万元 (10 000 yuan)	1998465	2051423	2329541	3015885	3288008	3749267
其他产值	Others	万元 (10 000 yuan)	357718	661100	722311	924525	745346	1530061
竣工产值	Value of Construction Completed	万元 (10 000 yuan)	7415119	7987351	8691856	12943615	12789160	13373476
房屋施工面积	Floor Space Completed	万平方米 (10 000 sq.m)	10293	11363	12984	14955	17090	19410
# 本年新开工	Started This year	万平方米 (10 000 sq.m)	3222	3694	4842	4705	5349	5621
房屋竣工面积	Floor Space Completed	万平方米 (10 000 sq.m)	2298	2280	2366	3418	3323	3730
# 住宅	Residential	万平方米 (10 000 sq.m)	1379	1258	1502	2170	1916	2247
所有者权益	Creditors'Equity	万元 (10 000 yuan)	4433678	5900444	6269077	8130630	7894051	9363017
利润总额	Total Profits	万元 (10 000 yuan)	573258	836297	810897	1051261	1087848	1360873
工资总额	Total wages	万元 (10 000 yuan)	1812042	2185631	3480056	3793574	3295738	3454592

13-2 建筑企业资产实力（2021 年）
Assets of Construction Enterprises(2021)

单位：万元

指标（总承包与专业承包）	Item	流动资产合计 Liquid Assets	# 存货 Inventory
总计	Total	39517611	3432147
其中：国有及国有控股企业	State-owned and State-controlled Enterprises	28840153	1444420
一、按登记注册类型分组	By Status of Registration		
内资企业	Domestic Invested Enterprises	39513226	3430255
国有企业	State-owned Enterprises	112080	10966
集体企业	Collective-owned Enterprises	105805	26434
股份合作企业	Cooperative Enterprises	105790	82721
联营企业	Joint-owned Enterprises	0	0
其他联营企业	Other Joint Ownership Enterprises	0	0
有限责任公司	Limited Liability Corporations	30536830	2064494
国有独资公司	State Sole-proprietorship Corporations	6830571	395261
其他有限责任公司	Other Joint Ownership Enterprises	23706259	1669233
股份有限公司	Share-holding Corporations Ltd.	905197	94720
私营企业	Private Enterprises	7747523	1150920
私营有限责任公司	Private Limited Liability Corporations	7737660	1149350
私营股份有限公司	Private Share-holding Corporations Ltd.	9863	1570
港、澳、台商投资企业	Enterprises with Investment from Hong Kong,Macao and Taiwan	0	0
外商投资企业	Foreign Invested Enterprises	4385	1893
中外合资经营企业	Joint-venture Enterprises	4385	1893
外商投资股份有限公司	Share-holding Corporations Ltd.	0	0
二、按国民经济行业分组	By Sector		
房屋建筑业	Construction of Buildings	11266563	1358691
土木工程建筑业	Civil Engineering	24460189	1542084
建筑安装业	Construction Installation	1810574	293910
建筑装饰装修和其他建筑业	Building Decoration and Other Construction	1980285	237462
三、按隶属关系分组	By Ownership		
中央	Central	16178466	497930
地方	Local	12865792	1257627
其他	Others	10473353	1676591
四、按企业资质等级分组	By Qualification Criteria		
施工总承包	Construction Contract	35867933	2937443
特级	Special Grade	23273457	1083565
一级	First Grade	7688487	768374
二级	Second Grade	2932827	714074
三级及以下	Third Grade and below	1973162	371431
专业承包	Professional Contract	3649678	494704
一级	First Grade	2054283	304311
二级	Second Grade	911758	105813
三级及以下	Third Grade and below	683636	84581

(10 000yuan)

固定资产原价 Original Value of Fixed Assets	资产合计 Fixed Assets	流动负债合计 Current Liabilities Total	非流动负债合计 Non-Current Liabilities Total	负债合计 Total Liabilitie	所有者权益合计 Total Creditors' Equity
2682482	47764560	36706503	1525413	38401543	9363017
1570551	35652749	28067519	1223290	29290981	6361768
2682482	47760176	36703426	1525413	38398467	9361709
18894	132191	97148	4854	102045	30146
14608	131462	89196	278	91018	40444
1641	110505	123354	0	123354	-12849
0	0	0	0	0	0
0	0	0	0	0	0
1790281	37534665	29409756	1318697	30791014	6743651
442166	8036112	6355891	396126	6752017	1284096
1348115	29498552	23053866	922571	24038997	5459555
44134	999082	664557	74489	739046	260036
812923	8852272	6319415	127095	6551991	2300281
811168	8839374	6312244	127095	6544820	2294553
1756	12898	7171	0	7171	5727
0	0	0	0	0	0
0	4385	3076	0	3076	1308
0	4385	3076	0	3076	1308
0	0	0	0	0	0
661933	12701050	9287471	414811	9795559	2905491
1557294	30589504	24306690	1009574	25327008	5262496
277289	2193729	1512302	34042	1560616	633113
185967	2280278	1600040	66987	1718360	561918
962252	20508580	16407720	672440	17080160	3428420
681449	15410356	11880933	601521	12485797	2924559
1038781	11845625	8417850	251452	8835587	3010038
2252164	43586067	33827219	1443150	35361343	8224724
1038408	28990898	23161102	982576	24143678	4847220
612457	8700644	6462136	259066	6721202	1979443
368067	3587996	2726556	45698	2837457	750540
233232	2306529	1477426	155810	1659007	647522
430318	4178493	2879283	82263	3040200	1138293
137362	2275608	1720552	20658	1752129	523479
105189	1041829	691078	10635	714134	327695
187766	861057	467653	50971	573937	287120

13-3 建筑业施工产值构成（2021 年）
Output Value of Construction Structure(2021)

单位：万元 (10 000 yuan)

指标（总承包与专业承包）	Item	合计 Total	建筑工程 Constructional Engineering	安装工程 Installation Project	其他产值 Other Value	竣工产值 Value of Construction Completed
总计	Total	41260343	35981015	3749267	1530061	13373476
其中：国有及国有控股企业	State-owned and State-controlled Enterprises	31035906	27738821	2353721	943364	8608792
一、按登记注册类型分组	By Status of Registration					
内资企业	Domestic Invested Enterprises	41258818	35981015	3747742	1530061	13373476
国有企业	State-owned Enterprises	85877	62321	0	23556	39357
集体企业	Collective-owned Enterprises	45080	44678	0	402	24917
股份合作企业	Cooperative Enterprises	41922	41746	0	176	3914
联营企业	Joint Ownership Enterprises	0	0	0	0	0
其他联营企业	Other Joint Ownership Enterprises	0	0	0	0	0
有限责任公司	Limited Liability Corporations	31854356	28357565	2500991	995800	8955276
国有独资公司	State Sole-proprietorship Corporations	9695597	8202470	1472860	20267	3189042
其他有限责任公司	Other Limited Liability Corporations	22158759	20155095	1028131	975532	5766234
股份有限公司	Share-holding Corporations Ltd.	579453	518769	59724	961	220157
私营企业	Private Enterprises	8652130	6955937	1187027	509166	4129856
私营有限责任公司	Private Limited Liability Corporations	8647665	6954099	1184400	509166	4129856
私营股份有限公司	Private Share-holding Corporations Ltd.	4465	1838	2627	0	0
港、澳、台商投资企业	Enterprises with Investment from Hong Kong,Macao and Taiwan	0	0	0	0	0
外商投资企业	Foreign Invested Enterprises	1525	0	1525	0	0
中外合资经营企业	Joint-venture Enterprises	1525	0	1525	0	0
外商投资股份有限公司	Share-holding Corporations Ltd.	0	0	0	0	0
二、按国民经济行业分组	By Sector					
房屋建筑业	Construction of Buildings	17771114	16627863	1028732	114519	8752237
土木工程建筑业	Civil Engineering	19764658	17086010	1514091	1164557	3069550
建筑安装业	Construction Installation	1609742	527124	1034143	48475	691738
建筑装饰装修和其他建筑业	Building Decoration and Other Construction	2114829	1740018	172301	202510	859951
三、按隶属关系分组	By Ownership					
中央	Central	21677643	19879925	1762197	35522	6111784
地方	Local	10417195	9025668	433522	958005	3772077
其他	Others	9165505	7075423	1553548	536534	3489616
四、按企业资质等级分组	By Qualification Criteria					
施工总承包	Construction Contract	37728678	33454772	2952084	1321822	11901000
特级	Special Grade	27075007	25518792	1541214	15002	8835671
一级	First Grade	7172477	5187646	1006749	978082	1819035
二级	Second Grade	1658533	1359515	149202	149817	604607
三级及以下	Third Grade and below	1822661	1388820	254920	178921	641688
专业承包	Professional Contract	3531665	2526243	797183	208239	1472476
一级	First Grade	2071763	1579283	392044	100436	824758
二级	Second Grade	982529	604535	310789	67205	461228
三级及以下	Third Grade and below	477373	342425	94349	40599	186490

13-4 建筑企业损益及分配(2021年)
Profit,Loss and Distribution of Construction Enterprises(2021)

单位：万元 (10 000yuan)

指标（总承包与专业承包）	Item	营业收入 Business Revenue	利税总额 Total Profits and Taxes	营业利润 Profits from Business	利润总额 Total Profits	应付职工薪酬（本年贷方累计发生额）Total Wages Payable
总计	Total	42958070	2120401	1340342	1360873	3454592
其中：国有及国有控股企业	State-owned and State-controlled Enterprises	32466339	1624251	1154869	1166234	2163249
一、按登记注册类型分组	By Status of Registration					
内资企业	Domestic Invested Enterprises	42955813	2120532	1340513	1361044	3454066
国有企业	State-owned Enterprises	107873	5556	2324	2496	10376
集体企业	Collective-owned Enterprises	81069	4504	-432	-518	13429
股份合作企业	Cooperative Enterprises	77511	4997	1248	1240	1339
联营企业	Joint Ownership Enterprises	0	0	0	0	0
其他联营企业	Other Joint Ownership Enterprises	0	0	0	0	0
有限责任公司	Limited Liability Corporations	33468126	1667176	1154469	1165337	2164403
国有独资公司	State Sole-proprietorship Corporations	9268209	457804	335210	339032	564802
其他有限责任公司	Other Limited Liability Corporations	24199917	1209372	819260	826304	1599601
股份有限公司	Share-holding Corporations Ltd.	589414	39811	25422	27207	66061
私营企业	Private Enterprises	8631822	398488	157482	165283	1198459
私营有限责任公司	Private Limited Liability Corporations	8624529	398752	158096	165845	1197586
私营股份有限公司	Private Share-holding Corporations Ltd.	7293	-264	-614	-562	873
港、澳、台商投资企业	Enterprises with Investment from Hong Kong,Macao and Taiwan	0	0	0	0	0
外商投资企业	Foreign Invested Enterprises	2257	-131	-172	-172	526
中外合资经营企业	Joint-venture Enterprises	2257	-131	-172	-172	526
外商投资股份有限公司	Share-holding Corporations Ltd.	0	0	0	0	0
二、按国民经济行业分组	By Sector					
房屋建筑业	Construction of Buildings	16349082	829638	547640	552779	1546273
土木工程建筑业	Civil Engineering	21986143	1051271	689298	699938	1561487
建筑安装业	Construction Installation	2143298	121240	51707	54925	204698
建筑装饰装修和其他建筑业	Building Decoration and Other Construction	2479548	118253	51696	53231	142135
三、按隶属关系分组	By Ownership					
中央	Central	22964084	907671	635884	641718	1196759
地方	Local	9757109	642505	457620	463694	1108816
其他	Others	10236877	570226	246838	255461	1149017
四、按企业资质等级分组	By Qualification Criteria					
施工总承包	Construction Contract	38570432	1894950	1242526	1259515	3149117
特级	Special Grade	28393500	1287307	918950	926541	1948157
一级	First Grade	6011246	372877	230655	234733	732271
二级	Second Grade	2054196	122092	56522	56880	251006
三级以下	Third Grade and below	2111491	112674	36399	41361	217684
专业承包	Professional Contract	4387638	225452	97816	101358	305476
一级	First Grade	2432691	129650	60502	61746	147656
二级	Second Grade	1151304	43755	13488	15266	102766
三级以下	Third Grade and below	803643	52047	23826	24346	55054

13–5 施工工程施工面积（2021 年）
Number of Floor Space Under Construction (2021)

单位：万平方米 (10 000sq.m)

指标（总承包与专业承包）	Item	房屋建筑施工面积 Floor Space under Construction	# 本年新开工面积 Started This Year	房屋建筑竣工面积 Floor Space Completed	# 住宅房屋 (Residential	竣工房屋价值（万元）Value of Construction Completed (10 000 yuan)
总计	Total	19410	5621	3730	2247	8587751
其中：国有及国有控股企业	State-owned and State-controlled Enterprises	12690	3354	1702	767	5697155
一、按登记注册类型分组	By Status of Registration					
内资企业	Domestic Invested Enterprises	19410	5621	3730	2247	8587751
国有企业	State-owned Enterprises	2	0	3	0	471
集体企业	Collective-owned Enterprises	8	3	1	0	2649
股份合作企业	Cooperative Enterprises	4	3	4	2	3914
有限责任公司	Limited Liability Corporations	12680	3542	1849	832	5835679
国有独资公司	State Sole-proprietorship Corporations	4151	940	537	237	1864303
其他有限责任公司	Other Limited Liability Corporations	8529	2602	1312	595	3971375
股份有限公司	Share-holding Corporations Ltd.	537	118	85	50	212271
私营企业	Private Enterprises	6178	1957	1787	1364	2532767
私营有限责任公司	Private Limited Liability Corporations	6178	1957	1787	1364	2532767
私营股份有限公司	Private Share-holding Corporations Ltd.	0	0	0	0	0
二、按国民经济行业分组	By Sector					
房屋建筑业	Construction of Buildings	16488	4579	2768	1472	7443719
土木工程建筑业	Civil Engineering	2567	765	533	422	1000175
建筑安装业	Construction Installation	167	146	250	233	51916
建筑装饰装修和其他建筑业	Building Decoration and Other Construction	189	131	179	121	91941
三、按隶属关系分组	By Ownership					
中央	Central	10554	2799	1229	487	4692723
省（自治区、直辖市）	Provincial	4480	1232	993	623	2285302
地区（州、盟、省辖市）及以下、其他	Region	4376	1590	1508	1138	1609725
四、按企业资质等级分组	By Qualification Criteria					
施工总承包	Construction Contract	18117	5106	2947	1551	8417893
特级	Special Grade	15118	4012	2105	991	6818440
一级	First Grade	2225	706	547	404	1122233
二级	Second Grade	429	179	155	96	297146
三级及以下	Third Grade and below	346	209	140	61	180073
专业承包	Professional Contract	1293	515	783	696	169858
一级	First Grade	1065	337	442	401	91723
二级	Second Grade	225	176	304	260	64905
三级及以下	Third Grade and below	3	2	37	35	13230

13-6 济南市建筑业特级、一级资质企业一览表(2021年)

Summary of Construction Enterprises with Grade 1 Qualification(2021)

企业名称 Name	资质等级 Ownership	经济类型 Economic Type	所属行业 Industry
山东省建设建工(集团)有限责任公司	特级	私营有限责任公司	住宅房屋建筑
中建八局第二建设有限公司	特级	其他有限责任公司	住宅房屋建筑
中建八局第一建设有限公司	特级	国有独资公司	住宅房屋建筑
济南二建集团工程有限公司	特级	其他有限责任公司	住宅房屋建筑
中铁十局集团建筑工程有限公司	特级	私营有限责任公司	住宅房屋建筑
济南四建(集团)有限责任公司	特级	其他有限责任公司	住宅房屋建筑
山东港基建设集团有限公司	特级	其他有限责任公司	住宅房屋建筑
山东平安建设集团有限公司	特级	私营有限责任公司	住宅房屋建筑
济南长兴建设集团有限公司	特级	私营有限责任公司	住宅房屋建筑
山东三箭建设工程股份有限公司	特级	股份有限公司	住宅房屋建筑
中儒科信达建设集团有限公司	特级	其他有限责任公司	住宅房屋建筑
山东省路桥集团有限公司	特级	其他有限责任公司	铁路、道路、隧道和桥梁工程建筑
中化学交通建设集团有限公司	特级	其他有限责任公司	铁路、道路、隧道和桥梁工程建筑
中铁十四局集团第三工程有限公司	特级	其他有限责任公司	铁路、道路、隧道和桥梁工程建筑
山东高速工程建设集团有限公司	特级	其他有限责任公司	铁路、道路、隧道和桥梁工程建筑
中铁十四局集团有限公司	特级	其他有限责任公司	铁路、道路、隧道和桥梁工程建筑
中铁十局集团有限公司	特级	其他有限责任公司	铁路、道路、隧道和桥梁工程建筑
中国电建集团山东电力建设第一工程有限公司	特级	国有独资公司	架线和管道工程建筑
中国电建集团核电工程有限公司	特级	其他有限责任公司	架线和管道工程建筑
济南城建集团有限公司	特级	国有独资公司	铁路、道路、隧道和桥梁工程建筑
山东天宝建设集团有限公司	一级	其他有限责任公司	住宅房屋建筑
山东高速齐鲁建设集团有限公司	一级	其他有限责任公司	其他房屋建筑业
瑞森新建筑有限公司	一级	私营有限责任公司	其他房屋建筑业
中国山东对外经济技术合作集团有限公司	一级	其他有限责任公司	住宅房屋建筑
山东省城建工程集团公司	一级	股份合作	住宅房屋建筑
山东鲁建工程集团有限公司	一级	其他有限责任公司	住宅房屋建筑
山东泰山建工发展集团有限公司	一级	其他有限责任公司	住宅房屋建筑
山东泉景建设有限公司	一级	其他有限责任公司	住宅房屋建筑
山东恒霖建设工程有限公司	一级	私营有限责任公司	住宅房屋建筑
济南华海建设集团有限公司	一级	私营有限责任公司	住宅房屋建筑
普利置业集团股份有限公司	一级	股份有限公司	住宅房屋建筑
山东中恒建设集团有限公司	一级	私营有限责任公司	住宅房屋建筑
济南建工总承包集团有限公司	一级	其他有限责任公司	住宅房屋建筑
济南一建集团有限公司	一级	国有独资公司	住宅房屋建筑
山东铁信建设集团有限公司	一级	其他有限责任公司	住宅房屋建筑
山东长箭建设集团有限公司	一级	私营有限责任公司	住宅房屋建筑
山东汇富建设集团有限公司	一级	私营有限责任公司	住宅房屋建筑
山东长泰建设集团工程有限公司	一级	私营有限责任公司	住宅房屋建筑
章丘市第二建筑安装(集团)有限责任公司	一级	其他有限责任公司	住宅房屋建筑
山东泰实建筑工程有限公司	一级	其他有限责任公司	住宅房屋建筑
中铁十四局集团建筑工程有限公司	一级	其他有限责任公司	住宅房屋建筑
山东三箭建设工程管理有限公司	一级	私营有限责任公司	住宅房屋建筑
山东莱芜建设集团有限公司	一级	国有独资公司	住宅房屋建筑
莱芜市庚鑫市政工程有限公司	一级	其他有限责任公司	管道和设备安装
山东正顺建设集团有限公司	一级	私营有限责任公司	住宅房屋建筑
济南市宏强建设有限公司	一级	私营有限责任公司	其他房屋建筑业
济南铸诚建筑工程集团有限公司	一级	私营有限责任公司	住宅房屋建筑
山东信达建设工程有限公司	一级	私营有限责任公司	其他房屋建筑业
中国电建集团山东电力建设有限公司	一级	其他有限责任公司	电力工程施工
中宝鼎盛建设集团有限公司	一级	私营有限责任公司	住宅房屋建筑
山东省建设集团有限公司	一级	私营有限责任公司	其他房屋建筑业
山东惠诚建筑有限公司	一级	私营有限责任公司	其他房屋建筑业
山东建华土木有限公司	一级	私营有限责任公司	住宅房屋建筑
国舜绿建科技有限公司	一级	其他有限责任公司	其他房屋建筑业
中铁十四局集团第四工程有限公司	一级	国有独资公司	铁路、道路、隧道和桥梁工程建筑
山东省公路桥梁建设集团有限公司	一级	其他有限责任公司	铁路、道路、隧道和桥梁工程建筑

13–6 续表 1 continued 1

企业名称 Name	资质等级 Ownership	经济类型 Economic Type	所属行业 Industry
山东省高速路桥养护有限公司	一级	其他有限责任公司	铁路、道路、隧道和桥梁工程建筑
山东省大通公路工程有限责任公司	一级	其他有限责任公司	铁路、道路、隧道和桥梁工程建筑
济南通达公路工程有限公司	一级	国有独资公司	铁路、道路、隧道和桥梁工程建筑
济南金曰公路工程有限公司	一级	其他有限责任公司	铁路、道路、隧道和桥梁工程建筑
山东泰东公路工程有限公司	一级	其他有限责任公司	铁路、道路、隧道和桥梁工程建筑
山东省齐鲁装饰设计院	一级	集体企业	建筑装饰和装修业
济南舜联建设集团有限公司	一级	私营有限责任公司	其他房屋建筑业
山东济铁工程建设集团有限公司	一级	私营有限责任公司	铁路、道路、隧道和桥梁工程建筑
山东水总有限公司	一级	国有独资公司	水利和水运工程建筑
山东黄河工程集团有限公司	一级	国有独资公司	水利和水运工程建筑
山东省水利工程局有限公司	一级	国有独资公司	水利和水运工程建筑
山东昌利建设工程有限公司	一级	私营有限责任公司	水利和水运工程建筑
山东黄河顺成水利水电工程有限公司	一级	国有独资公司	架线和管道工程建筑
山东大禹水务建设集团有限公司	一级	私营有限责任公司	水利和水运工程建筑
山东送变电工程有限公司	一级	国有独资公司	架线和管道工程建筑
山东电建建设集团有限公司	一级	其他有限责任公司	架线和管道工程建筑
山东兴发建筑工程有限公司	一级	私营有限责任公司	住宅房屋建筑
山东环城城建工程有限公司	一级	其他有限责任公司	其他未列明建筑业
济南易通城市建设集团股份有限公司	一级	股份有限公司	铁路、道路、隧道和桥梁工程建筑
济南普利供水工程有限公司	一级	其他有限责任公司	架线和管道工程建筑
山东顺河路桥工程有限公司	一级	其他有限责任公司	铁路、道路、隧道和桥梁工程建筑
中铁十四局集团隧道工程有限公司	一级	其他有限责任公司	铁路、道路、隧道和桥梁工程建筑
山东汇通建设集团有限公司	一级	国有独资公司	铁路、道路、隧道和桥梁工程建筑
济南黄河路桥建设集团有限公司	一级	国有独资公司	铁路、道路、隧道和桥梁工程建筑
山东汇友市政园林集团有限公司	一级	国有独资公司	其他未列明建筑业
中铁十局集团第一工程有限公司	一级	其他有限责任公司	铁路、道路、隧道和桥梁工程建筑
济南昊兴市政工程有限公司	一级	私营有限责任公司	架线和管道工程建筑
山东亿威市政工程有限公司	一级	其他有限责任公司	铁路、道路、隧道和桥梁工程建筑
济南能源工程集团有限公司	一级	国有独资公司	管道和设备安装
济南市市政工程建设集团有限公司	一级	其他有限责任公司	铁路、道路、隧道和桥梁工程建筑
山东省邮电工程有限公司	一级	其他有限责任公司	架线和管道工程建筑
山东宏业发展集团有限公司	一级	私营有限责任公司	架线和管道工程建筑
山东鑫联通信科技有限公司	一级	私营有限责任公司	电气安装
山东江森机电工程有限公司	一级	私营有限责任公司	管道和设备安装
山东省工业设备安装集团有限公司	一级	其他有限责任公司	其他建筑安装业
中铁十四局集团电气化工程有限公司	一级	国有独资公司	架线和管道工程建筑
中铁十局集团电务工程有限公司	一级	其他有限责任公司	铁路、道路、隧道和桥梁工程建筑
山东省建设高压容器有限公司	一级	其他有限责任公司	管道和设备安装
山东亚特尔集团股份有限公司	一级	股份有限公司	管道和设备安装
山东福源设备安装有限公司	一级	私营有限责任公司	管道和设备安装
山东福源建设集团有限公司	一级	私营有限责任公司	管道和设备安装
山东省深基建设工程总公司	一级	国有企业	住宅房屋建筑
济南岩土工程公司	一级	国有企业	其他土木工程建筑
山东正元建设工程有限责任公司	一级	其他有限责任公司	其他房屋建筑业
济南百士岩土工程有限公司	一级	其他有限责任公司	铁路、道路、隧道和桥梁工程建筑
山东省机械施工有限公司	一级	私营有限责任公司	建筑物拆除和场地准备活动
中铁济南工程技术有限公司	一级	其他有限责任公司	铁路、道路、隧道和桥梁工程建筑
山东建科特种建筑工程技术中心有限公司	一级	其他有限责任公司	其他房屋建筑业
山东建勘集团有限公司	一级	国有独资公司	建筑物拆除和场地准备活动
山东润豪建设工程有限公司	一级	私营有限责任公司	铁路、道路、隧道和桥梁工程建筑
山东昌舜岩土工程有限公司	一级	私营有限责任公司	建筑物拆除和场地准备活动
山东众联恒信工程集团有限公司	一级	私营有限责任公司	建筑物拆除和场地准备活动
济南振华岩土工程有限责任公司	一级	私营有限责任公司	提供施工设备服务
山东省亘基工程有限公司	一级	私营有限责任公司	其他房屋建筑业
山东航空港建设工程有限公司	一级	私营有限责任公司	其他土木工程建筑
山东省装饰集团有限公司	一级	国有独资公司	建筑装饰和装修业
济南百川建设装饰工程有限公司	一级	私营有限责任公司	建筑装饰和装修业
山东华森装饰工程有限公司	一级	私营有限责任公司	建筑装饰和装修业
鸿鑫工程有限公司	一级	私营有限责任公司	建筑装饰和装修业
山东展鸿华商装饰工程有限公司	一级	私营有限责任公司	建筑装饰和装修业

13-6 续表 2 continued 2

企业名称 Name	资质等级 Ownership	经济类型 Economic Type	所属行业 Industry
中炬装饰工程集团有限公司	一级	私营有限责任公司	建筑装饰和装修业
济南林海装饰工程有限公司	一级	私营有限责任公司	建筑装饰和装修业
山东豪庭建设集团有限公司	一级	私营有限责任公司	建筑装饰和装修业
山东省建设建工集团装饰装璜有限公司	一级	其他有限责任公司	建筑装饰和装修业
万得福实业集团有限公司	一级	其他有限责任公司	建筑装饰和装修业
山东德铭工程建设有限公司	一级	私营有限责任公司	建筑装饰和装修业
山东创达建设工程有限公司	一级	其他有限责任公司	建筑装饰和装修业
永隆装饰工程有限公司	一级	私营有限责任公司	建筑装饰和装修业
济南万泰建筑装饰工程有限公司	一级	私营有限责任公司	建筑装饰和装修业
山东同大装饰有限公司	一级	私营有限责任公司	建筑装饰和装修业
山东世纪装饰工程股份有限公司	一级	股份有限公司	建筑装饰和装修业
济南宏铁建筑装饰工程有限公司	一级	其他有限责任公司	建筑装饰和装修业
山东通海建设集团有限公司	一级	私营有限责任公司	建筑装饰和装修业
山东中大净化工程有限公司	一级	私营有限责任公司	其他建筑安装业
山东清尚建筑装饰设计工程有限公司	一级	私营有限责任公司	建筑装饰和装修业
风派特装饰工程有限公司	一级	私营有限责任公司	建筑装饰和装修业
辉瑞（山东）环境科技有限公司	一级	私营有限责任公司	建筑装饰和装修业
山东福缘来装饰有限公司	一级	私营有限责任公司	建筑装饰和装修业
山东福思特建筑装饰有限公司	一级	私营有限责任公司	建筑装饰和装修业
山东盛顺装饰有限公司	一级	私营有限责任公司	建筑装饰和装修业
沃尔德项目管理有限公司	一级	其他有限责任公司	建筑装饰和装修业
山东深装总装饰工程工业有限公司	一级	私营有限责任公司	建筑装饰和装修业
山东鲁控建设集团有限公司	一级	其他有限责任公司	住宅房屋建筑
山东黄金集团建设工程有限公司	一级	国有独资公司	住宅房屋建筑
山东鑫龙装饰工程有限公司	一级	私营有限责任公司	建筑装饰和装修业
山东国宸装饰工程有限公司	一级	其他有限责任公司	建筑装饰和装修业
山东欧瑞装饰有限公司	一级	私营有限责任公司	建筑装饰和装修业
山东洁昕建筑装饰工程设计有限公司	一级	私营有限责任公司	建筑装饰和装修业
山东莱芜创艺装饰集团有限公司	一级	其他有限责任公司	建筑装饰和装修业
山东青亦蓝装饰工程有限公司	一级	私营有限责任公司	建筑装饰和装修业
山东省鲁美建材装饰有限公司	一级	私营有限责任公司	建筑装饰和装修业
七彩建设发展有限公司	一级	私营有限责任公司	建筑装饰和装修业
中直科创股份有限公司	一级	股份有限公司	建筑装饰和装修业
万旭宏业集团有限公司	一级	私营有限责任公司	建筑装饰和装修业
山东百特展览工程有限公司	一级	国有独资公司	建筑装饰和装修业
阿郎装饰股份有限公司	一级	股份有限公司	建筑装饰和装修业
山东千业建设工程有限公司	一级	私营有限责任公司	建筑装饰和装修业
山东万林建设工程有限公司	一级	私营有限责任公司	建筑装饰和装修业
山东富力达建筑科技有限公司	一级	私营有限责任公司	建筑装饰和装修业
山东英士力装饰工程有限公司	一级	私营有限责任公司	建筑装饰和装修业
山东国创装饰工程有限公司	一级	私营有限责任公司	建筑装饰和装修业
山东嘉嘉装饰有限公司	一级	其他有限责任公司	建筑装饰和装修业
山东今生缘建筑装饰工程有限公司	一级	私营有限责任公司	建筑装饰和装修业
嘉林建设集团有限公司	一级	私营有限责任公司	建筑装饰和装修业
山东津单幕墙有限公司	一级	私营有限责任公司	建筑装饰和装修业
山东万和中盛幕墙有限公司	一级	私营有限责任公司	建筑装饰和装修业
山东天石集团有限公司	一级	私营有限责任公司	建筑装饰和装修业
济南佳宸装饰安装有限公司	一级	私营有限责任公司	建筑装饰和装修业
山东信兴建设发展有限公司	一级	其他有限责任公司	其他建筑安装业
和瑞消防工程有限公司	一级	私营有限责任公司	电气安装
山东奥深智能工程有限公司	一级	私营有限责任公司	其他未列明建筑业
山东宇宸建设工程有限公司	一级	私营有限责任公司	管道和设备安装
山东剑锋消防工程有限公司	一级	私营有限责任公司	管道和设备安装
山东费尔消防技术工程有限公司	一级	私营有限责任公司	电气安装
山东涌泉安全科技有限公司	一级	私营有限责任公司	其他建筑安装业
山东宏雁电子系统工程有限公司	一级	私营有限责任公司	电气安装
山东华森建筑消防项目管理有限公司	一级	私营有限责任公司	电气安装
济南凯诚消防自控设备有限公司	一级	私营有限责任公司	电气安装

13-6 续表 3 continued 3

企业名称 Name	资质等级 Ownership	经济类型 Economic Type	所属行业 Industry
山东坚瑞建设股份有限公司	一级	股份有限公司	其他未列明建筑业
山东深博建筑工程有限公司	一级	私营有限责任公司	管道和设备安装
山东润霖消防工程有限公司	一级	私营有限责任公司	电气安装
济南消防工程有限公司	一级	私营有限责任公司	电气安装
山东泰景楼宇安全技术有限公司	一级	私营有限责任公司	其他未列明建筑业
山东宏岳消防工程有限公司	一级	私营有限责任公司	其他建筑安装业
山东润诚机电工程有限公司	一级	私营有限责任公司	电气安装
山东中安消防设施维修有限公司	一级	私营有限责任公司	其他未列明建筑业
山东力盟电力电子有限公司	一级	私营有限责任公司	其他建筑安装业
山东启方科技有限公司	一级	其他有限责任公司	电气安装
山东飞马消防工程有限责任公司	一级	私营有限责任公司	电气安装
济南信高工程技术有限公司	一级	私营有限责任公司	电气安装
山东华尔泰建筑工程有限公司	一级	私营有限责任公司	电气安装
山东金岛消防安全工程有限公司	一级	私营有限责任公司	电气安装
山东华盛特克科技有限公司	一级	私营有限责任公司	电气安装
山东天翼安全技术有限公司	一级	私营有限责任公司	电气安装
山东佑安消防系统有限公司	一级	私营有限责任公司	其他建筑安装业
山东海瑞林装饰工程有限公司	一级	私营有限责任公司	建筑装饰和装修业
山东三盛防水工程有限公司	一级	私营有限责任公司	节能环保工程施工
山东凯罗福环保节能科技有限公司	一级	私营有限责任公司	建筑装饰和装修业
山东群雄建设工程有限公司	一级	私营有限责任公司	建筑装饰和装修业
秦恒建设科技有限公司	一级	私营有限责任公司	节能环保工程施工
山东洪雨防水工程有限公司	一级	私营有限责任公司	其他未列明建筑业
山东鼎森工程项目管理有限公司	一级	其他有限责任公司	住宅房屋建筑
山东志坚建筑工程有限公司	一级	私营有限责任公司	其他房屋建筑业
山东昶博建筑工程有限公司	一级	私营有限责任公司	其他房屋建筑业
济南四建集团智能消防工程有限责任公司	一级	其他有限责任公司	其他建筑安装业
中国铁路通信信号集团济南工程有限公司	一级	私营有限责任公司	架线和管道工程建筑
济南建设设备安装有限责任公司	一级	其他有限责任公司	管道和设备安装
山东科发建设工程有限公司	一级	其他有限责任公司	建筑装饰和装修业
雪山集团有限公司	一级	私营有限责任公司	管道和设备安装
山东铁迅建设工程有限公司	一级	私营有限责任公司	电气安装
山东宇顺建筑工程有限公司	一级	私营有限责任公司	住宅房屋建筑
山东华埠特克智能机电工程有限公司	一级	私营有限责任公司	其他未列明建筑业
山东宏晨智能工程有限公司	一级	私营有限责任公司	铁路、道路、隧道和桥梁工程建筑
山东圣恩城市建设工程有限公司	一级	私营有限责任公司	工矿工程建筑
山东鸿图科技有限公司	一级	私营有限责任公司	其他建筑安装业
山东蓝润建筑工程有限公司	一级	私营有限责任公司	电气安装
优士科技发展有限公司	一级	私营有限责任公司	电气安装
山东鲁光信息工程有限公司	一级	私营有限责任公司	电气安装
山东思达特信息科技有限公司	一级	私营有限责任公司	电气安装
山东双利电子工程有限公司	一级	其他有限责任公司	电气安装
中广核宏达环境科技有限责任公司	一级	其他有限责任公司	节能环保工程施工
山东太平洋环保股份有限公司	一级	股份有限公司	其他建筑安装业
山东水发鲁润水务科技有限公司	一级	其他有限责任公司	节能环保工程施工
山东安泰智能工程有限公司	一级	其他有限责任公司	电气安装
山东天启智能工程有限公司	一级	私营有限责任公司	其他未列明建筑业
山东奥邦交通设施工程有限公司	一级	其他有限责任公司	其他建筑安装业
山东博安智能科技股份有限公司	一级	股份有限公司	电气安装
济南金宇公路产业发展有限公司	一级	其他有限责任公司	铁路、道路、隧道和桥梁工程建筑
山东海威装饰工程有限公司	一级	私营有限责任公司	建筑装饰和装修业
山东省建设建工集团消防工程有限公司	一级	私营有限责任公司	电气安装
千庭景观建设有限公司	一级	私营有限责任公司	铁路、道路、隧道和桥梁工程建筑
山东彩旺建设有限公司	一级	私营有限责任公司	电气安装
奥斯福集团有限公司	一级	私营有限责任公司	电气安装
山东清华康利城市照明研究设计院有限公司	一级	其他有限责任公司	电气安装
济南东元改建加固工程有限公司	一级	私营有限责任公司	其他房屋建筑业

主要统计指标解释

建筑业总产值 指以货币表现的建筑业企业在一定时期内生产的建筑业产品和服务的总和。建筑业总产值包括建筑工程产值、安装工程产值和其他产值三部分内容，不包括境外产值。

建筑工程产值：指列入建筑工程预算内的各种工程价值。

安装工程产值：指设备安装工程价值以及将预制部品部件安装成建筑工程产品的价值。

其他产值：建筑业总产值中除建筑工程、安装工程以外的产值。包括房屋构筑物修理产值、非标准设备制造产值、总包企业向分包企业收取的管理费以及不能明确划分的施工活动所完成的产值。

房屋施工面积 指报告期内施工的全部房屋建筑面积。包括本期新开工的房屋建筑面积、上期跨入本期继续施工的房屋建筑面积、上期停缓建在本期恢复施工的房屋建筑面积、本期竣工的房屋建筑面积以及本期施工后又停缓建的房屋建筑面积。多层建筑应填各层建筑面积之和。

房屋竣工面积 指报告期内房屋建筑按照设计要求已全部完工，达到住人和使用条件，经验收鉴定合格或达到竣工验收标准，可正式移交使用的各栋房屋建筑面积的总和。

竣工面积以房屋单位工程（栋）为核算对象，在整栋房屋符合竣工条件后按其全部建筑面积一次性计算，而不是按各栋施工房屋中已完成的部分或层次分割计算。

营业收入 指企业从事销售商品、提供劳务和让渡资产使用权等生产经营活动形成的经济利益流入。包括“主营业务收入”和“其他业务收入”。根据会计“利润表”中“营业收入”项目的本年累计数填报。

营业利润 指企业从事生产经营活动所取得的利润。执行企业会计准则或《小企业会计准则》的企业，根据会计“利润表”中“营业利润”项目的本年累计数填报；执行其他企业会计制度的企业，根据会计“损益表”中“营业利润”项目、“投资收益”项目的本年累计数之和填报。

Explanatory Notes on Main Statistical Indicators

Gross output value of construction industry refers to the sum of construction products and services produced by construction enterprises in monetary terms in a certain period of time. The total output value of the construction industry includes the output value of construction projects, the output value of installation projects and other output values, excluding overseas output values.

Output value of construction projects: refers to various project values included in the construction budget.

Output value of installation projects: refers to the value of equipment installation projects and the value from installation of prefabricated parts into construction project products.

Other output value: refers to the output value other than that of the construction projects and installation projects of the total output value of the construction industry. This includes the output value of building structure repair, the output value of non–standard equipment manufacturing, the management fees charged by the general contractor to the subcontractors, and the output value of construction activities that cannot be clearly classified.

Housing construction area refers to the total housing construction area during the reporting period. This includes the newly–started housing construction area during the current period, the housing construction area transitioning to the current period to continue construction from the previous period, the housing construction area that was suspended in the previous period and resumed in the current period, the housing construction area that was completed during the current period, and the housing construction area that was suspended after commenced during the current period. Multi–storey buildings should be filled with the sum of areas of each floor.

Completed area of houses refers to the total building area of all houses that have been completed according to the design requirements, met the living and use conditions, passed the acceptance test or reached the completion acceptance standards during the reporting period, and can be officially handed over for use.

The completed area takes the housing unit project (building) for accounting. After the whole building meets the conditions for completion, it will be wholly calculated according to its total construction area, instead of being calculated according to the completed parts or floors of each building under construction.

Operating income refers to the inflow of economic benefits from the production and operation activities of enterprises such as selling commodities, providing labor services and transferring the right to use assets. This includes "major business income" and "other business income". It is listed according to the yearly cumulative "operating income" items in the accounting "income statement".

Operating profit refers to the profit acquired by an enterprise in its production and business activities. Enterprises that implement the Accounting Standards for Business Enterprises or the Accounting Standards for Small–sized Enterprises shall report it according to the yearly cumulative "operating profit" items in the accounting "income statement"; Enterprises that implement other enterprise accounting systems shall report it according to the sum of the yearly cumulative "operating profit" and "investment income" items in the accounting "income statement"

14

运输与邮电

TRANSPORTATION POST
AND TELECOMMUNICATIONS

14-1 邮电业务量
Business Volume of Postal Services and Telecommunication Services

指标	Item	单位 Unit	2016 年	2017 年	2018 年	2019 年	2020 年	2021 年
国内分类业务量	Domestic Classified Business Volume							
固定电话数	Number of Fixed Telephone	万户（10 000 subscribers）	155.90	153.10	135.27	148.82	144.78	145.31
年末市内电话	Urban Fixed Telephone Subscribers at Year-end	万户（10 000 subscribers）	135.89	132.55	118.70	136.30	127.65	-
年末农村电话	Rural Telephone Subscribers at Year-end	万户（10 000 subscribers）	19.07	19.23	16.47	12.20	2.78	-
年末住宅电话	Number of Fixed Telephone Subscribers at Year-end	万户（10 000 subscribers）	71.79	79.54	67.64	25.56	14.26	-
年末移动电话用户	Number of Mobile Telephone Subscriber at Year-end	万户（10 000 subscribers）	1087.71	971.10	1013.65	1122.86	1154.06	1216.34
4G 电话用户数	4G Mobile Phone Subscribers	万户（10 000 subscribers）	442.10	623.50	725.01	888.81	922.67	750.03
宽带互联网接入用户数	Subscribers of Broad Band Internet	户（subscriber）	2618800	2987500	3447000	3926200	4454800	4630400
每百人互联网用户数	Number of Internet User per 100 Population	户 / 百人 (subscriber/100 person)	41.38	46.81	53.05	49.63	55.56	57.05
邮电局所	Post & Telecommunication offices	处 (unit)	204	207	207	252	252	253
国际及港澳分类业务量	International.Hong kong and Macao Classified Business Volume							
函件	Letters	万件 (10 000 pieces)	16.10	27.67	51.95	45.75	13.02	3.54
包件	Packages	万件 (10 000 pieces)	1.24	1.35	0.76	0.60	0.60	3.72

注：按照山东省通信管理局发布的通信业发展情况，年末市内电话、年末农村电话、年末住宅电话等指标不再进行统计。
Note:According to the development of communication industry released by Shandong Communications Administration, data of local telephone, rural telephone and residential telephone indicators at the end of year are not counted.

14-2 交通运输业基本情况
Basic Conditions of Transport

指标	Item	2016 年	2017 年	2018 年	2019 年	2020 年	2021 年
客运量 （万人）	Passenger Traffic (10 000 persons)						
铁路	Railways	11923.7	13411.8	14547.7	15745.1	9797.4	12163.7
公路	Highways	3212.0	3192.0	3149.0	3244.0	1209.0	2024.0
民航	Civil Aviation	645.1	785.6	894.1	936.1	1238.5	1361.6
旅客周转量 （亿人公里）	Passenger-Kilometers (100 million passenger-km)						
铁路	Railways	703.8	754.6	784.6	795.3	431.9	523.9
公路	Highways	52.2	52.7	52.9	54.1	17.1	39.6
民航	Civil Aviation	272.9	334.3	368.5	376.5	256.3	268.6
货运量 （万吨）	Freight Traffic (10 000 tons)						
铁路	Railways	16749.1	17865.2	18728.0	20869.8	23188.8	22895.4
公路	Highways	21212.0	24058.0	25571.0	28064.0	22677.0	24669.0
民航	Civil Aviation	5.1	5.0	5.6	6.7	14.7	16.8
货物周转量 （亿吨公里）	Freight Ton-Kilometers (100 million ton-km)						
铁路	Railways	1153.0	1254.9	1288.4	1460.5	1566.1	1682.1
公路	Highways	419.0	459.5	474.0	561.4	516.4	577.4
公路通车里程（公里）	Length of Highways in Operation(km)						
公路通车里程	Length of Highways in Operation	12730.2	12856.8	12637.7	17770.9	18117.2	18200.1
#高速公路	Expressway	462.2	488.5	488.5	653.6	737.8	737.8
有铺装、简易铺装路面	Poved Roads	12603.9	12735.7	12579.4	17290.0	18117.2	18200.1
未铺装路面	UnPoved Roads	126.3	121.1	58.3	480.9	0.0	0.0
民用航空	Civil Aviation						
执行航线（条）	Perform Routes(line)	125	150	182	198	208	185
通航城市（个）	Navigable Cities(unit)	64	82	96	120	91	100
起飞架次（架次）	Plane Flights(Sorties)	100152	115529	126828	129994	102375	112746
民用车辆（辆）	Civil Vehicles(unit)						
民用汽车	Civil Vehicles	1742313	1949707	2160748	2584278	2794278	3025326
私人汽车	Private Vehicles	1573761	1764574	1948815	2332421	2512357	2705622
载客汽车	Passenger Vehicles	1592737	1783848	1978951	2370437	2556622	2759683
#大型	Large	12206	13539	14002	15767	15535	15330
载货汽车	Trucks	134741	151141	166277	194957	224713	250200
#重型	Heavy	27303	31632	36720	41904	46148	51609
其他汽车	Others	14835	14718	15520	18884		
专项作业车	Special Operation vehicles					12943	15443
摩托车	Motorcycles	73568	106168	133743	258382	329477	405497
挂车	Wheeler	8191	9102	9851	12538	14842	15590

注：1. 铁路系统统计数据来自中国铁路济南局集团有限公司。
2.2020 年起，因公安部“公安交通管理综合应用平台”调整，修改了机动车报表统计口径，增加“专项作业车”等部分车型的统计，不再提供“其他”类汽车保有量。
3.2020 年起，民航客运量、货运量统计口径调整为出港和进港合计数。
4.2021 年交通运输部采用新的公路货运统计方法，对 2020 年公路货运量、公路货物周转量数据进行了修正。

Notes:1.Statistical data of railway system comes from China Railway Jinan Group Co., Ltd.
2.Since 2020, due to the adjustment of the “Public Traffic Management Integrated Application Platform”, the statistical caliber of motor vehicles statement is varied, the statistics on “special motor vehicle” is supplemented, while “Population of Other Vehicles” is not listed longer.
3.Since 2020, the passenger transport volume of civil aviation, and the statistical caliber of freight traffic volume are adjusted as the total number of departures and arrivals.
4.In 2021, the Ministry of Transport adopted a new statistic method for road freight, and revised the data of road freight volume and road freight turnover in 2020.

14-3 规模以上交通运输、仓储和邮政业企业财务指标 (2021 年)
Main Financial Indicators of Transport,Storage and Postal Services above Designated Size(2021)

单位 : 万元 (10 000 yuan)

指标	Item	交通运输、仓储和邮政业 Transport,Storage and Postal Services
单位数（个）	Number(unit)	366
年初存货	Inventory at Beginning of year	288175
流动资产合计	Total Liquid Assets	14443376
其中：应收账款	Receivable	1551502
存货	Inventory	229305
固定资产原价	Original Value of Fixed Assets	45100035
本年折旧	Depreciation in the Year	1721543
资产总计	Total Assets	91715615
负债合计	Total Liabilities	45834387
所有者权益合计	Total Creditors'Equity	45881227
营业收入	Business Revenue	14546788
营业成本	Business Cost	13571222
税金及附加	Taxes and Other Surcharges	41827
销售费用	Sales Expenses	148401
管理费用	Management Expenses	656088
研发费用	Research and Development Expenses	20970
财务费用	Financial Expenses	900561
投资收益	Investment Interests	437168
其他收益	Other Revenues	433888
营业利润	Profits from Business	123521
营业外收入	Profits from Non-Business	74729
营业外支出	Expense from Non-Business	35526
利润总额	Total Profits	162724
所得税费用	Income Tax Expense	103467
应付职工薪酬（本年贷方累计发生额）	Total Wages Payable	3047295
应交增值税	Value-added Tax Payable	348777
期末用工人数（人）	Number of employees at the end of the period(person)	180531

14-4 分地区公路交通(2021 年)

Road Transportation by Region(2021)

单位: 公里 (km)

指标	Item	济南市 Ji'nan	其中 of which		
			市区 Urban	平阴县 Ping yin	商河县 Shang he
公路通车里程	Length of Highways in Operation	18200.1	14476.7	1036.6	2686.8
#高速公路	Expressway	737.8	644.3	60.8	32.7
有铺装、简易铺装路面	Poved Road	18200.1	14476.7	1036.6	2686.8
未铺装路面	UnPoved Road	0.0	0.0	0.0	0.0

主要统计指标解释

公路里程 指在一定时期内实际达到《公路工程技术标准JTJ01-88》规定的等级公路,并经公路主管部门正式验收交付使用的公路里程数。包括大中城市的郊区公路以及通过小城镇街道部分的公路里程和桥梁、渡口的长度,不包括大中城市的街道、厂矿、林区生产用道和农业生产用道的里程。两条或多条公路共同经由同一路段,只计算一次,不得重复计算里程长度。它是反映公路建设发展规模的重要指标,也是计算运输网密度等指标的基础资料。

民用航空航线里程 指民航运输定期班机飞行的航线长度的总和。航线长度按机场之间的距离计算,通常有两种计算方法:一是将每条航线长度相加称为重复计算航线里程;一是将两线或两条以上航线经过同一区段里程,只计算一次航线长度称为不重复计算航线里程。一般常用的是后者,它能确切反映民航运输网的规模,是表明民航事业为国民经济服务和方便人民生活程度的主要指标。

货(客)运量 指在一定时期内,各种运输工具实际运送的货物(旅客)数量。它是反映运输业为国民经济和人民生活服务的数量指标,也是制定和检查运输生产计划、研究运输发展规模和速度的重要指标。货运按吨计算,客运按人计算。货物不论运输距离长短、货物类别,均按实际重量统计。旅客不论行程远近或票价多少,均按一人一次客运量统计;半价票、小孩票也按一人统计。

货物(旅客)周转量 指在一定时期内,由各种运输工具运送的货物(旅客)数量与其相应运输距离的乘积之总和。它是反映运输业生产总成果的重要指标,也是编制和检查运输生产计划,计算运输效率、劳动生产率以及核算运输单位成本的主要基础资料。计算货物周转量通常按发出站与到达站之间的最短距离,也就是计费距离计算。计算公式为:

货物(旅客)周转量 = Σ(货物(旅客)运输量 × 运输距离)

移动电话用户 指在移动电话营业部门登记,通过移动电话交换机进入移动电话网、占有移动电话号码的电话用户。用户数量以实际办理登记手续进入邮电部门移动电话网的户数进行计算,一部或一台移动电话统计为一户。

电话用户 指接入国家公众固定电话网,并按固定电话业务进行经营管理的电话用户。1997 年以前,电话用户分为市内电话用户和农村电话用户。市内电话用户是指接入县城及县以上城市电话网上的电话用户;农村电话用户是指接入县邮电局农话台及县以下农村电话交换点,以县城为中心(除市话用户外)联通县、乡(镇)、行政村、村民小组的用户。从 1997 年起,电话用户数分组调整为以用户所在区域划分为"城市电话用户"和"乡村电话用户",与过去的按市内电话和农村电话划分方法不同。而电话用户数、电话机部数统计方法不变。

Explanatory Notes on Main Statistical Indicators

Length of Highways refers to the length of highways which are built in conformity with the grades specified in the Technical Standard JTJ01–88 for Highway Engineering within a certain period of time, and have been formally checked and accepted by the departments of highways and put into use. The length of highways includes that of the suburb highways at large and medium sized cities, highways passing through streets at small cities and towns, and also the length of bridges and ferries. It does not include the length of streets in big and medium sized cities and highways built for the production purpose at factories, mines, forest areas and agricultural areas. If two or more highways go to the same section of the way, the length of the section is only calculated for once and no duplication is allowed. The length of highways is an important indicator to show the development of the highway construction and to provide essential information to calculate the transport network density.

Mileage of Civil Aviation Routes refers to the sum of the length of the route of scheduled civil aviation flight. The length of the route is calculated as the distance between airports. There are usually two calculation methods: First, repeated calculation of route mileage is deemed in case of adding the length of each route; Second, no repeated calculation of route mileage is deemed if the length of the route is only calculated once when no less than two routes pass the same zone. The second one is usually used, as it can precisely show the size of the civil aviation network and also is the major indicator of indicating the extent of civil aviation serving the national economy and the people.

Freight (Passenger) Traffic refers to the volume or freight (passenger) transported with various means in a certain period. It provides a quantitative measure to show how the transportation industry serves the national economy and people, and is also an important indicator for planning the transport industry and for studying the development scale and speed of the transport industry. Freight transport is calculated in tons and passenger traffic is calculated in the number of persons. Despite the type of freight and traveling distance, the freight transport is calculated in the actual weight of the goods. And despite the traveling distance and ticket price, the passenger traffic is calculated by the principle that one person can be counted only once in one travel. The passengers who travel with a half–price ticket or a child ticket is also calculated as one person.

Tonnage Mileage (Passenger turnover) refers to the sum of the products of the volume of transported cargos (passengers) multiplying by the transport distance. It is an important indicator to reflect the achievement of transportation industry, to prepare and examine the transport plan and to measure the efficiency, the labor productivity and the unit cost of transport. Normally, the shortest distance between the departure station and the destination station (i.e., the payable distance) is the basis to calculate the Tonnage mileage. The formula is as follows:

Tonnage mileage (passenger turnover) = Σ(freight (passenger) traffic* distance of transportation)

Wireless Subscribers refer to persons who have registered at the mobile phone business department and hence connected with the mobile telephone communication network through the mobile telephone switchboards and occupy mobile telephone numbers. The number of subscribers is calculated in line with the number of users actually handling the registration procedures and entering the mobile telephone network of the post and telecommunications departments. One mobile telephone is deemed as one household.

Telephone Subscribers refer to telephone subscribers entering the national public fixed telephone network and undergoing operating management based on fixed telephone services. Before 1997, telephone subscribers were divided into local telephone subscribers and rural telephone subscribers. Local telephone subscribers refer to telephone subscribers accessing to the urban telephone network of county and above; Rural telephone subscribers refer to telephone subscribers accessing to the agricultural telephone station of the county post and telecommunications office and the rural telephone exchange of those below country, and connecting with county, township (town), administrative village and group of villagers based on the county as the center (except for city telephone users). From 1997, grouping of telephone users is adjusted to "city telephone subscribers" and "rural telephone subscribers" in light of regions where subscribers are, which is different from partition method –– local call and rural call in the past. The statistical approaches for counting telephone subscribers and telephones numbers remain unchanged.

15

国内贸易

DOMESTIC TRADE

15-1 各时期分行业社会消费品零售

Total Retail Sales of Consumer Goods by Section in Each Period

单位：万元 (10 000 yuan)

年份 Year	社会消费品零售总额 Retail Sale of Consumer Goods						
	总计 Total	批发零售业 Wholesale and Retail Trades	住宿业 Hotels Services	餐饮业 Catering Services	制造业 Manufacture	其他 Others	农民对非农业居民 Farmers to Non-agricultural Residents
1949	11426	7312		556	3514	–	44
1952	22248	16985		1223	3592	–	448
1957	34568	29279		1935	2381	3	970
1962	41436	35784		1655	2946	266	785
1965	40795	36470		1829	1856	287	353
1970	42993	39397		1537	1468	321	270
1975	60105	53239		2565	2914	1217	170
1978	81335	70661		2907	5120	2222	425
1979	96036	80703		4000	9060	823	1450
1980	119775	95121		4392	16489	1299	2474
“六五时期”							
1981	135236	103303		5388	21353	2157	3035
1982	152094	116241		8165	21398	2778	3512
1983	167948	127884		9225	23569	2953	4317
1984	200301	150233		11342	29563	4506	4657
1985	243080	181867		14823	32342	5535	8513
“七五时期”							
1986	294102	219730		17880	35565	5456	15471
1987	331504	240192		20305	45386	8963	16658
1988	425984	300090		30808	60463	12300	22323
1989	484392	343978		28634	71653	9729	30398
1990	528221	382047		25599	71505	10886	38184
“八五时期”							
1991	597989	424836		27443	78452	14186	53072
1992	711774	535080		37096	77951		61647
1993	985251	723914		56059	80101		125177
1994	1426472	1037687		86141	99621		203023
1995	1837618	1345321		133501	115105		243691
“九五时期”							
1996	2234590	1570947		176100	141201		346342

15-1 续表 continued

年份 Year	社会消费品零售总额 Retail Sale of Consumer Goods						
	总计 Total	批发零售业 Wholesale and Retail Trades	住宿业 Hotels Services	餐饮业 Catering Services	制造业 Manufacture	其他 Others	农民对非农业居民 Farmers to Non-agricultural Residents
1997	2568584	1744014		216727	177219		430624
1998	2834024	1893486		255616	207595		477327
1999	3092091	2043078		305333	225132		518548
2000	3444527	2287545		377550	233128		546304
"十五时期"							
2001	3857141	2574216		485494	237545		559886
2002	4321225	2935804		613178	231947		540296
2003	5115396	4373831		741565	–		–
2004	6689452	5691288	57973	940191	–		–
2005	7726458	6575543	66490	1084425	–		–
"十一五时期"							
2006	8974064	7571831	78098	1324135	–		–
2007	10526639	8791908	86322	1648409	–		–
2008	12922856	10684195	96391	2142271	–		–
2009	15254265	12710608	105378	2438279	–		–
2010	17254574	14022650	150810	3081114	–		–
"十二五时期"							
2011	20231045	16338362	175067	3717616	–		–
2012	23235965	18740304	187466	4308195	–		–
2013	26338714	22006709	177160	4154845	–		–
2014	28640303	24120903	182090	4337310	–	–	–
2015	31410419	26484428	193710	4732280	–	–	–
"十三五时期"							
2016	34350723	28971634	210316	5168774	–	–	–
2017	37525226	31658152	228909	5638165	–	–	–
2018	40910775	34521369	248418	6140988	–	–	–
2019	44204092	37604716	275686	6323691			
2020	44691335	38570115	255049	5866171	–	–	–
"十四五时期"							
2021	51260961	43881612	301524	7077825			

注：1992 年至 2019 年社会消费品零售总额及分组数据根据第四次全国经济普查数据进行了修订。
Note:Total retail volume of social consumption and grouping data from 1992 to 2019 are revised according to the fourth national economic census.

15-2 限额以上批发零售业法人企业商品销售情况(2021年)
Sales of Commo-dities by Enterprises above Designated Size of Wholesale and Retail Trade(2021)

单位:万元 (10 000 yuan)

指标	Item	商品销售总额 Total Sale Value		
		合计 Total	批发 Wholesale	零售 Retail
总计	Total	116078022.4	98922754.1	17155268.3
批发业	Wholesale Trade	101628260.0	98312135.5	3316124.5
农、林、牧、渔产品批发	Wholesale of Agricultural, Forestry, Livestock and Fishery Products	1319238.6	1284600.3	34638.3
食品、饮料及烟草制品批发	Wholesale of Food, Beverages and Tobaccos	5049940.8	4578526.6	471414.2
纺织、服装及家庭用品批发	Wholesale of Textiles, Wearing Apparel and Household Articles	2607081.4	2316694.0	290387.4
文化、体育用品及器材批发	Wholesale of Culture, Sports Appliances and Equipments	3550224.6	2670260.7	879963.9
医药及医疗器材批发	Wholesale of Medicines and Medical Appliances	9559664.2	9511834.1	47830.1
矿产品、建材及化工产品批发	Wholesale of Mineral Products, Building Materials and Chemical Products	66987785.5	65918585.2	1069200.3
机械设备、五金产品及电子产品批发	Wholesale of Machinery, Hardware and Electronic Products	11656396.0	11150987.0	505409.0
贸易经纪与代理	Trade Broker and Agency	190249.5	188295.9	1953.6
其他批发业	Other Wholesale not Classified Elsewhere	707679.4	692351.7	15327.7
内资企业	Domestic Invested Enterprises	94417106.9	91534416.8	2882690.1
国有企业	State-owned Enterprises	6979688.0	6949983.7	29704.3
集体企业	Collective-owned Enterprises	5700.6	5700.6	
股份合作企业	Cooperative Enterprises			
有限责任公司	Limited Liability Corporations	37770778.2	36053693.1	1717085.1
股份有限公司	Share-holding Corporations Ltd.	1845912.0	1643358.6	202553.4
私营企业	Private Enterprises	47785724.7	46852377.4	933347.3
其他企业	Other Enterprises	29303.4	29303.4	
港、澳、台商投资企业	Enterprises with Investment from Hong Kong, Macao and Taiwan	3090106.9	3090106.9	

15-2 续表 continued

指标	Item	商品销售总额 Total Sale Value		
		合计 Total	批发 Wholesale	零售 Retail
外商投资企业	Foreign Invested Enterprises	4121046.2	3687611.8	433434.4
零售业	**Retail Trade**	**14449762.4**	**610618.6**	**13839143.8**
综合零售	General Retail	2318088.5	79655.6	2238432.9
食品、饮料及烟草制品专门零售	Special Retail of Food, Beverages and Tobaccos	427359.3	33808.7	393550.6
纺织、服装及日用品专门零售	Special Retail of Textiles, Garments and Daily Consumer Articles	625271.3	68789.0	556482.3
文化、体育用品及器材专门零售	Special Retail of Culture, Sports Appliances and Equipments	385083.8	48045.2	337038.6
医药及医疗器材专门零售	Special Retail of Medicines and Medical Appliances	718073.0	28536.9	689536.1
汽车、摩托车、零配件和燃料及其他动力销售	Retail of Motor Vehicles, Motorcycles, Parts, and Fuel and Other Powers	6719743.2	155910.6	6563832.6
家用电器及电子产品专门零售	Special Retail of Household Electric Appliances and Electronic Products	1275563.5	51921.3	1223642.2
五金、家具及室内装饰材料专门零售	Special Retail of Hardware, Furniture and Interior Decoration Materials	113428.2	3470.6	109957.6
货摊、无店铺及其他零售业	Stalls, Non-shop and Other Retails	1867151.6	140480.7	1726670.9
内资企业	Domestic Invested Enterprises	12978650.6	585761.9	12392888.7
国有企业	State-owned Enterprises	443877.7	1255.2	442622.5
集体企业	Collective-owned Enterprises	26034.8		26034.8
股份合作企业	Cooperative Enterprises	18458.6	385.1	18073.5
有限责任公司	Limited Liability Corporations	3123969.5	201264.0	2922705.5
股份有限公司	Share-holding Corporations Ltd.	1011132.3	13512.0	997620.3
私营企业	Private Enterprises	8353360.0	369345.6	7984014.4
其他企业	Other Enterprises	1817.7		1817.7
港、澳、台商投资企业	Enterprises with Investment from Hong Kong, Macao and Taiwan	834965.8	3681.1	831284.7
外商投资企业	Foreign Invested Enterprises	636146	21175.6	614970.4

15-3 限额以上批发零售贸易企业资产实力(2021年)

Capital Power of Enterprises above Designated Size of Wholesale and Retail Trade(2021)

单位：万元

指标	Item	法人企业数(个) Number of Corporation Enterprises (unit)	流动资产合计 Total Working Capitals
总计	Total	4562	41014881.2
批发业	Wholesale Trade	3560	34149852.2
农、林、牧、渔产品批发	Wholesale of Agricultural, Forestry, Livestock and Fishery Products	75	728974.1
食品、饮料及烟草制品批发	Wholesale of Food, Beverages and Tobaccos	224	1947846.6
纺织、服装及家庭用品批发	Wholesale of Textiles, Wearing Apparel and Household Articles	175	1403815.0
文化、体育用品及器材批发	Wholesale of Culture, Sports Appliances and Equipments	108	1681300.3
医药及医疗器材批发	Wholesale of Medicines and Medical Appliances	372	5504221.0
矿产品、建材及化工产品批发	Wholesale of Mineral Products, Building Materials and Chemical Products	1739	16882580.3
机械设备、五金产品及电子产品批发	Wholesale of Machinery, Hardware and Electronic Products	815	5576836.8
贸易经纪与代理	Trade Broker and Agency	7	96120.0
其他批发业	Other Wholesale not Classified Elsewhere	45	328158.1
内资企业	Domestic Invested Enterprises	3534	30857413.3
国有企业	State-owned Enterprises	37	3168569.4
集体企业	Collective-owned Enterprises	1	1012.3
股份合作企业	Cooperative Enterprises		
联营企业	Joint Ownership Enterprises		
有限责任公司	Limited Liability Corporations	450	14357634.0
股份有限公司	Share-holding Corporations Ltd.	26	732510.7
私营企业	Private Enterprises	3016	12590825.8
其他企业	Other Enterprises	4	6861.1
港、澳、台商投资企业	Enterprises with Investment from Hong Kong, Macao and Taiwan	13	2361184.7
外商投资企业	Foreign Invested Enterprises	13	931254.2

(10 000 yuan)

其中 of which 存货 Inventory	固定资产原价 Original Value of Fixed Assets	累计折旧 Depreciation	其中 of which 本年折旧 Depreciation in the Year	资产总计 Total Assets	负债合计 Total Liabilities	所有者权益合计 Total Creditors' Equity	其中 of which 实收资本 Paid-up Capitall
6081458.5	3595790.6	1448150.6	227111.9	50696338.4	38590643.5	12028121.5	8893826.2
5066328.5	2415411.4	928486.3	142446.3	41508798.4	31113692.7	10326977.2	7576592.6
175955.8	64683.0	26012.9	2255.3	828031.2	686699.5	141331.7	123103.6
693483.0	296504.0	134274.8	13211.0	2269182.3	1541832.5	702007.7	300466.8
320114.8	136144.8	36928.2	6832.6	1680857.8	1428231.6	252626.2	153894.3
406062.3	348671.6	125536.8	13565.2	2356441.9	1535619.0	820636.8	251681.0
717922.5	373783.9	133886.3	27907.3	6231249.5	5166678.0	1062001.0	666328.9
1670804.6	771670.0	302939.4	36165.1	21486727.1	15305950.1	6144489.9	3845289.5
1026154.8	393924.7	162595.7	40904.7	6198065.2	5090251.0	1104071.5	2165197.7
11215.0	1577.1	746.6	103.1	100562.2	72242.5	28319.7	18980.0
44615.7	28452.3	5565.6	1502.0	357681.2	286188.5	71492.7	51650.8
4204864.7	2234046.2	853067.4	132952.1	37807237.4	30386210.2	7352898.6	6156062.8
723139.4	96373.1	23031.7	2788.5	3432868.9	2496748.9	910435.3	396560.3
50.3	48.3			1089.1	547.2	541.9	50.0
1574855.2	1281373.5	497156.3	68304.9	18665840.2	15070651.5	3572714.2	2396386.3
85018.6	49199.1	20405.6	2320.4	1297844.0	900231.9	397612.1	179793.3
1821635.5	806463.4	312432.3	59501.9	14402186.8	11912921.3	2469296.1	3182770.9
165.7	588.8	41.5	36.4	7408.4	5109.4	2299.0	502.0
673944.6	48543.2	13414.0	3290.2	2414838.5	2032194.0	382644.5	360897.0
187519.2	132822.0	62004.9	6204.0	1286722.5	-1304711.5	2591434.1	1059632.8

15-3 续表 continued

指标	Item	法人企业数（个）Number of Corporation Enterprises (unit)	流动资产合计 Total Working Capitals
零售业	Retail Trade	1002	6865029.0
综合零售	General Retail	76	3034761.0
食品、饮料及烟草制品专门零售	Special Retail of Food, Beverages and Tobaccos	92	212045.8
纺织、服装及日用品专门零售	Special Retail of Textiles, Garments and Daily Consumer Articles	76	275671.9
文化、体育用品及器材专门零售	Special Retail of Culture, Sports Appliances and Equipments	61	241099.0
医药及医疗器材专门零售	Special Retail of Medicines and Medical Appliances	64	433757.6
汽车、摩托车、零配件和燃料及其他动力销售	Retail of Motor Vehicles, Motorcycles, Parts, and Fuel and Other Powers	362	1766496.2
家用电器及电子产品专门零售	Special Retail of Household Electric Appliances and Electronic Products	144	495970.7
五金、家具及室内装饰材料专门零售	Special Retail of Hardware, Furniture and Interior Decoration Materials	24	46845.6
货摊、无店铺及其他零售业	Stalls, Non-shop and Other Retails	103	358381.2
内资企业	Domestic Invested Enterprises	979	6544813.1
国有企业	State-owned Enterprises	17	182406.3
集体企业	Collective-owned Enterprises	9	7060.8
股份合作企业	Cooperative Enterprises	5	6876.4
联营企业	Joint Ownership Enterprises		
有限责任公司	Limited Liability Corporations	192	1009747.1
股份有限公司	Share-holding Corporations Ltd.	11	2536280.9
私营企业	Private Enterprises	743	2802220.8
其他企业	Other Enterprises	2	220.8
港、澳、台商投资企业	Enterprises with Investment from Hong Kong, Macao and Taiwan	12	168204.7
外商投资企业	Foreign Invested Enterprises	11	152011.2

其中 of which	固定资产原价 Original Value of Fixed Assets	累计折旧 Depreciation	其中 of which	资产总计 Total Assets	负债合计 Total Liabilities	所有者权益合计 Total Creditors' Equity	其中 of which
存货 Inventory			本年折旧 Depreciation in the Year				实收资本 Paid-up Capitall
1015130.0	1180379.2	519664.3	84665.6	9187540.0	7476950.8	1701144.3	1317233.6
137046.6	588556.9	279867.0	39156.2	4101193.8	3639219.0	461974.8	298141.3
36855.3	67891.6	28554.3	2224.6	261331.6	197290.8	63251.8	51023.7
69426.7	44480.4	12721.0	2712.6	404433.9	354874.6	51555.1	142847.1
59581.1	31090.4	13374.9	2218.9	288435.3	160643.4	127791.9	54272.7
108459.8	25482.4	8821.7	3357.6	562649.0	384200.8	179247.2	67617.7
484105.5	328587.8	147327.8	30127.8	2429612.2	1829946.1	588904.0	514494.7
49987.6	11512.3	5078.6	481.8	608444.2	530605.5	77826.6	90382.2
10014.8	44321.3	10797.9	2313.3	112301.0	69166.0	43135.0	17121.8
59652.6	38456.1	13121.1	2072.8	419139.0	311004.6	107457.9	81332.4
946933.6	967478.4	425106.2	57431.0	8403824.0	7007244.2	1387134.9	1092363.7
38928.8	12192.2	4977.8	949.3	218994.8	178330.2	35351.3	24174.1
2045.2	1587.7	803.8	51.4	8354.4	3031.0	5323.4	844.4
3611.9	888.9	493.5	64.9	7690.1	5265.5	2424.6	922.6
183664.4	306672.4	116442.0	15094.9	1474381.9	1029044.8	440294.3	319359.6
60730.8	309559.6	152738.4	8647.4	3251989.6	2910829.2	341160.4	106334.3
657832.5	336477.6	149640.7	32613.1	3442165.9	2880617.4	562459.7	640648.7
120.0	100.0	10.0	10.0	247.3	126.1	121.2	80.0
32426.5	92002.1	49387.7	20950.2	249122.6	171179.3	77943.3	23550.8
35769.9	120898.7	45170.4	6284.4	534593.4	298527.3	236066.1	201319.1

15-4 限额以上批发零售贸易企业损益及分配(2021年)
Profit Loss and Distribution of Enterprises above Designated Size of Wholesale and Retail Trade (2021)

单位:万元

指标	Item	法人企业数(个) Number of Corporation Enterprises (unit)	主营业务收入 Revenue from Principal Business	营业成本 Cost of Business
总计	Total	4562	102598418.9	97946966.0
批发业	Wholesale Trade	3560	90541741.2	87328850.2
农、林、牧、渔产品批发	Wholesale of Agricultural, Forestry, Livestock and Fishery Products	75	1235462.6	1201314.5
食品、饮料及烟草制品批发	Wholesale of Food, Beverages and Tobaccos	224	4568707.8	4073995.1
纺织、服装及家庭用品批发	Wholesale of Textiles, Wearing Apparel and Household Articles	175	2271709.9	2171919.7
文化、体育用品及器材批发	Wholesale of Culture, Sports Appliances and Equipments	108	3320499.7	2958945.3
医药及医疗器材批发	Wholesale of Medicines and Medical Appliances	372	8529761.7	7739275.9
矿产品、建材及化工产品批发	Wholesale of Mineral Products, Building Materials and Chemical Products	1739	59187440.9	58410650.7
机械设备、五金产品及电子产品批发	Wholesale of Machinery, Hardware and Electronic Products	815	10609144.8	9995180.6
贸易经纪与代理	Trade Broker and Agency	7	183042.1	170923.6
其他批发业	Other Wholesale not Classified Elsewhere	45	635971.7	606644.8
内资企业	Domestic Invested Enterprises	3534	83976215.9	81032452.9
国有企业	State-owned Enterprises	37	6266830.8	6181289.1
集体企业	Collective-owned Enterprises	1	5056.9	4928.8
股份合作企业	Cooperative Enterprises			
联营企业	Joint Ownership Enterprises			
有限责任公司	Limited Liability Corporations	450	33520384.1	32415618.0
股份有限公司	Share-holding Corporations Ltd.	26	1604873.5	1542847.8
私营企业	Private Enterprises	3016	42552879.2	40865418.9
其他企业	Other Enterprises	4	26191.4	22350.3
港、澳、台商投资企业	Enterprises with Investment from Hong Kong, Macao and Taiwan	13	2911626.1	2779592.4
外商投资企业	Foreign Invested Enterprises	13	3653899.2	3516804.9

(10 000 yuan)

税金及附加 Taxes and Surcharges	销售费用 Cost of Sales	管理费用 Cost of Management	财务费用 Cost of Finance	营业利润 Profits from Business	利润总额 Total Profits	所得税费用 Income Tax Expense	应付职工薪酬（本年贷方累计发生额）Total Wages Payable	应交增值税 Value-added Tax Payable
290227.0	2916765.6	1418702.5	408794.7	902618.3	1957219.3	268584.1	1432997.8	658651.5
241866.1	1734437.0	1037597.5	336193.4	816677.5	1858520.9	217568.7	894461.9	468611.6
419.5	12484.5	17116.9	63777.6	2717.9	7770.5	873.1	11698.7	1687.3
123744.9	145140.3	155600.0	5812.9	157976.3	161383.3	32518.9	105529.4	51515.6
2416.7	93870.2	41786.1	−1367.2	19761.6	10088.1	5093.3	46822.7	15772.7
5234.5	137349.4	112527.1	−1403.4	109729.8	112165.1	6052.7	142105.6	6072.0
17521.7	477795.6	189495.2	53104.7	113119.2	113447.1	23979.3	178504.7	108867.7
49935.0	431430.4	310682.1	173743.4	312064.9	1333559.5	125070.4	193710.1	170914.5
41637.3	414833.1	198757.0	41640.7	98879.3	116490.2	23305.9	205896.4	109070.4
152.9	8382.9	1522.6	31.7	1939.9	2614.1	25.6	2255.7	714.9
803.6	13150.6	10110.5	853.0	488.6	1003.0	649.5	7938.6	3996.5
234818.4	1598563.1	935559.7	306830.9	765852.2	1796454.0	191320.3	832039.5	439902.0
2962.4	12837.8	20289.8	9238.3	−8338.3	−3174.7	−1976.0	24967.8	17135.8
1.6		28.9	−1.1	98.7	103.7	2.9	15.5	13.4
168923.8	547145.0	344523.4	178687.0	535014.9	1549912.0	141486.4	391785.7	188837.5
1726.7	36557.5	18973.6	16803.0	20912.2	21309.5	6403.9	18673.5	4747.5
61155.3	1000125.3	551555.1	102094.8	216467.8	226596.1	44973.9	396380.9	229161.0
48.6	1897.5	188.9	8.9	1696.9	1707.4	429.2	216.1	6.8
2772.1	70542.2	62366.7	22356.3	8823.9	9800.3	3523.2	29679.9	12055.7
4275.6	65331.7	39671.1	7006.2	42001.4	52266.6	22725.2	32742.5	16653.9

15-4 续表 continued

指标	Item	法人企业数（个）Number of Corporation Enterprises (unit)	主营业务收入 Revenue from Principal Business	营业成本 Cost of Business
零售业	Retail Trade	1002	12056677.7	10618115.8
综合零售	General Retail	76	1486727.2	1233432.6
食品、饮料及烟草制品专门零售	Special Retail of Food, Beverages and Tobaccos	92	406632.9	337464.7
纺织、服装及日用品专门零售	Special Retail of Textiles, Garments and Daily Consumer Articles	76	526335.1	426176.4
文化、体育用品及器材专门零售	Special Retail of Culture, Sports Appliances and Equipments	61	353826.6	295808.3
医药及医疗器材专门零售	Special Retail of Medicines and Medical Appliances	64	656160.2	509901.3
汽车、摩托车、零配件和燃料及其他动力销售	Retail of Motor Vehicles, Motorcycles, Parts, and Fuel and Other Powers	362	5999771.9	5581194.3
家用电器及电子产品专门零售	Special Retail of Household Electric Appliances and Electronic Products	144	870140.6	819615.3
五金、家具及室内装饰材料专门零售	Special Retail of Hardware, Furniture and Interior Decoration Materials	24	103780.5	76493.4
货摊、无店铺及其他零售业	Stalls, Non-shop and Other Retails	103	1653302.7	1338029.5
内资企业	Domestic Invested Enterprises	979	10760901.9	9539403.2
国有企业	State-owned Enterprises	17	389153.0	371436.0
集体企业	Collective-owned Enterprises	9	23070.0	21469.7
股份合作企业	Cooperative Enterprises	5	16336.7	13900.5
联营企业	Joint Ownership Enterprises			
有限责任公司	Limited Liability Corporations	192	2669922.4	2366525.3
股份有限公司	Share-holding Corporations Ltd.	11	404141.7	309769.6
私营企业	Private Enterprises	743	7256493.4	6454539.0
其他企业	Other Enterprises	2	1784.7	1763.1
港、澳、台商投资企业	Enterprises with Investment from Hong Kong, Macao and Taiwan	12	730236.0	654794.4
外商投资企业	Foreign Invested Enterprises	11	565539.8	423918.2

税金及附加 Taxes and Surcharges	销售费用 Cost of Sales	管理费用 Cost of Management	财务费用 Cost of Finance	营业利润 Profits from Business	利润总额 Total Profits	所得税费用 Income Tax Expense	应付职工薪酬（本年贷方累计发生额）Total Wages Payable	应交增值税 Value-added Tax Payable
48360.9	1182328.6	381105.0	72601.3	85940.8	98698.4	51015.4	538535.9	190039.9
12888.9	281278.1	79011.8	20113.4	28422.7	28902.4	9848.6	149876.0	24275.7
1519.8	23595.3	11617.3	697.5	37341.2	37699.7	7084.4	16310.7	8455.5
4119.1	84402.8	28108.4	6924.9	-11028.8	-6313.1	1325.4	40365.0	9484.1
4311.5	33249.9	14787.2	2288.7	8265.3	9640.5	1827.5	22123.8	5160.7
4485.2	115590.3	31799.4	2625.9	3676.0	2745.8	2383.3	70133.6	12201.6
15838.7	278720.2	131188.4	34453.0	64484.7	70192.8	23530.3	168255.6	96296.2
516.5	51259.9	24834.6	3646.2	-21862.3	-23320.6	140.4	22900.6	4627.5
932.6	12387.6	14196.2	1887.8	-2171.6	-1712.1	246.7	8262.1	2202.4
3748.6	301844.5	45561.7	-36.1	-21186.4	-19137.0	4628.8	40308.5	27336.2
41112.7	998297.4	341994.5	61537.6	73424.5	85993.3	41089.1	486756.2	172277.2
905.8	18983.3	7984.0	4133.0	-667.7	-471.4	931.5	15360.3	17644.5
210.5	779.3	1104.5	21.5	-414.1	-401.8	7.1	740.4	148.3
29.5	1803.1	614.9	36.3	77.5	97.2	32.9	672.0	133.6
9018.0	209332.7	84769.2	18659.8	55585.0	58972.6	19108.5	116139.2	34281.2
6760.4	115198.1	38631.5	7581.1	24197.5	24474.9	1690.2	62684.8	13336.3
24188.5	652200.9	208837.1	31105.9	-5355.0	3321.8	19285.9	291099.0	106733.3
		53.3		1.3		33.0	60.5	
4934.6	45906.3	6570.4	1437.3	32887.5	32686.6	8847.4	20144.0	5422.2
2313.6	138124.9	32540.1	9626.4	-20371.2	-19981.5	1078.9	31635.7	12340.5

15-5 限额以上餐饮业主要经济指标 (2021 年)

Main Economic Indicators of Enterprises above Designated Size of Catering Services (2021)

单位：万元

指标	Item	法人企业数（个）Number of Corporation Enterprises (unit)	资产总计 Total Assets	负债合计 Total Liabilities	所有者权益 Creditors'Equity
总计	Total	485	706724.3	522411.8	188777.8
正餐服务	Restaurant	295	488812.8	354031.1	139303.5
快餐服务	Fast Food	164	183869.2	133917.0	49895.7
饮料及冷饮服务	Beverages and Cold Drinks	4	3030.9	9724.1	-6693.2
餐饮配送及外卖送餐服务	Catering Distribution and Delivery Service	17	13055.0	7514.5	5540.5
其他餐饮业	Others	5	17956.4	17225.1	731.3
内资企业	Domestic Invested Enterprises	481	665857.2	471852.4	198470.1
国有企业	State-owned Enterprises	14	185326.5	54573.6	130752.9
集体企业	Collective-owned Enterprises	1	867.6	308.6	559.0
股份合作企业	Cooperative Enterprises	1	2362.8	1455.7	907.1
联营企业	Joint Ownership Enterprises	1	1510.3	24.9	1485.4
有限责任公司	Limited Liability Corporations	62	155394.2	108981.3	46976.2
股份有限公司	Share-holding Corporations Ltd.	2	6432.8	2363.5	4069.3
私营企业	Private Enterprises	399	313805.1	304086.9	13620.2
其他企业	Other Enterprises	1	157.9	57.9	100.0
港、澳、台商投资企业	Enterprises with Investment from Hong Kong, Macao and Taiwan	3	40732.4	49774.9	-9042.5
外商投资企业	Foreign Invested Enterprises	1	134.7	784.5	-649.8

(10 000 yuan)

其中 of which 实收资本 Paid-up Capital	主营业务收入 Revenue from Principal Business	营业成本 Cost of Business	销售费用 Expenses on Business	管理费用 Expenses on Management	财务费用 Expenses on Finance	营业利润 Profits from Business	利润总额 Total Profits	应付职工薪酬（本年贷方累计发生额）Total Wages Payable
123213.7	611045.6	332962.5	187198.2	103243.0	7022.2	−10577.0	−7168.4	152134.7
84399.3	395949.4	200477.2	123386.5	83268.7	5223.4	−14308.0	−11486.1	95402.1
34359.2	169199.6	97699.5	55044.9	14445.4	1674.0	4168.3	4652.4	46791.1
207.7	12047.5	7610.4	3089.9	1276.2	8.7	80.3	27.1	2525.6
3178.7	20644.5	17552.9	2982.1	2964.9	50.0	−589.6	−471.2	4496.6
1068.8	13204.6	9622.5	2694.8	1287.8	66.1	72.0	109.4	2919.3
118457.9	560416.9	314650.1	160789.0	100494.5	5587.5	−12242.4	−8887.8	133382.1
21682.4	27114.7	13933.2	7704.5	10549.5	−624.4	−2447.9	−2578.5	11976.3
300.0	493.8	82.4	7.7	192.6	104.3	93.3	94.0	81.5
876.8	1522.6	501.0	592.9	423.0	−7.3	10.7	21.0	446.9
1500.0	1370.0	1320.9	7.0	86.8	−1.1	−43.7	−14.6	539.8
28349.9	158075.7	104894.1	35897.8	26082.8	1656.0	−3764.3	−2560.0	39952.3
4185.0	3751.9	1101.0	815.7	2476.0	6.9	−660.2	17.4	1221.3
61563.8	367766.5	192671.9	115603.1	60683.8	4453.4	−5446.3	−3890.0	79095.0
	321.7	145.6	160.3		−0.3	16.0	22.9	69.0
4705.8	49814.0	18041.2	25861.8	2748.5	1429.7	1674.7	1723.2	18567.0
50.0	814.7	271.2	547.4		5.0	−9.3	−3.8	185.6

15-6 限额以上住宿业主要经济指标(2021年)
Main Economic Indicators of Enterprises above Designated Size of Hotels Services(2021)

单位：万元

指标	Item	法人企业数（个）Number of Corporation Enterprises (unit)	资产总计 Total Assets	负债合计 Total Liabilities	所有者权益 Owners' Equity
总计	Total	217	989355.9	942276.9	50050.4
旅游饭店	Tourist Hotel	56	672933.7	530846.5	144273.9
一般旅馆	General Hotels	144	201071.3	245199.6	-43343.6
民宿服务	Home Lodging Services				
露营地服务	Campground Services				
其他住宿业	Others	17	115350.9	166230.8	-50879.9
内资企业	Domestic Invested Enterprises	214	977081.1	932504.7	45309.8
国有企业	State-owned Enterprises	13	224933.4	108649.1	116284.3
集体企业	Collective-owned Enterprises	2	9495.6	12039.6	-2544.0
股份合作企业	Cooperative Enterprises	2	19975.1	18354.4	1620.7
联营企业	Joint Ownership Enterprises				
有限责任公司	Limited Liability Corporations	41	470676.2	556506.1	-85881.2
股份有限公司	Share-holding Corporations Ltd.	2	444.6	453.0	-8.4
私营企业	Private Enterprises	154	251556.2	236502.5	15838.4
其他企业	Other Enterprises				
港、澳、台商投资企业	Enterprises with Investment from Hong Kong, Macao and Taiwan	2	11736.5	8842.4	5132.1
外商投资企业	Foreign Invested Enterprises	1	538.3	929.8	-391.5

(10 000 yuan)

其中 of which 实收资本 Paid-up Capital	主营业务收入 Revenue from Principal Business	营业成本 Cost of Business	销售费用 Expenses on Business	管理费用 Expenses on Management	财务费用 Expenses on Finance	营业利润 Profits from Business	利润总额 Total Profits	应付职工薪酬（本年贷方累计发生额）Total Wages Payable
246410.0	327845.1	119707.4	138985.5	112956.6	5783.8	-33105.7	-30261.0	98376.0
89456.4	176648.9	67045.8	79729.1	60650.3	477.2	-15894.4	-13272.0	64357.6
152437.4	128497.5	42135.7	51463.2	41097.3	1773.1	-7708.1	-7331.4	28395.2
4516.2	22698.7	10525.9	7793.2	11209.0	3533.5	-9503.2	-9657.6	5623.2
241590.0	324123.8	119392.6	136877.4	110455.2	5794.8	-31932.0	-29044.9	96296.0
31375.3	73304.5	23038.2	37484.7	25024.4	-2422.0	-6352.4	-4395.9	29515.3
1883.4	4209.6	1160.3	3363.9	1054.2	7.3	-1359.8	-1306.2	1258.8
1416.4	3993.8	1873.5	970.6	1239.7	195.2	-299.8	-255.2	925.9
51568.7	114179.6	37624.6	55290.4	45941.4	2745.8	-16803.5	-16544.0	37948.3
480.0	883.9	297.9	686.3	23.9	1.3	-125.9	-122.3	415.6
154866.2	127552.4	55398.1	39081.5	37171.6	5267.2	-6990.6	-6421.3	26232.1
4320.0	3339.9	280.4	1406.0	2275.1	-10.6	-702.6	-769.2	1894.5
500.0	381.4	34.4	702.1	226.3	-0.4	-471.1	-446.9	185.5

15-7 限额以上住宿业和餐饮业法人企业经营情况（2021 年）

Main Indicators of Enterprises above Designated Size of Hotels and Catering Services(2021)

指标	Item	法人企业数（个）Number of Corporation Enterprises (unit)	从业人员期末人数（人）Engaged Persons at Year-end (person)	营业额（万元）Business Revenue (10 000yuan)
总计	Total	702	42700	994853.8
住宿业	Hotels	217	15154	354334.7
旅游饭店	Tourist Hotel	56	8520	193927.7
一般旅馆	General Hotels	144	5469	136313.1
民宿服务	Home Lodging Services			
露营地服务	Campground Services			
其他住宿业	Others	17	1165	24093.9
内资企业	Domestic Invested Enterprises	214	14955	350013.0
国有企业	State-owned Enterprises	13	3505	76682.0
集体企业	Collective-owned Enterprises	2	218	4499.2
股份合作企业	Cooperative Enterprises	2	181	4134.1
联营企业	Joint Ownership Enterprises			
有限责任公司	Limited Liability Corporations	41	5979	127721.1
股份有限公司	Share-holding Corporations Ltd.	2	74	926.8
私营企业	Private Enterprises	154	4998	136049.8
其他企业	Other Enterprises			
港、澳、台商投资企业	Enterprises with Investment from Hong Kong, Macao and Taiwan	2	166	3621.8
外商投资企业	Foreign Invested Enterprises	1	33	699.9
餐饮业	Catering Services	485	27546	640519.1
正餐服务	Restaurant	295	17400	409110.5
快餐服务	Fast Food	164	8124	180629.7
饮料及冷饮服务	Beverages and Cold Drinks	4	313	12677.0
餐饮配送及外卖送餐服务	Catering Distribution and Delivery Service	17	969	24590.3
其他餐饮业	Others	5	740	13511.6
内资企业	Domestic Invested Enterprises	481	23861	586915.9
国有企业	State-owned Enterprises	14	1964	30064.1
集体企业	Collective-owned Enterprises	1	14	513.5
股份合作企业	Cooperative Enterprises	1	82	1613.8
联营企业	Joint Ownership Enterprises	1	153	1452.2
有限责任公司	Limited Liability Corporations	62	5946	165257.5
股份有限公司	Share-holding Corporations Ltd.	2	375	4613.5
私营企业	Private Enterprises	399	15313	383064.5
其他企业	Other Enterprises	1	14	336.8
港、澳、台商投资企业	Enterprises with Investment from Hong Kong, Macao and Taiwan	3	3650	52754.2
外商投资企业	Foreign Invested Enterprises	1	35	849.0

其中 of which				客房数（间）Number of Room (room)	床位数（个）Number of Beds (bed)	餐位数（位）Number of Dining-seats (seat)	年末餐饮营业面积（平方米）Operating Area of Catering Enterprises at Year-end (sq.m)
客房收入 From Hotel Rooms	餐费收入 From Meals	商品销售收入 Revenue from Commodities	其他收入 Other Revenue				
246140.9	656573.6	18611.0	73528.3	49354	75160	300038	1563034
190614.8	109208.5	8324.5	46186.9	38515	56023	72561	747783
77829.4	80643.2	6952.6	28502.5	10231	15981	55376	307329
97574.9	20578.2	1050.9	17109.1	25925	36556	13970	405566
15210.5	7987.1	321.0	575.3	2359	3486	3215	34888
188549.7	108291.1	8313.2	44859.0	38086	55373	71721	743683
28478.6	34701.5	4924.2	8577.7	2771	4289	8734	94327
2162.8	2299.5		36.9	454	789	2450	7707
1128.1	2830.8		175.2	337	660	1600	2400
62927.8	38602.4	2248.3	23942.6	11699	17594	45641	209152
827.8	89.4	9.6		277	413	206	9046
93024.6	29767.5	1131.1	12126.6	22548	31628	13090	421051
1397.2	899.2		1325.4	330	490	800	1600
667.9	18.2	11.3	2.5	99	160	40	2500
55526.1	547365.1	10286.5	27341.4	10839	19137	227477	815251
55373.2	329572.9	4038.7	20125.7	10811	19085	171227	652186
	173390.5	2603.0	4636.2			38256	113783
	11939.7	386.9	350.4			292	586
152.9	18950.4	3257.9	2229.1	28	52	164	20576
	13511.6					17538	28120
55526.1	496731.0	9051.0	25607.8	10839	19137	219894	783523
11443.8	15402.6	555.2	2662.5	1847	3383	8407	61343
513.5				118	240	500	7000
813.0	775.3	25.5		140	266	380	1000
	1452.2					8000	12000
9593.1	140910.7	5266.3	9487.4	1812	3261	45881	148453
785.8	1706.4	237.2	1884.1	245	320	680	3840
32376.9	336147.0	2966.8	11573.8	6677	11667	155980	549572
	336.8					66	315
	49785.1	1235.5	1733.6			7359	29728
	849.0					224	2000

15-8 销售过亿元的商品交易市场一览表(2021年)

Summary of Consumer Goods Markets with Annual Transaction Value Above 100 Million Rmb Yuan(2021)

市场类别 Category	市场数量 (个) Market Quantity (unit)	市场总摊位 (个) Number of booths (unit)	年末出租摊位数 (个) Number of rent booths at Year-End (unit)	年末营业面积 (平方米) Operating Area at Year-End (sq.m)	年成交额 (万元) Annual Turnover (10 000 yuan)
总计	27	19497	18270	1704153	6598846
工业消费品综合市场	3	3736	3542	125515	220463
农产品综合市场	2	2595	2545	177800	339402
金属材料市场	2	182	170	45000	533890
水产品市场	2	2012	1772	121200	3630000
蔬菜市场	3	1664	1644	95810	342959
干鲜果品市场	1	241	241	110000	112240
茶叶市场	2	800	620	90000	155400
服装市场	1	2760	2750	199000	177571
鞋帽市场	1	889	811	19925	128000
小商品市场	1	1510	1505	45500	112328
家具市场	6	2103	1918	447465	317433
汽车市场	1	70	70	130000	307160
机动车零配件市场	2	935	682	96938	222000

主要统计指标解释

社会消费品零售总额　指企业（单位、个体户）通过交易直接售给个人、社会集团非生产、非经营用的实物商品金额，以及提供餐饮服务所取得的收入金额。个人包括城乡居民和入境人员，社会集团包括机关、社会团体、部队、学校、企事业单位、居委会或村委会等。

商品销售额　指对本单位以外的单位和个人出售的商品金额（包括售给本单位消费用的商品，含增值税），在批发和零售业中，本指标反映在国内市场上销售商品以及出口商品的总价。

商品销售包括：（1）售给个人和社会集团消费用的商品；（2）售给农业、工业、建筑业、服务业等国民经济各行业用于生产、经营用的商品，包括售予批发和零售业作为转卖或加工后转卖的商品；（3）对国（境）外直接出口的商品。

商品销售不包括：（1）未通过买卖行为付出的商品，如因机构变动移交给其他企业单位的商品、借出的商品、归还受其他单位委托代保管的商品、付出的加工原料和赠送给其他单位的样品等；(2)促销返券所销售的、不计入营业收入的商品；(3)经本单位介绍，由买卖双方直接结算，本单位只收取手续费的业务；(4)未发生所有权转移的商品预付卡销售，如加油卡；(5)汽车维修、电话卡销售等服务性经济活动；（6）购货退回的商品；（7）商品损耗和损失；（8）出售本单位自用的废旧物资；（9）期货交易商品；（10）自来水供应企业、电力企业、天然气供应企业提供的水、电、气。

批发额　指售给国民经济各行业用于生产、经营用的商品金额。

商品批发包括：（1）售给农业、工业、建筑业等行业用于生产的各种机器设备、工具、原料、材料、燃料、建筑材料，售给农民的农业生产资料，售给交通运输、仓储和邮政业用于业务活动的设备、车辆和燃料等；（2）售给信息传输、软件和信息技术服务，科学研究和技术服务业，水利、环境和公共设施管理业等行业用于生产经营、勘察设计、科研试验等业务经营使用的商品，售给批发和零售业、住宿和餐饮业使用的各种设备、工具、原材料、燃料、仓储运输用的商品；（3）售给居民服务、修理和其他服务业各种营业用品，如售给理发业的理发工具、毛巾等，日用品修理业的设备、工具、材料、零配件等，售给民政部门救灾用的商品等；（4）售给批发和零售业作为转卖用的商品；售给餐饮业用于烹饪、调制加工后出售的商品和转卖的商品；售给服务业转卖的商品；（5）出口的商品。

零售额　指售给个人用于生活消费和社会集团用于公共消费的商品金额。

商品零售包括：（1）售给城乡居民和入境外国人、华侨、港澳台同胞的各类生活消费品；（2）售给行政事业单位、社会团体、军队和武警等机构的商品，以及以零售方式售给各类企业的商品。具体包括：用于非生产和社会交往的办公用品，如通讯设备、计算器具和设备、电讯网络设备、文印设备、音像视听器材和设备、纸张、本册、文具及装订文印材料、家具、日用电器、针纺织品、清洁卫生用品、文体用品、奖品、纪念品、礼品等；供内部人员乘坐的交通工具和燃料；用于办公设施修缮的各类配件、材料、工具等；用于取暖和防暑降温的设备、燃料、材料及食品等；专用于教学的用品和设备；非专用的劳动保护用品；不对外营业的内部食堂用的餐具、炊具、设备、清洁卫生工具和食品、燃料等；军队、武警用于其人员生活的衣着品和个人用品；其他各类非生产性设备和用品。

商品零售不包括：（1）售给城乡居民已确知是用于生产、经营的商品；（2）售给各类农业生产者的生产资料类商品，如农机、农药化肥、农膜、种子饲料等商品；（3）售给企业单位生产用具及生产上专用的劳动保护用品；（4）专用于科研的用品和设备；（5）售给医疗机构的中、西药品、中药材和医疗设备器材；（6）以投资为目的的商品，如黄金、收藏品等。

住宿餐饮业营业额　指住宿和餐饮业单位在经营活动中，因提供服务或销售商品等取得的全部收入（含增值税），收入主要来源于提供客房、餐费服务、商品销售和其他服务，如商务服务。不包括多产业法人企业附营的其他行业产业活动单位的餐费收入、商品销售收入等各项收入。

Explanatory Notes on Main Statistical Indicators

Total Retail Sales of Consumer Goods refer to the amount obtained by enterprises (units, self-employed individuals) through the direct sales of non-production & non-business physical commodity to individuals, social institutions, and the revenue from providing catering services. Individuals include rural and urban households, population from abroad, social institutions include government agencies, social organizations, military units, schools, institutions. neighborhood or village committees.

Total Sales of Commodities refers to value of commodities sold by the establishments to other establishments and individuals (including commodities sold to their own establishments for consumption, including VAT). This indicator is used to show the total value of sales of commodities at domestic markets and export.

The commodities includes: (1) commodities sold to urban and rural residents and social groups for their consumption; (2) commodities sold to establishments in agriculture, industry, construction, service and various sectors of national economy for their production and operation, including commodities sold to wholesale and retail establishments for re-selling with or without further processing; (3) commodities for directing export to other countries.

Commodities exclude: (1) Commodities given not based on purchase and sale activities, such as commodities handed over to other enterprises due to the change in the institution, commodities lent, commodities which are kept by other unit based on entrustment returned, raw materials for processing given and samples given away to other units; (2) Commodities sold based on promotion coupons and not included into operating income; (3) Businesses introduced by the unit based on direct settlement by the buyer and the seller for which the unit only charges for the service charges; (4) Sales of the prepaid card of commodities without transfer of ownership (such as oil filling card); (5) Service economic activities such as vehicle maintenance and repair and sales of phone card; (6) Commodities returned; (7) Commodity loss and damage; (8) Sale of self-used waste and old materials of the unit; (9) Futures trading commodity; (10) Water, electricity and gas provided by the tap water supply enterprise, the power enterprise and the natural gas supply enterprise.

Wholesale Amount refers to the amount of commodities sold to all industries of national economy for production and operation.

The wholesale includes: (1) Various machines and equipment, tools, raw materials, materials, fuel and building materials sold to agriculture, industry and construction industry, etc. for production as well as equipment, vehicles and fuel sold to transportation, warehousing and mail business for business activities; (2) Commodities sold to information transmission, software and information technology services, scientific research and technological services, water conservancy, environment and public facilities management for production, operation, survey and design, scientific research and test, various equipment, tools, raw materials and fuel sold to the wholesale and retail and accommodation and catering industries for use as well as commodities for warehousing and transportation; (3) Various operating supplies sold to neighborhood services, repair and other service industries, such as barber tools and towels sold to the hairdressing industry; equipment, tools, materials and spare and accessory parts for the commodity repair industry and commodities sold to the civil administration department for relieving the victims of a disaster; (4) Commodities sold to wholesale and retail industries for reselling; commodities sold to the catering industry for cooking, selling after processing and reselling; commodities sold to the service industry for reselling; (5) Exported commodities.

Retail Sales refer to the amount of commodities sold to individuals for living consumption and social groups for public consumption.

Commodity retail includes: (1) Various consumer goods sold to urban and rural residents, inbound foreigners, overseas Chinese and compatriots from Hong Kong, Macao and Taiwan; (2) Commodities sold to such institutions as administrative institution, social organization, army and armed police as well as commodities sold to various enterprises in the form of retails. Specifically include: Office supplies not for production and social interaction, such as communication equipment, calculation appliances and equipment, telecommunication network equipment, printing equipment, audio-visual devices and equipment, paper, books, stationery, binding and printing materials, furniture, household electrical appliance, knitwear and textile, sanitary articles, stationery and sporting goods, prizes, souvenirs and presents; communication media for internal personnel and fuel; various accessories, materials and tools for repair of office facilities; equipment, fuel, materials and food for heating and heatstroke prevention; supplies and equipment for teaching; non-special labor protection appliances; tableware, cooking utensils, equipment, cleaning and sanitation tools, food and fuel for internal canteen only; clothing and personal belongings for personnel from the army and armed police living; all other kinds of nonproductive equipment and supplies.

Commodity retail excludes: (1) Commodities sold to urban and rural residents, having been confirmed to be used for production and operation; (2) Means of production (such as agricultural machinery, pesticide and fertilizer, agricultural film and seed feed) sold to various agricultural producers; (3) Production equipment sold to enterprises and special labor protection articles for production; (4) Supplies and equipment for scientific research; (5) Traditional Chinese and Western medicines, traditional Chinese medicinal materials, and medical equipment and supply sold to medical establishments; (6) Commodities for investment, such as gold and collection.

Sales Revenue of Accommodation and Catering industry refers to the total revenue (included VAT) received by accommodation and catering industries from services provided and goods sold, where the main sources are: guest rooms provided, catering services, goods sold and other services such as business services, other than catering income, goods sold income or income from other activities of other industry activity units additive by multi-industry corporate enterprises.

16

对外贸易与国际旅游

FOREIGN TRADE AND INTERNATIONAL TOURISM

16-1 海关进出口商品总额
Total Value of Imports and Exports by Category of Commodities

单位：万美元 (10 000 USD)

指标	Item	2021年进出口总额 Total Value of Imports and Exports in 2021	其中 of which 出口 Export	其中 of which 进口 Import	2020年进出口总额 Total Value of Imports and Exports in 2020	其中 of which 出口 Export	其中 of which 进口 Import
总额	Total	3003034	1818852	1184182	1998749	1089426	909323
按贸易方式分	By Trade						
一般贸易	General Trade	2590983	1597762	993221	1725078	977785	747292
援助物资	Aid Material	705	705		508	508	
捐赠物资	Donation Material	6	6		495	302	192
补偿贸易	Compensation Trade						
来料加工装配贸易	Processing and Assembling Trade with Sent Materials	59551	28137	31414	11492	6889	4603
进料加工贸易	Processing Trade with Imported Materials	61413	46805	14608	46415	34747	11668
对外承包工程出口货物	Export of Contracted projects	16904	16904		18892	18892	
投资设备	Investment Goods				276		276
出料加工贸易	Export Processing Trade	421	118	303	35	13	22
海关特殊监管区域进口设备	Import of Equipment in Special Customs Supervision Area	2912		2912	2		2
海关特殊监管区域物流货物	Logistics Freight of Equipment in Special Customs Supervision Area	193999	96898	97100	101044	20045	80999
易货贸易	Barter Trade						
保税监管场所进出境货物	Bonded Supervision Entry and Exit Goods	60657	26908	33749	84554	27269	57285
来料加工装配进口设备	Imported Equipment for Processing Incoming Materials						
租赁贸易	Leasing Trade	9000		9000	5378		5378
其他贸易	Other Trade	6483	4608	1875	4582	2976	1606
按运输方式分	By Ways of Transport						
水路运输	Waterway Transport	1907055	1298080	608975	1267202	825059	442143
铁路运输	Railway Transport	52574	41049	11525	34193	25893	8300
公路运输	Road Transport	480124	95500	384623	338755	45683	293072
航空运输	Air Transport	447506	278333	169172	349862	190450	159412
邮件运输	Mail Transport	4500	3617	884	2917	2053	864
其他运输	Others	111275	102273	9002	5616	181	5435
按企业性质分	By Natural of Enterprises						
国有企业	State-owned Enterprises	535528	54929	480599	372105	36545	335560
集体企业	Collective-owned Enterprises	132501	36683	95818	100158	25779	74379
外商投资企业	Foreign Funded Enterprises	575302	424111	151190	353576	259099	94477
中外合资	Joint-venture Enterprises	147062	114148	32914	127583	94178	33406
中外合作	Cooperation Enterprises	1347	1347		466	466	
外商独资	Wholly Foreign-owned Enterprises	426892	308616	118276	225526	164455	61071
其他	Others	4505	3603	902	2889	2038	852

16-2 主要国别（地区）海关进出口商品总额
Total Value of Imports and Exports of Main Countries or Territories by Categoty of Commodities

单位：万美元 (10 000 USD)

国别（地区）	Country (region)	2021年进出口总值 Total Value of Imports and Exports in 2021	其中 of which 出口 Export	其中 of which 进口 Import	2020年进出口总值 Total Value of Imports and Exports in 2020	其中 of which 出口 Export	其中 of which 进口 Import
总额	Total	3003034	1818852	1184182	1998544	1089319	909225
亚洲	Asia	1456614	892916	563698	932197	496657	435540
中国香港	Hong kong	76806	76660	147	21701	21523	178
印度	India	69230	48972	20259	48580	35178	13402
印度尼西亚	Indonesia	49056	41975	7081	37621	32827	4794
日本	Japan	117113	62878	54234	97861	55087	42774
马来西亚	Malaysia	195194	97008	98186	138171	23932	114238
巴基斯坦	Pakistan	26960	26944	15	14435	14355	80
菲律宾	Philippines	74305	53232	21073	43533	32606	10927
卡塔尔	Katar	3984	3723	262	3126	2764	362
沙特阿拉伯	Saudi Arabia	40291	34872	5419	16469	10986	5483
新加坡	Singapore	61122	50751	10372	67133	60418	6715
韩国	Republic of Korea	144128	108777	35351	69279	39390	29889
泰国	Thailand	94887	26083	68804	68239	12954	55285
土耳其	T ü rkiye	15475	15125	350	10674	10387	287
阿拉伯联合酋长国	The United Arab Emirates	47454	44205	3250	23484	21178	2306
越南	Vietnam	87131	72482	14648	41707	35930	5777
中国台湾	Taiwan	146026	29957	116069	94720	15791	78928
非洲	Africa	225055	209351	15704	144905	124208	20698
埃及	Egypt	12055	11990	66	10332	10322	10
南非	South Africa	25570	14691	10878	12556	6988	5568
尼日利亚	Nigeria	38311	38131	180	15985	15982	3

16-2 续表 continued

国别（地区）	Country (region)	2021 年进出口总值 Total Value of Imports and Exports in 2021	其中 of which		2020 年进出口总值 Total Value of Imports and Exports in 2020	其中 of which	
			出口 Export	进口 Import		出口 Export	进口 Import
欧洲	**Europe**	**470155**	**332983**	**137172**	**365097**	**229887**	**135210**
比利时	Belgium	10419	9624	795	6872	5715	1157
英国	United Kingdom	41315	36404	4910	23770	15824	7946
德国	Germany	102427	52244	50184	93406	38337	55068
法国	France	26098	20211	5888	30665	26464	4201
意大利	Italy	24316	18013	6304	20474	15012	5462
荷兰	Netherlands	33880	24602	9279	25759	19111	6648
西班牙	Spain	25269	18696	6573	23744	17358	6386
芬兰	Finland	3133	2015	1118	2329	1463	866
瑞典	Sweden	8670	2630	6040	7467	2609	4858
瑞士	Switzerland	8346	1818	6528	5782	1591	4191
俄罗斯	Russia	81821	71166	10655	47235	38073	9162
拉丁美洲	**Latin America**	**299353**	**119216**	**180138**	**180651**	**74436**	**106216**
阿根廷	Argentina	14424	7659	6765	11600	4247	7353
巴西	Brazil	137045	32170	104875	88100	17062	71038
智利	Chile	52816	11833	40984	19116	6597	12520
墨西哥	Mexico	21223	20002	1221	16040	14541	1500
北美洲	**North America**	**302882**	**218852**	**84031**	**226942**	**141360**	**85582**
加拿大	United States	56433	38694	17739	53849	33888	19961
美国	Canada	242830	180130	62700	168289	107451	60838
大洋洲	**Oceanic**	**248095**	**45535**	**202561**	**147861**	**22772**	**125089**
澳大利亚	Australia	224624	37561	187063	134841	17614	117227
新西兰	New Zealand	19696	4459	15238	10450	2588	7863

16-3 海关进出口商品分类金额

Value of Imports and Exports by Category of Commodities

单位：万美元 (10 000 USD)

商品类别	Commodity	2021年		2020年	
		出口 Export	进口 Import	出口 Export	进口 Import
总额	Total	1818852	1184182	1089319	909225
活动物；动物产品	Live Animals; Animal Products			705	67378
活动物	Live Animals				
肉及食用杂碎	Meat and Edible Met Offal		65057		47136
鱼、甲壳动物、软体动物及其他水生无脊椎动物	Fish and Crustacean,Mollusc and Other Aquatic Invertebrates		17161	54	16072
乳品；蛋品；天然蜂蜜；其他食用动物产品	Dairy Produce; Birds' Eggs; Natural Honey; Edible Products of Animal Origin, not Elsewhere Specified or Included			49	4068
其他动物产品	Products of Animal Origin, not Elsewhere Specified or Included	1169	131	601	102
植物产品	Vegetable Products			75154	15391
活树及其他活植物；鳞茎、根及类似品；插花及装饰用簇叶	Live Tree and Other Plants; Bulbs, Roots and the Like; Cut Flowers and Ornamental Foliage			4	46
食用蔬菜、根及块茎	Edible Vegetable and Certain Roots and Tubers	35467	150	38863	66
食用水果及坚果；柑桔属水果或甜瓜的果皮	Edible Fruit and Nuts; Peel of Citrus Fruit or Melons	19806	188	19357	53
咖啡、茶、马黛茶及调味香料	Coffee, Tea, Mate and Spices	14164	3213	16697	2892
谷物	Cereals		4247		5856
制粉工业产品；麦芽；淀粉、菊粉；面筋	Products of The Milling Industry; Malt; Starches; Inulin; Wheat Gluten			49	1736
含油子仁及果实；杂项子仁及果实；工业用或药用植物；稻草、秸秆及饲料	Oil Seeds and Oleaginous Fruits; Miscellaneous Grains, Seeds and Fruit; Industrial or Medicinal Plants; Straw and Fodder			145	4714
虫胶；树胶、树脂及其他植物液、汁	Lac; Gums, Resins And Other Vegetable Saps and Extracts	64	33	20	7
编结用植物材料；其他植物产品	Vegetable Plaiting Materials; Vegetable Products Not Elsewhere Specified or Included			18	22
动、植物油、脂及其分解产品；精制的食用油脂；动、植物蜡	Animal or Vegetable Fats and Oils and their Cleavage Products; Prepared Edible Fats; Animal or Vegetable Waxes	22	1746	254	2012
动、植物油、脂及其分解产品；精制的食用油脂；动、植物蜡	Animal or Vegetable Fats and Oils and their Cleavage Products; Prepared Edible Fats; Animal or Vegetable Waxes	22	1746	254	2012
食品；饮料、酒及醋；烟草、烟草及烟草用品的制品	Prepared Foodstuffs; Beverages, Spirits And Vinegar; Tobacco and Manufactured Tobacco Substitutes			21641	6103
肉、鱼、甲壳动物、软体动物及其他水生无脊椎动物的制品	Preparations of Meat,of Fish or of Crustaceans,Molluscs or other Aquatic Invertebrates			144	
糖及糖食	Sugars and Sugar Confectionery	388	524	142	150
可可及可可制品	Cocoa and Cocoa Preparations	31	121		253
谷物、粮食粉、淀粉或乳的制品；糕饼点心	Preparations of Cereals, Flour, Starch or Milk; Pastry-Cooks' Products	3585	22	3796	21
蔬菜、水果、坚果或植物其他部分的制品	Preparations of Vegetable, Fruit, Nuts or Other Parts of Plants	19969	785	13509	1158
杂项食品	Miscellaneous Edible Preparations	2651	611	3273	1627
饮料、酒及醋	Beverages, Spirits and Vinegar	34	1923	240	2710
食品工业的残渣及废料；配制的动物饲料	Residues and Waste from The Food Industries; Prepared Animal Fodder	833	124	537	186
烟草、烟草及烟草代用品的制品	Tobacco and Manufactured Tobacco Substitutes				
矿产品	Mineral Products			331	218620
盐；硫磺；泥土及石料；石膏料、石灰及水泥	Salt; Sulphur; Earths and Stone; Plastering Materials, Lime and Cement	583	1453	190	877
矿砂、矿渣及矿灰	Ores, Slag and Ash	2	295918	2	173741
矿物燃料、矿物油及其蒸馏产品；沥青物质；矿物蜡	Mineral Fuels, Mineral Oils and Products of Their Distillation; Bituminous Substances; Mineral Waxes	110	17841	140	44003
化学工业及其相关工业的产品	Products of The Chemical or Industries Allied			120322	9957

16-3 续表 1 continued 1

商品类别	Commodity	2021 年		2020 年	
		出口 Export	进口 Import	出口 Export	进口 Import
无机化学品；贵金属、稀土金属、放射性元素及其同位素的有机及无机化合物	Inorganic Chemicals; Organic or Inorganic Compounds of Precious Metals, of Rare-Earth	5927	487	2191	488
有机化学品	Organic Chemicals	75904	3247	56970	2046
药品	Pharmaceutical Products	29431	1505	29587	2607
肥料	Fertilizers	1061		948	
鞣料浸膏及染料浸膏；鞣酸及其衍生物；染料、颜料及其他着色料；油漆及清漆；油灰及其他类似胶粘剂；墨水、油墨	Tanning or Dyeing Extracts; Tannins and Their Derivatives; Dyes, Pigments and Other Colouring Matter; Paints and Varnishes; Putty and Other Mastics; Inks	19323	618	10753	646
精油及香膏；芳香料制品及化妆盥洗品	Essential Oils and Retinoid; Perfumery, Cosmetic or Toilet Preparations	854	245	109	177
肥皂、有机表面活性剂、洗涤剂、润滑剂、人造蜡、调制蜡、光洁剂、蜡烛及类似品、塑型用膏、“牙科　用蜡”及牙科用熟石膏制剂	Soap,Organic Surface-Active Agents,Washing Preparations, Lubricating Preparations, Artificial Waxes, Prepared Waxes, Polishing or Scouring Preparations, Candles and Similar Articles, Modelling Pastes, "Dental Waxes" And Dental Preparations With a Basis of Plast	1371	489	1198	563
蛋白类物质；改性淀粉；胶；酶	Albuminoidal Substances; Modified Starches; Glues; Enzymes	1809	1322	1175	570
炸药；烟火制品；火柴；引火合金；易燃材料制品	Explosives; Pyrotechnic Products; Matches; Pyrophoric Alloys; Certain Combustible Preparations				
照相及电影用品	Photographic or Cinematographic Goods	96	384	41	190
杂项化学产品	Miscellaneous Chemical Products	18006	5007	17349	2670
塑料及其制品；橡胶及其制品	**Plastics and Articles Thereof Rubber and Articles Thereof**				
塑料及其制品	Plastics and Articles Thereof	68832	23052	39144	23257
橡胶及其制品	Rubber and Articles Thereof	9084	4362	33614	20080
生皮、皮革、毛皮及其制品；鞍具及挽具；旅行用品、手提包及类似容器、动物肠线（蚕胶丝除外）制品	**Raw Hides and Skins, Leather, Fur Skins and Articles Thereof; Saddlery and Harness; Travel Goods,Handbags and Similar Containers; Articles of Animal Gut (Other Than Silk-Worm Gut)**			3943	74
生皮（毛皮除外）及皮革	Raw Hides and Skins(Other Than Fur Skins) and Leather	72	118	1	30
皮革制品；鞍具及挽具；旅行用品、手提包及类似容器；动物肠线（蚕胶丝除外）制品	Articles of Leather; Saddlery and Harness; Travel Goods, Handbags and Similar Containers; Articles of Animal Gut(Other Than Silk-Worm Gut)	17592	36	1924	43
毛皮、人造毛皮及其制品	Fur Skins and Artificial Fur; Manufactures Thereof	2239		2019	
木及木制品；木炭；软木及软木制品；稻草、秸秆、针茅或其他编结材料制品；蓝筐及柳条编结品	**Wood and Articles of Wood; Wood Charcoal;Cork and Articles of Cork; Manufactures of Straw, of Esparto or of Other Plaiting Materials; Basket Ware and Wickerwork**			8095	4186
木及木制品；木炭	Wood and Articles of Wood; Wood Charcoal	8172	11590	6371	4186
软木及软木制品	Cork and Articles of Cork	11		15	
稻草、秸秆、针茅或其他编结材料制品；蓝筐及柳条编结品	Manufactures of Straw, of Esparto or of Other Plaiting Materials; Basket Ware and Wickerwork	2821		1709	
木浆及其他纤维状纤维素浆；回收（废碎）纸或纸板；纸、纸板及其制品	**Pulp of Wood or of Other Fibrous Cellulosic Material; Waste and Scrap of Paper or Paperboard; Paper and Paperboard and Articles Thereof**			4054	42781
木浆及其他纤维状纤维素浆；回收（废碎）纸或纸板	Pulp of Wood or of Other Fibrous Cellulosic Material; Waste and Scrap of Paper or Paperboard	43	43197	3827	3000
纸及纸板；纸浆、纸或纸板制品	Paper and Paperboard; Articles of Paper Pulp, of Paper or Paperboard	12505	4962	194	144
书籍、报纸、印刷图画及其他印刷品；手稿、打字稿及设计图纸	Printed Books, Newspapers, Pictures and Other Products of The Printing Industry; Manuscripts, Typescripts and Plans	1087	154		
纺织原料及纺织制品	**Textiles and Textile Articles**			104078	3257
蚕丝	Silk	20			
羊毛、动物细毛或粗毛；马毛纱线及其机织物	Wool, Fine or Coarse Animal Hair;Horsehair Yarn and Woven Fabric	18	33	9	3
棉花	Cotton	4968	2157	2138	1289

16-3 续表 2 continued 2

商品类别	Commodity	2021 年		2020 年	
		出口 Export	进口 Import	出口 Export	进口 Import
其他植物纺织纤维；纸纱线及其机织物	Other Vegetable Textile Fibres; Paper Yarn and Woven Fabrics of Paper Yarn	48	1	5	
化学纤维长丝	Man-Made Filaments	5406	262	4255	168
化学纤维短纤	Man-Made Short Fibres	9142	547	6792	393
絮胎、毡呢及无纺织物；特种纱线；线、绳、索、缆及其制品	Wadding, Felt and Nonwoven; Special Yarns; Twine, Cordage, Ropes and Cables and Articles Thereof	7648	381	7237	429
地毯及纺织材料的其他铺地制品	Carpets and Other Textile Floor Coverings	4415	42	3056	7
特种机织物；簇绒织物；花边；装饰毯；装饰带；刺绣品	Special Woven Fabrics; Tufted Textile Fabrics; Lace; Tapestries; Trimmings; Embroidery	1759	75	335	83
浸渍、涂布、包覆或层压的纺织物；工业用纺织制品	Impregnated, Coated, Covered or Laminated Textile Fabrics; Textile Articles of a Kind Suitable for Industrial Use	1504	57	1371	88
针织物或钩编织物	Knitted or Crocheted Fabrics	1143	86	283	76
针织或钩编的服装及衣着附件	Articles of Apparel and Clothing Accessories, Knitted or Crocheted	35505	32	7816	95
非针织或非钩编的服装及衣着附件	Articles of Apparel and Clothing Accessories, not Knitted or Crocheted	46225	160	15095	238
其他纺织制成品；成套物品；旧衣着及旧纺织品；碎织物	Other Made Up Textile Articles; Sets; Worn Clothing And Worn Textile Articles; Rags Articles; Rags	22067	51	55682	389
鞋、帽、伞、杖、鞭及其零件；已加工的羽毛及其制品；人造花；人发制品	**Footwear, Headgear, Umbrellas, Sun Umbrellas, Walking-Sticks, Seat-Sticks, Whips, Riding-Crops and Parts Thereof; Prepared Feathers and Articles Made Therewith; Artificial Flowers; Articles of Human Hair**			**3266**	**106**
鞋靴、护腿和类似品及其零件	Footwear, Gaiters and The Like; Parts of Such Articles	10674	86	693	93
帽类及其零件	Headgear and Parts Thereof			393	13
雨伞、阳伞、手杖、鞭子、马鞭及其零件	Umbrellas, Sun Umbrellas, Walking-Sticks, Seat-Sticks, Whips, Riding-Crops And Parts Thereof	335	1	43	
已加工羽毛、羽绒及其制品；人造花；人发制品	Prepared Feathers and Down and Articles Made of Feathers or of Down; Artificial Flowers; Articles of Human Hair	9727		2137	1
石料、石膏、水泥、石棉、云母及类似材料的制品；陶瓷产品；玻璃及其制品	**Articles of Stone, Plaster, Cement, Asbestos, Mica or Similar Materials; Ceramic Products; Glass and Glassware**			**26177**	**2222**
石料、石膏、水泥、石棉、云母及类似材料的制品	Articles of Stone, Plaster, Cement, Asbestos, Mica or Similar Materials	10493	188	6620	103
陶瓷产品	Ceramic Products	11429	2022	3728	868
玻璃及其制品	Glass and Glassware	24381	1151	15830	1251
天然或养殖珍珠、宝石或半宝石、贵金属、包贵金属及其制品；仿手饰；硬币	**Natural or Cultured Pearls, Precious or Semi-Precious Stones, Precious Metals, Metals Clad With Precious Metal and Stones, Precious Metals, Metals Clad With Precious Metal and Articles Thereof; Imitation Jewellery; Coin**	**8330**	**90**	**50**	**14**
天然或养殖珍珠、宝石或半宝石、贵金属、包贵金属及其制品；仿手饰；硬币	Natural or Cultured Pearls, Precious or Semi-Precious Stones, Precious Metals, Metals Clad With Precious Metal and Stones, Precious Metals, Metals Clad With Precious Metal and Articles Thereof; Imitation Jewellery; Coin	8330	90	50	14
贱金属及其制品	**Base Metals and Articles of Base Metal**	**213947**	**46916**	**117428**	**11235**
钢铁	Iron and Steel	70726	524	25265	2955
钢铁制品	Articles of Iron or Steel	107645	2710	73701	2590
铜及其制品	Copper and Articles Thereof	3897	36398	2122	2731
镍及其制品	Nickel and Articles Thereof	37	1161	13	27
铝及其制品	Aluminium and Articles Thereof	15173	4612	12082	1973

16-3 续表 3 continued 3

商品类别	Commodity	2021 年		2020 年	
		出口 Export	进口 Import	出口 Export	进口 Import
铅及其制品	Lead and Articles Thereof	24	1	6	2
锌及其制品	Zinc and Articles Thereof	102	32	39	21
锡及其制品	Tin and Articles Thereof	2		2	
其他贱金属、金属陶瓷及其制品	Other Base Metals; Cermets; Articles Thereof	251	261	105	169
贱金属工具、器具、利口器、餐匙、餐叉及其零件	Tools, Implements, Cutlery, Spoons and Forks, of Base Metal; Parts Thereof of Base Metal	8060	963	2240	454
贱金属杂项制品	Miscellaneous Articles of Base Metal	8030	254	1853	313
机器、机械器具、电气设备及其零件；录音机及放声机、电视图像、声音的录制和重放设备及其零件、附件	Machinery and Mechanical Appliances; Electrical Equipment; Parts Thereof; Sound Recorders and Reproducers, Television Image and Sound Recorders and Reproducers; and Parts and Accessories of Recorders and Reproducers; and Parts and Accessories of Such Artic	573016	519589	355130	430736
核反应堆、锅炉、机器、机械器具及其零件	Nuclear Reactors, Boilers, Machinery and Mechanical Appliances; Parts Thereof	343994	343127	263456	246488
电机、电气设备及其零件；录音机及放声机、电视图像、声音的录制和重放设备及其零件、附件	Electrical Machinery and Equipment and Parts Thereof; Sound Recorders and Reproducers, Television Image and Sound Recorders and Reproducers, and Parts and Accessories of Such Articles	229023	176462	91674	184248
车辆、航空器、船舶及有关运输设备	Vehicles, Aircraft, Vessels And Associated Transport Equipment	302843	16008	169915	11322
铁道及电车道机车、车辆及其零件；铁道及电车道轨道固定装置及其零件、附件；各种机械（包括电动机械）交通信号设备	Railway or Tramway Locomotives, Rolling-Stock and Parts Thereof; Railway or Tramway Track Fixtures And Fittings and Parts Thereof; Mechanical(Including Electro-Mechanical) Traffic Signalling Equipment of All Kinds	796	356	1896	436
车辆及其零件、附件，但铁道及电车道车辆除外	Vehicles Other Than Railway or Tramway Rolling-Stock, and Parts and Accessories Thereof	296777	1850	164016	2115
航空器、航空器及其零件	Aircraft, Spacecraft, and Parts Thereof	4160	13771	3301	8735
船舶及浮动结构体	Ships, Boats and Floating Structures	1111	31	702	36
光学、照相、电影、计量、检验、医疗或外科用仪器及设备、精密仪器及设备；钟表；乐器；上述物品的零件、附件	Optical, Photographic, Cinematographic, Measuring, Checking, Precision, Medical or Surgical Instruments and Apparatus; Clocks And Watches; Musical Instruments; Parts and Accessories Thereof	30400	59741	14337	59148
光学、照相、计量、检验、医疗或外科用仪器及设备、精密仪器及设备；上述物品的零件、附件	Optical, Photographic, Cinematographic, Measuring, Checking, Precision Medical or Surgical Instruments and Apparatus; Parts and Accessories Thereof	26470	59725	13577	59127
钟表及其零件	Clocks and Watches and Parts Thereof	2435	15	72	9
乐器及其零件、附件	Musical Instruments; Parts and Accessories of Such Articles	1495	1	689	12
武器、弹药及其零件、附件	Arms and Ammunition; Parts and Accessories Thereof	1	405		
武器、弹药及其零件、附件	Arms and Ammunition; Parts and Accessories Thereof	1	405		
杂项制品	Miscellaneous Manufactured Articles	92063	99	22632	494
家具；寝具、褥垫、弹簧床垫、软坐垫及类似的填充制品；	Furniture; Bedding, Mattresses, Mattress Supports, Cushions and Similar Stuffed Furnishings	44661	30	13724	390
玩具、游戏品、运动用品及其零件、附件	Toys, Games and Sports Requisites; Parts and Accessories Thereof	39687	69	7364	32
杂项制品	Miscellaneous Manufactured Articles	7715		1544	73
艺术品、收藏品及古物	Works of Art, Collectors' Pieces and Antiques	33		13	54
特殊交易品及未分类商品	Commodities and Transactions not Classified According to Kind	10464	950	2245	877

16-4 按企业性质分海关进出口商品总额（2021年）
Import and Export Value of Commodities by Ownership(2021)

单位：万美元 (10 000 USD)

指标	Item	合计 Total	国有企业 State-owned Enterprises	外商投资企业 Foreign Funded nterprises				集体企业 Collective -owned Enterprises	其他 Others
				小计 Total	中外合作 Cooperation Enterprises	中外合资 Joint-venture Enterprises	外商独资 Wholly Foreign-owned		
进口商品总额	**Total Value of Imports**	1184182	480599	151190		32914	118276	95818	902
一般贸易	General Trade	993221	3024201	433665		77621	356044	620936	2343400
来料加工装配贸易	Processing and Assembling Trade with Sent Materials	31414		31104		57	31047		310
进料加工贸易	Processing Trade with Imported Materials	14608	694	4333		1881	2452		9581
租赁贸易	Leasing Trade	9000		9000		9000			
海关特殊监管区域进口设备	Import of Equipment in Special Customs Supervision Area	2912		2900		1	2899		12
海关特殊监管区域物流货物	Logistics Freight of Equipment in Special Customs Supervision Area	97100	10854	19133		12	19121		67113
投资设备	Investment Goods								
保税监管场所进出境货物	Bonded Supervision Entry and Exit Goods	33749	536	17532		9928	7604		15680
国际无偿援助和捐赠物资	International Aid and Material Donations								
其他贸易	Others	1875	601	180		52	128		1094
出口商品总值	**Total Value of Exports**	1818852	54929	424111	1347	114148	308616	36683	3603
一般贸易	General Trade	1597762	29839	332075	1347	83104	247624	35996	1199852
国际无偿援助和捐赠物资	International Aid and Material Donations	705	257					346	101
来料加工装配贸易	Processing and Assembling Trade with Sent Materials	28137		27302		712	26589		835
进料加工贸易	Processing Trade with Imported Materials	46805		17379		9498	7882	82	23485
对外承包工程出口货物	Export of Contracted projects	16904	4537					258	12109
保税监管场所进出境货物	Bonded Supervision Entry and Exit Goods	26908		26904		20780	6123		5
海关特殊监管区域物流货物	Logistics Freight of Equipment in Special Customs Supervision Area	96898	14304	20044			20044		62550
其他贸易	Others	4608	133	408		54	353		4067

16-5 历年海关进出口总额

Total Imports and Exports by Category(Customs Statistics)

单位：万美元 (10 000 USD)

年份 Year	进出口总额 Total Value of Imports and Exports	进口总额 Total Value of Imports	出口总额 Total Value of Exports
1993	27446	21371	6075
1994	41746	23579	18167
1995	66587	29812	36775
1996	91347	48193	43154
1997	104230	52862	51368
1998	79943	45096	34847
1999	96125	60199	35926
2000	143935	86827	57108
2001	150143	90746	59397
2002	149264	79755	69509
2003	201554	117980	83545
2004	304678	167373	137305
2005	376213	198370	177843
2006	438930	194981	243949
2007	621804	278277	343527
2008	802699	342979	459720
2009	565704	260998	304706
2010	743776	338888	404888
2011	1041422	436966	604456
2012	913286	341844	571442
2013	957442	409126	548316
2014	1048867	442950	605917
2015	911424	311763	599661
2016	1086259	352229	734030
2017	1130449	379887	750562
2018	1318209	463119	855090
2019	1630123	695064	935059
2020	1998749	909323	1089426
2021	3003034	1184182	1818852

16-6 利用外资情况
Utilization of Foreign Capital

指标	Item	2016 年	2017 年	2018 年	2019 年	2020 年	2021 年
新批外商投资企业个数（个）	Newly established Foreign Investment Enterprises(unit)	104	110	239	228	203	330
外商直接投资	Foreign Direct Investments	104	110	239	228	203	330
合同外资金额（万美元）	Total Amount of Contracted Foreign Capita(10 000 USD)	179479	218692	556119	683441	585244	968530
外商直接投资	Foreign Direct Investments	179479	218692	556119	683441	585244	968530
实际使用外资（万美元）	Total Amount of Foreign Capital Actually Utilized(10 000 USD)	171625	187623	272847	224249	192456	265840
外商直接投资	Foreign Direct Investments	171625	187623	272847	224249	192456	265840

16-7 对外经济技术合作
Technological Cooperation with Foreign Countries or Territories

指标	Item	单位 Unit	2016 年	2017 年	2018 年	2019 年	2020 年	2021 年
对外承包和劳务合作合同金额	Foreign Contracted Projects and Service Contrate	万美元 (10 000 USD)	539589	539598	565706	573114	439945	660562
对外承包	Contracted Projects with Foreign Countries or Regions	万美元 (10 000 USD)	539589	539598	565706	573114	439945	660562
对外承包和劳务合作营业额	Foreign Contracted Projects and Service Contrate	万美元 (10 000 USD)	350099	373739	408427	408820	427206	410022
对外承包	Contracted Projects with Foreign Countries or Regions	万美元 (10 000 USD)	350099	373739	408427	408820	427206	410022
外派劳务人数	Number of Persons Sent out	人 (person)	6976	7037	6586	8047	11996	8608
境外投资企业数	Numberof Overseas Investment Enterprises	个 (unit)	55	42	50	79	77	60
中方实际投资额	China Actual Investment	万美元 (10 000 USD)	70175	83760	102434	110798	191321	174208

注："中方实际投资额"，2016 年以前为"中方协议投资额"口径。
Note:"China's actual investment" was the caliber of "agreed investment amount of China" before 2016.

16-8 出口 1000 万美元以上企业一览 (2021 年)

Summary of Enterprises with Annual Exports Value Above 10 Million Dollar(2021)

单位名称 Name of Enterprises	单位名称 Name of Enterprises
中国重汽集团进出口有限公司	济南智德电子商务有限公司
贝斯济钢（山东）钢板有限公司	济南中船设备有限公司
费斯托气动有限公司	济南中恩电子商务有限公司
福士汽车零部件（济南）有限公司	济南中海炭素有限公司
瀚瑞森（中国）汽车悬挂系统有限公司	济南中尼海合进出口贸易有限公司
华熙生物科技股份有限公司	济南中外运国际物流有限公司
环磨科技控股（集团）有限公司	济南中雅电子商务有限公司
济钢（济南）国际供应链管理有限公司	济南综保保税物流有限公司
济南阿美利娅跨境电子商务有限公司	金雷科技股份公司
济南艾伯特商贸有限公司	九阳股份有限公司
济南艾拉进出口贸易有限公司	康阳贸易（山东）有限公司
济南爱达进出口有限公司	莱芜钢铁集团银山型钢有限公司
济南爱诺特种防护制品有限公司	莱芜鲁蒙食品股份有限公司
济南奥本贸易有限公司	莱芜市华赢塑胶有限公司
济南澳海炭素有限公司	莱芜市金雨地进出口有限公司
济南澳利进出口有限公司	莱芜市聚佳服装有限公司
济南柏源贸易代理有限公司	莱芜泰丰食品有限公司
济南邦德激光股份有限公司	莱芜泰禾生化有限公司
济南邦和工贸有限公司	莱芜万兴果菜食品加工有限公司
济南博雅电子商务有限公司	莱芜旭佳经贸有限公司
济南博意达商贸有限公司	莱芜英拓进出口有限公司
济南博展运进出口有限公司	莱芜长荣食品有限公司
济南采明木业有限公司	临工集团济南重机有限公司
济南畅腾贸易代理有限公司	鲁达顺（山东）国际供应链有限公司
济南超凡进出口有限公司	迈大食品（山东）有限公司
济南创凯科技有限公司	玫德集团有限公司
济南创全贸易有限公司	明铭鸣跨境电子商务（济南）有限公司
济南达事进出口有限公司	铭茂（山东）国际贸易有限责任公司
济南大自然新材料有限公司	平阴县盛凯润贸易有限公司
济南德复川国际贸易有限公司	平阴县远顺供应链有限公司
济南东进皮草有限公司	齐鲁安替制药有限公司
济南东然电子商务有限公司	齐鲁制药有限公司
济南东烨国际贸易有限公司	柔裕（济南）跨境电子商务有限公司
济南恩惠电子商务有限公司	森峰（济南）进出口有限公司
济南二机床集团有限公司	山东爱地高分子材料有限公司
济南飞德电子商务有限公司	山东爱国锻造有限公司
济南飞科进出口有限公司	山东安诺康跨境电子商务有限公司

16-8 续表 1 continued 1

单位名称 Name of Enterprises	单位名称 Name of Enterprises
济南飞腾进出口有限公司	山东安信制药有限公司
济南丰劲贸易代理有限公司	山东百利通亚陶科技有限公司
济南富相贸易有限公司	山东贝邦国际贸易有限公司
济南海航化工有限公司	山东贝创国际贸易有限公司
济南海智进出口有限公司	山东程拓实业有限公司
济南好创进出口有限公司	山东大鲁阁织染工业有限公司
济南弘正科技有限公司	山东德融汽车销售有限公司
济南宏创博展汽车销售有限公司	山东电力建设第一工程公司
济南虹缤贸易代理有限公司	山东电力设备有限公司
济南虹智贸易代理有限公司	山东东铁铸锻有限公司
济南鸿天服装有限公司	山东恩吉尔电子商务有限公司
济南华辰实业有限责任公司	山东凡克特电子商务有限公司
济南华景电子商务有限公司	山东钢铁股份有限公司莱芜分公司
济南华耀进出口有限公司	山东港口陆海国际物流集团有限公司
济南黄台煤气炉有限公司	山东高速路桥国际工程有限公司
济南汇达电子商务有限公司	山东冠世时装加工有限公司
济南家明进出口有限公司	山东海纳供应链有限公司
济南嘉亚经贸发展有限公司	山东弘泉贸易有限公司
济南健科进出口有限公司	山东泓泽电子商务有限公司
济南江凯贸易代理有限公司	山东华宸进出口贸易有限公司
济南今发顺进出口有限公司	山东华民钢球股份有限公司
济南金宝塑业有限公司	山东华青科技有限公司
济南金富山跨境电子商务有限公司	山东汇瀚通国际贸易有限公司
济南金麒麟刹车系统有限公司	山东汇金股份有限公司
济南金腾利电子商务有限公司	山东汇通达国际贸易有限公司
济南金威刻科技发展有限公司	山东慧恩跨境电子商务有限公司
济南锦罗贸易代理有限公司	山东集森电子科技有限公司
济南巨丰电子商务有限公司	山东济阳机械厂股份有限公司
济南恺丽贸易代理有限公司	山东建盛贸易有限公司
济南康悦贸易有限公司	山东锦朔贸易有限公司
济南莱福瑞制冷配件有限公司	山东晋煤日月化工有限公司
济南力平进出口有限公司	山东璟铭国际货运代理有限公司
济南利衡贸易代理有限公司	山东聚德顺电子科技有限公司
济南溧松供应链管理有限公司	山东俊发电子科技有限公司
济南临港国际贸易有限公司	山东郡嘉国际贸易有限公司
济南霖信贸易代理有限公司	山东凯莱（国际）贸易有限公司
济南麟发电子商务有限公司	山东凯信达工贸有限公司
济南隆祥进出口有限公司	山东科赛怡锐化工有限公司

16-8 续表 2 continued 2

单位名称 Name of Enterprises	单位名称 Name of Enterprises
济南鲁东耐火材料有限公司	山东科兴生物制品有限公司
济南鲁韵进出口有限公司	山东科源制药股份有限公司
济南陆港保税物流有限公司	山东兰杜新材料有限公司
济南迈科管道科技有限公司	山东朗灿国际贸易有限公司
济南玫泓国际贸易有限公司	山东浪潮进出口有限公司
济南美慧贸易代理有限公司	山东力诺光伏高科技有限公司
济南敏桦贸易代理有限公司	山东力诺特种玻璃股份有限公司
济南敏捷贸易代理有限公司	山东历诚意航跨境电子商贸有限公司
济南南北潭电子商务有限公司	山东立达进出口公司
济南尼克焊接技术有限公司	山东链上自贸国际供应链管理有限公司
济南诺德金瑞国际贸易有限公司	山东领品机械科技有限公司
济南欧博雅供应链有限公司	山东鲁电国际贸易有限公司
济南帕萨迪纳装饰材料有限公司	山东鹿嗷嗷跨境电子商务有限公司
济南齐泰电子商务有限公司	山东洛坤国际贸易有限公司
济南启骅贸易代理有限公司	山东绿霸化工股份有限公司
济南秦工国际贸易有限公司	山东绿健生命科技股份有限公司
济南轻骑标致摩托车有限公司	山东铭宇跨境电子商务有限公司
济南轻骑大韩摩托车有限责任公司	山东宁泉漳电子商务有限公司
济南轻骑对外贸易有限责任公司	山东欧锐激光科技有限公司
济南轻骑铃木摩托车有限公司	山东鹏森供应链管理有限公司
济南清尔雅贸易代理有限公司	山东齐发药业有限公司
济南荣锦进出口有限公司	山东齐鲁医药进出口有限公司
济南荣续供应链有限公司	山东仟鹤电子商务服务有限公司
济南锐灿贸易代理有限公司	山东瑞升国际货运代理有限公司
济南瑞泰克制冷设备有限公司	山东睿彦新材料科技有限公司
济南森峰科技有限公司	山东润科国际贸易有限公司
济南深济祥商贸有限公司	山东润农果蔬有限公司
济南深南电子商务有限公司	山东三维商贸有限公司
济南圣泉倍进陶瓷过滤器有限公司	山东山左控股集团有限责任公司
济南圣泉集团股份有限公司	山东商龙经贸有限公司
济南盛世阳光机械零部件有限公司	山东省汇通达企业服务有限公司
济南盛亚电子商务有限公司	山东省万兴食品有限公司
济南实达紧固件有限公司	山东省冶金设计院股份有限公司
济南市迪刚秀国际贸易有限公司	山东省永信非织造材料有限公司
济南市钦邦跨境电子商务有限公司	山东圣泉新材料股份有限公司
济南市速通电子商务有限公司	山东胜晔磨球有限公司
济南市冶金科学研究所有限责任公司	山东晟贺国际货运代理有限公司
济南双科国际贸易有限公司	山东史泰丰肥业有限公司
济南思晗韵贸易代理有限公司	山东思诚供应链管理有限公司

16-8 续表 3 continued 3

单位名称 Name of Enterprises	单位名称 Name of Enterprises
济南思迈迩制衣有限公司	山东太古飞机工程有限公司
济南松杨供应链管理有限公司	山东泰成食品有限公司
济南台有玻璃制品有限公司	山东泰丰食品有限公司
济南腾伦贸易代理有限公司	山东天博志工贸有限公司
济南天杰进出口有限公司	山东天泰啤酒设备有限公司
济南万方炭素进出口有限公司	山东通和供应链有限公司
济南维亚贸易有限公司	山东通翔国际物流有限公司
济南沃德汽车零部件有限公司	山东万煜电子商务服务有限公司
济南西门子变压器有限公司	山东威明汽车产品有限公司
济南溪化生物科技有限公司	山东希诺金属材料有限公司
济南翔渝贸易代理有限公司	山东湘华国际贸易有限公司
济南芯嘉集运供应链有限公司	山东享赢化工进出口有限公司
济南新天科技有限公司	山东信敏惠供应链管理有限公司
济南鑫瑞进出口有限公司	山东耀华玻璃有限公司
济南鑫晟源国际贸易有限公司	山东晔霖食品有限公司
济南星辉数控机械科技有限公司	山东一达通企业服务有限公司
济南幸福森林食品有限公司	山东一品农产集团有限公司
济南雄尊贸易代理有限公司	山东益鑫泰国际贸易有限公司
济南迅吉安保税物流有限公司	山东银丰纳米新材料有限公司
济南雅晨贸易代理有限公司	山东钰珑跨境电子商务有限公司
济南雅洁地毯有限公司	山东臻真然国际贸易有限公司
济南燕飞电子商务有限公司	山东智晟电子商务有限公司
济南伊禾进出口有限公司	山东中农联合生物科技股份有限公司
济南易安达保税物流有限公司	山东中天重工有限公司
济南易得顺供应链有限公司	山东重诺锻造有限公司
济南易威进出口有限公司	斯凯孚（济南）轴承与精密技术产品有限公司
济南易逊通国际贸易有限公司	桃乐桃电子商务(山东)有限公司
济南易源进出口有限公司	卧龙电气（济南）电机有限公司
济南奕鑫商贸有限公司	伊莱特能源装备股份有限公司
济南益庆贸易有限公司	源和电站股份有限公司
济南银亮贸易代理有限公司	悦通（山东）供应链管理有限公司
济南赢辉商贸有限公司	章丘美华进出口贸易有限公司
济南颖威贸易代理有限公司	章丘市台头特种钢球厂
济南永富跨境电子商务有限公司	章丘市铜铝铸造厂
济南永景贸易代理有限公司	智辉新云跨境电子商务（济南）有限公司
济南永俊贸易代理有限公司	中地国际贸易（山东）有限公司
济南宇凯贸易代理有限公司	中海油石化工程有限公司
济南域潇集团有限公司	中能华辰集团有限公司
济南裕兴化工有限责任公司	中铁十局集团有限公司
济南哲宏贸易代理有限公司	卓锦（山东）供应链管理有限公司

16-9 旅游住宿单位接待入境游客
Received Inbound Tourists by Hotels

指标	Item	2015 年	2016 年	2017 年	2018 年	2019 年	2020 年
入境游客人数（人次）	**Number of Inbound Tourists(person-time)**	332942	351526	375469	398721	456585	108524
外国人	Foreigners	205477	216899	232260	247086	285071	90926
日本	Japan	22154	21972	21967	23123	28653	2674
菲律宾	Philippines	2215	2357	2622	2901	3500	1446
新加坡	Singapore	14837	15586	16588	17503	18092	2729
韩国	Republic of Korea	34238	36137	34695	37432	41390	5536
加拿大	Canada	5697	5558	6445	6970	7859	1836
英国	United Kingdom	9693	10286	10918	11602	12910	7623
德国	Germany	14688	15608	16543	17706	19384	2557
法国	France	6694	7041	7532	8000	8893	1555
意大利	Italy	4086	4330	5190	5524	6069	583
瑞士	Switzerland	986	1051	1119	1216	1348	156
澳大利亚	Australia	8934	9456	10089	10762	12422	3783
新西兰	New Zealand	1625	1825	1958	2078	2113	815
美国	United States	21396	23187	24797	26325	29556	20623
港澳和台湾同胞	Compatriots from Hong Kong Macao and Taiwan	127465	134627	143209	151635	171514	17700
# 台湾同胞	Compatriots from Taiwan	61726	65050	68839	72667	87086	4355
入境游客人天数（人天）	**Number of Days on Inbound Tourists(person-day)**	786451	829300	878238	1086701	1276852	265436
外国人	Foreigners	460937	483753	513621	683730	806837	187665
港澳和台湾同胞	Compatriots from Hong Kong and Macao	325514	345547	364617	402971	959122	77773
# 台湾同胞	Compatriots from Taiwan	172776	178839	187351	265047	317730	45873
旅游外汇收入（亿美元）	**Foreign Exchange Income of Tourism (100 million USD)**	1.84	1.96	2.08	2.23	2.75	0.33
# 商品性收入	Commecial Income	0.53	0.51	0.54	0.6	0.7	0.08
附：平均每天来济国际旅游人数（人次）	Number of Tourists Per Day(person-time)	912	963	1029	1092	1251	296.51
星级宾馆客房出租率（%）	Star Hotel Room Rate(%)	61.0	64.5	64.56	63.4	62	47.51

注：1.2018 年起接待入境游客包含了过夜游客和一日游游客。
2. 根据省文化和旅游厅统一安排，2021 年起暂停测算、公布和使用入境旅游数据。

Notes:1.Starting in 2018, inbound tourists include overnight visitors and day-trippers.
2.According to the unified arrangement of the Provincial Department of Culture and Tourism, the measurement, publication and use of inbound tourism data have been suspended since 2021.

16-10 济南与国外结成友好城市一览表（2021 年末）
Foreign Friendly Cities of Jinan(End of 2021)

国别	Country	城市	City	缔结日期 Day
日本	Japan	和歌山市（和歌山县首府）	Wakayama	1983.01.14
英国	United Kingdom	考文垂市（英国汽车工业故乡，制造业中心之一）	Coventry	1983.10.03
日本	Japan	山口市（山口县首府）	Yamaguchi	1985.09.20
美国	United States	萨克拉门托市（加利福尼亚州首府）	Sacramento	1985.05.29
加拿大	Canada	里贾纳市（萨斯喀彻温省省会）	Regina	1987.08.10
巴布亚新几内亚	Papua New Guinea	莫尔斯比港（巴布亚新几内亚首都）	Port Moresby	1988.09.28
韩国	Republic of Korea	水原市（京畿道首府）	Suwon	1993.10.27
俄罗斯	Russia	下诺夫哥罗德市（下诺夫哥罗德州首府）	Nizhny novgorod	1994.09.25
芬兰	Finland	万达市（欧洲机场城市、芬兰第四大城市）	Vantaa	2001.08.27
法国	France	雷恩市（布列塔尼大区首府）	Renne	2002.07.17
澳大利亚	Australia	郡德勒普市（西澳洲新兴教育科技中心）	Draper	2004.09.04
德国	Germany	奥格斯堡市（施瓦本地区首府）	Augsburg	2004.10.10
乌克兰	Ukraine	哈尔科夫市（哈尔科夫州首府）	Kharkov	2007.05.23
以色列	Israel	卡法萨巴市（沙龙地区中心城市）	Kafassaba	2009.05.11
白俄罗斯	Belorussia	维捷布斯克市（维捷布斯克州首府）	Vitebsk	2009.09.20
佛得角	Cape Verde	普拉亚市（佛得角首都）	Praia	2009.09.22
巴西	Brazil	波多韦柳市（朗多尼亚州首府）	Bothoweri	2011.10.13
土耳其	Turkey	马尔马里斯市（地中海沿岸港口城市和旅游胜地）	Marmaris	2011.10.21
白俄罗斯	The Republic of Belarus	明斯克市苏维埃区（白俄罗斯首都明斯克市历史最悠久的区之一）	Savetski (Soviet) District , Minsk	2012.08.03
印度尼西亚	Indonesia	徐图利祖市（东爪哇省泗水市机场城市、新兴经济城市）	Xu Tzu Chi City	2012.09.21
保加利亚	Bulgaria	卡赞勒格市（保加利亚玫瑰精油生产中心）	Kazanlak	2013.08.29
墨西哥	Mexico	萨博潘市（哈利斯科州经济首府）	Saab Pan	2014.05.20
格鲁吉亚	Georgia	库塔伊西市（格鲁吉亚西部历史名城和第二大工业城市）	Kutaisi	2016.05.26
意大利	Italy	奇维塔韦基亚市（欧洲第三大客运港）	Civitavecchia	2016.06.20
印度	India	那格浦尔市（印度地理中心城市、马哈拉施特拉邦第二首府）	Nagpur	2017.12.08
埃塞俄比亚	Ethiopia	阿尔巴门奇市（埃塞俄比亚西南部重要城镇，格穆戈法州首府）	Arba Minch	2018.09.06
斯洛文尼亚	Slovenia	马里博尔（斯洛文尼亚第二大城市、重要的工业中心）	Maribor	2019.09.26

16-11 济南市与各友好城市交流
Basic Statistics of Transmission Between Foreign Friendly Cities and Jinan

单位：批数、人次 (batch.person-time)

指标	Item	2016 年	2017 年	2018 年	2019 年	2020 年	2021 年
因公出访交流考察	Business Trip						
批　数	Batch	780	747	781	718	7	6
人　次	Number	1907	1906	2107	1798	15	26
接待来访团组	Receive Visitors						
批　数	Batch	204	207	206	–	–	–
人　次	Number	1352	1829	1730	–	–	–

注：本表指标为“–”的，部门相关统计制度中已经不在进行统计。
Note:The Item “–” in this table means statistics are no longer in the relevant statistical system of the department.

主要统计指标解释

海关进出口商品总额 指实际进出我国关境的货物总金额。包括对外贸易实际进出口货物，来料加工装配进出口货物，国家间、联合国及国际组织无偿援助物资和赠送品，华侨、港澳台同胞和外籍华人捐赠品，租赁期满归承租人所有的租赁货物，进料加工进出口货物，边境地方贸易及边境地区小额贸易进出口货物，中外合资企业、中外合作经营企业、外商独资经营企业进出口货物和公用物品，到、离岸价格在规定限额以上的进出口货样和广告品（无商业价值、无使用价值和免费提供出口的除外），从保税仓库提取在中国境内销售的进口货物，以及其他进出口货物。该指标可以观察一个国家在货物贸易方面的总规模。我国规定出口货物按离岸价格统计，进口货物按到岸价格统计。

利用外资 指我国各级政府、部门、企业和其他经济组织通过对外借款、吸收外商直接投资以及用其他方式筹措的境外现汇、设备、技术等。

外商直接投资 指外国企业和经济组织或个人（包括华侨、港澳台胞以及我国在境外注册的企业）按我国有关政策、法规，用现汇、实物、技术等在我国境内开办外商独资企业、与我国境内的企业或经济组织共同举办中外合资经营企业、合作经营企业或合作开发资源的投资（包括外商投资收益的再投资）。即“外方投资者的投资股本”和总投资与注册资本差额部分的“外方股东对企业的直接贷款”。

对外承包工程 指各对外承包公司以招标议标承包方式承揽的下列业务：（1）承包国外工程建设项目，（2）承包我国对外经援项目，（3）承包我国驻外机构的工程建设项目，（4）承包我国境内利用外资进行建设的工程项目，（5）与外国承包公司合营或联合承包工程项目时我国公司分包部分，（6）对外承包兼营的房屋开发业务。对外承包工程的营业额是以货币表现的本期内完成的对外承包工程的工作量，包括以前年度签订的合同和本年度新签订的合同在报告期内完成的工作量。

对外劳务合作 指以收取工资的形式向业主或承包商提供技术和劳动服务的活动。我国对外承包公司在境外开办的合营企业，中国公司同时又提供劳务的，其劳务部分也纳入劳务合作统计。劳务合作营业额按报告期内向雇主提交的结算数（包括工资、加班费和奖金等）统计。

入境游客 指报告期内来中国（大陆）观光、度假、探亲访友、就医疗养、购物、参加会议或从事经济、文化、体育、宗教活动的外国人、港澳台同胞等游客（即入境旅游人数）。

外国人 指属外国国籍的人，加入外国国籍的中国血统华人也计入外国人。

旅游外汇收入 入境游客在中国（大陆）境内旅行、游览过程中用于交通、参观游览、住宿、餐饮、购物、娱乐等全部花费。

Explanatory Notes on Main Statistical Items

Total Value of Customs Export–import Commodities refer to the value of commodities actually imported or exported across the border of China. They include the actual imports and exports through foreign trade, imported and exported goods under the processing and assembling trades and materials, supplies and gifts as aid given gratis between governments and by the United Nations and other international organizations, and contributions donated by overseas Chinese, compatriots in Hong Kong and Macao and Chinese with foreign citizenship, leasing commodities owned by tenant at the expiration of leasing period, the imported and exported commodities processed with imported materials, commodities trading in border areas, the imported and exported commodities and articles for public use of the Sino–foreign joint ventures, cooperative enterprises and ventures with sole foreign investment. Also included are import or export of samples and advertising goods for which CIF or FOB value are beyond the permitted ceiling (excluding goods of no trading or use value and free commodities for export), imported goods sold in China from bonded warehouses and other imported or exported goods. The indicator of the total imports and exports at customs can be used to observe the total size of external trade in a country. In accordance with the stipulation of the Chinese government, exports are calculated at FOB, while imports are calculated at CIF.

Utilization of Foreign Capital refers to remittance, equipment and technology financed from abroad, by foreign loans, attracting foreign direct investment and other forms undertaken by the Chinese governments at all levels, by various departments, enterprises and other economic organizations.

Foreign Direct Investment refers to investments by exclusively foreign–owned enterprises established by foreign enterprise and economic organization or individual (including overseas Chinese, Hong Kong, Macao and Taiwan compatriots and China's enterprise registered abroad) in China according to related policies and regulations of China based on spot exchange, material object and technology, joint venture with Chinese and foreign investment, cooperative enterprise or cooperative development resources jointly organized by enterprises or economic organizations in China, (including reinvestment of foreign direct investment income), namely "direct loan from foreign shareholders to enterprises" of the balance between "investment capital of foreign investors" and total investment as well as registered capital.

Contract Foreign Projects refer to the following business undertaken by all foreign contract companies based on the method of contract through bidding negotiation: (1) Contracting foreign construction projects, (2) Contracting China's foreign economic assistance projects, (3) Contracting construction projects of China's institution functioning abroad, (4) Contracting projects constructed based on foreign capital in China, (5) Subcontracting part of China's company at the time of joint operation with foreign contracting company or united contracting of the project, and (6) Contracting the housing development business operated concurrently. Turnover of contract foreign projects is the workload of contract foreign projects completed in the current period embodied with currency, including workload of the contract signed in previous year and the contract newly signed in this year which is completed in the reporting period.

Foreign Labor Cooperation refers to the activities of providing technology and labor services for owners or contractors in the forms of receiving salaries and wages. China's foreign contract companies refer to cooperative enterprises established outside the border with labor service provided by Chinese company at the same time whose labor service is included into labor service cooperation statistics as well. The business volume of labor service cooperation shall be counted in accordance with the settlement amount (wages and salaries, overtime pay, bonuses and other remuneration) submitted to the employers during the reporting period.

Entry Visitors refer to foreigners and compatriots from Hong Kong, Macao and Taiwan coming to China (Chinese Mainland) for sightseeing, vacation, visiting relatives and friends, medical treatment, shopping, attending the meeting or engaging in economic, cultural, sports and religious activities in the reporting period (namely the number of inbound travelers).

Foreigners refer to persons with foreign nationality and ethnic Chinese with Chinese descent and foreign nationality is also included into foreigners.

Income from Tourism Foreign Exchange refers to total cost spent by entry visitors on transportation, sightseeing, accommodation, catering, shopping and entertainment, etc. in the process of travelling and sightseeing in China (Chinese Mainland).

17

科技

SCIENCE AND TECHNOLOGY

17-1 科技综合情况
Basic Statistics on Science and Technology

指标	Item	单位 Unit	2013 年	2014 年	2015 年	2016 年	2017 年	2018 年	2019 年	2020 年
R&D 活动单位	R&D Activity Units	个 (unit)	573	660	803	890	964	821	1089	1209
R&D 活动全时人员	Full-time R&D Personnel	人年 (man-years)	41643	46796	51297	52395	57506	59995	52153	53677.5
R&D 活动经费内部支出	Internal Expenditure on R&D	万元 (10 000 yuan)	1111522	1205441.6	1330543.8	1567365	1851538.7	2085980.1	2255264.6	2654629.1
# 基础研究	Basic Research	万元 (10 000 yuan)	77918	81092.8	106229	128504.7	152909.2	144105.1	173425.2	184501.6
# 应用研究	Applied Research	万元 (10 000 yuan)	127176	142847.5	136507.2	151841.2	208526.4	246533.3	304343.7	414305.5
# 试验发展	Experimental Development	万元 (10 000 yuan)	906428	981501.4	1087807.6	1287019.1	1490103.1	1695281.7	1777495.7	2055822.1
# 日常性支出	Daily Expenditure	万元 (10 000 yuan)	967345	1068380.6	1161517.8	1376837.7	1636821.4	1843653.3	2010202.7	2373932.1
人员劳务费	Staff Service Fee	万元 (10 000 yuan)	320273	376372.8	470989.9	522676.7	616187.2	763134.5	695510.6	864042.4
# 资产性支出	Capital Expenditure	万元 (10 000 yuan)	144177	137061	169026	190527.3	214717.4	242326.8	233015.5	277874.7
仪器设备	Instrument and Equipment	万元 (10 000 yuan)	135607	126101.9	160989.5	185967.8	188836.8	236760.3	218192.1	263337.9
R&D 活动经费外部支出	External expenditure on R&D	万元 (10 000 yuan)	46679	57993	42612	62140.8	70569.2	79731.3	107132.1	218149.6
科技成果情况	Scientific Achievements									
专利申请数	Patent Applications	件 (piece)	10221	12196	14178	15490	19645			
# 发明专利申请数	Inventions	件 (piece)	4755	6234	8454	9138	12027			
拥有发明专利数	Number of Invention Patents	件 (piece)	6087	7712	10007	13808	20059			
科技项目（课题）情况	Scientific Projects									
项目（课题）数	Number of Projects	项 (item)	17683	18811	21177	22570	27666			
项目参加人员折合全时当年	Number of Participants	人年 (man-years)	39557	43828.2	46715	44188	46457.1			

注：1. 2018 年数据为行政区划调整前口径，以下各表同。
2. “科技成果情况” 2018 年起，省统计局未反馈相关数据。

Notes:1.Data used in 2018 is the statistical scale before the adjustment of administrative division (the same below).
2."Scientific and Technological Achievements" since 2018, the Shandong provincial Bureau of Statistics has not provided relevant data.

17–2 科技投入情况（2020 年）
Basic Statistics on Scientific and Technological Funds(2020)

指标	Item	单位 Unit	合计 Total	科研机构 Research Institutions	高等院校 colleges and universities	规模以上工业企业 Industrial Enterprises above Designated Size	其他 Others
有 R&D 活动单位数	Number of Enterprises with R&D Activities	个 (unit)	1209	59	65	811	274
R&D 人员	R&D Personnel	人 (Person)	83032	5836	26636	33732	16828
# 研究人员	Research Personnel	人 (Person)	48531	4804	22470	13211	8046
R&D 人员折合全时人员	Full–time Equivalent of R&D Personnel	人年 (man–years)	53678	4845	13217.1	23416	12199
基础研究	Basic Research	人年 (man–years)	8941	1335	7079.5	103	424
应用研究	Applied Research	人年 (man–years)	10919	1952	5748.6	444	2774
试验发展	Experimental Development	人年 (man–years)	33818	1558	389	22869	9002
R&D 经费内部支出	Internal Expenditure on R&D	万元 (10 000 yuan)	2654629	267416	337806	1514651	534756
基础研究	Basic Research	万元 (10 000 yuan)	184502	33987	131054	2723	16737
应用研究	Applied Research	万元 (10 000 yuan)	414306	144423	195678	19623	54580
试验发展	Experimental Development	万元 (10 000 yuan)	2055822	89005	11074	1492305	463438
日常性支出	Routine Expenses	万元 (10 000 yuan)	2373932	136362	276781	1451936	508853
# 人员劳务费	Labor Cost	万元 (10 000 yuan)	864042	73669	54546	428802	307026
资产性支出	Assets Expenditure	万元 (10 000 yuan)	277875	131054	61025	62715	23080
# 仪器和设备	Instrument and Equipment	万元 (10 000 yuan)	263338	124611	57535	60002	21191

17-3 规模以上工业企业科技活动情况(2020年)

Main Items of Industrial Enterprises Above Designated Size(2020)

单位:个 (unit)

指标	Item	企业数 Number of Industial Enterprises	# 有 R&D 活动的单位数 Number of Units with Research and Development Activities	企业办科技机构数 Number of Technology Institutions Run By Enterprises
总计	Total	2218	811	297
按登记注册类型分	By Status of Registration			
内资企业	Domestic Funded Enterprises	2074	751	270
国有企业	State-owned Enterprises	29	4	1
集体企业	Collective-owned Enterprises	7	1	1
股份合作企业	Cooperative Enterprises	4	1	1
联营企业	Joint Ownership Enterprises	1		
有限责任公司	Private Limited Liability Corporations	552	224	90
国有独资公司	State Sole funded Corporations	40	21	8
其他有限责任公司	Other Limited Liability Corporations	512	203	82
股份有限公司	Share-holding Corporations Ltd.	89	63	41
私营企业	Private Enterprises	1391	457	136
私营独资企业	Private-funded Enterprises	39	1	2
私营合伙企业	Private Partnership Enterprises	1	1	
私营有限责任公司	Private Limited Liability Corporations	1280	406	117
私营股份有限公司	Private Share-holding Corporations Ltd.	71	49	17
其他企业	Other Enterprises	1	1	
港、澳、台商投资企业	Enterprises with Funds from Hong Kong,Macao and Taiwan	59	19	9
合资经营企业	Joint-venture Enterprises	31	12	5
合作经营企业	Cooperative Enterprises	1		
独资经营企业	Enterprises with Sole Investment	27	7	4
投资股份有限公司	Share-holding Corporations Ltd.			
其他港澳台投资企业	Other Enterprises with Funds from Hong Kong,Macao and Taiwan			
外商投资企业	Foreign Funded Enterprises	82	39	17
中外合资经营企业	Joint-venture Enterprises	34	21	6
中外合作经营企业	Cooperation Enterprises	2	1	
外资企业	Enterprises with Sole Fund	42	14	10
外商投资股份有限公司	Share-holding Corporations Ltd. with Foreign Investment	4	3	1
其他外商投资企业	Other Foreign Funded Enterprises			
按工业行业大类分	By Sector			
煤炭开采和洗选业	Mining and Washing of Coal	3		
石油和天然气开采业	Extraction of Petroleum and Natural Gas	3		
黑色金属矿采选业	Mining and Processing of Ferrous Metal Ores	9	2	1
有色金属矿采选业	Mining and Processing of Non-Ferrous Metal Ores			
非金属矿采选业	Mining and Processing of Nonmetal Ores	10		1
开采专业及辅助性活动	Professional and Support Activities for Mining			
其他采矿业	Mining of Other Ores			

17-3 续表 continued

指标	Item	企业数 Number of Industial Enterprises	# 有 R&D 活动的单位数 Number of Units with Research and Development Activities	企业办科技机构数 Number of Technology Institutions Run By Enterprises
农副食品加工业	Processing of Food from Agricultural Products	85	15	7
食品制造业	Manufacture of Foods	67	23	5
酒、饮料和精制茶制造业	Manufacture of Wine, Drinks and Refined Tea	17	4	2
烟草制品业	Manufacture of Tobacco	1		
纺织业	Manufacture of Textile	47	16	5
纺织服装、服饰业	Manufacture of Textile Wearing Apparel and Finery	22	2	2
皮革、毛皮、羽毛及其制品和制鞋业	Manufacture of Leather, Fur, Feather & Its Products and Footwear	4	1	
木材加工和木、竹、藤、棕、草制品业	Processing of Timbers, Manufacture of Wood,Bamboo, Rattan, Palm, and Straw Products	11	2	1
家具制造业	Manufacture of Furniture	14		
造纸和纸制品业	Manufacture of Paper and Paper Products	39	10	
印刷和记录媒介复制业	Printing, Reproduction of Recording Media	40	8	6
文教、工美、体育和娱乐用品制造业	Manufacture of Culture, Education,Arts and crafts, Sport and Entertainment Goods	22	9	4
石油、煤炭及其他燃料加工业	Processing of Petroleum, Coal and Other Fuels	15	6	3
化学原料和化学制品制造业	Manufacture of Chemical Raw Material and Chemical Products	105	45	20
医药制造业	Manufacture of Medicines	68	39	29
化学纤维制造业	Manufacture of Chemical Fiber	10	5	1
橡胶和塑料制品业	Manufacture of Rubber and Plastic	58	18	6
非金属矿物制品业	Manufacture of Non-metallic Mineral Products	282	71	23
黑色金属冶炼和压延加工业	Manufacture and Processing of Ferrous Metals	36	16	6
有色金属冶炼和压延加工业	Manufacture & Processing of Non-ferrous Metals	25	7	3
金属制品业	Manufacture of Metal Products	241	66	25
通用设备制造业	Manufacture of General Purpose Machinery	252	127	26
专用设备制造业	Manufacture of Special Purpose Machinery	205	110	33
汽车制造业	Manufacture of Automotive	120	39	15
铁路、船舶、航空航天和其他运输设备制造业	Manufacture of Railroad,Marine,Aerospace and Other Transportation Equipment	28	9	4
电气机械和器材制造业	Manufacture of Electrical Machinery & Equipment	137	63	26
计算机、通信和其他电子设备制造业	Manufacture of Computer, Communications and Other Electronic Equipment	62	39	19
仪器仪表制造业	Manufacture of Measuring Instrument	72	41	18
其他制造业	Other Manufacture	4	2	
废弃资源综合利用业	Comprehensive Utilization of Waste	8	1	
金属制品、机械和设备修理业	Metal Products, Machinery and Equipment Repair Industry	5	2	3
电力、热力生产和供应业	Production and Supply of Electric Power and Heat Power	49	7	1
燃气生产和供应业	Production and Supply of Gas	21	1	
水的生产和供应业	Production and Supply of Water	18	3	1

17-4 规模以上工业企业技术改造及引进吸收（2020 年）

Innovation and Resorb of Industrial Enterprises Above Designated Size（2020）

单位：万元 (10 000 yuan)

指标	Item	技术改造经费支出 Technical Reform Expenditure	引进国外技术经费支出 Acquisition of Foreign Technology Expenditure	引进技术的消化吸收经费支出 Expenditure for Assimilation Technology	购买国内技术经费支出 Expenditurefor Purchase Domestic Technology
总计	Total	403854	12603	16	12112
按登记注册类型分	By Status of Registration				
内资企业	Domestic Funded Enterprises	341725	4220	16	12112
国有企业	State-owned Enterprises	767			
集体企业	Collective-owned Enterprises	84			
股份合作企业	Cooperative Enterprises				
联营企业	Joint Ownership Enterprises				
有限责任公司	Private Limited Liability Corporations	195021	4005		11579
国有独资公司	State Sole funded Corporations	6238	336		
其他有限责任公司	Other Limited Liability Corporations	188784	3669		11579
股份有限公司	Share-holding Corporations Ltd.	102484	138	16	319
私营企业	Private Enterprises	43368	77		213
私营独资企业	Private-funded Enterprises	3			
私营合伙企业	Private Partnership Enterprises				1
私营有限责任公司	Private Limited Liability Corporations	34295			117
私营股份有限公司	Private Share-holding Corporations Ltd.	9071	77		95
其他企业	Other Enterprises				
港、澳、台商投资企业	Enterprises with Funds from Hong Kong,Macao and Taiwan	1261			
合资经营企业	Joint-venture Enterprises	923			
合作经营企业	Cooperative Enterprises				
独资经营企业	Enterprises with Sole Investment	338			
投资股份有限公司	Share-holding Corporations Ltd.				
其他港澳台投资企业	Other Enterprises with Funds from Hong Kong,Macao and Taiwan				
外商投资企业	Foreign Funded Enterprises	8736	8383		
中外合资经营企业	Joint-venture Enterprises	5063	5903		
中外合作经营企业	Cooperation Enterprises				
外资企业	Enterprises with Sole Fund	260	2481		
外商投资股份有限公司	Share-holding Corporations Ltd. with Foreign Investment	3413			
其他外商投资企业	Other Foreign Funded Enterprises				
按工业行业大类分	By Sector				
煤炭开采和洗选业	Mining and Washing of Coal				
石油和天然气开采业	Extraction of Petroleum and Natural Gas				
黑色金属矿采选业	Mining and Processing of Ferrous Metal Ores				
有色金属矿采选业	Mining and Processing of Non-Ferrous Metal Ores				
非金属矿采选业	Mining and Processing of Nonmetal Ores				
开采专业及辅助性活动	Professional and Support Activities for Mining				
其他采矿业	Mining of Other Ores				

17-4 续表 continued

指标	Item	技术改造经费支出 Technical Reform Expenditure	引进国外技术经费支出 Acquisition of Foreign Technology Expenditure	引进技术的消化吸收经费支出 Expenditure for Assimilation Technology	购买国内技术经费支出 Expenditurefor Purchase Domestic Technology
农副食品加工业	Processing of Food from Agricultural Products	1865			27
食品制造业	Manufacture of Foods	4000			
酒、饮料和精制茶制造业	Manufacture of Wine, Drinks and Refined Tea	212			20
烟草制品业	Manufacture of Tobacco				
纺织业	Manufacture of Textile	1816			1
纺织服装、服饰业	Manufacture of Textile Wearing Apparel and Finery		77		50
皮革、毛皮、羽毛及其制品和制鞋业	Manufacture of Leather, Fur, Feather & Its Products and Footwear				
木材加工和木、竹、藤、棕、草制品业	Processing of Timbers, Manufacture of Wood,Bamboo, Rattan, Palm, and Straw Products	29			
家具制造业	Manufacture of Furniture				
造纸和纸制品业	Manufacture of Paper and Paper Products	1			
印刷和记录媒介复制业	Printing, Reproduction of Recording Media	2211			
文教、工美、体育和娱乐用品制造业	Manufacture of Culture, Education,Arts and crafts, Sport and Entertainment Goods	16			
石油、煤炭及其他燃料加工业	Processing of Petroleum, Coal and Other Fuels	24482			199
化学原料和化学制品制造业	Manufacture of Chemical Raw Material and Chemical Products	72001			
医药制造业	Manufacture of Medicines	18844	3335		9317
化学纤维制造业	Manufacture of Chemical Fiber				
橡胶和塑料制品业	Manufacture of Rubber and Plastic	2412			
非金属矿物制品业	Manufacture of Non-metallic Mineral Products	11933	434		1
黑色金属冶炼和压延加工业	Manufacture and Processing of Ferrous Metals	144626			
有色金属冶炼和压延加工业	Manufacture & Processing of Non-ferrous Metals	2411			
金属制品业	Manufacture of Metal Products	19212			
通用设备制造业	Manufacture of General Purpose Machinery	6624	473	16	
专用设备制造业	Manufacture of Special Purpose Machinery	10712	1774		
汽车制造业	Manufacture of Automotive	8270	707		
铁路、船舶、航空航天和其他运输设备制造业	Manufacture of Railroad,Marine,Aerospace and Other Transportation Equipment	60	5469		1
电气机械和器材制造业	Manufacture of Electrical Machinery & Equipment	3576	143		82
计算机、通信和其他电子设备制造业	Manufacture of Computer, Communications and Other Electronic Equipment	1447	191		373
仪器仪表制造业	Manufacture of Measuring Instrument	5282			146
其他制造业	Other Manufacture	275			275
废弃资源综合利用业	Comprehensive Utilization of Waste				
金属制品、机械和设备修理业	Metal Products, Machinery and Equipment Repair Industry	913			
电力、热力生产和供应业	Production and Supply of Electric Power and Heat Power	8232			1621
燃气生产和供应业	Production and Supply of Gas				
水的生产和供应业	Production and Supply of Water	260			

17-5 规模以上工业企业技术资源(2020年)
Technical Resources of Industrial Enterprises Above Desitnated Size (2020)

指标	Item	R&D经费内部支出合计(万元) Internal Expenditure on R&D (10 000 yuan)	新产品销售收入(万元) Output Value of New Products (10 000 yuan)	研究与试验发展(R&D)人员(人) R&D Personnel (Person)	R&D人员折合全时当量(人年) Full-time Equivalent of R&D Personnel (man-years)
总计	Total	1514651	28315004	33732	23416
按登记注册类型分	By Status of Registration				
内资企业	Domestic Funded Enterprises	1209671	22113524	29261	20318
国有企业	State-owned Enterprises	8152	67172	162	85
集体企业	Collective-owned Enterprises	317	39784	20	11
股份合作企业	Cooperative Enterprises	916.0	4864	56	56
联营企业	Joint Ownership Enterprises				
有限责任公司	Private Limited Liability Corporations	608912	6702004	12506	9409
国有独资公司	State Sole funded Corporations	72062	546641	2665	2065
其他有限责任公司	Other Limited Liability Corporations	536850	6155363	9841	7344
股份有限公司	Share-holding Corporations Ltd.	316844.5	12356957	7048	4951
私营企业	Private Enterprises	274101	2942697	9439	5780
私营独资企业	Private-funded Enterprises	675	5538	16	16
私营合伙企业	Private Partnership Enterprises	148		7	1
私营有限责任公司	Private Limited Liability Corporations	236993	2232495	8021	4761
私营股份有限公司	Private Share-holding Corporations Ltd.	36285	704664	1395	1001
其他企业	Other Enterprises	429	46	30	26
港、澳、台商投资企业	Enterprises with Funds from Hong Kong,Macao and Taiwan	246582	4885796	2175	1598
合资经营企业	Joint-venture Enterprises	54203	974619	903	713
合作经营企业	Cooperative Enterprises				
独资经营企业	Enterprises with Sole Investment	192380	3911177	1272	885
投资股份有限公司	Share-holding Corporations Ltd.				
其他港澳台投资企业	Other Enterprises with Funds from Hong Kong,Macao and Taiwan				
外商投资企业	Foreign Funded Enterprises	45622	1226824	2055	1290
中外合资经营企业	Joint-venture Enterprises	20366	451401	708	481
中外合作经营企业	Cooperation Enterprises	302	408	8	7
外资企业	Enterprises with Sole Fund	12904	229045	1046	661
外商投资股份有限公司	Share-holding Corporations Ltd. with Foreign Investment	12050	545970	293	140
其他外商投资企业	Other Foreign Funded Enterprises				
按工业行业大类分	By Sector				
煤炭开采和洗选业	Mining and Washing of Coal				
石油和天然气开采业	Extraction of Petroleum and Natural Gas				
黑色金属矿采选业	Mining and Processing of Ferrous Metal Ores	3710		340	279
有色金属矿采选业	Mining and Processing of Non-Ferrous Metal Ores				
非金属矿采选业	Mining and Processing of Nonmetal Ores		2143		
开采专业及辅助性活动	Professional and Support Activities for Mining				
其他采矿业	Mining of Other Ores				

17-5 续表 continued

指标	Item	R&D 经费内部支出合计（万元）Internal Expenditure on R&D (10 000 yuan)	新产品销售收入（万元）Output Value of New Products (10 000 yuan)	研究与试验发展 (R&D) 人员（人）R&D Personnel (Person)	R&D 人员折合全时当量（人年）Full-time Equivalent of R&D Personnel (man-years)
农副食品加工业	Processing of Food from Agricultural Products	6606	97029	219	119
食品制造业	Manufacture of Foods	9517	176797	890	633
酒、饮料和精制茶制造业	Manufacture of Wine, Drinks and Refined Tea	1287	36307	79	37
烟草制品业	Manufacture of Tobacco				
纺织业	Manufacture of Textile	10785	141474	402	295
纺织服装、服饰业	Manufacture of Textile Wearing Apparel and Finery	1007	368	88	79
皮革、毛皮、羽毛及其制品和制鞋业	Manufacture of Leather, Fur, Feather & Its Products and Footwear	375	7939	40	39
木材加工和木、竹、藤、棕、草制品业	Processing of Timbers, Manufacture of Wood,Bamboo, Rattan, Palm, and Straw Products	1424	20598	26	21
家具制造业	Manufacture of Furniture		1672		
造纸和纸制品业	Manufacture of Paper and Paper Products	5162	94264	138	77
印刷和记录媒介复制业	Printing, Reproduction of Recording Media	5992	145320	303	252
文教、工美、体育和娱乐用品制造业	Manufacture of Culture, Education,Arts and crafts，Sport and Entertainment Goods	3186	38304	165	101
石油、煤炭及其他燃料加工业	Processing of Petroleum, Coal and Other Fuels	16050	216056	526	248
化学原料和化学制品制造业	Manufacture of Chemical Raw Material and Chemical Products	49122	1237363	1474	897
医药制造业	Manufacture of Medicines	246269	1875623	3822	3111
化学纤维制造业	Manufacture of Chemical Fiber	4271	2463	141	85
橡胶和塑料制品业	Manufacture of Rubber and Plastic	5752	68695	334	240
非金属矿物制品业	Manufacture of Non-metallic Mineral Products	35724	497807	1172	688
黑色金属冶炼和压延加工业	Manufacture and Processing of Ferrous Metals	239617	2054165	2986	1455
有色金属冶炼和压延加工业	Manufacture & Processing of Non-ferrous Metals	3308	45269	227	184
金属制品业	Manufacture of Metal Products	79139	1103144	2243	1542
通用设备制造业	Manufacture of General Purpose Machinery	113919	1100597	4975	3468
专用设备制造业	Manufacture of Special Purpose Machinery	88083	1097807	2616	1882
汽车制造业	Manufacture of Automotive	221476	9464002	2846	1900
铁路、船舶、航空航天和其他运输设备制造业	Manufacture of Railroad,Marine,Aerospace and Other Transportation Equipment	8623	254905	231	148
电气机械和器材制造业	Manufacture of Electrical Machinery & Equipment	77411	1852545	2479	1870
计算机、通信和其他电子设备制造业	Manufacture of Computer, Communications and Other Electronic Equipment	209956	6078106	2710	2248
仪器仪表制造业	Manufacture of Measuring Instrument	27406	351763	1286	837
其他制造业	Other Manufacture	698	242	26	19
废弃资源综合利用业	Comprehensive Utilization of Waste	60		3	2
金属制品、机械和设备修理业	Metal Products, Machinery and Equipment Repair Industry	3481	65524	254	204
电力、热力生产和供应业	Production and Supply of Electric Power and Heat Power	20633	97114	360	227
燃气生产和供应业	Production and Supply of Gas	80		29	1
水的生产和供应业	Production and Supply of Water	1745	742	61	18

17-6 规模以上工业企业科技活动项目（2020 年）
Technology Project Activities of Industrial Enterprises Above Designated Size(2020)

指标	Item	R&D 活动项目经费内部支出（万元）Internal Expenditure on R&D (10 000 yuan)	新产品开发项目数（项）Number of on new products Development (unit)	新产品开发经费支出（万元）Expenditure on new products Development (10 000 yuan)
总计	Total	1514651	8085	1572210
按登记注册类型分	By Status of Registration			
内资企业	Domestic Funded Enterprises	1209671	7141	1246168
国有企业	State-owned Enterprises	8152	44	9170
集体企业	Collective-owned Enterprises	317		
股份合作企业	Cooperative Enterprises	916.0	6	906
联营企业	Joint Ownership Enterprises			
有限责任公司	Private Limited Liability Corporations	608912	2803	619405
国有独资公司	State Sole funded Corporations	72062	371	66510
其他有限责任公司	Other Limited Liability Corporations	536850	2432	552895
股份有限公司	Share-holding Corporations Ltd.	316844.5	923	287252
私营企业	Private Enterprises	274101	3348	328641
私营独资企业	Private-funded Enterprises	675	20	1045
私营合伙企业	Private Partnership Enterprises	148		
私营有限责任公司	Private Limited Liability Corporations	236993	2898	275928
私营股份有限公司	Private Share-holding Corporations Ltd.	36285	430	51668
其他企业	Other Enterprises	429	17	794
港、澳、台商投资企业	Enterprises with Funds from Hong Kong,Macao and Taiwan	246582	303	253858
合资经营企业	Joint-venture Enterprises	54203	152	53228
合作经营企业	Cooperative Enterprises			
独资经营企业	Enterprises with Sole Investment	192380	151	200630
投资股份有限公司	Share-holding Corporations Ltd.			
其他港澳台投资企业	Other Enterprises with Funds from Hong Kong,Macao and Taiwan			
外商投资企业	Foreign Funded Enterprises	45622	428	56246
中外合资经营企业	Joint-venture Enterprises	20366	184	25722
中外合作经营企业	Cooperation Enterprises	302	9	458
外资企业	Enterprises with Sole Fund	12904	144	16781
外商投资股份有限公司	Share-holding Corporations Ltd. with Foreign Investment	12050	91	13286
其他外商投资企业	Other Foreign Funded Enterprises			
按工业行业大类分	By Sector			
煤炭开采和洗选业	Mining and Washing of Coal			
石油和天然气开采业	Extraction of Petroleum and Natural Gas			
黑色金属矿采选业	Mining and Processing of Ferrous Metal Ores	3710	6	1034
有色金属矿采选业	Mining and Processing of Non-Ferrous Metal Ores			
非金属矿采选业	Mining and Processing of Nonmetal Ores		1	110
开采专业及辅助性活动	Professional and Support Activities for Mining			
其他采矿业	Mining of Other Ores			

17-6 续表 continued

指标	Item	R&D 活动项目经费内部支出（万元）Internal Expenditure on R&D (10 000 yuan)	新产品开发项目数（项）Number of on new products Development (unit)	新产品开发经费支出（万元）Expenditure on new products Development (10 000 yuan)
农副食品加工业	Processing of Food from Agricultural Products	6606	73	7238
食品制造业	Manufacture of Foods	9517	169	12055
酒、饮料和精制茶制造业	Manufacture of Wine, Drinks and Refined Tea	1287	24	2231
烟草制品业	Manufacture of Tobacco			
纺织业	Manufacture of Textile	10785	107	14645
纺织服装、服饰业	Manufacture of Textile Wearing Apparel and Finery	1007	8	1043
皮革、毛皮、羽毛及其制品和制鞋业	Manufacture of Leather, Fur, Feather & Its Products and Footwear	375	3	167
木材加工和木、竹、藤、棕、草制品业	Processing of Timbers, Manufacture of Wood,Bamboo, Rattan, Palm, and Straw Products	1424	13	1758
家具制造业	Manufacture of Furniture		1	227
造纸和纸制品业	Manufacture of Paper and Paper Products	5162	48	4275
印刷和记录媒介复制业	Printing, Reproduction of Recording Media	5992	75	7529
文教、工美、体育和娱乐用品制造业	Manufacture of Culture, Education,Arts and crafts, Sport and Entertainment Goods	3186	55	3750
石油、煤炭及其他燃料加工业	Processing of Petroleum, Coal and Other Fuels	16050	21	6767
化学原料和化学制品制造业	Manufacture of Chemical Raw Material and Chemical Products	49122	453	64743
医药制造业	Manufacture of Medicines	246269	909	235637
化学纤维制造业	Manufacture of Chemical Fiber	4271	38	8533
橡胶和塑料制品业	Manufacture of Rubber and Plastic	5752	89	7045
非金属矿物制品业	Manufacture of Non-metallic Mineral Products	35724	376	41961
黑色金属冶炼和压延加工业	Manufacture and Processing of Ferrous Metals	239617	259	171590
有色金属冶炼和压延加工业	Manufacture & Processing of Non-ferrous Metals	3308	37	2726
金属制品业	Manufacture of Metal Products	79139	589	84695
通用设备制造业	Manufacture of General Purpose Machinery	113919	1168	140837
专用设备制造业	Manufacture of Special Purpose Machinery	88083	981	103510
汽车制造业	Manufacture of Automotive	221476	488	238684
铁路、船舶、航空航天和其他运输设备制造业	Manufacture of Railroad,Marine,Aerospace and Other Transportation Equipment	8623	96	22782
电气机械和器材制造业	Manufacture of Electrical Machinery & Equipment	77411	782	115775
计算机、通信和其他电子设备制造业	Manufacture of Computer, Communications and Other Electronic Equipment	209956	439	193313
仪器仪表制造业	Manufacture of Measuring Instrument	27406	436	44423
其他制造业	Other Manufacture	698	17	608
废弃资源综合利用业	Comprehensive Utilization of Waste	60	4	622
金属制品、机械和设备修理业	Metal Products, Machinery and Equipment Repair Industry	3481	36	5607
电力、热力生产和供应业	Production and Supply of Electric Power and Heat Power	20633	64	9609
燃气生产和供应业	Production and Supply of Gas	80		
水的生产和供应业	Production and Supply of Water	1745	7	745

17-7 规模以上工业企业 R&D 经费情况 (2020 年)

R&D Funds of Industrial Enterprises Above Designated Size (2020)

单位：万元

指标	Item	合计 Total	按支出用途分组 By Object of Expenditure	
			经常费支出 Daily Expenditure	资产性支出 Capital Expenditure
总计	Total	1514651	1451936	62715
按登记注册类型分	By Status of Registration			
内资企业	Domestic Funded Enterprises	1209671	1151593	58078
国有企业	State-owned Enterprises	8152	8151	1
集体企业	Collective-owned Enterprises	317	290	27
股份合作企业	Cooperative Enterprises	916	892	24
联营企业	Joint Ownership Enterprises			
有限责任公司	Private Limited Liability Corporations	608912	570837	38076
国有独资公司	State Sole funded Corporations	72062	68677	3385
其他有限责任公司	Other Limited Liability Corporations	536850	502160	34691
股份有限公司	Share-holding Corporations Ltd.	316845	306474	10370
私营企业	Private Enterprises	274101	264522	9579
私营独资企业	Private-funded Enterprises	675	675	
私营合伙企业	Private Partnership Enterprises	148	148	
私营有限责任公司	Private Limited Liability Corporations	236993	228380	8613
私营股份有限公司	Private Share-holding Corporations Ltd.	36285	35319	966
其他企业	Other Enterprises	429	429	0
港、澳、台商投资企业	Enterprises with Funds from Hong Kong,Macao and Taiwan	246582	243847	2735
合资经营企业	Joint-venture Enterprises	54203	52086	2116
合作经营企业	Cooperative Enterprises			
独资经营企业	Enterprises with Sole Investment	192380	191760	619
投资股份有限公司	Share-holding Corporations Ltd.			
其他港澳台投资企业	Other Enterprises with Funds from Hong Kong,Macao and Taiwan			
外商投资企业	Foreign Funded Enterprises	45622	43949	1673
中外合资经营企业	Joint-venture Enterprises	20366	19756	610
中外合作经营企业	Cooperation Enterprises	302	302	
外资企业	Enterprises with Sole Fund	12904	12096	808
外商投资股份有限公司	Share-holding Corporations Ltd. with Foreign Investment	12050	11795	255
其他外商投资企业	Other Foreign Funded Enterprises			
按工业行业大类分	By Sector			
煤炭开采和洗选业	Mining and Washing of Coal			
石油和天然气开采业	Extraction of Petroleum and Natural Gas			
黑色金属矿采选业	Mining and Processing of Ferrous Metal Ores	3710	3710	
有色金属矿采选业	Mining and Processing of Non-Ferrous Metal Ores			
非金属矿采选业	Mining and Processing of Nonmetal Ores			
开采专业及辅助性活动	Professional and Support Activities for Mining			
其他采矿业	Mining of Other Ores			

(10 000 yuan)

R&D 经费内部支出 Internal Expenditure on R&D				R&D 经费外部支出 External expenditure on R&D
按资金来源分组 By Capital Source				
政府资金 Government Appropriation Funds	企业资金 Self-raised Funds by Enterprises	境外资金 Foreign funds	其他资金 Other Funds	
20337	1493617	320	377	149048
18458	1190826	11	377	115255
	7873		279	
	317			
50	866			
7634	601216		62	25175
1173	70889			512
6461	530327		62	24663
6153	310681	11		84701
4622	269444		35	5338
	675			
	148			
2599	234359		35	4574
2023	34262			764
	429			40
1262	245320			12693
1237	52965			12693
25	192355			
561	44751	309		611
509	19548	309		56
	302			
32	12872			555
20	12030			
	3710			18

17-7 续表 continued

指标	Item	合计 Total	按支出用途分组 By Object of Expenditure 经常费支出 Daily Expenditure	资产性支出 Capital Expenditure
农副食品加工业	Processing of Food from Agricultural Products	6606	6127	479
食品制造业	Manufacture of Foods	9517	9347	170
酒、饮料和精制茶制造业	Manufacture of Wine, Drinks and Refined Tea	1287	1256	31
烟草制品业	Manufacture of Tobacco			
纺织业	Manufacture of Textile	10785	10375	410
纺织服装、服饰业	Manufacture of Textile Wearing Apparel and Finery	1007	1005	3
皮革、毛皮、羽毛及其制品和制鞋业	Manufacture of Leather, Fur, Feather & Its Products and Footwear	375	374	1
木材加工和木、竹、藤、棕、草制品业	Processing of Timbers, Manufacture of Wood,Bamboo, Rattan, Palm, and Straw Products	1424	1424	
家具制造业	Manufacture of Furniture			
造纸和纸制品业	Manufacture of Paper and Paper Products	5162	5143	19
印刷和记录媒介复制业	Printing, Reproduction of Recording Media	5992	5837	155
文教、工美、体育和娱乐用品制造业	Manufacture of Culture, Education,Arts and crafts，Sport and Entertainment Goods	3186	2634	552
石油、煤炭及其他燃料加工业	Processing of Petroleum, Coal and Other Fuels	16050	16030	20
化学原料和化学制品制造业	Manufacture of Chemical Raw Material and Chemical Products	49122	47526	1596
医药制造业	Manufacture of Medicines	246269	224536	21732
化学纤维制造业	Manufacture of Chemical Fiber	4271	3967	303
橡胶和塑料制品业	Manufacture of Rubber and Plastic	5752	5462	289
非金属矿物制品业	Manufacture of Non-metallic Mineral Products	35724	34659	1066
黑色金属冶炼和压延加工业	Manufacture and Processing of Ferrous Metals	239617	238750	867
有色金属冶炼和压延加工业	Manufacture & Processing of Non-ferrous Metals	3308	2997	311
金属制品业	Manufacture of Metal Products	79139	75351	3789
通用设备制造业	Manufacture of General Purpose Machinery	113919	104020	9899
专用设备制造业	Manufacture of Special Purpose Machinery	88083	84132	3952
汽车制造业	Manufacture of Automotive	221476	219071	2405
铁路、船舶、航空航天和其他运输设备制造业	Manufacture of Railroad,Marine,Aerospace and Other Transportation Equipment	8623	7558	1065
电气机械和器材制造业	Manufacture of Electrical Machinery & Equipment	77411	76488	924
计算机、通信和其他电子设备制造业	Manufacture of Computer, Communications and Other Electronic Equipment	209956	201558	8398
仪器仪表制造业	Manufacture of Measuring Instrument	27406	26102	1304
其他制造业	Other Manufacture	698	698	
废弃资源综合利用业	Comprehensive Utilization of Waste	60	60	
金属制品、机械和设备修理业	Metal Products, Machinery and Equipment Repair Industry	3481	3273	208
电力、热力生产和供应业	Production and Supply of Electric Power and Heat Power	20633	18096	2537
燃气生产和供应业	Production and Supply of Gas	80	80	
水的生产和供应业	Production and Supply of Water	1745	1745	0

R&D 经费内部支出 Internal Expenditure on R&D				R&D 经费外部支出 External expenditure on R&D
按资金来源分组 By Capital Source				
政府资金 Government Appropriation Funds	企业资金 Self-raised Funds by Enterprises	境外资金 Foreign funds	其他资金 Other Funds	
190	6416			80
148	9339		30	88
43	1244			90
36	10749			188
221	786			102
	375			
	1424			
	5162			
38	5954			10
	3186			
	16050			610
967	48155			1133
4433	241825	11		23888
	4271			
119	5632			
222	35503			335
252	239365			710
	3308			60
640	78500			135
2782	111075		62	1933
2135	85944		5	2242
101	221096		279	38059
586	7728	309		85
979	76433			3331
5121	204835			52204
1156	26250			2615
	698			94
	60			
	3481			
113	20520			549
	80			
	1745			

17-8 规模以上工业企业办科技机构情况（2020年）

Science and Technology Institutions of Industrial Enterprises Above Designated Size (2020)

指标	Item	机构数（个）Number (unit)	机构人员（人）Research Personnel(Person) 合计 Total	博士毕业 Doctor	硕士毕业 Master	机构经费支出（万元）Agency Expenditure (10 000 yuan)	仪器和设备原价（万元）Original price of Equipment (10 000 yuan)
总计	Total	434	23727	390	4139	1280010	728888
按登记注册类型分	By Status of Registration						
内资企业	Domestic Funded Enterprises	398	18862	317	3210	1037581	591959
国有企业	State-owned Enterprises	1	6		1	100	10
集体企业	Collective-owned Enterprises	1	92			1341	182
股份合作企业	Cooperative Enterprises	1	70		8	917	1432
联营企业	Joint Ownership Enterprises						
有限责任公司	Private Limited Liability Corporations	147	8757	183	1883	529870	361513
国有独资公司	State Sole funded Corporations	18	1644	37	364	52800	125490
其他有限责任公司	Other Limited Liability Corporations	129	7113	146	1519	477070	236023
股份有限公司	Share-holding Corporations Ltd.	76	5032	98	951	318921	125845
私营企业	Private Enterprises	172	4905	36	367	186432	102977
私营独资企业	Private-funded Enterprises	2	23		2	292	31
私营合伙企业	Private Partnership Enterprises						
私营有限责任公司	Private Limited Liability Corporations	141	3758	19	251	154586	79930
私营股份有限公司	Private Share-holding Corporations Ltd.	29	1124	17	114	31554	23016
其他企业	Other Enterprises						
港、澳、台商投资企业	Enterprises with Funds from Hong Kong,Macao and Taiwan	11	3110	32	775	207301	18586
合资经营企业	Joint-venture Enterprises	7	1110	1	52	50491	13248
合作经营企业	Cooperative Enterprises						
独资经营企业	Enterprises with Sole Investment	4	2000	31	723	156810	5338
投资股份有限公司	Share-holding Corporations Ltd.						
其他港澳台投资企业	Other Enterprises with Funds from Hong Kong,Macao and Taiwan						
外商投资企业	Foreign Funded Enterprises	22	1550	34	104	33943	102720
中外合资经营企业	Joint-venture Enterprises	7	472	3	28	9458	13230
中外合作经营企业	Cooperation Enterprises						
外资企业	Enterprises with Sole Fund	10	849	6	72	13108	55904
外商投资股份有限公司	Share-holding Corporations Ltd. with Foreign Investment	5	229	25	4	11377	33587
其他外商投资企业	Other Foreign Funded Enterprises						
按工业行业大类分	By Sector						
煤炭开采和洗选业	Mining and Washing of Coal						
石油和天然气开采业	Extraction of Petroleum and Natural Gas						
黑色金属矿采选业	Mining and Processing of Ferrous Metal Ores	1	97			1585	2133
有色金属矿采选业	Mining and Processing of Non-Ferrous Metal Ores						
非金属矿采选业	Mining and Processing of Nonmetal Ores	1	6		1	100	10
开采专业及辅助性活动	Professional and Support Activities for Mining						
其他采矿业	Mining of Other Ores						

17-8 续表 continued

指标	Item	机构数（个）Number (unit)	机构人员（人）Research Personnel(Person)			机构经费支出（万元）Agency Expenditure (10 000 yuan)	仪器和设备原价（万元）Original price of Equipment (10 000 yuan)
			合计 Total	博士毕业 Doctor	硕士毕业 Master		
农副食品加工业	Processing of Food from Agricultural Products	9	78	6	22	1485	3331
食品制造业	Manufacture of Foods	5	729		2	8101	33604
酒、饮料和精制茶制造业	Manufacture of Wine, Drinks and Refined Tea	3	124	2	5	1502	1282
烟草制品业	Manufacture of Tobacco						
纺织业	Manufacture of Textile	7	133	2	2	4449	6533
纺织服装、服饰业	Manufacture of Textile Wearing Apparel and Finery	2	43	3	5	588	153
皮革、毛皮、羽毛及其制品和制鞋业	Manufacture of Leather, Fur, Feather & Its Products and Footwear						
木材加工和木、竹、藤、棕、草制品业	Processing of Timbers, Manufacture of Wood,Bamboo, Rattan, Palm, and Straw Products	1	14			247	30
家具制造业	Manufacture of Furniture						
造纸和纸制品业	Manufacture of Paper and Paper Products						
印刷和记录媒介复制业	Printing, Reproduction of Recording Media	6	347		3	7179	9115
文教、工美、体育和娱乐用品制造业	Manufacture of Culture, Education,Arts and crafts, Sport and Entertainment Goods	4	46		4	1029	1319
石油、煤炭及其他燃料加工业	Processing of Petroleum, Coal and Other Fuels	4	109	2	4	17937	4124
化学原料和化学制品制造业	Manufacture of Chemical Raw Material and Chemical Products	29	1373	16	122	52237	41421
医药制造业	Manufacture of Medicines	51	4460	129	1361	267709	161591
化学纤维制造业	Manufacture of Chemical Fiber	1	15	1	2	204	325
橡胶和塑料制品业	Manufacture of Rubber and Plastic	8	210	2	11	3051	3756
非金属矿物制品业	Manufacture of Non-metallic Mineral Products	26	735	4	30	20474	32049
黑色金属冶炼和压延加工业	Manufacture and Processing of Ferrous Metals	6	1207	35	110	215177	44091
有色金属冶炼和压延加工业	Manufacture & Processing of Non-ferrous Metals	3	95		2	1222	1133
金属制品业	Manufacture of Metal Products	38	1138	28	26	55597	44223
通用设备制造业	Manufacture of General Purpose Machinery	40	2334	16	340	49236	88661
专用设备制造业	Manufacture of Special Purpose Machinery	39	1589	21	224	52462	34042
汽车制造业	Manufacture of Automotive	20	2532	40	766	167297	11205
铁路、船舶、航空航天和其他运输设备制造业	Manufacture of Railroad,Marine,Aerospace and Other Transportation Equipment	4	444	4	55	12877	6829
电气机械和器材制造业	Manufacture of Electrical Machinery & Equipment	33	1109	9	145	43799	72505
计算机、通信和其他电子设备制造业	Manufacture of Computer, Communications and Other Electronic Equipment	28	2516	25	605	248221	56160
仪器仪表制造业	Manufacture of Measuring Instrument	45	1371	12	148	28209	11354
其他制造业	Other Manufacture						
废弃资源综合利用业	Comprehensive Utilization of Waste						
金属制品、机械和设备修理业	Metal Products, Machinery and Equipment Repair Industry	6	498		32	5935	6340
电力、热力生产和供应业	Production and Supply of Electric Power and Heat Power	10	159	26	60	10886	35632
燃气生产和供应业	Production and Supply of Gas						
水的生产和供应业	P roduction and Supply of Water	1	11		2	31	313

17-9 规模以上工业企业自主知识产权及相关情况(2020年)
Independent Intellectual Property Rights of Industrial Enterprises Above Designated Size(2020)

指标	Item	专利申请数 (件) Patent Applications (piece)
总计	Total	11041
按登记注册类型分	By Status of Registration	
内资企业	Domestic Funded Enterprises	8628
国有企业	State-owned Enterprises	60
集体企业	Collective-owned Enterprises	7
股份合作企业	Cooperative Enterprises	8
联营企业	Joint Ownership Enterprises	
有限责任公司	Private Limited Liability Corporations	3080
国有独资公司	State Sole funded Corporations	316
其他有限责任公司	Other Limited Liability Corporations	2764
股份有限公司	Share-holding Corporations Ltd.	1918
私营企业	Private Enterprises	3551
私营独资企业	Private-funded Enterprises	40
私营合伙企业	Private Partnership Enterprises	15
私营有限责任公司	Private Limited Liability Corporations	3091
私营股份有限公司	Private Share-holding Corporations Ltd.	405
其他企业	Other Enterprises	4
港、澳、台商投资企业	Enterprises with Funds from Hong Kong,Macao and Taiwan	470
合资经营企业	Joint-venture Enterprises	179
合作经营企业	Cooperative Enterprises	
独资经营企业	Enterprises with Sole Investment	291
投资股份有限公司	Share-holding Corporations Ltd.	
其他港澳台投资企业	Other Enterprises with Funds from Hong Kong,Macao and Taiwan	
外商投资企业	Foreign Funded Enterprises	1568
中外合资经营企业	Joint-venture Enterprises	126
中外合作经营企业	Cooperation Enterprises	3
外资企业	Enterprises with Sole Fund	165
外商投资股份有限公司	Share-holding Corporations Ltd. with Foreign Investment	1274
其他外商投资企业	Other Foreign Funded Enterprises	
按工业行业大类分	By Sector	
煤炭开采和洗选业	Mining and Washing of Coal	6
石油和天然气开采业	Extraction of Petroleum and Natural Gas	
黑色金属矿采选业	Mining and Processing of Ferrous Metal Ores	35
有色金属矿采选业	Mining and Processing of Non-Ferrous Metal Ores	
非金属矿采选业	Mining and Processing of Nonmetal Ores	7
开采专业及辅助性活动	Professional and Support Activities for Mining	
其他采矿业	Mining of Other Ores	

# 发明专利 （件） Inventions (piece)	有效发明专利数 （件） Effective Invention Patent (piece)	拥有注册商标数 （件） Registered Trademarks (piece)	形成国家或行业标准数 （项） Industry or National Standards (unit)
3773	12199	11219	398
3025	9684	9387	303
20	22	5	
2	15	1	
2	1	8	
1172	3428	4593	119
151	258	145	20
1021	3170	4448	99
1065	3338	1826	66
764	2874	2940	118
	16	27	5
668	2303	2610	102
96	555	303	11
	6	14	
191	315	345	15
119	128	297	4
72	187	48	11
280	1020	206	42
26	216	168	38
	2		
98	97	15	
156	705	23	4
1			

17-9 续表 continued

指标	Item	专利申请数（件）Patent Applications (piece)
农副食品加工业	Processing of Food from Agricultural Products	81
食品制造业	Manufacture of Foods	150
酒、饮料和精制茶制造业	Manufacture of Wine, Drinks and Refined Tea	25
烟草制品业	Manufacture of Tobacco	8
纺织业	Manufacture of Textile	121
纺织服装、服饰业	Manufacture of Textile Wearing Apparel and Finery	25
皮革、毛皮、羽毛及其制品和制鞋业	Manufacture of Leather, Fur, Feather & Its Products and Footwear	
木材加工和木、竹、藤、棕、草制品业	Processing of Timbers, Manufacture of Wood,Bamboo, Rattan, Palm, and Straw Products	23
家具制造业	Manufacture of Furniture	10
造纸和纸制品业	Manufacture of Paper and Paper Products	46
印刷和记录媒介复制业	Printing, Reproduction of Recording Media	101
文教、工美、体育和娱乐用品制造业	Manufacture of Culture, Education,Arts and crafts， Sport and Entertainment Goods	101
石油、煤炭及其他燃料加工业	Processing of Petroleum, Coal and Other Fuels	38
化学原料和化学制品制造业	Manufacture of Chemical Raw Material and Chemical Products	251
医药制造业	Manufacture of Medicines	544
化学纤维制造业	Manufacture of Chemical Fiber	39
橡胶和塑料制品业	Manufacture of Rubber and Plastic	136
非金属矿物制品业	Manufacture of Non-metallic Mineral Products	518
黑色金属冶炼和压延加工业	Manufacture and Processing of Ferrous Metals	616
有色金属冶炼和压延加工业	Manufacture & Processing of Non-ferrous Metals	48
金属制品业	Manufacture of Metal Products	746
通用设备制造业	Manufacture of General Purpose Machinery	1271
专用设备制造业	Manufacture of Special Purpose Machinery	988
汽车制造业	Manufacture of Automotive	576
铁路、船舶、航空航天和其他运输设备制造业	Manufacture of Railroad,Marine,Aerospace and Other Transportation Equipment	172
电气机械和器材制造业	Manufacture of Electrical Machinery & Equipment	2053
计算机、通信和其他电子设备制造业	Manufacture of Computer, Communications and Other Electronic Equipment	1079
仪器仪表制造业	Manufacture of Measuring Instrument	589
其他制造业	Other Manufacture	2
废弃资源综合利用业	Comprehensive Utilization of Waste	15
金属制品、机械和设备修理业	Metal Products, Machinery and Equipment Repair Industry	16
电力、热力生产和供应业	Production and Supply of Electric Power and Heat Power	207
燃气生产和供应业	Production and Supply of Gas	
水的生产和供应业	Production and Supply of Water	23

# 发明专利 （件） Inventions (piece)	有效发明专利数 （件） Effective Invention Patent (piece)	拥有注册商标数 （件） Registered Trademarks (piece)	形成国家或行业标准数 （项） Industry or National Standards (unit)
20	149	85	1
35	203	244	2
7	12	81	1
3	25		
21	51	13	4
3	5	34	1
	2	7	1
1	2	5	
	29		
8	24	7	
11	79	71	6
27	51	10	1
3	72	10	
79	831	2780	15
376	808	4089	30
11	11	9	
32	60	40	7
104	495	90	41
236	824	41	13
8	31	15	1
186	498	299	29
273	1072	541	24
274	888	459	31
169	562	128	10
105	584	4	
469	1729	313	73
779	1417	336	14
194	387	219	44
2			1
	15		
8	41	2	
48	60	6	7
3	2		3

主要统计指标解释

科技活动 是指在自然科学、农业科学、医药科学、工程与技术科学、人文与社会科学领域（简称科学技术领域）中，与科技知识的产生、发展、传播和应用密切相关的有组织的活动。在企（事）业中只有列入单位工作计划的科技活动才予以统计，而独立发明人等在企（事）业外或计划外进行的科技活动不在统计范围之内。科研活动可分为研究与试验发展（简称 R&D，包括基础研究、应用研究和试验发展）、研究与试验发展（R&D）成果应用及相关的科技服务三类活动。

基础研究 是指为了获得关于现象和可观察事实的基本原理的新知识（揭示客观事物的本质、运动规律，获得新发现、新学说）而进行的实验性或理论性研究。基础研究属于科学研究范畴。从研究目的看，基础研究不以任何专门或特定的应用或使用为目的，它只是通过试验分析或理论性研究对事物的特性、结构和各种关系进行分析，加深对客观事物的认识，解释现象的本质，揭示物质运动的规律或提出和验证各种设想、理论和定律。从研究结果看，基础研究的结果具有一般的或普遍的正确性，通常表现为一般的原则、理论和规律，其成果以科学论文和科学著作为主要形式。

应用研究 是指为获得新知识而进行的创造性研究，主要针对某一特定的目的或目标。应用研究也属于科学研究范畴。从研究目的看，应用研究是探索基础研究成果的可能用途，或是为达到预定的目标探索应采取的新方法（原理性）或新途径，为解决实际问题提供科学依据。从研究结果看，应用研究的成果一般只影响科学技术的某些领域和有限范围，并具有专门的性质，针对具体的领域、问题或情况，其成果形式以科学论文、专著、原理性模型或发明专利等为主。

试验发展 是指利用从基础研究、应用研究和实际经验所获得的现有知识，为产生新的产品、材料和装置，建立新的工艺、系统和服务，以及对已产生和建立的上述各项做实质性的改进而进行的系统性工作。在社会科学领域，试验发展是指通过把基础研究、应用研究获得的知识转变成可以实施的计划（包括为检验和评估实施示范项目）的过程。

专利申请数 指企业在报告期内向国内外知识产权行政部门提出专利申请并被受理的件数。

专利申请数中发明专利 指企业在报告期内向国内外知识产权行政部门提出发明专利申请并被受理的件数。

新产品产值 指报告期企业生产的新产品的产值。新产品是指采用新技术原理、新设计构思研制、生产的全新产品，或在结构、材质、工艺等某一方面比原有产品有明显改进，从而显著提高了产品性能或扩大了使用功能的产品。新产品产值、新产品销售收入既包括经政府有关部门认定并在有效期内的新产品，也包括企业自行研制开发，未经政府有关部门认定，从投产之日起一年之内的新产品。

拥有注册商标 指企业在报告期末拥有的注册商标件数。包括在境内和境外注册的商标件数，一件商标在境内外同时注册时只统计一件。

技术改造经费支出 指企业在报告期进行技术改造而发生的费用支出。技术改造指企业在坚持科技进步的前提下，将科技成果应用于生产的各个领域（产品、设备、工艺等），用先进工艺、设备代替落后工艺、设备，实现以内涵为主的扩大再生产，从而提高产品质量、促进产品更新换代、节约能源、降低消耗，全面提高综合经济效益。

Explanatory Notes on Main Statistical Items

Scientific and Technological Activities refer to organized activities closely related to generation, development, dissemination and application of knowledge of science and technology in natural science, agricultural science, pharmaceutical science, engineering and technical science, humanities and social sciences field (called as science and technology field for short). Only scientific and technological activities listed into the work plan of the enterprise (institution) will be included, while scientific and technological activities by independent inventors outside the enterprise (institution) or the plan are out of the statistics scope. Scientific research activities can be divided into three categories -- research and experimental development (called as R&D for short, including fundamental research, application research and experimental development), application of results of research and experimental development (R&D) and related science and technology services.

Fundamental Research refers to empirical or theoretical research aiming at obtaining new knowledge on the fundamental principles of phenomena of observable facts to reveal the nature and law of movement of objects and to acquire new discoveries or new theories. Fundamental research falls into scientific research. From the perspective of research purpose, fundamental research takes no specific or designated application as the aim of the research which only involves analysis on features, structures and various relationships of things by experimental analysis or theoretical research to deepen the understanding of objective things, explain the nature of the phenomenon and reveal the laws of the motion of matter or put forward and verify various assumptions, theories and laws. From the perspective of research result, the result of fundamental research is of general or universal correctness, usually presented as general principle, theory and law. Results of fundamental research are mainly released or disseminated in the form of scientific papers or monographs.

Applied Research refers to creative research aiming at obtaining new knowledge on a specific objective or target. Applied research also falls into scientific research. From the perspective of research purpose, purpose of the applied research is to identify the possible use of results from basic research, or to explore new (fundamental) methods or new approaches as well as provide scientific basis for solving practical problems. From the perspective of research result, achievements of application research only influence some fields and limited scope of science and technology generally and are of a specialized nature and expressed in the form of scientific papers, monographs, fundamental models or invention patents on the basis of specific field, problem or situation.

Experiments and Development refer to systematic activities aiming at using the knowledge from fundamental and applied researches or from practical experience to develop new products, materials and equipment, to establish new production process, systems and services, or to make substantial improvement on the existing products, process or services. In social sciences, experiment and development activities refer to the process of converting the knowledge from or applied researches into feasible programs (including conduct of demonstration projects for assessment and evaluation).

Quantity of Patents Applied refers to the quantity of patents accepted with application for a patent filed by the enterprise to intellectual property administrative departments at the home and abroad in the reporting period.

Quantity of Invention Patent in the Patents Applied refers to the quantity of patents for invention accepted with application for an invention patent filed by the enterprise to intellectual property administrative departments at the home and abroad in the reporting period.

Output Value of New Products refers to output value of new products produced by enterprises in the reporting period. New products refer to new products developed or produced by new know-why and design concept and products with properties of products obviously improved or use function expanded due to the obvious improvement in structure, texture or technology in comparison to those of original products. Output value of new products and sales revenue from new products include new products approved by relevant government departments whose valid term fails to expire and new products developed independently by the enterprise and not approved by relevant government departments which exist for less than one year as of the date of going into operation.

Possession of Registered Trademark refers to the quantity of registered trademarks owned by the enterprise at the end of the reporting period, including quantity of trademark registered at home and abroad. Statistics of a trademark are only conducted once at the moment of being registered at the home and abroad at the same time.

Expenditure on Technological Transformation refers to the expenditure incurred by technological transformation by the enterprise in the reporting period. Technological transformation refers to the enterprise applying scientific and technological achievements to all fields of production (product, equipment and technology, etc.) and replacing backward technology and equipment with advance technology and equipment to realize intention-based expanded reproduction, thus to improve product quality, promote product upgrading, save energy, lower consumption and comprehensively enhance composite economic results in the premise of insisting on scientific and technological progress.

18

教育与文化

EDUCATION AND CULTURE

18-1 教育事业基本情况
Basic Statistics on Education

指标	Item	1952 年	1957 年	1962 年	1965 年	1970 年
学校数（所）	Number of Schools(unit)	2679	3106	3731	4318	5359
# 驻济高等学校	Colleges and Universities in Ji'nan	5	4	12	8	2
中等教育	Secondary Education	37	67	112	410	1204
# 中等职业学校	Vocational Secondary Education	16	16	15	15	17
普通中学	Ordinary middle school	21	51	93	159	1024
小学	Elementary school	2636	3034	3606	3899	4152
专任教师（人）	Full-time Teachers(person)	8555	13452	19606	26760	32508
# 驻济高等学校	Colleges and Universities in Ji'nan	671	1325	2598	2451	922
中等教育	Secondary Education	1108	2569	3418	5321	9607
# 中等职业学校	Vocational Secondary Education	311	787	765	685	914
普通中学	Ordinary middle school	797	1782	2629	3502	8445
小学	Elementary school	6773	9550	13571	18971	21954
在校学生（万人）	Total Enrollment(10 000 persons)	26.87	31.95	49.82	68.27	80.20
# 驻济高等学校	Colleges and Universities in Ji'nan	0.43	0.82	1.65	1.40	0.30
中等教育	Secondary Education	2.73	5.14	5.80	10.43	18.97
# 中等职业学校	Vocational Secondary Education	0.69	0.93	0.51	0.65	0.12
普通中学	Ordinary middle school	2.04	4.21	5.22	7.50	17.81
小学	Elementary school	23.70	25.98	42.35	56.42	60.91
各类学校毕业生数（万人）	Graduates(10 000 persons)	4.38	8.58	10.60	10.45	12.09
# 驻济高等学校	Colleges and Universities in Ji'nan	0.14	0.11	0.31	0.43	–
中等教育	Secondary Education	0.60	1.14	1.72	1.90	1.02
# 中等职业学校	Vocational Secondary Education	0.13	0.14	0.32	0.03	–
普通中学	Ordinary middle school	0.46	1.00	1.40	1.80	0.38
每一教师负担学生数（人）	Each Teacher Burden Number of Students(person)	31.41	23.75	25.41	23.27	24.67
# 驻济高等学校	Colleges and Universities in Ji'nan	6.41	6.19	6.35	5.71	3.25
中等教育	Secondary Education	24.64	20.01	16.97	19.60	19.75
# 中等职业学校	Vocational Secondary Education	22.33	11.84	6.64	9.51	1.36
普通中学	Ordinary middle school	25.63	23.64	19.84	21.41	21.09
小学	Elementary school	34.99	27.20	31.21	29.74	27.74
平均每万人口在校学生（人）	Number of Enrollment Per 10000 Population(person)	843	922	1418	1829	1968
# 大学生	Undergraduate	14	24	47	38	7
中专生	Secondary Students	22	27	14	17	3
中学生	Middle School Students	64	122	150	256	463
小学生	Elementary School Students	743	750	1206	1513	1494

注：1. 驻济高等学校在校生含普通专本科、成人本专科、研究生在校生。
2. 驻济高等学校毕业生为普通本专科毕业生。
3. “中等职业学校”中相关教师、学生数据不含技工学校。

1975 年	1980 年	1985 年	1990 年	1995 年	2000 年	2005 年	2010 年	2015 年	2019 年	2020 年	2021 年
5412	**5066**	**4511**	**3924**	**3360**	**1725**	**1251**	**1025**	**946**	**1110**	**1108**	**1464**
4	11	16	16	16	16	59	66	72	52	52	52
922	759	593	529	440	423	348	302	280	375	390	373
21	30	40	39	41	40	91	73	41	40	41	66
783	710	491	417	312	297	247	209	214	312	320	332
4485	4295	3899	3368	2890	1273	832	645	582	683	666	641
42432	**49608**	**46806**	**55978**	**58779**	**62869**	**77334**	**83106**	**88487**	**118342**	**121438**	**123004**
2468	3744	4614	7245	7500	8269	24341	29526	31693	40627	42202	41894
15274	19062	17530	21618	23946	26817	27435	28370	30589	41112	42017	42643
985	1338	2367	2890	2941	2916	4738	4511	4068	4058	3642	4040
13571	17294	13572	16065	17621	20585	21915	21943	23643	34177	34796	35587
24654	26775	24579	26922	27417	27417	25201	24801	25795	36067	37219	38467
90.28	**83.56**	**78.38**	**79.48**	**91.69**	**95.79**	**129.28**	**144.60**	**153.71**	**182.68**	**201.27**	**183.14**
0.61	1.58	3.02	3.73	5.66	9.30	48.71	64.25	71.40	76.20	89.85	69.40
25.43	20.24	25.34	28.08	36.64	44.99	42.50	41.76	40.77	52.24	54.41	52.74
0.58	0.31	1.92	2.51	4.79	5.75	9.88	8.10	5.93	5.68	6.28	6.40
23.86	19.63	21.49	22.45	27.15	33.82	30.91	30.18	30.16	39.35	39.84	40.70
64.22	61.47	49.98	47.57	49.23	41.40	37.88	38.40	41.44	54.14	57.01	61.00
22.66	**18.07**	**17.31**	**17.12**	**20.88**	**23.65**	**33.58**	**38.10**	**39.83**	**55.99**	**43.89**	**41.35**
0.20	0.03	0.45	1.03	1.68	1.55	13.49	17.57	19.48	17.07	18.37	17.86
11.83	8.41	7.36	8.24	10.39	10.80	14.03	13.55	14.22	16.47	17.12	15.27
0.20	0.46	0.52	0.62	1.16	1.84	3.29	3.13	2.75	2.05	1.73	1.72
11.58	7.89	6.39	6.66	7.78	8.16	10.40	9.20	10.23	12.30	12.97	12.28
21.28	**16.84**	**16.75**	**14.20**	**15.60**	**15.24**	**16.72**	**17.40**	**17.37**	**15.44**	**16.58**	**14.89**
2.47	4.22	6.55	5.15	7.54	11.25	20.01	21.76	22.53	18.76	21.29	16.57
16.65	10.62	14.46	12.99	15.30	16.78	15.49	14.72	13.33	12.71	11.00	12.37
5.95	2.29	8.12	8.69	16.30	18.84	20.86	17.96	14.58	14.00	17.24	15.80
17.58	11.35	15.83	13.98	15.41	16.43	14.10	13.75	12.76	11.51	11.45	11.43
26.05	22.96	20.33	17.67	18.20	15.10	15.03	15.48	16.07	15.01	15.32	15.87
2062	**1822**	**1605**	**1518**	**1691**	**1702**	**2177**	**2395**	**2465**	**2505**	**2510**	**1962**
14	34	62	71	104	165	820	1064	1145	1040	1121	743
13	7	39	48	88	102	195	192	170	178	182	565
566	429	473	473	553	601	521	500	484	542	497	436
1466	1339	1024	908	908	736	638	636	664	745	711	653

Notes:1.Students under high education in Jinan include regular college students, regular junior college students, adult college students, adult junior students and postgraduate students.

2.Graduates under high education in Jinan are Undergraduates and Short-cycle Courses in Regular HEIs.

3.Data related to teachers and students in the "Secondary Vocational Schools" do not include Skilled Workers Schools.

18-2 普通高等院校一览（2021 年）

Basic Statistics on Institutions of Higher Education(2021)

单位：人 (person)

名称 Name	普通本专科在校学生数 Total Enrollment	普通本专科毕业生数 Graduates	普通本专科招生数 New Enrollment	教职工人数 Teachers and Staff	# 专任教师 Full-time Teachers		
					合计 Total	# 正高级 Senior	# 副高级 Sub-Senior
总计	658281	174989	197541	55510	39573	5984	12889
综合性大学	110211	26189	30489	13181	8536	2315	3146
山东大学	41565	9828	10169	8434	4929	1822	1859
济南大学	33724	8737	8267	2853	2182	362	835
山东青年政治学院	18304	3468	6152	1030	801	69	229
山东女子学院	16618	4156	5901	864	624	62	223
理工院校	83298	22563	22859	8584	5909	838	2139
山东建筑大学	23946	6506	5967	2266	1704	296	667
山东科技大学	2584	735	607	234	200	11	49
齐鲁工业大学	29360	7128	7794	3582	2278	384	806
山东交通学院	23785	7376	7181	1865	1482	119	503
山东电力高等专科学校	3623	818	1310	637	245	28	114
医药院校	57020	16449	15849	5521	3650	690	1315
山东第一医科大学	22333	5517	5781	3201	1811	297	719
山东中医药大学	18317	4457	4124	1529	1315	314	390
山东医学高等专科学校	9900	4626	3600	352	283	52	122
济南护理职业学院	6470	1849	2344	439	241	27	84
师范院校	51763	14232	13446	4359	3288	475	971
山东师范大学	26870	8206	6128	2824	2077	381	656
齐鲁师范学院	17727	4497	5094	975	829	91	247
济南幼儿师范专科学校	7166	1529	2224	560	382	3	68
财经院校	33274	9118	7546	2909	2087	329	791
山东财经大学	27068	7063	6526	2456	1690	261	625
山东财经大学燕山学院	6206	2055	1020	453	397	68	166
政法院校	25064	5697	7441	1760	1157	110	330
山东警察学院	5432	995	1500	569	308	36	127
山东司法警官职业学院	8292	1811	2875	285	159	2	40
山东政法学院	11340	2891	3066	906	690	72	163
体育院校	8067	2028	1837	725	593	60	215
山东体育学院	8067	2028	1837	725	593	60	215
艺术院校	16255	4387	4297	1794	1438	147	494
山东艺术学院	8830	2576	2251	1029	876	83	300
山东工艺美术学院	7425	1811	2046	765	562	64	194
职业技术学院	273329	74326	93777	16677	12915	1020	3488
山东协和学院	30832	5790	10495	1513	1362	115	404
山东商业职业技术学院	16607	4685	6453	1127	930	45	235
山东劳动职业技术学院	12819	3852	4814	705	554	27	125
山东职业学院	13263	5197	3503	688	615	38	199
山东圣翰财贸职业学院	9043	2431	2315	581	364	4	75
山东艺术设计职业学院	4365	886	1642	451	344	15	55
山东英才学院	21201	5736	6314	1261	1020	93	276
山东旅游职业学院	9539	2664	3364	520	441	20	79
济南工程职业技术学院	13358	4084	4979	702	587	62	161
山东电子职业技术学院	9908	3227	3765	595	457	9	129
济南职业学院	14233	4769	5762	986	754	59	279
山东现代学院	19555	5580	7790	1036	703	51	237
山东工程职业技术大学	19263	2961	6765	1062	891	136	224
山东城市建设职业学院	13762	4362	5032	701	588	10	184
山东管理学院	10232	3636	2959	798	598	42	123
齐鲁理工学院	20049	4556	6566	1586	1065	189	277
山东农业工程学院	12067	3610	3273	884	581	52	152
山东特殊教育职业学院	1398	404	472	192	101	11	30
山东传媒职业学院	10503	2408	3309	542	447	16	73
莱芜职业技术学院	11332	3488	4205	747	513	26	171

18-3 中等专业学校一览(2021 年)

Basic Statistics on Specialized Secondary Schools (2021)

单位：人 (person)

名称 Name	在校学生数 Total Enrollment	毕业生数 Graduates	招生数 New Enrollment	教职工人数 Teachers and Staff	# 专任教师 Full-time Teachers		
					合计 Total	# 副高级 Sub-Senior	# 中级 Middle
总计	13302	3019	4602	1364	1013	287	463
工科学校							
济南信息工程学校	3249	887	1121	200	173	55	91
济南电子机械工程学校	2446	491	837	221	176	59	73
济南铁路学校	200	57	82	46	46	15	11
山东冶金中等专业学校	773	223	217	138	57	29	21
财经学校							
山东省济南商贸学校	2242	547	1097	233	196	58	98
体育学校							
济南市体育运动学校	1025	203	319	116	54	18	18
济南市第二体育运动学校	248	42	55	30	30	8	16
山东体育学院附属中学	1368	298	468				
艺术学校							
山东省文化艺术学校	869	83	144	184	110	10	56
山东工艺美术学院附属中等美术学校	147	40	49	23	20	4	4
济南艺术学校	735	148	213	173	151	31	75

18-4 分县区儿童学前教育基本情况(2021 年)

Student Enrollment in Pre-school Education (2021)

单位：人 (person)

地区	Region	幼儿园数(所) Number of Kindergartens (unit)	在园人数 Enrolment	入园人数 Entrants	教职工数 Teachers and Staff	# 专任教师 Full-timeTeachers
全市	Total	2227	369201	117649	46591	26319
历下区	Li xia	132	35162	10580	5311	2877
市中区	Shi zhong	184	36490	11817	5581	3103
槐荫区	Huai yin	166	36752	11765	5038	2599
天桥区	Tian qiao	176	32702	10759	4635	2248
历城区	Li cheng	223	51855	18305	6453	3546
长清区	Chang qing	130	18045	5326	1894	1142
章丘区	Zhang qiu	205	28882	10773	3541	2042
济阳区	Ji yang	159	20330	5595	1949	1175
莱芜区	Lai wu	335	36099	10204	3922	2733
钢城区	Gang cheng	80	10785	3247	1204	807
济南高新区	Ji'nan Gao xin	104	21744	7053	2984	1458
南部山区	Nan shan	69	7107	2377	858	443
平阴县	Ping yin	55	11088	3171	1050	780
商河县	Shang he	209	22160	6677	2171	1366

18-5 文化事业机构和人员
Number of Institutions and Persons in Culture

指标	Item	2016年	2017年	2018年	2019年	2020年	2021年
机构数（个）	Number(unit)						
电影业	Movies	44	52	54	65	64	65
艺术业	Arts	27	27	27	25	27	26
文物业	Cultural Relics	48	48	48	67	64	80
图书馆业	Libraries	12	12	12	14	14	14
群众文化业	Mass Culture	155	153	153	175	174	174
艺术教育业	Art Education	1	1	1	1	1	1
文艺科研业	Culture Research	1	1	1	1	1	1
从业人员数（人）	Personnel(person)						
电影业	Movies	913	936	1380	1075	641	588
艺术业	Arts	1557	1569	1537	1475	1512	1492
文物业	Cultural Relics	1173	1158	1068	1365	844	1637
图书馆业	Libraries	447	462	472	507	567	756
群众文化业	Mass Culture	710	719	695	745	801	723
艺术教育业	Art Education	164	167	170	175	181	180
文艺科研业	Culture Research	51	49	47	47	50	49

注：电影业机构、从业人员数据为城市电影院线数据，不含农村。
Note:The data of the film industry institutions and employees are urban cinema line data, excluding rural areas.

主要统计指标解释

普通高等学校 指按照国家规定的设置标准和审批程序批准举办，通过国家统一招生考试，招收高中毕业生为主要培养对象，实施高等教育的全日制大学、独立设置的学院和高等专科学校、短期职业大学。

文化事业机构 指从事专业文化工作和为专业文化工作服务的独立建制的单位。不包括这些单位另外举办独立核算的其他机构和各部门的业余文化组织。

Explanatory Notes on Main Statistical Items

Regular Institutions of Higher Education refer to educational establishments that set up according to the government evaluation and approval procedures, enrolling graduates from senior secondary schools and providing higher education courses and training for senior professionals. They include full time universities, colleges and high professional schools which set up independently as well as short-term vocational colleges.

Cultural Institutions refer to units which have their own organizational system, work on professional culture work and serve the professional culture work, excluding other institutions for independent accounting established by such units separately and amateur cultural organizations of all departments.

体育与卫生

SPORTS AND PUBLIC HEALTH

19-1 体育事业
Statistics of Sports Instituons

指标	Item	2016 年	2017 年	2018 年	2019 年	2020 年	2021 年
体育部门职工人数（人）	Number of Persons of Physical System(person)	724	720	591	672	677	550
# 业余体育学校	Spare-time Sports School	221	9	423	402	410	375
总计中：教练员	Referees	151	231	191	183	181	251
等级裁判员（人）	Number of Referees in Grades(person)						
一级裁判员	First Grade Referees		7				
二级裁判员	Second Grade Referees	122	153	268	344	155	169
三级裁判员	Third Grade Referees		55				
二级运动员发展人数（人）	Number of Second Grade Sportsmen(person)	401	465	279	534	564	637
少年儿童业余体校在校学生（人）	Enrollment Spare-time Sports School(person)	1036	845	1140	1286	1010	1961
业余体校（所）	Spare-time Sports School(unit)	5	7	5	10	10	10
运动员获奖牌数（枚）	Number of Medals Won by Athletes(unit)	1110	1188.5	1186	1353	715.5	784
# 世界级　金牌	World　Gold Medals	12	1	3	13	0	3
银牌	Silver Medals	4	2	1	7	0	0
铜牌	Copper Medal	4	1	2	8	0	2
# 洲际　金牌	Intercontinental　Gold Medals	7	3	3	10	0	1
银牌	Silver Medals	4	3	2	11	0	0
铜牌	Copper Medal	4	0	1	7	0	1
# 全国　金牌	Country　Gold Medals	43	85	50	100	15	39
银牌	Silver Medals	29	61	36	91	7	28
铜牌	Copper Medal	16	100	41	132	10	27
# 全省　金牌	Province　Gold Medals	402	395.5	430	442	285.5	298
银牌	Silver Medals	292	273	319	248	182	162
铜牌	Copper Medal	293	264	288	284	216	223
体育设施（个）	Sports Facility(unit)						
体育场	Stadium	12	6	12	14	14	124
体育馆	Gymnasium	9	17	9	10	11	28
游泳馆	Natatorium	5	11	5	9	10	79
室内外游泳池	Indoor Swimming Pool	2	5	4	10	10	90
有固定看台的灯光球场	Light Count With Fixed Stand	2	7	2	5	5	8

注：1. 等级裁判员为当年新评定的人数。
2. 2017 年体育设施统计口径为市、区县体育部门主管的设施数量。
3. 2017 年业余体育学校统计口径只指学位，不包括业训网点。

Notes:1.The number of referees is the number of new assessments in the current year.
2.The number of sports facilities in 2017 is the number of facilities in charge of the sports department of the city, district and county.
3.In 2017, the statistical caliber of amateur sports schools only refers to degree, excluding amateur training outlets.

19-2 各时期卫生事业情况
Statistics of Health Institutions in Major Years

年份 Year	卫生机构(个) Number of Health Institutions (unit)		卫生工作人员(人) Medical Technical Personnel (person)		卫生机构床位(张) Number of Health Institutions Beds (set)	
	小计 Total	# 医院及卫生院 Hospitals and Township Hospitals	小计 Total	# 卫生技术人员 Medical Technical Personnel	小计 Total	# 医院及卫生院 Hospitals and Township Hospitals
1952	208	22	6277	4778	3160	1906
1957	708	45	10740	7991	5972	3401
1962	1191	98	13705	9648	7917	5662
1965	1144	114	18885	14881	9035	6438
1970	682	130	13273	10341	7878	6462
1975	934	137	20021	14956	9066	8050
1978	1017	148	24949	19198	11496	9856
1979	1078	152	26385	20110	11902	10781
1980	1091	151	27843	21295	12301	11052
"六五"时期						
1981	1188	152	29597	22559	12428	11436
1982	1159	151	30636	22814	12379	11383
1983	1177	156	31924	23948	12966	11674
1984	1160	157	32967	24502	13728	12960
1985	1175	165	34232	26185	14356	13791
"七五"时期						
1986	1184	167	35803	27360	14757	14165
1987	1137	166	37129	28159	15457	14721
1988	1103	171	38384	29167	16165	15580
1989	1137	180	39926	29878	16698	16176
1990	1300	178	41444	31130	18214	17216
"八五"时期						
1991	1233	177	40957	30815	18439	17538
1992	1331	180	41996	31541	18818	18178
1993	1285	193	43274	32871	20243	19320
1994	1228	213	43630	33007	20001	19064
1995	1185	216	43648	32848	20747	19534
"九五"时期						
1996	1674	214	45765	35219	20428	19716

19–2 续表 continued

年份 Year	卫生机构（个）Number of Health Institutions (unit)		卫生工作人员（人）Medical Technical Personnel (person)		卫生机构床位（张）Number of Health Institutions Beds (set)	
	小计 Total	# 医院及卫生院 Hospitals and Township Hospitals	小计 Total	# 卫生技术人员 Medical Technical Personnel	小计 Total	# 医院及卫生院 Hospitals and Township Hospitals
1997	1567	220	44664	34188	21422	20706
1998	1574	227	45110	34596	21965	21130
1999	1570	226	45121	34000	21735	21086
2000	1414	231	45166	35669	21698	20830
"十五"时期						
2001	1414	231	45296	35790	21906	21033
2002	1708	243	39386	31945	21576	21042
2003	1868	246	41925	33803	22674	22262
2004	1917	243	41625	33998	24044	22588
2005	2138	246	41499	34129	24695	23524
"十一五"时期						
2006	2285	240	43023	35124	27695	26101
2007	2265	243	42513	34579	26055	25328
2008	5092	286	44416	36143	28939	27555
2009	5163	281	46311	37648	30920	28749
2010	5086	277	54711	39366	31947	29844
"十二五"时期						
2011	5159	262	58590	42116	34920	31545
2012	5239	243	60426	44331	38834	35194
2013	5368	255	76955	57700	45465	41287
2014	5784	265	84515	63604	48280	44058
2015	5947	269	89117	71778	49311	45195
"十三五"时期						
2016	6188	270	92060	76447	52191	47524
2017	5770	289	97663	76273	54855	50142
2018	6030	293	104347	82834	57460	51207
2019	7487	351	122370	97532	66623	59697
2020	7514	343	126681	102172	68831	62072
"十四五"时期						
2021	7515	336	131269	108401	72832	66258

注：2015 年及 2016 年的卫生技术人员为注册卫生技术人员，其他年份为在岗卫生技术人员。
Note:Health technicians in 2015 and 2016 are registered health technicians, and other years are on–the–job health technicians.

19-3 卫生事业机构及床位
Number of Health Institutions and Beds

指标	Item	2016 年	2017 年	2018 年	2019 年	2020 年	2021 年
各类卫生机构数（个）	Number of Health Institutions (unit)	6188	5770	6030	7487	7514	7515
医院	Hospital	217	238	246	289	284	279
社区卫生服务中心（站）	Health Service Center for Community	286	283	314	352	379	385
卫生院	Health Centers	53	51	47	62	59	57
门诊部	Outpatient Department	89	115	135	156	163	177
急救中心（站）	First-Aid Center	2	1	1	1	1	1
采血供应机构	Pick and Supply Blood Institution	4	2	2	3	2	2
妇幼保健院（所、站）	Women and Children Care Agencies	12	12	12	15	15	15
专科疾病防治院（所、站）	Specialized Disease Prevention &Treatment Institution	10	10	11	13	9	8
疾病预防控制中心（防疫站）	Center for Disease Control and Prevention	12	12	12	15	14	14
医学科学研究机构	Medical Science Research Institutes	2	2	2	2	2	2
其他卫生机构	Other Medical Institutions	18	27	29	39	32	30
各类卫生机构病床数（张）	Number of Health Institutions Beds(set)	52191	54855	57460	66623	68831	72832
医院	Hospital	44526	47575	48843	56315	58790	62887
社区卫生服务中心（站）	Health Service Center for Community	2946	3195	3361	3791	3899	3873
卫生院	Health Centers	2998	2567	2364	3382	3282	3371
门诊部	Outpatient Department	112	46	65	33	43	138
妇幼保健院（所、站）	Women and Children Care Agencies	1243	1126	1158	1444	1533	1592
专科疾病防治院（所、站）	Specialized Disease Prevention	366	346	1669	1658	1284	932
千人拥有量（张、人）	Number Per 1000 Population(set.person)						
平均每千人拥有病床	Number Of Beds Per 1000 Population	7.22	7.49	7.70	7.48	7.48	7.80
每千人拥有卫生技术人员	Number Of Medical Technical Personnel Per 1000 Population	10.57	10.42	11.10	10.95	11.10	11.61
每千人拥有医生	Number Of Doctors Per 1000 Population	4.75	3.97	4.31	4.30	4.37	4.55
每千人拥有护士	Number Of Nurses Per 1000 Population	5.82	4.62	5.03	4.91	4.97	5.30

19-4 分地区卫生事业机构及床位(2021年)
Number of Health Institutions and Beds by District(2021)

指标	Item	全市 Total	市区 Urban	平阴县 Ping yin	商河县 Shang he
各类卫生机构数(个)	**Number of Institutions(unit)**	7515	6809	251	455
医院	Hospital	279	269	4	6
疗养院	Health Service Center for Community				
社区卫生服务中心(站)	Health Centers	385	369	8	8
卫生院	Outpatient Department	57	40	6	11
门诊部	Outpatient Department	177	171		6
诊所、卫生所、医务室	Infirmaries and Clinics	2876	2730	64	82
急救中心(站)	First-Aid Center	1	1		
采血供应机构	Pick and Supply Blood Institution	2	2		
妇幼保健院(所、站)	Women and Children Care Agencies	15	13	1	1
专科疾病防治院(所、站)	Specialized Disease Prevention &Treatment Institution	8	7	1	
疾病预防控制中心(防疫站)	Center for Disease Control and Prevention	14	12	1	1
卫生监督所	Medical Supervision Institution	14	12	1	1
医学科学研究机构	Medical Science Research Institutes	2	2		
其他卫生机构	Other Medical Institutions	30	30		
各类卫生机构病床数(张)	**Number of Institutions Beds(set)**	72823	67697	2450	2676
医院	Hospital	62887	59119	1736	2032
疗养院	Sanatorium				
社区卫生服务中心(站)	Health Service Center for Community	3873	3792	20	61
卫生院	Health Centers	3371	2229	568	574
门诊部	Outpatient Department	138	138		
妇幼保健院(所、站)	Women and Children Care Agencies	1592	1577	6	9
专科疾病防治院(所、站)	Specialized Disease Prevention&Treatment Institution	932	812	120	
千人拥有量(张、人)	**Number Per 1000 Population(set.person)**				
平均每千人拥有病床	Number Of Beds Per 1000 Population	7.80	8	7.45	5.07
每千人拥有卫生技术人员	Number Of Medical Technical Personnel Per 1000 Population	11.61	12.15	7.54	5.46
每千人拥有医生	Number Of Doctors Per 1000 Population	4.55	4.76	2.80	2.19
每千人拥有护士	Number Of Nurses Per 1000 Population	5.30	5.54	3.50	2.45

19-5 医疗机构年收入与支出 (2021 年)

Revenue and Expenditure in Health Institutions (2021)

单位：万元 (10 000yuan)

机构分类	Institutions	总收入 Total Income			
		合计 Total	财政补助收入 Financial Subsidy Income	上级补助收入 Grant From Higher Authority	业务收入 / 事业收入 Business Income
合计	Total	7066575.7	853802.8	42489.7	5813713.6
医院	Hospital	5951823.9	498343.2	11919.0	5182950.7
社区卫生服务中心 (站)	Health Service Center for Community	265647.0	79362.3	4508.3	175337.6
卫生院	Health Centers	121861.8	62549.3	2448.0	55604.0
门诊部	Outpatient Department	45289.4	0.0	0.0	40675.4
诊所 . 卫生所 . 医务室	Infirmaries and Clinics	79222.9	0.0	0.0	69874.5
急救中心 (站)	First-Aid Center	2367.8	2271.8	0.0	94.0
妇幼保健院 (所、站)	Women and Children Care Agencies	216333.5	49367.3	441.0	156290.8
专科疾病防治院 (所、站)	Specialized Disease revention&Treatment Institution	21305.3	10956.7	355.1	9625.7

19-5 续表 continued

机构分类	Institutions	总支出 Total Expenditure			总费用中：人员费用 Staff Expenditure
		合计 Total	单位管理费 Unit Management Fee	业务活动费 Business Activity Fee	
合计	Total	6301885.9	727868.7	5291042.0	2171579.8
医院	Hospital	5385056.5	629125.3	4613798.7	1806765.3
社区卫生服务中心 (站)	Health Service Center for Community	256000.3	9236.5	237128.3	93500.6
卫生院	Health Centers	117435.0	3109.3	110520.2	54649.8
门诊部	Outpatient Department	28745.0	0.0	0.0	13767.0
诊所 . 卫生所 . 医务室	Infirmaries and Clinics	50793.8	0.0	0.0	28900.8
急救中心 (站)	First-Aid Center	2648.8	416.3	2232.5	1268.9
妇幼保健院 (所、站)	Women and Children Care Agencies	185224.8	26133.3	157477.2	85588.9
专科疾病防治院 (所、站)	Specialized Disease revention&Treatment Institution	9250.2	1381.1	7866.8	5255.5

注：门诊部及诊所、卫生所、医务室不填报财政补助收入、上级补助收入、单位管理费、业务活动费四项指标。
Note:Outpatient department and clinic,Health clinic,The medical office does not report four Items: financial subsidy income, superior subsidy income, Unit Management Fee, Business Activity Fee.

19-6 医院、卫生院工作情况
Basic Statistics on Hospitals and Health Institutions

指标	Item	2016 年	2017 年	2018 年	2019 年	2020 年	2021 年
医院	Hospital						
单位数（个）	Unit Number(unit)	217	238	246	289	284	279
诊疗人次数（万人次）	Visits (10 000 person–times)	2865	3157	3309	3922	3397	3993
#门诊人次数	OutPatients	2570	2779	2960	3449	3018	3504
急诊人次数	Emergency Patients	165	207	228	300	235	327
健康检查人数（万人次）	check–up(10 000 person–times)	154	166	201	260	235	271
入院人数（万人）	Inpatients(10 000 persons)	127.9	140.4	150.0	182.2	172.3	204.3
出院人数（万人）	Discharged(10 000 persons)	127.3	139.7	149.4	181.5	171.8	203.6
平均开放病床数（张）	Average Bed Opened(set)	41402	44400	45132	52359	54692	58399
病床使用率（%）	Utilization Rate of Beds(%)	86.12	87.52	87.28	87.27	77.71	82.71
病床周转次数（次）	Turnover of Beds(time)	30.70	31.50	33.10	34.70	31.40	34.90
出院者平均住院日（日）	Average Stay Days in Hospital(day)	10.10	9.90	9.40	9.20	9.10	8.50
卫生院	Health Centers						
单位数（个）	Unit Number(unit)	53	51	47	62	59	57
诊疗人次数（万人次）	Visits (10 000 person–times)	233.4	208.1	195.2	301.9	304.1	349.4
#门诊人次数	OutPatients	224.6	197.6	190.3	292.1	292.7	334.2
急诊人次数	Emergency Patients	3.4	6.5	3.3	3.6	5.0	4.5
健康检查人数（万人次）	Check–up(10 000 person–times)	23.0	20.2	20.4	35.8	25.5	28.3
入院人数（万人）	Inpatients(10 000 persons)	6.6	5.3	4.4	7.2	5.8	6.5
出院人数（万人）	Discharged(10 000 persons)	6.5	5.3	4.4	7.2	5.7	6.5
平均开放病床数（张）	Average Bed Opened(set)	2907	2479	2277	3187	3203	3240
病床使用率（%）	Utilization Rate of Beds(%)	54.54	52.00	54.85	58.03	47.37	51.77
病床周转次数（次）	Turnover of Beds(time)	22.40	21.40	19.40	22.70	17.90	20.00
出院者平均住院日（日）	Average Stay Days in Hospital(day)	8.40	8.30	9.70	7.80	8.50	8.80

19-7 分地区卫生技术人员分类情况（2021 年）
Medical Technical Personnel by Region(2021)

单位：人 (person)

指标	Item	全市 Total	市区 Urban	平阴县 Ping yin	商河县 Shang he
各类卫生机构工作人员合计	Total of Personnel in Health Care Institutions	131269	124124	3130	4015
# 卫生技术人员小计	Health Technical Personnel	108401	103036	2480	2885
医生	Licensed Doctors	42474	40398	922	1154
注册护士	Registered Nurse	49446	47004	1151	1291
其他	Others	16481	15634	407	440

主要统计指标解释

等级裁判员人数 指经考核正式批准授予等级裁判员称号的人数。裁判员等级分为国际裁判、国家级裁判、一级裁判、二级裁判、三级裁判。

体育场 指有 400 米跑道（中心含足球场），有固定道牙，跑道 6 条以上，并有固定看台的室外田径场地。体育场按看台容纳观众人数分为：甲级 25000 人以上，乙级 15000-25000 人，丙级 5000-15000 人，丁级 5000 人以下。

体育馆 指有固定看台，可供篮球、排球、羽毛球、乒乓球、体操等项目训练比赛活动用的室内运动场地。体育馆按看台容纳观众人数分为：甲级 6000 人以上，乙级 4000-6000 人，丙级 2000-4000 人，丁级 2000 人以下。

医院 包括综合医院、中医医院、中西医结合医院、民族医医院、各类专科医院和护理院，不包括专科疾病防治院、妇幼保健院和疗养院，包括医学院校附属医院。

卫生技术人员 包括执业医师、执业助理医师、注册护士、药师（士）、检验及影像技师（士）、卫生监督员和见习医（药、护、技）师（士）等卫生专业人员。

医生 指取得医师执业证书且实际从事临床工作的人。

卫生机构 指从卫生（卫生健康）行政部门取得《医疗机构执业许可证》《中医诊所备案证》《计划生育技术服务许可证》或从民政、工商行政、机构编制管理部门取得法人单位登记证书，为社会提供医疗服务、公共卫生服务或从事医学科研和学在职培训等工作的单位。

Explanatory Notes on Main Statistical Items

Number of Grade Referees refers to the number of referees formally approved upon evaluation to be granted with the title of grade referee. Referees are divided into international referee, national referee, Level I referee, Level II referee and Level III referee.

Stadium refers to outdoor athletic field with 400m track (football field in the center), fixed kerbs, more than 6 tracks and fixed stands. Stadiums can be divided as follows as per the quantity of spectators contained by the standard: Class A stadium for above 25,000 persons, Class B stadium for 15,000–25,000 persons, Class C stadium for 5,000–15,000 persons and Class D stadium for less than 5,000 persons.

Gymnasium refers to indoor sports ground with fixed stands which can be used for training and competition of basketball, volleyball, badminton, table tennis and gymnastics. Gymnasium can be divided as follows as per the quantity of spectators contained by the standard: Class A gymnasium for above 6,000 persons, Class B gymnasium for 4,000–6,000 persons, Class C gymnasium for 2,000–4,000 persons and Class D gymnasium for less than 2,000 persons.

Hospital includes general hospital, traditional Chinese medicine hospital, hospital of traditional Chinese and Western medicine, ethnic medical hospital, various specialized hospital and nursing home and affiliated hospital of medical college other than specialized disease prevention and maternity and child care center and nursing home.

Medical Technical Personnel refers to health professionals such as medical practitioner, assistant medical practitioner, registered nurse, pharmacist, senior pharmacist (assistant pharmacist), inspection and imaging technician (assistant technician), health supervisor and medical intern (trainee medical assistant), pharmacy intern (probationary pharmacist), trainee nurse (practice nurse) or medical trainee (apprentice technician).

Doctors refer to persons getting the medical practitioner certificate and actually engaging in clinical work.

Health Care Institution refers to units getting Practicing License of Medical Institution, Registration Certificate of TCM Clinic and Family Planning Technical Service License from the administrative department of health (hygiene and health) or getting the registration certificate of legal entity from civil affairs, industrial and commercial administration, institutional establishment management departments, providing the society with medical service and public health service or engaging in medical scientific research and studying on–the–job training.

20

民政、司法和其他

SOCIAL WELFARE CIVIL ADMINISTRATION AND JUSTICE

20-1 社会治安主要指标
Main Indicators of Public Order

指标	Item	2016 年	2017 年	2018 年	2019 年	2020 年	2021 年
刑事案件（件）	Criminal Cases(case)						
当年全部立案数	Put on Record	21142	19648	18594	25382	32965	40583
破获当年刑事案件数	Cracked the Number of Criminal Cases	7610	8571	7103	9259	18983	17316
治安案件（件）	Public Security Cases(case)						
受理数	Cases Accepted	71868	66375	75393	79355	68614	64550
查处数	Cases Punished	68439	63734	73700	72593	60633	58043
城市交通事故	Traffic Accidents						
交通事故（起）	Number of Traffic Accidents(case)	2944	3075	3071	3334	3313	3317
伤亡人数（人）	Number of Injuries and Deaths(person)	3573	3219	3618	3925	3747	3631
#死亡人数（人）	Number of Deaths(person)	403	421	419	472	465	447
损失折款（万元）	Direct Losses(10 000 yuan)	875.2	1020.3	947.4	905.48	1006.2	1206.72
火灾事故	Fires						
火灾起数（起）	Number of Fire Accidents(case)	1825	1752	1539	4577	4319	5907
伤亡人数（人）	Number of Injuries and Deaths(person)	15	11	12	12	16	35
#死亡人数（人）	Number of Deaths(person)	13	10	10	10	13	24
损失折款（万元）	Direct Losses(10 000 yuan)	1903	599	827	1529	2153	6231.8

20–2 分地区社会治安主要指标(2021年)
Main Indicators of Public Order by District(2021)

指标	Item	全市 Total	其中 of which 市区 Urban	平阴县 Ping yin	商河县 Shang he
刑事案件(件)	Criminal Cases(case)				
当年全部立案数	Put on Record	40583	38676	799	1108
破获当年刑事案件数	Cracked the Number of Criminal Cases	17316	16331	438	547
治安案件(件)	Public Security Cases(case)				
受理数	Cases Accepted	64550	57477	4553	2520
查处数	Cases Punished	58043	51734	4545	1764
城市交通事故	Traffic Accidents				
交通事故(起)	Number of Traffic Accidents(case)	3317	3185	89	43
伤亡人数(人)	Number of Injuries and Deaths(person)	3631	3474	106	51
#死亡人数(人)	Number of Deaths(person)	447	412	23	12
损失折款(万元)	Direct Losses(10 000 yuan)	1206.7	1193	5	8
火灾事故	Fires				
火灾起数(起)	Number of Fire Accidents(case)	5907	5312	252	343
伤亡人数(人)	Number of Injuries and Deaths(person)	35	33	0	2
#死亡人数(人)	Number of Deaths(person)	24	23	0	1
损失折款(万元)	Direct Losses(10 000 yuan)	6231.8	5456	379	397

20-3 社会保障和救济
Basic Statistics on Social Security and Receiving Relief Flinds

指标	Item	2016 年	2017 年	2018 年	2019 年	2020 年	2021 年
优抚情况（人）	Veteran Benefit and Placement(person)						
享受定期抚恤金人数	Number of Receiving Periodic Pensions	907	831	784	914		
在乡复员军人	Demobilized Soldiers in Countryside	2319	1892	1486	1727		
参战退役人员	Veterans	4741	4705	4630	5636		
社会救济情况（人）	Social Relief(person)						
城镇居民最低生活保障人数	Number of Urban Residents for Minimum Livelihood Guarantee	19742	16742	13364	15491	14159	13063
农村居民最低生活保障人数	Number of Rural residents for Minimum Livelihood Guarantee	80147	77121	64271	73305	84209	84367
民政经费（万元）	Civil Affairs Expenditures(10 000 yuan)						
城市居民最低生活保障费	Urban Residents for Minimum Livelihood Guarantee	11573	10966	9563	9657	11030	11774
农村最低生活保障费	Rural residents for Minimum Livelihood Guarantee	24938	26929	26439	26039	39218	51177
其他社会救助费	Other Social Assistance Expenses	6614	5757	3088	1158	1175	1367
社会福利费	Social Welfare Funds	35898	32194	47654	60731	69771	92454
退役安置费（万元）	Decommissioning Costs(10 000 yuan)	96164	134557	12656	13538		
自然灾害生活救助费（万元）	Natural Disaster Assistance Expenses (10 000 yuan)	654	259	69	2450	–	
医疗救助费（万元）	Medical Assistance Expenses(10 000 yuan)	7245	8396	7175	3680	9280	10409
社会保障及扶贫（个、元）	Social Security and Poverty Alleviation(unit.yuan)						
建立社会保障服务网络的乡镇数	Number of Towns With Social Security Service Network	39	29	29	40	29	29
城市市区居民最低生活保障金标准	Minimum Living Standards for Urban Residents	580	596	616	685	821	904

注：本表指标为“–”的，部门相关统计制度中已经不再进行统计。
Note:The Item “–” in this table means statistics are no longer in the relevant statistical system of the department.

20-4 分地区社会保障和救济(2021 年)
Basic Statistics on Social Security and Receiving Relief Flinds by District(2021)

指标	Item	济南市(汇总) Total	济南市(市本级) Cities	历下区 Li xia	市中区 Shi zhong	槐荫区 Huai yin	天桥区 Tian qiao	历城区 Li cheng	长清区 Chang qing	章丘区 Zhang qiu	济阳区 Ji yang
社会救济情况(人)	Social Relief(person)										
城镇居民最低生活保障人数	Number of Urban Residents for Minimum Livelihood Guarantee	13063		1496	1789	1213	2940	392.0	596	609	76
农村居民最低生活保障人数	Number of Rural residents for Minimum Livelihood Guarantee	84367			1223	414	512	1770.0	10294	18297	5719
民政经费(万元)	Civil Affairs Expenditures (10 000 yuan)										
城市居民最低生活保障费	Urban Residents for Minimum Livelihood Guarantee	11773.5		1405.3	1733.2	1173.9	2869.3	409.0	456.5	553.2	58.0
农村最低生活保障费	Rural residents for Minimum Livelihood Guarantee	51176.9			1172.7	372.0	462.1	1702.5	5914.5	10699.8	3266.5
其他社会救助费	Other Social Assistance Expenses	1367.4		135.4	209.4	246.5	25.9	198.5		401.8	83.4
社会福利费	Social Welfare Funds	92453.6	26594.2	5381.0	3496.2	2761.4	3015.1	4366.4	2546.5	7710.3	6323.8
社会保障及扶贫(个、元)	Social Security and Poverty Alleviation(unit.yuan)										
建立社会保障服务网络的乡镇数	Number of Towns With Social Security Service Network	29							2	1	2
城市市区居民最低生活保障金标准	Minimum Living Standards for Urban Residents	904.0		904.0	904.0	904.0	904.0	904.0	904.0	904.0	904.0

20-4 续表 continued

指标	Item	莱芜区 Lai wu	钢城区 Gang cheng	济南高新区 Ji'nan Gao xin	济南起步区(直管) Ji'nan Start-up Area (Directly under)	南部山区 Nan shan	平阴县 Ping yin	商河县 Shang he
社会救济情况(人)	Social Relief(person)							
城镇居民最低生活保障人数	Number of Urban Residents for Minimum Livelihood Guarantee	2598	651	19	116	48	158	362
农村居民最低生活保障人数	Number of Rural residents for Minimum Livelihood Guarantee	16641	3634	926	2261	4628	4067	13981
民政经费(万元)	Civil Affairs Expenditures (10 000 yuan)							
城市居民最低生活保障费	Urban Residents for Minimum Livelihood Guarantee	1942.2	586.8	19.7	133.5	49.7	143.8	239.4
农村最低生活保障费	Rural residents for Minimum Livelihood Guarantee	9912.7	2393.0	841.5	1541.4	3427.2	2304.4	7166.6
其他社会救助费	Other Social Assistance Expenses			11.9			30.7	23.9
社会福利费	Social Welfare Funds	7323.0	7885.8	3092.7	1503.6	1550.6	3997.6	4905.3
社会保障及扶贫(个、元)	Social Security and Poverty Alleviation(unit.yuan)							
建立社会保障服务网络的乡镇数	Number of Towns With Social Security Service Network	7					6	11
城市市区居民最低生活保障金标准	Minimum Living Standards for Urban Residents	904.0	904.0	904.0	904.0	904.0	904.0	904.0

20-5 律师、公证、司法基本情况（2021年）
Basic Statistics on Law,Notarizations and Mendiation(2021)

指标	Item	单位 Unit	全市 Total	市区 Urban	平阴县 Ping yin	商河县 Shang he
律师工作	Lawyers					
律师事务所	Number of Law Offices	个 (unit)	474	465	7	2
执业律师	Number of Lawyers	人 (person)	7898	7827	53	18
担任常年法律顾问	Permanent Legal Advisor	家 (unit)	10853	10662	161	30
民事诉讼代理	Civil Agent	件 (case)	92956	91684	870	402
刑事诉讼辩护及代理	Criminal Defense and Agent	件 (case)	10081	9694	164	223
行政诉讼代理	Administrative Agent	件 (case)	5777	5752	19	6
非诉讼法律事务	Non-litigation Legal Matters	件 (case)	18760	18751	9	
公证工作	Notarization					
公证处	Number of Notary Offices	个 (unit)	15	13	1	1
公证处人员	Personnel of Notary Offices	人 (person)	527	510	10	7
# 公证员	Notaries	人 (person)	153	147	4	2
办理公证总数	Number of Notarized Affair	件 (case)	246097	238187	1782	6128
# 国内民事公证	Domestic Civil Notarization	件 (case)	149263	147276	1357	630
国内经济公证	Domestic Commerce Notarization	件 (case)	96834	90911	425	5498
涉外公证	Foreign-related Notarization	件 (case)	57581	57510		71
办理经济公证涉及金额	Money ofCommerce Notarization	亿元 (100 million yuan)	0.90	0.884	0.01	0.01
基层司法行政工作	Basic Judicical Administration					
人民调解委员会	People's Mediation Committee	个 (unit)	6036	5133	347	556
人民调解员	People's Mediators	人 (person)	23477	19610	1278	2589
调解纠纷总数	Number of Mediation Disputes	件 (case)	27322	23087	1018	3217
# 调解成功	Success Mediation	件 (case)	26807	23483	108	3216
法律服务所	Legal Service Office	个 (unit)	150	138	9	3
基层法律工作者	Grassroots Legal Workers	人 (person)	861	814	34	13
担任法律顾问	Legal Advisor	家 (unit)	735	653	74	8
民事诉讼代理	Civil Agent	件 (case)	8114	6734	463	917
非诉讼代理	Non-litigation Agent	件 (case)	2417	2250	142	25
法律援助工作	Legal Aid					
法律援助机构	Legal Aid Institution	个 (unit)	14	12	1	1
执业人员	Practitioners	人 (person)	164	143	10	11
办理法律援助案件	Legal Aid Cases	件 (case)	21074	19035	259	1280

主要统计指标解释

律师 指受聘参加法律顾问处工作，担任法律顾问、刑（民）事代理人、刑事辩护人，办理非诉讼事件、解答法律询问，代写法律事务文书等主要从事律师业务的专职法律工作者和兼职律师。

公证人员 指在国家公证机关依法办理公证事务的司法人员，包括公证员、助理公证员和在公证处工作的其他人员。

调解人员 指在人民调解委员会担负调解民间一般民事纠纷和轻微违法行为引起纠纷的工作人员，包括调解委员会的委员和调解小组的调解员。

立案 指检察机关对犯罪线索进行初步调查后，认为存在职务犯罪事实并需要追究刑事责任时，依法决定作为刑事案件进行侦查的诉讼活动，是追究犯罪的开始。

Explanatory Notes on Main Statistical Items

Lawyers refer to full–time legal workers and part–time lawyers hired to work in the legal advisory office, serving as legal adviser, criminal (civil) agent and criminal advocate and mainly engaging in law practice (such as handling non–contentious matter, answering legal questions and ghostwriting legal papers).

Notary Personnel refers to judicial personnel legally handling notarial affairs at the state notary organ, including notary, assistant notary and other personnel working in the notary office.

Mediation Personnel refers to staff taking charge of mediating ordinary civil disputes among the people and disputes arising from minor infraction at the people's mediation committee, including the member of the mediation committee and the mediator of the mediation team.

Case Filing refers to the litigious activity involving investigation of criminal case according to law when existence of duty–related crimes is deemed and it is necessary to investigate the criminal responsibility after preliminary investigation of crime clues by the investigating and prosecuting apparatus. It is the start of the investigation of crime.

附录

APPENDIX

附录一 山东省十六城市主要经济指标(2021 年)
Main Indicators of 16 Cities in Shandong(2021)

单位：亿元

城市名称	Region	地区生产总值 Gross Domestic Product	第一产业 Primary Industry	第二产业 Secondary Industry	第三产业 Tertiary Industry	固定资产投资比上年增长(%) Growth Rate Investment in Fixed Assets (%)	房地产开发投资额 Estate Development Investment	一般公共预算收入 General Public Budget Revenue	一般公共预算支出 General Public Budget Expenditure	金融机构本外币存款余额 The Balance of RMB and Foreign Currency Deposits in Financial Institutions
全省	Total	83095.9	6029.0	33187.2	43879.7	6.0	9819.7	7284.5	11709.1	130482.1
济南市	Ji'nan	11432.2	408.8	3964.1	7059.4	11.5	1928.0	1007.6	1293.1	23437.0
青岛市	Qingdao	14136.5	470.1	5070.3	8596.1	4.1	1981.8	1368.3	1705.7	22374.9
淄博市	Zibo	4200.6	180.6	2073.1	1947.0	22.1	414.2	369.0	520.7	6167.6
枣庄市	Zaozhuang	1951.6	185.8	795.4	970.3	6.5	310.3	158.9	273.8	2590.8
东营市	Dongying	3441.7	181.9	1988.4	1271.4	12.5	193.2	261.8	301.5	4610.5
烟台市	Yantai	8711.8	626.1	3598.5	4487.1	0.2	803.1	646.6	802.9	11013.5
潍坊市	Weifang	7010.6	628.4	2831.4	3550.9	16.0	875.2	656.9	879.8	11217.8
济宁市	Jining	5070.0	583.8	2034.6	2451.6	12.4	584.9	440.5	727.2	7257.7
泰安市	Taian	2996.7	327.4	1166.5	1502.8	−29.4	281.2	230.5	428.2	4947.9
威海市	Weihai	3463.9	349.2	1355.1	1759.6	6.0	382.5	266.9	343.3	5246.0
日照市	Rizhao	2212.0	194.7	903.6	1113.7	3.0	210.5	187.5	270.6	3306.1
临沂市	Linyi	5465.5	484.1	2116.8	2864.6	11.4	703.6	409.5	806.6	8960.3
德州市	Dezhou	3488.7	366.9	1435.0	1686.8	−19.6	329.6	234.1	492.4	4777.0
聊城市	Liaocheng	2642.5	374.2	968.5	1299.8	12.9	322.0	230.3	487.8	4898.8
滨州市	Binzhou	2872.1	279.3	1212.0	1380.8	15.3	156.8	287.3	478.2	3767.0
菏泽市	Heze	3976.7	390.9	1653.3	1932.5	15.8	342.9	283.9	632.8	5619.7
济南位次	Position	2	6	2	2	8	2	2	2	1

注：本表内其他城市数据根据内部资料整理，不做正式发布，仅供参考。各项指标最终数据，敬请关注各城市官方发布机构。

Note:The data regarding other cities in this table is sorted out according to internal data which is for reference only instead of being released officially. As for final data regarding various indicators, refer to official release mechanism in each city.

(100 million yuan)

# 住户存款 House–hold Deposits	金融机构本外币贷款余额 The Balance of RMB and Foreign Currency Loans in Financial Institutions	社会消费品零售总额比上年增长(%) Growth Rate Total Retail Sales of Consumer Goods (%)	货物进出口总额 Total Import & Export	# 出口总额 Total Export	实际使用外资(亿美元) Actual Use of Foreign Capital (100 million USD)	城镇居民人均可支配收入(元) Per Capita Disposable Income of Urban Households (yuan)	城镇居民人均消费支出(元) Per Capita Consumption Expenditure of Urban Households (yuan)	农村居民人均可支配收入(元) Per Capita Disposable Income of Rural Households (yuan)	农村居民人均消费支出(元) Per Capita Consumption Expenditure of Rural Households (yuan)	居民消费价格指数(%) Consumer Price Indices (%)
72609.8	111035.4	15.3	29304.1	17582.7	215.2	47066	29314	20794	14299	101.2
8620.5	23313.2	14.7	1944.2	1174.1	26.6	57449	36866	22580	14591	101.5
9152.9	24089.1	14.8	8498.4	4921.3	61.7	60239	38574	26125	17021	101.5
4004.0	4287.7	15.4	1192.4	725.1	8.2	50096	31675	23010	16850	101.0
1831.9	2011.2	16.0	315.1	292.0	4.5	37843	22030	19553	12692	101.1
2451.6	3412.7	15.8	2011.9	555.0	6.4	56625	33526	22255	16593	101.2
6470.3	7477.1	15.4	4115.0	2448.6	26.5	53169	34178	24574	17472	101.4
6913.3	8873.0	16.4	2657.0	1861.7	13.2	46616	28498	24007	15511	101.5
4838.0	5600.9	15.6	678.7	485.5	11.3	41256	24051	20747	13119	100.7
3478.7	3579.9	13.6	291.1	193.2	4.1	41741	24696	21769	13979	100.9
3274.2	4048.3	15.5	2032.5	1494.0	14.5	54264	33752	25692	15537	100.8
2010.8	3365.5	12.0	1165.7	403.0	5.2	39380	23559	20154	10598	100.8
5894.7	8170.0	15.9	1766.8	1584.8	13.8	42606	20367	17783	11370	101.1
3459.7	2903.0	14.8	513.6	333.6	4.5	31927	19091	19020	14878	101.5
3484.3	3135.4	14.5	530.4	366.4	4.6	32262	19012	17512	12576	100.9
2273.3	3067.6	14.7	1023.1	462.2	5.1	41566	26513	20539	13975	100.9
4451.0	3457.3	17.0	568.2	282.3	5.0	31872	20319	16872	13554	100.7
2	2	12	6	6	2	2	2	6	8	1

附录二 十五副省级城市主要经济指标（2021 年）

Main Indicators of 15 Vice-provincial Cities(2021)

单位：亿元

城市名称	Region	地区生产总值 Gross Dmoestic Product	第一产业 Primary Industry	第二产业 Secondary Industry	第三产业 Tertiary Industry	固定资产投资比上年增长 (%) Growth Rate Investment in Fixed Assets (%)	房地产开发投资比上年增长 (%) Growth Rate Estate Development Investment (%)	一般公共预算收入 General Public Budget Revenue	一般公共预算支出 General Public Budget Expenditure	金融机构本外币存款余额 The Balance of RMB and Foreign Currency Deposits in Financial Institutions
济南	Ji'nan	11432.2	408.8	3964.1	7059.4	11.5	12.9	1007.6	1293.1	23437.0
沈阳	Shenyang	7249.7	326.3	2570.3	4353.0	4.1	−1.1	773.0	1032.5	19374.9
大连	Dalian	7825.9	513.3	3301.6	4011.0	1.2	−3.2	737.6	980.1	17081.5
长春	Changchun	7103.1	523.7	2960.5	3618.9	11.6	1.6	617.1	966.5	15467.3
哈尔滨	Harbin	5351.7	628.2	1239.2	3484.3	4.2	−14.6	365.8	992.1	14655.4
南京	Nanjing	16355.3	303.9	5902.7	10148.7	6.2	3.4	1729.5	1817.7	44708.7
杭州	Hangzhou	18109.0	333.0	5489.0	12287.0	9.0	1.5	2387.0	2393.0	61044.0
宁波	Ningbo	14594.9	356.1	6997.2	7241.6	11.0	14.1	1723.1	1944.4	27228.9
厦门	Xiamen	7033.9	29.1	2882.9	4121.9	11.3	1.3	881.0	1060.0	14767.5
青岛	Qingdao	14136.5	470.1	5070.3	8596.1	4.1	3.1	1368.3	1705.7	22374.9
武汉	Wuhan	17716.8	444.2	6208.3	11064.2	12.9	17.2	1578.6	2219.3	33775.9
广州	Guangzhou	28232.0	306.4	7722.7	20202.9	11.7	10.1	1883.2	3020.7	74988.9
深圳	Shenzhen	30664.9	26.6	11338.6	19299.7	3.7	−15.4	4257.8	4570.2	112545.2
成都	Chengdu	19917.0	582.8	6114.3	13219.9	10.0	10.4	1697.9	2237.6	47968.0
西安	Xi'an	10688.3	308.8	3585.2	6794.3	−11.6	−7.0	856.0	1474.9	28510.0
济南位次	Position	9	7	9	9	4	3	9	10	9

注：1. 为便于排序，厦门、广州、成都实际使用外资数据根据人民币口径和年均汇率推算。
2. 本表内其他城市数据根据内部资料整理，不做正式发布，仅供参考。各项指标最终数据，敬请关注各城市官方发布机构。

Notes:1.To facilitate ranking, the data regarding foreign investment actually used by Xiamen Guangzhou and Chengdu is calculated as per RMB caliber and average ann
2.The data regarding other cities in this table is sorted out according to internal data which is for reference only instead of being released officially. As for final data regarding various indicators, refer to official release mechanism in each city.

(100 million yuan)

金融机构本外币贷款余额 The Balance of RMB and Foreign Currency Loans in Financial Institutions	社会消费品零售总额 Total Retail Sales of Consumer Goods	货物进出口总额 Total Import & Export	# 出口总额 Total Export	实际使用外资（亿美元） Actual Use of Foreign Capital (100 million USD)	城镇居民人均可支配收入（元） Per Capita Disposable Income of Urban Households (yuan)	农村居民人均可支配收入（元） Per Capita Disposable Income of Rural Households (yuan)	居民消费价格指数(%) Consumer Price Indices (%)
23313.2	5126.1	1944.2	1174.1	26.6	57449	22580	101.5
19230.2	3985.1	1416.0	484.9	8.2	50566	21662	101.3
13540.3	1909.7	4248.5	1931.7	16.7	50531	23763	101.4
15907.1	2219.2	1179.8	165.9	4.7	43281	18473	100.5
13839.9	2380.3	344.6	171.3	3.8	42745	21512	100.6
43305.4	7899.4	6366.8	3989.9	50.1	73593	32701	101.5
56275.0	6744.0	7369.0	4647.0	81.7	74700	42692	101.3
29045.5	4649.1	11926.1	7624.3	32.7	73869	42946	102.1
15316.7	2584.1	8876.5	4307.3	28.9	67197	29894	101.2
24089.1	5975.4	8498.4	4921.3	61.7	60239	26125	101.5
40825.4	6795.0	3359.4	1929.0	125.6	55297	27209	100.6
61399.6	10122.6	10825.9	6312.2	84.1	74416	34533	101.1
77240.8	9498.1	35435.6	19263.4	109.7	70847	–	100.9
46425.0	9251.8	8222.0	4841.2	78.2	52633	29126	100.5
29411.3	4963.4	4400.0	2361.9	87.1	46931	17389	101.7
10	8	12	12	11	8	10	3

附录三　二十六省会城市主要经济指标(2021年)
Main Indicators of 26 Provincial Capitals (2021)

单位：亿元

城市名称	Region	地区生产总值 Gross Dmoestic Product	第一产业 Primary Industry	第二产业 Secondary Industry	第三产业 Tertiary Industry	固定资产投资比上年增长(%) Growth Rate Investment in Fixed Assets (%)	房地产开发投资比上年增长(%) Growth Rate Estate Development Investment (%)	一般公共预算收入 General Public Budget Revenue	一般公共预算支出 General Public Budget Expenditure	金融机构本外币存款余额 The Balance of RMB and Foreign Currency Deposits in Financial Institutions
济南	Ji'nan	11432.2	408.8	3964.1	7059.4	11.5	12.9	1007.6	1293.1	23437.0
石家庄	Shijiazhuang	6490.3	504.8	2107.1	3878.4	–5.6	2.7	681.4	1152.5	17951.7
太原	Taiyuan	5121.6	44.8	2113.1	2963.7	7.9	–6.9	423.4	629.0	15924.0
呼和浩特	Hohhot	3121.4	137.1	1052.6	1931.7	12.3	9.6	228.9	419.0	6683.7
沈阳	Shenyang	7249.7	326.3	2570.3	4353.0	4.1	–1.1	773.0	1032.5	19374.9
长春	Changchun	7103.1	523.7	2960.5	3618.9	11.6	1.6	617.1	966.5	15467.3
哈尔滨	Harbin	5351.7	628.2	1239.2	3484.3	4.2	–14.6	365.8	992.1	14655.4
南京	Nanjing	16355.3	303.9	5902.7	10148.7	6.2	3.4	1729.5	1817.7	44708.7
杭州	Hangzhou	18109.0	333.0	5489.0	12287.0	9.0	1.5	2387.0	2393.0	61044.0
合肥	Hefei	11412.8	351.1	4171.2	6890.5	3.5	–5.2	844.2	1223.7	20605.7
福州	Fuzhou	11324.5	637.0	4289.8	6397.7	5.9	8.6	749.9	925.7	19117.3
南昌	Nanchang	6650.5	238.3	3218.1	3194.1	11.1	0.4	484.8	870.0	14757.4
郑州	Zhengzhou	12691.0	181.7	5039.3	7470.0	–6.2	–9.9	1223.6	1624.4	27094.0
武汉	Wuhan	17716.8	444.2	6208.3	11064.2	12.9	17.2	1578.7	2219.3	33775.9
长沙	Changsha	13270.7	425.6	5251.3	7593.9	8.2	19.7	1188.3	1543.3	25348.5
广州	Guangzhou	28232.0	306.4	7722.7	20202.9	11.7	10.1	1883.2	3020.7	74988.9
南宁	Nanning	5120.9	606.8	1198.8	3315.4	3.1	–1.3	391.8	775.4	12100.0
海口	Haikou	2057.1	85.4	346.8	1624.9	8.4	2.0	208.3	274.8	5839.7
成都	Chengdu	19917.0	582.8	6114.3	13219.9	10.0	10.4	1697.9	2237.6	47968.0
贵阳	Guiyang	4711.0	193.4	1681.3	2836.3	–7.1	–8.1	426.7	681.5	13441.4
昆明	Kunming	7222.5	333.1	2287.7	4601.7	–7.8	–5.1	689.1	928.2	–
西安	Xi'an	10688.3	308.8	3585.2	6794.3	–11.6	–7.0	856.0	1474.9	28510.0
兰州	Lanzhou	3231.3	62.5	1113.9	2054.9	7.7	8.8	276.7	483.6	9577.7
西宁	Xining	1548.8	58.9	518.2	971.6	6.8	–1.7	153.9	343.8	4710.8
银川	Yinchuan	2263.0	83.8	1028.3	1150.8	–3.6	4.6	171.2	292.2	4705.7
乌鲁木齐	Urumqi	3691.6	28.1	1039.8	2623.7	1.4	–1.9	377.9	419.6	10322.6
济南位次	Position	8	9	10	8	5	3	8	9	9

注：1. 为便于排序，福州、广州和成都实际使用外资数据根据人民币口径和年均汇率推算。
2. 本表内其他城市数据根据内部资料整理，不做正式发布，仅供参考。各项指标最终数据，敬请关注各城市官方发布机构。

(100 million yuan)

金融机构本外币贷款余额 The Balance of RMB and Foreign Currency Loans in Financial Institutions	社会消费品零售总额 Total Retail Sales of Consumer Goods	货物进出口总额 Total Import & Export	# 出口总额 Total Export	实际使用外资（亿美元） Actual Use of Foreign Capital (100 million USD)	城镇居民人均可支配收入（元） Per Capita Disposable Income of Urban Households (yuan)	农村居民人均可支配收入（元） Per Capita Disposable Income of Rural Households (yuan)	居民消费价格指数(%) Consumer Price Indices (%)
23313.2	5126.1	1944.2	1174.1	26.6	57449	22580	101.5
14657.3	2501.2	1481.2	857.1	19.2	43024	18676	100.9
16589.0	1873.9	1852.4	1153.1	1.7	41377	21551	101.0
9606.6	1104.7	159.8	80.6	1.6	53026	22435	100.9
19230.2	3985.1	1416.0	484.9	8.2	50566	21662	101.3
15907.1	2219.2	1179.8	165.9	4.7	43281	18473	100.5
13839.9	2380.3	344.6	171.3	3.8	42745	21512	100.6
43305.4	7899.4	6366.8	3989.9	50.1	73593	32701	101.5
56275.0	6744.0	7369.0	4647.0	81.7	74700	42692	101.3
20322.4	5111.7	3324.8	2029.2	37.5	53208	26856	101.7
21484.1	4549.4	3321.5	2200.6	12.5	53421	25201	100.6
17621.0	2878.7	1293.6	897.7	44.0	50447	22913	101.0
32356.3	5389.2	5892.1	3552.8	48.6	45246	26790	101.1
40825.4	6795.0	3359.4	1929.0	125.6	55297	27209	100.6
27235.1	5111.6	2780.3	1977.5	20.1	62145	38195	101.1
61399.6	10122.6	10825.9	6312.2	84.1	74416	34533	101.1
18100.0	2364.2	1231.9	582.0	5.8	41394	17808	101.4
6839.2	1057.0	476.4	110.5	25.7	43605	19267	100.5
46425.0	9251.8	8222.0	4841.2	78.2	52633	29126	100.5
17284.1	2546.7	478.7	374.6	23.0	43876	20565	101.6
–	3386.4	1716.3	935.1	7.2	52523	19507	100.2
29411.3	4963.4	4400.0	2361.9	87.1	46931	17389	101.7
14231.8	1757.7	141.8	36.8	0.7	43244	16191	101.3
5487.6	621.1	22.5	9.3	–	39251	14948	101.3
6156.4	788.7	132.1	109.5	1.2	42412	18170	101.4
9811.0	1171.9	385.5	259.8	0.5	46142	24878	101.3
9	7	11	11	10	5	12	4

Notes:1.To facilitate ranking, The data regarding foreign investment actually used by Fuzhou Guangzhou and Chengdu is calculated as per RMB caliber and average annual rate.

2.The data regarding other cities in this table is sorted out according to internal data which is for reference only instead of being released officially. As for final data regarding various indicators, refer to official release mechanism in each city.

附录四

中华人民共和国统计法

Statistical Law of The People's Republic of China

（1983 年 12 月 8 日第六届全国人民代表大会常务委员会第三次会议通过 根据 1996 年 5 月 15 日第八届全国人民代表大会常务委员会第十九次会议《关于修改〈中华人民共和国统计法〉的决定》修正 2009 年 6 月 27 日第十一届全国人民代表大会常务委员会第九次会议修订）

目 录

第一章 总 则

第一条 为了科学、有效地组织统计工作，保障统计资料的真实性、准确性、完整性和及时性，发挥统计在了解国情国力、服务经济社会发展中的重要作用，促进社会主义现代化建设事业发展，制定本法。

第二条 本法适用于各级人民政府、县级以上人民政府统计机构和有关部门组织实施的统计活动。

统计的基本任务是对经济社会发展情况进行统计调查、统计分析，提供统计资料和统计咨询意见，实行统计监督。

第三条 国家建立集中统一的统计系统，实行统一领导、分级负责的统计管理体制。

第四条 国务院和地方各级人民政府、各有关部门应当加强对统计工作的组织领导，为统计工作提供必要的保障。

第五条 国家加强统计科学研究，健全科学的统计指标体系，不断改进统计调查方法，提高统计的科学性。

国家有计划地加强统计信息化建设，推进统计信息搜集、处理、传输、共享、存储技术和统计数据库体系的现代化。

第六条 统计机构和统计人员依照本法规定独立行使统计调查、统计报告、统计监督的职权，不受侵犯。

地方各级人民政府、政府统计机构和有关部门以及各单位的负责人，不得自行修改统计机构和统计人员依法搜集、整理的统计资料，不得以任何方式要求统计机构、统计人员及其他机构、人员伪造、篡改统计资料，不得对依法履行职责或者拒绝、抵制统计违法行为的统计人员打击报复。

第七条 国家机关、企业事业单位和其他组织以及个体工商户和个人等统计调查对象，必须依照本法和国家有关规定，真实、准确、完整、及时地提供统计调查所需的资料，不得提供不真实或者不完整的统计资料，不得迟报、拒报统计资料。

第八条 统计工作应当接受社会公众的监督。任何单位和个人有权检举统计中弄虚作假等违法行为。对检举有功的单位和个人应当给予表彰和奖励。

第九条 统计机构和统计人员对在统计工作中知悉的国家秘密、商业秘密和个人信息，应当予以保密。

第十条 任何单位和个人不得利用虚假统计资料骗取荣誉称号、物质利益或者职务晋升。

第二章 统计调查管理

第十一条 统计调查项目包括国家统计调查项目、部门统计调查项目和地方统计调查项目。

国家统计调查项目是指全国性基本情况的统计调查项目。部门统计调查项目是指国务院有关部门的专业性统计调查项目。地方统计调查项目是指县级以上地方人民政府及其部门的地方性统计调查项目。

国家统计调查项目、部门统计调查项目、地方统计调查项目应当明确分工，互相衔接，不得重复。

第十二条 国家统计调查项目由国家统计局制定，或者由国家统计局和国务院有关部门共同制定，报国务院备案；重大的国家统计调查项目报国务院审批。

部门统计调查项目由国务院有关部门制定。统计调查对象属于本部门管辖系统的，报国家统计局备案；统计调查对象超出本部门管辖系统的，报国家统计局审批。

地方统计调查项目由县级以上地方人民政府统计机构和有关部门分别制定或者共同制定。其中，由省级人民政府统计机构单独制定或者和有关部门共同制定的，报国家统计局审批；由省级以下人民政府统计机构单独制定或者和有关部门共同制定的，报省级人民政府统计机构审批；由县级以上地方人民政府有关部门制定的，报本级人民政府统计机构审批。

第十三条 统计调查项目的审批机关应当对调查项目的必

要性、可行性、科学性进行审查，对符合法定条件的，作出予以批准的书面决定，并公布；对不符合法定条件的，作出不予批准的书面决定，并说明理由。

第十四条 制定统计调查项目，应当同时制定该项目的统计调查制度，并依照本法第十二条的规定一并报经审批或者备案。

统计调查制度应当对调查目的、调查内容、调查方法、调查对象、调查组织方式、调查表式、统计资料的报送和公布等作出规定。

统计调查应当按照统计调查制度组织实施。变更统计调查制度的内容，应当报经原审批机关批准或者原备案机关备案。

第十五条 统计调查表应当标明表号、制定机关、批准或者备案文号、有效期限等标志。

对未标明前款规定的标志或者超过有效期限的统计调查表，统计调查对象有权拒绝填报；县级以上人民政府统计机构应当依法责令停止有关统计调查活动。

第十六条 搜集、整理统计资料，应当以周期性普查为基础，以经常性抽样调查为主体，综合运用全面调查、重点调查等方法，并充分利用行政记录等资料。

重大国情国力普查由国务院统一领导，国务院和地方人民政府组织统计机构和有关部门共同实施。

第十七条 国家制定统一的统计标准，保障统计调查采用的指标涵义、计算方法、分类目录、调查表式和统计编码等的标准化。

国家统计标准由国家统计局制定，或者由国家统计局和国务院标准化主管部门共同制定。

国务院有关部门可以制定补充性的部门统计标准，报国家统计局审批。部门统计标准不得与国家统计标准相抵触。

第十八条 县级以上人民政府统计机构根据统计任务的需要，可以在统计调查对象中推广使用计算机网络报送统计资料。

第十九条 县级以上人民政府应当将统计工作所需经费列入财政预算。

重大国情国力普查所需经费，由国务院和地方人民政府共同负担，列入相应年度的财政预算，按时拨付，确保到位。

第三章 统计资料的管理和公布

第二十条 县级以上人民政府统计机构和有关部门以及乡、镇人民政府，应当按照国家有关规定建立统计资料的保存、管理制度，建立健全统计信息共享机制。

第二十一条 国家机关、企业事业单位和其他组织等统计调查对象，应当按照国家有关规定设置原始记录、统计台账，建立健全统计资料的审核、签署、交接、归档等管理制度。

统计资料的审核、签署人员应当对其审核、签署的统计资料的真实性、准确性和完整性负责。

第二十二条 县级以上人民政府有关部门应当及时向本级人民政府统计机构提供统计所需的行政记录资料和国民经济核算所需的财务资料、财政资料及其他资料，并按照统计调查制度的规定及时向本级人民政府统计机构报送其组织实施统计调查取得的有关资料。

县级以上人民政府统计机构应当及时向本级人民政府有关部门提供有关统计资料。

第二十三条 县级以上人民政府统计机构按照国家有关规定，定期公布统计资料。

国家统计数据以国家统计局公布的数据为准。

第二十四条 县级以上人民政府有关部门统计调查取得的统计资料，由本部门按照国家有关规定公布。

第二十五条 统计调查中获得的能够识别或者推断单个统计调查对象身份的资料，任何单位和个人不得对外提供、泄露，不得用于统计以外的目的。

第二十六条 县级以上人民政府统计机构和有关部门统计调查取得的统计资料，除依法应当保密的外，应当及时公开，供社会公众查询。

第四章 统计机构和统计人员

第二十七条 国务院设立国家统计局，依法组织领导和协调全国的统计工作。

国家统计局根据工作需要设立的派出调查机构，承担国家统计局布置的统计调查等任务。

县级以上地方人民政府设立独立的统计机构，乡、镇人民政府设置统计工作岗位，配备专职或者兼职统计人员，依法管理、开展统计工作，实施统计调查。

第二十八条 县级以上人民政府有关部门根据统计任务的需要设立统计机构，或者在有关机构中设置统计人员，并指定统计负责人，依法组织、管理本部门职责范围内的统计工作，实施统计调查，在统计业务上受本级人民政府统计机构的指导。

第二十九条 统计机构、统计人员应当依法履行职责，如实搜集、报送统计资料，不得伪造、篡改统计资料，不得以任何方式要求任何单位和个人提供不真实的统计资料，不得有其他违反本法规定的行为。

统计人员应当坚持实事求是，恪守职业道德，对其负责搜集、审核、录入的统计资料与统计调查对象报送的统计资料的一致性负责。

第三十条 统计人员进行统计调查时，有权就与统计有关的问题询问有关人员，要求其如实提供有关情况、资料并改正不真实、不准确的资料。

统计人员进行统计调查时，应当出示县级以上人民政府统计机构或者有关部门颁发的工作证件；未出示的，统计调查对象有权拒绝调查。

第三十一条 国家实行统计专业技术职务资格考试、评聘制度，提高统计人员的专业素质，保障统计队伍的稳定性。

统计人员应当具备与其从事的统计工作相适应的专业知识和业务能力。

县级以上人民政府统计机构和有关部门应当加强对统计人员的专业培训和职业道德教育。

第五章 监督检查

第三十二条 县级以上人民政府及其监察机关对下级人民政府、本级人民政府统计机构和有关部门执行本法的情况，实施监督。

第三十三条 国家统计局组织管理全国统计工作的监督检查，查处重大统计违法行为。

县级以上地方人民政府统计机构依法查处本行政区域内发生的统计违法行为。但是，国家统计局派出的调查机构组织实施的统计调查活动中发生的统计违法行为，由组织实施该项统计调查的调查机构负责查处。

法律、行政法规对有关部门查处统计违法行为另有规定的，从其规定。

第三十四条 县级以上人民政府有关部门应当积极协助本级人民政府统计机构查处统计违法行为，及时向本级人民政府统计机构移送有关统计违法案件材料。

第三十五条 县级以上人民政府统计机构在调查统计违法行为或者核查统计数据时，有权采取下列措施：

（一）发出统计检查查询书，向检查对象查询有关事项；

（二）要求检查对象提供有关原始记录和凭证、统计台账、统计调查表、会计资料及其他相关证明和资料；

（三）就与检查有关的事项询问有关人员；

（四）进入检查对象的业务场所和统计数据处理信息系统进行检查、核对；

（五）经本机构负责人批准，登记保存检查对象的有关原始记录和凭证、统计台账、统计调查表、会计资料及其他相关证明和资料；

（六）对与检查事项有关的情况和资料进行记录、录音、录像、照相和复制。

县级以上人民政府统计机构进行监督检查时，监督检查人员不得少于二人，并应当出示执法证件；未出示的，有关单位和个人有权拒绝检查。

第三十六条 县级以上人民政府统计机构履行监督检查职责时，有关单位和个人应当如实反映情况，提供相关证明和资料，不得拒绝、阻碍检查，不得转移、隐匿、篡改、毁弃原始记录和凭证、统计台账、统计调查表、会计资料及其他相关证明和资料。

第六章 法律责任

第三十七条 地方人民政府、政府统计机构或者有关部门、单位的负责人有下列行为之一的，由任免机关或者监察机关依法给予处分，并由县级以上人民政府统计机构予以通报：

（一）自行修改统计资料、编造虚假统计数据的；

（二）要求统计机构、统计人员或者其他机构、人员伪造、篡改统计资料的；

（三）对依法履行职责或者拒绝、抵制统计违法行为的统计人员打击报复的；

（四）对本地方、本部门、本单位发生的严重统计违法行为失察的。

第三十八条 县级以上人民政府统计机构或者有关部门在组织实施统计调查活动中有下列行为之一的，由本级人民政府、上级人民政府统计机构或者本级人民政府统计机构责令改正，予以通报；对直接负责的主管人员和其他直接责任人员，由任免机关或者监察机关依法给予处分：

（一）未经批准擅自组织实施统计调查的；

（二）未经批准擅自变更统计调查制度的内容的；

（三）伪造、篡改统计资料的；

（四）要求统计调查对象或者其他机构、人员提供不真实的统计资料的；

（五）未按照统计调查制度的规定报送有关资料的。

统计人员有前款第三项至第五项所列行为之一的，责令改正，依法给予处分。

第三十九条 县级以上人民政府统计机构或者有关部门有下列行为之一的，对直接负责的主管人员和其他直接责任人员由任免机关或者监察机关依法给予处分：

（一）违法公布统计资料的；

（二）泄露统计调查对象的商业秘密、个人信息或者提供、泄露在统计调查中获得的能够识别或者推断单个统计调查对象身份的资料的；

（三）违反国家有关规定，造成统计资料毁损、灭失的。

统计人员有前款所列行为之一的，依法给予处分。

第四十条 统计机构、统计人员泄露国家秘密的，依法追究法律责任。

第四十一条 作为统计调查对象的国家机关、企业事业单位或者其他组织有下列行为之一的，由县级以上人民政府统计机构责令改正，给予警告，可以予以通报；其直接负责的主管人员和其他直接责任人员属于国家工作人员的，由任免机关或者监察机关依法给予处分：

（一）拒绝提供统计资料或者经催报后仍未按时提供统计资料的；

（二）提供不真实或者不完整的统计资料的；

（三）拒绝答复或者不如实答复统计检查查询书的；

（四）拒绝、阻碍统计调查、统计检查的；

（五）转移、隐匿、篡改、毁弃或者拒绝提供原始记录和凭证、统计台账、统计调查表及其他相关证明和资料的。

企业事业单位或者其他组织有前款所列行为之一的，可以并处五万元以下的罚款；情节严重的，并处五万元以上二十万元以下的罚款。

个体工商户有本条第一款所列行为之一的，由县级以上人民政府统计机构责令改正，给予警告，可以并处一万元以下的罚款。

第四十二条 作为统计调查对象的国家机关、企业事业单位或者其他组织迟报统计资料，或者未按照国家有关规定设置原始记录、统计台账的，由县级以上人民政府统计机构责令改正，给予警告。

企业事业单位或者其他组织有前款所列行为之一的，可以并处一万元以下的罚款。

个体工商户迟报统计资料的，由县级以上人民政府统计机构责令改正，给予警告，可以并处一千元以下的罚款。

第四十三条 县级以上人民政府统计机构查处统计违法行为时，认为对有关国家工作人员依法应当给予处分的，应当提出给予处分的建议；该国家工作人员的任免机关或者监察机关应当依法及时作出决定，并将结果书面通知县级以上人民政府统计机构。

第四十四条 作为统计调查对象的个人在重大国情国力普查活动中拒绝、阻碍统计调查，或者提供不真实或者不完整的普查资料的，由县级以上人民政府统计机构责令改正，予以批评教育。

第四十五条 违反本法规定，利用虚假统计资料骗取荣誉称号、物质利益或者职务晋升的，除对其编造虚假统计资料或者要求他人编造虚假统计资料的行为依法追究法律责任外，由作出有关决定的单位或者其上级单位、监察机关取消其荣誉称号，追缴获得的物质利益，撤销晋升的职务。

第四十六条 当事人对县级以上人民政府统计机构作出的行政处罚决定不服的，可以依法申请行政复议或者提起行政诉讼。其中，对国家统计局在省、自治区、直辖市派出的调查机构作出的行政处罚决定不服的，向国家统计局申请行政复议；对国家统计局派出的其他调查机构作出的行政处罚决定不服的，向国家统计局在该派出机构所在的省、自治区、直辖市派出的调查机构申请行政复议。

第四十七条 违反本法规定，构成犯罪的，依法追究刑事责任。

第七章 附 则

第四十八条 本法所称县级以上人民政府统计机构，是指国家统计局及其派出的调查机构、县级以上地方人民政府统计机构。

第四十九条 民间统计调查活动的管理办法，由国务院制定。

中华人民共和国境外的组织、个人需要在中华人民共和国境内进行统计调查活动的，应当按照国务院的规定报请审批。

利用统计调查危害国家安全、损害社会公共利益或者进行欺诈活动的，依法追究法律责任。

第五十条 本法自 2010 年 1 月 1 日起施行。

附录五

中华人民共和国统计法实施条例

Regulations for the Implementation of the Statistics Law of the People's Republic of China

中华人民共和国国务院令

第 681 号

《中华人民共和国统计法实施条例》已经 2017 年 4 月 12 日国务院第 168 次常务会议通过，现予公布，自 2017 年 8 月 1 日起施行。

总理　李克强

2017 年 5 月 28 日

中华人民共和国统计法实施条例

第一章　总　则

第一条　根据《中华人民共和国统计法》（以下简称统计法），制定本条例。

第二条　统计资料能够通过行政记录取得的，不得组织实施调查。通过抽样调查、重点调查能够满足统计需要的，不得组织实施全面调查。

第三条　县级以上人民政府统计机构和有关部门应当加强统计规律研究，健全新兴产业等统计，完善经济、社会、科技、资源和环境统计，推进互联网、大数据、云计算等现代信息技术在统计工作中的应用，满足经济社会发展需要。

第四条　地方人民政府、县级以上人民政府统计机构和有关部门应当根据国家有关规定，明确本单位防范和惩治统计造假、弄虚作假的责任主体，严格执行统计法和本条例的规定。

地方人民政府、县级以上人民政府统计机构和有关部门及其负责人应当保障统计活动依法进行，不得侵犯统计机构、统计人员独立行使统计调查、统计报告、统计监督职权，不得非法干预统计调查对象提供统计资料，不得统计造假、弄虚作假。

统计调查对象应当依照统计法和国家有关规定，真实、准确、完整、及时地提供统计资料，拒绝、抵制弄虚作假等违法行为。

第五条　县级以上人民政府统计机构和有关部门不得组织实施营利性统计调查。

国家有计划地推进县级以上人民政府统计机构和有关部门通过向社会购买服务组织实施统计调查和资料开发。

第二章　统计调查项目

第六条　部门统计调查项目、地方统计调查项目的主要内容不得与国家统计调查项目的内容重复、矛盾。

第七条　统计调查项目的制定机关（以下简称制定机关）应当就项目的必要性、可行性、科学性进行论证，征求有关地方、部门、统计调查对象和专家的意见，并由制定机关按照会议制度集体讨论决定。

重要统计调查项目应当进行试点。

第八条　制定机关申请审批统计调查项目，应当以公文形式向审批机关提交统计调查项目审批申请表、项目的统计调查制度和工作经费来源说明。

申请材料不齐全或者不符合法定形式的，审批机关应当一次性告知需要补正的全部内容，制定机关应当按照审批机关的要求予以补正。

申请材料齐全、符合法定形式的，审批机关应当受理。

第九条　统计调查项目符合下列条件的，审批机关应当作出予以批准的书面决定：

（一）具有法定依据或者确为公共管理和服务所必需；

（二）与已批准或者备案的统计调查项目的主要内容不重复、不矛盾；

（三）主要统计指标无法通过行政记录或者已有统计调查资料加工整理取得；

（四）统计调查制度符合统计法律法规规定，科学、合理、

可行;

（五）采用的统计标准符合国家有关规定;

（六）制定机关具备项目执行能力。

不符合前款规定条件的，审批机关应当向制定机关提出修改意见;修改后仍不符合前款规定条件的，审批机关应当作出不予批准的书面决定并说明理由。

第十条 统计调查项目涉及其他部门职责的，审批机关应当在作出审批决定前，征求相关部门的意见。

第十一条 审批机关应当自受理统计调查项目审批申请之日起20日内作出决定。20日内不能作出决定的，经审批机关负责人批准可以延长10日，并应当将延长审批期限的理由告知制定机关。

制定机关修改统计调查项目的时间，不计算在审批期限内。

第十二条 制定机关申请备案统计调查项目，应当以公文形式向备案机关提交统计调查项目备案申请表和项目的统计调查制度。

统计调查项目的调查对象属于制定机关管辖系统，且主要内容与已批准、备案的统计调查项目不重复、不矛盾的，备案机关应当依法给予备案文号。

第十三条 统计调查项目经批准或者备案的，审批机关或者备案机关应当及时公布统计调查项目及其统计调查制度的主要内容。涉及国家秘密的统计调查项目除外。

第十四条 统计调查项目有下列情形之一的，审批机关或者备案机关应当简化审批或者备案程序，缩短期限:

（一）发生突发事件需要迅速实施统计调查;

（二）统计调查制度内容未作变动，统计调查项目有效期届满需要延长期限。

第十五条 统计法第十七条第二款规定的国家统计标准是强制执行标准。各级人民政府、县级以上人民政府统计机构和有关部门组织实施的统计调查活动，应当执行国家统计标准。

制定国家统计标准，应当征求国务院有关部门的意见。

第三章 统计调查的组织实施

第十六条 统计机构、统计人员组织实施统计调查，应当就统计调查对象的法定填报义务、主要指标涵义和有关填报要求等，向统计调查对象作出说明。

第十七条 国家机关、企业事业单位或者其他组织等统计调查对象提供统计资料，应当由填报人员和单位负责人签字，并加盖公章。个人作为统计调查对象提供统计资料，应当由本人签字。统计调查制度规定不需要签字、加盖公章的除外。

统计调查对象使用网络提供统计资料的，按照国家有关规定执行。

第十八条 县级以上人民政府统计机构、有关部门推广使用网络报送统计资料，应当采取有效的网络安全保障措施。

第十九条 县级以上人民政府统计机构、有关部门和乡、镇统计人员，应当对统计调查对象提供的统计资料进行审核。统计资料不完整或者存在明显错误的，应当由统计调查对象依法予以补充或者改正。

第二十条 国家统计局应当建立健全统计数据质量监控和评估制度，加强对各省、自治区、直辖市重要统计数据的监控和评估。

第四章 统计资料的管理和公布

第二十一条 县级以上人民政府统计机构、有关部门和乡、镇人民政府应当妥善保管统计调查中取得的统计资料。

国家建立统计资料灾难备份系统。

第二十二条 统计调查中取得的统计调查对象的原始资料，应当至少保存2年。

汇总性统计资料应当至少保存10年，重要的汇总性统计资料应当永久保存。法律法规另有规定的，从其规定。

第二十三条 统计调查对象按照国家有关规定设置的原始记录和统计台账，应当至少保存2年。

第二十四条 国家统计局统计调查取得的全国性统计数据和分省、自治区、直辖市统计数据，由国家统计局公布或者由国家统计局授权其派出的调查机构或者省级人民政府统计机构公布。

第二十五条 国务院有关部门统计调查取得的统计数据，由国务院有关部门按照国家有关规定和已批准或者备案的统计调查制度公布。

县级以上地方人民政府有关部门公布其统计调查取得的统计数据，比照前款规定执行。

第二十六条 已公布的统计数据按照国家有关规定需要进行修订的，县级以上人民政府统计机构和有关部门应当及时公布修订后的数据，并就修订依据和情况作出说明。

第二十七条 县级以上人民政府统计机构和有关部门应当及时公布主要统计指标涵义、调查范围、调查方法、计算方法、抽样调查样本量等信息，对统计数据进行解释说明。

第二十八条 公布统计资料应当按照国家有关规定进行。公布前，任何单位和个人不得违反国家有关规定对外提供，不得利用尚未公布的统计资料谋取不正当利益。

第二十九条 统计法第二十五条规定的能够识别或者推断单个统计调查对象身份的资料包括:

（一）直接标明单个统计调查对象身份的资料;

（二）虽未直接标明单个统计调查对象身份，但是通过已标明的地址、编码等相关信息可以识别或者推断单个统计调查对象身份的资料;

（三）可以推断单个统计调查对象身份的汇总资料。

第三十条 统计调查中获得的能够识别或者推断单个统计调查对象身份的资料应当依法严格管理，除作为统计执法依据外，不得直接作为对统计调查对象实施行政许可、行政处罚等具体行政行为的依据，不得用于完成统计任务以外的目的。

第三十一条 国家建立健全统计信息共享机制，实现县级以上人民政府统计机构和有关部门统计调查取得的资料共享。制定机关共同制定的统计调查项目，可以共同使用获取的统计资料。

统计调查制度应当对统计信息共享的内容、方式、时限、渠道和责任等作出规定。

第五章　统计机构和统计人员

第三十二条　县级以上地方人民政府统计机构受本级人民政府和上级人民政府统计机构的双重领导，在统计业务上以上级人民政府统计机构的领导为主。

乡、镇人民政府应当设置统计工作岗位，配备专职或者兼职统计人员，履行统计职责，在统计业务上受上级人民政府统计机构领导。乡、镇统计人员的调动，应当征得县级人民政府统计机构的同意。

县级以上人民政府有关部门在统计业务上受本级人民政府统计机构指导。

第三十三条　县级以上人民政府统计机构和有关部门应当完成国家统计调查任务，执行国家统计调查项目的统计调查制度，组织实施本地方、本部门的统计调查活动。

第三十四条　国家机关、企业事业单位和其他组织应当加强统计基础工作，为履行法定的统计资料报送义务提供组织、人员和工作条件保障。

第三十五条　对在统计工作中做出突出贡献、取得显著成绩的单位和个人，按照国家有关规定给予表彰和奖励。

第六章　监督检查

第三十六条　县级以上人民政府统计机构从事统计执法工作的人员，应当具备必要的法律知识和统计业务知识，参加统计执法培训，并取得由国家统计局统一印制的统计执法证。

第三十七条　任何单位和个人不得拒绝、阻碍对统计工作的监督检查和对统计违法行为的查处工作，不得包庇、纵容统计违法行为。

第三十八条　任何单位和个人有权向县级以上人民政府统计机构举报统计违法行为。

县级以上人民政府统计机构应当公布举报统计违法行为的方式和途径，依法受理、核实、处理举报，并为举报人保密。

第三十九条　县级以上人民政府统计机构负责查处统计违法行为；法律、行政法规对有关部门查处统计违法行为另有规定的，从其规定。

第七章　法律责任

第四十条　下列情形属于统计法第三十七条第四项规定的对严重统计违法行为失察，对地方人民政府、政府统计机构或者有关部门、单位的负责人，由任免机关或者监察机关依法给予处分，并由县级以上人民政府统计机构予以通报：

（一）本地方、本部门、本单位大面积发生或者连续发生统计造假、弄虚作假；

（二）本地方、本部门、本单位统计数据严重失实，应当发现而未发现；

（三）发现本地方、本部门、本单位统计数据严重失实不予纠正。

第四十一条　县级以上人民政府统计机构或者有关部门组织实施营利性统计调查的，由本级人民政府、上级人民政府统计机构或者本级人民政府统计机构责令改正，予以通报；有违法所得的，没收违法所得。

第四十二条　地方各级人民政府、县级以上人民政府统计机构或者有关部门及其负责人，侵犯统计机构、统计人员独立行使统计调查、统计报告、统计监督职权，或者采用下发文件、会议布置以及其他方式授意、指使、强令统计调查对象或者其他单位、人员编造虚假统计资料的，由上级人民政府、本级人民政府、上级人民政府统计机构或者本级人民政府统计机构责令改正，予以通报。

第四十三条　县级以上人民政府统计机构或者有关部门在组织实施统计调查活动中有下列行为之一的，由本级人民政府、上级人民政府统计机构或者本级人民政府统计机构责令改正，予以通报：

（一）违法制定、审批或者备案统计调查项目；

（二）未按照规定公布经批准或者备案的统计调查项目及其统计调查制度的主要内容；

（三）未执行国家统计标准；

（四）未执行统计调查制度；

（五）自行修改单个统计调查对象的统计资料。

乡、镇统计人员有前款第三项至第五项所列行为的，责令改正，依法给予处分。

第四十四条　县级以上人民政府统计机构或者有关部门违反本条例第二十四条、第二十五条规定公布统计数据的，由本级人民政府、上级人民政府统计机构或者本级人民政府统计机构责令改正，予以通报。

第四十五条　违反国家有关规定对外提供尚未公布的统计资料或者利用尚未公布的统计资料谋取不正当利益的，由任免机关或者监察机关依法给予处分，并由县级以上人民政府统计机构予以通报。

第四十六条　统计机构及其工作人员有下列行为之一的，由本级人民政府或者上级人民政府统计机构责令改正，予以通报：

（一）拒绝、阻碍对统计工作的监督检查和对统计违法行为的查处工作；

（二）包庇、纵容统计违法行为；

（三）向有统计违法行为的单位或者个人通风报信，帮助其逃避查处；

（四）未依法受理、核实、处理对统计违法行为的举报；

（五）泄露对统计违法行为的举报情况。

第四十七条　地方各级人民政府、县级以上人民政府有关部门拒绝、阻碍统计监督检查或者转移、隐匿、篡改、毁弃原始记录和凭证、统计台账、统计调查表及其他相关证明和资料的，由上级人民政府、上级人民政府统计机构或者本级人民政府统计机构责令改正，予以通报。

第四十八条 地方各级人民政府、县级以上人民政府统计机构和有关部门有本条例第四十一条至第四十七条所列违法行为之一的，对直接负责的主管人员和其他直接责任人员，由任免机关或者监察机关依法给予处分。

第四十九条 乡、镇人民政府有统计法第三十八条第一款、第三十九条第一款所列行为之一的，依照统计法第三十八条、第三十九条的规定追究法律责任。

第五十条 下列情形属于统计法第四十一条第二款规定的情节严重行为：

（一）使用暴力或者威胁方法拒绝、阻碍统计调查、统计监督检查；

（二）拒绝、阻碍统计调查、统计监督检查，严重影响相关工作正常开展；

（三）提供不真实、不完整的统计资料，造成严重后果或者恶劣影响；

（四）有统计法第四十一条第一款所列违法行为之一，1年内被责令改正3次以上。

第五十一条 统计违法行为涉嫌犯罪的，县级以上人民政府统计机构应当将案件移送司法机关处理。

第八章 附 则

第五十二条 中华人民共和国境外的组织、个人需要在中华人民共和国境内进行统计调查活动的，应当委托中华人民共和国境内具有涉外统计调查资格的机构进行。涉外统计调查资格应当依法报经批准。统计调查范围限于省、自治区、直辖市行政区域内的，由省级人民政府统计机构审批；统计调查范围跨省、自治区、直辖市行政区域的，由国家统计局审批。

涉外社会调查项目应当依法报经批准。统计调查范围限于省、自治区、直辖市行政区域内的，由省级人民政府统计机构审批；统计调查范围跨省、自治区、直辖市行政区域的，由国家统计局审批。

第五十三条 国家统计局或者省级人民政府统计机构对涉外统计违法行为进行调查，有权采取统计法第三十五条规定的措施。

第五十四条 对违法从事涉外统计调查活动的单位、个人，由国家统计局或者省级人民政府统计机构责令改正或者责令停止调查，有违法所得的，没收违法所得；违法所得50万元以上的，并处违法所得1倍以上3倍以下的罚款；违法所得不足50万元或者没有违法所得的，处200万元以下的罚款；情节严重的，暂停或者取消涉外统计调查资格，撤销涉外社会调查项目批准决定；构成犯罪的，依法追究刑事责任。

第五十五条 本条例自2017年8月1日起施行。1987年1月19日国务院批准、1987年2月15日国家统计局公布，2000年6月2日国务院批准修订、2000年6月15日国家统计局公布，2005年12月16日国务院修订的《中华人民共和国统计法实施细则》同时废止。

附录六

统计违法违纪行为处分规定

Statistics Regulation Violations of Law

中华人民共和国监察部
中华人民共和国人力资源和社会保障部　令
国家统计局

第 18 号

《统计违法违纪行为处分规定》已经监察部2009年2月9日第一次部长办公会议、人力资源社会保障部2008年12月30日第十六次部务会议、国家统计局2008年11月6日第十八次局务会议审议通过。现予公布，自2009年5月1日起施行。

监察部部长 马馼
人力资源社会保障部部长 尹蔚民
国家统计局局长 马建堂
二〇〇九年三月二十五日

统计违法违纪行为处分规定

第一条　为了加强统计工作，提高统计数据的准确性和及时性，惩处和预防统计违法违纪行为，促进统计法律法规的贯彻实施，根据《中华人民共和国统计法》、《中华人民共和国行政监察法》、《中华人民共和国公务员法》、《行政机关公务员处分条例》及其他有关法律、行政法规，制定本规定。

第二条　有统计违法违纪行为的单位中负有责任的领导人员和直接责任人员，以及有统计违法违纪行为的个人，应当承担纪律责任。属于下列人员的（以下统称有关责任人员），由任免机关或者监察机关按照管理权限依法给予处分：

（一）行政机关公务员；

（二）法律、法规授权的具有公共事务管理职能的事业单位中经批准参照《中华人民共和国公务员法》管理的工作人员；

（三）行政机关依法委托的组织中除工勤人员以外的工作人员；

（四）企业、事业单位、社会团体中由行政机关任命的人员。

法律、行政法规、国务院决定和国务院监察机关、国务院人力资源社会保障部门制定的处分规章对统计违法违纪行为的处分另有规定的，从其规定。

第三条　地方、部门以及企业、事业单位、社会团体的领导人员有下列行为之一的，给予记过或者记大过处分；情节较重的，给予降级或者撤职处分；情节严重的，给予开除处分：

（一）自行修改统计资料、编造虚假数据的；

（二）强令、授意本地区、本部门、本单位统计机构、统计人员或者其他有关机构、人员拒报、虚报、瞒报或者篡改统计资料、编造虚假数据的；

（三）对拒绝、抵制篡改统计资料或者对拒绝、抵制编造虚假数据的人员进行打击报复的；

（四）对揭发、检举统计违法违纪行为的人员进行打击报复的。

有前款第（三）项、第（四）项规定行为的，应当从重处分。

第四条　地方、部门以及企业、事业单位、社会团体的领导人员，对本地区、本部门、本单位严重失实的统计数据，应当发现而未发现或者发现后不予纠正，造成不良后果的，给予警告或者记过处分；造成严重后果的，给予记大过或者降级处分；造成特别严重后果的，给予撤职或者开除处分。

第五条　各级人民政府统计机构、有关部门及其工作人员在实施统计调查活动中，有下列行为之一的，对有关责任人员，给予记过或者记大过处分；情节较重的，给予降级或者撤职处分；情节严重的，给予开除处分：

（一）强令、授意统计调查对象虚报、瞒报或者伪造、篡改统计资料的；

（二）参与篡改统计资料、编造虚假数据的。

第六条 各级人民政府统计机构、有关部门及其工作人员在实施统计调查活动中，有下列行为之一的，对有关责任人员，给予警告、记过或者记大过处分；情节较重的，给予降级处分；情节严重的，给予撤职处分：

（一）故意拖延或者拒报统计资料的；

（二）明知统计数据不实，不履行职责调查核实，造成不良后果的。

第七条 统计调查对象中的单位有下列行为之一，情节较重的，对有关责任人员，给予警告、记过或者记大过处分；情节严重的，给予降级或者撤职处分；情节特别严重的，给予开除处分：

（一）虚报、瞒报统计资料的；

（二）伪造、篡改统计资料的；

（三）拒报或者屡次迟报统计资料的；

（四）拒绝提供情况、提供虚假情况或者转移、隐匿、毁弃原始统计记录、统计台账、统计报表以及与统计有关的其他资料的。

第八条 违反国家规定的权限和程序公布统计资料，造成不良后果的，对有关责任人员，给予警告或者记过处分；情节较重的，给予记大过或者降级处分；情节严重的，给予撤职处分。

第九条 有下列行为之一，造成不良后果的，对有关责任人员，给予警告、记过或者记大过处分；情节较重的，给予降级或者撤职处分；情节严重的，给予开除处分：

（一）泄露属于国家秘密的统计资料的；

（二）未经本人同意，泄露统计调查对象个人、家庭资料的；

（三）泄露统计调查中知悉的统计调查对象商业秘密的。

第十条 包庇、纵容统计违法违纪行为的，对有关责任人员，给予记过或者记大过处分；情节较重的，给予降级或者撤职处分；情节严重的，给予开除处分。

第十一条 受到处分的人员对处分决定不服的，依照《中华人民共和国行政监察法》、《中华人民共和国公务员法》、《行政机关公务员处分条例》等有关规定，可以申请复核或者申诉。

第十二条 任免机关、监察机关和人民政府统计机构建立案件移送制度。

任免机关、监察机关查处统计违法违纪案件，认为应当由人民政府统计机构给予行政处罚的，应当将有关案件材料移送人民政府统计机构。人民政府统计机构应当依法及时查处，并将处理结果书面告知任免机关、监察机关。

人民政府统计机构查处统计行政违法案件，认为应当由任免机关或者监察机关给予处分的，应当及时将有关案件材料移送任免机关或者监察机关。任免机关或者监察机关应当依法及时查处，并将处理结果书面告知人民政府统计机构。

第十三条 有统计违法违纪行为，应当给予党纪处分的，移送党的纪律检查机关处理。涉嫌犯罪的，移送司法机关依法追究刑事责任。

第十四条 本规定由监察部、人力资源社会保障部、国家统计局负责解释。

第十五条 本规定自 2009 年 5 月 1 日起施行。

附录七

济南市统计局2021年统计大事要事

Chronicle of Events of Jinan Statistical Undertaking

1月6日，山东省统计局党组书记、局长辛树人一行4人，到魏家庄万达广场开展工作调研。市统计局党组书记、局长苑子建陪同调研。

1月7日，济南市局举办《山东省重大行政决策程序规定》专题培训班。

1月8日，济南市局组织局班子成员、市管干部、总经济师、各处室负责人30余人集中收看全国统计工作视频会议。

1月11日至15日，济南市第十七届人民代表大会第三次会议胜利召开，济南市局高度重视，积极准备，圆满完成"人代会"现场统计咨询服务工作。

1月17日，济南市局参加市委、市政府2020年省市一体化推进济南加快发展考评工作现场答辩，圆满完成省市一体化推进济南加快发展考评工作任务。

1月22日，济南市局与市地方金融监管局联合召开2020年度金融业运行分析座谈会，人民银行济南分行、山东银保监局、山东证监局、省金融局、济南市税务局、齐商行、中泰证券、鲁证期货、泰山保险等单位参加会议。

1月26日，济南市委市政府举行新闻发布会，通报2020年全市经济社会运行情况。市统计局党组副书记、市社会经济调查中心主任、新闻发言人唐军参加新闻发布会并回答记者提问。

1月27日，济南市局召开2020年度党支部书记抓党建述职评议会。局党组书记、局长苑子建参加会议，市直机关工委宣传部毕京利到会指导工作。

2月2日，市统计局党组成员、副局长张兴利，党组成员、正处级领导干部沈桂欣带领办公室、组织人事处、机关党委有关人员，到第一书记帮扶村莱芜区雪野街道狂山村开展"我们的节日·春节"送温暖献爱心主题活动。

2月3日，市统计局党组成员、副局长张谨国，党组成员、正处级领导干部周光萍带领市统计局第四党支部开展"情系基层、冬送温暖，我为群众办实事"活动，走访慰问双报到定点单位洪北社区困难群众家庭，为他们送上慰问金和慰问品，带去市统计局关怀与新春祝福。

2月4日，市统计局党组成员、副局长谈友军，在市社情民意调查中心主任题宗阳的陪同下，到济阳区市民中心看望慰问市统计局派出干部许晓霞所在的市派济阳四进工作二组。

2月6日，市统计局党组副书记、市社会经济调查中心主任、新闻发言人唐军作为发布嘉宾参加了由济南市委宣传部、济南市政府新闻办公室与中国新闻社山东分社、济南日报报业集团、济南广播电视台联合举办的"2020济南十大新闻、十大新名片"发布活动。

2月7日，市统计局党组召开2020年度民主生活会。会议由党组书记、局长苑子建主持，市委第十五督导组组长李英涛带领督导组全体成员到会指导并作点评讲话，市纪委监委有关同志到会监督，局机关党委专职副书记列席会议。

2月9日，市统计局党组副书记、市社会经济调查中心主任、市统计局工作人员绩效考核领导小组办公室主任唐军带队开展节前工作纪律和办公安全检查。

2月16日，济南市人普办下发《关于做好全市第七次全国人口普查工作总结及技术业务总结的通知》（济人普办字〔2021〕2号），要求各区县普查机构全面梳理第七次全国人口普查截至目前的各项工作情况，各阶段重点工作和业务技术方面的创新性做法、经验、成效、存在的问题、不足及启示性建议等，认真组织开展本地区人口普查工作总结及技术业务总结。

2月26日，济南市局召开2020年工作总结会议。党组书记、局长苑子建作工作报告，党组副书记、市社会经济调查中心主任唐军主持会议并讲话。市纪委监委派驻第六纪检监察组组长郭尚兰受邀到会指导并讲话。

3月4日，济南市组织召开全市升规纳统工作专班会议。市发展和改革委、市工业和信息化局、市住房和城乡建设局、市商务局、市统计局负责调查单位升规直报工作的分管负责人和业务处室负责人参加会议。市统计局党组书记、局长苑子建出席会议并讲话。

3月9日，济南市局召开全市统计工作会议，传达学习全国、全省统计工作会议精神，总结2020年全市统计工作，分析当前形势，研究部署2021年重点工作任务，并为入选省第二届基层统计人才培育工程人选、2020年度升规直报工作先进集体和先进个人颁发了奖牌和证书。市统计局党组书记、局长苑子建作了题为《立足新起点 展现新作为 奋力谱写统计现代化改革新篇章》的工作报告。

3月9日，济南市统计系统全面从严治党暨党风廉政建设工作会议召开。市统计局党组书记、局长苑子建，市纪委监委派驻第六纪检监察组组长郭尚兰出席会议并讲话。市统计局党组副书记、市社会经济调查中心主任唐军主持会议。

3月10日至11日，山东省统计局工业统计处处长傅相国一行，来济调研重点工业企业经济运行情况。市统计局党组成员、副局长张兴利，高新区发改科经部副部长张晋菊等陪同调研。

3月11日，国家统计局人事司一级巡视员李文海一行4人，到济南调研统计人才队伍建设情况。人事司人才处副处长李恩来、事业单位人事处四级调研员李强在我局组织召开调研座谈会。党组书记、局长苑子建，党组副书记、市社会经济调查中心主任唐军，部分处室主要负责人及年轻干部代表参加座谈会。省统计局党组成员、副局长周尊考，人事处处长、二级巡视员李涛及有关同志陪同调研。

3月12日，山东省统计局二级巡视员王志珍带领核算处相关人员到山东力创科技股份有限公司调研。济南市统计局党组成员、副局长张谨国，莱芜区统计局党组书记卢诗献等陪同调研。

3月15日，济南市统计执法监察支队支队长李中亮带队赴钢城区和莱芜区就两区统计执法难点和热点，统计基层基础建设现状及创新情况进行调研。

3月17日，济南市局召开全市农村统计工作暨县域社会经济统计培训会议。市统计局党组成员、副局长孙夕良出席会议并讲话。

3月15日至19日，市统计局党组成员、副局长谈友军一行10人，先后到宁波市、厦门市、广州市学习考察“一套表”调查单位管理工作。

3月25日，国家统计局能源司副司长于新华一行3人。到济南调研新旧动能转换及清洁能源发展情况。山东省统计局副局长周尊考、能源处副处长辛超，市统计局副局长孙夕良陪同调研。

3月31日，国家统计局副局长鲜祖德到济南市统计局调研，并看望慰问干部职工。

3月31日，济南市局召开党史学习教育动员大会，深入学习习近平总书记在党史学习教育动员大会上的重要讲话精神，部署全局党史学习教育工作。党组书记、局长苑子建出席会议并作动员讲话，党组副书记、市社会经济调查中心主任唐军主持会议。

4月2日，济南市统计局党组副书记、市社会经济调查中心主任唐军带领40余名党员到泺口九烈士纪念碑祭奠革命先烈。

4月9日，济南市局组织副处级以上干部集体观看《监督保障执行 促进完善发展——山东正风肃纪反腐2020》《检徽下的交易——巩盛昌严重违纪违法案件警示录》等警示教育片。

4月9日，济南市委党史学习教育第七巡回指导组李伟组长一行来济南市局指导党史教育工作。市统计局党组书记、局长苑子建就目前党史学习教育开展情况、近期工作计划及整体进度安排向指导组作了汇报。

4月12日，济南市局举行市统计局“颂歌献给党”——庆祝中国共产党成立100周年合唱活动启动仪式。市统计局党组副书记、机关党委书记、市社会经济调查中心主任唐军主持启动仪式并作动员报告。

4月13日，济南市统计执法监察支队支队长李中亮结合党史学习教育到市中区开展题为“法为坐标　扬帆数海”的专题统计普法宣传教育。

4月13日至14日，济南市局组织召开全市名录业务培训会议。市统计局党组成员、副局长谈友军出席会议并讲话。

4月15日，济南市局组织干部职工走上街口巷陌、走进人海车流，开展文明交通志愿服务。市统计局党组成员、副局长张谨国到经十路奥体西路路口督导工作、慰问志愿者。

4月16日，济南市统计局党组书记、局长苑子建参加市政府系统跨部门业务培训大课堂暨全市统计业务知识培训会，并做《立足万亿起点 熟悉统计规则 以真实可靠的统计数据服务强省会建设》专题授课。

4月21日，中共济南市委、市政府印发《关于表扬优化营商环境工作优秀单位和优秀个人的通报》，市统计局获得优秀单位通报表扬，李玉祥、许明智两名同志被评为优秀个人。

4月27日，济南市局召开2021年一季度区（县）级生产总值统一核算专题会议。市统计局党组书记、局长苑子建出席会议并讲话。

4月28日，山东省统计局贸易处处长王慕然一行3人，到济南调研民宿发展情况。市统计局党组成员、副局长张谨国陪同调研。

4月29日，济南市委市政府举行新闻发布会，通报2021年一季度全市经济社会运行情况。市统计局党组副书记、市社会经济调查中心主任、新闻发言人唐军出席新闻发布会，并就一季度经济运行情况回答媒体记者提问。

5月6日，济南市统计局党组理论学习中心组组织第8次集体学习，对新民主主义革命时期历史进行专题学习研讨。党组书记、局长苑子建主持会议并对党史学习提出明确要求，党组副书记、市社会经济调查中心主任唐军领学部分篇目，党组成员、副局长张谨国、谈友军围绕新民主主义革命时期历史作重点发言。

5月6日，济南市统计局党组副书记、市社会经济调查中心主任唐军同志以“从百年党史里汲取精神营养 在真抓实干中践行初心使命”为题，为市统计局机关第二党支部全体党员上了一堂生动的专题党课。

5月8日，济南市局召开党史学习教育工作推进会。党组书记、局长苑子建，党组副书记、市社会经济调查中心主任唐军，党史学习领导小组办公室全体成员参加会议，党组成员、党史学习领导小组办公室主任沈桂欣主持会议。

5月10日，济南市统计局党组理论学习中心组组织第9次集体学习，对社会主义革命和建设时期历史进行集体学习研讨。党组书记、局长苑子建主持学习会议，党组副书记、市社会经济调查中心主任唐军，党组成员、副局长李士营、卜繁钢作重点发言，党组成员、副局长谈友军，党组成员、正处级领导干部沈桂欣领学《中国共产党简史》社会主义革命和建设时期有关篇目。

5月10日，济南市局组织全市跨境电商发展情况部门座谈会。市统计局党组成员、副局长李士营出席会议。

5月12日，国家统计局社科文司副司长韩静一行3人，来济调研医养结合工作开展情况。省统计局党组书记、局长辛树人、省统计局一级巡视员刘银田、省统计局二级巡视员姜西海，市统计局党组书记、局长苑子建，历下区和天桥区领导同志等陪同调研。

5月13日，济南市局在局党组副书记、市社会经济调查中心主任唐军带领下，联合洪北社区党总支开展“传承红色基因，弘扬沂蒙精神”主题党日暨“双报到”活动，组织党员观看红色主旋律影片《沂蒙红嫂俺的娘》。

5月20日，济南市统计局党组理论学习中心组组织第10次集体学习，对改革开放以来历史进行专题学习研讨。党组书记、局长苑子建主持会议，党组副书记、市社会经济调查中心主任唐军领学部分篇目。市委党史学习教育第七巡回指导组副组长郭木及有关同志到会指导。

5月27日，济南市统计局党组书记、局长苑子建主持党组理论学习中心组第11次集体学习研讨，重点学习习近平《论中国共产党历史》。

5月28日，济南市局组织干部职工走上街口巷陌、走进人海车流，开展文明交通志愿服务，把党史学习的成果转化为为人民服务的效果，扎实为人民群众办实事，为创建文明城市做贡献。市统计局党组书记、局长苑子建到经十路奥体西路路口慰问志愿者。

5月28日，济南市委市直机关工委副书记解胜利带领第六调研组一行5人，来市统计局调研机关党建工作。市统计局党组书记、局长苑子建参加调研活动。

6月1日、3日，济南市统计局党组成员、副局长李士营一行4人，分赴历下区和济南高新区督导统计督察整改工作推进情况，并听取两区上半年经济运行情况汇报。

6月2日，济南市统计局党组书记、局长苑子建一行赴历城区督导检查统计督察整改推进情况，调研上半年经济运行情况，参观党史展览馆开展党史学习教育，并为历城区统计局党员代表讲党课。

6月2日，济南市统计局党组成员、正处级领导干部沈桂欣一行4人，赴章丘区统计局督导检查统计督察整改工作推进情况，开展上半年经济运行情况调研，并以“传承红色基因 践行党员使命”为题，为章丘区统计局党员代表讲党课。

6月2日，济南市局正处级领导干部李登杰一行5人到新旧动能转换起步区，对统计督察反馈意见整改推进情况进行督导，并到光大环保能源（济南）有限公司进行上半年经济运行情况调研。

6月3日，济南市统计局党组成员、副局长谈友军到市中区、天桥区统计局对统计督察整改推进情况督导检查，调研上半年经济运行情况，并以《学党史、悟思想、办实事、开新局》为题，分别给市中区、天桥区统计局党员干部讲党课。

6月3日，济南市统计局党组成员、正处级领导干部周光萍一行5人，赴商河县统计局对统计督察整改推进情况进行督导检查，开展上半年经济运行情况调研。

6月3日，济南市统计执法监察支队支队长李中亮一行3人，赴长清区督导统计督察整改工作推进情况，调研上半年经济运行情况，并以“学习习近平法治思想 推进统计法治建设”为主题，为长清区统计局党员及业务骨干讲党课。

6月3日至4日，济南市统计局党组成员、副局长张谨国一行，赴槐荫区、济阳区统计局对统计督察整改推进情况进行督导检查，开展上半年经济运行情况调研，并以《汲取党史智慧，贡献统计力量》为题，为槐荫区统计局党员干部讲党课。

6月3日至4日，济南市统计局党组成员、正处级领导干部张秀玲一行，赴平阴县开展统计督察整改情况督导及上半年经济运行情况调研，并以“学党史明理增信 开新局展现新作为”为题，为平阴县统计局党员代表讲党课。

6月8日，济南市统计局党组成员、副局长张兴利一行4人，赴莱芜区、钢城区统计局对统计督察整改推进情况进行督导检查，开展上半年经济运行情况调研，并以“风雨苍黄百年路 高歌奋进新征程”为题，为莱芜区统计局党员干部讲党课。

6月10日，济南市统计局党组成员、正处级领导干部沈桂欣一行30名党员干部，赴济南美术馆参观“学党史 庆华诞 强省会—庆祝建党100周年书画摄影展”。

6月11日至12日，省统计局党组成员、副局长周尊考带领省煤炭消费压减工作督导专班，对莱芜区和钢城区的四家重点耗能企业的煤炭消费情况进行核查。市统计局局长苑子建，副局长孙夕良，钢城区区委副书记、区长郅颂，莱芜区、钢城区相关人员陪同。

6月18日，省统计局设管处处长刘东华一行3人，先后到平阴县和长清区调研统计基层基础建设情况。市统计执法监察支队支队长李中亮陪同调研。

6月18日，市委党史学习教育第七巡回指导组李伟组长一行，到市统计局开展现场督导。市统计局党组副书记、市社会经济调查中心主任唐军就党史学习教育开展情况向指导组做汇报。

6月21日，国家发展改革委副主任兼国家统计局党组书记、局长宁吉喆围绕“铭记百年历史 传承红色基因 全面开启统计现代化改革新征程”讲专题党课。市统计局班子成员、副处级以上干部以视频会议方式集中收听收看了党课。

6月21日，济南市局举行处级干部党史学习教育专题学习培训班开班式，党组书记、局长苑子建作动员讲话，党组副书记、市社会经济调查中心主任唐军主持会议。局领导班子成员、局机关及局属事业单位副处级以上干部参加会议，市委第七巡回指导组组长李伟及有关同志到会指导。

6月23日，中共济南市委市直机关工作委员会下发《中共济南市委市直机关工作委员会关于表彰市直机关优秀共产党员、优秀党务工作者和先进基层党组织的决定》。市统计局机关党委作为“市直机关先进基层党组织”，李婷同志作为“市直机关优秀共产党员”，林清同志作为“市直机关优秀党务工作者”受到中共济南市委市直机关工作委员会表彰。

6月28日，济南市统计局党组书记、局长苑子建带领80余名党员干部，参观“庆百年华诞、讲身边故事，济南市市直机关‘百名身边榜样’主题展”，为在全局营造学党史、看榜样、见行动的浓厚氛围作出了表率。

6月29日，济南市统计局党组书记、局长苑子建，党组成员、副局长谈友军，党组成员、副局长卜繁钢，党组成员、副局长孙夕良，党组成员、副局长张兴利分别走访看望了12名“光荣在党50年”离退休老党员，为他们送去党的关怀和温暖，感谢他们为党的事业和统计事业作出的积极贡献，并为他们颁发了“光荣在党50年”纪念章。

7月1日，济南市局组织全体干部职工收听收看庆祝中国共产党成立100周年大会直播，聆听习近平总书记重要讲话。

7月1日，济南市统计局党组成员、副局长李士营以“在服务业经济社会发展中践行初心使命”为题，为第四党支部全体党员干部上党课。

7月5日，济南市局召开党组（扩大）会议，专题传达学习习近平总书记在庆祝中国共产党成立100周年大会上的重要讲话。党组书记、局长苑子建主持会议并讲话，党组成员和其他市管干部、总经济师、一级调研员、各处室（单位）主要负责人参加会议。

7月7日，国家统计局设管司副司长吕庆喆带队一行3人，来济南市调研统计制度修订工作和统计制度方法改革的有关情况。省统计局副局长陈汉臻、设管处处长刘东华、市统计局局长苑子建、市统计执法监察支队支队长李中亮陪同调研。

7月7日，济南市统计局党组副书记、市社会经济调查中心主任、局机关党委书记唐军带队参观济南市庆祝中国共产党成立100周年主题展览，张谨国、谈友军、卜繁钢、孙夕良、张兴利、沈桂欣、周光萍等7名局党组成员参加活动。

7月22日，济南市统计局与济南市地方金融监管局联合召开2021年上半年金融业运行分析座谈会。市统计局党组成员、副局长张谨国主持会议。

7月28日，济南市统计局党组成员，副局长张谨国带领核算处、投资处、贸易处、服务业处负责同志到历下区调研经济运行情况。历下区区委副书记、区长杨传军主持会议，区委常委、副区长续明，相关部门负责人参加座谈。

8月3日，济南市局组织开展“学史力行 践行初心”无偿献血活动。缪爱斌、赵巍、任绪勇、赵玉栋、柳青等5名同志用汩汩热血表达爱党爱国的赤子之心。

8月9日，省统计局党组书记、局长辛树人一行，到山东产业技术研究院开展座谈调研。市统计局党组书记、局长苑子建，济南高新区管委会副主任陈安彪等陪同调研。

8月11日，省统计局党组书记、局长辛树人一行4人，到济南对家居市场进行专题调研。市统计局党组书记、局长苑子建，天桥区区委书记韩伟等陪同调研。

8月9日至13日，济南市局举办党组理论学习中心组专题读书班。市统计局党组书记、局长苑子建作开班动员讲话，市统计局党组副书记、市社会经济调查中心主任唐军主持开班式。

8月24日，济南市委第四巡察组对市统计局党组巡察“回头看”工作动员会召开。市委第四巡察组组长陈敏作动员讲话，对做好巡察工作提出要求，市统计局党组书记、局长苑子建主持会议并作表态发言。

8月25日，省统计局总经济师官照华一行5人，到济南市历下区调研督导“双随机”执法检查工作。市统计局党组副书记、市社会经济调查中心主任唐军，市统计执法监察支队支队长李中亮陪同。

8月31日，济南市局召开全市“上规入库”工作专题推进会议。市统计局党组书记、局长苑子建出席会议并讲话。市发展改革委、市工业和信息化局、市住房城乡建设局、市商务局、市税务局、市行政审批服务局分管负责人和相关处室负责人，各区县（功能区）统计部门主要负责人、分管负责人，市统计局相关处室人员参加会议。

8月31日，省统计局设管处处长刘东华带队来济南新旧动能转换起步区调研统计制度建设情况。市委副书记、济南新旧动能转换起步区党工委副书记、管委会主任边祥慧接见了调研组一行。市统计执法监察支队支队长李中亮陪同调研。

9月1日，济南市审计局负责全市重点项目的审计组成员，到市统计局就全市重点项目推进与纳统情况进行座谈交流。市统计局党组成员、副局长卜繁钢参加座谈。

9月2日，济南市统计局党组书记、局长苑子建带队上线济南广播电视台《作风监督热线》栏目，回应群众关注热点问题，并就统计工作情况与听众、网友交流。

9月6日至9日，济南市发展改革委、济南市统计局对21个市级行业主管部门和部分区县行业主管部门开展了为期4天的服务业行业发展精准培训。市统计局党组书记、局长苑子建出席会议并讲话。

9月8日至9日，省“四进”攻坚工作组到济南市平阴县、槐荫区、济阳区、历城区检查及调研升规纳统工作开展情况。市统计局党组成员、副局长谈友军陪同调研。

9月9日，国家统计局“赓续红色血脉 奋进统计未来”主题第十二届“中国统计开放日”在福建福州举行启动仪式。市统计局组织各处室、各区县统计局干部职工收看现场直播。

9月15日，在中秋佳节到来前夕，市统计局党组书记、局长苑子建带队到局派第一书记帮扶村——莱芜区雪野街道狂山村，开展“走进帮扶村，我为群众办实事”主题活动，扎实推进党史学习教育落在实处。党组副书记、市社会经济调查中心主任唐军，党组成员、副局长孙夕良，党组成员、正处级领导干部沈桂欣，莱芜区委副书记、区长秦蕾，区统计局党组书记魏永振，雪野街道办事处党工委书记邹振儒等一同参加活动。

9月22日，省统计局投资处副处长、二级调研员潘光臣一行来市中区开展专题调研。市统计局党组成员、副局长卜繁钢，市中区委常委、副区长程伟，区统计局主要负责人陪同调研。

10月9日，济南市委副书记、市长孙述涛对市统计局报送的《企业发展势头良好 制约因素不容忽视——2020年济南市部分重点农业产业化龙头企业调研报告》作出批示。

10月9日，省统计局二级调研员张圣红、科研所副所长曹亮一行赴基层基础工作联系点章丘区调研基层统计工作。

10月11日，济南市委第四巡察组组长陈敏一行，到天桥区调研基层统计网格化管理工作。市统计局党组书记程伟，天桥区委书记韩伟，区委副书记、区长亓伟陪同调研。

10月13日，济南市局在济南西客站东广场举行第十二届“中国统计开放日”活动。省统计局总经济师官照华，市统计局党组书记程伟，槐荫区委副书记、区长孙常建出席活动。

10月13日，济南市局组织党员干部到四五党性教育基地开展“赓续红色血脉 奋进统计未来”主题党日活动，接受党性教育。市统计局党组副书记、市社会经济调查中心主任唐军及其他班子成员，市纪委监委派驻第六纪检监察组组长郭尚兰参加活动。

10月14日，济南市直机关纪律作风检查组张晟副组长一行3人，到市统计局开展工作纪律作风互查互评。

10月15日，济南市统计局党组成员、副局长孙夕良带队赴商河县调研新能源发展和生猪生产情况，同时，对能源统计知识进行了培训。商河县统计局局长张元香陪同调研。

10月19日至20日，济南市统计局党组成员、副局长孙夕良带队赴章丘、钢城两区进行农村统计调查基础工作专题调研。章丘、钢城两区统计局的负责同志参加调研活动。

10月20日，济南市局参加全省1—3季度市级生产总值统一核算视频会议，市统计局党组书记程伟在分会场参加会议。

10月20日，济南市统计局与济南市地方金融监管局联合召开三季度金融业运行分析座谈会。市统计局、市地方金融监管局分管领导及相关处室负责人参加座谈。

10月21日，济南市统计局党组成员、副局长谈友军带队赴章丘区调研上规入库工作。市发展改革委、市工业和信息化局、市住房城乡建设局、市商务局等上规入库专班成员单位相关同志参加调研，章丘区统计局主要领导陪同调研。

10月28日，济南市局机关党委召开党务干部培训暨党建工作推进会，对支部书记、支部委员开展党建业务基础知识培训，对支部标准化、规范化建设工作再部署、再推动。市统计局党组副书记、市社会经济调查中心主任、机关党委书记唐军同志主持会议。

10月29日，济南市局联合市发展改革委、市工业和信息化局、市住房城乡建设局、市商务局召开全市年度调查单位“上规入库”工作推进暨业务培训会。市统计局党组成员、副局长谈友军出席会议并讲话。

11月5日，省统计局人口处处长、一级调研员张定新一行5人，到济南调研1%人口抽样调查工作开展情况。市统计局党组成员、副局长卜繁钢陪同调研。

11月4日至5日，济南市统计局党组成员、副局长张兴利带队到章丘区、济南高新区、莱芜区进行工作调研，并与科兴生物、神思电子、泰钢集团等重点工业企业负责人进行座谈。

11月11日，省统计局核算处处长彭丽芳一行，到济南调研经济运行情况。市统计局党组书记、局长程伟陪同调研。

11月15日，济南市局组织副处以上干部集中观看《强化政治监督》《党史的清廉故事》《远离家庭腐败》《围猎·行贿者说》等廉政教育系列参考片。

11月19日，济南市局召开创新创优工作专题会。市统计局党组书记、局长程伟出席会议并讲话。

11月19日，济南市统计局党组成员、副局长谈友军一行，到天桥区调研“准四上”监测系统平台建设情况。天桥区统计局党组书记、局长王俊参加座谈。

11月23日，济南市委副书记边祥慧对市统计局报送的《济南市农业现代化与农村发展现状和典型做法》作出批示。

11月23日，省统计局农村处二级调研员于永健一行，到济南调研现代高效农业发展情况。市统计局党组成员、副局长孙夕良陪同调研。

11月22日至23日，济南市局召开全市农村统计制度培训会议。省统计局二级调研员于永健到会指导，市统计局党组成员、副局长孙夕良参加会议并讲话。

11月24日，济南市统计局党组成员、副局长张兴利带队到历下区、槐荫区进行工作调研，并与中国石油化工股份有限公司济南分公司、济南二机床集团有限公司、九阳股份有限公司主要负责人进行座谈。

11月29日，济南市统计局召开学习贯彻党的十九届六中全会精神专题党课会议。市统计局党组书记、局长程伟为全局干部职工作专题党课辅导。

12月1日，济南市社情民意调查中心正式启动2021年度市属事业单位服务高质量发展绩效考核服务对象评价电话调查工作。

12月2日，济南市统计局党组成员、正处级领导干部张秀玲以《改革创新，主动作为，全面提升统计工作水平》为题，为局机关第一党支部全体党员上党课。

12月7日，济南市局召开全市年度“上规入库”工作推进暨“准四上”单位跟踪监测系统布置会议，市统计局党组成员、副局长谈友军出席会议并讲话。

12月8日，济南市局联合天桥区统计局举办2021年济南市法治宣传月启动仪式。市统计局党组成员、副局长卜繁钢带队参加活动。

12月8日，济南市局召开省市一体化推进济南加快发展工作会议，总结安排省市一体化各项工作。局领导张谨国、张秀玲、李亮参加会议。

12月10日，山东省统计局党组书记、局长辛树人一行，到济南调研统计基层基础建设和经济运行情况。市委副书记边祥慧，市委常委、副市长王宏志，市统计局党组书记、局长程伟，章丘区委、区政府主要负责人陪同调研。

12月10日，“省四进”驻济南中心组到商河县调研“四新”经济入库纳统工作。市统计局党组成员、副局长谈友军陪同调研。

12月8日至10日，济南市局举办全市服务业调查制度和统计业务培训班。市统计局党组成员、副局长李士营出席会议并讲话。

12月15日，济南市统计局党组成员、副局长卜繁钢带队赴历城区统计局调研经济社会发展情况和统计工作开展情况。

12月16日，济南市委第四巡察组在市统计局召开巡察“回头看”情况反馈会议。市委第四巡察组组长陈敏向市统计局党组反馈巡察“回头看”情况，市委巡察工作领导小组成员、市委巡察办主任李敬德出席会议并对抓好巡察整改工作提出要求。市统计局党组书记、局长程伟主持会议并作表态发言。

12月17日，省统计局普查中心主任袁晓勇一行，到济南调研“准四上”单位跟踪监测系统、调查单位“上规入库”及基本单位名录库日常维护工作。市统计局党组成员、副局长谈友军陪同调研。

12月22日，济南市局举办处级干部党的十九届六中全会精神专题学习班开班式。市统计局党组书记、局长程伟出席开班式并作动员讲话，党组副书记、市社会经济调查中心主任唐军主持开班式。

12月24日，济南市局举办学习宣传贯彻党的十九届六中全会精神宣讲报告会。市直机关宣讲团成员、山东省党建研究会特邀研究员，济南市党建研究会常务理事、副秘书长，市委讲师团成员，市委党校李琳教授作宣讲报告。市统计局党组成员、副局长李士营主持报告会，市委党史学习教育第七巡回指导组毕秀廷处长参加宣讲活动。

12月28日，国家统计局以视频形式召开全国统计工作会议，济南市统计局党组书记、局长程伟在分会场参加会议。

12月29日，市委党史学习教育第七巡回指导组组长李伟一行，到济南市局开展党史学习教育评估工作。

12月28日至30日，济南市局召开全市贸易专业统计报表制度培训暨商业综合体会议。